NORTHWEST BEST PLACES

Restaurants, Lodgings, and Touring
in Oregon, Washington, and British Columbia

David Brewster
Stephanie Irving

Sasquatch Books
Seattle

Library of Congress Catalog Card Number 88-655110

Copy Editor: Alice Copp Smith
Editorial Assistants: Penny Herbst, Rebecca Wilkinson
Contributors: Joan Anderman, Karen Brooks, Carol Brown, Jo Brown, Todd
Campbell, Jacalyn Cohen, Connie Cooper, Anne Depue, Tom Douglas, Susan
English, Doris and Bob Evans, Stephanie and Lawrence Feeney, Rich Fencsak,
Terrin Haley, Kitty Harmon, Phyllis Hayes, Joan Herman, Laurel Helton, John
Hughes, Griggs Irving, Eve Johnson, Jennifer and Louis Jurcik, Lauren
Kessler, Gene Laverty, Serena Sinclair Lesley, Francesca Lindstrom, Rhonda
May, Marnie McPhee, Gail Norton, Kim Osborn, J. Kingston Pierce, Rose
Pike, Pam Pruitt, Nancy Pryor, John S. Robinson, Kathryn Robinson, Junius
Rochester, Eric Scigliano, Marilyn and Fred Tausend, Cleve Twitchell, Laurie
Underwood, Colleen Whaley

Design: Jane Rady
Maps: Karen Schober
Production: Weekly Typography and Graphic Design
Proofreaders: Barry Foy and Don Roberts

The Best Places guidebooks have been published continuously since 1975. Books
in the Best Places series read as personal guidebooks, but our evaluations are based
on numerous reports from locals and traveling inspectors. Final judgments are made
by the editors. Our inspectors never identify themselves (except over the phone)
and never take free meals or other favors. Readers are advised that places listed
in previous editions may have closed or changed management, or are no longer
recommended by this series. The editors welcome information conveyed by users
of this book, as long as they have no financial connection with the establishment
concerned. A report form is provided at the end of the book. *Northwest Best Places*,
Seattle Best Places, and other Sasquatch books are available at bulk discounts for
corporate gifts, conventions, and fund-raising sales for clubs and organizations. See
order form in back of book.

Sasquatch Books
1931 Second Avenue
Seattle, Washington 98101
(206) 441-5555

Contact us for a catalog of our regional titles on travel, gardening, food,
history, and sports.

CONTENTS

HOW TO USE THIS BOOK
v

OREGON
1

WASHINGTON
153

HOW TO USE THIS BOOK

Books in the Best Places series read like personal guidebooks, but our evaluations are based on numerous reports from local and traveling inspectors. Final judgments are made by the editors. Our inspectors never identify themselves (except over the phone) and never accept free meals or other favors.

Rating System. We rate establishments on value, performance measured against goals, uniqueness, enjoyability, loyalty of local clientele, cleanliness, and professionalism of service.

(no stars) Worth knowing about, if nearby

★ A good place

★★ Excellent; some outstanding qualities

★★★ Distinguished; many wonderful features

★★★★ The very best in the region

Price Range. Prices are based on high-season rates; when they range between two categories (for instance, moderate to expensive) the lower one is given.
► *Expensive* indicates a tab of more than $75 for dinner for two, including wine (but not tip), and more than $90 for one night's lodging for two.
► *Moderate* falls between expensive and inexpensive.
► *Inexpensive* indicates a tab of less than $25 for dinner, and less than $50 for lodgings for two. Prices throughout the British Columbia section are in Canadian dollars and are classified according to Canadian value.

Checks and credit cards. Most establishments that accept checks also require a major credit card for identification. American Express is abbreviated as AE, Diners Club as DC, MasterCard as MC, Visa as V.

Maps. New to this edition are about 50 town maps, though directions (or sometimes coordinates) are included in every entry. Whenever possible, you should call ahead; many of the B&Bs are private homes and discourage drop-in visits. There is a map for each region in the book, normally found at the beginning of each geographic section, though some maps are combined to include several regions. All maps are oriented with north at the top of the page.

Indexes. All restaurants, lodgings, town names, and some tourist attractions are listed alphabetically at the back of the book. New to this edition is an activities index.

Calendar. This section is a month-by-month listing of Northwest events, from jazz festivals to tennis tournaments to slug races.

Reader reports. At the end of the book is a report form. We receive hundreds of these reports from readers, suggesting new finds or agreeing or disagreeing with our assessments. They greatly help in our evaluations. We encourage readers to respond.

OREGON

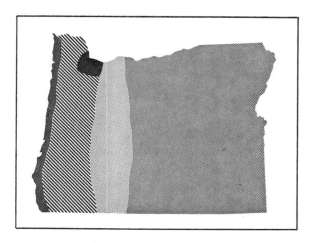

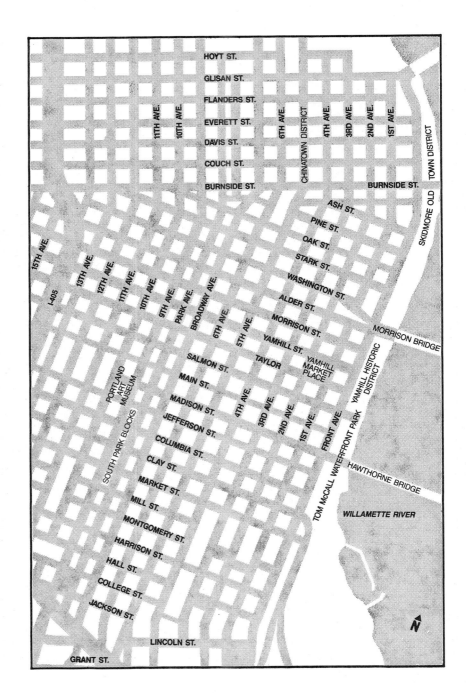

PORTLAND
AND ENVIRONS

*Including outlying areas: Beaverton, Hillsboro, and Tigard to the west,
Lake Oswego to the south, and Gresham to the west.*

Bit by bit, kicking and screaming and aw-shucksing, Portland is being dragged to
major metropolitan status. During the last few years of the '80s and the first few
of the '90s, the city that doesn't want to be a city has acquired, or is about to: a
nationally noted light-rail service; a small jewel of a downtown performing-arts center,
which attracted a resident company from the Oregon Shakespeare Festival and
ecstatic reviews from national media; a new downtown shopping complex starring
a Saks Fifth Avenue; and a major convention center that will probably bring a new
headquarters hotel in its wake. Then there was the downtown riverfront development that was so popular people tried to move an interstate freeway to match it
on the other bank, and there's the attraction that residents would probably rate
above any of the rest: a giant bronze statue of Portlandia, leaning off the new
municipal building as though trying to play tag with the city buses.

The secret may be getting out, but Portlanders still insist that a city is not
for networking or catching planes to other places, but for living. What they prize
about the place is not its per capita income but its rivers, its neighborhoods, its
live jazz, its microbreweries, and its pro basketball Trailblazers. The last may be
an acquired taste, but all the rest comes naturally—one of Portland's favorite words.

THE ARTS

Music. Nothing ever did so much for this city's aural offerings as the Arlene
Schnitzer Concert Hall, and by this time Portlanders are packing the place 52 weeks
a year. Besides the essential house "given"—the Oregon Symphony Orchestra, under
conductor James DePreist—the "Schnitz" has expanded Portland's musical agen-
da significantly. Chamber Music Northwest presents a five-week-long summer festival
spanning four centuries of music, (503) 223-3202. From Johnny Mathis to Bad Company to Queen Ida, the importation of upscale entertainment is suddenly reality
in a town that once struggled to maintain a local opera company.

Theatre. Neighboring Schnitzer Hall is the recently completed Performing Arts
Center. The most notable impact of this addition containing three performance
spaces has been the full-time residence of Portland Center Stage, a northern offshoot of the acclaimed Oregon Shakespeare Festival in Ashland. Portland Repertory continues to put out quality productions; Storefront is the operation taking
risks; New Rose offers a traditional package; Artists Repertory is the best small
company; and musicals of any caliber land at the Portland Civic (home of the Portland
Opera, now in its 25th year).

Visual Arts. The Portland art scene continues to grow, and the former exodus
of local talent is only a memory. Gallery walks the first Thursday of every month
haven't hurt the expansion of that community: The Portland Art Museum, Augen,

Blue Sky, Blackfish, Elizabeth Leach, Jamison/Thomas, Laura Russo, Northwest Artists Workshop, and Quartersaw are the hot showcases of both local and national work.

Dance. Ballet in Portland has two competent representatives, Pacific Ballet Theatre and Ballet Oregon. Nancy Matchek's Contemporary Dance Season at Portland State University brings in the hottest out-of-town dance action, and probably the most watched prospect on the horizon is Mary Oslund Van Liew's contemporary dance company.

Literature. The first time people see Powell's Books, they react like stout Cortez discovering the Pacific—except that the Pacific doesn't have nearly as good a history section. Besides this superpower of used bookstores, Portland has a flock of other strong hardcover contenders, including Cameron's, for back-issue magazines; the Catbird Seat, in the center of the city; Annie Bloom's Books, especially for Judaica; and Murder by the Book, which is to mysteries what Powell's is to everything else. Any of these, or a local church or college, might on any day be presenting readings by local or visiting writers, and Portland Arts and Lectures produces a growing number of lectures by nationally known literary figures.

Architecture. Between Pietro Belluschi's glass-box Equitable Building, Michael Graves' controversial postmodern Portland Building, Will Martin's swank, complexly designed Pioneer Courthouse Square, A.E. Doyle's spectacularly ornate Old US Bank Building, Zimmer Gunsul Frasca's KOIN Center, and the city's most recent architectural entry, ZGF's blue-reflective One Financial Center, Portland's downtown skyline has become dramatically sophisticated in recent years. Several resurrected historic sites are worth checking out; the waterfront district comes to mind.

OTHER THINGS TO DO

Nightlife. Portland's jazz community is picking up a national reputation: Remo's, Brasserie Montmartre, The Hobbit, and DJs Village Jazz are the favored options. The Portland Art Museum is another hot spot; its After Hours gigs are each Wednesday evening. Rock fans get their best licks at Key Largo, Pine Street Theatre, and Starry Night. Music on or past the edge—and habitues of the same—can be found at Satyricon in Old Town, north of Burnside between the river and Fifth Street.

Sports. The town's only big-league action is the Portland Trailblazers basketball team. While they usually manage to make the finals, the Blazers have a penchant for fizzling in the playoffs, and fans are stuck with the memory of the '77 championship. Baseball fans like to follow the Portland Beavers (they made the minor-league playoffs in 1988 for the first time in six years). The Beavers play half of their 142-game schedule in the Portland Civic Stadium. Individual sports thrive in the region: runners have access to over 50 manicured miles of trail in the 5,000-acre Forest Park complex; rowers are guaranteed miles of flat water on the Willamette; and bicyclists use more than 100 miles of off-street paved bike path in the greater Portland area.

Parks and Gardens. There are nearly 150 parks in the city besides the sprawling and primitive Forest Park. The Hoyt Arboretum, close to the Washington Park Zoo, has the most impressive collection of native and exotic flora, as well as the best-kept trails. More formalized grounds are the International Rose Test Garden, the Japanese Gardens, and the Rhododendron Gardens. A new World Forestry Center Building, also next to the zoo, has ongoing displays worth checking. And the largest memorial of its kind in the nation, the Vietnam Veterans Living Memorial, is an inspiring outdoor cathedral commemorating the Oregon victims of that conflict.

Shopping. Crafts and renaissance-style goods can be found at Saturday Market under the Burnside Bridge; upscale specialty shops and eateries are found at the Yamhill Market, The Galleria, New Market Theater, The Water Tower, Lloyd Center, and Holiday Market. Northwest Portland's 23rd Avenue and Southeast Hawthorne Blvd between 35th and 45th feature great neighborhood merchants. Antiques are found in Sellwood, in the city's southeast corner.

Transportation. The city's public transportation system, Tri-Met, runs throughout the metropolitan area and is free in the downtown core area. The light-rail system, MAX, is a speedy conduit to the eastside, going as far as Gresham. Once a day Amtrak heads north, south, and east. Plans are under way for a west-moving rail line, which should be completed in the next few years. The airport is a $20 cab ride (or less than half that on shuttle buses from major hotels). Portland is one of those cities where the meters must be fed on Saturdays.

RESTAURANTS

Genoa

From downtown Portland, Morrison Bridge will become SE Belmont, then continue east until the 2800 block, (503) 238-1464
2832 SE Belmont Street, Portland
Moderate; wine; AE, DC, MC, V
Dinner Mon-Sat

There's a constant debate over which is the best restaurant in town, Genoa or L'Auberge. Neither is perfect, but at their best, no place in Portland can equal either. For atmosphere and flexibility, choose L'Auberge. For the most ambitious meal in town, Genoa wins hands down—provided you like an intimate atmosphere, Northern Italian food made with care and skill, and meals that span three hours without running out of imagination.

There's no view to act as drawing card: the windowless dining room is without much illumination, and it may be a couple of courses before you know with whom you are dining. By then, however, you may hardly care; saffron-inflected fish soup, seafood ravioli, or spinach dumplings overshadow all other thoughts. Of the seven courses—appetizer, soup, pasta, fish, entree, dessert, and fruit—not all will be spectacular, but a couple will certainly be—and the rest will be very good. The only choice of the evening comes with the entrees, where you're offered dishes such as pork tenderloin in a tomato and Marsala sauce or veal scallops in Madeira and morels. Yes, you can also choose dessert from a trayful of tortes and gelati—but there's really only one showstopper: boccone dolce, a baroque layering of meringue, chocolate, berries, and whipped cream. Some diners have been known to sob audibly over it.

Outbursts and other singularities are well handled by a knowledgeable staff who carefully explain the food and know the well-thought-out wine list. Theatergoers will be pleased with the abridged version of dinner (antipasto, pasta, entree, dessert) served 5:30–6pm and complete by curtain time.

L'Auberge

I-405, US 30/St. Helen's exit, (503) 223-3302
2601 NW Vaughn Street,

Those who think French restaurants are stuffy should wander into the bar here on Sunday nights. In a setting known for high-style informality, an innovative, eclectic menu, and—Sunday nights only—free screenings of

Portland
Expensive; full bar; AE,
DC, MC, V
Dinner every day, bar
menu every day

classic movies, you'll discover terrific cheeseburgers and what might be the best barbecued ribs this side of the Mississippi. Welcome to L'Auberge bar, a softly lit den of elegant rusticity and upscale hipness, with a well-stoked hearth in the winter, a homey outdoor dining deck in the summer and, in all seasons, a witty, personable staff. L'Auberge bar is easily the most relaxing and attractive retreat in town. Changing every two weeks, the bar menu is replete with great finds, such as grilled swordfish with cilantro pesto and a salad of wild edible greens cultivated on a farm in southern Oregon.

The sunken, split-level dining room downstairs is given over to more serious pretensions. The execution is fairly understated—this is not a place to look for the shock of the new—and the dinners are among the most expensive in town. But L'Auberge, which celebrated its 20th birthday in 1989, is distinguished by consistently high standards of excellence. Three- or six-course dinners are offered six nights a week in a country-inn atmosphere punctuated by contemporary touches. The kitchen emphasizes fresh, local ingredients: entrees usually include local game birds, veal, beef, or fresh fish. Options run from grilled quail with prune custard to rack of lamb marinated in pomegranate juice. Service is highly informed, the wine list astutely selected.

Bread and Ink Cafe
36th and Hawthorne,
(503) 234-4756
3610 SE Hawthorne
Blvd, Portland
Inexpensive; beer and
wine; MC, V
Breakfast, lunch, dinner
Mon-Sat, brunch Sun

Tracing the Hawthorne area's boom over the last decade, you might almost call Bread and Ink a neighborhood restaurant that created its neighborhood around it. The idiosyncratic menu boasts everything from the city's best homemade blintzes to a wild salad (with some 17 greens and flowers) to burgers in which all the condiments—mayo, mustard, and ketchup—are made on the premises. Blackboard specials venture successfully into neo-American, Mediterranean, and Mexican specialties. Any place where lunch can consist of spring rolls, chicken enchiladas, and a sublime Italian cassata for dessert—before things get more ambitious at dinner—has both nerve and style and, unsurprisingly, a large and loyal clientele. Wonderful homemade cookies and silken chocolate pots de creme are mainstays of the dessert selection. For breakfast, there are delicious, billowing omelets, assorted homemade breads, and great coffee. On Sunday, bring *The New York Times* and settle in for a soul-satisfying four-course Yiddish brunch.

Cafe des Amis
20th and NW Kearny,
(503) 295-6487
1987 NW Kearny Street,
Portland

From its beginnings as a down-home French cafe, the now upscale Cafe des Amis has dimmed a bit from what it was, but it still produces mostly satisfying meals that are surprisingly reasonable. The fragrant soups and hearty stews of provincial France and the Spanish

Moderate; full bar;
AE, MC, V
Dinner Mon-Sat

Pyrenees are still around, and the duck terrine with pistachios and the chicken-liver pate redolent with figs and port still glisten. When mussels are in top form, they emerge in a marvelous soup enriched with curry and cream. Add a salad tossed with toasted walnuts, a basket of terrific oven-fresh French rolls, and one of the many bottles of good wine, and you have the makings of a light but satisfying meal. Recent entrees include quail in a honey-lime duck reduction, and a fillet of salmon, sauteed and then poached, in a sauce of creme fraiche and shallots. Chef Denis Baker also makes the best steak in town: a buttery, two-inch-thick filet in a sauce that is an alchemy of port and garlic. The dessert tray always merits serious consideration, and the serving staff can be relied upon to assess the day's offerings candidly.

Eddie Lee's
2nd and Stark
in Old Town,
(503) 228-1874
409 SW Second Street,
Portland
Inexpensive; full bar;
AE, MC, V
Lunch, dinner Mon-Sat

Often, restaurants open impressively and then taper off. Eddie Lee's opened impressively and keeps getting better. From a solid opening in 1987, with stunning sandwiches such as roast pork loin with fruit mustard and sweet onion relish on focaccia, and lighter entrees such as Portuguese mussels with chorizo, the restaurant has extended its hours and broadened its menu. Now nighttime means dishes like grilled duck breast with smoked tea butter, and the establishment's own bouillabaisse. The atmosphere—two small dining rooms crowded with director's chairs across a lobby from each other—not only makes the late-night effect more dramatic, it keeps prices down. The excitement here is not only to consume an impressive meal but to see what the place has come up with now.

The Heathman Restaurant and Bar
SW Broadway at Salmon,
(503) 241-4100
1009 SW Broadway,
Portland
Expensive; full bar;
AE, DC, MC, V
Breakfast, lunch, dinner
every day

This is the local leader in the Pacific Northwest cuisine movement. Since taking over the kitchen in 1985, chefs Greg Higgins and George Tate have turned this once-hohum eatery into a showcase of regional excellence: a stately place with a marble-top bar, big leather chairs, and a wall of Andy Warhol paintings. Under their guidance, native bounty has become more the specialty of the house: local seafood, game, and seasonal produce are some of the highlights. A dinner menu might feature Chinook salmon sharpened with Sichuan spices. On another night, quail comes in a nest of fresh rosemary, and sturgeon is delivered in a fire of Thai curry.

Breakfast is served in a setting of turquoise elegance with great attention to taste and detail. Eggs Benedict take on a Northwest flavor with smoked salmon replacing ham; waffles come with a hint of malt and a mound of seasonal fruit; and cornmeal cakes with fresh blueberry compote exalt the notion of griddle food. The bar, a rich, glinting affair of marble and brass, features tapas and a fine selection from Portland's best microbreweries.

Indigine

*Between Powell and
Hawthorne on SE Divi-
sion, (503) 238-1470
3725 SE Division Street,
Portland
Moderate; beer and wine;
MC, V
Dinner Tues-Sat*

The regulars who fill this small, unpretentious eatery are
a casually dressed group for whom eating out is serious
business. They put great stock in the wizardry of owner-
chef Millie Howe, whose highly maverick style and obsession with quality guarantee nothing here shall be routine
or prepackaged. For example, when Howe serves brunch
—a once-a-month event—she makes the bagels, as well
as the cream cheese, and cures the lox. Saturdays are
reserved for a blowout East Indian feast. The four-course
extravaganza starts with something unexpected, perhaps
mango mousse and homemade goat cheese in phyllo.
There's a choice of entrees, typically a searing rabbit
"vindaloo," lamb curry, seafood curry, or a collection of
vegetarian options. It's not unusual to find a stunning
selection of Howe's chutneys on the side. Weeknight suppers carry Latin American, European, or Pacific Northwest overtones: roast chicken stuffed beneath the skin
with wildly garlicked pesto; a lovely salad basket overflowing with greens, and seafood enchiladas with hot chiles
and cream. While there are numerous dessert offerings,
Howe's pies are hard to beat.

Ron Paul Catering
and Charcuterie

*Corner of NW 23rd and
Everett, (503) 223-2121
2310 NW Everett Street,
Portland
Moderate; beer and wine;
MC, V
Lunch, dinner every day*

For such a small operation, Ron Paul's packs in the options; you can eat indoors, outdoors, or get the goods to
go. Located inside this smart-looking Northwest place
(part produce stand, part flower shop, part eatery), Ron
Paul turns out a range of distinctive dishes: individualized
pizzas, great barbecued chicken, a spicy Moroccan orzo
salad with dates, and some of the best specialty breads
in town (try the rich, dark walnut wheat). Desserts, from
the rhubarb pie with phyllo crust to the ultra-rich Black
Angus cookies to the carrot cake with ricotta and raisins,
rank high. Quality control here is an obvious priority:
the kitchen cures the salmon, smokes the sausages, and
assembles the pates. On Friday nights the counter
becomes a tapas bar with an array of Spanish appetizers,
and on Fridays and Saturdays a mesquite grill is fired
up outside. And if you're looking for a morning spot, you
won't find better coffee or rum-glazed bran muffins
anywhere. Bring a sweater; the concrete floors and glass
walls keep the place cool.

Alexis

*Between 2nd and 3rd on
Burnside, (503) 224-8577
215 W Burnside Street,
Portland
Moderate; full bar;
AE, DC, MC, V
Lunch Mon-Fri, dinner
every day*

No place in Portland is quite like Alexis—a temple to good
times which has evolved over the last nine years into
something far beyond a little Greek eatery. The environment is a worthy evocation of Old Athens. Seven nights
a week, members of the Alexis Bakouros family and their
loyal staff patrol the premises with a professionalism all
too rare on the West Coast. They welcome you exuberant-
ly like a long-lost relative from their native Filiatra on
the Peloponnesus. The bear hug is the house greeting,

lightning service the house pace, and loud laughter the house music. Expect the staff to move to the same beat, occasionally belting out a spontaneous "Opa!!" There's never a dearth of action, from lawyers' conventions to Old World folk dancing to Aurelia, the region's hottest Middle Eastern dancer. The food is authentic and of consistent quality. Some think you won't find better calamari this side of the Aegean, and the bronzed oregano chicken is full of robust flavors. Complete dinners will give you the most for your buck, but regulars also find the makings of a meal in the appetizers. Plan to dip into everything with Portland's finest house bread—the crusty wedges are essential for scooping up the lusty drippings.

Atwater's
30th floor of Bancorp Tower, (503) 275-3600
111 SW Fifth Avenue, Portland
Expensive; full bar; AE, DC, MC, V
Dinner every day, brunch Sun

Five years ago, Atwater's appeared atop the US Bancorp Tower in a cloud of rolling vistas and culinary confusion. Recently, with the arrival of chef George Poston, Atwater's is beginning to have menus to match its mountain views. The menu changes every season, but always relies on Northwest seafood, game, wild mushrooms, and fruit, although the original fascination with cranberries has ebbed. The six-course formal dinner is $35, but the three-course version for $22.50 is a bargain. The all-you-can-eat Sunday buffet has been a particular hit, with groaning tables piled with a vast assortment of traditional and contemporary items, chefs whipping out omelets, and only a few steam-table perennials. The star is the space itself, with an etched-glass wine cellar rising in the middle of the peach-toned dining room and hundreds of miles of Oregon and Washington stretching outside the windows.

B. Moloch/The Heathman Bakery and Pub
At the north end of the South Park blocks, (503) 227-5700
901 SW Salmon Street, Portland
Moderate; beer and wine; AE, MC, V
Breakfast, lunch, dinner every day

This offshoot of the Heathman Restaurant and Bar is the brainchild of chef Greg Higgins. He designed everything from the modestly priced bistro menu to the industrial-chic decor. One of the big attractions here is a 25-ton wood-burning brick oven, embellished with a copper hood and Old Dutch tiles, where some of the city's best pizzas and breads are born. A seafood calzone, stuffed with smoked mussels, shrimp, and plenty of ricotta, was wonderful. Salmon, peppered ham, and sun-dried tomatoes are cured in a cold-smoker in back of the massive baking furnace. There's a take-out counter for on-the-go types, and if leisure is a habit, the microbrew bar has some of the region's finest malt happenings on tap. The new breakfast menu, which kicked off in the spring of '89, is a homage to culinary creativity: hazelnut and stout (yes, as in beer) waffles with marionberry syrup, and "eggs in purgatory" (eggs stirred in marinara sauce and

Would you like to order a copy of Best Places for a friend? There's an order form at the back of this book.

spiked with the pub's homemade Italian sausage). With stuff like that, you can expect lines.

Bangkok Kitchen

*Corner of Belmont and
26th, (503) 236-7349
2534 SE Belmont Street,
Portland
Inexpensive; beer and
wine; no credit cards;
checks ok
Lunch Mon-Fri, dinner
Mon-Sat*

Outstanding and friendly service makes up for any dearth of decor. The setting here is kitschy cafe, but authentic Thai offerings and the wacky good humor of owner-chef Sirchan Miller and her family bring in a loyal coterie of fans. They come for the heat treatment—the array of searing house soups, peanut sauces, and salads of fresh shrimp and lime. One of the popular specials is a whole fried fish covered in a feverish chile paste and deeply sauteed peppers, all decorated with basil leaves and other artful trimmings. If you want to have fun along with good food at moderate prices, this is the ticket.

Bush Garden

*Corner of 9th and
Morrison, (503) 226-7181
900 SW Morrison Street,
Portland
Moderate; full bar;
AE, MC, V
Lunch Mon-Sat,
dinner every day*

Some of the city's best practitioners of sushi art pass through these doors. Chefs here have turned out versions of sushi not found elsewhere: a brilliant flounder sushi elevated with chile peppers, sake, and soy sauce, for example; and a mackerel with jelly-textured kombu and toasted sesame seeds. When they're available, try the hand-rolled seaweed cones holding small bouquets of radish sprouts and salmon-skin shavings. Regular Japanese fare is offered in tatami rooms; however, some of the entrees are thoroughly stripped of authentic character. Others, such as the tea on rice, and jellyfish salad, are so authentic they can only be meant for the Japanese business crowd. You figure it out.

Cajun Cafe and Bistro

*Corner of Lovejoy and
21st, (503) 227-0227
2074 NW Lovejoy Street,
Portland
Moderate; full bar;
AE, DC, MC, V
Lunch Mon-Fri,
dinner every day*

After an episode of nonstop blackening, the Cajun Cafe has headed off on the Santa Fe Trail, and the trip was worth it. Solid renditions of jambalaya and crawfish etouffee are now joined by "terminator" green chile and black bean cake with salsa fresca and goat cheese. The changes have been accomplished without loss of the original Cajun core, and the examples here are earthy yet sophisticated, with enough heat to justify repeated applications of Dixie beer and Cajun martinis. The kitchen is not afraid to experiment with the two cuisines—the leg of lamb in a ginger-hoisin marinade and the grilled venison with wild mushrooms, hazelnuts, and tarragon may be hard to place, but they're easy to swallow. The servers are reliable and competent guides. As we go to press, Chef John Huyck has stepped over to Casa-U-Betcha, and we're not confident about the effects of this transition.

Chang's Yangtze

*Corner of 10th and
Morrison, 3rd floor of
Galleria, (503) 241-0218
921 SW Morrison Street,*

Chi Wei Chang, who also owns Chang's Mongolian Grill, has been a mover and shaker in Portland's Oriental cooking scene for more than a decade. He figured out years ago that Sinophiles expect fiery sauces, exotic touches, and authentic ingredients. This is the fare at the Yangtze,

*Portland
Moderate; full bar;
MC, V
Lunch Mon-Sat,
dinner every day*

★ ★

a stylish but casual little place with a hot and cool interior of pink, turquoise, and red. His menu includes favorites from the six major culinary regions of China, and his chicken dishes—especially the onion chicken and the five-flavored chicken—are considered the best around. Pass up the routine appetizers and concentrate on the house specials. Also not to be missed is sesame beef on crisp white noodles—a stunning blend of chile heat and high flavor.

Chen's Dynasty

*Between Broadway and
6th, (503) 248-9491
622 SW Washington
Street, Portland
Moderate; full bar;
AE, DC, MC, V
Lunch Mon-Sat,
dinner every day*

★ ★

The 12-page menu must be one of the most complete anywhere this side of the People's Republic—you could explore culinary China here for years without repetition. Several dishes are rarities for these parts: sweet and pungent fish with honey-roasted pine nuts, squid cut to look like clusters of flowers and perfumed with Sichuan peppercorns, and pheasant, Hunan-style. Standbys such as kung pao shrimp and General Tsao's chicken are usually treated with respect. The ambience belies the notion that Chinese restaurants must look like Fu Manchu sets. Among the nice touches is a rendering of the Great Wall that winds from the doorway to the dining room entrance, festooned with soft cotton serpent sculptures.

Esplanade at RiverPlace (Alexis Hotel)

*Off of Front,
(503) 295-6166
1510 SW Harbor Way,
Portland
Expensive; full bar;
AE, DC, MC, V
Breakfast, dinner every
day, lunch Mon-Fri,
brunch Sun*

★ ★

From high-price, low-success beginnings, Esplanade continues to improve, although it still has a way to go. The strengths are still there: a lovely room, a wide-angle-lens view of the Willamette, and a formality of service that can convince you that something special is going on. And on the menu, instead of silly amalgamations created solely for the sake of appearances, there now seems to be an honest attempt to create something actually edible. Soups such as lobster bisque and apple/broccoli are outstanding, and salads—especially the endive-and-Stilton salad with apple slices and Calvados vinaigrette—are impressive and imaginative. Appetizers and entrees are less consistent, but a fine meal is certainly possible here. Service is attentive without being intrusive. The fixed-price Sunday brunch, which includes an appetizer platter, breads and brioche, your choice of entree, and a selection from the dessert tray, is far superior to all-you-can-eat offerings at the same price.

Fong Chong

*Corner of 4th and
Everett, (503) 220-0235
301 NW Fourth Avenue,
Portland
Inexpensive; full bar;
checks ok
Lunch, dinner every day*

★ ★

The setting, a cacophony of Chinese and Caucasian voices, clattering teacups, and clicking chopsticks, is far from sedate. From 10am to 3pm daily, young waiters scurry from table to table, hawking their handmade morsels on miniature saucers. Welcome to Portland's finest dim sum parlor, where an array of steamed buns and savory dumplings are dispatched with manifest gusto. Come here with an adventurous spirit; dishes are inexpensive enough for you to discard the occasional one that fails to please. Order by simply pointing at what looks interesting. At night, Fong Chong is transformed into a quiet Cantonese eatery, with average preparations and a few surprises.

Jake's Famous Crawfish

1 block south of Burnside on 12th,
(503) 226-1419
401 SW 12th Avenue,
Portland
Moderate; full bar;
AE, DC, MC, V
Lunch Mon-Fri, dinner every day

The length of its daily fresh list keeps this brass-and-mahogany Portland landmark on top of the Portland seafood restaurant list. No other local establishment of any kind can compete with it for style, atmosphere, and nonstop social scene. The faithful—and on some nights, one suspects, the unfaithful—pack the bar for hand-built drinks. In the dining room, the reservationless don't seem to mind the hour's wait for one of the coveted tables; they know their patience will be rewarded with some of the best seafood in the city and a grand old time. For sure satisfaction, order from the fresh sheet—local crawfish are available May through September, and every August Jake's takes on a New Orleans restaurant in a crawfish cook-off. Items on the regular menu, as well as some of the stabs at Cajun, can be inconsistent. But when the restaurant is hot—the bouillabaisse, packed with fish and fennel, is one example—it's hot. The ultra-rich truffle cake leads the desserts, but the peach-and-pear crisp has its loyal supporters.

Opus Too

Corner of 2nd and Couch in Old Town,
(503) 222-6077
33 NW Second Avenue,
Portland
Moderate; full bar;
AE, DC, MC, V
Lunch Mon-Sat, dinner every day

The rendezvous here is between fish and fire; grilled seafood is so expertly accomplished at this small operation that it has earned a devoted following even from the area's most diligent dieters. Great slabs of fresh seafood come away from the mesquite-fueled flames dripping with one of the restaurant's eight different sauces, from Bearnaise to beurre rouge. The decor is urban cool—tile floor, dark wood booths, and a long swivel-chair bar overlooking the open kitchen and grills. The exuberant environment has inspired a respectable wine list, some fine desserts, and piles of vividly flavored fettuccine. A terrific sourdough bread comes with the deal.

Papa Haydn

8 blocks north of Bybee and Milwaukie,
(503) 232-9440
5829 SE Milwaukie,
Portland
Inexpensive; beer and wine; AE, MC, V
Lunch, dinner Mon-Sat

This chocolate empire continues to expand: there are pasta, good chicken dishes, and imaginative sandwiches, with the northwestern outpost more serious in its outlook than the original southeast Portland outlet. But the core is still the display of towering, intense desserts, led by the autumn meringue—layers of chocolate mousse and baked meringue festooned with chocolate leaves—and the boccone dolce, a mountain of whipped cream, meringue, chocolate, and fresh berries. There are also subtler temptations, including a shocking purple blackberry ice and dense shortbread cookies. There are decent wine and beer lists, and a full bar in the northwest location. The clientele there tends toward the upscale, while southeast owes more to the cerebral Reed crowd, but both have lines running out the door. The northwest branch: 701 NW 23rd, (503) 228-7317 (where they serve brunch on Sunday).

The Ringside

22nd and W Burnside,
(503) 223-1513
2165 W Burnside Street,
Portland
Moderate; full bar;
AE, MC, V
Dinner every day

The mythically juicy steaks here might not bowl over those beef connoisseurs in Kansas, but in this territory they're hard to beat: for texture, color, flavor, and character, they're everything you could want from a hunk of steer. The menu has recently expanded into ocean fare, but the rib steak still rules. The degree of cooking is as requested and deviations are slight. Still, it's the plump, batter-light, and slightly salty onion rings, made from Walla Walla sweets, that single-handedly made The Ringside famous; an order is essential. Other house specialties include crackling fried chicken and nicely charred burgers. Appetizers and salads are limited, although the marinated herring deserves attention; the desserts do not. You may have French fries or cottage cheese with your entree, but opt for the baked potato. It has a crisp skin and a firm, piping-hot interior into which you can insert sour cream studded with chives. The dignified black-jacketed and bow-tied waiters are eminently professional, even when 30-odd musicians from the Northwest Chamber Music Festival flock in for a late-night summer meal.

Ristorante Medici

Near the corner of 30th
and Burnside,
(503) 232-9022
2924 E Burnside Street,
Portland
Moderate; full bar;
AE, MC, V
Dinner Tues-Sun

Northern Italian cuisine in Portland took a great leap forward in 1988, when Nick Medici decided to depose his Duchess of Burnside restaurant and reopen it with the family name and the family recipes. The resulting new menu was a stunning victory for family values and a considerable expansion of Portland options. A meal beginning with polenta cups filled with toasted pine nuts and Gorgonzola, continuing through a thick veal T-bone marinated in olive oil, herbs, and balsamic vinegar, and ending with a fresh cherry cake doused in Frangelico would be a triumph anywhere. Though recently we've seen some inconsistency—meals have been verging on average and our mussels sandy. Gentle, helpful service, 40 Oregon pinot noirs, and a view overlooking Burnside Street complete the experience.

Salty's on the Columbia

Take the Marine Drive
East Exit off I-5,
(503) 288-4444
3839 NE Marine Drive,
Portland
Moderate; full bar;
AE, DC, MC, V
Lunch Mon-Sat, dinner

The new Salty's washed up on a wave of doubt, created by the mediocre performance of Salty's on the Willamette. But the new operation is not only on a more exciting river, it has a considerably more exciting menu, served up with consistency and style. There is a daily fresh list of about 20 items, but the regular menu is even more impressive, including cioppino, and catfish fried in cornmeal batter. The restaurant is usually jammed, both the din-

every day, brunch Sun

Sumida's

Corner of Sandy and
68th, (503) 287-9162
6744 NE Sandy Blvd,
Portland
Moderate; beer and wine;
MC, V
Dinner Wed-Sun

Vat & Tonsure

Near Taylor and Yamhill,
(503) 227-1845
822 SW Park Avenue,
Portland
Inexpensive; beer and
wine; checks ok
Lunch, dinner Mon-Sat

Yen Ha

Sandy Blvd and NE
68th, (503) 287-3698
6820 NE Sandy Blvd,
Portland
Inexpensive; beer and
wine; MC, V
Lunch, dinner Tues-Sun

Zell's: An American Cafe

Corner of SE 13th and
Morrison, (503) 239-0196
1300 SE Morrison Street,

ing room downstairs and the upper deck lounge, and the view is only part of the reason.

Etsuo Sumida is nothing less than the patron saint of Portland's sushi scene, and his restaurant is where you come to satiate the raw fish fetish. Just watching this master's virtuoso knife work is an event: he's the Bruce Lee of seafood carving. Everything in this cozy neighborhood eatery is impeccably fresh, from the raw tuna strips to uni with quail's eggs. And Sumida has also mastered the fine art of sushi rice preparation: the vinegared rice must be sticky enough inside to hold fish, avocado, and such, but stick-free on the outside to ease handling. This difficult balance is something of a litmus test for true sushi chefs—rare in the Northwest. If your taste for the raw is limited, most of the grilled seafood is reliable here, and familiar items like tempura and teriyaki chicken are well executed.

The original impetus for this kind of place was the coffeehouse of the late '50s to mid-'60s—a scene for earnest conversation and thoughtful dialogue. But that era passed, and it has since become difficult to find a sanctuary of intellectual discourse where the food and spirits are in sync with the '70s and '80s sophistication of American dining. If there's an answer to that dilemma, this is it. The high-backed wooden booths on the upper and lower decks of this split-level eatery are filled with a cerebral and arty crowd (and, not surprisingly, plenty of smoke) that waxes moody to the aural background of classical music. Owner Mike Quinn runs the bar and offers one of the town's most complete wine cellars. His wife, Rose-Marie, handles the kitchen, turning out some fine stuffed Cornish hens, sauteed prawns, and lamb chops. Service can be slightly aloof with newcomers, but advice, once obtained, is reliable.

Last year, Duck Van Tran inherited this branch of Yen Ha from his celebrated culinary cousin now stationed in Beaverton, and he's made it his own: Yen Ha east is a bustling Vietnamese cafe with an innovative kitchen. Try the superb soups, the succulent salt-fried Dungeness crab in tangy sauce, or the hot pot with seafood vegetables and Asian exotica. This is a menu worth exploring, and service is better than found in most Vietnamese operations.

Now, this is breakfast! Smoked sturgeon omelet, spring Chinook salmon and scrambled eggs, huckleberry pancakes, homebaked scones and two jams. The powerful coffee and fresh-squeezed orange juice are the kind of

Portland
Inexpensive; beer and
wine; AE, MC, V
Breakfast, lunch every day

touches that make getting up in the morning seem worth-while. This establishment can also boast one of the few soda fountains around that isn't a campy imitation of the original goods: Zell's is a converted '50s drugstore whose owners wisely spared the fountain counter from the remodeler's saw. Finally, if you can't deny recklessly sweet things in the morning, try the German pancakes with apples.

Al-Amir

Between 2nd and 3rd on
Stark, (503) 274-0010
223 SW Stark Street,
Portland
Inexpensive; beer and
wine; AE, MC, V
Lunch, dinner Mon-Sat

The Bishop's House, complete with crosses and crenella-tions, seems an unlikely place to have baba ghanooj as part of its destiny. But Al-Amir, a solid Middle Eastern restaurant with both range and consistency, has finally conquered the original building. In addition to pungent kabobs, the menu includes *kharouf muammar*, a huge pile of moist, faintly sweet lamb chunks, and *dujaj musahab*, a charcoal-grilled chicken breast in lemon and olive oil. Holding everything together are creamy pools of buttery hummus and baba ghanooj. Prices are reasonable, and a little Lebanese beer can make the light through the stained glass windows shine even more brightly.

Bijou Cafe

Pine and 3rd,
(503) 222-3187
132 SW Third Street,
Portland
Inexpensive; beer and
wine; checks ok
Breakfast, lunch daily

It's lost a little of its cult status, but the lines stretching out onto the street on Saturday morning still testify to the Bijou's early-morning power. Grilled cinnamon bread, specialty muffins, and oatmeal with helpful garnishes lead the list, and the Bijou is still one of only two places in Portland that can scramble an egg. The sandwiches and salads might not make your day, but the burgers are solid—try the one with cheese, ham, and egg—and the milk shakes are top of the line. Breakfasts are served long past the time when some people start to think about lunch.

Cafe de Paris

On 2nd between Pine and
Ash, (503) 274-2773
112 SW Second Avenue,
Portland
Expensive; full bar;
MC, V
Lunch, dinner Tues-Sat

A straightforward, pleasant, and expensive French restaurant. Up front, the tone is understated elegance, with dusky pillars against dove gray walls, banquettes of firm, pleated cloth, and soft oval chairs. Farther back, the mood is Parisian cafe. The cooking is pre-trendy French traditional, the way it was before flowers were moved from the table vase to the plate. Owner-chef Jacky Michel turns out great luncheon steaks, and his omelets are exemplary. At dinner, the sausage of salmon mousse and the hot fish pate appetizer are more than worthwhile.

(CLOSED)

Casa-U-Betcha

Between Hoyt and Irving,
(503) 227-3887
612 NW 21st Street,
Portland
Moderate; full bar;

Welcome to Portland's first taco club. This wild and crazy eatery has become one of northwest Portland's most "happening" restaurants. One of the reasons is the in-terior, best described as hardware sci-fi. Galvanized stovepipe doubles for industrial-art cacti and sprouts from

AE, MC, V
Lunch Mon-Fri,
dinner every day

glitzy Formica banquettes and metal-topped tables, beneath an electric orange sunset of corrugated fiberglass deck roofing. The bar is a psychedelicized tile affair, invariably inhabited by punkos and preppies. The cumin jalapeno cheesecake is only one example of the restaurant's neo-Mex cuisine. Specials are ambitious if not always successful. Regular attempts, by new chef John Huyck, at Brazilian and Chilean cooking express the understanding that "south of the border" need not be restricted to Tijuana. A Seattle branch, at 2212 First Avenue, was just opening at press time.

Chang's Mongolian Grill
3rd and Burnside,
(503) 243-1991
#1 SW Third Avenue,
Portland
Inexpensive; beer and
wine; MC, V
Lunch, dinner every day

If you'd like to cook your own meal but can't be troubled to stock a cupboard full of esoteric ingredients, this is the place. You move along a buffet stocked with fresh fixings—meats, seafoods, and vegetables, plus a full range of seasonings, oils, and spices—and select whatever combination your mood dictates. Your creation is then stir-fried to perfection atop a half-ton convex grill manned by two cooks. Back at the table, you enclose your concoction, burrito-style, in thin Chinese pancake wrappers. You're the boss here, which means the experience won't be disappointing. All this in a setting with an outstanding expression of restaurant art: a 3-D depiction of warring Mongol horsemen galloping through fiery fluorescent lights across a neon blue sky.

Crepe Faire
Corner of 2nd and Pine,
(503) 227-3365
133 SW Second Avenue,
Portland
Moderate; full bar;
AE, DC, MC, V
Breakfast, lunch,
dinner Mon-Sat

This gracious establishment, with large arched windows, exposed brick, and crimson and gray tones, is one of the few places in town that continues to take the almost-vanished genre of crepes seriously. Ironically, except for some permutations on the dessert list, crepes are among the least interesting option here. (The brown sugar and sour cream crepe is no longer on the menu, but the kitchen will make it up if you ask.) Breakfast features impressive muffins; the spinach and mushroom gateau is always around, and the evening features a stylish green peppercorn chicken and a good beef filet with even better pommes frites. Chocolate chestnut torte is a grand finale, and the wine list is one of the better and more reasonably priced in Portland. Crepe Faire is a place for romantic tete-a-tetes, high-minded brokerages, or just a good, leisurely meal with attentive service, especially at the sidewalk tables on nice days.

Greek Deli and Grocery
E Burnside and 18th,
(503) 232-0274
1740 E Burnside Street,
Portland
Inexpensive; beer and
wine; MC, V

The quintessential "great find": the city's most gregarious grocery store, home of the best souvlaki and gyros in town, and purveyor of perfect pistachios (imported from the family farm in Greece). The owners are typically Greek—warm and welcoming. Where else can you get a guided tour of aisles packed with Aegean specialties?

Lunch, dinner Mon-Sat

It's also the only spot in Portland where you can take a break from shopping and dive into authentic ethnic eats dished up fresh from the operation's small deli. A fun place full of surprises.

Hands On Cafe
Follow Burnside south until it turns into Barnes, (503) 297-5544
8245 SW Barnes Road, Portland
Inexpensive; no alcohol; checks ok
Lunch Mon-Fri, dinner Mon-Thurs, brunch Sun

At this rustic little dining room, which operates under the auspices of the Oregon School of Arts and Crafts, you can dine off handmade pottery, as carefully crafted as the artwork from the adjoining school. The everchanging lunch menu is low on selection but high on innovation: Basque bean and pumpkin potage, fresh tomato and pesto tart, Kenyan chicken stew, and pear custard tart are typical offerings. The place really lights up—and fills up—for Sunday brunch, when the inspiration can range from the Pacific Northwest to New Orleans to Peru. Good sticky cinnamon rolls, fresh fruit, and French bread come with your choice of entrees. Expect to wait, but there are certainly things to look at while you do.

Hunan
Between Washington and Alder on Park, (503) 224-8063
515 SW Broadway, Portland
Moderate; full bar; MC, V
Lunch, dinner every day

Visit Hunan if you want to become acquainted with some of the more fervid aspects of Chinese cooking. Except for an occasional misfire, it's one of the most consistently on-target Chinese eateries in town. Among the standouts: Hunan beef, Lake T'ung T'ing shrimp, and minced Sichuan chicken wrapped in pancakes. The restaurant's versions of the spicy standards—General Tso's chicken, twice-cooked pork, chicken in tangy sauce—are pungent and massively popular. Service comes in one mode: fast and impersonal.

Jarra's Ethiopian Restaurant
1 block from the Morrison Bridge on Belmont, (503) 230-8990
607 SE Morrison Street, Portland
Inexpensive; beer and wine; MC, V
Lunch Wed only, dinner Mon-Sat

Nothing, not those four-alarm Texas chiles nor those palate-flogging peppers from Thailand, packs the wallop of this kitchen's wat stews. Made of chicken, lamb, or beef, they are deep red, oily, and packed with peppery afterkicks. Full dinners come with assorted stewed meats and vegetables, all permeated with vibrant spices and mounded on enjura—the spongy Ethiopian bread that doubles as plate and fork. The variety is not extensive, but this is the area's unequaled heat champ. Be sure to take time to chat with the friendly owners, Petros Jarra and Ainalem Sultessa, who will explain the origin of the food, give you an Abyssinian history lesson, and debate Ethiopian politics. Take it all in with plenty of cold beer, the logical beverage with this cuisine.

Koji Osakaya Fish House
5 minutes south of downtown on corner of Texas, (503) 293-1066
7007 SW Macadam Avenue, Portland

High on atmosphere, low on frills, and with enough noise to drown out a fraternity party, this is the Japanese answer to the neighborhood tavern. Koji's is also where you come to catch up on the latest in sumo wrestling—Nippon's most popular sport is broadcast on a television

Moderate; full bar; AE, DC, MC, V
Lunch Mon-Fri, dinner every day

perched above the sushi bar. Sushi fans pack the 23-seat raw fish counter to watch dueling behemoths ritualize the physics of overfed flesh. Most of the standard sushi preparations can be had here, as well as a few rarities such as the pungent plum-mint rolls. It's a busy place, and service can be—how you say—leisurely.

Macheesmo Mouse
Between Park and Broadway, (503) 228-3491
723 SW Salmon Street, Portland
Inexpensive; beer and wine; checks ok
Lunch, dinner every day

One of the attractions here is wall art by local film celeb Gus Van Sant. Flying sombreros, houses falling out of the sky, and checkered lassos whirling above empty prairie highway might not recall anything about Mexican chow—the culinary Mouse theme—but they do convey a feeling of lightness. And that mood fits perfectly with the health-consciousness of this futuristic fast-food outlet. The menu is small and stays within the boundaries of cheese-chicken-black-bean-tortilla territory. The patrons come for the quality, if not the hip neo-industrial decor; and offerings are geared to the fast-lane crowd—low-fat, high-protein stuff made to wolf down with confidence in its nutritional high octane. There are a number of other outlets, but this is best.

Marco's Cafe and Espresso Bar
Multnomah and 35th, (503) 245-0199
7910 SW 35th Avenue, Portland
Inexpensive; beer and wine; MC, V
Breakfast, lunch, dinner Tues-Sat; breakfast, lunch Sun

In a luncheonette space in Multnomah Village, Marco's is actually two restaurants, and for Multnomah, they're both impressive. Mornings and noontimes, it produces solid lunches and breakfasts, especially a continental breakfast featuring home-baked croissants, Black Forest ham, fresh orange juice, and cappuccino. Evenings it turns into an imaginative and accomplished dinner operation, with menus changing nightly, and the chef using chicken breasts, pork medallions, and inspirations ranging from Italy to Thailand.

McCormick & Schmick's Oak Street Restaurant
1st and Oak, (503) 224-7522
235 SW First Avenue, Portland
Moderate; full bar; AE, DC, MC, V
Lunch Mon-Fri, dinner every day

We try. We try, but we seldom get past the appetizers. The house oyster arrangement combines a half-dozen species from various waters, which says something about priorities here. There are at least two dozen seafood possibilities, as well as the fresh list—and that's just to start. Those who do break the appetizer-barrier will enjoy the creations of adventurous chef Bill King. The baked sockeye salmon with basil-avocado cream exemplifies the new order of inspiration. And we'll return again to sample the Pacific yellowfin tuna, Columbia River sturgeon, and Alaska prawns. For all of its attention to food that swims, M&S's also manages to dish up great cheeseburgers and golden fries.

Love a good bargain? Then you'll really like Seattle Cheap Eats, *a compendium of 230 terrific bargain eateries in and around Seattle, brought to you by the same folks who bring you the* Best Places *series.*

The Original Pancake House

Intersection of 24th and Barbur, (503) 246-9007
8600 SW Barbur Blvd, Portland
Inexpensive; no alcohol; checks ok
Breakfast, lunch Wed-Sun

The name says everything. This landmark operation does all its sourdough flapjacks from scratch, and there are nearly 20 species—from wine-spiked cherries to wheat-germ to a behemoth apple variety with sticky cinnamon glaze. A good bet is the ultra-thin egg-rich Dutch baby, dusted with powdered sugar and served with fresh lemon, essential to its overall flavor. Drawbacks are a painfully long wait to get seated (bring a copy of *War and Peace* if you're thinking of weekend breakfast), a 90-decibel interior, and the town's weakest coffee. Once you're seated, the service is rushed and aloof.

Plainfield's Mayur

Corner of 21st and Taylor, (503) 223-2995
852 SW 21st Avenue, Portland
Moderate; full bar; AE, DC, MC, V
Lunch Mon-Fri, dinner every day

This is the only spot in Portland with an authentic tandoor oven. The style is basically Mogul, with an emphasis on subtle flavors and aromatic spices; the setting is sparse and somewhat formal, with bone china, crystal, candles, and linen-covered tables. Portions are small and tariffs a bit steeper than one usually expects for this cuisine. For starters, bypass the traditional offerings for something unusual, such as tomato coconut soup. The tandoori offerings—roasted prawns in tandoori jhinga for one—are outstanding.

Winterborne

42nd and Fremont, (503) 249-8486
3520 NE 42nd, Portland
Moderate; beer and wine; AE, MC, V
Dinner Wed-Sat

A sense of '60s solemnity still seems to pervade Portland's first nonsmoking restaurant. For years it has been quietly turning out some of the most respectable fish in town. No pretensions to elegance here—there's not a pastry wagon nor a maitre d' in sight. Instead, plain dishware, low lights, classical music, and a few lithographs set the tone. Chef-owner Dwight Bacon's menu is small, and meals are complemented by fresh whole-wheat bread, a simple salad, and a fragrant fish soup. Half a dozen entrees, all seafood, are never overwhelmed by their simple sauces. Pan-fried oysters with homemade tartar sauce make an excellent starter. For dessert, try the thick, bittersweet chocolate mousse.

Yamhill Book Merchants

Between Yamhill and Taylor, (503) 242-0087
818 SW First Avenue, Portland
Moderate; beer and wine; MC, V
Breakfast Sat-Sun, lunch every day

There are dozens of New York and San Francisco restaurants doubling as bookstores, but there's only one in Portland. The literature in this operation is on the ground floor, and the loft is a modest but forward-looking American cafe. An extensive menu includes earthy soups, hearty salads, hot and cold pastas, and well-constructed sandwiches. Works by local artists change monthly on the back wall. If you're coming to eat rather than read, try the hot Greek sandwich—shreds of roasted chicken, warm feta, and black olives on fine-crusted, homemade bread. Weekends offer a decent breakfast. Don't hesitate to delve with committed abandon into a Sunday paper.

Send us your opinions and tips on the report form at the back of this book.

Brasserie Montmartre

Between Alderwood and Morrison, (503) 224-5552
626 SW Park Avenue, Portland
Moderate; full bar; AE, DC, MC, V
Lunch Mon-Fri, dinner every day

This is a place where spiked heels compete with spiked coifs in droves. It's also the only game in town for late-night eats—on weekends you can graze until 3am. A hot repertoire of local jazz (no cover) is also a plus. Some of the pastas are in the same league as the operation's ambitions—linguine with pesto and scallops, for example —but the salmon with lingonberry sauce is the real triumph here. There are a few decent desserts; try the chocolate gateau with almonds and currants. The setting is artsy/decadent Paris of the '30s, which has, unfortunately, influenced a much-to-be-desired service.

Delphina's

21st and Kearny, (503) 221-1195
2112 NW Kearny Street, Portland
Moderate; full bar; AE, DC, MC, V
Lunch Mon-Fri, dinner every day

People go here because other people go here. Exposed brick, big open arches, high ceilings, and a contemporary bar are the setting for only one recommendable menu item—a thick-crust pizza that is often quite tasty. Although the kitchen cranks out its own pasta, much of it is overpriced and less than authentic. There are a handful of desserts, a decent wine list, and zealous service that has been known to come on like a long-lost in-law. Salvation here is with recently hired chef Naomi Knori. If the kitchen will let her inspired ideas bloom, the place can advance beyond the status of a pretty hangout to a bona fide and commendable restaurant.

LODGINGS

The Heathman Hotel

SW Broadway at Salmon, (503) 241-4100;
(800) 551-0011
1009 SW Broadway, Portland, OR 97205
Expensive; AE, DC, MC, V

This is *the* place to stay in town—afternoon tea each day, exquisite marble bar, elegant rooms, and one of Portland's finest restaurants (see review). The Heathman is also an historic landmark, restored about a decade ago by the Stevenson family (from the Washington town of the same name). One of the recent additions is the Elizabeth Leach Mezzanine Gallery, opening new shows quarterly and furnished with a small dining arrangement. The most notable feature of the interior is the generous use of Burmese teak paneling—the owner is a timber magnate. Small guest rooms are furnished with leather-bound rattan chairs, marble-topped bathroom pieces with brass fittings, chintz window shades, Oriental celadon lamps, and original prints and paintings. Color themes are soft green, rose, and cream. Among the amenities are more than 150 complimentary movies, European soaps, bathrobes, and a nightly turndown service. One of the Heathman's nicest qualities is the service—its employees are low-key (a highly valued quality in Oregon—indeed, in all the Northwest) but meticulously attentive. Guests feel well taken care of but not fussed over. Inside rooms are best; the hotel is on downtown Portland's busiest street. Rooms (double) start at $120.

RiverPlace Alexis Hotel
City Center exit off I-5;
Harbor Way off Front,
(503) 228-3233
1510 SW Harbor Way,
Portland, OR 97201
Expensive; AE, DC,
MC, V

The Portland counterpart to Seattle's elegant Alexis Hotel is situated in Portland's showcase riverfront district. It features 10 chic apartments, 74 rooms, specialty shops, two restaurants, scenic jogging paths, and an upscale nightclub. Inside are many distinguishing features: plush furnishings, postmodern colors, televisions concealed in armoires, complimentary sherry in the bar, smashing views of the river, and a lively night scene. The best rooms face the Willamette River or look north across the park lawns to the downtown cityscape. A jogging path, extending along the riverfront from the hotel's front door to downtown, is so popular with guests that hotel management has added to its complimentaries list the loan of jogging suits and athletic shoes. The use of the adjacent RiverPlace Athletic Club facilities is an extra $5.

The hotel restaurant, Esplanade, is strong in New American cuisine (see review); and the bar is staffed by one of the most knowledgeable wine stewards around.

Heron Haus B&B
25th and Johnson,
(503) 274-1846
2545 NW Westover Road,
Portland, OR 97210
Expensive; AE, MC, V

One usually doesn't choose a hostelry on the merits of its bathrooms, but you won't find more luxurious wallowing than at this striking, three-story renovated home in the northwest hills overlooking Portland. Built in 1904 for a local cranberry baron, Heron Haus maintains many original touches, including parquet flooring on the main level. Updated amenities, however, are no less pleasant; one of the five rooms has an elevated spa offering a view of the city below. Another has turn-of-the-century plumbing, featuring a seven-nozzle shower. This is a spacious operation for a B&B: 7,500 square feet. Perhaps too spacious—there are reports of many overlooked details: dirty windows, warm mineral water, and mediocre breakfasts. Still, there's a living room with modern furniture, a handsome, well-stocked library, a TV room, an enclosed sun room, and a year-round outside pool. If you're visiting in late summer, you'll get in on the harvest from a mini-orchard of pear, apple, and cherry trees. Another plus is the location—two blocks from the city's most popular specialty shop district. Double occupancy begins at $85.

MacMaster House
Below Washington Park,
near corner of Burnside
and Vista,
(503) 223-7362
1041 SW Vista Avenue,
Portland, OR 97205
Moderate; MC, V

This colonial is two blocks from the largest municipal park in the country—the Washington Park–Forest Park complex, which incorporates Portland's renowned Rose Gardens and Hoyt Arboretum. Hiking and jogging possibilities are almost endless and include over 50 miles of groomed trail, several stands of old-growth fir, and a two-layered canopy of deciduous growth that is as close as the Northwest gets to the chromatic fantasy of a New England fall. MacMaster is a recently restored B&B, with a massive portico set off by Doric columns—a spacious manse with seven fireplaces, leaded glass windows, and a magnificent collection of Oriental rugs and European antiques. There are several works by local artists on the walls, and the six guest rooms begin at $70 for a double. All rooms have queen beds and cable TV, and two have fireplaces. The suite, however, is choicest, with three rooms, fireplace, private bath, and balcony. Breakfast is served communally in the stately dining room.

Mumford Manor

Follow Burnside west to 22nd (King), (503) 243-2443 1130 SW King Avenue, Portland, OR 97205 Moderate; MC, V

The city's newest B&B, the Mumford is a fully restored Queen Anne from the turn of the century. The blue-shuttered, three-story beige structure is ideally located in the heart of the commercial triangle—walking distance from the business hub of downtown, the indulgence shops of the northwest district, and the sequestered beauty of Washington Park. The master suite is Victorian throughout (if you don't count the electric towel warmer), done in reds and chintz and with a fireplace. The three other rooms are equally stylish, from their designer wallpaper and goosedown pillows and comforters to the antique pedestal sinks in the bathrooms. A wholesome breakfast is served on fine china and crystal.

Portland's White House

Take the Coliseum exit from I-5, near Lloyd Center, (503) 287-7131 1914 NE 22nd Avenue, Portland, OR 97212 Moderate; MC, V

Another local timber baron, Robert F. Lytle, built what is now this popular B&B to last—it's constructed with solid Honduras mahogany. From the outside it's an imposing white mansion with all the trappings of Brahmin taste—fountain, carriage house, and grand circular driveway. Inside are six roomy units, exquisite Oriental rugs, and other elegant appointments. The Canopy Room has a private bath, its own balcony, and a large canopied bed. Another room, equally romantic, has a vintage brass bed and delicate lace curtains.

The Westin Benson

Corner of Broadway and Oak, (503) 228-9611 309 SW Broadway, Portland, OR 97205 Expensive; AE, DC, MC, V

Simon Benson was a philanthropic lumber tycoon who in 1913 built the Benson Hotel, giving orders to spare no expense. The creation was a noble 13-story affair of brick and marble (the latter has by now acquired a pale green patina), with a palatial lobby featuring a stamped tin ceiling, mammoth chandeliers, stately columns, a generous fireplace, and encompassing panels of carved Circassian walnut imported from Russia. For decades this was the only lodging in town with noteworthy class. Competition has ended the Benson's exclusive status. Rooms in the original 200-room section are generally small, jammed with furniture, and fitted with bathrooms that seem to be inserted into former closets. Nor are they noise-proofed, and the traffic din of adjacent Broadway becomes a shared experience. The newer portion of the building—the South Wing—has the more forgiving accommodations. There are two pricey restaurants within the hotel—the London Grill and Trader Vic's.

Allenhouse B&B

*10 blocks north of
Burnside, near 23rd,
(503) 227-6841
2606 NW Lovejoy Street,
Portland, OR 97210
Moderate; AE, MC, V*

Barbara Allen is a sophisticated arbiter of interior design. The guest rooms in her 1914 refurbished Northwest home suggest the presence of nature at peace. Warm hues of wood mingle with shades of forest green and sky blue. In the North Room, a canopy bed and a white peacock chair are set off by wallpaper adorned with exotic birds. Bursts of sunlight enter the private deck adjoined to the master room, the largest on the premises. Downstairs, a spacious living room is outfitted with retro furnishings and modest family heirlooms. In the back yard is a well-kept flower-bedecked garden, the perfect spot for relaxing. Allen's reputation for innovative breakfasts and good cheer has earned her a strong local following.

Corbett House

*Call for directions, 3
miles south of city center,
(503) 245-2580
7533 SE Corbett,
Portland, OR 97219
Moderate; AE, DC,
MC, V*

A mere drive by won't do this mustard-colored two-story building justice. This is one of Portland's oldest B&Bs, and among the most originally decorated. Owner, artist, and forager Sylvia Malagamba displays her sculptures and paintings throughout—and her handpicked edibles at breakfast. There's a large collection of 1920s European Art Deco, a literal forest of potted plants, and some fascinating Moroccan wall hangings. Each of the three rooms is eclectically themed, and in the fashion of any artist's digs, prone to spontaneous revisions. The place radiates Sylvia's warmth. The cookie jar is always full, and a light breakfast of marionberries (she picks and freezes them for year-round treats), good oat and strawberry muffins, and a smooth cup of coffee awaits you in the morning—no matter how early you depart.

General Hooker's B&B

*¾ mile south of the Marriott Hotel, between 1st
and 2nd, (503) 222-4435
125 SW Hooker Street,
Portland, OR, 97201
Moderate; AE, MC, V*

Happy Hooker, an Abyssinian cat, greets you at the door of this gracious Victorian B&B in a quiet southwest neighborhood. The General's house offers three rooms with handmade batik quilts and other homey touches, including a large wood stove, an eclectic library, hanging metal artwork by owner Lori Hall's mother, and a sun deck. There's a VCR in each room, complete with Hall's personal movie selections, and the building has central air conditioning. The best unit is the Rose Room, with a king-size bed, private entrance, and skylit bath. Wine is served to guests nightly on the roof decks, and there is complimentary use of the close-by Metro YMCA. Duniway Park track, Terwilliger Boulevard bike path, and Lair Hill public tennis courts are also within walking distance. Downtown is five minutes by car and also accessible by bus.

Mallory Motor Hotel

*Corner of SW 15th and
Yamhill, (503) 223-6311
729 SW 15th Avenue,*

This place is an older building in every sense of the word—from the massive hunks of ornate wooden furniture to the clientele to the senior staff. It's also one of the best bargains in town, starting at $37 for a double and with

Portland, OR 97205
Inexpensive; AE, DC,
MC, V

vast suites going for $70. While rooms are spacious, they're also short on chic features. On the other hand, this is one of the few areas bordering downtown Portland that is genuinely quiet. Parking is easy to find and mostly meter-free, and several of the rooms have good views of the city or the west hills. The bar, a kind of bizarre hybrid of '50s dark-plushy and '60s eccentric-cutesy, is not the major attraction here. Another drawback is the pervasive irritation of Muzak in every corner of the ground floor. Those flaws, however, are easily forgotten in view of simple, charming touches such as the small, lace-trimmed pillow with needle, thread, and an array of buttons left in your room and the almost motherly service.

Marriott Hotel
Between Clay and
Columbia facing the river,
(503) 226-7600
1401 SW Front Avenue,
Portland, OR 97201
Expensive; AE, DC,
MC, V

This big, urban place looks like your standard convention lodging in every big city in the country. Redeeming that is its location overlooking the Willamette River. There are 503 rooms in the 14-story structure, and facilities include a health club, an indoor pool, two restaurants, and two bars. This is the kind of operation where callers can expect a chirpy-voiced clerk to put them on hold for five minutes, then field rate queries in terms of "current, tomorrow, and weekend." Double occupancy begins at $85.

HILLSBORO
RESTAURANTS

Helvetia Tavern
2½ miles north of Sunset
Highway, (503) 647-5286
Helvetia Road, Hillsboro
Inexpensive; beer and
wine; cash only
Lunch, dinner every day

Polished sports cars and motorcycles share space in the parking lot of this regular joint, where locals and highway travelers pack the premises and there's much backslapping between staff and patrons. Hamburgers and fries are the establishment's raison d'etre—beyond these options, proceed at your own risk. Burgers are topped with mildly sauteed onion rings, crisp lettuce, and tomatoes, and finished with a light mayonnaise sauce—a decent old-fashioned burger. The fries are terrific, long and lean with brown skins intact, and heaped into a mound that covers half the plate like a golden haystack.

BEAVERTON
RESTAURANTS

Chen's China Clipper
Near the Scholl's Ferry
Road, (503) 292-4898
6750 SW Beaverton-

In the middle of 1988 chef Chi-siung Chen jumped his proverbial Portland ship. Departing downtown for the suburbs, he opened a restaurant specializing intensely in seafood, including 28 different shrimp dishes, and a

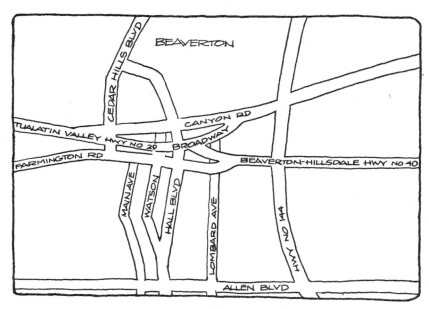

Hillsdale Highway,
Beaverton
Moderate; full bar;
AE, DC, MC, V
Lunch, dinner every day

giant papier-mache fish hanging from the ceiling. The results are sometimes uneven, but often brilliant, and usually well worth getting your feet wet. Shanghai Harbor Crab, a whole Dungeness in a hoisin sauce flecked with ginger and scallions, is a strong example of what the place is like at its best. Chiang siu, whole crispy fish and scallops in the nest—Hunan-style—depict the effectiveness of a melange of Northwestern seafood and Far Eastern inspiration. Be warned: you're going to pay more than you might expect for Chinese food, and when Chen himself is not in the kitchen, the food dips toward the waterline.

Yen Ha
Corner of 87th and
Canyon Road,
(503) 292-0616
8640 SW Canyon Road,
Beaverton
Moderate; full bar; AE,
MC, V
Lunch, dinner every day

Talented Vietnamese chef Bach Tuyet has moved her popular operation to the suburbs. Her new purple-labyrinth digs are spacious enough to feed most of the large West Slope community. The food is still the same great offering that wowed *The New Yorker*'s food essayist Calvin Trillin on a recent Portland sojourn. While there's much to recommend, the classic is *bo noung vi*. In this amazing do-it-yourself dish, you plunge slivers of marinated beef into a pool of hot oil on a stove placed on your table. Once cooked to taste, the beef is wrapped with assorted fresh greens and mint into pliable, edible rice paper. A frisky anchovy sauce is the finishing touch that brings out all of the succulent bundle's exotic flavor. There are also a wonderful shrimp salad garnished with crushed peanuts and a wide selection of chef's specials. Try the won ton soup, full of plump dumplings and Vietnamese herbs. The original outlet at 6820 NE Sandy Boulevard, (503) 287-3698, is in the competent hands of Tuyet's kin.

McCormick's Fish

Off Highway 217, 1½ miles east of Beaverton, (503) 643-1322 9945 SW Beaverton-Hillsdale Highway, Beaverton Moderate; full bar; AE, DC, MC, V Lunch Mon-Fri, dinner every day

This rough version of the downtown operation of McCormick and Schmick's lacks the fine touches of its progenitor. The seafood dishes are solid, if low on risk. Poached salmon and sauteed scallops are the kind of basics that work in the 'burbs. But the bar, like its cousin in the big city, is an occasion for good business anywhere.

Tara Thai House

Corner of SW Farmington and Watson, (503) 626-2758 4545 SW Watson Avenue, Beaverton Inexpensive; beer and wine; MC, V Lunch Mon-Fri, dinner Tues-Sat

This is perhaps the only restaurant in Portland's large contingent of Southeast Asian operations that regularly serves Laotian dishes. In her artistically arranged specials, owner-chef Lavanny Phommaneth fuses local ingredients with native techniques and flavorings: fresh salmon spiked with red or green curry paste, clams graced with a pungent Thai chile sauce, or swordfish wrapped as sausage and soaked in powerful Asian spices. Another standout is *ho mok kai*—steamed chicken shredded in coconut sauce and laced with fresh basil. Portions are somewhat small and service is somewhat friendly.

TIGARD

LODGINGS

Embassy Suite Hotel

Take the Progress Street exit off Highway 217, (503) 644-4000 9000 SW Washington Square Road, Tigard, OR 97223 Expensive; AE, DC, MC, V

This is the westside equivalent of the Marriott. Large (253 rooms) and complete with atrium, the Embassy is urban-moderno, right down to its location—across from the sprawling Washington Square shopping complex, about 15 minutes driving time from Portland. The only recommendation here is for the traveler needing quick access to Oregon's "Silicon Valley" business district in the flat plains between Beaverton and Tigard. Complimentary full breakfast, athletic club use, and mall limo service. The usual Denny's-gone-velvet restaurant and lounge found in all hotels of this genre. Double occupancy begins at $99.

Wondering about our standards? We rate establishments on value, performance measured against the place's goals, uniqueness, enjoyability, loyalty of clientele, cleanliness, excellence and ambition of the cooking, and professionalism of the service. For an explanation of the star system, see the Introduction.

LAKE OSWEGO
RESTAURANTS

Thai Villa
*1 block south of A
Avenue, (503) 635-6164
340 N First Street,
Lake Oswego
Inexpensive; beer and
wine; MC, V
Lunch Mon-Fri, dinner
every day*

Hidden away in a corner of a municipal parking lot next to the Lake Oswego fire station is a Thai restaurant with few matches but a lot of fire. Thai Villa specializes in pungent soups swirling in a moat around a pillar of flame, and a wide range of seafood dishes. The spicing is up to you, but the highest level of heat is called "volcano," and they're not kidding. The chef also calls upon basil, garlic, and subtle hints of sweetness, and the prices are reasonable, especially on a cost-per-tingle basis.

GRESHAM
RESTAURANTS

Main Street Restaurant
*Half a block north of
Powell, (503) 661-7877
120 N Main Street,
Gresham
Moderate; beer and wine;
AE, MC, V
Breakfast, lunch Mon-Sat,
dinner Tues-Sat; brunch
Sun*

Smack in the middle of Portland's most conservative suburb, this progressive little operation has somehow managed not only to survive but to thrive. The ambience is artsy, and the setting is a hybrid of California commune mercantile and New York City loft: big storefront windows, exposed brick, and high ceilings, punctuated by braided garlic bulbs, wicker baskets, and fresh flowers. Dinner offers some predictable appetizers and pasta, and a few ambitious projects like the chicken en croute—a boneless breast baked in herbed cream sauce and tucked into phyllo dough. There's also a nice variation on the theme of Oregon quail.

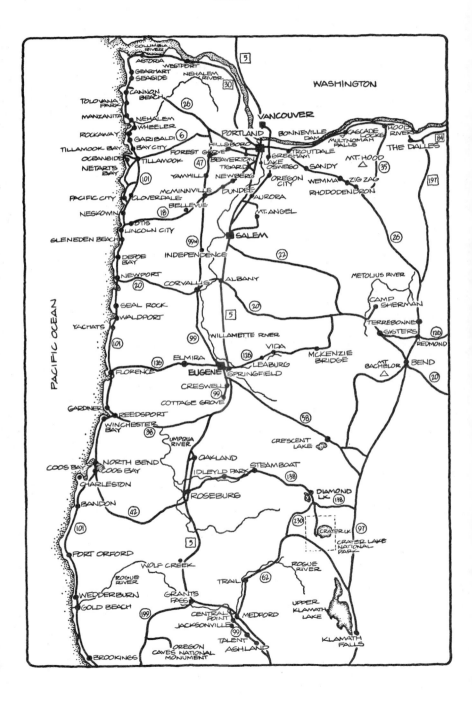

OREGON COAST

▲

*From Westport (on the Columbia River, some 30 miles inland), a southward
route down the coast.*

WESTPORT
LODGINGS

King Salmon Lodge
*At the ferry dock,
(503) 455-2400
Mail: PO Box 511,
Westport, OR 97016
Moderate; no alcohol; V
Lunch, dinner by
reservation; brunch Sun*

Westport is the tiny Columbia River town connected to
Puget Island by ferry, then by bridge to Cathlamet,
Washington, and the Washington mainland. The King
Salmon Lodge, formerly a barracks for Chinese salmon-
cannery workers, is now a bed and breakfast with a
restaurant. The setting, on a gurgling creek lined with
alders and maples, is idyllic. Lunch and dinner are open
to non-guests, though you must call ahead to guarantee
a spot. A $7.50 all-you-can-eat buffet lunch might include
some decent lasagne and pretty good clam chowder. Dinners are more elaborate, at $12 to $18, and might feature
prime rib, steak, or calamari, with soup, salad, and dessert
included. A Sunday-only brunch is another all-you-can-
eat opportunity.

Bed-and-breakfast prices are reasonable at $60, with
a $90 suite that sleeps five. If time permits, take the
15-minute ferry ride to Puget Island. You might spot deer,
elk, and even a bald eagle enroute.

ASTORIA

A fishing and cannery town never known for tourism, Astoria, founded in 1811,
lays claim as the first permanent American settlement west of the Rockies. Recently,
the city has begun touting its historical attractions, and visitors from Portland and
Puget Sound are discovering that the North Coast has more to offer than sandy
beaches.

Boston's Robert Gray first sailed into the Columbia in May of 1792 (Oregon
and Washington are planning a 200th anniversary celebration for 1992) and named
the river for his ship. In 1805–06, explorers Lewis and Clark spent a miserably
rainy winter at the now-restored Fort Clatsop, six miles southwest of town. Noting
that only 12 of 106 days were without rain, these two intrepid explorers gave the
Northwest coast its permanent reputation for dampness. Five years later, New Yorker

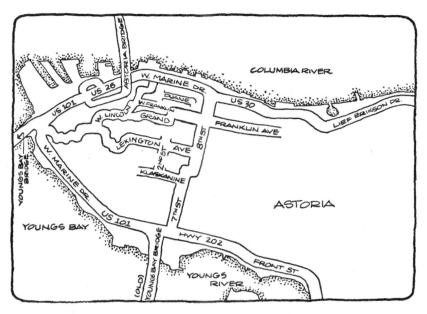

John Jacob Astor, one of America's wealthiest individuals, sent out the fur-trading company that founded Fort Astoria (now partially restored at 15th and Exchange streets).

The city really dates to the late 1840s, when it began to thrive as a customs-house town and shipping center. The well-maintained Victorian homes lining the harbor hillside at Franklin and Grand avenues provide glimpses of that era. Now Astoria is a museum without walls, an unstirred mix of the old and new that finds common ground along the busy waterfront—once the locale for canneries and river steamers, now an active port for oceangoing vessels and Russian fish-processing ships. Salmon- and bottom-fishing trips leave from here; biggest is **Thunderbird Charters**, (503) 325-7990.

The Columbia River Maritime Museum is the best maritime museum in the Northwest. Located at the foot of 17th Street along Marine Drive, (503) 325-2323, the museum boasts a Great Hall with restored small craft and seven thematic galleries, each depicting a different aspect of the Northwest's maritime heritage: sailing vessels, river commerce, marine safety, etc. The lightship *Columbia*, the last of its kind on the Pacific coast, is moored outside the museum and is included in the admission price.

Fort Clatsop National Memorial, six miles southwest of Astoria off Highway 101, reconstructs Lewis and Clark's 1805–06 winter encampment. A visitor center features audiovisual displays about the Lewis and Clark expedition, limited exhibits, and a small collection of books and souvenirs.

Captain George Flavel House/Heritage Museum. Operated by the Clatsop County Historical Society, these two museums feature local historical displays. The Flavel House, named after a prominent 19th-century businessman and river-barge pilot, is the city's best example of ornate Queen Anne architecture; Eighth and Duane streets, (503) 325-2563. The recently restored Heritage Museum,

(503) 325-2203, is eight blocks away at 1618 Exchange Street.

The Astoria Column, atop the city's highest point, Coxcomb Hill, offers an endless view of the Columbia River estuary out to the Pacific and beyond. Well worth the 160-plus-step climb. Spiral murals of the region's history wrap around the column. To get there, drive up to the top of 16th Street and follow the signs.

Sixth Street River Park has an always-open, covered observation tower providing the best vantage point to view river commerce, observe bar and river pilots board tankers and freighters, and watch seals and sea lions looking for a free lunch.

Josephson's Smokehouse, 106 Marine Drive, (503) 325-2190, prepares alder-smoked salmon that's as good as you'll find anywhere. Other smoked fish include tuna and sturgeon. Third-generation owners Linda and Mike Josephson are good sources for local information.

Fort Stevens State Park, 20 minutes southwest of Astoria off Highway 101, is a 3,500-acre outdoor wonderland of uncrowded beaches—including the permanent resting spot of the hulk of the *Peter Iredale*, wrecked in 1906. With 605 camping sites, Fort Stevens is Oregon's largest publicly owned campground.

The South Jetty lookout tower, located at Oregon's northwesternmost point, is a supreme storm-watching spot. It also marks the start of the Oregon Coast Trail, the 62-mile trail along the beach and coastal hill to Tillamook Bay.

Ricciardi Gallery, the newest kid on the 10th Street block—108 10th Street, (503) 325-5450—offers a nice selection of regional art displayed in an airy, attractive setting. Espresso, juices, fruit smoothies, and desserts are offered up front.

RESTAURANTS

Columbian Cafe
Corner of 11th and Marine Drive,
(503) 325-2233
1114 Marine Drive,
Astoria
Moderate; beer and wine;
checks ok
Breakfast, lunch Mon-Sat,
dinner Wed-Fri

Inside this vegetarian, nonsmoking joint that appears to be firmly entrenched in the late '60s, the person seated on the stool next to you might be the city manager, the drummer from the coast's hottest garage band, or a kid who thinks "hippies" means too much rear flab. Label it anything you want, but sample the delicately crafted crepes, sumptuous cream of oyster soup, excellent omelets, and luscious desserts at the Columbian Cafe, and you'll definitely call it pretty darn good.

Cramped quarters, uneven service, and an eccentric chef come with your meal. Walk in, sit down, and you might wait 10 minutes before you see a menu and another half-hour before you eat; or you might be served right away. While you're waiting, chef Uriah Hulsey might engage you in stimulating conversation, offer up-to-the-minute tidbits on Astoria happenings, or totally ignore you. So just order the crepe of the day, chock-full of wholesome ingredients such as avocado, broccoli, cream cheese, and mushrooms, and forget about the lack of etiquette. The Border Town Burrito Bar now occupies the space next door and offers fabulous burritos, beers, and Italian sodas.

Pacific Rim
Next to the WWI monument,
(503) 325-4481

In a city aching to tap into the East Asian trade scene, it's appropriate that a restaurant with a view of oceangoing vessels be named the *Pacific Rim*. But don't expect

*229 W Marine Drive,
Astoria
Inexpensive; full bar;
MC, V
Lunch, dinner every day*

any Oriental cuisines. Here, the rim of choice is the chewy, doughy crust encircling the handmade pizzas. You can choose between a traditional New York–style pie and a thicker, more filling Sicilian square. Toppings include San Francisco Italian sausage and pepperoni, along with the usual array of veggies and such. Lasagne, spinach and cheese ravioli, and some tasty Italian soups also are worth trying. Service can be spotty, especially on summer weekends when the smallish Rim gets crowded. Diverse diners (you might spot a Beamer squeezed in between two log trucks out front) seem to appreciate the absence of the canned mushrooms and pre-fab dough found in most coastal pizzerias.

The Ship Inn

*Off Marine Drive,
at west end of town,
(503) 325-0033
1 Second Street, Astoria
Moderate; full bar;
MC, V
Lunch and dinner
every day*

For the past 15 years English expatriates Jill and Featon Stokeld have been focusing on what they do best: fish and chips. The halibut is double-dipped in a delicately seasoned batter and cooked moist in fresh oil, while the chips are made from large potato slices. Neither is greasy. If you're really starving, start with a bowl of clam chowder and then eat your way through a combination seafood platter. Wash it down with a pint of Watney's ale, served on tap.

The properly cheery innkeepers keep you informed and entertained. Ask what seafood is freshest, and what the kitchen may have prepared as a special that day (such as Cornish pasties). There's a congenial (but smoky) bar up front—a wonderful place to enjoy a brew, take in some local chit-chat, or listen to the occasional live acoustic music. But the nicest tables are in back, next to the windows, where you can watch the ship traffic in the channel just a hundred yards away. There's almost always a wait.

LODGINGS

Franklin Street Station

*Between 11th and 12th
on Franklin,
(503) 325-4314
1140 Franklin Avenue,
Astoria, OR 97103
Moderate; MC, V*

Jim and Renee Caldwell have done a magnificent job of converting a solid but nondescript structure into an exemplary bed and breakfast. The location, three blocks from downtown, on a rather ordinary street, could be better, but not much else could; everything is done with style, elegance, and attention to detail, in keeping with what seems to be the Caldwells' quiet pursuit of perfection. The building was constructed in the 1900s by a local shipbuilder for his son; rich woodwork attests to dad's fondness for local forest products. Local art—a soft-hued watercolor of an Astoria hillside, a Columbia River scene rendered in acrylics—decorates the hallways, sleeping rooms, and parlor. The five guest rooms (one is a two-bedroom suite), all with private baths, are exquisitely appointed with Victorian furnishings. Renee and her mother, Karen Nelson (who operates her own B&B six blocks away), sewed every frilly drapery, cherry-patterned quilt, and pillowcase in the house. The Astor Suite has a claw-footed tub, a wet bar, and a deck—a fine honeymoon suite.

Franklin House
Franklin and 17th,
(503) 325-5044
1681 Franklin Avenue,
Astoria, OR 97103
Moderate; MC, V

Matronly innkeeper Karen Nelson scurries around this remodeled Victorian B&B, looking after her guests like an indulgent grandmother. Towering sequoias and other evergreens dominate the grounds, and the quiet residential location just down the street from some of Astoria's finest Victorians ensures serenity.

Inside, the furnishings—including a rich wrought-iron fireplace with paneled mirrors—were chosen with meticulous care. Mrs. Nelson named each of the home's five spacious guest rooms after a Northwest lighthouse; each has a private bath, including the beautiful burgundy-tiled washroom in the Cape Flattery Room (which doubles as the bridal suite upon request). The home's only basement room, Grays Harbor, is the largest, darkest, and least attractive, but the best choice for families with children.

K.C.'s Mansion-by-the-Sea
Duane and 37th,
(503) 325-6172
3652 Duane Street,
Astoria, OR 97103
Expensive; MC, V

Something of a misnomer—the sea being eight miles distant—this B&B is nonetheless housed inside a spectacular, restored Victorian structure, decked out in a frilly golden color. Spacious landscaped grounds, wide-open views and sounds of the Columbia River (ships' booming foghorns at night sound like they're right outside your bedroom window, and almost are), and unrestrained service add to the total experience. There are four guest rooms, all with private baths. Owner/operator Cher Jenkins will attend to your every need, so kick back and enjoy the luxury. The ample breakfast, prepared and served by Cher and fiance Gus Karas, keeps pace with the other amenities.

Crest Motel
2 miles east of downtown,
on Highway 30,
(503) 325-3141
5366 Leif Erikson Drive,
Astoria, OR 97103
Moderate; AE, DC, MC, V

Small and tidy, this well-maintained motel perches on a bluff overlooking the Columbia River. In the large back yard, guests may recline in lawn chairs and enjoy a bird's-eye view of the international shipping traffic, or unwind in a gazebo-enclosed whirlpool. The motel's original 36 rooms come equipped with coffeepots; some have views. The 10 new nonsmoking rooms all face the river.

GEARHART

Gearhart should win the prize for having the most examples of "Oregon Coast" architecture on the shore, with large, weathered-wood homes in shades of gray and white. Fashionable Portlanders first put their summer cottages here—some of which are substantial dwellings—when the coast was "discovered." Unlike other coastal towns, Gearhart is mostly residential. Razor-clam digging is popular here, and many gas stations rent shovels. The wide beach is backed by lovely dunes.

Gearhart Golf Course, opened in 1892, is the second-oldest course in the West—a 6,089-yard layout with sandy soil that dries quickly; open to the public, (503) 738-5248.

RESTAURANTS

Pacific Way Bakery and Cafe

Corner of Cottage and Pacific downtown,
(503) 738-0245
601 Pacific Way,
Gearhart
Moderate; beer and wine;
MC, V
Breakfast, lunch, dinner
Wed-Sun

★

There are two kinds of bakery treats: the cloyingly sweet ones and the scrumptious, wholesomely concocted kind that you can't stop eating. The Pacific Way deals solely in the latter—purveying breads, croissants, sandwiches, pizza, and tons of nectarous delights to an odd mix of suspender-and-clam-shovel locals and Bass-Weejuns-and-Patagonia "gearheads" (the BMW and summer-beach-front-home crowd). The cinnamon rolls, French apple turnovers, pecan buns, cheesecake, and other mouth-watering concoctions aren't the only worthwhile fare. At press time the dinner menu was being revamped, but we can recommend as solid lunch choices the good Oregon shrimp sandwich served on a croissant, and the Greek sandwich with salami, olives, feta, and mozzarella on French bread.

The year-old Pacific Way is airy and impeccably clean, with hardwood floors, lots of windows, white wooden walls, minimalist service but hip waiters, cool sounds, and hot espresso.

SEASIDE

One hundred years ago, affluent Portland beachgoers rode Columbia River steamers to Astoria, then hopped a stagecoach to Seaside, the Oregon Coast's first resort town. Seemingly, the place has become more crowded every year. Destination resort hotels, shops, and tourist amenities of all sorts are springing up at a rapid pace. The crowds mill along Broadway, eyeing the entertainment parlors, the taffy concession, and the bumper cars, then emerge at the Prom, the two-mile-long cement "boardwalk" that's ideal for strolling.

Fishing. Surf fishing is popular here. Your best bet lies at the south end of town in the cove area (also frequented by surfers). Steelhead and salmon are taken only from the Necanicum River, which flows through town. Seaside has good razor-clam beaches.

Hiking. The trailhead for the six-mile hike over Tillamook Head is at the end of Sunset Boulevard at the town's south end. The spectacular and rugged trail ends at Indian Beach in Ecola State Park near Cannon Beach.

Art. The Weary Fox Gallery in Sand Dollar Square on Broadway, (503) 738-3363, features Northwest arts and crafts.

RESTAURANTS

Dooger's

Broadway and Franklin,
(503) 738-3773
505 Broadway, Seaside
Moderate; beer and wine;
MC, V
Lunch, dinner every day

Okay, so you're determined to have clam chowder and maybe some razor clams while in Seaside. Get in line. This is the best stop in town for clam chowder, sandwiches, or quick seafood dinners. Stick with the simpler offerings and avoid anything that didn't come from Northwest waters. Order a microbrewery libation to round out your meal. Dooger's recently opened a second restaurant in Cannon Beach, 1371 S Hemlock, (503) 436-2225. Both establishments are nonsmoking.

LODGINGS

The Boarding House

N Holladay and 3rd,
(503) 738-9055
208 N Holladay Drive,
Seaside, OR 97138
Moderate; MC, V

As its name implies, this circa-1898 Victorian retains many of the features of a traditional boarding house: fir tongue-and-groove walls, beamed ceilings, and paneling. The location fronts busy Holladay Drive in Seaside, but the back yard slopes gently down to the shores of the Necanicum. Every room has a private bath, TV, and a beachy feeling. There's also a miniature Victorian cottage with one bedroom, living quarters, fully equipped kitchen, and a loft with a river view that, at $85, is a good deal for families.

Gaston's Beachside Bed & Breakfast

Avenue I and the Prom,
(503) 738-8320
921 S Prom, Seaside,
OR 97138
Inexpensive; checks ok

This place falls into the "great deal" category. Consider the location on Seaside's Prom. Okay, so there are only two rooms, but the place sports panoramic ocean views and direct access to one of Seaside's less crowded stretches of beach. Proprietor Helen Gaston sets a mean breakfast table that might include interesting egg dishes or waffles, fresh fruits, and various baked goodies. Although guests share a bath, rates run only $40 to $50, and children are welcome. If you've a family or just want more privacy, rent both rooms for only $65.

Gilbert Inn B&B

Beach Drive and Avenue
A, (503) 738-9770
341 Beach Drive, Seaside,
OR 97138
Moderate; MC, V

The only Queen Anne–style Victorian in Seaside, the popular Gilbert Inn is currently doubling its five-guest-room capacity. The original building dates to 1880, and we hope the new addition (scheduled for summer '89 completion) and the new owners (formerly of the Boarding House) will be true to its Victorian heritage. For now, ask for one of the light, cheery turret rooms, located on the original structure's second floor. Private baths and full breakfasts are standard, but color TVs seem out of character with the turn-of-the-century architecture. The beach is only a block away.

Riverside Inn B&B

1½ blocks south of
Broadway at S Holladay,
(503) 738-8254

The total package is more like a lodge than an intimate B&B. This comfortable lodging combines an inn-with-cottages and a recently built annex, totaling 11 guest accommodations. The setting along Seaside's Necanicum

*430 S Holladay Drive,
Seaside, OR 97138
Moderate; MC, V*

River is removed from the main-street action but also is a good walk from the beach. Each unit, furnished with country flavor, includes TV and private bath; some have kitchens. Fruit, juices, and baked goods are put out for breakfast nibbles. Rates are reasonable, with off-season cottages as low as $35. Located nearby, just a half-block from the beach, is another cottage that accommodates up to five, with kitchen, Franklin stove in the living room, washer-dryer in the basement, and barbecue out back.

Shilo Inn

*N Prom and Broadway,
(503) 738-9571, toll-free
(800) 222-2244
30 N Prom, Seaside, OR
97138
Expensive; AE, DC,
MC, V*

We're wary of glitzy establishments that hog the shore, but this one has a good and well-deserved reputation. The setting is excellent, on the beach at Broadway in downtown Seaside. The public areas (lobby and restaurant) are upbeat and stylish, and all the usual amenities expected in a full-service resort hotel are here: indoor swimming pool, steam room, sauna, workout room, and therapy pool. Choicest rooms are the ones on the west side, with fireplaces, full kitchens, and private patios; they're priced accordingly.

The Shilo frequently hosts conventions, but it does offer ample covered parking. The on-premises restaurant is overpriced and mediocre.

CANNON BEACH

Cannon Beach is the Carmel of the Northwest, an arts community with a hip ambience and strict building codes that prohibit neon and ensure that only aesthetically pleasing structures of weathered cedar and assorted wood products are built here.

Still, the town is tourist-oriented, and during the summer it explodes with visitors who come to browse through its galleries and crafts shops or rub shoulders with coastal intelligentsia on crowded Hemlock Street. Its main draw is the spectacular beach—wide, inviting, and among the prettiest anywhere.

Haystack Rock, one of the world's largest coastal monoliths, dominates the long, sandy stretch. It's impressive enough just to gaze at, but check it out at low tide and observe the rich marine life in the tidal pools.

Ecola State Park (on the town's north side) has fine overlooks, picnic tables, and good hiking trails. If you hike to Tillamook Head, you can see the Tillamook Rock Light Station, a lighthouse built offshore under severe conditions more than 100 years ago and abandoned in 1957. Today it is a columbarium (a facility where cremated remains are stored) called "Eternity at Sea." No camping along the trail, except for summer campsites atop the Head.

Haystack Program in the Arts, (503) 464-4812, offered through Portland State University, conducts arts workshops.

Coaster Theater hosts good summer plays, as well as local and out-of-town shows in the winter; 108 N Hemlock, (503) 436-1242.

Galleries abound in the area, all on Hemlock, the main drag. Two especially good ones are the White Bird, which has a range of arts and crafts, (503) 436-2681, and the Haystack Gallery, with photography too, (503) 436-2547.

Other shops of interest, also on Hemlock, include Once Upon a Breeze, a kite store at the north end of town, (503) 436-1112; Osburn's Ice Creamery & Deli, with excellent picnic and take-out supplies and ice cream, (503) 436-2234; Cannon Beach Baker, with one of the few remaining brick oil-fired hearth ovens on the West Coast, supplying a good assortment of breads, cookies, and pastries, (503) 436-2592; Cannon Beach Book Company, with a surprisingly extensive selection and an owner who lets customers browse indefinitely, (503) 436-1301; and El Mundo Ltd. Clothing for Women and El Mundo Ltd. for Men, with natural-fiber clothing in chic, youthful styles, (503) 436-1572 (women's), (503) 436-1002 (men's).

RESTAURANTS

Cafe de la Mer
*Hemlock and Dawes in
Haystack Square,
(503) 436-1179
1287 S Hemlock Street,
Cannon Beach
Expensive; beer and wine;
AE, MC, V
Dinner Wed-Sun
(summer; varies in winter)*

★ ★ ★

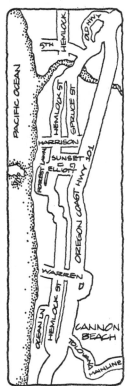

In step with Cannon Beach's changing times (bear in mind this was originally a logging town) the upscale Cafe de la Mer has won a considerable following among Valley visitors and the moneyed old guard with vacation homes in Tolovana Park and Gearhart. Husband-and-wife owners Ron Schiffman and Pat Noonan have seen the handwriting in the sand and transformed a post-'60s coffeehouse into one of the beach's best eating establishments. An open kitchen divides 15 or so tables into two dining areas—a glassed-in patio and a homey wood-paneled room. Patrons receive pampered but purposeful service. Even in the '90s, you don't expect to find a place this fine along the Oregon coastline.

There's a price to pay for all this attention. A la carte dinners, with entrees ranging from bouillabaisse to veal, cost $15 to $20, and portions have been small. Soup or salad will set you back an extra $2.50 to $3.50. An extensive wine list with a formidable French section is also expensive. A bottle of Northwest pinot noir that went for $10 less down the street cost $30. Along with these prices, be prepared for an evening tainted by a subtle but refined Cannon Beach hauteur that may either amuse or offend you.

Nevertheless, the food is glorious. A hearty bowl of country mushroom soup smelled like an Oregon coast autumn forest and tasted as earthy as fresh-picked chanterelles. The bouillabaisse contained a lusty mix of Dungeness crab, salmon, and whitefish chunks in an excellent bread-dipping broth: flavorful and not overdone. Tender slices of veal were served with a copious quantity of melted blue cheese (but there could have been more veal). An accompanying wild brown rice mixture was a robust contrast to the melt-in-your-mouth morsels. The kitchen exhibits inspired artistry with specials such as seafood pasta "moutarde" and oysters in fish-shaped puff pastry with tarragon sauce. Desserts extend dinner's caloric count into the stratosphere.

The Bistro

*In downtown Cannon
Beach opposite Spruce,
(503) 436-2661
263 N Hemlock Street,
Cannon Beach
Expensive; full bar;
MC, V
Lunch Sat-Sun, dinner
Thurs-Tues*

Cannon Beach native Matt Dueber's The Bistro has all the quaintness of an inn on the coast of Brittany. Of course, the patrons here speak Cannon Beach chic instead of French, and the cuisine is best described as Northwest eclectic. Matt, a recent California Culinary Institute graduate, has worked hard to provide patrons with a worthwhile alternative to run-of-the-mill beach restaurants.

The intimate interior has a dozen closely spaced tables with an adjacent cozy bar. Soft chamber music, flower boxes and an herb garden out back set a quaint country-inn mood, but a full house can make this place noisy. In step with the times, the Bistro is a nonsmoking establishment, except for the bar.

Dinners are imaginatively prepared and usually involve four courses: an appetizer plate of lightly dressed veggies with cheese and meat; a choice of soup, including a hearty Hungarian mushroom; a well-dressed salad; and an entree that might be prawns on a bed of rice with herbs and chopped carrots (a spicy Cajun sauce was too peppery for most palates) or a healthy number of oysters sauteed in butter and lemon. (The latter won't challenge The Ark's, in Nahcotta, Washington, for best in the universe, but are nevertheless wonderful.) The chocolate peanut-butter pie is a heavenly after-treat.

Service can be spotty. On our last visit, the maitre d' and bartender was the person most in tune with our needs, while the waitresses were sometimes out in left field. But everyone tries to please, and Matt frequently visits tables to ensure that his guests are satisfied. The Bistro is getting better all the time, on its way to perhaps three-stardom and the top echelon of Oregon Coast restaurants.

The Brass Lantern

*Hemlock and Gower,
(503) 436-2412
1116 S Hemlock Street,
Cannon Beach
Moderate; beer and wine;
cash only
Dinner Tues-Sat
(summers); Thurs-Sat
(winters)*

Don't let the Brass Lantern's average-Americana interior fool you; the food here is exotic and the preparation daring. A limited menu offers a culinary grand tour, with selections from Italy, North Africa, the Middle East, as well as the Northwest.

Iranian owner/chef Reza Kamali keeps diners enthusiastic and dinners enticing with a rotating specials board that might include North Coast razor clams, scampi, and intriguing lamb preparations such as shashlik and rice—lamb marinated in olive oil, dill, and curry and broiled on a skewer. Omelets, of all things, occasionally appear on the menu, including a rarely seen eggplant.

Scallops, fresh and plump, arrive simmering in a subtle herb-and-wine sauce. A lightly breaded and sizeable Oregon snapper fillet is quickly pan-fried and served moist and fresh. A large number of unbreaded and sauteed oysters did minimum time on the stove. Vegetables such as mushrooms, artichokes, broccoli, and zucchini accompany the entrees and are prettied with sauces. An Arab-style rice mixture with mushrooms, raisins, cinnamon, ginger, red peppers, and a potpourri of varying ingredients rounds out almost every meal. Desserts are scrumptious—try the strawberry pie, with a light custard filling and a round of fresh berries.

Lazy Susan Cafe
Hemlock and 1st,
(503) 436-2816
126 N Hemlock Street,
Cannon Beach
Moderate; beer and wine;
checks ok
Breakfast, lunch every
day; dinner summer only
(call for hours)

Everyone in town seems to gather at this airy, sunny, double-decker restaurant in a courtyard opposite the Coaster Theater. The nonsmoking interior is bright with natural wood, plants hanging from the balcony, and local art on the walls. Very Oregon. Definitely Cannon Beach.

Breakfast is the best time here, when you can order omelets, oatmeal, waffles topped with fresh fruit and yogurt, and excellent coffee to prolong your stay. Eggs are correctly cooked, and fresh home fries make a nice accompaniment. Lunch includes quiche and some interesting specials. Expect long waits on sunny weekends.

LODGINGS

Surfview Resort
Hemlock and Sunset,
(503) 436-1566,
(800) 345-5676
1400 S Hemlock Street,
Mail: PO Box 547,
Cannon Beach,
OR 97110
Expensive; AE, DC,
MC, V

The proximity to Haystack Rock and the expansive, sandy beach at this three-level, cedar-shake motel is outstanding, and the view from the deck rooms presents a Canada-to-Mexico horizon. The large structure has been designed and decorated in a more luxurious style than most Oregon Coast destinations, but reports of uneven service suggest that the Surfview has developed some of the liabilities that seem to go with size.

The 129 rooms are tastefully decorated and all have refrigerators; many have fireplaces and kitchens. *The Oregonian* is delivered to each room every morning. Beds are comfortable, and a supply of firewood is provided. Other amenities include a sunny, greenhouselike enclosure with indoor heated pool, hot tubs, and sauna. There are even a weight room for workout advocates and a kiddie pool for the little ones.

**Tern Inn Bed
and Breakfast**
Hemlock (the Beach
Loop), (503) 436-1528
3663 S Hemlock Street,
Mail: PO Box 952,
Cannon Beach, OR
97110
Moderate; checks ok

A small, two-room B&B, Tern Inn sits on a rise two blocks from the beach and well away from Cannon Beach's tourist congestion. The spacious rooms, both with private baths, are for the most part tastefully and comfortably appointed. One is actually two rooms (with a glassed-in sun room); the other has a fireplace. Queen-size beds with down comforters help to capture the home-away-from-home feeling. The full breakfast features European-style breads, pastries, and meat or veggie casseroles.

If you've found a place that you think is a Best Place, send in the report form at the back of this book. If you're unhappy with one of the places, please let us know why. We depend on reader input.

TOLOVANA PARK

Nestled on Cannon Beach's south side, Tolovana Park is more laid back, less crowded. Leave your vehicle at the **Tolovana Park Wayside** (with parking and restrooms) and stroll an uncluttered beach, especially in the off-season. At low tide you can walk all the way to Arch Cape, some five miles south. (Be careful; the incoming tide might block your return.) **Hane's Bakery**, 3116 S Hemlock, sells myriad varieties of muffins, cheesecakes, French bread, and croissants; (503) 436-1719.

LODGINGS

Sea Sprite Motel
*Nebesna and Ocean
Front, (503) 436-2266
Mail: PO Box 66,
Tolovana Park, OR 97145
Moderate; MC, V*
★

Tidy and cute, this ocean-front motel has six small units on the beach, each with a color TV and kitchen and most with fireplaces. The location is quiet and private. Owner Stephen Tuckman also owns the Hearthstone Inn in Cannon Beach, worth asking about if the Sea Sprite is full.

MANZANITA

Resting mostly on a sandy peninsula with undulating dunes covered in beach grass, shore pine, and Scotch broom, Manzanita is a lazy community gaining popularity as a second home for well-to-do Portlanders. The attractions are obvious: the adjacent Nehalem Bay area is fast becoming a windsurfing mecca; **Nehalem Bay State Park**, just south of town, offers hiking and bike trails, as well as miles of little-used beaches; and overlooking it all, nearby Neahkahnie Mountain, with a steep, switchbacked trail leading to the 1,600-foot summit, boasts the best viewpoints on Oregon's north coast.

Oswald State Park, just north of town, has one of the finest camping grounds on any coast in the world. You walk a half mile from the parking lot to tent sites among old-growth trees; the ocean, with a massive cove and tidepools, is a short walk further on. No reservations, but the walk deters the crowds who would otherwise come; call (503) 238-7488 for advance word on availability.

RESTAURANTS

Blue Sky Cafe
*1 block from the beach at
Laneda and 2nd,
(503) 368-5712
154 Laneda Avenue,
Manzanita
Moderate; beer and wine;
MC, V
Breakfast, lunch Fri-Tues;
dinner Fri-Tues (summer),
Fri-Sun (winter)*

Old-timers in these parts still speculate about the legendary loot supposedly buried on nearby Neahkahnie Mountain by the survivors of a wrecked 17th-century Spanish galleon. You're not likely to uncover any of this treasure, but if you look hard enough in downtown Manzanita, you'll discover an array of gourmet riches inside the Blue Sky Cafe.

A block and a half off the beach, the two-year-old Blue Sky is an unglitzy restaurant that offers no outward clues to the culinary excitement within. Two separate rooms make up the dining area, about a dozen tables in all and each with salt and pepper shakers sporting a different plant or animal motif. The atmosphere is akin to a hippie cafe turned upscale, but without the pretensions or stratospheric prices. Let the witty, knowledgeable, and off-the-wall Bob Bersan and his wife, Julie, advise you about the wine list, explain the origin of the fresh fish, and maybe reveal the recipe for the scrumptious brown bread.

Appetizers include steamer clams, crab cocktails, and a couple of oyster choices, all artfully prepared. Soup might be a cream of carrot—more a nectarlike porridge than a soup, and a good excuse to partake of yet another piece of brown bread. The entrees are hearty, as evidenced by the seafood stir-fry, a collection of mid-sized shrimp, tender bay scallops, and bits of whitefish in a vegetable medley on a bed of brown rice. The seafood fettuccine includes shellfish mingled with wide, perfectly cooked egg noodles covered with a thick, cheesy, but not overpowering sauce. Pesto prawns are large, succulent crustaceans with a light touch of basil and garlic. Meateaters can partake of two beef selections and a couple of chicken dishes. Generous portions leave little room for dessert. You might be able to do without the potato cheesecake, but good luck passing up the chocolate-peanut-butter-fudge pie or the mocha ice cream. Willy Wonka never had it so good.

Creative Catering & Deli
Manzanita Road and US Highway 101,
(503) 368-5595
630 Manzanita Road, Manzanita
Inexpensive; no alcohol; checks ok
Lunch, dinner every day

Ever been driving along remote stretches of the north Oregon coast and had a hankering for a tasty take-out pizza? Used to be you had to look a long ways—sometimes as far as Portland. Now you need search no further than Manzanita and Fawn de Turk's handcrafted pies, featuring a zesty sauce, gobs of mozzarella cheese, and a light and doughy crust. Hefty sandwiches and over-the-counter burritos are reasonably priced. Huge, gooey cinnamon rolls are a weekend specialty. Fawn's own spicy salsa is as good as any we've had.

WHEELER

Two miles south of Nehalem at Wheeler, the Nehalem River widens into an estuary. Although you'd never know it today, Wheeler once was touted as a potential San Francisco of the Northwest. It became a retirement community and a stopover for recreational fishermen and crabbers.

RESTAURANTS

River Sea Inn
Just off Highway 101 at Marine Drive,
(503) 368-5789
380 Marine Drive, Wheeler
Moderate; full bar;

There's a surprising variety of dishes offered at this Nehalem Bay–front restaurant just off Highway 101. Chicken, veal, prime rib, a Mexican combination plate, and Italian fare are just some of the ambitious menu's many choices. The Sunday brunch is a good deal at $4.95; it includes a glass of champagne, a choice of eggs

MC, V
Breakfast, lunch, dinner
every day (summer); hours
vary off-season

prepared several ways (with chopped sirloin or oysters, for example), and homemade muffins. There's even a Chateaubriand for two at $29.95, served on Sunday evenings (or otherwise with a day's advance notice).

ROCKAWAY

RESTAURANTS

Karla's Krabs 'n' Quiche Delight
At the north end of
Rockaway on Highway
101, (503) 355-2362
2010 Highway 101 N,
Rockaway Beach
Moderate; no alcohol;
MC, V
Lunch, dinner Tues-Sun

At 50mph Karla's appears as just another shell-shop/greasy-spoon combo on the northern reaches of the Rockaway strip. Not so. Even the Governor, Neil Goldschmidt, puts on his brakes here. Karla and her partner Amelia dole out good old-fashioned home cooking in as friendly an atmosphere as you're likely to find. No fast-food mediocrity here, just casual quick service.

You'd expect to find the red snapper or halibut fish and chips plopped on a pile of hand-hewn fries and the ample sandwiches in a down-home diner of this sort. But wait; there's also a full seafood dinner menu, with excellent clam chowder and bouillabaisse, oyster stew, and quiche (baked on the premises, of course). A hot sweet potato pie was more than enough for two ($3).

GARIBALDI/BAY CITY

The Tillamook bayfront is one of the seasonal homes for the summer salmon fleet. If you don't mind wading through an RV park, greasy-spoon restaurants, and tacky surroundings, there are several Garibaldi establishments that sell the area's freshest seafood, including salmon, shrimp, sole, bottom fish, and crab. **Miller Seafood** on Highway 101 is the easiest to find. Fresh salmon, ling cod, and bottom fish are featured; (503) 322-0355. **Smith's Pacific Shrimp Co.** sells fine shrimp at 608 Commercial Street; (503) 322-3316. **Hayes Oysters** is the best place to buy oysters (check whether the rare and wondrous Kumamoto oysters are available); on Highway 101 in Bay City; (503) 377-2210.

RESTAURANTS

Downie's Cafe
5th & C, (503) 377-2220
9230 Fifth Street,
Bay City
Inexpensive; no alcohol;
local checks only
Breakfast, lunch, dinner
every day

Downie's is right off the set of the '60s television show *Mayberry R.F.D.*, so don't be surprised if Andy Griffith strolls in during your meal and sits in the booth behind you. Clean, tidy, unpretentious, and small (one lit cigarette would fill the room), Downie's offers down-home service and food, specializing in fresh fish from nearby Tillamook Bay and ocean waters. Formica tabletops with plastic booths and a tiny counter offer seating for 25 or so. Clam chowder is a can't-miss: a rich, creamy potion of potatoes, celery, and thick chunks—not bits—of clams. Although the toasted bread and hand-hewn chips are greasy, the fish (lingcod), fried in light batter, is not. Avoid the bland coleslaw.

TILLAMOOK

Tillamook is dairy country par excellence, where cows are more likely to hold a convention than people. On the north end of town along US Highway 101 sits the home of Tillamook cheese, the **Tillamook County Creamery Association**. Inside the creamery (under expansion at press time), a self-guided tour offers only a glimpse of the cheese-making process, along with minuscule cheese samples, schlocky tourist trappings, overpriced Tillamook cheese, and too many tourists; (503) 842-4481.

Instead, about one mile south on 101 is the **Blue Heron French Cheese Factory**. Blue Heron is less kitschy and better stocked than the Tillamook Creamery and offers a variety of cheeses, including a made-on-the-premises Brie. The establishment also has a Knudsen Erath wine-tasting room, where visitors may sip the Oregon-made wine; (503) 842-8281.

Pioneer Museum occupies three floors of the 1905 county courthouse. Displays recreate the pioneer past and document wildlife; Second and Pacific, (503) 842-4553.

Clamming is very good at Netarts Bay, west of Tillamook.

RESTAURANTS

La Casa Medello
North end of Tillamook on Highway 101,
(503) 842-5768
1160 Highway 101 N,
Tillamook
Inexpensive; full bar;
MC, V
Lunch, dinner every day

Along the Oregon Coast, good Mexican restaurants are as rare as 90-degree days. La Casa Medello won't make you forget south-of-the-border cooking, but it's worth a look. The restaurant is situated in an old house with a homey atmosphere: wooden floors, spacious dining area, fireplace—even a giant succulent. A large menu features standard Cal-Mex choices, but they're reasonably priced and hearty and they taste, well, maybe like San Diego. Dinners are served with beans, rice, and the requisite chips and salsa. "Hot" is pretty darn hot.

LODGINGS

Whiskey Creek B&B
Follow signs toward Cape Lookout State Park,
(503) 842-2408
7500 Whiskey Creek Road, Tillamook,
OR 97141
Moderate; checks ok

Want to really get away? On the outskirts of the Netarts/Oceanside environs, on a little cove in Netarts Bay in the lee of Cape Lookout, sits Whiskey Creek B&B. Sea birds will likely be your only bayfront visitors as you enjoy the view at one of the nation's most pristine estuaries. There are only two rooms: the larger downstairs room includes a kitchen and living quarters ($65); the upstairs accommodations ($55) are pretty austere.

OCEANSIDE

Eight miles west of Tillamook, Oceanside is part of 22-mile **Three Capes scenic drive**, one of Oregon's—and perhaps the world's—most beautiful stretches of coastline. The narrow, winding road skirts the outline of Tillamook Bay, climbs over Cape Meares, traverses the shores of Netarts Bay, and runs over Cape Lookout, the westernmost headland on the north Oregon coast. The trail from the parking lot at the cape's summit meanders through primeval forests of stately cedar and Sitka spruce. Spectacular ocean vistas fill the lower side of the drive. Back at sea level, the desertlike landscape of sandy dunes presents a stark contrast to Cape Lookout's densely forested slopes. The road to Pacific City and the route's third cape, Kiwanda, runs through lush, green dairy country.

RESTAURANTS

Roseanna's
On the west side
of Highway 131,
(503) 842-7351
1440 Pacific, Oceanside
Moderate; beer and wine;
MC, V
Breakfast, lunch, dinner
every day; closed Mondays
in winter

The gradual evolution of Roseanna's from grocery-store-with-sandwiches to mellow, upscale cafe continues, and the menu is increasingly ambitious. The ambience is pleasant and laid back, with George Winston on the turntable by day and an aspiring musician plunking the establishment's piano at night. Service is up and down.

The clientele appear happy to have discovered this small culinary treasure. Seafood dinners dominate the menu of well-prepared and generally satisfying meals. The restaurant offers a nice selection of home-baked desserts, including the Toll House pie topped with Tillamook ice cream—an outstanding choice.

LODGINGS

Three Capes
Bed and Breakfast
10 miles west of
Tillamook on Maxwell
Mountain Road,
(503) 842-6126
1685 Maxwell Mountain
Road, Oceanside,
OR 97134
Moderate; checks ok

The two guest rooms in this contemporary hillside house overlook the ocean and have private entrances, private baths with claw-footed tubs, and period furnishings. Breakfast, served upstairs in the dining room or out on the deck (from which the views are truly spectacular), is continental during the week, with an entree—perhaps a shrimp-and-scallop souffle—added on weekends.

House on the Hill
Maxwell Mountain Road,
Maxwell Point,
(503) 842-6030
Mail: PO Box 187,
Oceanside, OR 97134
Moderate; MC, V

Three two-story buildings, each containing five units, make up this clean, beachy, out-of-the-way outpost. The setting is gorgeous, overlooking Three Arch Rocks and the blue Pacific, but the trapezoidal architecture is unusual at best. Inside, furnishings are tacky—orange Naugahyde, Formica, and plastic—and awkwardly arranged. Outside, wooden walls block much of the lovely view. Choose a unit with a kitchen and stock up with groceries from Tillamook or Garibaldi, since local pickings are rather slim.

PACIFIC CITY

The fleet comes home to Pacific City, where salmon-fishing boats are launched from trailers in the south lee of Cape Kiwanda. This town is lately known for another kind of fleet: hang gliders, which swoop off the slopes of the cape and land on the sandy expanses below. The region's second Haystack Rock (Cannon Beach has the other) sits a half mile offshore. Even if you've never visited before, this area may look familiar: nationally acclaimed Oregon photographer Ray Atkeson has made Cape Kiwanda the most-photographed spot on the Oregon coast. **Robert Straub State Park**, worth visiting, sits at the south end of town and occupies most of the Nestuca beach sandspit.

RESTAURANTS

Riverhouse Restaurant
¼ mile north of the stoplight on Brouten,
(503) 965-6722
34450 Brouten Road,
Pacific City
Moderate; full bar;
MC, V
Lunch, dinner every day
(Wed-Sun in winter)

You might see a great blue heron perched on a log on the Nestuca River, which flows idly to the sea right outside the window. The Riverhouse is a cozy, calming stop, three miles off 101 in the little town of Pacific City, and many people go far out of their way to come here. It's small—11 tables—with hanging plants and a piano in the corner for the local folk musicians who perform here on weekends. Everything's homemade: soup might be a chunky fresh vegetable or French onion. Salads with creamy dressings and deluxe hamburgers are consistently good. Try the apple pie with cinnamon sauce for dessert; this is an apple-pie sort of place.

CLOVERDALE

LODGINGS

Hudson House
Bed & Breakfast
2½ miles south of
Cloverdale,
(503) 392-3533
37700 Highway 101 S,
Cloverdale, OR 97112
Moderate; MC, V

Perched on a bluff in the middle of nowhere is the historic Hudson House, built in 1906. Staying here evokes memories of a country weekend at Grandma's house, and the Case family reinforces a warm, friendly atmosphere. The downstairs parlor features an elegant divan and an upright piano. Up the antique staircase are three (soon to be four) sleeping rooms, simply appointed in early-century country style with a few choice hardwood furnishings. But ahhh, the beds. With imposing headboards of brass and wood, and covered with luxurious quilts, these beds surely kept Grandpa and Grandma Hudson comfortable through the years. Bedroom windows reveal a pastoral scene of Holsteins and Herefords grazing contentedly across the road. The farmhouse kitchen downstairs produces morning meals of fresh eggs, home-baked breads or biscuits, and heaping bowls of fruit.

NESKOWIN

LODGINGS

The Chelan
Breakers Blvd,
off Salem Blvd,
(503) 392-3270

An attractive, substantial, cream-colored adobe structure houses nine condominium units, all with lovely ocean views. Each unit has two bedrooms, a well-equipped kitch-

48750 Breakers Blvd,
Mail: PO Box 732,
Neskowin, OR 97149
Moderate; MC, V

Pacific Sands
Breakers Blvd and Amity,
(503) 392-3101
48250 Breakers Blvd,
Mail: PO Box 356,
Neskowin, OR 97149
Moderate; MC, V

en, and a big living room with a picture window and a large brick fireplace. Ground-floor units have a double doorway leading out to the small back yard; upstairs accommodations have private balconies. The front lawn and gardens are most inviting; in fact, the whole place has a cared-for, welcoming look.

This small, well-maintained resort motel with an average, bland exterior and spacious rooms enjoys a spectacular setting—literally a stone's throw from breaking waves. The preferred rooms occupy the beach side. Some have fireplaces, and all, unfortunately, have tacky furnishings. But that's a small price to pay for an ideal getaway spot with miles of sandy beach just outside your door and primitive Cascade Head just a short distance to the south. Considering the location, it's a good deal. Pets okay with a deposit.

OTIS
RESTAURANTS

Otis Cafe
Otis Junction,
(503) 994-2813
Highway 18, Otis
Inexpensive; beer and
wine; checks ok
Breakfast, lunch every
day; dinner Thurs-Sun

The Otis Cafe does all the things small-town cafes all over America used to do—only better. Even the prices are a bit old-fashioned. Proprietors Gale and Jim Powers cook up beefy burgers, soups, and complete breakfasts. Dinner specials are also available. Try the huge malts and milk shakes, wonderful throwbacks to soda fountain days and a deal for under $2—still. As a concession to our times, a small selection of wines is available, including a featured white each week. Baked items are surprisingly good and available to go. The black bread is simply delicious. Rumor has it that a *New York Times* restaurant critic recently visited and went gaga over the pie selections.

LINCOLN CITY

Picture the Oregon Coast without any land-use planning laws. It would be only slightly worse than the 10 miles of strip development collectively known as Lincoln City. With a few notable exceptions, Lincoln City offers little in the way of outstanding lodgings or restaurants, and if you're coming to the coast to escape the rat race, beware the congested stretch of Highway 101 between Lincoln City and Newport during the summer.

Lacey's Doll and Antique Museum displays more than 4,000 dolls, some of them very old, plus some antiques and curios; daily, 3400 NE Highway 101; (503) 994-2392.

Barnacle Bill's seafood store is famous for smoked fish: salmon, sturgeon, albacore tuna, and black cod. It also sells fresh seafood; 2174 NE Highway 101, (503) 994-3022.

Cascade Head, three miles north of Lincoln City, is a tall promontory of rain forests, meadows, and rocky cliffs, reachable only on foot. **The Sitka Center for**

Art and Ecology operates here and offers summer classes on many subjects, plus numerous concerts, talks, and exhibits. It's well worth checking; (503) 994-5485.

Mossy Creek Pottery in Kernville, just south of Lincoln City, sells some of the best high-fired stoneware and porcelain made by local artists; (503) 996-2415.

Catch the Wind Kite Shop is the headquarters of a successful coast kite manufacturing and sales company, with outlets along the Oregon coast from Seaside to Florence. The operators often fly some of their more spectacular designs, weather permitting, at the D River beach wayside, across the highway from the shop, and at Agate Bay, north of Newport; Highway 101; (503) 994-9500.

RESTAURANTS

Bay House
¼ mile south of Lincoln City, (503) 996-3222
5911 SW Highway 101, Lincoln City
Expensive; full bar;
MC, V
Dinner Wed-Sun

Just out of reach of the glitzy tourist trade, on the banks of Siletz Bay, you'll find the Bay House. Inside, virtually every table possesses a splendid view of the bay's shores, covered with old-growth driftwood logs bleached by 80 years of sun and salt water. Imaginative local art graces the walls.

You share the riches, though, for the award-winning Bay House gets crowded and, at times, a bit noisy. We've become familiar with the menagerie of distractions in the well-thought-out waiting room: a bowl of walnuts and filberts, a cappuccino maker, and a phone. Go ahead, call—you're here for the night.

Once seated at your table, you'll want to take your time. The food is sublime and the service well paced and professional. We've enjoyed many delectable offerings here in the past couple of years. And so far, we're confident that chef Jean Kovacki (in training the night we visited) will carry on the delectable traditions of now-departed chef Barbara Lowry. Soup one night was French onion with tiny shrimp. The overall effect was deliciously mellow and creamy, with a hint of sweetness. The tangy raspberry vinaigrette salad dressing made a mix of assorted greens come alive. Prawns Santa Fe—as sweet a shellfish as the Gulf Coast has to offer—were prepared in a spicy, tomato- and cumin-based sauce and served with black beans. A generous portion of correctly cooked razor clams—a rarity even on the coast that spawns them—was matched with crunchy baby asparagus spears and boiled red potatoes. Lowry's crab cannelloni was a mixture of crab, spinach, and cheeses wrapped in a thin crepe and baked in a mild, creamy sauce. The changing menu might also feature Winchester Bay oysters, Oregon lamb, a pasta special—fettuccine with escargots, on one occasion—duckling, chicken, and a couple of beef choices. Desserts are equally excellent, particularly a spectacular lemon-almond cheesecake.

Time your reservations with sunset and experience the Siletz Bay's daily dusk light show—like the food, a treat worth savoring.

Road's End Dory Cafe

Next to the State Park,
(503) 994-5180
Locan Road, one mile off
US Highway 101,
Lincoln City
Inexpensive; beer and
wine; MC, V
Lunch, dinner every day

Very popular with the locals; a covered walkway is proof that appreciative throngs stand in line rain or shine for hamburgers (including a half-pound monster), clam chowder, grilled fish, homemade cream pies, and carrot cake. It's near the Road's End Wayside State Park, a good clamming beach.

GLENEDEN BEACH
RESTAURANTS

Chez Jeannette

¼ mile south of Salishan
Lodge, (503) 764-3434
7150 Old Highway 101,
Gleneden Beach
Expensive; beer and wine;
MC, V
Dinner Tues-Sun (closed
Sun in winter)

Flower boxes by the windows and whitewashed brick walls in an intimate, woodsy setting, with trees pressed right up to the building, give this restaurant the appearance of a French country inn. As at Salishan, just half a mile away, the clientele is upscale, yet the ambience here is noticeably less formal. Two fireplaces, usually blazing away in the cooler months, add to the coziness.

The working owners—Larry is the maitre d' and Joan, formerly of Salishan, the head waitress—make sure that no detail is overlooked. Chef Randy Tobias uses the Northwest's finest ingredients in his French provincial offerings, which are skillfully prepared in sometimes unorthodox but always innovative ways. Each course will challenge your senses but never your sensibilities.

For example, soup one night was a cream of potato with tiny shrimp—smooth and sumptuous, with a soft-crusted French bread the perfect accompaniment. Another time, bay shrimp highlighted a vegetable curry soup. A salad with greens, artichoke hearts, olives, radishes, and pear slices, topped with a sprightly Dijon vinaigrette, tingled the imagination as well as the taste buds. Fish entrees might include salmon, halibut, or sea bass with a shrimp-and-caper cream sauce (the last a dish not recommended for cholesterol-counters). Veal, pork, lamb, and chicken are always on the menu, but carnivorous overachievers should opt for the carpetbagger steak, stuffed with Yaquina Bay oysters, wrapped in bacon and served with a sauce of creme fraiche, bacon, spinach, and scallions. Accompanying vegetables might be carrots and mangoes, cabbage with walnuts and onions, or creamy sauteed eggplant.

LODGINGS

Salishan Lodge

Highway 101, Gleneden
Beach, (503) 764-2371,

This world-famous resort is the dream of Portland industrialist John Gray, who engineered a resort as posh as it is respectful of the Oregon landscape. Buildings are

*toll-free (800) 547-6500
(outside Oregon)
Mail: PO Box 118,
Gleneden Beach,
OR 97388
Expensive; full bar;
AE, DC, MC, V
Dinner every day*

scattered far enough apart not to harm the delicate ecology; they are low-lying and faced with local wood, so that they seem to retreat into the landscape; the placement of rocks and trees and covered walkways exhibits an almost Japanese sensitivity. You stay in eightplex units, spread around the lush fairways of the lovely Fred Federspiel-designed golf course. Because distances inside the resort are considerable, you should specify your desired locale: Spruce, Fairway, Chieftain House South, and Sunset Suite overlook the golf links; Chieftain House North and the aptly named Tennis House are close to indoor and outdoor courts; best views of Siletz Bay and the Pacific Ocean can be had from Blue Heron and Tide units; Sandpiper is nearest to the children's play area. Rooms are spacious and tastefully furnished but not extravagant, with brick fireplaces, view balconies, splashes of regional art, and individual covered carports. Those designated "Chieftain" are larger, with refrigerators and separate bedrooms. Prices range from $85 for an off-season guest room to $184 for a summer Chieftain; larger parties get better deals.

Here couples slip into the gentle rhythm of the place, partaking of golf on the par-72 course, a game of tennis, or a dip in the indoor pool. You can walk on the nature trails and paved paths looping throughout the 750-acre forest preserve, or fly-fish in the catch-and-release trout pond. The beach, a half mile away, is a splendid strand of driftwood and gulls. Putting the lodge this far away was a bold stroke of ecological wisdom, but it also is the one possible drawback of staying here. Service continues to be some of the most professional on the coast, from the bellman to the reading room in the main lodge, thoughtfully stocked with newspapers and periodicals.

Unfortunately, the food in the main dining room, although good, doesn't maintain the standard of excellence achieved in the rest of the resort. You dine on one of three levels, all within view of large picture windows looking out on the bay. After being seated, you're immediately handed Salishan's highly touted wine list, representing a cellar stocked with almost 20,000 bottles. Wine steward Phil deVito is usually on hand, hobnobbing about the dining room offering good advice and waxing eloquent about his superlative collection—a nice way to help fill the long wait between courses. There's a good selection of hot and cold appetizers, from terrine of seasoned vegetables to Columbia River caviar, from oysters to escargots. Entrees are priced high for the coast ($13 to $22) but have lately expanded, with more seafood and beef selections, along with venison, lamb, and chicken. Preparations sometimes include unorthodox ingredients that don't always work together (asparagus soup with almonds and chicken) or are unassertive, even bland

(paella with dry, almost tasteless prawns and scampi totally overpowered by chunks of chorizo). In this place, at
these prices, you expect the best of what the coast has
to offer. Alas, prepare yourself for some disappointments.

Across Highway 101 and a maze of specialty shops
sits Salishan's other restaurant, the Marketplace. Edibles
here are ordinary, but shop browsing is worthwhile.

DEPOE BAY

Once a charming coastal community, Depoe Bay today is only an extension of Lincoln City's strip development. Driving down Highway 101, it's hard to tell where
one community ends and the other begins. Fortunately, however, some of the original
Depoe Bay, including its tiny harbor, remains intact. During the gray whale migratory season (December through April), the leviathans cruise within hailing distance
of the headlands.

Deep Sea Trollers, located on the sidewalk in front of the Spouting Horn
Restaurant on Highway 101, is one of several operations offering whale-watching
cruises; theirs are an hour long ($7 for adults, less for children); (503) 765-2248.

Depoe Bay Aquarium and Shell Shop has a simulation of an undersea cave,
plus harbor seals in a grotto. The Shell Shop is notable; Highway 101 at Bay Drive;
(503) 765-2259.

Cape Foulweather is reached by the Otter Crest Loop, two miles south of town.
It has an inspiring viewpoint for watching birds, sea lions, and surf. Adjoining is
the **Lookout Gift Shop and Observatory**, a rarity: the gifts are carefully selected
items from craftspeople around the world; (503) 765-2270.

RESTAURANTS

Sea Hag
Highway 101 and Bay,
(503) 765-7901
58 E Highway 101,
Depoe Bay
Moderate; full bar;
AE, MC, V
Breakfast, lunch,
dinner every day

The Sea Hag's the old standby around these parts, and
the staff encourages its fishing-oriented clientele by opening before sunrise. Sack lunches are available for those
going on charter trips. The *New York Times Cookbook*
has used the Hag's chowder recipe; but as served here,
a bowlful tastes just above average. A popular, all-you-
can-eat seafood buffet for $13.95 on Friday evenings is
ample. Expect to wait for a dinner table during summer
season.

LODGINGS

The Inn at Otter Crest
Otter Crest Loop, 2 miles
south of Depoe Bay,
(503) 765-2111, toll-free
(800) 547-2181 outside
Oregon
Mail: PO Box 50,
Otter Rock, OR 97369
Expensive; AE, MC, V

The 100-acre parklike setting of this attractive destination resort on Cape Foulweather is exquisitely and lushly
landscaped with rhododendrons, evergreens, and coastal
shrubs—a seeming oasis of serenity with an isolated
beach and a breathtaking view. What could be better?

A number of things. For starters, there's a history
of less-than-topnotch service—such as reservations being misplaced—that detracts from the positive attributes.
The Inn is so large (over 200 rooms and suites) that
sometimes the personal touch is lacking. The many con-

ventions held here can be intrusive. The tennis facilities —two indoor and two outdoor courts—are inadequate for the resort's size; the golf course is three miles south. Only the first fireplace log is complimentary. Still, most of the rooms enjoy marvelous ocean views from private decks (be sure to request one of these) and are part of fourplex and eightplex units that blend in well with the surrounding countryside. You leave your car a short distance away and hop a shuttle van to your room. Many have fireplaces and fully equipped kitchens. The restaurant is ordinary and does not match the surroundings. All in all, a nice but expensive alternative to beach-front motel life.

By the way, Cape Foulweather was named by famous British mariner Captain James Cook when he sailed by in 1778, evidently unimpressed by the situation overhead. It's an apt description: fog often enshrouds the cape, even though sunny skies may beam just north and south.

Channel House
Foot of Ellingston,
(503) 765-2140
Mail: PO Box 56,
Depoe Bay, OR 97341
Expensive; MC, V

The house feels more like a small motel than a bed and breakfast, but the setting is spectacular, perched on the edge of a cliff overlooking the Pacific Ocean and Depoe Bay. The three new, large suites all face the ocean, with gas fireplaces, hot tubs on their decks, and kitchenettes. They also cost ($140). The six rooms in the main house are smaller (smallest, "The Crow's Nest," runs $48), although three have decks and hot tubs and are priced accordingly. Bring your binoculars, especially during whale-watching season.

NEWPORT

One of the most popular tourist destinations on the Oregon coast, Newport demonstrates the pitfalls of development fulfilled. The place has grown—in some instances, not attractively. Veer off Highway 101's commercial sprawl and seek out the real Newport.

The bay front is a working waterfront going full tilt, where fishing boats of all types—trollers, trawlers, shrimpers, and crabbers—berth year-round. Nearby, take a drive out on the **South Jetty Road** for sea-level views of harbor traffic. A walk through the friendly **Nye Beach** area offers glimpses of the old and the new in Newport, a potpourri of neo-professionals, tourists, writers, and fishermen.

Art galleries. Oceanic Arts Center, 444 SW Bay Boulevard, (503) 265-5963, and the Wood Gallery, 818 SW Bay Boulevard, (503) 265-6843, both on the bay front, offer fine selections—the former primarily jewelry, paintings, and sculpture, the latter functional sculpture, woodwork, pottery, and weaving.

Fishing charters. Most provide bait and tackle, clean and fillet your catch, and even smoke or can it for you. Many charter operators have initiated whale-watching excursions, as well as half- and full-day fishing trips. Sea Gull Charters, 343 SW Bay Boulevard, (503) 265-7441, and Newport Sport-fishing, 1000 SE Bay Boulevard, (503) 265-7558, are two popular operators.

Hatfield Marine Science Center offers displays, a facsimile tidepool, educa-

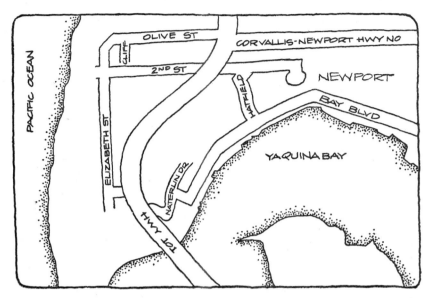

tional programs, and a full range of free nature walks, field trips, and films, especially during the summer Seatauqua program. Marine Science Drive on the south side of the bay in South Beach; (503) 867-3011.

RESTAURANTS

Canyon Way Restaurant and Bookstore

1 block up the hill off Bay Boulevard and Fall at Canyon Way,
(503) 265-8319
1216 SW Canyon Way, Newport
Moderate; full bar;
AE, MC, V
Lunch Mon-Sat, dinner Tues-Sat, every day in summer

An appealing bookstore–gift shop—where books are shelved alongside cards, records, toys, and trinkets— shares space with an intimate restaurant, one of the area's favorites.

Pasta and seafood fill the lunch menu, as well as freshly baked croissants stuffed with a variety of fillings—beef Wellington, for example—bouillabaisse, ginger-garlic chicken, a good chef's salad, and tasty omelets served with pan-fried red potatoes. Desserts are made daily; the banana cream torte remains memorable. Dinners are more elaborate and expensive but not always as successful. Forgo the sometimes-overcooked and fancy-sounding selections (such as trout stuffed with scallop mousse) for the simpler seafood preparations.

Service is efficient and friendly. On sunny days, request an outdoor table overlooking the bay. A carry-out store featuring homemade pasta, bread, and pastries is located in the entry adjacent to the bookstore.

The Whale's Tale

SW Bay and SW Fall,
(503) 265-8660
452 SW Bay Boulevard,

Owner Dick Schwartz may well be found jigging to live Celtic dulcimer music in the corner of his restaurant, taking small breathers to stroll and jaw with the locals and

*Newport
Moderate; beer and wine;
AE, DC, MC, V
Breakfast, lunch, dinner
every day; closed Wed in
winter*

tourists who fill the place to brimming. Breakfasts are sumptuous, the best in Newport, with fresh jalapeno omelets, oyster omelets, mushroom-and-cheese-stuffed biscuits the size of small barges, and filling poppyseed pancakes. Coffee is fresh and strong, the perfect jolt to set you in motion after such rib-sticking food.

Lunch is a combo of vegetarian and meat dishes, and often highly seasoned. A Reuben, a whopper veggie-burger, and fresh soups—spicy fisherman's stew among the best—are featured. Reasonably priced dinners might include razor clams Romano, catfish Provencal, a baby coho salmon poached in champagne and finished with hollandaise, or Dick's memorable moussaka. Wine and beer selections, plentiful and reasonably priced, are updated often as the owners discover new favorites. If you can find room, split a piece of rich chocolate cake with a friend and sip some espresso.

LODGINGS

**Ocean House
Bed & Breakfast**
*Just off Highway 101 N,
(503) 265-6158
4920 NW Woody Way,
Newport, OR 97365
Moderate; MC, V*

The first bed and breakfast in Lincoln County, Ocean House is arguably as good as any on the north Oregon coast. Although the setting overlooking the surf at Agate Beach is spectacular, the Ocean House is neither elegant nor luxurious. Rather, it is just about the most comfortable place you could ever want to stay.

Bob and Bette Garrard are gracious and helpful, but unobtrusive. Having lived here 24 years, they are more than qualified to comment on the Newport scene. You can curl up with a good book and relax in Bob's sheltered garden on a cliff, or retire to your room and snuggle beneath thick comforters while a storm brews outside. A short trail leads from the garden to one of Newport's less crowded beaches in the lee of Yaquina Head, with Yaquina Lighthouse towering nearby.

The Garrards serve a full breakfast in the spacious living room or on the porch, weather permitting. Bob's waffles are covered with fresh strawberries and whipped cream, accompanied by bacon and a slice of honeydew melon topped with a peppermint sprig.

Sylvia Beach Hotel
*Take Route 20 next to
NW Cliff,
(503) 265-5428
267 NW Cliff, Newport,
OR 97365
Moderate; beer and
wine; MC, V
Breakfast, dinner
every day*

The 77-year-old hotel currently basks in what must be its happiest and most imaginative incarnation. Owners Goody Cable (of Portland's Rimsky–Korsakoffee House) and Sally Ford have dedicated their bluff-top hotel to bookworms and their literary heroes/heroines. They gave several like-minded friends the task of decorating each of the 20 rooms, and the results are rich in whimsy and fresh, distinct personality. Most luxurious is the Agatha Christie suite, decorated in lush green English chintz, with a tiled fireplace, a large deck facing out over the seacliff below, and—best of all—clues from the writer's many murders: men's shoes peeking from beneath a curtain, notes on the walnut secretary, bottles labeled "poison" in the medicine cabinet, a suspicious-looking blob of wax on the rug, even a monocle on the door. Peeks into other rooms reveal mosquito netting slung over the Tennessee Williams bed; a mechanized pendulum swinging over the Edgar Allan Poe bed (consider the possibilities); and porcelain cats, lace, and plumped pillows in Colette's boudoir. The Dr. Seuss room has twin beds Books abound in the cozy upstairs library—as do cello solos, poetry readings, and other elevated impromptu entertainments, compliments of fellow guests. Hot wine is served nightly at 10pm. Breakfast (open to non-guests by reservation) is included in the price of a room. Prepare for a stay sans phones, TVs (if you're desperate, a portable may be had), and stress; long beach walks, good reads, and a decidedly un-hotel atmosphere are the order of the day.

Dinners in the hotel's Tables of Content restaurant, located downstairs and just above the beach, are family-style, prix-fixe affairs, open to the public on a reservation-only basis. Meals are eight or so "chapters" long and cost about $15, probably less than you'd pay for a good book. On our recent visit, we began with zesty crab-cake appetizers and a big, rather ordinary, bowl of green salad. Flaky and tender halibut was, unfortunately, smothered in a Dijonnaise sauce. Veggies and pasta, both okay but not outstanding, were also served. A spice torte with chocolate glaze rounded out the meal. Service is friendly and relaxed. Overall, dinner makes for a good read.

Oar House Bed & Breakfast

1 block west off Highway 101 on 2nd,
(503) 265-9571
520 SW Second Street,
Newport, OR 97365
Moderate; checks ok

The name is a delicate play on words: the place was once a bordello. It boasts a centralized location, and a pleasant—if distant—view of the ocean in Newport's Nye Beach area. The 5,600-square-foot establishment's two guest rooms have private baths, one with a bidet. The nautical motif is a bit overstated, but the overall effect is pleasing.

Guests have use of an indoor spa and sauna, a protected sun deck (where smoking is permitted), and a fireside room. The roof has a lookout tower with a widow's walk and an exhilarating 360-degree view. Full breakfasts are served. During our stay we enjoyed eggs Benedict, homemade bran muffins, and local blackberries.

Embarcadero

West off Highway 101 on Bay Blvd,
(503) 265-8521
1000 SE Bay Blvd,
Newport, OR 97365

This huge complex, situated right on the bay, is quite attractive. The facility offers all the amenities one might expect of a destination resort, including heated pool, sauna, whirlpool, children's play area, outdoor crab cooker, and even a private marina. But the best feature of all is

Expensive; AE, DC, MC, V

the sweeping view of the harbor, the Newport Bay bridge, and the blue Pacific beyond. Each roomy unit has tasteful furnishings, a skylight, a deck, and a view. Kitchen units have fireplaces as well. The grounds are well landscaped, the architecture well conceived. The restaurant has a pleasant bar view, plus a Sunday champagne brunch.

SEAL ROCK
LODGINGS

**Blackberry Inn
Bed & Breakfast**
*12 miles south of
Newport at Seal Rock,
(503) 563-2259
6575 Pacific
Coast Highway,
Mail: PO Box 188,
Seal Rock, OR 97376
Moderate; MC, V*

Unfortunately, this small, homey, two-room B&B is located on the wrong side of Highway 101 amid very average surroundings. Otherwise, hosts Bob and Barbara Tarter run a class act in their 1938 Cape Cod–style dwelling. Rooms are appointed with antique oak furniture, down comforters, and private baths. There's a private wing with wood stove, sitting room, and a hot tub on an outside deck. Breakfast might be Dutch babies with fresh apple filling, maple-flavored link sausage, and a parfait of fruit, granola, and yogurt. Outside, there's a picnic area, walking trails, and a horseshoe pit.

WALDPORT

This small, unpretentious, quiet town at the Alsea River mouth was named in the 1870s by German settlers who floated downriver to what was formerly an Alsi Indian burial ground. At one time, the area had several sawmills and salmon canneries. There's still good clamming and crabbing in the bay, and equipment can be rented at the dock in the Old Town section, on the water just east of Highway 101.

Fudge, Highway 101, Seal Rock, is a tiny storefront selling varieties of scrumptious light and dark fudge. Good ice cream is also available; (503) 563-2766.

LODGINGS

**The Cliff House
Bed & Breakfast**
*1 block west off Highway
101 at Adahi Road,
(503) 563-2506
Mail: PO Box 436,
Waldport, OR 97394
Expensive, MC, V*

Call them magicians. It wasn't by chance that Gabriella Duvall and D.J. Novgrad opened this utterly romantic B&B on Valentine's Day 1988. It took them over two years of their own handiwork to turn this dilapidated structure into a whimsical retreat. The house is exactly where it claims to be—perched on a cliff above eight miles of beach, affording ocean views that end only at the horizon. Turn 90 degrees and there's the bay; another 90 degrees, the Alsea River; again, the Coast Range. For starters, every room in the house has an ocean view (okay, so two of the five bathrooms look out at the bay). Each of the five bedrooms has a balcony, a full bath, and a chandelier.

We stayed in the loft, appropriately named the Redwood Room, which is akin to sleeping in a comfy, padded cedar chest. The bridal suite is luxurious—with a skylight, a Jacuzzi, and, ahem, a fully mirrored bathroom (floors, ceilings, and walls). You almost get dizzy. Breakfast is first-rate: a yogurt cup with papaya, strawberries, kiwi fruit, and granola, followed by a fluffy souffle topped with sugar, lemon, blueberries, and sour cream. At press time, a hot tub was being installed outside on the deck, and a sauna was queued up to be next. No wish goes un-answered—a massage for both of you, croquet in the front yard, or a candlelight dinner in your room. But most of the magic of this place is that good things, under the direc-tion of two visionary women, just seem to happen.

Cape Cod Cottages
2½ miles south of Waldport, (503) 563-2106
4150 SW Pacific Coast Highway, Waldport, OR 97394
Moderate; MC, V

These cozy spic-and-span duplexes a couple of miles south of Waldport are usually packed. There are four two-bedroom duplexes and four one-bedroom units, each with kitchen, some with a garage. Decks on the ocean side and fireplaces in which to burn the real logs provided by the owners.

Edgewater Cottages
2½ miles south of Waldport on Highway 101, (503) 563-2240
3978 SW Pacific Coast Highway, Waldport, OR 97394
Inexpensive; checks ok

Each unit has good beach access and views, deck, wind-breaks from the summer winds, TV, fireplace, and kitch-en. They range from a duplex and a fourplex to separate cottages that sleep two to eight, and the crow's nest, a honeymoon cottage.

YACHATS

Yachats (pronounced Ya-Hots) is a tiny settlement straddling the mellow Yachats River on the bare basaltic marine terrace tucked between mountains and sea. In fact, the name Yachats means "at the foot of the mountain." Nearby, the most un-trammeled and dramatic rocky beaches in Oregon yield rich tidepools, wildlife breeding grounds, whooshing geysers, and near-shore whale-watching. It's little wonder that Yachats has dubbed itself "The Gem of the Oregon Coast."

Cape Perpetua. The newly remodeled Visitors Center offers films and dioramas to orient you to the surrounding natural formations. Under Highway 101 at Cook's chasm, the ocean churns in a deep cleft. From the Visitors Center you can drive or hike to the highest point on the Oregon Coast. The 19-mile auto tour begins three miles south of Yachats on Highway 101; (503) 547-3289.

RESTAURANTS

La Serre
Downtown Yachats, (503) 547-3420
Second and Beach streets, Yachats
Moderate; full bar; AE, MC, V

The skylight-domed, arched ceiling, whitewashed walls, and lace-curtained windows create an airy, open frame in this country French eatery. Antiques and healthy plants add warmth. Until recently, though, the food just hasn't measured up to the decor. Fortunately, with new, more-involved management, it's consistently good; add a bit of panache and it could be great. Shrimp omelets, pop-

*Lunch, dinner every day,
brunch Sun*

pyseed pancakes, and good espresso are morning favorites. For lunch, stick with the entree salads and seafood specials. There's even a Distraction Plate of fruit chunks for children. Candlelight softens the room at night. Try the clam puff appetizers, prawns sauteed in butter, almost any fresh fish special, and the zesty cioppino. The spinach salad is a meal in itself. Accompany your meal with the wine of the week. And top it off with summer's freshest fruit pie, the chocolate-raspberry cake, or a cordial in the Bistro bar with live folk music on weekends.

New Morning Coffeehouse
*Across from the bank,
Highway 101 and 4th,
(503) 547-3848
Fourth Street and
Highway 101, Yachats
Inexpensive; no alcohol;
checks ok
Breakfast, lunch every day*

Blythe Collins adopted this previously vacant building in May 1988. She let in the sun through sparkling panes of beveled glass, softened the space with plants and handmade quilts, and allowed the cathedral ceiling to show off its handsome blond beams. But it's not only the company or the solitude that draws locals and travelers to Blythe's. Boy, can she bake! Our carrot cake was unforgettable, the marionberry pie superb. The light menu, which seems to be continually growing, features very good soups, salads, and sandwiches on homemade bread.

LODGINGS

The Adobe Motel
*Downtown Yachats,
(503) 547-3141
1555 Highway 101,
Mail: PO Box 219,
Yachats, OR 97498
Moderate; AE, DC, MC, V
Breakfast, lunch Mon-Sat,
dinner every day, brunch
Sun*

This resort—both the original section and the newer complex—was built with respect for the landscape. The Adobe fans out around the edge of a basalt-bumpy shore. Waves crash onto the rocks; their thunder echoes into the rooms. Oddly, given this wet climate, the original rooms were made out of the resort's namesake: local adobe bricks. Those rooms—knotty pine, beamed ceilings, fireplaces, and ocean views—are still popular. Forty-two units in two newer wings have refrigerators and coffeemakers; some have fireplaces. There's a six-person Jacuzzi and a sauna for all. Except for a few oversights (one room had a torn bedspread), the resort is exquisitely maintained, down to the careful pruning of wind-bent trees.

Recently the Adobe hired a new chef. He's retained old favorites while adding French-styled American food, emphasizing fresh fish and produce. Breakfasts facing the ocean are decadent; dinners at sunset are delightful. Service is slow, but with so much window gazing you barely notice. The bar has a full ocean view, but the loft is the perfect perch for a drink or snack while watching whales (March–April), waves, stars, and storms. Children are welcome, and with advance notice so is your dog.

Oregon House
*8 miles south of Yachats,
on Highway 101,
(503) 547-3329*

Joyce and Bob Freeman deserve kudos for transforming the Oregon House into the lovely oceanside retreat it always should have been. The nonsmoking rooms are

94288 Highway 101,
Yachats, OR 97498
Moderate; MC, V

artful-country style, spotlessly clean, and colored with fresh flowers from the Freemans' 3½ acres. There are eight separate units, all different. Couples will be comfortable in the one-room cabin done in red-and-white gingham; families should reserve the larger unit that sleeps six. A path (lit at night) takes you to a private beach. For those who don't want to cook breakfast or go out, the Freemans will serve a full meal for just $10 extra per couple. No pets, but children are welcome to pet the farm's goat, chickens, and ducks.

Ziggurat

6½ miles south of
Yachats on Highway 101,
(503) 547-3925
95330 Highway 101,
Yachats, OR 97498
Moderate; checks ok

A visiting professor named this stunning glass-and-wood four-story pyramid after an ancient Sumerian pyramid found near Babylon. Its radical triangular design works well—as a beach house and as a well-placed sculpture. Owners Mary Lou Cavendish (who took over contracting and interior design from the original architect) and Irv Tebold will gladly discuss its architectural fine points, such as the spectacular views from all 40 windows.

Guests share the 1,800-square-foot first-floor living and reading rooms complete with refrigerator, books, and games. Two more guest bedrooms upstairs share a bath-cum-sauna. A tiled solarium wraps around the second floor, providing a wind-free spot for everyone to read or weather-watch. The hosts will serve you breakfast wherever you please.

Gull Haven Lodge

7 miles south of Yachats
on Highway 101,
(503) 547-3583
Mail: 94770 Highway
101, Florence, OR 97439
Inexpensive; MC, V

Mary Fike picks up her mail in Florence, but her popular haven for beachcombers is technically in Yachats. The main lodge sits on a bluff overlooking the ocean—and so do most of the rooms (with private baths and kitchen privileges). The rooms are reasonably priced, though for $35 you might consider the Shag's Nest, a separate cabin with 180-degree ocean views, a fireplace, and a kitchen. The only problem: it has no bath (and it's a 30-yard dash to the lodge). But reserve it early anyway, as it's usually booked well in advance. There's a separate unit with a commercial kitchen—ideal for meetings.

Shamrock Lodgettes

On Highway 101 S, just
south of Yachats,
(503) 547-3312
Mail: PO Box 346,
Yachats, OR 97498
Moderate; AE, DC, MC, V

The name says green and cozy, and the Shamrock Lodgettes deliver. Rustic cabins and newer motel units are nicely spaced on immaculate grounds adjacent to the mouth of the Yachats River. Kids race on the grass and dig in the sand on the protected beach. Bring friends and stay in one of the well-maintained but older log cabins with cedar paneling, fireplaces, and two-burner kitchenettes. Less private but nicely appointed are the newer motel rooms with fireplaces and ocean or bay views. The deluxe units have kitchenettes and Jacuzzi bathtubs.

As an extra, non-exclusive luxury, owners Bob and Mary Oxley added a separate spa building with sauna,

Jacuzzi, and exercise room (no equipment, though). As Bob makes his morning rounds, he deposits a copy of *The Oregonian* at your front door.

FLORENCE

Florence is surrounded by the beauty of the Oregon Dunes National Recreation Area, the Siuslaw River, several large freshwater lakes, and in May, a lei of bright pink native rhododendron flowers. Old Town is the heart of Florence: a continually upgraded few blocks of shops, restaurants, and some of the town's oldest structures on Bay Street east of Highway 101 along the banks of the Siuslaw. Though it does draw tourists, the traffic won't crush you. You can rent crab rings and catch your dinner right off the city dock in Old Town. The **Old Town Coffee Company** is the daytime hangout. **Catch the Wind Kite Shop** displays airborne creations. And Ken Kesey modeled his mythical bar "The Snag," in *Sometimes a Great Notion*, after the **Fisherman's Wharf**.

The Oregon Dunes National Recreation Area. Orient yourself to this intriguing ecosystem at the Oregon Dunes Overlook, 12 miles south of town. Hike or ride a dune buggy into a land of 600-foot-high dunes, dark lakes, and tree islands. Dune buggies are available at **Sand Dunes Frontier**, 83960 Highway 101 S, (503) 997-3544; **Sandland Adventures Inc.**, Highway 101 at 10th Street, (503) 997-8087; or **Gary's ATC Rental**, 586 Highway 101, (503) 997-6755.

Heceta Head Lighthouse and the light-keeper's home, 12 miles north, offer *the* postcard shot on the coast. The supposedly haunted but truly lovely light-keeper's home can be reserved for college classes or unusual weddings, (503) 997-8444.

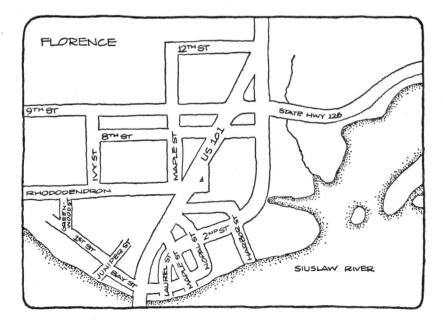

Sea Lion Caves, (503) 547-3111, 10 miles north, may be the largest sea grotto in the world and is the only known mainland breeding colony of the Steller's sea lion.

Darlingtonia Botanical Wayside is a bog five miles north of town with insect-eating plants called cobra lilies. Look for their unusual burgundy flowers in May.

The Toy Factory, five miles north, sells the finest local and imported toys, (503) 997-8604.

Indian Forest, (503) 997-3677, four miles north, has buffalo and deer grazing near authentic models of Native American structures.

RESTAURANTS

Windward Inn

*1½ miles north of Florence on Highway 101, (503) 997-8243
3757 Highway 101 N, Florence
Moderate; full bar; AE, DC, MC, V
Breakfast, lunch, dinner every day (closed Mon in winter)*

The pride of Florence, this large, handsome, though somewhat pretentious restaurant is the town's best, containing a coffee shop, a library-like room, a formal hall with a grand piano, and most recently, a spacious courtyard lounge.

Owner David Haskell has added a dozen or so seafood items. Regulars claim the wild mussels (from California) are the best they've had since their last trip to Paris. Others wouldn't go so far. On the right night, however, you'll be in for a treat. Dinner favorites include oysters grilled with Pernod, garlic, and butter; veal in Madeira cream; and superb boudin blanc made with chicken. The inn is exceptionally proud of its breads and pastries, baked on the premises, and its sumptuous dark chocolate truffles.

LODGINGS

**Johnson House
Bed & Breakfast**

*1 block north of the river, (503) 997-8000
216 Maple Street,
Mail: PO Box 1892,
Florence, OR 97439
Moderate; MC, V*

Jayne and Ron Fraese bring wit, curiosity, and high aesthetic standards to this perennially popular Victorian B&B in Old Town. Built in 1892, it once comprised the entire town. Reflecting the Fraeses' interests (he's a political science prof; she's an English teacher), the library is strong on local history, natural history, politics, and collections of essays, letters, cartoons, and poetry. They even sell old, unused postcards from their extensive collection. Each of the five bedrooms is pillowed in down; two have private baths. Jayne uses asparagus, blueberries, rhubarb, cherries, and herbs from the garden in her full breakfasts that include fresh muffins and fresh-squeezed orange juice. And they'll loan you crabbing gear for the day, or sell their own conserves for guests to take home.

The well-kept secrets, however, are the two independent cottages run by the Fraeses: Moonset, a two-person octagonal cabin facing Lily Lake (nine miles up the road) and the Coast House, 10 miles north at the water's edge. The latter is a remodeled artist's shack (five levels high), clinging to a cliff with two skylit sleeping lofts, an ocean-viewing bath with a claw-footed tub, an exceptional library and tape collection, and a living room with wood stove. This is guaranteed to be the only place on the coast where you can watch tufted puffins or gray whales from a wind-protected outdoor shower. Two-night minimum.

Driftwood Shores Surfside Resort Inn
3 miles north of Florence, on Heceta Beach Road off Highway 101, (503) 997-8263, toll-free, (800) 824-8774 (outside Oregon) 88416 First Avenue, Florence, OR 97439 Moderate; AE, DC, MC, V

This is one of the few places on the south central coast where you can stay right on the beach—actually, 10 miles of uninterrupted beach. The four-story resort contains 136 plain but tasteful rooms. All have views and balconies; most have kitchens. Groups can get large units with fireplaces, kitchens, and up to three bedrooms for about $120. Amenities include an indoor pool, sauna, and Jacuzzi.

The Surfside Restaurant and Lounge serves acceptable food in extraordinary surroundings. Some dinner favorites: scampi flambe, rack of lamb, Chateaubriand, and the Captain's Plate. Breakfasts are standard, but portions are quite substantial.

GARDINER

LODGINGS

Gardiner Guest House
Front at Jewett Lane, (503) 271-4005 401 Front Street, Mail: PO Box 222, Gardiner, OR 97441 Moderate; checks ok

★

Even though it's near the center of Gardiner (notorious for its pulp mill), winds tend to carry odors away from this lovely 1883 Victorian built by Reedsport's namesake. The two upstairs guest rooms overlook the town and the Umpqua River. The front room has redwood paneling and gas lamps, and there's an indoor Jacuzzi. Big breakfasts may include anything from eggs to pancakes. The per-night fee goes up in the summer, although proprietors Guy and Dixie Hash are willing to negotiate for stays longer than two days.

REEDSPORT

This port town on the Umpqua River has gained a new attraction: the **Dean Creek Elk Reserve**, about four miles east of town on Route 38, where you can observe a wild herd grazing on protected land.

In the summer the **Oregon Dunes National Recreation Area** at the intersection of Highway 101 and Route 38 offers educational programs on this country's highest coastal dunes, (503) 271-3611.

WINCHESTER BAY

RESTAURANTS

Seven Seas Cafe
4th and Beach Blvd, Winchester Bay, no phone

Cram into this colorful 34-seat maritime diner opposite the harbor for simple, homemade food and Jim and Marilyn Fleming's rambunctious good humor. Nautical

Inexpensive; no alcohol; local checks only
Breakfast, lunch Tues-Sat

knowledge comes in handy here, for passing Marilyn's trivia quiz. It's the right combo on a beachy day. The menu runs the gamut of short-order specialties, from fresh seafood (deep-fried or grilled) to hamburgers.

NORTH BEND
RESTAURANTS

The Brass Rail

On Highway 101 S,
(503) 756-2121
2072 Sherman Avenue,
North Bend
Inexpensive; beer and
wine; AE, MC, V
Breakfast Sat-Sun,
lunch every day

Forget the highway and breeze into the quiet garden courtyard of North Bend's best eatery. Deli sandwiches, seafood, fresh soups, special salads (try the orange-almond), and daily specials such as stuffed cabbage rolls and enchiladas keep the regulars coming. Not to mention the desserts, about 50 of them—notably the lemon meringue, coconut-apricot, and French silk pies.

LODGINGS

Highlands Bed & Breakfast

5 miles east of Highway
101 on Ridge Road,
(503) 756-0300
608 Ridge Road,
North Bend, OR 97459
Moderate; checks ok

It's the view of the Coast Range (and Coos Bay), the deer (and an occasional elk), and the steelhead (but not the skunks) that lure people to these five acres of highlands. Not to mention the comfortable 2,000-square-foot lower level of Marilyn and Jim Dow's contemporary cedar home. There's a huge living room with a soapstone stove and wraparound windows. Both bedrooms have private baths and use of the kitchen. Breakfast is best on the wraparound deck, with Marilyn's marvelous baked French toast with fresh fruit. If you want to try your hand at crabbing, the Dows will loan you their crab ring and cook what good creatures you reap. No children under 10, please.

Sherman House

Southbound Highway
101, 3 blocks above the
old town center,
(503) 756-3496
2380 Sherman Avenue,
North Bend, OR 97459
Moderate; checks ok

The house is Pennsylvania Dutch and the hostess is from Arkansas, but you're very much in Oregon, three blocks above North Bend's old town district. There are three bedrooms (two with city or harbor views), all decorated in Jennifer and Phillip Williams' antiques. Guests have free run of the top two floors of this three-story home; upstairs there's a sitting room, downstairs a full kitchen, dining room with fireplace, and living room. Business meetings, however, can be held in complete privacy. Jennifer Williams dishes up biscuits and gravy (true to her Southern roots), omelets, or lighter fare for breakfast, depending on your appetite.

CHARLESTON

Charleston's docks moor the bay's commercial fishing fleet. Fresh fish is inexpensive, the pace is slow, and there's lots to do.

Visit the **Oregon Institute of Marine Biology**, the University of Oregon's respected research station, (503) 888-2581; the **South Slough National Estuarine Reserve**, the first of 21 such reserves in the US, and **Qualman Oyster Farms**, 4898 Crown Point Road, (503) 888-3145.

To the west, a trio of state parks. **Sunset Bay** features a large cove with fossil-filled sandstone walls, a sandy beach, and ample camping space. **Shore Acres Botanical Gardens'** spectacular geology, crazy surf, and quiet pocket beach convinced timber baron Louis J. Simpson to build his estate here. The mansions are gone, but the views and the gardens (Japanese, formal, and rose) remain. Farther south, listen for and observe Steller's and California sea lions and harbor seals on tiny islands offshore from **Cape Arago State Park**.

RESTAURANTS

Portside
Follow Cape Arago Highway, right at drawbridge, right again at Captain John's,
(503) 888-5544
8001 Kingfisher Road, Charleston
Moderate; full bar; AE, DC, MC, V
Lunch Mon-Fri, dinner every day

From your table, watch tidal fluctuations and the boat traffic in the mouth of the Charleston Boat Basin. Fish, direct from the boat and simply prepared, is the specialty. Try the Dungeness crab steamed with melted butter; the calamari sauteed in garlic, wine, and butter; the grilled Empire clams; or the refreshing combination of shrimp, crab, and smoked salmon in cucumber dressing, served in a hollowed-out cucumber. Owner Joe Tan expresses his Chinese heritage in the sumptuous Friday seafood buffet. For $12.95 you can sample hot-and-spicy octopus, shrimp egg rolls, and chilled steamed shrimp, plus steamer clams, pickled herring, oysters on the half shell, and cold cracked crab. Of course, you'll see a few meat entrees (including barbecued ribs) in the line-up, but why bother?

COOS BAY

As the largest natural harbor between San Francisco and Seattle, surrounded by some of the richest forests in the world, Coos Bay has long been a busy port. Ships carrying logs, lumber, and wood chips to Asian markets have kept local tugboat companies and longshoremen busy. Ship crews have infused cultural diversity into this Scandinavian/German town.

But the forests have been felled and the big mills have closed, so Coos Bay's base may be shifting from trees to tourists. As a result, the town is undergoing a facelift. The downtown mall is being remodeled, and a San Francisco architect is helping redesign the waterfront. Riverboat, harbor, and charter cruises are available in the area; contact the Chamber of Commerce.

Coos Bay hosts the **Oregon Coast Music Festival** in July, the **Blackberry Arts Festival** in August, and the **Bay Area Fun Festival** (including a 10K run) in September. The **Coos Bay Art Museum**, 235 Anderson Avenue, (503) 267-3901, brings in high-quality displays. The **Marshfield Sun Printing Museum** has been restored (Highway 101 and Front Street). And the **Playwrights' American Conservatory Theatre** has improved local theatre—Broadway Theater, 226 S Broadway, (503) 269-2501.

RESTAURANTS

Blue Heron Bistro
Highway 101 and Commercial,
(503) 267-3933
100 Commercial Street,
Coos Bay
Moderate; beer and wine; MC, V
Breakfast, lunch every day, dinner Mon-Sat

Although Wim de Vriend has changed the name of his restaurant (formerly the Hurry Back! Cafe), and readjusted the interior, he hasn't monkeyed with his successful formula. His consistency, from-scratch recipes, and European flair keep his cafe bustling. Dinners are more eclectic than before: try the Indonesian grilled chicken with a spicy peanut sauce or the bay scallops, shrimp, and snow peas on homemade spinach fettuccine. De Vriend handles fish so that the herbs, wine, and sauces enhance rather than overpower the subtleties. His homemade pastas are al dente, with vibrant sauces. Salads are as fresh and innovative as local supply allows. His soups are superb, especially a recent beer-cheese potage and the just-spicy chicken soup with green chiles.

Breakfasts will satisfy any appetite, with freshly made croissants, cinnamon rolls, and danishes or more filling entrees. Two new omelets stand out: the beefy stroganoff and the Lollobrigida (salami, cream cheese, pesto, mushrooms, and onions). You won't need any potato salad after one of the deli-style sandwiches—although served warm (Dutch style) with homemade mayonnaise, it might tempt you to consider skipping the sandwich. There are lots of desserts to choose from, but the apple pie is the best bet.

Kum-Yon's
On the main drag,
(503) 269-2662
835 S Broadway,
Coos Bay
Moderate; beer and wine; MC, V
Lunch, dinner every day

Kum-Yon transformed a former fast-food eatery into a showcase of her native South Korean plus Japanese and Sichuan specialties. Food is still fast but very fresh. Sushi, dim sum, hot and sour soup, and Sichuan entrees stand out in a menu that also includes Mongolian beef, shrimp tempura, and beef teriyaki. Japanese traders (among the many knowledgeable diners) order off the menu. Kum-Yon's American mother-in-law bakes the desserts. Kum-Yon has opened a new eatery in Newport (1006 S Coast Highway).

LODGINGS

Captain's Quarters
Bed & Breakfast
West side of the bay,
(503) 888-6895
265 S Empire Blvd, Coos Bay, OR 97420
Moderate; checks ok

Captain John McGenn, known fondly as the "Poet of the Pacific," built this home in 1892. Over the past few years, owners Jean and John Griswold have tracked McGenn's relatives and have assembled his history, including some of his poetry. The two guest bedrooms overlook the bay: they cost about $45 per night. Johnny's seven-grain waffles are a hit in the dining room or on the sunny porch next to the rose garden. No smoking inside, please.

This Olde House

Corner of 2nd, downtown
Coos Bay, (503) 267-5224
202 Alder Avenue, Coos
Bay, OR 97420
Moderate; checks ok

Edward and Jean Mosieur decorated their 1893 Victorian with love (including the lampshades they made themselves) and humor; the Mosieurs' "instant family" consists of secondhand portraits they've hung inside antique frames Jean's collected for about 60 years. The trees surrounding this B&B (just four blocks from the heart of downtown) keep it quiet. They have four bedrooms, one with a private bath. French toast for breakfast, along with Edward's superb bran muffins. There's room for kids but no pets.

BANDON

Some locals believe Bandon sits on a "ley line," a focus of powerful cosmic energies. Certainly there's magic here: this little community at the mouth of the Coquille River bustles. North of town are **Whiskey Run Wind Turbine Project**, Oregon's first wind energy "farm," and the **Coquille River Lighthouse**, accessible through **Bullards Beach State Park**.

In town, sample the famous Cheddar cheeses (especially the squeaky cheese curds) at **Bandon's Food**, which reopened in 1988 at 680 E Second Street, (503) 347-2456. For another treat, try the *New York Times*–touted handmade candies at **Cranberry Sweets**, (503) 347-9475, First and Chicago streets. Bandon's cranberry bogs make it the nation's fifth-largest producer. Call (503) 347-3230 for a tour.

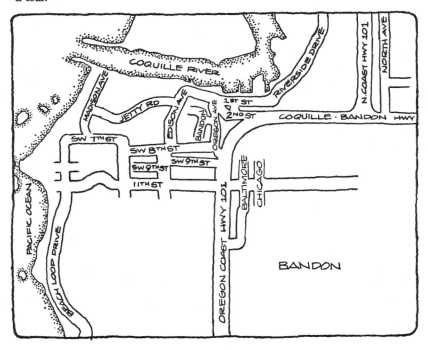

Old Town features **Harbor Hall**, which books ballet to blues and is the home of the Encore Presenters acting troupe, (503) 347-4404. There are also **Second Street Gallery** and other fine crafts shops and at least 11 food purveyors. **Southern Oregon Sailboards** rents surfing and windsurfing equipment and gives lessons, (503) 347-WAVE. And the sternwheeler *Dixie Lee* takes slow-paced trips up the Coquille River.

The south jetty has the best beach access: **Coquille Point** (also the center of a development controversy) at the end of 11th street or the **Face Rock Viewpoint** on Beach Loop Road. Six miles south of Bandon is the **West Coast Game Park Safari**, a special "petting" park where you can pet lions and tigers and elk, among others, (503) 347-3106.

RESTAURANTS

Andrea's
1 block west of the waterfront, (503) 347-3022
160 Baltimore Street, Bandon
Moderate; beer and wine; checks ok
Breakfast, lunch Mon-Sat, dinner Fri-Sat, brunch Sun

Andrea Gatov's eclectic south coast restaurant continues to be one of the most popular in the area. Breakfasts are filling and bargain-priced (even her Sunday brunches with heaps of huevos rancheros and rich berry blintzes). Substantial sandwiches on homemade whole-grain breads, soups, and pizza by the slice round out the lunch menu. On Friday nights, locals descend on the place for a dynamite pizza.

Expect almost anything for dinner—Andrea draws on many traditions, from Cajun to Russian. She's strong on seafood cooked any of six different ways, from blackened to fat-free. Her ginger-sherry crab legs have garnered national attention; however, recent dinner reports of overcooked lamb and bland sauces lead us to think the locals are right in concentrating on the pizza.

Bandon Boatworks
Follow the river road out to the jetty, (503) 347-2111
South Jetty Road, Bandon
Moderate; beer and wine; AE, DC, MC, V
Lunch, dinner Tues-Sun (closed January)

Always a local favorite, the Boatworks takes advantage of its location near the south jetty on the Coquille River to provide fine dining with an equally fine view. The restaurant has expanded, with seating downstairs overlooking the river. If the restaurant is packed, wait anyway for a table upstairs; it's a shame to miss the sunset on the river and ocean. Dinner selections include baked butterflied shrimp served in a light and tangy mustard sauce; fresh oysters roasted in anisette; slabs of prime rib on weekends; an excellent rack of lamb; and seafood tossed with homemade fettuccine. The decent salad bar includes warm loaves of sweet cranberry bread (cranberries are an important local crop). For lunch, the sauteed squid is especially good. On Sundays the Boatworks features brunch and an above-average Mexican dinner, on top of all the rest. Desserts are fair; service is excellent.

LODGINGS

Cliff Harbor Guest House
Beach Loop Road at 9th, (503) 347-3956

This modern ocean- and bay-fronting home sits on a bluff overlooking the Pacific and Coquille River Harbor. The Harbor Suite features a bedroom, sitting room, window

*Mail: PO Box 769,
Bandon, OR 97411
Expensive; checks ok*

seat, bath, sun deck, and private entrance with wheelchair access, for $75. Upstairs, the Cliffside Studio has two double beds, kitchen, bath, fireplace, window seat, and private entrance for $85. The open floorplan and panoramic view appeal to all ages. Katherine Haines and her husband Douglas have made a few changes: Douglas, a master craftsman who built the lovely contemporary home, has remodeled the Cliffside Studio. He's also the chef. His creations are health-conscious, using organically grown meats and produce. He's added Spanish-sauced eggs, seafood omelets, crepes, and whole-wheat croissants. Cliffside guests get a serve-yourself natural-food breakfast from the well-stocked fridge. Use the sunning deck or follow the path to the beach strewn with petrified wood and agates.

Lighthouse Bed and Breakfast
*Turn left at 1st in Old Town, (503) 347-9316
650 Jetty Road, Mail: PO Box 24, Bandon, OR 97411
Moderate; MC, V*

Wood heat warms this spacious, appealing contemporary with windows opening toward the Coquille River, its lighthouse, and the ocean. Guests can watch fishing boats, seals, and seabirds nearby or stroll into Old Town. Hosts Linda and Bruce Sisson slice local organically grown strawberries for the morning's meal of French toast. In summer the Sissons offer four rooms, all with private baths; two view the ocean, the others look at the river and town. Three rooms with queen beds run about $65; the fourth (with king bed and whirlpool tub) gets $75. From November to February the Sissons migrate upstairs, and, for $70, rent out their downstairs two-bedroom apartment with river view.

Inn at Face Rock
*2 miles south of Bandon, turn right at Seabird Lane, (503) 347-9441
3225 Beach Look Drive, Bandon, OR 97411
Moderate, AE, MC, V
Lunch, dinner every day (summers, breakfast daily)*

★

Bandon's only resort is just across the road from the beach. Choose from one-bedroom, two-bath suites with kitchens, queen hideabeds, fireplace, and balconies. Many rooms have views (except for the 24 newer units in back). Prices vary as dramatically as the weather ($35–$105). The rooms are large, comfortable, and very attractive. There are two nonsmoking king units. The Jacuzzi is exclusive to guests; the nine-hole golf course, restaurant, and bar are not. The resort's golf pros can give you a lesson in coping with the often-irritating winds. The ocean-view dining room is inviting, but the quality of the meals flip-flops. The bar is relaxing, especially on a stormy night.

Sea Star Hostel and Guest House
*Take 2nd off Highway 101 into Old Town, (503) 347-9632
375 Second Street, Bandon, OR 97411*

We'd like this place even if it weren't $8 a night. Okay, so it's a hostel; but it's a hostel in the loosest sense of the word—and the most popular one on the West Coast. Jim Kennett's genius is in treating travelers like adults; there's no curfew. As a result, many guests often extend their Bandon stay for weeks. The oft-remodeled hostel has small men's and women's dorms, private rooms for

Inexpensive; MC, V

couples and families, a wood-stove–heated common room, kitchen, secluded courtyard, and sun decks.

The Guest House (connected to the hostel by a courtyard) with natural wood interior, skylights, and harbor-view deck, offers a relatively lavish alternative to its less formal neighbor ($25–$35). Apartments have an open floorplan with a queen hideabed, kitchen, living room, and deck ($40–$55). For an additional $5, Fido can join.

Kennett's new coffeehouse is busy serving simple homemade meals, snacks, and European-style desserts to locals and transients alike (8am–midnight).

Windermere Motel
1½ miles south of Bandon, west on Seabird Lane, (503) 347-3710
3250 Beach Loop Road, Bandon, OR 97411
Moderate; MC, V

Many guests wouldn't change a thing about this quintessential family motel. Where else can you find wonderfully battered oceanside cottages with kitchenettes and room for kids to run for $47–$72 in summer? It's nothing fancy, even a little run-down. The rooms are clustered in units of three or four. The best are those with sleeping lofts; but all rooms have truly magnificent ocean views and access to an uncrowded beach.

PORT ORFORD

It's got history (the oldest townsite on the Oregon coast), location (prime views and beaches with summer wind protection), mild climate, natural resources, and talented residents. Sheep ranching, fishing, sea-urchin harvesting, and cranberries dominate. Due to an engineering error, the harbor silts in; boats are launched by a crane on the main dock.

Several surprises await. **Cape Blanco State Park**, six miles north of town, is the westernmost park in the contiguous US, with empty beaches, a scenic lighthouse, and the nearby historic **Hughes House**; the **Elk** and **Sixes** rivers are prime fishing streams.

One warning: from here south, poison oak grows close to the ocean. Watch out for it on Battle Rock.

RESTAURANTS

The Whale Cove
Across from Battle Rock Park, (503) 332-7575
190 Sixth Street (Highway 101 S), Port Orford
Moderate; full bar; AE, MC, V
Lunch, dinner every day (dinner Tues-Thurs in winter); brunch Sun

It's a treasure, though you'd hardly suspect it from the unassuming gray exterior. First there's a casually elegant ambience: a wide-open Pacific view, handpainted silk ceiling waves and fish created by co-owner Donna Roselius; live baroque music on Monday nights; fresh flowers; and the genuine warmth of the Roseliuses and their chef, Michael Petchekovitch.

And the food! Petchekovitch, himself equal parts Russian, Irish, and painter, wanders freely among many cuisines and plays with color and taste. He chooses the best local ingredients, including organically grown fruits, herbs, and vegetables, and wild mushrooms, berries, and fish. He concocts cranberry and strawberry vinaigrettes, cream of cilantro soup with peppers and rose petals, rich seafood bisques, herb-flavored vegetarian pastas. He'll roast a wild boar or stuff a savory baked quail into a pear half. We've yet to find a bland morsel of veal, beef, or chicken. Strictly fresh salmon is slow-broiled and served with butter enhanced with wasabi or lime. Petrale sole is served with green shrimp sauce en papillote. The cioppino is worthy of a photograph.

Petchekovitch's flair carries over to his dessert creations: a crepe de myrtle, subtly flavored with myrtle leaves; a dark chocolate creme brulee (mousse in a sweet crust topped with whipped cream and strawberries) or an exceptional Grand Marnier souffle. If there is a fault, it's that dishes are sometimes too rich; once a chocolate-crusted custard pie garnished with fresh fruit daunted even a committed dessertaholic. To top it off, it doesn't cost an arm and a leg. Visit the gallery in the back, where you'll see some more of Petchekovitch's work—on the wall!

Truculent Oyster Restaurant and Peg Leg Saloon
Highway 101 at the south end of town,
(503) 332-9461
236 Sixth Street,
Port Orford
Moderate; full bar;
AE, DC, MC, V
Lunch, dinner every day

Enter the dark nautical interior of the Truculent Oyster through the Peg Leg Saloon, its bar affiliate. The fresh oyster shooters, homemade soups (split pea with ham), weekend prime rib, and mild Mexican entrees are the strong points of the eclectic menu. Try the shrimp-stuffed baked potato for lunch. Or for lunch or dinner, choose El Camaron en Queso, two large flour tortillas wrapped around fresh shrimp, avocado, and green chiles and covered with sour cream. The slow-broiled Chinook salmon (seasonal) can be outstanding. Portions are sizeable, service prompt.

LODGINGS

Castaway by the Sea (formerly the Neptune Motel)
Between Ocean and
Harbor Drives on W 5th,
(503) 332-4502
545 W Fifth, Port
Orford, OR 97465
Moderate; AE, MC, V

This bluff-top motel sits on history: ancient Indian artifacts; the former site of Fort Orford, the oldest military installation on the Oregon coast, and the Castaway Lodge, once frequented by Jack London. Owners Donna and Rosy Roselius continue to upgrade the 14-unit, two-story motel. The two three-bedroom units have kitchenettes and glassed-in sundecks with harbor and ocean views ($35–$85). A remnant wing of the former Neptune is favored by scuba divers because it sleeps up to 10. Avoid the dank older section under the office, except in a pinch. It's an easy stroll to the beach, harbor, or shops. Look for off-season specials, including dinner at the Roseliuses' Whale Cove Restaurant.

Gwendolyn's Bed & Breakfast
Oregon at Highway 101,
(503) 332-4373

Like roadside guest homes of the past, Gwendolyn's provides home-style comfort in a gingerbread-cute 1921 home next to Highway 101 in downtown Port Orford. All three bedrooms have brass beds. Hostess Gwendolyn

735 Oregon Street,
Mail: PO Box 913,
Port Orford,
OR 97465
Inexpensive; MC, V

★

Guerin enjoys serving her salmon and crab pie and fresh-baked breads. She can also arrange for a Victorian buggy tour of Port Orford. Children and smoking are okay, but pets aren't.

GOLD BEACH

This is famous as the town at the ocean end of the Rogue River, a favorite with Zane Grey and one of the most wild and scenic rivers in the US. It's also a supply town for hikers heading into the remote Kalmiopsis Wilderness Area.

Fishing. The river is famous for steelhead and salmon. You might want to visit some of the lodges favored by fisherfolk to pick up tips, or rent clam shovels and fishing gear at the **Rogue Outdoor Store**, 560 N Ellensburg Avenue (Highway 101), (503) 247-7142.

Jet boat trips. Guides will discuss the area's natural history and stop to observe wildlife on these thrilling trips from 64 to 104 miles up the Rogue River. You'll even get a hearty lunch or dinner, with local sweet corn and tomatoes, at one of the inns along the way. One caution: prepare for sun exposure in these open boats. Call **Court's White Water Trips** at Jots Resort, 94360 Wedderburn Loop, Box J, Gold Beach, OR 97444, (800) 367-5687; **Jerry's Rogue Jets**, Port of Gold Beach, PO Box 1011, Gold Beach, OR 97444, (503) 247-7601 for information or (800) 451-3645 for reservations; and **Mail Boat Hydro-Jets**, PO Box 1165-G, Gold Beach, OR 97444, (503) 247-7033 for information or (800) 458-3511 for reservations.

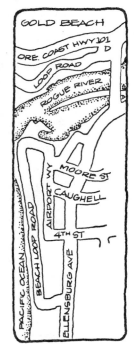

Whitewater trips. Traffic on the all-too-popular wild and scenic part of the Rogue is controlled. People interested in unsupervised trips must sign up for a lottery—the first six weeks in the new year—with the Galice Ranger District; (503) 479-3735.

Hiking. Trails cut deep into the Kalmiopsis Wilderness or the Siskiyou National Forest, or follow the Rogue River. The new 1¼-mile Old Growth Trail winds through an increasingly rare virgin forest. A jet boat can drop you off to explore part or all of the 40-mile-long Rogue River Trail along the river's north bank. Spring is the best time for a trek, before 90-degree heat makes the rockface trail intolerable. Stay at any or all of seven remote lodges, where—for prices ranging from $40 to $75 per night—you end your day with a hot shower, dinner, and bed, and begin with breakfast and sack lunch for the next day. (Reservations are a must.)

In the Agness area the lodges are **Cougar Lane Lodge**, 04219 Agness Road, Agness, OR 97406, (503) 247-7533; and **Illinois River Cabins**, PO Box 561, North Bend, OR 97459, (503) 756-2420 or (503) 267-7460.

In the Rogue River Wilderness contact **Clay Hill Lodge** and **Wild River Lodge**, PO Box 18, Agness, OR 97406, (503) 247-6215; **Singing Springs Ranch**, 34501 Agness–Illahee Road, Agness, OR 97406, (503) 247-6162, **Half Moon Bar Lodge**, 719 NW Third Street, Grants

Pass, OR 97526, (503) 476-4002, or **Paradise Lodge**, PO Box 456, Gold Beach, OR 97444, (503) 247-6022. For information about trails contact the Gold Beach Ranger District, 1225 S Ellensburg Avenue, Gold Beach, OR 97444, (503) 247-6651. The Rogue–Pacific Interpretive Center (920 S Ellensburg Avenue) prepares you for your trip with an overview of the area.

RESTAURANTS

The Captain's Table
South end of town,
(503) 247-6308
1295 S Ellensburg
Avenue, Gold Beach
Moderate; full bar;
MC, V
Dinner every day

This is Gold Beach's old favorite, though recent reports of poorly prepared seafood have been registered. The corn-fed beef from Kansas City is beef you can't often get this far west. One nice touch: the salad is served family style and you can help yourself to as much as you want. The dining area is moderately small, furnished with antiques, and can get smoky from the popular bar. Both dining room and bar have nice ocean views. The staff is courteous, enthusiastic (if a bit hovering), and speedy.

Nor'Wester
On the waterfront,
(503) 247-2333
Port of Gold Beach,
Gold Beach
Moderate; full bar;
AE, MC, V
Dinner every day

From the windows of the Nor'Wester you may watch fishermen delivering your meal: local sole, snapper, halibut, ling cod, and salmon. Most seafood is served simply: broiled or sauteed, perhaps sprinkled with some almonds. Richer concoctions are adequate. If you've had enough fish lately, try a spinach salad; the classic with bacon and chopped egg or the house recipe, with mandarin oranges, shrimp, and avocado in a tangy orange dressing.

LODGINGS

Tu Tu Tun Lodge
Follow the Rogue River
up the north bank,
(503) 247-6664
96550 North Bank
Rogue, Gold Beach,
OR 97444
Expensive; full bar;
MC, V
Breakfast, lunch,
dinner every day

Tucked into the tall, mist-cloudy trees on the north shore of the Rogue River, the lodge is one of the loveliest on the coast, though you are seven miles inland. The building is handsomely designed, with such niceties as private porches overlooking the river, racks to hold fishing gear, and stylish, rustic decor throughout. You can choose among 16 units in the two-story main building, or two larger, noisier kitchen suites in the lodge; all face the river. You may bring Fido: $3 charge.

Owners Dirk and Laurie Van Zante are excellent guides to the area. Jet boats up the Rogue stop here to pick up people, and you can swim in the heated lap pool, use the four-hole pitch-and-putt course, play horseshoes, relax around the mammoth rock fireplace, or hike. Most people come to fish, of course, since the Chinook salmon and steelhead are famous in this area.

Three meals a day are served in the lodge or on the patio, family style from lazy susans. Dinner begins with hors d'oeuvres in the bar, compliments of the Van Zantes. Your own fish might be the entree, or perhaps prime rib, or chicken breasts with a champagne sauce, with freshly made soup, salad, bread, and dessert. The no-choice meals are well cooked, and outsiders can dine here if they make advance reservations. The wine list is ordinary. Tu Tu Tun is open May through October only; however, two fully equipped river suites are available in winter.

Fair Winds Bed and Breakfast

Call for directions, (503) 247-6753
Mail: PO Box 1274, Gold Beach, OR 97444
Inexpensive; checks ok

One of the few coast spots where the ocean's not necessarily the draw, although you can glimpse it through the forest; gardens, paths, kids' treehouse (yes, they're invited), and Jacuzzi in the outdoor gazebo are the real draw. There's a bedroom with an antique double bed, a library with a single bed. The bath is shared. Hostess Marion ("Butch") Jarman will dish up breakfast on a whim: lemon bread or sheepherder's bread, cheeses, local Black Forest ham, fruit, and fresh-ground coffee, or Dutch babies and decadent French toast. She's a delightful woman who will gladly share stories from her travels and her love of reading.

Nicki's Country Place

4 miles up north bank of Rogue River,
(503) 247-6037
31780 Edson Creek Road, Mail: PO Box 1065, Gold Beach, OR 97444
Moderate; MC, V

You'll feel at home here (even if home isn't a chateau on 11 acres); Nicki Fass makes sure of it by accommodating almost any wish. Once she switched bedrooms with guests who were enchanted with her loft. Another time she moved to her mother's to give honeymooners full privacy. She'll also adjust to your morning appetite. Breakfasts can be oversized country-style (German pancakes with apples, Denver omelets, bran muffins, or biscuits and gravy) or continental. She'll serve indoors or out on the deck backed by the Siskiyou Mountains. She'll freeze your catch, pack you a lunch, or prepare dinner (with at least a little advance notice). Flexibility is her forte.

Ireland's Rustic Lodges, Inc.

South of town off Highway 101,
(503) 247-7718
1120 S Ellensburg Avenue, Gold Beach, OR 97444
Moderate; checks ok

The original eight cabins live up to the name they got when the Irelands owned the place: rustic log structures with driftwood handrails and nice stonework set amid lovely, well-maintained gardens. They have one or two bedrooms and fireplaces, but unfortunately no kitchens. Maybe that's because Mrs. Ireland once brought $6 steak dinners to the rooms. But no more. Under the present owners there are new cabins and about 27 motel rooms; all have queen beds, fireplaces, and decks overlooking the Pacific. Two complete three- and four-bedroom houses are available for $65. Nonsmoking rooms available upon request. The landscaping, always lovely, is renowned.

Jot's Resort

At the Rogue River Bridge, (503) 247-6676; (800) FOR-JOTS
94630 Waterfront Loop, Mail: PO Box J, Gold

The manicured grounds of this lovely resort spread out on the north bank of the Rogue River near the historic Rogue River Bridge; the lights of Gold Beach (and the traffic) are just across the river. The 140 rooms are spacious, tastefully decorated, and well furnished. Sum-

Beach, OR 97444
Moderate; AE, DC,
MC, V

mer rates range from about $59 for a standard room to $145 for a two-bedroom condo accommodating six. There's an outdoor pool and an indoor spa. Rent a bike (or a boat!) to explore the riverfront. Rogue River jet boats and guided fishing trips leave right from the resort's docks. Unprepared? The lodge will rent you all the necessary gear.

BROOKINGS

Brookings sits in Oregon's "banana belt," just six miles north of the California line: it enjoys the state's mildest winter temperatures. In addition, the town is bookended by breathtaking beauty. To the northwest are the Samuel H. Boardman and Harris Beach State Parks. To the east are the verdant Siskiyou Mountains, deeply cut by the Chetco and Winchuck rivers. Brookings also boasts the safest harbor—and therefore a busy port—on the Oregon Coast.

Chetco Valley Historical Museum. The standard pioneer items are here, plus a haunting iron casting of a face, which may have been left by Sir Francis Drake in 1579. Near the museum is the nation's largest cypress tree. Highway 101 south of town, (503) 469-6651.

Azalea State Park just east of 101. Fragrant Western azaleas bloom in May, alongside wild strawberries, fruit trees, and violets; you can picnic amid all this splendor on hand-hewn myrtlewood tables. Myrtlewood, which grows here and in Palestine, can be seen in groves in Loeb Park, eight miles north of town off 101, or carved up into far too many souvenir knickknacks.

Outdoor activities. Fishing is usually good here: a small fleet operates at the south end of town. And there's access from Brookings to trails into the Kalmiopsis Wilderness Area and the Siskiyou National Forest. The Redwood Nature Trail winds through one of the few remaining groves of coastal redwoods in Oregon.

RESTAURANTS

Mama's Authentic Italian Food
The Central Mall Building on Highway 101, (503) 469-7611 703 Chetco Avenue, Brookings
Inexpensive; beer and wine; MC, V
Lunch, dinner every day

Octogenarian "Mama" (Antonia Lucarini Vallejo) means authentic: she slow-simmers her *real* sauces and hand-makes her pasta, pizza, and bread. She may be 82 and petite, but she's a dynamo. She cooks *and* waits table *and* buses the dishes. And visits with you as if this were her dining room at home. She and her extended family keep this no-frills place humming with true warmth. Her no-fuss food is good, and cheap. Try the ravioli with meatballs and hand-thrown pizzas. "Aglio and olio" will provide a proper garlic hit; a full plate costs less than $6, served with Mama's crisp and garlicky breadsticks and salad.

Plum Pudding
At the north end of town, (503) 469-6961 1011 Chetco Avenue, Brookings
Inexpensive; no alcohol;

The bad news is that Plumm Smith sold her popular restaurant. The good news is that her 11-year employee, Karen Kemp, bought it. Plumm's touch is still evident, right down to her favorite calligraphed motto: "Eat dessert first, life is uncertain." Certainly the warm

checks ok
Breakfast, lunch Tues-Sat

chocolate torte, made with two pounds of chocolate and served topped with whipped cream, bears out the maxim. But you'll be hard-pressed to finish any of the luncheon specials, such as spinach lasagne or spinach quiche, if you follow this advice. Try the chicken enchirito—a large flour tortilla filled with chicken, potato chunks, onions, and olives in a mild Mexican sauce, covered with Cheddar cheese, baked, and served with sour cream and salsa. Breakfasts run from light to overwhelming, such as Eggs Arielle, a toasted English muffin topped with cream cheese, Canadian bacon, fluffy herbed eggs, tomato, Cheddar cheese, and hollandaise. Everything comes off wonderfully here, and Kemp's commitment to freshness is always evident.

Rubio's
At the north end of town,
(503) 469-4919
1136 Chetco Avenue,
Brookings
Moderate; beer and wine;
AE, MC, V
Lunch, dinner Tues-Sat

The salsa is outstanding; you can buy bottles of it here and elsewhere in Brookings. But the restaurant itself is the only place you can get Rubio's incredible chiles rellenos and chile verde. And—wow—the Combination Seafood a la Rubio blends fresh ling cod, scallops, and prawns in a butter, garlic, wine, and jalapeno sauce. The 10 tables at this drive-in-ish eatery don't provide much seating room, so patrons have grown accustomed to taking the food out.

LODGINGS

Chetco River Inn
Follow North Bend Road
17 miles, turn left after
4th bridge,
(503) 469-4628;
(800) 327-2688
21202 High Prairie
Road, Brookings,
OR 97415
Moderate; MC, V

Owners Clay and Sandra Brugger studied B&Bs they stayed at and, after buying these 35 acres, planned and built their own. Clay's architect cousin has never seen the structure he and Clay designed over the phone, but their collaboration has succeeded. Expect a culture shock.

The fishing retreat sits on a peninsula wrapped by the turquoise Chetco River, 17 miles east of Brookings and 6 miles from a phone. There's a radio-phone operator, but forget privacy. Others often overhear *and* interrupt your conversation—it's almost a sport around here. The lovely deep-green marble floors are a practical choice for muddy boots. All rooms view river or forest, but the place is not so remote that you can't read by safety propane lights and watch TV via satellite (there's even a VCR). The large, open main floor offers views of the river, myrtlewood groves, and wildlife. Porch overhangs and clerestory windows keep the building cool in summer; solid construction (Clay's a general contractor) and a wood stove provide winter warmth.

A fisherman-sized breakfast comes with a night's stay; however, packages include early-riser breakfast service, a deluxe sack lunch, and an exemplary five-course dinner, which might include fresh salmon or steelhead. For extra enjoyment there are a library, games, and horseshoes. All told, this is getting away from it in fishing style.

Chetco Inn

In town behind the Shell station, (503) 469-9984 417 Fern Street, Mail: PO Box 1386, Brookings, OR 97415
Inexpensive; MC, V

For years nobody but vagrants would touch this once-elegant 1915 hotel. In 1985 the Roberts and Schroder families bought the big blue building in the middle of town, rolled up their sleeves, and threw everything out. It's taken four years to restore it to the comfortable grandeur that once attracted Clark Gable and Carole Lombard to downtown Brookings. And it may take another four years before landscaping and all are complete. For now, it's a vast improvement, and the grandest place in town. Period antiques and handcrafted items decorate the 35 rooms; 10 have ocean views, most have private baths, and a half dozen come with kitchenettes. A complimentary fruit basket in the parlor is always full. Take an apple and hop on a rental bike to the harbor front.

The Ward House Bed & Breakfast

2 blocks north of the Chetco Bridge, (503) 469-5557 516 Redwood Street, Mail: PO Box 86, Brookings, OR 97415
Moderate; MC, V

Owners Shell and Gro Lent graciously share this spacious antique-filled inn in one of downtown Brookings' oldest homes. Gro will share traditions and delicacies of her native Norway—maybe even some seaweed in your breakfast eggs. (No joke—it's good!) Put your feet up in the expansive but cozy living room, in the private indoor hot tub and sauna, or on the outdoor sundeck. The large upstairs bedrooms have ocean views, queen beds, and private baths. And if you need a lift to or from the airport, the Lents will accommodate you at no extra charge.

WILLAMETTE VALLEY AND SOUTHERN OREGON

North to south along the I-5 corridor from Yamhill and Washington counties in the north to the Rogue River Valley in Southern Oregon.

OREGON CITY

Native Americans settled here some 3,000 years ago, taking advantage of the Willamette River's shallow falls for fishing. By the 1830s the falls provided water power for a flour mill. A decade later Oregon City became the state's first capital (and the first incorporated city west of the Mississippi). Dr. John McLoughlin, who ran the Hudson's Bay Company, retired here; his home is one of several attractions in a local historic district on the bluff above the downtown business district (North America's only municipal elevator runs up and down the bluff). At 500 Washington Street you'll find an interpretive center that marks the end of the 2,000-mile Oregon Trail.

AURORA

The whole town, midway between Portland and Salem on the east bank of the Willamette, is a well-preserved turn-of-the-century village that's been put on the National Register of Historic Places. Two dozen or so clapboard and Victorian houses line the highway; many contain antique shops. The Ox Barn Museum recounts the German Christian communal history of the town, (503) 678-5754.

RESTAURANTS

Chez Moustache
Corner of Highway 99E and Main,
(503) 678-1866
21527 Highway 99E,
Aurora
Moderate; full bar; MC, V
Dinner Tues-Sat

Until the town gets a new sewer system, no new restaurant will be allowed to open. So Chez Moustache has the market to itself. Chez Moustache began life as a tavern, taking its name from a Frenchman who migrated up from California. Barbara Kretz runs the place by herself, seating the guests at oilcloth-covered tables in a series of small rooms and verandahs. She spends nothing on advertising, preferring to put money into fresh ingredients. Lunches, for just over $4, include a stuffed schnitzel, beef burgundy, and breast of chicken. Three-course dinners (about $13) begin with a soup, followed by a salad with a marvelous (and secret) vinaigrette. The main course might be a filet mignon with morels or fresh oyster mushrooms, with a generous side serving of homemade pasta topped with scampi. The best desserts consist of fresh fruit.

WILLAMETTE VALLEY WINERIES

Yamhill County is a region in transition. This quiet agricultural area is being challenged by the migration of urbanites lured by its peaceful beauty less than 40 minutes from Portland. Once best known for its filbert and prune crops, the valley now boasts some of the finest vineyards on the West Coast and has a growing international reputation for pinot noir. Local produce stands still dot the roadside in summer, but increasingly it's the wineries, antique shops, and B&Bs that draw visitors to these lush green hills. A good starting place for collectibles is **Lafayette School**, Lafayette, (503) 864-2720, a large antique mall in an old schoolhouse.

Oregon has designated Highway 99W as the state's official wine road. A dozen wineries are now open to the public and ready to let you sample their products, including bottles that have won worldwide renown. Some of the best stops along Highway 99W between Portland and Eugene, north to south: **Rex Hill Vineyards**, Newberg, (503) 538-0666, has one of the state's best visitor facilities as well as some of its better pinot noirs. **Veritas Vineyard**, Newberg, (503) 538-1470, is a more modest facility across the highway from Rex Hill. Enjoy good chardonnay as well as samples from Eyrie and Adelsheim, which don't have tasting rooms of their own. **Autumn Wind Vineyard**, Newberg, (503) 538-6931, is a brand-new winery already gaining attention for its first pinot noirs. **Knudsen Erath Winery**, Dundee, (503) 538-3318, one of Oregon's largest and highest-quality producers, offers excellent pinot noir and a variety of more affordable, "good value" wines. Just up the hill from Crabtree Park, a good picnic site. **Sokol Blosser Winery**, Dundee (503) 864-2282, another large producer, also makes noteworthy pinot noir and chardonnay. Picnic facilities. **Chateau Benoit Winery**, Lafayette, (503) 864-2991, Oregon's premier sparkling-wine producer, has a fine view of the valley and an arbor for shaded picnics. **Elk Cove Vineyards**, Gaston, (503) 985-7760, presents fine pinot noir, superb late harvest rieslings, and a lovely setting in the woods. There's a second tasting room in Dundee. **Arterberry Winery**, McMinnville, (503) 472-1587, is a small working winery producing traditional sparkling wines and pinot noir. **Yamhill Valley Vineyards**, Oldsville Road off Highway 18, McMinnville (503) 843-3100, offers an attractive setting and fine pinot noir and pinot gris. **Amity Vineyards**, Amity, (503) 835-2362, features excellent gewurztraminer, pinot noir, and dry white riesling. **Bethel Heights Vineyard**, Salem, (503) 581-2262, offers estate-bottled pinot noir, chardonnay, and dry chenin blanc. **Alpine Vineyards**, Alpine, (503) 424-5851, specializes in off-dry rieslings, chardonnay, and cabernet sauvignon. **Tyee Wine Cellars**, Corvallis, (503) 753-8754, features pinot noir and pinot gris from vineyards near ancient Indian campsites.

In addition to the Willamette Valley wineries, several excellent wineries operate in the Tualatin Valley, due west of Portland: **Ponzi Vineyards**, Beaverton, (503) 628-1227, first-rate pinot noir and pinot gris; **Tualatin Vineyards**, Forest Grove, (503) 357-5005, excellent estate-bottled wines and a second tasting room in Dundee; **Shafer Vineyard Cellars**, Forest Grove, (503) 357-6604, noteworthy chardonnays; **Laurel Ridge Winery**, Forest Grove, (503) 359-5436, excellent dry gewurztraminer and sparkling wines; **Oak Knoll Winery**, Hillsboro, (503) 648-8198, award-winning pinot noir. For a booklet with maps to most of the wineries, suggested tour routes, and hours they are open to the public, contact the Oregon Winegrowers Association at 1359 W Fifth, Eugene, OR 97402, (503) 233-2377.

DUNDEE

RESTAURANTS

Pinot Pete's
Next to the AM/PM Mini Market, (503) 538-6758, (800) 422-1186
760 Highway 99W, Dundee
Inexpensive; wine and beer; MC, V
Breakfast, lunch, dinner Wed-Mon

Here's a fun place. Interesting food, available for take-out, to enjoy on all those picnic tables you see outside all those wineries you've been visiting. Peter Hale's deli/wineshop in an old diner features sandwiches, salads, soups, entrees, homemade bread, and rich desserts. The always-changing menu reflects seasonal specialties. Limited seating is available, and you can choose from an interesting selection of Oregon wines offered by the glass. If you forget to make a purchase at your favorite winery, don't despair—Pete's has a great selection with the best prices around. An especially useful service: call ahead on their toll-free number and have your picnic waiting for you en route to the wineries or the lovely Oregon coast, or even on your way back from the beach. It's true one-stop shopping.

Alfie's Wayside Country Inn
Take the Tigard exit off I-5 and follow it into Dundee, (503) 538-9407
1111 SW Highway 99W, Dundee
Moderate; full bar; AE, DC, MC, V
Lunch every day, dinner Tues-Sun, brunch Sun

Alfie's was once probably the best the area had to offer, but there are better restaurants in the valley now. The decor in this converted country home on Highway 99 is a cluttered mishmash, and so is much of the food, reflecting the eclectic personal style of owner Alfie Tahan. Prices here are on the high side, and preparations are burdened with unnecessary ingredients. Opt for the seafood, which is usually thoughtfully prepared. Fresh razor clams were lightly breaded and pan-fried with lemon juice and shallots, and garnished with capers (lots of capers—something of a theme at Alfie's). The clams were tender and flavorful. Desserts include a fine hazelnut pie—using local filberts—in a phyllo crust.

YAMHILL

LODGINGS

Flying M Ranch
10 miles west of Yamhill; watch for signs
(503) 662-3222
23029 NW Flying M Road, Yamhill, OR 97148
Moderate; AE, DC, MC, V

Several years ago the heart of this remote spot, a rustic lodge built a generation ago by the Bryce Mitchell family, burned to the ground, but the Mitchells, undaunted, rebuilt. The lodge itself contains a Western-style lounge (the bar is made from a six-ton log) and a restaurant that serves decent breakfasts and straightforward steaks.

But you don't come here for the food. Instead, you enjoy the clean, restful setting and the modest accommodations: a rather primitive "motel" that looks like a dude-ranch bunkhouse (but with Hershey kisses on the pillows at night), one of several simple cabins under alder and maple trees, or even shaded campsites at the confluence of Hanna Creek and the North Yamhill River. Or just come up for the day: enjoy the plentiful picnic grounds for families and enormous picnic shelters for large groups—and swim in the huge pond.

There's an airstrip in case you have your own plane, and stables if you want to bring your own horse. For a fee, local cowboys can take you on the trail on one of Flying M's horses. "Steak Fry" rides on summer evenings are a change of pace for city dwellers; you ride your horse down the trail (or hitch a ride on the hay wagon) to a picnic site where chefs in cowboy garb serve up T-bones with all the trimmin's. Breakfast rides are offered too.

Getting here is an adventure in itself: you drive through miles of spectacular scenery in the foothills of the Coast Range, following little red M's with wings posted along the winding country roads.

McMINNVILLE

RESTAURANTS

Lavender's Blue, A Tea Room
1 block east of Highway 99W on Cowls,
(503) 472-4594
535 N Cowls Street, McMinnville
Inexpensive; no alcohol; no credit cards, checks ok
Lunch, tea, dinner
Tues-Sat

An elegant and genteel tearoom named for an old children's song in a lovely neighborhood a few blocks from downtown McMinnville. After a long search, Terese and Keith Blanding moved from their native Montana, purchased this fine old home (they're the second owners in nearly 50 years), and decorated it—inside and out—in subtle shades of lavender and Wedgwood blue. Terese's lace collection hangs on the walls, her favorite books are on every table, and the menu shows off her splendid calligraphy. Tea here, served on fine china and silver, is a soothing respite during a weekend of wine tasting. You can enjoy cream or ginger scones, an excellent prune walnut spice cake, hazelnut torte, or, if you wish, afternoon tea with scones, savories, and dessert, all freshly made by Terese. If she has time, she'd love to talk to you about books, calligraphy, old lace, and life in Montana. By bringing together the threads of her varied passions, this remarkable woman has created the best tearoom in the Northwest.

Nick's Italian Cafe
Off Highway 99W, across from the movie theater,
(503) 434-4471
521 E Third Street, McMinnville
Moderate; beer and wine; no credit cards; checks ok
Dinner Tues-Sun

People who travel far to eat at Nick's—and some have been known to trek in from Seattle just for a meal—always remark how extraordinary it is to find a superb restaurant in such a small, out-of-the-way burg. They miss the point. Nick's would be extraordinary wherever it were—Seattle, San Francisco, even New York—for it combines two qualities rarely found in one restaurant: outstanding food and total lack of pretension. Nick Peirano is an inventive but mercifully untrendy Northern Italian cook who has created a friendly, relaxed atmosphere in which to eat marvelous meals. The elegance of the food is in its preparation, not its presentation. A piece of Nick's extraordinary lasagne, for example, comes to you naked on a plate, unadorned by even a sprig of parsley. The waiter who brings it wears corduroys and a sports shirt. He doesn't tell you his name, and he doesn't work overtime to impress you with his culinary knowledge. He doesn't have to. It's clear he knows everything that goes on in Nick's kitchen.

Nick's level-headed approach to service and atmosphere (the cafe is a renovated luncheonette) puts the food in sharp focus, where it belongs. The five-course, fixed-price menu changes nightly but always includes a second-course tureen of Nick's grandmother's rich, garlicky minestrone (alone worth the drive to McMinnville), followed by a fresh, simply dressed green salad and chewy, dense French bread from Ken Piontek's outstanding bakery in Willamina. The fourth course is always pasta, always homemade, and always delicious—from spaghetti with rosemary sauce to delicate, airy spinach ravioli. Dinner might begin with fresh asparagus, lightly steamed, then grilled quickly on a hot griddle for a·magnificent, nutty flavor. The pasta course could be hazelnut-filled ravioli in a Gorgonzola sauce or lasagne, meltingly tender with paper-thin layers, creamy middle, and slices of homemade sausage. Entree choices might be fresh halibut grilled in butter and olive oil with a light pesto sauce or sirloin steak with capers. If you have room, Nick's offers a delightful array of homemade pastries for dessert, including Italian specialties created by Nick's mother. Appropriately for a restaurant located in the heart of Oregon's wine country (and a perfect spot to dine after a day of tasting), the wine list includes an impressive array of local bottlings at very reasonable prices, and the knowledgeable staff won't steer you wrong.

La Maison Surrette
On 3rd near Ford,
(503) 472-6666
729 E Third Street,
McMinnville
Moderate; beer and wine;
AE, MC, V
Dinner Fri-Sat

This immaculately restored Victorian house, complete with antique furnishings, is the setting for chef John Surrett's restaurant (he added the final "e" to make the restaurant sound more French). The prix-fixe meal begins with a simple appetizer, followed by soup, perhaps seafood bisque (more of a chowder really, studded with bay scallops and potatoes). Main courses might range from fresh halibut with sauce Bearnaise to filet mignon with hunter sauce or medallions of pork with a white wine-butter–Dijon sauce. Desserts are prepared by Surrett's wife, Carol, who doubles as the waitstaff. Choices could be a rich, bittersweet chocolate cheesecake or fresh apple pie. This leisurely, moderately priced meal is available only on weekends; your hosts have full-time careers in Portland.

Roger's
*Corner of 27th and
Highway 99W,
(503) 472-0917
2121 E 27th Street,
McMinnville
Moderate; full bar;
AE, DC, MC, V
Lunch Mon-Fri, dinner
every day*

Tucked below Highway 99 on the outskirts of town, Roger's grew out of an adjoining seafood market, which still provides both the basis for the restaurant's menu and the rationale for the dining room's nautical motif. The decor is enhanced by bentwood chairs and fresh carnations and, above all, by the calm setting: a quiet stream running through natural greenery just outside. In good weather you can eat out on the patio; at night the trees twinkle with hundreds of tiny lights.

The execution of Roger's deep-fried items—especially the fish and chips—can be ideal, but it's not a sure thing, according to local reports. Baked and sauteed items show a steadier hand. A dish of snapper arrived hot from the oven, topped with a tarragon glaze, accompanied by perfectly done fries (crunchy outside, moist inside). The soup at a recent meal was a floury cream of asparagus, but the highlight, surprisingly, was a delightful homemade pine-nut torte, moist without being gooey or cloying.

LODGINGS

Mattey House
*¼ mile south of Lafayette
on Highway 99W,
(503) 434-5058
10221 NE Mattey Lane,
McMinnville, OR 97128
Moderate; MC, V*

Mattey House was the first B&B in the Willamette Valley, and it's still the best. Standing behind its own little vineyard—an acre of Muller Thurgau—like a remote French manor house, it's actually an 1890s Victorian mansion, beautifully restored by Gene and Susan Irvin. Each of the four guest rooms is named for a wine variety (pinot noir, chardonnay), and three are decorated with antiques. Extra touches include fresh flowers, plush bathrobes, bedtime chocolates, and an afternoon glass of wine in the parlor. The Irvins are perfect hosts and knowledgeable, enthusiastic guides to the local wine scene. The hearty homemade breakfasts are a perfect send-off for a day of wine-sampling in the nearby Red Hills.

Safari Motor Inn
*At the intersection of
19th and Highway 99W,
(503) 472-5187
345 N Highway 99W,
McMinnville, OR 97128
Inexpensive; AE, DC,
MC, V*

Just off Highway 99 as it enters McMinnville, this unassuming motor lodge doesn't offer anything fancy, but it's ideally located for visitors who shy from the B&B scene. The Safari offers relatively new, perfectly quiet rooms with wonderfully comfortable beds. A small exercise facility with Jacuzzi is available, and the coffee shop is fine for breakfasts.

Steiger Haus
*Turn east of Highway 99
at the hospital on Cowles,
(503) 472-0821
360 Wilson Street,
McMinnville, OR 97128*

This large contemporary home is located right in McMinnville, only minutes from some of the area's best wineries and restaurants. Two rooms downstairs (at press time, a third was being refinished) are comfortable and attractive and overlook a private park. The decor reflects the owners' hobbies—spinning, weaving, making leaded glass. Merino Morningsun Room ($55) is small and direct-

Moderate; no credit cards; checks ok

ly below the kitchen, so you can hear breakfast being prepared as you awake. Finnsheep Fireside Room ($75) is of particular note—an elegant, spacious suite with fireplace, private bath, and its own deck. Separating the two rooms is a comfortable common room for reading or watching the large color TV. Doris and Lynn Steiger are friendly hosts, ready to steer you to their favorite wineries and restaurants. They'll serve you a hearty breakfast in the bright kitchen to start your day off right.

BELLEVUE/SHERIDAN

Bellevue (a little bump on the road) is the site of three fine establishments, all under one roof. The **Oregon Wine Tasting Room**, (503) 843-3787, 11:30–5:30 daily, offers tastes of the best bottlings from two dozen Oregon wineries. **The Lawrence Gallery**, (503) 843-3633, 10–5:30 daily, is an excellent showcase of fine regional talent in all media. Upstairs is **Augustine's**, one of the region's better restaurants.

RESTAURANTS

Augustine's
*Highway 18, 7 miles west of McMinnville,
(503) 843-3225
19706 Highway 18,
Bellevue
Moderate; full bar;
MC, V
Lunch, dinner Wed-Sun;
brunch Sun*

Augustine's was purchased by owner-chef Jeff Quatraro in early 1988, and the restaurant has been steadily improving ever since. The clean, open space has views out to the farmland on one side and down into the Lawrence Gallery on the other side.

You could start your meal with a smoked seafood platter (salmon, mussels, halibut, and cream cheese) or some of the excellent creamy clam chowder. Soup or a pleasant green salad is included with the entree. For the main course, there are pasta dishes, filet mignon, and lamb chops, but seafood is a real focus at Augustine's (Quatraro worked at the Couch Street Fishhouse in Portland). Poached salmon was a huge fillet served with a simple herb butter. Fresh sturgeon fillet piccata was tender and delicious. Desserts are deservedly popular. The legendary hazelnut cheesecake is rich, light, and not too sweet; citrus tart (orange, lemon, and grapefruit curd) is tangy and refreshing. The all-Oregon wine list is reasonably priced. Many fine vintages are offered by the glass, particularly new releases. Sunday brunch with live classical music in the background is especially popular. With assured, knowledgeable service and fine fresh ingredients carefully and imaginatively prepared, Augustine's has become a real star in the Willamette Valley dining scene.

LODGINGS

Sheridan Country Inn
1 mile west of Sheridan on Highway 18,

This old house is now an inn, located in sleepy Sheridan. There are ten rooms, six in the funky but spacious mansion (formerly a private residence) and four in the outside

(503) 843-3151
1330 W Main, Sheridan,
OR 97378
Moderate; DC, MC, V

duplexes. The rooms ($35–$55) are large and comfortable, with views of the acre of grounds surrounding the house. All have private bath, phone, TV, and a small refrigerator to chill your latest wine discoveries. Room 7 ($95) is a huge suite with a private Jacuzzi. The location isn't particularly convenient to the wineries, but the rates are reasonable, and kids are welcome, making the inn a nice alternative to a motel. During summer, you can relax in the outdoor Jacuzzi. A serve-yourself continental breakfast is included.

MOUNT ANGEL

The town stages a Bavarian folk festival in mid-September that's enthusiastically supported by neighboring residents.

Mount Angel Abbey, a Benedictine seminary for the last hundred years, is a fully accredited college atop a butte the Indians considered sacred. The campus is worth a visit, not only for the view but for the architecture (the library is a gem by the Finnish architect Alvar Aalto). For hours, call (503) 845-3030.

SALEM

Oregon's capital city has nearly 100,000 residents and is home to the Northwest's oldest college, Willamette University. The capitol building, dedicated in 1938, is one of the country's newest; you get a good view of the campus and the river from its dome. Astride the top stands a statue of the Oregon Pioneer, cast in bronze and finished in gold leaf. Salem's less visible feature is Mill Creek, which meanders through town toward the river; it originally provided power to the manufacturing plants along its path.

Mission Mill Village, 1313 Mill Street SE, (503) 585-7012, is an impressive 4½-acre cluster of restored buildings from the 1800s: a woolen mill, a parsonage, a Presbyterian church, and several homes. The mill itself—which drew its power from Mill Creek—houses a museum that literally makes the sounds of the factory come alive. The Jason Lee House, dating from 1841, is the oldest remaining frame house in the Northwest; regular tours of the premises run from 10 to 4:30, Tuesday–Saturday. Picnic along the stream and feed the ducks, if you like. The Salem Visitor Information Center is part of the complex, as are several shops selling handcrafted clothing, gifts, and antiques.

Bush House, 600 Mission Street SE, (503) 363-4714, is a genuine Victorian home built in 1877–78 by pioneer newspaper publisher Asahel Bush. It sits on an 89-acre park, complete with conservatory, rose gardens, hiking paths, and a barn-turned-art-gallery. Tours of the house every half hour.

The downtown business district, for the most part, has now been restored. The three-story Reed Opera House at Liberty and Court streets is one of the earliest examples; the original offices have been partitioned into a maze of shops and restaurants.

Old-fashioned ferries. These cable-operated barges still traverse the Willamette River in a few places, supplementing the few bridges and offering brief—but restful—scenic rides. Under county jurisdiction, they're inexpensive (50 cents for passengers,

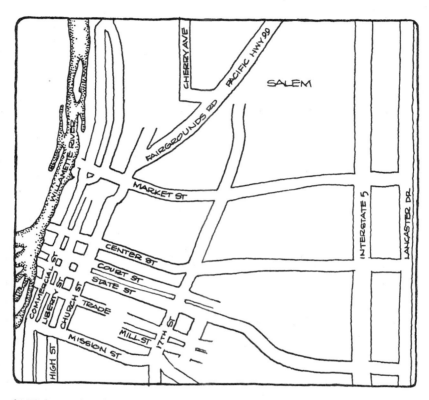

$1.50 for cars) and treat travelers to panoramic views upriver and down as they churn across. The Canby ferry, west of Highway 99E, is the most northerly, (503) 655-8521. Another is about 12 miles north of Salem at Wheatland, (503) 588-5304; a fine, forested picnic spot on the western shore is Maud Williamson State Park. The Buena Vista ferry, halfway between Salem and Albany, is no longer running.

RESTAURANTS

Alessandro's Park Plaza
Trade and High streets,
(503) 370-9951
325 High Street, Salem
Moderate; full bar; AE,
DC, MC, V
Lunch Mon-Fri, dinner
Mon-Sat

Alessandro Fasani has returned to Salem (and still manages to look after his place in Portland, Alessandro's, as well) to take over the restaurant he started here, overlooking Mill Creek Park—a lovely urban oasis. You will feel out of place here if you don't dress up. The interior is handsome: layers of red, white, and green napery give the two-story interior an elegant Italian look (Fasani calls it Roman); wildflowers add a nice touch to the tables, contrasting with the just-short-of-pretentious service and supercilious menu. ("The names of some of the dishes are unpronounceable. It is permissible to point.")

One particularly good dish is oysters amandine,

served freshly sauteed in an almond crust with a relish of eggplant, coriander, and green pepper. The hearty bouillabaisse is laced with saffron and studded with shellfish and chunks of tomato. Three different multicourse dinners are offered daily: the staff asks only if there's a particular dish you don't like, and they surprise you with the rest. For a $15 tariff you might get a hot appetizer (salmon over linguine, for instance), a salad, a plate of chicken forestiere, and a fresh fruit dessert. For $20, a cold appetizer and a hot appetizer, with a veal Marsala and a more elaborate dessert. At $25, three appetizer courses, the entree, and a choice of desserts.

Inn at Orchard Heights

On Highway 221 north of Salem, (503) 378-1780
695 Orchard Heights Road NW, Salem
Moderate; full bar;
AE, DC, MC, V
Dinner Mon-Sat

It took a sense of humor to turn the inside of this 1937-vintage home overlooking Salem into a thoroughly slick restaurant full of glass, chrome, and mirrors, then adorn the outside with enough twinkling lights to illuminate the capitol building. You sit in the bar, sipping a glass of fragrant Yamhill Valley Vineyards elderblossom wine, and see a gray deer in the bushes: it's a fake, made from twigs and vineyard clippings.

Recent reports claim the kitchen has been relying more on pretensions than on quality—not going the extra step we know they're capable of. When they're on, the preparations can be first-rate, beginning with homemade appetizers such as freshly marinated herring in sour cream. Follow that up with an unusual soup (cream of dill pickle, Cheddar cheese au gratin). Then proceed to the entrees, many stuffed seafood and pasta dishes as well as sautes and curries of veal and pork; Swiss-style schnitzels show up as well. Owner-chef Hans d'Alessio's continental sauces go well with the local wines; try a Sokol Blosser chardonnay with appetizers or fish. There's a conventional pastry tray if you still have room for dessert, as well as espresso drinks from the comfortable bar.

Kwan's

Commercial and Mission, (503) 362-7711
835 Commercial Street SE, Salem
Inexpensive; full bar;
MC, V
Lunch Sun-Fri, dinner every day

A schematic diagram of the water system is not the first thing you'd expect to see in Salem's best Chinese restaurant; however, Kam Sang Kwan is very proud of his restaurant's pure water and his rebellion against, as he calls it, the "Chinese syndrome" (he uses no chemicals, no animal fat, and no MSG). As a matter of fact, he's so conscious of what goes into your body, he's put the dietary needs (and allergies) of his regular customers into a database. You can count on the numerous seafood dishes being fresh (and the garlic squid being oh-so-tender). All the beef is sliced from top sirloin, and all the chicken is skinned. Kwan's touch leans toward the spicy, but it rarely overpowers the entree itself.

All places in this book are recommended; even "no stars" are worth knowing about.

Pilar's

In the Reed Opera House
in Court Liberty,
(503) 363-7578
189 Liberty Street N,
Salem
Inexpensive; full bar; AE,
MC, V
Lunch, dinner Tues-Sat

If you don't like garlic or olive oil, this is not for you—but enough people do to warrant the new bigger location (only a name change away from the former Via Florencia). Pilar Thompson makes pasta for take-out, but why leave when there's space for all in any of the three different rooms (one's all nonsmoking) where Pilar serves the freshest of pasta dishes on heirloom china. A remarkable woman, Pilar (born in Spain) cooks with a zeal that borders on religious devotion and comes up with inspired tastes: raviolis that melt in your mouth, linguine with pesto, fresh walnuts, and garlic. The extravagant salad bar—full of a variety of pasta salads as well as greens—is locally famous, as are the low prices and great service.

Off Center Cafe

17th and Center,
(503) 363-9245
1741 Center NE, Salem
Inexpensive; no alcohol;
no credit cards; checks ok
Breakfast Tues-Sat, lunch
Tues-Fri, dinner Thurs-
Sat, brunch Sun

A throwback to the '60s, the Off Center Cafe features a genuine soda fountain, demure classical music or rock 'n' roll (depending on the chef's mood), a clientele ranging from aging hippies to professors grading papers to bankers in three-piece suits, and intriguing food: scrambled tofu for breakfast, black Cuban beans and rice at lunch, fresh halibut with lime at dinner, and fruit pies all day long. It's not a fancy place, but one that offers "real food" and prides itself on serving its customers well. Many have their own special concoctions listed on the menu: try Ed's Cooler, a mixture of ice cream, mocha, and Pepsi. Mmmmm.

LODGINGS

State House B&B

21st and State,
(503) 588-1340
2146 State Street, Salem,
OR 97301
Inexpensive; MC, V

Behind Mike Winsett and Judy Uselman's B&B you'll discover a handsomely landscaped garden: a wide spot along Mill Creek with its own gazebo, hot tub, ducks, and geese. You can barely hear the traffic as you sit in the shade of red maples, and you begin to understand why the owners have made grand plans for this site: a small boat dock, rose bushes, a grape arbor, and eventually a cafe with a terrace overlooking the creek.

The four-bedroom B&B boasts queen beds, brass fixtures, chandeliers, and terrycloth bathrobes. Two spacious "standard" rooms share a bath; two suites (one with a kitchenette) have private baths. New to the property are two bungalows, one a two-bedroom cottage with fireplace, the other containing two separate units that can be combined to form a three-bedroom spread. Both cottages have kitchenettes.

Breakfasts feature bacon or ham that Mike, a trained butcher, cuts himself, plus virtually anything else you'd like (eggs Benedict, crepes, a breakfast casserole).

Chumaree

Market Street exit off I-5,

Of all the motels near the capitol buildings, this one has the most to offer. The rooms are what you'd expect—

(503) 370-7888,
(800) 248-6273
3301 Market Street NE,
Salem, OR 97303
Moderate; AE, DC,
MC, V

except the luxury suites with Jacuzzis. Still, it's the courtesy car to the airport, direct-dial phones, and the indoor garden—all free to all guests—that place this convention-oriented motel one step above the others.

INDEPENDENCE

As long as anyone can remember, **Taylor's Fountain & Gift**, on the corner of Main & Monmouth, has been serving up old-fashioned sodas, burgers, and breakfasts. Marge Taylor, her daughter, and two granddaughters run the place and haven't changed it much in its 44 years.

RESTAURANTS

Amador's Alley
Hoffman and Main,
(503) 838-0170
870 N Main Street,
Independence
Inexpensive; beer and
wine; MC, V
Lunch, dinner Mon-Sat

Here's a little gem: a place just north of the restored main part of town, tucked into a fading strip mall, that produces some of the most honest Mexican fare we've tasted in years. Brothers Manuel and Antonio Amador do the cooking while their families (down to the youngest children, no more than 10 years old) wait on the customers. Nothing elaborate in the way of decor: a whitewashed space, a few Mexican fans, paper flowers, a painted parrot on the floor. But you know it's going to be good as soon as the first basket of chips arrives (thick, crunchy, homemade), along with a fresh salsa; you can taste the corn and the tomatoes.

Choices here look like basic Tex-Mex, but everything from tacos to enchiladas is exquisitely fresh, piping hot, and lavishly garnished with sour cream, avocado, fresh tomatoes, and green onions. The refried beans, just short of soupy, are especially noteworthy. The side dish of hot sauce is flecked with fiery red peppers. Because everything tastes so clean, so natural, you may find yourself wishing for a hint of subtle spicing—a pinch of cumin, perhaps—in the chicken enchilada. But Amador's is doing too well to risk a challenge to their regular patrons; Manuel and Antonio are so popular they've already expanded twice in four years.

ALBANY

Historic districts. Just far enough away from the freeway to have escaped the bulldozer, Albany's downtown commercial and residential areas have been restored to Victorian splendor. A self-guided tour of the scores of historic homes and business buildings displays 13 distinct architectural styles in the 50-block, 368-building Monteith Historic District alone. Then there are the Hackelman District (28 blocks, 210 buildings) and Downtown (9½ blocks, 80 buildings). Many of the buildings are open for inspection on annual tours—the last Saturday in July and the Sunday evening before Christmas Eve. A handy guide is available free of charge from the Albany Convention and Visitors Commission, 435 W First Avenue, (503) 926-1517, and guided tours through Experience Albany, 2697 NW Quince, (503) 926-5652 or (503) 926-1517.

Covered bridges. In 1930, more than 300 covered bridges spanned streams and rivers in western Oregon. Today only 50-some remain, most of them in the Willamette Valley counties of Lane, Lincoln, and Linn, but that's more than in any state west of the Mississippi. Many have aged gracefully, while others—sagging precariously—are candidates for restoration by the Covered Bridge Society of Oregon. Best jumping-off places for easy-to-follow circuits of the bridges are Albany, Eugene, and Cottage Grove; in addition, many handsome bridges dot the woods of the Oregon Coast Range. For details and maps of wooden bridges, send SASE with 45 cents postage to the Covered Bridge Society of Oregon, PO Box 1804, Newport, OR 97365, or call (503) 265-2934.

RESTAURANTS

Novak's Hungarian Paprikas
Take exit 233B toward town, (503) 967-9488
2835 Santiam Highway, Albany
Inexpensive; no alcohol; MC, V
Lunch Sun-Fri, dinner every day

Refugees from Pecs in south-central Hungary, Joe and Matilda Novak run this roadside restaurant with help from their family: daughter Karen bakes the desserts, son Ed helps with the sausages, big Joe dispenses the bear hugs. And another brother may soon be on the plane from Hungary, importing another Novak talent, no doubt.

Dinners begin with a tasty chicken-and-vegetable soup and a salad of chopped lettuce covered with a house dressing, which falls somewhere between French and Italian (dry packets are now available for take-out). Then come the Hungarian specialties, well executed though on the bland side: beef *szelet* and *pariszi* (pork) *szelet* are tender cutlets, battered and fried to crisp perfection; *kolbasz* are mild homemade sausages served with deliciously tangy sweet-and-sour shredded cabbage; *szekely toltot kapposzta* is a cabbage roll stuffed with lean pork and topped with a dollop of sour cream. Everything tastes fine, if a bit underseasoned; you long for a bold, assertive hand in the kitchen, or at least for a glass of wine to spice up the meal. For dessert, choose the Dobos torte over Mama's Favorite.

LODGINGS

Lilla's
Ellsworth and 7th, (503) 928-9437
206 Seventh Avenue SW, Albany, OR 97321
Moderate; AE, MC, V
Lunch, dinner Tues-Sat, brunch Sun

Located amid the grand old homes of Albany's Monteith Historic District, Lilla's is one of the best-preserved Victorian mansions in town. There's a respectable restaurant downstairs and four guest rooms upstairs.

You might think you're visiting friends at a vintage beach house with hooked rugs on the plank floors, comfortable bedding, and a claw-footed tub with a ring shower; yet the place is lacking in some of the amenities you'd expect at home—no bedside tables or lamps, for instance. Breakfasts are filling: fresh orange juice; homemade nut and raisin bread; an omelet with mushrooms, Italian sausage, red and green peppers, basil, and two cheeses.

Chuck and Nancy Gilliam, who worked for the original owners, have taken over Lilla's; Nancy does the baking and acts as chef for lunch and dinner. The Gilliams don't live in the house, so be sure to ask for a key if you (or your children) plan to stay out late.

CORVALLIS

Very cosmopolitan for its small size and slow pace, Corvallis gets its intellectual stimulation from the influx of academic events at Oregon State University (a land-grant college that specializes in agriculture). "Beaver" football and basketball games are a big deal; Parker Stadium holds enough seats for the entire town. The student union displays the best of the student artwork, and the **Horner Museum** in Gill Coliseum houses a rambling collection of antiques, Native American artifacts, and natural history pieces, plus a new crafts gift shop, (503) 754-2951. **Corvallis Art Center,** located in a renovated 1889 Episcopal church off Central Park, displays local crafts and hosts weekly lunchtime concerts, (503) 754-1551. Corvallis is ideal for biking and running; most streets include a wide bike lane, and routes follow both the Willamette and Marys rivers. **Avery Park**, 15th Street and US 20, offers a maze of wooded trails as well as prime picnic sites and a rose garden.

RESTAURANTS

The Gables
Follow Harrison to 9th,
(503) 752-3364
1121 NW 9th Street,
Corvallis
Moderate; full bar; AE,
DC, MC, V
Dinner every day

For years, this was *the* only place to go for dinner in Corvallis. And even with increased competition today, The Gables continues to be a mainstay of the community. The atmosphere is homey with dark-wood furnishings, low beams, and a fireplace, and the staff is courteous. The menu features tried-and-true American fare: prime rib, lamb chops, teriyaki chicken, and, more recently, seafood. Dinners are huge (especially given the price) and come with all the trimmings of sourdough bread, relish tray, salad or chicken bisque, veggies, and rice or potato. Fresh herbs from The Gables' own garden enhance the meals. The prime rib has a reputation as the best in town, and the seafood saute we tried was a generous crock full of prawns, scallops, salmon, and halibut in a delicate lemon-butter-and-wine sauce. A heaping bowlful of homemade garlic croutons comes to your table for soup and salad. The wine cellar is often used for special occasions.

Nearly Normal's
Near the corner of
Monroe and 15th,
(503) 753-0791
109 NW 15th Street,
Corvallis
Inexpensive; beer and

Normal's is not normal. It's funk: a gigantic mural of orchids out front, a fine collection of pink plastic flamingos on the back porch, and sometimes-barefoot waiters in shorts. Inside, Normal's is a noisy den of mismatched tables and chairs crowded with OSU folk enjoying generous helpings of the restaurant's "gonzo cuisine"—

*wine; no credit cards;
checks ok
Breakfast, lunch, dinner
Mon-Sat*

vegetarian fare prepared with gusto. Variations of the oversized burritos are the specialty, but Normal's also dabbles in pastas, stir-fries, and Middle Eastern dishes. The falafel is a hearty mix of spicy garbanzo patties packed into pita with fresh veggies and a cool yogurt sauce, and the Sunburger (made with sunflower seeds, eggs, and veggies on a whole-wheat bun) satisfies even the most skeptical carnivore. There's live music Wednesday, Thursday, and Saturday nights, but there's never any smoking, and there's a suggested two-drink maximum.

Oscar's
*Behind the courthouse,
between 4th and 5th,
(503) 753-7444
559 Monroe Avenue,
Corvallis
Inexpensive; no alcohol;
MC, V
Breakfast, lunch Mon-Sat,
dinner Tues-Sun, brunch
Sun*

Known for its big breakfasts served till noon, Oscar's is a bustling weekend spot for waffles, French toast, and egg specialties. Design-your-own omelets can be ordered throughout the day. At lunch the hot and cold sandwiches, stuffed potatoes, quiche of the day, and a slew of salads are best when you carry them across the street to the park.

LODGINGS

Hanson Country Inn
*5 minutes west of town
on Western,
(503) 752-2919
795 SW Hanson Street,
Corvallis, OR 97333
Moderate; DC, MC, V*

★★

You follow a country road to a grand wood-and-brick 1928 farmhouse on a knoll overlooking the Willamette Valley. Formerly a prosperous poultry-breeding ranch, it's now, thanks to an extensive renovation by San Franciscan Patricia Covey, a registered historic home. A hand-carved staircase of imported New Zealand gumwood leads up to the four guest rooms with original hardwood floors and built-in cabinetry. The living room (with piano and fireplace), sun room, and library are often used for weddings. Upstairs in the best suite, you will find a queen-size four-poster bed, a private bath and a study. After a gourmet breakfast, explore the grounds and the original egg house. Bring the kids, but not the dog; the chickens, sheep, and rabbits are company enough.

Madison Inn
*Corner of 7th and
Madison, near the
University,
(503) 757-1274
660 Madison Avenue,
Corvallis, OR 97330
Moderate; MC, V*

A stately five-story Tudor opposite Central Park, downtown. Owner Paige Down grew up in the house (which her mother, Kathryn Brandis, began as a bed and breakfast in 1980), and the seven guest bedrooms are named after Paige and her siblings. Furnished with antique beds and woolen patchwork quilts, the wood-floored rooms have a rustic, cozy feel. Request the Kathryn Room on the top floor for a cathedral ceiling and the best view of the park, or the Matt & Mike Room for a private entry (it's the only one with a private bath). Paige and husband Richard prepare a full breakfast for guests that includes such daily specialties as quiche, scones, or Dutch babies.

After more than a decade as a bed and breakfast, the inn has secured a solid reputation in the area, and reservations should be made well in advance.

ELMIRA

LODGINGS

McGillivray's Log Home Bed and Breakfast
*14 miles west of Eugene off Highway 126,
(503) 935-3564
88680 Evers Road,
Elmira, OR 97437
Moderate; MC, V*

This peaceful, spacious log home has two huge guest rooms, both with private baths. Skylights let the sun into the upstairs room (with a king-size bed and two twins—great for families). A pancake and baked-egg-and-bacon breakfast is prepared on the wood cookstove with an antique griddle. But contemporary comforts are not forgotten—the log building is both air-conditioned and wheelchair-accessible.

EUGENE

Oregon's second-largest city has finally pulled itself up out of an almost-decade-long, timber-related economic slump. Nowadays there is renewed civic energy and more commercial activity than the city has seen since its heyday in the mid-'70s. Major new construction is planned for downtown. The historic district is expanding. New restaurants are opening. The downtown mall that, at a low point in the early '80s, looked more like a ghost town than the civic showcase it was designed to be, is prosperous once again.

Still a study in contrasts, Eugene is an odd mix of cultured urbanites, backcountry loggers, and persevering hippies—possibly one of the few places on earth where a 10-block skyline includes both a grain elevator and a world-class performing arts center. Home to the state's flagship institution of higher learning, the University of Oregon, the area also includes one of Weyerhaeuser's largest mills and a thriving alternative community. Eugene has its own symphony, theater, ballet, and opera companies.

Hult Center for the Performing Arts is a top concert facility with two architecturally striking, acoustically perfect halls. The 24-hour concert line is (503) 342-5746.

University of Oregon has an art museum with a permanent collection of noteworthy Oriental pieces, a new natural history museum, and an array of films, speakers, and events.

Wistech, a hands-on science and technology museum coupled with a planetarium, is the place to take kids on rainy afternoons; open Tuesday–Sunday afternoons, 2300 Centennial Boulevard, (503) 484-9027.

Lane County Museum offers a large homesteading collection and excellent historical photography; open Tuesday–Sunday, 740 W 13th, (503) 687-4239.

Saturday Market is a not-to-be-missed Eugene experience. This thriving open-air crafts and food fair features nonstop entertainment and the best people-watching in town; open April–December, 9am–6pm, High Street at Broadway.

Fifth Street Public Market has three levels of shops surrounding a lovely brick courtyard and fountain. Jazz, classical, and folk musicians perform on most weekend afternoons. There's ample opportunity for inspired snacking (Italian, Greek, nouvelle cuisine) as you read any number of out-of-town newspapers (from Marketplace Books)

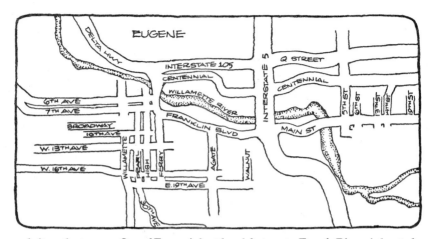

and sit on the terrace. One of Eugene's best breakfast spots, **Terry's Diner**, is located in the market, as is the area's newest Thai restaurant, **Mekala's**.

Outdoors. Two rivers run through town, the Willamette and the McKenzie, and, thanks to the farsighted environmentalism of the late governor Tom McCall, they run clear and clean. Rafting and canoeing are favorite summertime activities, from easy, flat-water runs (great for families) between Eugene and Harrisburg on the Willamette to more challenging whitewater treks on the McKenzie. Hikers will find miles of pristine forest trails just outside the city limits. Runners—Eugene is known as the nation's track capital—will love the well-groomed, packed running paths that cut through parks and follow the river.

Parks. **Prefontaine Trail** is a 6.3K running trail along the banks of the Willamette in Alton Baker Park. At **Amazon Park** in south Eugene is a slough-side 1.6K track. **Hendricks Park** is the city's oldest, with an outstanding 10-acre rhododendron garden (best blooms are May and early June) and a view of the city. **Skinner Butte Park**, which follows the Willamette north of downtown, has nice picnic grounds, several playgrounds, a lovely rose garden, and the Greenway Loop bike trail (12 miles with five bridges). **Spencer's Butte** at the south end of town offers sweeping urban and pastoral views. Two relatively easy trails wend their way to the top.

RESTAURANTS

Chanterelle

Corner of 5th and Pearl,
(503) 484-4065
207 E Fifth Avenue,
Eugene
Moderate; full bar; AE,
MC, V
Dinner Tues-Sat

Chef Rolf Schmidt never fails. Working alone in a kitchen the size of a walk-in closet, he turns out meal after superb meal, showing equal skill with hearty venison and beef dishes and delicate seafood offerings. The printed menu is always enhanced by a sometimes staggering number of chef's seasonal specials, from marlin to sturgeon, buffalo to antelope. In the spring, there are dishes showcasing Chinook salmon, local lamb, and fresh asparagus. In the winter, there's Rolf's wonderfully full-bodied onion soup. When the mood hits him, he'll buy venison from New Zealand, escargots from France, or tuna from Hawaii. Trust this man to make anything well.

Ditto for Mrs. Schmidt, the pastry chef: the desserts are lovely. Expect excellent service at this intimate and subdued restaurant, and little pretension.

Cafe Central

Corner of W 13th and
Lawrence, (503) 343-9510
384 W 13th Street,
Eugene
Moderate; full bar;
MC, V
Lunch Mon-Fri, dinner
Mon-Sat

This pretty storefront restaurant offers quiet dining in a small, skylit room or more spirited interaction at the friendly oak bar or front tables. The service is careful but unobtrusive, the presentation is always lovely, and the poached chocolate cheesecake and persimmon-brandy mousse are the two best desserts in town—which, in Eugene, is saying a lot.

That's the good news. The bad news is that it's possible to encounter some real duds on the seasonally changing menu. On a recent visit, the mesquite-grilled leeks were unpleasantly mushy, and rubbery pieces of fish floated in the otherwise nicely flavored bouillabaisse. On the other hand, the ahi tuna was grilled to perfection and finished with a wonderful beurre rouge, and the spring lamb chops were tender and juicy. The Northwest and international wine selection is commendable.

The Excelsior Cafe

E 13th across from the
Sacred Heart Hospital,
(503) 342-6963
754 E 13th Avenue,
Eugene
Moderate; full bar; AE,
DC, MC, V
Lunch Mon-Fri, dinner
every day, brunch Sun

The grande dame of Eugene's sophisticated dining scene, the Excelsior has gotten neither lazy with age nor complacent with success. It continues to offer inventive nouvelle and Northwest cuisine in an informal yet elegant atmosphere. Located in an attractive Victorian one block west of the University of Oregon campus, the restaurant and its small, bustling bar (plus a new nonsmoking bar) are extremely popular with the university crowd.

The eclectic menu changes monthly to reflect inseason fish and produce and locally raised lamb or beef. The soups—always superb—range from a light, delicate carrot soup to a hearty French onion gratinee. The standout salad is fresh greens with pear, hazelnuts, Oregon blue cheese, and raspberry vinaigrette. On a recent visit, the Oriental duck with chiles and black mushrooms was succulent in a deep sherry and soy sauce. The lasagne with smoked salmon, Italian cheeses, and dill bechamel sauce represented Excelsior's daring but almost always successful flights of culinary fancy. Desserts are very good here.

For lunch, the place is a bit too bustling for good digestion. Nonetheless, the Sunday brunches are a great way to experience the Excelsior, with a variety of omelets, crepes and waffles, and a lovely basket of homemade pastries.

Zenon Cafe

Corner of E Broadway
and Pearl,
(503) 343-3005

Eugene's most spirited, urban eatery, Zenon is an active, noisy, upbeat place with an ever-changing, ever-international menu. A recent menu featured Cajun, Greek, Italian, East Indian, North African, homespun American,

898 Pearl Street, Eugene
Moderate; beer and wine;
MC, V
Breakfast, lunch, dinner
Mon-Sat

and Northwest nouvelle offerings. You would think it's too much to pull off, but Zenon's large kitchen staff (eight cooks under chef-co-owner Mike West) does an always-credible, sometimes inspired job. Pasta dishes are inventive and good: ravioli filled with wonderfully garlicky pesto and topped with fresh crab and a very light tomato sauce. For an entree, the Satay Kaming Madura—tender, juicy Indonesian broiled lamb marinated in soy, garlic, hot peppers, peanuts and molasses—worked well, and the sauce was hot enough to make you sit up and take notice. The Ozark Mountain Barbecued Pork Chops (made with local pork) were nicely seared, but the barbecue sauce was overpowering. Regional wines, many by the glass, are well represented on the wine list. Desserts, temptingly displayed in a pastry case at the entrance, are a big deal here. Save room.

For breakfast eaters with truly hearty appetites, there are chilaquiles con huevos (a wonderful combination of tortillas, eggs, chorizo, cheese, and green chiles) and a variety of other dishes including omelets, frittatas, and Belgian waffles.

Ambrosia

Corner of Broadway and
Pearl, (503) 342-4141
1174 E Broadway,
Eugene
Inexpensive; full bar;
MC, V
Lunch Mon-Sat, dinner
every day

Despite a sign that looks as though it belongs on a teenage disco and mediocre oak antiques inherited from the previous occupant (Accuardi's Old Town Pizza), this place has a lot going for it. Pizza is the specialty here, with wonderfully crisp crust (thanks to the huge wood-burning ovens), rich plum-tomato sauce, and an inspired choice of ingredients (prosciutto, roasted eggplant, grilled chicken, kalamata olives, for example). There's also a good, solid minestrone, some very nice appetizers, a dozen out-of-the-ordinary pasta dishes, and a selection of Northern Italian seafood, chicken, and veal entrees. Try the spaghetti saporiti, fresh pasta tossed with sea scallops sauteed in olive oil, herbs, garlic, and pancetta. What else but a gelato for dessert?

Anatolia

Corner of 10th
and Willamette,
(503) 343-9661
992 Willamette, Eugene
Inexpensive; beer and
wine; MC, V
Lunch Mon-Fri, dinner
every day

Fans of the old Poppi's hail this reincarnation. The former Greek taverna has reopened with an expanded Mediterranean menu in a location away from the University but convenient to downtown. Poppi Cottam continues to serve hearty, unpretentious "peasant" food to a more professional clientele, but with the same convivial atmosphere. The favorites from the old Poppi's remain: spanakopita (spinach and feta in phyllo) and moussaka (traditional lamb or vegetarian). With the new digs comes a variety of curry dishes and other Indian and North African fare.

deFrisco's

Head south on
Willamette, turn right on

Here's a surprise: an erstwhile tavern transformed into a credible, full-service restaurant. Long a popular watering hole known for its great beer selection and cozy,

*10th, (503) 484-2263
99 W 10th, Eugene
Inexpensive; full bar; AE,
MC, V
Lunch, dinner every day,
brunch Sat-Sun*

paneled rooms, deFrisco's has tripled in size and made a quantum leap into the local restaurant scene. You can still go in just for a drink—but try the tempura rock shrimp or the baked Brie with apple as an accompaniment. Better yet, stay for dinner. The seafood pasta's excellent, with scallops and rock shrimp in a light, lemony sauce over fresh fettuccine. The salads and chicken dishes are equally matched. You shouldn't leave without a bite—and we doubt it will be just one bite—of the chocolate coffee torte, with its crushed pecan crust, mocha mousse, dense chocolate layer, and coffee-flavored whipped cream.

Genghis Khan

*Jefferson exit off I-5 to
W 7th and Blair,
(503) 687-2130
900 W Seventh Street,
Eugene,
Inexpensive; full bar; AE,
MC, V
Lunch Mon-Fri, dinner
every day*

You'd never expect it among the gas stations and used-car lots of west Eugene, but inside is an attractive restaurant of two candlelit rooms filled with bamboo furniture. The main draw is the Mongolian grill, a thick slab of iron heated to 800 degrees, which allows food to be cooked in seconds, sealing in the juices. The Mongolian barbecue comes mild, spicy, or quite hot, and with seafood, chicken, pork, or beef. At $7, this place is a real deal. You can watch the chef's pyrotechnics in the Mongolian grill room, but you'll probably need a reservation.

Lou & Ev's

*Indirectly across from
Gilbert Shopping Center
on Old Highway 99,
(503) 688-5553
1295 Pacific Highway
99N, Eugene
Inexpensive; full bar;
MC, V
Dinner every day*

Lou & Ev's should be next door to Ralph's Pretty Good Grocery and down the street from the Chatterbox Cafe; but it's in north Eugene and has been for close to 45 years. Lou & Ev's makes world-class fried chicken. There are other items on the menu, but the fried chicken is what brings 'em in. The chicken's served with a wonderful twice-baked potato, terrible salad, and, oddly enough, a stack of toast.

Mekala's

*In the Public Market at
5th, (503) 342-4872
296 E Fifth Street,
Eugene
Inexpensive; beer and
wine; MC, V
Lunch, dinner every day*

Chef Payvrig Van Styke and her husband, John, were the owners of Kuraya's in Springfield—the area's first Thai restaurant—and now they're the owners of the area's newest. With this venture, they've improved both their atmosphere and their service. Mekala's features an almost dauntingly extensive menu—six full pages with more than 20 vegetarian dishes. In the small, pretty dining area or, in the warm months, outside on the brick terrace overlooking the Fifth Street Public Market courtyard, you can enjoy everything from conventional (but nonetheless delicious) marinated, skewered, charbroiled chicken or beef satay to *tom kah gai*, an oddly pleasing rich, peppery soup made with coconut milk, fresh mushrooms, and lemon grass. Try the Angel Wings (deboned chicken wings stuffed with ground pork, glass noodles, and bean sprouts) or *khung phat kopote* (fresh shrimp, baby corn, and mushrooms stir-fried in an earthy red wine sauce).

The Thai cool down their palates with a dish of light but creamy homemade coconut ice cream; we suggest you do too.

North Bank

West of the Ferry Street Bridge, (503) 343-5622 22 Club Road, Eugene, Moderate; full bar; AE, DC, MC, V Dinner every day

Notable for its beautiful view of the Willamette River, relaxed ambience, lively bar, and reasonable prices, this is the place to go if you want a pleasant meal with little fuss. The serve-yourself homemade soup and salad bar is varied and fresh—no pallid greens or bland offerings here. The seafood (varies seasonally) is cooked nicely, but the beef and chicken dishes are rather standard. Drinks on the deck overlooking the river are a must on summer evenings.

Yen Jing

Chamber Street Connector, right at traffic light, (503) 484-6496 1775 W Sixth, Eugene Inexpensive; full bar; AE, DC, MC, V Lunch Tues-Fri, dinner every day

Eugene has dozens of Chinese restaurants, most of which serve MSG-laced, Americanized dishes that have virtually nothing to do with the provincial cuisines of China. Yen Jing, while not entirely authentic, is about as close as one can get in this town. The featured Mandarin, Sichuan, and Hunan dishes are carefully spiced and made with fresh ingredients. The usual mu-shu pork and kung pao chicken are indeed offered, but you'll also find such delights as sauteed Happy Family (a lovely mixture of scallops, shrimp, abalone, and six different vegetables), rich, garlicky chicken tossed with mushrooms and water chestnuts, and dumpling-like crabmeat Rangoon. Vegetarians will not leave hungry either.

Jamie's

Corner of 18th and Chambers, (503) 343-0485 1810 Chambers Street, Eugene Inexpensive; no alcohol; AE, MC, V Lunch, dinner every day

Take the kids to Jamie's, where they (and you) can get terrific burgers (11 varieties), inspired onion rings, and real—yes, real—milk shakes. There's also a great chargrilled chicken sandwich and just-like-Mom's grilled cheese sandwich. Avoid the ordinary fries. Kids can play on the red Vespa and sidecar displayed in the center of the restaurant while you listen to tunes from the '50s jukebox and wait for your order. There's a second location at 2445 Hilyard Street; (503) 342-2206.

LODGINGS

Campus Cottage

1 block south of the University on 19th, (503) 342-5346 1136 E 19th, Eugene, OR 97403 Moderate; checks ok

Eugene's original bed and breakfast is still the area's premier establishment: classy, cozy, and comfortable. The three guest rooms, all with private baths, are beautifully furnished with antiques. "The cottage," a private retreat with its own entrance (and its own price range), features a vaulted ceiling and bay windows overlooking a private deck and garden. Just a block from the University of Oregon campus, it's a favorite with visiting faculty and professionals. Innkeeper Ursula Bates and her assistant Kim serve a fine breakfast on elegant china.

Lorane Valley Bed and Breakfast

Almost a mile west of Chambers on Lorane Highway, (503) 686-0241 86621 Lorane Highway, Eugene, OR 97405 Moderate; MC, V

For those who want quiet, solitude, and lovely pastoral views, this is the place. Guests stay in a separate, self-contained apartment on the first level of this striking Northwest contemporary, located on 22 acres of wooded hillside and meadow just four miles from the heart of downtown. The 900-square-foot apartment (which sleeps up to four) features a comfortable living room, a fully equipped kitchen (including microwave), a full bath with deep Jacuzzi tub, and a pretty bedroom with a window seat and greenhouse window. Innkeepers Esther and George Ralph provide fresh flowers, fruit, and a split of champagne on arrival; come morning there is a full breakfast with fresh-squeezed orange juice in their dramatic dining room with 180-degree valley views.

Valley River Inn

Exit 194B off I-5 to west 105, exit #3 to the Valley River Center, (503) 687-0123 1000 Valley River Way, Eugene, OR 97401 Expensive; AE, DC, MC, V

Although next to a regional shopping mall, this sprawling complex effectively creates a world of its own, with pretty inner courtyards, lovely plantings, and an inviting pool area. The best rooms face the Willamette River. All rooms are large and tastefully decorated. The food's nothing special, but the public spaces offer river views, and the lobby provides a good selection of West Coast newspapers.

Eugene Hilton

Exit 194B off I-5, then exit 1 to the City Center, (503) 342-2000 66 E Sixth Avenue, Eugene, OR 97401 Expensive; AE, DC, MC, V

An excellent downtown location and terrific city views save this from being just another stamped-from-the-same-mold Hilton. The Hult Center for the Performing Arts is across a brick courtyard; the city's convention center is attached; the downtown mall is a block away. The 275 rooms are spacious and comfortable, but predictable. Amenities include an indoor pool, sauna/Jacuzzi, and game room. Ask about the special "bed and breakfast" rates.

Mapletree Inn

4 blocks from the University, on the main strip, (503) 344-8807 412 E 13th Avenue, Eugene, OR 97401 Moderate; checks ok

They had just booked their first wedding, rolled out the new lawn, and were busily finishing up the last couple of rooms on our first visit; but we have high hopes for this 85-year-old Queen Anne with six bedrooms (four with baths) and a sleeping porch that's a perfect place for up to three kids. Innkeeper Andy Fick and his family are at the end of a three-year renovation, and it's looking good: antique oak furnishings, custom wallpaper, and Victorian accents throughout. The University-area location and continental breakfast are good perks too.

The Best Western New Oregon Motel

Across the street from the University, (503) 683-3669

The free sports center and location just across from the University of Oregon put this place in a slightly different class than other strip motels. The 128 rooms are a cut above motel standards. The sports facility includes an

*1655 Franklin Blvd,
Eugene, OR 97403
Moderate; AE, DC,
MC, V*

indoor pool, Jacuzzi, two saunas, and two racquetball courts.

SPRINGFIELD
RESTAURANTS

Kuraya's
*Centennial and Mohawk,
(503) 746-2951
1410 Mohawk Blvd,
Springfield
Inexpensive; beer only;
MC, V
Lunch, dinner every day*

The area's first (and only) Thai restaurant, which opened in 1987, is constantly crowded. The menu is varied and inventive, featuring five very different curries and a number of traditionally fiery dishes. For appetizers, try the divine Angel Wings, deboned chicken wings stuffed with glass noodles, bean sprouts, blade mushrooms, and ground pork. Dinner might include mint leaves and chili, a tolerably spicy mix of pork, beef, or chicken stir-fried with onion, bell pepper, mint leaves, and chiles; or seafood basket, shrimp and scallops in a bracingly hot, wonderfully coconutty sauce. The servers are hard pressed to keep up with demand.

LEABURG
LODGINGS

Marjon Bed & Breakfast
*See review for directions,
(503) 896-3145
44975 Leaburg Dam
Road, Leaburg, OR
97489
Moderate; MC, V*

Three miles east of Leaburg on McKenzie Highway (and 24 miles from Eugene), turn right at the Leaburg Dam Road (milepost 24). Don't worry about the "dead end" signs—you're on the right track. Nestled at the edge of the blue-green McKenzie River is Marjorie Haas' contemporary home.

The house itself is an immaculate blend of Oriental and French provincial. The junior room, at $60 a night, is a nice-sized bedroom with his-and-hers bathrobes so that you can cross the hall to the bathroom (complete with fishbowl shower). The master suite ($80 a night) has a 7-by-12-foot bed, an adjoining bath with sunken tub, and a Japanese garden view. She calls her house the oyster and the grounds the pearl—she's right; it's a lovely, landscaped property.

CRESWELL
RESTAURANTS

Emerald Valley Restaurant and Lounge
*10 miles south of Eugene,
(503) 485-6796
83293 N Dale Kuni*

A recent change of ownership hasn't lowered the quality of food here, but the surroundings will be undergoing some major changes over the next few years, turning Emerald Valley into a major resort community, complete with homes, a hotel, and a shopping center. So far, the

Road, Creswell
Moderate; full bar; AE,
DC, MC, V
Dinner Wed-Sun,
brunch Sun

elegant steak-and-seafood restaurant remains the center-piece, with its panoramic view of the adjoining 18-hole championship golf course and the Cascade foothills. Business dinners are very popular here, and the food served at large meetings is excellent for the genre. The Sunday brunch is bountiful, the prime rib widely praised, and the Northwest wines on the card are extensive. A lounge hums with live music Friday and Saturday nights. In short, a very nice spot, particularly if you've had a successful round of golf.

COTTAGE GROVE

Mining country. There once was gold fever in these parts, and although the old steam engine The Goose is no longer running, you can still tour the old mines and mining towns by car or bus; you head east toward Bohemia, on roads that can be quite treacherous; call **Lane Ventures,** (503) 942-8241.

Old houses. Tour along the River Road, south from Main Street. **Cottage Grove Historical Museum** has more memorabilia, particularly from the mining era. Birch Avenue at H Street, (503) 942-8175 for irregular hours.

LODGINGS

Village Green Motor Hotel
I-5 at Cottage Grove exit,
(503) 942-2491,(800) 343-
ROOM (outside Oregon)
PO Box 277, Cottage
Grove, OR 97424
Moderate; AE, DC,
MC, V

It's a self-contained little resort, nicely laid out, small (96 rooms), and yet with lots of facilities: tennis, a playground, a heart-shaped pool, lawn games. Rates are reasonable and rooms diverse: try a poolside suite with a family room and fireplace. The restaurant is nothing special.

OAKLAND

RESTAURANTS

Tolly's
Exit 138 off I-5 to middle
of Oakland,
(503) 459-3796
115 Locust Street,
Oakland
Moderate; full bar; AE,
MC, V
Lunch every day, dinner
Tues-Sun

Here's an oddity: an ice-cream parlor downstairs, with authentic fixtures and a dandy candy counter; upstairs is a room reached by a curved red-oak staircase, where you sit among antiques and have an elegant—or romantic—dinner. A couples-only dining room overlooks the antique shop.

Chef Phil Mason cooks such entrees as peppercorn steak, five-spice chicken, and oysters Rockefeller. We had a generously spiced serving of plump scallops and butterflied prawns seasoned with garlic and fresh mint. The tender veal saltimbocca was stuffed with prosciutto and Swiss cheese. Desserts range from fresh fruit pies to velvet-smooth chocolate truffles. Birthdays are a big deal here.

LODGINGS

**Pringle House Bed
and Breakfast**
*Locust and 7th,
Oakland, OR*
(503) 459-5038
*PO Box 578, Oakland,
OR 97462*
*Inexpensive; no credit
cards; checks ok*

The home stands like a grand Victorian citadel at the end of Main Street, seeming to guard the quaint village. Historic Pringle House has two guest rooms decorated with antiques. Breakfast features freshly ground coffee, freshly squeezed orange juice, fruit compote with honey-yogurt dressing, croissants with homemade apple butter, and—what a send-off—a creme caramel.

STEAMBOAT

LODGINGS

Steamboat Inn
*38 miles east of Roseburg
on Highway 138,*
(503) 498-2411
*Steamboat Inn,
Steamboat, OR 97447*
Moderate; MC, V

On the banks of a fly-only fishing stream is the plain-seeming lodge. Linked by a long verandah on the North Umpqua River are eight small cabins for guests; rooms have knotty-pine walls, a bath, and just enough space. And tucked away in the woods you will find four secluded cottages, complete with living rooms and kitchens. The view of the river is the main plus, in addition to the attractive grounds. Prices are fair, starting at $67 for a double along the stream.

The main building serves some remarkably good food each night a half-hour after dark, by reservation only. The menu will begin with aperitifs and an appetizer, perhaps ham-and-cheese-stuffed phyllo with fruit, or maybe spinach balls with mustard sauce. From there it might go this way: chilled avocado soup, tomato-basil salad and herbed bread, chicken breast, fettuccine with sharp cheeses, pea pods, and a peach crisp with maple cream for dessert. The price of this feed, including the wine, is $20 per person. The cooking of chef Sharon Van Loan is delicious, and the company—gathered around big wooden slab tables to hear fishing stories of the day and lubricated by the social hour before—will be most congenial. No dinners winter weekdays.

ROSEBURG

The Roseburg area now has four **wineries**, open for tours and tastings. They are: **Davidson Winery**, 2637 Retton Road, (503) 679-6950; **Girardet Wine Cellars**, 895 Reston Road, (503) 679-7252; **Henry Winery**, Highway 9, Umpqua, (503) 459-5120; **HillCrest Vineyards**, 240 Vineyard Lane, (503) 673-3709.

Wildlife Safari allows you to drive through rolling country to see a quasi-natural wildlife preserve, with predators discreetly fenced from their prey, and to watch baby animals close up. Daily 9am–8pm, shorter hours in winter; Route 99, four miles west of I-5, exit 119, (503) 679-6761.

Douglas County Museum imaginatively displays logging, fur-trapping, and pioneer items in one of the handsomest contemporary structures you'll find. Open Tuesday–Sunday; free; off I-5 at the fairgrounds, exit 123, (503) 440-4507.

K&R's Drive Inn dishes out huge scoops of Umpqua ice cream. One scoop is really two; two scoops is actually four. Located 20 miles north of Roseburg, at the Rice Hill exit off I-5; the parking lot is full from before noon to after dark, year-round.

RESTAURANTS

Cafe Espresso
Corner of Douglas and Jackson, (503) 672-1859
368 SE Jackson, Roseburg
Inexpensive; no alcohol; MC, V
Breakfast, lunch Mon-Fri

It's a smart, sunny cafe with black-and-white tiled floor, red-and-white-checked tablecloths, and Roseburg's only decent espresso bar. They have good coffee and croissants at breakfast and Italian sodas, soups, and salads for lunch. Daily specials range from beef stroganoff to quiche to lasagne. Low prices and weekday-only hours confirm our hunch that the locals want to keep this place all to themselves.

WOLF CREEK

LODGINGS

Wolf Creek Tavern
Exit 76 off I-5,
(503) 866-2474
100 Railroad Avenue,
Mail: PO Box 97, Wolf Creek, OR 97497
Moderate; MC, V

An old stagecoach stop, this inn was purchased by the state and restored in 1979, thus saving an authentic Classic Revival inn that dates back to the 1850s. There are eight guest rooms, seven that rent for about $42 and one larger one for $52. All have private baths. Downstairs there's an attractive parlor and a dining room open to the public for all meals. The fare is standard but hearty and inexpensive. It's open year-round (except sometimes in early January). Children are okay; pets are not.

GRANTS PASS

The Rogue is one of Oregon's most beautiful rivers, chiseled into the coastal mountains from here to Gold Beach, protected by the million-acre Siskiyou National Forest, flecked with abandoned gold-mining sites, and inhabited by splendid steelhead and roaming Californians. Three companies offer jet boat tours. **Hellgate Excursions,** (503) 479-7204, and **Rogue Jetboat Excursions,** (503) 476-2628, both depart from the Riverside Park–Riverside Inn vicinity in Grants Pass. **Jet Boat River Excursions,** (503) 582-0800, leaves from the city of Rogue River, eight miles upstream. One guide that conducts wild and daring whitewater trips is **Orange Torpedo Trips,** (503) 479-5061. Or you can hike the Rogue, a very hot trip in the summer; see Gold Beach listing.

RESTAURANTS

Pongsri's
Take the North Grants Pass exit off I-5, continue 1 mile, (503) 479-1345

You don't need to dress up or bring much money to Don and Pongsri Von Essen's Thai restaurant. Still, you can choose from more than 75 dishes. Hot and spicy dishes such as *massamam* (beef curry with peanuts and potatoes,

1571 NE Sixth Street,
Grants Pass
Inexpensive; beer and
wine; MC, V
Lunch, dinner Tues-Sun

onions, and coconut milk) are marked on the menu with an asterisk. Order a two-asterisk dish like *pla kung*—spicy shrimp salad—and be prepared for an adventure. A safer choice, popular with the locals, is phad Thai—pan-fried noodles with shrimp, eggs, peanuts, and vegetables. A second branch, with an identical menu, is in the Medford suburb of Central Point.

R Haus

Cross the river from 6th,
turn left on Rogue River
Highway, (503) 476-4287
2140 Rogue River
Highway, Grants Pass
Moderate; full bar; AE,
DC, MC, V
Dinner every day

The portions aren't as gigantic as they were nearly 20 years ago, but the locals still flock to this restaurant in an old mansion near the Rogue River. Fare is both Italian and of the steak-and-seafood style—nothing spectacular, but good, basic food. You are probably best off ordering one of the 10 or more specials listed on a blackboard. The scampi sauce is notable. There may be a wait for a table, but the upstairs lounge with its antiques is a good place to pass the time.

LODGINGS

Paradise Ranch Inn

Take the Hugo or Merlin
exit off I-5,
(503) 479-4333
7000-D Monument Drive,
Grants Pass, OR 97526
Expensive; MC, V
Breakfast, dinner Tues-
Sun (every day in
summer)

Here's a divine place for a getaway, right in the heart of the Rogue Valley. Paradise, once a working dude ranch, has been transformed into a full-service resort. Activities abound: fishing for trout or bass, swimming in a heated pool, boating on a three-acre lake, playing tennis on two lighted courts, riding bicycles or hiking along miles of trails, relaxing in a hot tub. Three holes of an eventual 18-hole golf course have opened. With all this planned action, you might expect a sprawling modern resort, but Paradise Ranch Inn defies that image. There are only 18 guest rooms. The emphasis is on peace and quiet. No TVs or phones in the rooms. The green lawns and three ponds present a restful image. Rooms are large and furnished in Early American style; best are those that overlook one of the ponds. The four-bedroom Sunset House in the back 40 is a good choice for a couple of families to share.

Mattie and Oliver Raymond, who once owned the place, have stayed on as managers and are personable, enthusiastic hosts. The dining room is open to non-guests, with fresh fish, fresh pasta, veal, and shrimp among the dishes on a changing menu. There's outdoor dining in season. All in all, this is a winning Northwest resort.

The Handmaidens' Inn

3 miles south of town,
call for directions,
(503) 476-2932
230 Red Spur Drive,
Grants Pass, OR 97527
Moderate; AE, MC, V

★

You don't come to this 1983 three-story home to find the ambience of a Victorian B&B. You come to be pampered by Bette and Jody Hammer, who are the perfect companions on a weary day. There are three guest rooms, one with private bath and its own balcony. The hot tub does wonders too. The women will cook you a delightful breakfast—and dinner too, upon request.

Lawnridge House
From Highway 99,
Savage and Lawnridge,
(503) 479-5186
1304 NW Lawnridge,
Grants Pass, OR 97526
Moderate; checks ok

This restored historic-home-turned-B&B permits easy access to Ashland (45 minutes) or Jacksonville (25 minutes). The place has two suites, each with private bath. One is designed for families; the other has a king-size hand-made curtained canopy bed. Breakfasts are Northwest hearty: baked salmon, crab cakes, croissants, and quiche. Innkeeper-chef Barbara Head makes an effort to accommodate special dietary requests, so speak up.

The Washington Inn
Exit 58 from I-5, turn
right on Evelyn,
(503) 476-1131
1002 NW Washington
Boulevard, Grants Pass,
OR 97526
Moderate; AE, MC, V

In an 1864 National Historic Place, this B&B offers nostalgia as its theme. The three guest rooms are named for the children of owners Maryan and Bill Thompson: Linda's Love Nest, Pattie's Parlor, and Sally's Sunny View. The first two have fireplaces; the last has a canopy bed and, yes—on nice days—a sunny view. Two have private baths; the third shares. For breakfast Maryan makes things like Norwegian breakfast cookies and banana splits (minus the ice cream).

JACKSONVILLE

The town started with a boom when gold was discovered in Rich Gulch in 1851. Then the railroad bypassed it, and the tidy little city struggled to avoid becoming a ghost town. Much of the 19th-century city has been restored; Jacksonville now boasts 85 historic homes and buildings open to the public. The strip of authentic Gold Rush–era shops, hotels, and saloons along California Street has become a popular stage set for films, including *The Great Northfield, Minnesota Raid*, and the recent TV movie *Inherit the Wind*. Jacksonville is renowned for antique shops and is opening its first microbrewery this June.

Britt Festival, an outdoor music and arts series, runs from late June through September on the hillside field where Peter Britt, a famous local photographer and horticulturist, used to have his home. Listeners gather on benches or flop onto blankets on the grass to enjoy open-stage performances of jazz, bluegrass, folk, country, classical music, musical theatre, and dance. Quality of performances varies, but the series includes big-name artists from the various categories, and listening to the music under a twinkling night sky makes for a memorable evening. Begun in 1963, the festival now draws some 50,000 viewers through the summer. For tickets and information call the Britt Festival Office, (503) 773-6077.

Jacksonville Museum, housed in the stately 1883 courthouse, follows the history of the Central Oregon Railroad in the Rogue Valley with plenty of photos and artifacts, plus train sound effects and tales of the great train robberies. Another section displays works of Peter Britt. The adjacent children's museum lets kids walk through various miniaturized pioneer settings (jail, tepee, schoolhouse) and features a collection of the cartoons and memorabilia of Pinto Colvig, the Jacksonville kid who became Bozo the Clown and the voice of Disney's Pluto, Goofy, and three of the Seven Dwarfs. (503) 899-1847.

Books in the Best Places *series read like personal guidebooks, but our evaluations are based on numerous reports from local experts. Final judgments are made by the editors. Our inspectors never identify themselves (except over the phone) and never accept free meals or other favors. Be an inspector. Send us a report.*

RESTAURANTS

Jacksonville Inn

On California, the town's main thoroughfare, (503) 899-1900
175 E California Street, Jacksonville
Moderate; full bar; AE, DC, MC, V
Lunch Mon-Sat, dinner every day, brunch Sun

Ask a native to name the area's best, and the answer will often be the Jacksonville Inn. It is certainly the best the Rogue Valley has to offer: the staff is considerate, and the antique-furnished dining room, housed in the original 1863 building, is elegant and intimate. Executive chef Diane Menzie expertly creates the full realm of continental cuisine: steak, seafood, pasta, plus the recent addition of health-minded low-cholesterol fare and an expanded variety of vegetarian entrees. Leave plenty of time for a leisurely meal. Dinners come as a seven-course feast or a la carte; we suggest the latter, which includes salad, rice or potato, and vegetables. Try the veal piccata or shrimp with basil cream sauce. Jerry Evans boasts one of the best-stocked wine cellars in Oregon, with more than 600 domestic and imported labels on hand. You can save room for one of the lovely European dessert creations by ordering from the lighter, less expensive bistro menu in the lounge. Weekday lunch and Sunday brunch are popular with locals, as are twice-monthly Opera Pops dinner shows in the upstairs dining room.

Upstairs, eight refurbished rooms are decorated with 19th-century details: antique four-poster beds, patchwork quilts, and original brickworking on the walls. Modern amenities include private bathrooms and air conditioning (a boon in the 100-degree summer swelter). The rooms, especially the sought-after corner room overlooking the street, are a bit noisy—street sounds easily penetrate the walls. Guests enjoy a full breakfast with choice of waffles, eggs, omelets, fresh fruit, juices, and coffee. Reserve rooms in advance, especally during the Britt Festival.

Trombino's

Just off California on 5th, (503) 899-1340
605 N 5th Street, Jacksonville
Moderate; full bar; MC, V
Dinner every day (closed Mon-Tues in winter)

★

Jacksonville's best Italian restaurant may look boarded up, but it's far from closed. The building—like owner Sal Trombino (a Brooklyn native)—has a lot of personality. The menu leans toward ethnic dishes, like fettuccine tutto mare, sufritto, fried calamari, and risotto. Veal Ambrosia is our favorite of the six veal entrees. The homemade pasta is notable. And it's the only place in the area where you can get live Maine lobster, if you're into that sort of thing. There's not much to the decor—you come for the food—but try the rear dining room, which used to be a latticed-over courtyard.

LODGINGS

Livingston Mansion

Take Oregon Street past the city limits to Liv-

Dating from 1915, the fanciest of the local B&Bs is a mansion with three large rooms (and soon two smaller ones), private baths, and a swimming pool. Families are wel-

ingston, (503) 899-7107
PO Box 1476, Jackson-
ville, OR 97530
Moderate; MC, V

come. The Regal Room offers a fireplace, two sofas, and two baths, plus a louvered-off area that will sleep up to three kids.

Owner Sherry Lossing is locally renowned for her "breakfast cookies," big, rich treats loaded with granola, raisins, seeds, and nuts. Her full breakfasts may also feature eggs Benedict or German pancakes, plus fresh fruit and muffins. The view of the Rogue Valley is extraordinary. Rates $10 lower in winter.

McCully House Inn
*Follow the signs from I-5
to corner of 5th and E
California,*
(503) 899-1942
*240 E California Street,
Jacksonville, OR 97503
Moderate; beer and wine;
MC, V*

One of the first six homes in the city, McCully House was built in 1861 for Jacksonville's first doctor and later housed the first girls' school. It's elegant inside, with hardwood floors, fresh paint, lace curtains, and lovely antiques. The three guest rooms each have private baths, and the McCully room features a fireplace, a claw-footed pedestal tub, and the original black walnut furnishings that traveled round the horn with J.W. McCully. Downstairs, the new owner and inn manager, Patricia Gott, a Culinary Institute of America chef, will be opening the cafe to the public, serving homemade waffles and pancakes in the morning and American-style lamb, salmon, and a mixed grill for dinner.

CENTRAL POINT

RESTAURANTS

Mon Desir
*Exit 32 off I-5, east ½
mile to Hamrick, turn
left, (503) 664-6661
4615 Hamrick Road,
Central Point
Moderate; full bar; AE,
DC, MC, V
Dinner every day,
brunch Sun*

The mansion was built in 1910 by a Chicago millionaire who had married an actress; naturally, no expense was spared. Since it became a restaurant it has at times traded more on its decor and rose gardens than on its food. Current owners Russ and Betty Walters have made things less formal than before. Three generations of the Walters family run the place. Although Russ and Betty are vegetarians, the menu focus is mainly on steak and seafood, but there are some vegetarian offerings, such as quiche, broccoli crepes, and cheese lasagne. The cream of zucchini soup has acquired a following. The atmosphere is still grand: chandeliers, ornate bars, Victorian furniture, and the three acres of manicured lawn and rose gardens.

SHADY COVE/TRAIL

The Upper Rogue area, between Medford and Crater Lake, offers some of the region's most invigorating scenery—rugged mountains, timbered hillsides, and whitewater rapids.

Looking for a particular place? Check the index at the back of this book for individual restaurants, hotels, B&Bs, parks, and more.

RESTAURANTS

Bel Di's

After crossing Shady Cove's bridge going north, take the driveway immediately after the Mobil Station, (503) 878-2010 21900 Highway 62, Shady Cove Moderate; full bar; DC, MC, V Dinner Tues-Sun

Stan and Tommie Smith, former owners of Mon Desir, came out of retirement to turn this riverside country dinner house into a special place. The dining room has a grand view of the Rogue River. Try the scampi or the Louisiana Stuffed Prawns. When it comes time for dessert, ask whether Stan has prepared his famous bread pudding that evening.

Rogue River Lodge

25 miles from Medford on Highway 62, (503) 878-2555 24904 Highway 62, Trail Moderate; full bar; AE, MC, V Dinner every day

Tucked into the wild southern Oregon countryside is the oldest dinner house (more than 50 years) in Jackson County. Owner and ex-Navy man Ken Meirstin has had it for more than a decade now. The walls are decorated with his collection of ship paintings. Ken has been spread a bit thin of late since taking on a second restaurant (Oak Knoll in Ashland), but Dory, his wife, still supervises the cooking here and maintains a high standard of consistent quality with a somewhat predictable menu: steaks, scampi, teriyaki chicken, and prime rib (on weekends). The view of the Rogue isn't as good as at Bel Di's, down the road, but the locals like the place.

MEDFORD

Southern Oregon's largest city may not win any contests with nearby towns for prettiness, but it is the center of things in this part of the world. The city is well known in the nation due to the marketing efforts of Harry and David, the mail-order giant known for its pears, other fruit, and condiments.

Harry and David's Original Country Store, Highway 99 south of town, offers "seconds" from gift packs and numerous other items, as well as tours of the complex, which is also home of **Jackson & Perkins**, the world's largest rose growers. The firm ships from Medford, although most of the flowers are grown in California, (503) 776-2277.

River rafting on a nearby stretch of the Rogue, between Gold Hill and the city of Rogue River, is safe for beginners. You can rent a raft at River Trips in Gold Hill, (503) 855-7238, or try one of the shop's Rogue Drifters, a large sack filled with styrofoam balls.

The Oregon Vortex at the House of Mystery, between Medford and Grants Pass, is a "whirlpool of force" that causes some people to experience strange phenomena such as an inability to stand erect and changes in the laws of perspective; 18 miles northwest of Medford on Sardine Creek Road, Gold Hill, (503) 855-1543. Closed in winter.

Love a good bargain? Then you'll really like Seattle Cheap Eats, *a compendium of 230 terrific bargain eateries in and around Seattle, brought to you by the same folks who bring you the* Best Places *series.*

RESTAURANTS

Hungry Woodsman

In town just down the road from the Rogue Valley Mall,
(503) 772-2050
2001 N Pacific Highway, Medford
Moderate; full bar; AE, DC, MC, V
Lunch Mon-Fri, dinner every day

Bob LaFontaine, owner of a Medford hardware store, tired of the rowdy nightclub next door, bought it 17 years ago, tore it down, and erected the Hungry Woodsman. The building is a testimonial to the forest products industry. Old saws, photos, and other logging memorabilia adorn the walls. The menu is pretty basic: steak, prime rib, shrimp, crab, lobster. You're probably best off with a steak or English cut of prime rib; crab tends to be too pricey here. Locals like the Woodsman, as they call it. Few patrons dress up; the waiters wear jeans.

The Sandpiper

Take the Barnett Road exit east off I-5,
(503) 779-0100
1841 Barnett Road, Medford
Moderate; full bar; AE, DC, MC, V
Dinner every day

Although part of a chain (four of the five other Sandpipers are in Idaho), the Medford branch offers the sincere service and quality food that one associates with smaller operations. The "fresh sheet" here is the area's best. Salmon and lingcod are mainstays. Swordfish is often prepared with crab, zucchini, olives, and tomato. On the regular menu, try the brandied pork or Steak Sandpiper, a classic filet served with both Bearnaise and burgundy sauces. The pretty, split-level dining room has lots of flowers and soft lighting. The lounge is popular with young singles, so you may want to avoid weekends or late dining.

LODGINGS

Under the Greenwood Tree

Exit 27 off I-5, follow Steward for 3 miles, right on Bellinger,
(503) 776-0000
3045 Bellinger Lane, Medford, OR 97501
Expensive; MC, V

This bed and breakfast, which opened in 1985 halfway between Medford and Jacksonville, offers green lawns, 300-year-old trees, and a 10-acre farm setting complete with an orchard and riding area. The main house has four guest rooms, each with private bath. Its name refers to a popular Elizabethan song that appears in *As You Like It.*

Innkeeper Renate Ellam, a Cordon Bleu chef, goes all out. Guests who arrive by 4:30pm enjoy a British-style afternoon tea with sandwiches, breads, fruit, tea, and Madeira. Three-course breakfasts may include dishes like vanilla-poached pears with Chantilly cream; smoked ham with white potatoes, tomatoes, onions, and eggs, topped with sour cream; and strawberry blintzes with eggs-and-yogurt filling and strawberry preserves.

Red Lion Inn

Right off I-5; look for the signs, (503) 779-5811
200 N Riverside Avenue, Medford, OR 97501
Moderate; AE, DC, MC, V

Relax; it's only a Red Lion, smack in the middle of Motel Row and smack in the middle of the price range. But it's the best of its kind. Some units overlook a small creek, which in turn overlooks Interstate 5. A better strategy is to get a room facing the small inner courtyard with garden and pool. The restaurant isn't bad. The fare improved dramatically under chef Brad Toles, but he has left; still, nothing keeps the locals from their favorite Sunday brunch.

TALENT

RESTAURANTS

Chata

Talent exit off I-5; watch for signs, (503) 535-2575
1212 S Pacific Highway, Talent
Moderate; full bar; MC, V
Dinner every day

The name (pronounced HAH-tah) means "cottage" in Polish, but the restaurant is neither small nor strictly Polish. The eastern and central European menu features dishes like bigos, Polish hunter's stew, and *mamaliga de aur* (bread of gold)—Romanian cornmeal cakes sprinkled with cheese and served in a sauce of mushrooms, cream, and wine. Owners Jozef and Eileen Slowikowsky have the smooth service and splendid consistency in the food down to a practiced art—which they are now gradually turning over to their children. The change might explain Chata's broadening appeal (they've added some Cajun dishes and Chicago-style pizza). On our last visit we chose the pirogi, dumplings filled with meat or vegetables and topped with a sour cream sauce. Our lamb selection—braised with wine and herbs—was another fine dish. Soups are special, with choices like tomato brandy and lamb lentil. Blackboard specials augment the regular menu.

The wine list presents Oregon labels side by side with white riesling from Yugoslavia, among others from that region. And, of course, there's Polish vodka, Serbian plum brandy, and a brownish nectar from Hungary called "the wine of the emperors."

Arbor House

Take Talent to the railroad tracks, then west on Wagner,
(503) 535-6817
103 W Wagner Street, Talent
Moderate; beer and wine; checks ok
Dinner Wed-Sun

The exterior, recently enhanced by a Japanese garden, is still modest enough to fool you. Aging granola types consider this place a find. It is one of the most surprising, warmest places in the Rogue Valley. The menu ranges the world—vegetarian plates, curries, sauerbraten, jambalaya, enchiladas, eggplant parmigiana, and good old American steak. Chef/owner Patrick Calhoun loves to talk. If he's not first-naming everyone at the table by meal's end, you've done something seriously wrong. Delicious and fun—but allow plenty of time for this leisurely, offbeat dining experience. Another note: Calhoun's menu lists no prices. You have to ask, or trust. Don't be alarmed. At last report, no dinner exceeded $14.95.

ASHLAND

The remarkable success of the Oregon Shakespeare Festival, now over 50 years old, has transformed this sleepy town into the one with, per capita, the best tourist amenities in the region. The Ashland season now draws a total audience of nearly 350,000 through the eight-month season, filling its theatres to an extraordinary 94 percent of capacity. Visitors pour into this town of 15,000, creating fine shops

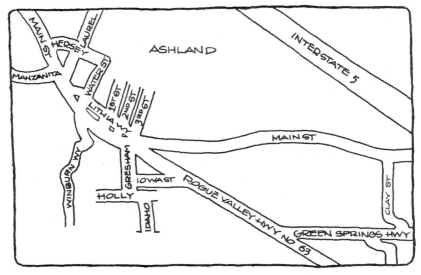

restaurants, and bed and breakfast places as they do. Amazingly, the town still has its soul: for the most part, it seems a happy little college town, set amid lovely ranch country, that just happens to house the fifth-largest theatre company in the land.

The Festival mounts plays in three theatres. In the outdoor Elizabethan Theatre, which seats 1,200, appear the famous and authentic nighttime productions of Shakespeare (three different plays) each summer. Stretching from February to October, the season for the two indoor theatres includes comedies, contemporary fare, and some experimental works; in these the large repertory company is more likely to excel, for Shakespeare outdoors takes a toll on voices and subtlety. Visit the Exhibit Center, where you can clown around in costumes from plays past. There are also lectures and concerts at noon, excellent backstage tours each morning, Renaissance music and dance nightly in the courtyard—plus all the nearby daytime attractions of river-rafting, picnicking, and historical touring. The best way to get information and tickets (last-minute tickets in the summer are rare) is through a comprehensive agency: Southern Oregon Reservation Center, (503) 488-1011, (800) 547-8052 (outside Oregon); PO Box 477, Ashland, OR 97520. Festival box office is (503) 482-4331.

Actor's Theatre of Ashland, Ashland's growing experimental theatre productions (often called **Off Shakespeare**), is worth checking into. Festival actors often join in these small companies, giving audiences a chance to see Shakespearean actors having a bit of fun and going out on a theatrical limb. A full listing of productions is available at the Chamber of Commerce, 110 E Main, (503) 482-3486.

Touring. The Rogue River Recreation Area has fine swimming for the sizzling summer days, as does the lovely valley of the Applegate River. Twenty-two scenic miles up Dead Indian Road is Howard Prairie Lake Resort, where you can camp, park your trailer, shower, rent a boat, and fish all day, (503) 482-1979.

Mount Ashland Ski Area, (503) 482-2897, 18 miles south of town, offers 22 runs for all classes of skiers, Thanksgiving to April.

Lithia Park. Designed by the creator of San Francisco's Golden Gate Park, Ashland's central park runs for 100 acres behind the outdoor theatre, providing a lovely mix of duck ponds, Japanese gardens, grassy lawns, playgrounds, groomed or dirt trails for hikes and jogging, and the pungent mineral water that gave the park its name. Great for picnicking, especially after stocking up at nearby Greenleaf Deli (49 N Main, 482-2808).

Manna From Heaven Bakery is a distinguished old-world bakery famous for elaborate breads and pastries, plus good coffee. Definitely worth a visit for breakfast. 358 E Main Street, (503) 482-5831.

Jazmin's Bistro & Sidewalk Cafe is the place to go dancing in town. It's a small spot, generally jam-packed on weekend nights, especially when musicians on their way to Portland or San Francisco stop in. 180 C Street, (503) 488-0883.

Mark Antony Hotel. This downtown landmark is of some historic interest but has fallen on hard economic times in recent years. Ownership seems to change almost yearly, with corresponding closures and reopenings; 212 E Main Street, (503) 482-1721.

Weisinger Ashland Winery and **Rogue Brewery & Public House** are new additions to the Ashland area. The winery is the perfect spot to sample the products of Oregon. Snuggled in a Bavarian-style building, the winery gift shop offers jams, jellies, sauces, and, of course, their wines for sale; Highway 99 just outside of Ashland, (503) 488-5989. Wash down a sandwich or a pizza with a Golden Ale at the Brewery, located at 31 B Water Street—a good place to unwind after a day of theatre; (503) 488-5061.

RESTAURANTS

Chateaulin
Down the walkway from the Angus Bowmer Theatre, (503) 482-2264 50 E Main Street, Ashland Moderate; full bar; AE, DC, MC, V Dinner every day

Locals say the best food in Ashland is a toss-up between Chateaulin and the Winchester Inn, but this small spot wins hands-down in the category of charm. Located less than a block from the theatres, it's a romantic cafe reminiscent of New York's upper West Side; the dark-wood-and-brick dining rooms (one is nonsmoking) are accented with copper kettles hung from the ceiling and displays of vintage wine bottles. Bits of ivy wind right through the brickwork in the main dining room. During the Shakespeare season, the place bustles with before- and after-theatre crowds gathered for the fine French cuisine or for drinks at the bar. House specialties are pates and veal dishes, but seafood is also impressive; the delicate butterflied shrimp in a subtle sauce of sherry, cream, leeks, and garlic, were delicious. Chef-owners David Taub and Michael Donovan change the menu seasonally and several daily specials feature seasonal entrees prepared with classical French flair.

The after-show "cafe menu" features lighter fare, desserts, and coffees. Our plate of baked goat cheese marinated in olive oil was served on featherweight squares of toast with a carafe of white Burgundy chosen from the excellent wine list. The restaurant also serves the best soupe a l'oignon this side of the Atlantic: a bubbling crockful of rich, sweet-salty broth under a thick sponge of French bread topped with melted cheese. Service is polished and smooth even during the rush of theatre crowds.

The Winchester Country Inn

Half a block from Main,
(503) 488-1113
35 S Second Street,
Ashland
Moderate; full bar;
MC, V
Dinner Tues-Sun,
brunch Sun

Pay a visit to the Winchester when you feel like being pampered. You sit amid crisp country furnishings on the slightly sunken ground floor of this century-old Queen Anne–style home and look out on tiers of neatly snipped garden outside. The staff attends to your every need, and, best of all, new chef Charles Barker creates from an ambitious range of entrees, from roast duck with mango bigarade sauce to Vietnamese marinated broiled *teng dah* beef to lamb du jour. Our meal began with the house soup—a savory blend of just-steamed vegetables laced with Parmesan—and while the broiled chicken breast in Chinese plum sauce was a bit sweet, the trout dipped in almond batter, lightly fried and dabbed with lime butter, was perfect. The baked apple in a pretty puff pastry was a perfect encore to the meal, and we had plenty of time for the two-block stroll to the theatre.

In addition to its renown as one of Ashland's two best restaurants, the Winchester provides seven antique-furnished guest rooms upstairs. Guests are treated to full breakfasts in the dining room or in the open patio in the summertime.

Bayou Grill

Half a block from Angus
Bowmer Theatre,
(503) 488-0235
139 E Main Street,
Ashland
Moderate; full bar;
MC, V
Dinner Tues-Sun
(Wed-Sun in summer)

Ashland may have been slow to jump on the blackened-redfish bandwagon, but the Bayou Grill is a welcome addition to the range of cuisines on the downtown dining strip. Formerly the beloved Change of Heart, the restaurant opted for a change of concept in 1988 when chef Candy Durham left town. The restaurant has kept its slick mix of classy brick walls, oversized ceiling fans, wicker furnishings, and vividly painted portraits on the walls. Try for a table near the windows overlooking Ashland's main drag—especially pleasant on sticky summer nights. The menu has all the basics of Cajun cuisine: shrimp etouffee, chicken creole, jambalaya, blackened sirloin, snapper pappadeaux, and even Cajun barbecued frog legs. The chicken Creole we tried was too lightly spiced, but the crawfish linguine was a perfect dish of pasta and the sweet crustaceans in a velvet-smooth cream sauce. For dessert, the pralines 'n' cream ice cream was delectable, and the French pot de creme is famous locally. Owner Beasy McMillan knows his restaurant stuff; in addition to the Bayou, he runs Beasy's Back Room, a favorite hangout for beer and barbecued steaks, the Thai Pepper (see listing), and an Italian trattoria called Macaroni's—newly opened in spring of 1989. Running sucessful restaurants in a town this competitive is exceptional. Running three simultaneously is amazing.

Green Springs Inn

17½ miles east of
Ashland on Highway 66,

Here's an escape from the tourist crowds of Ashland—a cozy, rustic spot dishing up Italian specialties in the midst of the splendid hills overlooking the Rogue Valley.

(503) 482-0614
11470 Highway 66,
Ashland
Moderate; beer and wine;
AE, MC, V
Breakfast, lunch, dinner
every day

(Guaranteed not to be filled with Californians, the restaurant also doubles as a neighborhod store, supplying necessities to those living in the area: bread, milk, videos.) The 35-minute drive through the red soil hills, jutting cliffs, and thick evergreens is worth the trip in itself, especially if you want to hike or cross-country ski along the Pacific Crest Trail that runs ¼ mile from the restaurant. The hearty soups, sandwiches, and 12 different pasta dishes make this a welcome stopping point. Our black bean soup was a generous dish, rich and lightly garlicked—perfect when lapped up with sweet, just-baked brown bread.

Thai Pepper

Downtown near Water
and the creek,
(503) 482-8058
84 N Main Street,
Ashland
Moderate; beer and wine;
MC, V
Dinner every day

True Thai connoisseurs might cringe while perusing the "Thai" offerings on the menu, but locals don't seem to mind that not a word of Thai appears on the menu or that the dishes listed would be rarities in Bangkok. Even if it's not entirely authentic, entrees like the Thai-style sweet-and-sour shrimp with Granny Smith apples, cucumber, and pineapple have made the restaurant a favorite since it opened in the winter of 1988.

Geppetto's

Main between 2nd and
3rd, (503) 482-1138
345 E Main, Ashland
Inexpensive; full bar;
MC, V
Breakfast, lunch,
dinner every day

The favorite hangout for many local folk, Geppetto's is well loved for its friendly, casual atmosphere and health-conscious food. (Geppetto's owns its own farm to supply the restaurant with organic fruits and vegetables). The dinner menu offers a conglomeration of Italian, Asian, and American dishes, with plenty of tasty vegetarian entrees. Sandwiches and veggieburgers are specialties at lunch; omelets and baked goods are the best bets for breakfast. The quirky but famous won ton appetizers—crispy won tons filled with spinach, feta, and cream cheese and dipped in mustard sauce—have their on and off days. Lately, they've been good. Geppetto's gets downright noisy during the lunch and dinner hours, and you can sometimes be ignored—especially on weekend nights.

LODGINGS

Chanticleer Bed & Breakfast Inn

2 blocks from the library
off Main, (503) 482-1919
120 Gresham Street,
Ashland, OR 97520
Expensive; MC, V

Despite growing competition, Chanticleer has maintained its roost as the preferred B&B through nearly a decade of Shakespeare seasons now—mostly due to hosts Jim and Nancy Beaver's extraordinarily high standards. The home has an uncluttered country charm with open-hearth fireplace in the spacious sitting room and carefully chosen antiques throughout, plus the plush extras of fresh-cut flowers, imported soaps and lotions in the rooms, and scripts of all the shows playing at the Shakespeare Festival. In the morning, a lavish breakfast is served in the dining room or (on request) brought to your room for breakfast in bed. It's a setting that promises to rejuvenate your soul. . .and your romance.

The inn offers seven rooms: Aerie and Fleur overlook Bear Creek Valley and the foothills of the Cascade range, and the Chanticleer Suite provides guests with two bedrooms with queen beds, a full kitchen, parlor stove, private bath, and a private garden outside. Situated in a quiet neighborhood, Chanticleer is four blocks from the theatre. This is a sought-after spot, so make reservations early. Rates are reduced during the winter, and a business rate is offered. No smoking.

Arden Forest Inn

On Hersey at Laurel,
(503) 488-1496
261 Hersey Street,
Ashland, OR 97520
Moderate; MC, V

A refreshing change of pace from the antique motif that abounds in Ashland's bed and breakfasts, this remodeled folk farmhouse and carriage house is modern, light and airy inside. The common living room and each of the five guest rooms are decorated with lovely examples of artist and host Audrey Sochor's vividly hued tapestries and paintings. Husband Art Sochor's extensive theatre library is available for guests' perusal, and the Shakespeare teacher and longtime theatre jack-of-all-trades welcomes chats with his theatre-bound guests. Meals are set according to guests' dietary needs, and the hosts have made the common room and three of the bedrooms wheelchair-accessible (a first in the Ashland B&Bs we visited). The two carriage-house rooms offer separate entrances and optimum privacy, and all rooms have private baths, air conditioning, reading lamps, and phones. In the summer, the three-course breakfast is served on the back deck which opens onto a half-acre of crabapple trees, rose gardens, and berry bushes. Shakespeare is within walking distance. Children are welcome. No smoking inside or out.

Fox House Inn

2nd and B off Main,
(503) 488-1055
269 B Street, Ashland,
OR 97520
Expensive; no credit cards;
checks ok

The two-bedroom inn offers guests the utmost privacy; the rooms are well spaced on separate floors, and each has its own entrance and its own phone (antique "candlestick" phones, of course). Oriental rugs on the oak floor, velvet drapery and a freestanding wood stove grace the common sitting room, and the two bedrooms are furnished with brass beds with half-canopies and private baths with claw-footed tubs. The larger Garden Room downstairs, highlighted with stained and etched glasswork, opens onto an enclosed flower garden. We recommend Annabel's Suite upstairs for a romantic getaway: guests have the entire second story, with private sitting room and dressing room, and a lavish bedroom featuring a lovely ivory satin-and-lace comforter on the bed.

Send us your opinions and tips on the report form at the back of this book.

Mt. Ashland Inn

*Exit 5 off I-5, follow
signs to Mt. Ashland Ski
Area for 5¼ miles,
(503) 482-8707
550 Mt. Ashland Road,
Ashland, OR 97520
Moderate; MC, V*

Wind your way up Mt. Ashland Road through several miles of gargantuan evergreens and you discover a huge, custom-made two-story log cabin. This is the dream home of Jerry and Elaine Shanafelt, who designed and built the lodge in 1987, using some 275 cedar trees cut from their 160-acre property in the Siskiyous. (Jerry is a designer and builder by trade; Elaine is a nurse-practitioner-turned-innkeeper who says, "Now I see people because they *want* to see me.")

Smack in the middle of the Pacific Crest trails and just a few minutes from Mt. Ashland Ski Area, the home is a magnificent work of architecture created with painstaking attention to quality. The inn is more posh than rustic, inside; the incense-cedar logs have been stripped and oiled to a light, golden color, and the spacious, airy feel is enhanced by open beam ceilings, large windows, and a huge stone fireplace. Examples of Jerry's handiwork seem to fill every nook of the home: stained glass windows decorate the entryway, a spiral cedar staircase with madrona railing connects the kitchen to the second story, and each of the five guest-room doors is carved with its mountain namesake. Guests sleep in antique beds covered with elaborate patchwork quilts handmade by Elaine, and each room has a private bath. Try for the newly opened McLoughlin Suite for a king-size bed and a sitting room, plus a view of Mt. Shasta and Mt. McLoughlin. Be prepared for snow (November to April) and plan at least a two-day stay. For longer stays, you might prefer the private guest house a quarter mile away, with an octagonal floor plan and a hot tub on the deck.

Romeo Inn

*At the end of the first
block on Idaho from Iowa,
(503) 488-0884
295 Idaho Street,
Ashland, OR 97520
Expensive; MC, V*

This imposing Cape Cod home has five spacious and plush guest rooms decorated in contemporary and antique furnishings. All rooms have king-size beds and private baths; the Canterbury Room features its own stone fireplace. There's a baby grand piano in the living room, and the heated pool and hot tub on the large back deck are open year-round. The newest addition, the Stratford Suite, is a separate structure with its own bedroom, bath, and kitchen; it features a vaulted ceiling with skylight, a marble-tiled fireplace, and a raised whirlpool bathtub-for-two. The generous breakfast of baked fruit, specialty main course, and fresh baked goods is said to satisfy through dinnertime.

Country Willows

*4 blocks down Clay from
Siskiyou Blvd,
(503) 488-1590
1313 Clay Street,
Ashland, OR 97520*

Set on five acres of farmland six minutes from downtown Ashland, this rebuilt 1896 country home offers peace and quiet and a lovely view of the hills. Bill and Barbara Huntley offer four freshly carpeted and painted rooms with air conditioning and private baths, plus a swimming pool and newly built hot tub on the large back deck.

Moderate to expensive;
MC, V

Breakfast is served on a pretty sunporch. The grounds outside offer running and hiking trails; a brook runs through the back yard, and the owners keep a host of ducks, geese, and horses on the property.

Cowslip's Belle
3 blocks north of the
theatre on Main,
(503) 488-2901
159 N Main, Ashland,
OR 97520
Moderate; MC, V

Named after a song in *A Midsummer-Night's Dream*, the home has a cheery charm with its swing chair on the front porch, vintage furniture and fresh flowers inside. There are two reasonably priced bedrooms in the main house, and a separate carriage house in the back offers extra privacy. Downtown and Lithia Park are three blocks away.

Morical House
Exit 19 from I-5, turn
left onto Highway 99,
(503) 482-2254
668 N Main, Ashland,
OR 97520
Moderate; MC, V

This large farmhouse dates back to the 1880s, but a full renovation has left the inside freshly painted and papered, with the original hardwood floors and stained glass windows restored. The five bedrooms are furnished with antiques, handmade quilts, and family heirlooms. The inn's proximity to busy Main Street takes away somewhat from its ambience, but the bedrooms are carefully soundproofed and provide back-yard views of the fields and mountains beyond. New owners Patricia and Peter Dahl run a tight ship, from the polished brass bathroom fixtures to the tray of refreshments available throughout the day. At breakfast, guests sample fresh fruit, home-baked goods, and Morical House "smoothies" on the sunporch overlooking the acre of flower gardens. Throughout the day, guests are encouraged to enjoy the books, current magazines, and games in the parlor, to set up a game of lawn croquet, or to practice their golf on the putting green.

CAVE JUNCTION

The daily tours of **Oregon Caves National Monument** are a bit strenuous and can be crowded, and the caves are chilly. But the marble and limestone formations are intriguing. Children under six are excluded; babysitting service is available. Open year-round. Arrive early during summer, or you may have a long wait. (503) 592-3400.

LODGINGS

Oregon Caves Chateau
Route 46, 20 miles east of
Cave Junction; look for
signs, (503) 592-3400
PO Box 128, Cave
Junction, OR 97523
Moderate; checks ok

This fine old wooden lodge is set among tall trees and a deep canyon. Doors don't always close properly, but the place is restful. The sound of falling water from numerous nearby mountain streams will help lull you to sleep. Views are splendid, the public rooms have the requisite massive fireplaces, and the down-home cooking in the dining room is quite good. The wine list features lots of local bottlings. There are 22 rooms in the lodge—nothing fancy, but clean. Open early June through early September.

OREGON CASCADES

The Columbia River Gorge—Troutdale to The Dalles—followed by two easterly Cascade crossings: Sandy to Mount Hood in the north, McKenzie Bridge to Bend mid-state. Finally, a southward progression through the heart of the mountains to Klamath Falls.

COLUMBIA RIVER GORGE

The Gorge was once more a terror than a scenic wonder because of the narrow, winding highway. But now most of the traffic is out on I-84, leaving beautiful old Route 30 for the take-your-time wanderers. The scenery is partly magnificent waterfalls, partly dramatic cliffs and rock formations cut by the country's second-largest river (but, unlike the Mississippi, one with a rapid, downhill surge). Watch the river for colorful practitioners of the burgeoning sailboard craze, for which this windy stretch of the Columbia has become world renowned (see Hood River introduction).

The old Scenic Gorge Highway is an easy 20-mile trip from Troutdale on. **Crown Point**, 725 feet above the river, features an English Tudor vista house. Below, at Rooster Rock State Park, one of the attractions is a nude-bathing beach. **Larch Mountain**, 14 miles upriver from Crown Point, is even more spectacular than the more famous overlooks. **Multnomah Falls** ranks second highest in the country, at 620 feet (in two steps). **Multnomah Falls Lodge**, at the foot of the falls, was designed in 1925 by Albert E. Doyle, of Benson Hotel fame, in a rustic-stone style. Now a National Historic Landmark, the lodge houses a naturalists' and visitors' center and a large restaurant and snack bar offering decent food, but does not have overnight facilities. Check out the new Falls Room Lounge; (503) 695-2376. **Oneonta Gorge** is a narrow, dramatic cleft through which a slippery half-mile trail winds to secluded Oneonta Falls; this rugged trail, mostly through the streambed itself, is suitable only for the adventurous. **Bonneville Dam**, the first Federal dam on the Columbia, offers tours of the dam, the fish ladders (seen through underwater viewing windows), and the navigational locks; (503) 374-8820. You can tour the Bonneville Fish Hatchery (next to the dam) year-round; however, the best time is in September and November when the Chinook are spawning; (503) 374-8393.

TROUTDALE

RESTAURANTS

**Tad's
Chicken 'n' Dumplings**
*1 mile east of Troutdale
on Highway 30,*

A down-home country restaurant, 20 miles east of Portland heading up the Columbia Gorge, this decades-old Oregon institution is popular with kids, bargain-hungry families, tourists—and fanciers of chicken. You can make

(503) 666-5337
943 SE Crown Point
Highway, Troutdale
Inexpensive; full bar;
AE, MC, V
Dinner Mon-Sat; Sun
dinner from 2 pm

quite an evening of it: a drink on the back deck, dinner at a window table where you can watch the sunset, a family-style meal (you should know what to order), topped off with ice cream or homemade pie. The place is usually packed, so call ahead to get on the waiting list, particularly for Sunday dinner.

CASCADE LOCKS

Bridge of the Gods, in the old river town of Cascade Locks, has a fine little museum that explains the Indian myth of the legendary rock-arch bridge over the Columbia that collapsed into the river long ago. **Columbia Gorge Sternwheeler** departs three times daily in the summer from the locks, stopping at Bonneville Dam and Stevenson Landing; (503) 374-8427.

RESTAURANTS

CharBurger Restaurant
Just east of the Bridge of
the Gods (Cascade Locks
exit off I-84),
(503) 374-8477
714 SW Wa-Na-Pa
Street, Cascade Locks
Moderate; beer and wine;
MC, V
Breakfast, lunch, dinner
every day, brunch Sun

Service is cafeteria-style in this barny place high on a bluff; get a window table for the view through the trees to the river below. Amid hokey, Old West decor choose from a truck-stop standard menu. Enjoy portions of all-American roadhouse food at a reasonable price. Best is the bakery, in which you can buy warm, homemade cinnamon and pecan rolls for just a buck apiece, and marvelous cookies.

LODGINGS

Scandian Motor Lodge
Wa-Na-Pa in the middle
of the Columbia Gorge
Center, (503) 374-8417
Mail: PO Box 398,
Cascade Locks,
OR 97014
Inexpensive; AE,
DC, MC, V

The Pacific Northwest, with its Ingmar Bergman–like winter light, has been attractive to Scandinavians, but rarely does this heritage go on public display. Here's an exception: a strikingly designed motel with brightly printed bedspreads, Norwegian wall decorations, tiled bathrooms in authentic Scandinavian styles, natural-wood furniture, and Norwegian-style telephone-showers. One room even has its own sauna. Try for an upstairs room, where the river views are better. Even there, the rates are quite reasonable.

HOOD RIVER

Much of the Northwest's bounty converges in this agreeable town of 4,000 souls. Fruit orchards are everywhere, benignly supervised by 11,245-foot Mount Hood, 30 miles to the south, and nourished by the Columbia River, rushing alongside the northern edge of town. From the town itself, however, the views are of Mount Adams on the Washington side, looking down upon the Columbia and its ubiquitous sailboarders through a fortuitous cleft in the bluff.

In summer you can't miss the "boardheads," dotting the river with their brilliant

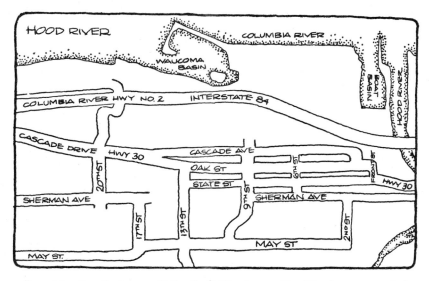

sails and lending the town a distinctly Californian quality. They've come, only in about the last half-decade, because of the roaring winds that blow opposite to the current—sailboarding perfection.

Right in town are two fine spectator spots, the **West Jetty** and **Port Marina Park**, although sailboarders will head for any number of other roadside launching spots east and west of here (and on the Washington side) when changing wind conditions warrant. For information on wind conditions, sailboard rentals, launching spots, or lessons, a multitude of sailboard equipment shops, including **Sailboard Warehouse**, 315 Oak Street, (503) 386-1699, can assist.

As locals will (strongly) attest, however, there was life in Hood River before the sailboarders descended. At **Hood River County Museum** (Port Marina Park, 503-386-6772, open Wednesday through Sunday until 4pm or when the flags are flying), exhibits depict, among other things, Native American artifacts of the region. The town's **Visitor Information Center** adjoins; (503) 386-2000.

The region's main draw has always been the orchards and vineyards of the fertile valley, celebrated in a wonderful small-town **Blossom Festival** held every year in mid-April. The **Mount Hood Railroad**, Hood River Depot, (503) 386-3556, makes four-hour round trips from the quaint Hood River Depot and into the heart of orchard country, May through October. You can buy the fruit of the orchards at **The Fruit Tree** near the Columbia Gorge Hotel, or sip a little grape in tasting rooms of the **Three Rivers Winery**, 275 Country Club Road, (503) 386-5453, or **Hood River Vineyards**, 4693 Westwood Drive, (503) 396-3772, the latter known for its pear and raspberry dessert wines. There's even a brewery in town now, the **WhiteCap BrewPub**, 506 Columbia Street, (503) 386-2247, home of the hand-crafted Full Sail Ales. The outdoor deck (with live music on weekends) of the pub provides a fitting place for tired sailboarders to unwind while still keeping the river in their sights.

Panorama Point, half a mile south on Highway 35, has the best view of the Hood River Valley leading to Mount Hood. Or, heading east out of Hood River, the **Rowena Crest Viewpoint** off old Highway 30 reveals a grandstand vista of the slow-moving Columbia.

RESTAURANTS

Stonehedge Inn
Exit 62 off I-84,
(503) 386-3940
3405 Cascade Drive,
Hood River
Moderate; full bar;
DC, MC, V
Dinner Wed-Sun

Originally constructed as a summer house in the early years of the century, the Inn is now a very cozy and somewhat remote (a quarter-mile up a gravel road) dining hideaway with one dressy, dark-paneled room, a homey library, a long porch room with a view, and an intimate bar. Owner Jean Harmon plays the part of roving proprietor well, greeting her guests and really chatting up the locals. We were quite delighted to find that such a lovely place doesn't just ride on hospitality or reputation, however, but produces subtle, beautiful food.

Nothing new or startling on the list; it's the usual classical array of pate (wonderful presentation) and escargots to begin with, then rack of lamb, lobster tails, filet mignon, veal, or seafood (fresh Oregon scallops, salmon, halibut). Oysters on the half shell are served when available. Chef Patrick Edwards shows marvelous restraint in dishes like a delicate poached salmon in an orange beurre blanc, presented in generous portion with vegetables and a twice-baked potato. Attention to extras—warm rosemary bread, sincere service, and exquisite cheesecake for dessert—tell us that Stonehedge isn't resting on its laurels. Easy-listening music in the background provides the only annoyance.

Chianti's Restaurant
6th and Cascade,
(503) 386-5737
509 Cascade Street,
Hood River
Moderate; beer and wine;
AE, MC, V
Dinner every day

The casual congeniality of a drop-in Italian restaurant fits snugly into this town. Chianti's is a bustling, active, and very youthfully staffed (your waiter might be too busy rhapsodizing about that day's wind to remember to bring out your bread) second-story roost, with a menu of about eight pastas, a half-dozen meat or seafood specials, and a few salads. It's all no-nonsense food: a robust, creamy Caesar; pollo fettuccine, fragrant with rosemary; big, chunky bowls of hearty spaghetti-for-two. And we hear the bread is good, anyway. Stick with gelato for dessert (the chocolate mousse pie tasted like Sara Lee's), and hang around awhile with your coffee: the day's best sailboarding stories are sure to be overheard from the next table.

Reflections of the Past
On the corner of 13th
and B, (503) 386-2111
1302 13th Street,
Hood River
Moderate; beer and wine;
MC, V
Lunch, dinner Tues-Sun,
brunch Sun

In this town where charming old houses almost automatically metamorphose into bed and breakfasts when they grow up, here's one off the main drag in upper Hood River that became a restaurant. It's an elegantly turned-out, family-run place, full of honest food like lightly creamy broccoli soup and thick turkey sandwiches and homemade German chocolate cake for dessert. Although we've tried only lunch here, reports are similarly glowing about dinner, when you can choose from a slightly more international menu (steak Diane to fajitas) at one of the more intimate upstairs tables. Danger: a basket of the addicting crispy-chewy criss-cross fries will put you off potato chips for the rest of your life.

Bette's Place

Take the west exit in Hood River, follow Highway 30 east, (503) 386-1880 416 Oak Street, Hood River Inexpensive; no alcohol; no credit cards; checks ok Breakfast, lunch Sat-Sun, dinner Mon-Fri

Where the boardheads go. Bette's is the last of the carbo-load coffee shops, with big plates of fresh hash browns and thick omelets and homemade blueberry muffins (or legendary cinnamon rolls if it's Wednesday) and, what the heck, a piece of pie to finish. Things like surimi in the seafood omelet don't seem to bother anybody a bit, but if they bother you, come at lunch and order a Barge Burger. You can't complain when your mouth is this full.

LODGINGS

Columbia Gorge Hotel

1 hour east of Portland on I-84, (503) 386-5566, toll-free (800) 345-1921, 4000 Westcliff Drive, Hood River, OR 97031 Expensive; AE, DC, MC, V

In 1921, lumber baron Simon Benson built a luxury hotel here, brought his famous chef Henry Thiele in for the opening, and thereby capped his successful completion of the Columbia Gorge Scenic Highway in 1920. Restored and reopened in 1979 after several non-hotel incarnations, the hotel has since enjoyed the starry-eyed attentions of countless tour-bus and honeymoon trippers. It's a handsome, expensive, and somewhat spoiled landmark.

Public and guest rooms are elegant, with dark wood antiques, French doors, a cheery rust-and-apricot decor, and floral prints blooming everywhere. Each room has its own color scheme. Aim for a gorgeside room—numbers 336 and 340 have the most glorious beds, but any of the corner rooms over here are quite desirable—since traffic noise from I-84 leaks through the windows on the non-view side. (Besides, the landscaping along the entrance resembles nothing so much as a pitch 'n' putt mini-golf course.) On a recent visit we had some difficulty regulating the thermostat in the room, and the bathroom faucets were rather unresponsive, but we were appeased somewhat by the complimentary basket of soaps and bath oils—a nice touch. Indeed, the service is of the ingratiatingly formal school, with all staff well trained in the art of the scraping bow. Rates for all this run from around $100, including a seven-course breakfast.

Though locals swear they often eat well here, we still find the restaurant to be disappointing. Service is the worst kind of flawless (the fawning staff is all over you), and the food is way overpriced for its quality (plan on at least $75 for two). On one visit, an entree of chicken breast breaded with pistachios, covered with apples and Tillamook cheese, and draped in a silky apple cream sauce was strange at best; the strong flavors fought with one another and thoroughly masked the delicate sauce. A pretty green salad was drowning in dressing, and shrimp in a saute was rubbery. The legendary seven-course farm breakfasts ($16.95 if you're not a guest), complete with "honey from the sky," are still little more than eat-fests, but if you're there at the right time of the year you can gobble up the sweet local berries. Do whatever it takes to get a window seat in this room; the grand view remains the best part of the meal.

Lakecliff Estate

Exit 62 off I-84, ½ mile
west of Hood River,
(503) 386-7000
3820 Westcliff Drive,
Hood River, OR 97031
Moderate; MC, V

Everyone's favorite Hood River bed and breakfast, the former Barkheimer House, is under new ownership but still delivers the same fine hospitality in the same outstanding surroundings. The forest green house, just a short jog off I-84 but shrouded by woods to create a sense of seclusion and quiet, commands an astonishing view of the Columbia River below. Built in 1908 by architect Albert E. Doyle, who designed Multnomah Falls Lodge and the Benson Hotel in Portland, Lakecliff features five stone fireplaces, a large, rustic living room, sun porch, and an elegant dining room where breakfast is served. Three of the four well-appointed rooms have fireplaces (which the owners keep stocked with wood); three rooms have river views. New owners Bruce and Judy Thesenga have gussied up the grounds and often use them for weddings.

State Street Inn

Near corner of State and
10th, (503) 386-1899
1005 State Street,
Hood River, OR 97031
Moderate; MC, V

This is the way to do a B&B. Amy Goodbar and Mac Lee are the young innkeepers of this impeccable jewel, located on a residential street near the center of things, which boasts (among other things) a dead-center view of Mount Adams. Four rooms (sharing two baths) are beautifully adorned to fit their names: the Massachusetts Room in Colonial style, Colorado with a hint of the Southwest, Maryland with Southern charm (and an extra bed), and—everyone's favorite—California, with bright colors and a picture window framing Mount Adams. Breakfast might be whole-wheat waffles, eaten with other guests around the big table in the dining room. A pleasure.

Duckwall House

State and Oak,
(509) 386-6635
811 Oak Street,
Hood River, OR 97031
Moderate; AE

Jack and Doris Kent and their guests occupy this tidy home close to the center of things on Oak Street. Four rooms (sharing only one bath) are done up in peaches and pinks and pretty antiques, and rent for a reasonable $50 a night. Unfortunately, the room with the best view of the river also has the most traffic noise. A lack of bedside lamps is the other complaint. Aside from these things, however, the best part of the stay revolves around Doris and Jack's gracious, but not obsequious, hospitality. Breakfast is a big treat: baked eggs, fresh fruit, potatoes, cinnamon buns, orange juice, and coffee.

Vagabond Lodge
Exit 62 off I-84,
(503) 386-2992
4070 Westcliff Drive,
Hood River, OR 97031
Inexpensive; MC, V

Ignore the motel exterior and the first nondescript row of highway-facing units, for behind these are a string of perfectly serviceable, tidy little rooms overlooking the river through lovely cliffside woodland gardens. There's also a newer two-story building. It's family-run, very reasonable ($35 to $52), and you can bring your pet. Three of the units have large stone fireplaces.

THE DALLES

The Dalles is *the* historical stop along this stretch. Here the Oregon Trail ended: goods from wagons were loaded onto barges for the final float to Portland. Here was Celilo Falls, where Indians fished for salmon until the dam submerged the falls. Here stood Fort Dalles, built in a peculiarly ornate style by an interesting American architect, Andrew Jackson Downing, whose 1850 surgeon's house still remains as a museum (15th and Garrison streets), with exceptional relics from the pioneer trails. Architecturally, the town is much more interesting than others nearby, with nicely maintained examples of Colonial, Gothic Revival, Italianate, and American Renaissance styles.

The best way to crown an afternoon of contemplating the past is to picnic at **Sorosis Park**, a large, shady park that is the highest overlook on the Scenic Drive through the Gorge. Or visit the new **River Front Park**, adjacent to I-84, for river access and tamer sailboarding winds.

RESTAURANTS

Ole's Supper Club
Take exit 84 off I-84,
go west 1 mile,
(503) 296-6708
2620 W Second Street,
The Dalles
Moderate; full bar;
MC, V
Dinner Tues-Sat

Ole's isn't glamorous, and those seeking the yuppie experience in the Gorge wouldn't single it out. In fact, they might have a hard time finding the place in the industrial west end of The Dalles. But the consistent quality of the food and the commitment to good wine make it notable—in spite of the fact that it looks like a double-wide mobile home.

The house special turns out to be one of the best cuts of prime rib we've tasted anywhere. Everything is included: delicious homemade soup, a standard salad, an individual loaf of hot homemade bread, a potato or vegetable. Although the restaurant has established its reputation on beef, it features chicken, seafood, and lamb also. It treats fresh razor clams well, when they're available. The wine list is notable because the bar is one of the few in Oregon that doubles as a wine shop; it's known regionally for a wide selection, and wine prices in the restaurant are just over retail.

LODGINGS

Williams House Inn
Corner of Trevett and
6th, (503) 296-2889
608 W Sixth Street,

A manicured three-acre arboretum surrounds this elaborate Victorian house, built in 1899, which has been in the Williams family for over 60 years. A few years ago Don and Barbara Williams opened it as a bed and break-

The Dalles, OR 97058
Moderate; AE, MC, V

fast; now guests clamor to return. Nicaraguan mahogany decorates the walls and Oriental rugs cover the floor of the large living room, which contains a piano and a fireplace. Two of the three rooms are upstairs, each with its own balcony. We liked the downstairs Elizabeth Suite with its separate bedroom, writing desk, and private bath with a marble-top wash basin and a claw-footed tub. The Williamses serve a fine breakfast of their own canned fruits—or fresh ones when they're perfectly ripe—home-roasted granola, muffins, and eggs. Don Williams is an encyclopedia of local lore.

SANDY

A pleasant town on the way to Mount Hood, Sandy (named for the nearby river) offers a white-steepled church, quaint shops, a weekend country market, and big fruit stands purveying the local fruits, vegetables, Oregon wines, juices, and filberts. In short—a nice stop before heading into the mountains.

The Oregon Candy Farm has added a line of Bavarian truffles to their 100 varieties of candies: caramels, barks, chocolate-covered prunes, apricot-walnut jellies, and on and on. Kids can watch the candy-makers in the kitchen. It's 5½ miles east of Sandy on Highway 26, (503) 668-5066.

Oral Hull Park is designed for the blind, with splashing water and plants to smell or touch; it is a moving experience even for the sighted. (503) 668-6195.

RESTAURANTS

Calamity Jane's
Highway 26, 1 mile east
of Sandy, (503) 668-7817
42015 Highway 26,
The Dalles
Inexpensive; beer
and wine; MC, V
Lunch, dinner every day

Take your choice of 15 different hamburgers while seated amid Wild West decor. The old-fashioned shakes, served in the big stainless steel shaker, are very good. A modest dinner menu with lots of different steaks and some fish and chips is also available.

CLOSED

WEMME (aka WELCHES)

This pretty little town is known as Wemme on maps and as Welches at the Post Office, because so many Welches settled here. Whatever you call it, it's full of the famous Oregon congeniality. **The Weavery** is a fine place to inspect pottery, paintings, and cards from the many artists who live in this region; Emma Wheeler, who weaves colorful plaids, is the proprietor; (503) 622-4693.

RESTAURANTS

Chalet Suisse
Highway 26 and
Welches Road
(503) 622-3600
24371 E Welches

If you can hold off your hunger until you get to Wemme, you'll be in for a treat that satisfies both your appetite and your palate. This chalet seems out of place for a town filling up with malls and condos, but inside, old cowbells

Road, Welches
Moderate; full bar; AE,
DC, MC, V
Dinner Wed-Sun

hang from the ceiling and waitresses in peasant dresses serve hard-to-find Swiss specialties from a kitchen with consistently high standards. Owner-chef Kurt Mezger prepares excellent buendnerfleisch (paper-thin folds of salt-cured beef), zurcher geschnitzeltes (a preparation of veal with mushrooms and cream sauce), and tender medallions of beef with chanterelles in a tarragon cream sauce. Chalet Suisse seats only 75 persons, so make reservations a day in advance, especially during the peak summer season and on any weekend.

LODGINGS

Rippling River Resort
1 hour east of Portland
on Highway 26,
(503) 622-3101, toll-free
(800) 547-8054
68010 E Fairway
Avenue, Welches,
OR 97067
Expensive; AE, DC,
MC, V

It's under new ownership—*again*—but we have faith; there's not much that could harm such a gracious layout. The complex still has 204 motel-style and condominium rooms, two dining rooms and lounges, a 1,000-person-capacity convention center, two pools, and two Jacuzzis. The condominiums, with private patios, are the best choice here (though all of the rooms resemble ordinary motel spaces); king rooms have kitchens. Mount Hood is 20 miles away, but if you don't want to go that far, Rippling River offers 27 holes of golf, six tennis courts (two with lights), and rental bikes. One dining room, Forest Hills, is particularly lovely, offering Sunday brunch and a continental dinner.

ZIG ZAG

RESTAURANTS

Salazar's
Highway 26, 1 mile east
of Zig Zag,
(503) 622-3775
71545 E Highway 26,
Rhododendron,
Moderate; full bar;
AE, DC, MC, V
Dinner every day

All three dining rooms have been filled with the fruits of owner-chef Al Salazar's 30-odd years of collecting: antique lamps, tapestries, stained glass, ornate carving knives, a huge collection of doorknobs, and so on. The effect is as disconcerting as it is fascinating.

The cuisine is equally eclectic and somewhat uneven: blackened cod, Oriental duck, lamb shanks, Swiss steak. The wine list is adequate. Our advice is to order a tender steak, dine in the upstairs loft for the view (particularly if there's a snowscape), and be sure to enjoy the doorknob collection.

Barlow Trail Inn
Highway 26, ½ mile east
of Thriftway,
(503) 622-3877
69580 E Highway 26,
Zig Zag
Moderate; full bar;
AE, MC, V
Breakfast, lunch, dinner
every day

Warm and friendly, this log lodge caters to the locals, serving up breakfasts, big burgers, thick steaks, and nothing unexpected. Have fried chicken or a burger, and sit outside. The place is so popular that the owners recommend reservations for breakfast.

MOUNT HOOD

At 11,245 feet, Hood may not be the highest in the chain of volcanoes in the Cascades, but it is one of the best-developed. The **Timberline Day Lodge** at the 6,000-foot level has plenty of facilities to equip the mountaineer, hiker, or skier (see listing). Chair lifts take you to the Palmer Snowfield, up in the glaciers, where you can ski in the middle of summer. The lower parts are ablaze with rhododendrons (peaking in June) and wildflowers (peaking in July); all are easily reachable from trails that spread out from the lodge. One of the best trails leads 4½ miles west from the lodge to flower-studded Paradise Park. Like Rainier, the mountain is girt by a long trail (called Timberline Trail), a 40-mile circuit of the entire peak that traverses snowfields as well as ancient forests.

Mid-May to mid-July is the prime time for climbing Mount Hood, a peak that looks easier than it is, since the last 1,500 feet involve very steep snow-climbing. Timberline Mountain Guides, in the Timberline Day Lodge, equip and conduct climbers to the summit; (503) 548-1888.

LODGINGS

Timberline Lodge
Off Highway 26, east of Zig Zag, (503) 272-3311, toll-free (800) 547-1406 (outside Oregon)
Mail: Timberline Lodge, Timberline, OR 97028
Moderate; AE, MC, V
Breakfast, lunch, dinner every day

Built in 1937 as a WPA project, Timberline Lodge is a wonderland of American crafts—carved stone, worked metal, massive beams with adze marks plain to see, rugged fireplaces everywhere, and a huge, octagonal lobby that is an inspiring centerpiece for the steep-roofed hotel. In 1975 an organization called Friends of Timberline was formed to supervise and finance restoration of the magnificent craftsmanship; since then, many of the upholsteries, draperies, rugs, and bedspreads in the public and guest rooms have been rewoven to their original patterns, in some cases with the help of the original craftspersons. When the lodge was declared a National Historic Landmark in 1978, a full-time curator was employed to ensure maintenance and care for every stick of furniture within the museumlike lodge. With the opening of the Wy'East day lodge in 1981, much of the traffic was diverted from the historic lodge, which permitted a return to its original hotel purpose. The personality of the place is best captured, perhaps, by Heidi II, the latest in a long succession of faithful St. Bernard greeters at the inn.

Visits here are quite special. It's worth it to book a room with a fireplace, at upwards of $120 for a double. Each restored room is differentiated by bold colors and motifs, and even the unrestored rooms are attractive. Activities include some of the Northwest's best downhill and cross-country skiing, shuffleboard, and springtime hiking and picnicking. There's also a sauna. The lobby doesn't offer enough light to read or play cards very well, which is a shame—it's a great place to be.

The restaurant menu, though good, hasn't changed in several years; best are the simple seafood dishes and pastas. The Ram's Head Bar downstairs is now open on weekdays, and fast food is available in the Wy'East lodge.

Inn at Cooper Spur

Head east from Portland on I-84, take Highway 35 south 23 miles,
(503) 352-6692 (lodging) or (503) 352-6037 (restaurant)
10755 Cooper Spur Road, Mount Hood, OR 97041
Expensive; full bar; MC, V
Breakfast, lunch, dinner every day

This new resort is located between the sleepy town of Hood River and the summit of Mount Hood. You can stay in a sleeping room in the main lodge, but get a cabin instead: each has two bedrooms (with queen-size beds), sleeping lofts with three single beds, a fully equipped kitchen, 1½ baths, and all the wood you could want for the huge fireplace. Tennis, basketball, and croquet await warm-weather guests. In the winter, midweek ski packages are available. Either season, you have the use of your own hot tub. Beware the plastic mattress covers.

The adjacent Cooper Spur Inn menu offers dinner starting at $7.95; a queen-size prime rib goes for $12.95 and filet mignon for around $30. Lunch is a bit less pricey, with entrees ranging from $3.95 to $7.95. The food is all highly touted by locals but was no great shakes on a recent visit. The grounds have been nicely sculpted since our last visit: green lawns and picnic tables in the summer, lovely snowscape in winter.

McKENZIE RIVER

The highway through this river valley is the most beautiful of all the Cascade crossings. Following Highway 126 from Eugene, you pass farm country alongside the green water of the McKenzie River. Soon you see lovely campgrounds and come to waterfalls and amazingly transparent lakes. At Foley Springs you catch Highway 242 for the pass (opens about July 1 each year). You will be in volcanic country, with vast lava beds that cooled off only 2,000 years ago.

McKenzie River-runs. Long celebrated for trout fishing, the McKenzie has become known for river-runs in rafts or the famous McKenzie River boats, rakish dories with upturned bows and sterns. **Dave Helfrich River Outfitter**, in Vida, conducts springtime day trips on the river and also arranges for fly-fishing expeditions in drift boats; (503) 896-3786.

McKENZIE BRIDGE

Tokatee Golf Course, three miles west of McKenzie Bridge, is commonly rated one of the five finest in the Northwest: lots of trees, rolling terrain, and concentration-distracting views of the scenery; (503) 822-3220.

RESTAURANTS

Log Cabin Inn

50 miles east of I-5 on Highway 126,
(503) 822-3432
56483 McKenzie Highway, McKenzie Bridge
Inexpensive; MC, V
Breakfast, lunch, dinner every day

The fundamentals of home cooking and clean, comfortable lodging (closed January and February) are enshrined here. You can opt for a continental breakfast ($4 extra) or you can order from the menu at the going rate. Dinners are popular and offer a range as broad as cod, wild boar, buffalo, and more traditional prime rib. They come from miles around to top it all off with marionberry cobbler for dessert.

LODGINGS

Holiday Farm

McKenzie River Drive,
3 miles west of McKenzie
Bridge, (503) 822-3715
54455 McKenzie River
Drive, Blue River,
OR 97413
Moderate; full bar; no
credit cards; checks ok
Breakfast, lunch, dinner
every day

First-time visitors to Holiday Farm wouldn't know at a glance that the resort encloses 90 acres and a hidden lake or three. They would find a freshly painted main house (an old stagecoach stop), pleasant dining in the restaurant, and some amiable riverside cottages with knockout views of the McKenzie. It's open April through November.

All of the cabins feature decks and bright windows—some are older green and white (with a rebuilt porch here and there); others are cedar-sided and more contemporary. Low foot-lamps light the path that connects them. Big and Little Rainbow is a large and modern unit that can be joined for a larger group (two families) or split for individual parties.

The restaurant, open to tourists passing through, makes a very pleasant stop; you dine on a porch overhanging the river. Burgers are typical fare for lunch; steaks, seafood, and game for dinner.

Loloma Lodge

½ mile east of McKenzie
Bridge on Highway 126
(503) 822-3267
56687 McKenzie
Highway, McKenzie
Bridge, OR 97413
Moderate; no credit cards;
checks ok

Don't be worried that the access to this restful resort is right off busy Highway 126. The road becomes luxuriantly overgrown and soon breaks out into a sunny clearing, where you'll find four cabins on the banks of the McKenzie. The units belie their age and boast decks, barbecues, and chaise lounges. Inside, high ceilings top great view windows; there are fully supplied kitchenettes, radiantly heated floors, extra-thick mattresses on the queen-size hideabed, extra-long twins in the bedroom, cable TV, fresh towels daily, and maid service every fourth day. Add to that a bench swing down by the river. On acreage out of sight of the cabins is a larger vacation home, with three bedrooms and three baths, comfortably accommodating eight.

CAMP SHERMAN

LODGINGS

House on the Metolius

Forest Service Road 1420,
2½ miles north of Camp
Sherman, (503) 595-6620
Mail: PO Box 601,
Camp Sherman,
OR 97730
Expensive; MC, V

★★

This private fly-fishing resort is open all year now (and it's still hard to get into), set in 200 acres of gorgeous scenery, with the Metolius River nearby. The cabins are lovely, fully equipped with fireplace, kitchenette, and king, double, or twin beds. Reservations needed at least a week in advance. Well-behaved pets okay. Don't forget your fly rod.

Lake Creek Lodge

4 miles north of Highway

The resort has been here for over 60 years, popular with families who want a knotty-pine cabin from which to en-

20 at Camp Sherman turnoff, (503) 595-6331 Star Route, Sisters, OR 97759 Expensive; no credit cards; checks ok

joy the fishing, the pond, and the hearty food at the lodge. Best choice is a lodge house, a cheerful, open-ceilinged home with two or three bedrooms, one or two baths, possibly a fireplace, a complete kitchen, living room, and screened porch; less expensive are the two-bedroom cottages, which have no kitchens. The cabins are spread around grassy grounds dotted with pines, overlooking the small lake made from a dammed stream. Facilities are extensive: tennis (two courts), fishing, hiking and biking, and children's activities like the Friday night fireboat races with small pitch-covered bark boats.

The lodge serves excellent breakfasts and dinners, and if it's not too busy with guests, it is also open for outsiders. There's no choice on a given night, but you can call ahead to see if it's salmon, barbecued steak, or lamb for that evening; bring your own wine.

SISTERS

Named after the three mountain peaks that dominate the horizon (Faith, Hope, and Charity), this little community is becoming a bit of a mecca for tired urban types looking for a taste of cowboy escapism. On a clear day (and there are about 250 of them a year), Sisters is exquisite. Surrounded by mountains, trout streams, and pine and cedar forests, this little town is beginning to capitalize on the influx of winter skiers and summer camping and fishing enthusiasts.

There's mixed sentiment about the pseudo-Western storefronts that are thematically organizing the town's commerce, but then again, Sisters does host 50,000 visitors for its annual June rodeo. If cowboy isn't your style, there are a very good art gallery at the corner of Elm and Main, a mini-mall called Barclay Square (with a nice tile boutique), and a knowledgeable mountain-supply store.

While the population is about 750, more than 4,000 folks get mail at the Sisters P.O. come summer. Many of them run boarding and ranch facilities. The most famous ranch is **The Patterson Ranch,** breeders of Polish Arabian horses and South American llamas. Call (503) 549-3831 for information.

RESTAURANTS

Hotel Sisters and Bronco Billy's Saloon
Cascade and Fir, (503) 549-RIBS 101 Cascade Street, Sisters Moderate; full bar; MC, V Breakfast, lunch, dinner every day (breakfast Sat-Sun only in winter)

The social centerpiece of Western-theme Sisters, this bar and eatery serves up Western-style ranch cooking, with good burgers and some Mexican fare as well. It's stringties all around on the friendly and diligent waitstaff. Seafood is fresh (deliveries thrice weekly from Salem), but we recommend you stay with the chicken and ribs and avoid the odd taco-shell preparations dredged in Parmesan and paprika.

Owners John Keenan, Bill Reed, and John Tehan have succeeded in turning old friendships into a going business consortium, re-creating the look of a first-class hotel, circa 1900. The old upstairs hotel rooms are now private meeting rooms, and photos of early Sisters enhance the pleasant dining decor downstairs. Drop-ins often eat in the saloon or on good days take a drink on the deck.

Papandrea's Pizza

*East end of town
on the main drag,
(503) 549-6081
Cascade Highway, Sisters
Inexpensive; beer and
wine; MC, V
Lunch, dinner every day*

Oregonians love this place. The original link in a growing chain of pizzerias, Papandrea's has built a quality reputation on fresh dough, homemade sauce, real cheese, and fresh vegetables. Because of all this freshness, the place does seem to abide by its disclaimer sign—"We will not sacrifice quality for speed, so expect to wait a little longer." Actually, you wait quite a bit longer for the original thick-crust pies, but they've added an express thin crust if you really can't wait and a You-Bake line for take-home.

The Gallery

*Corner of Cascade and
Hood, (503) 549-2631
230 W Cascade Street,
Sisters
Inexpensive; full bar;
MC, V
Breakfast, lunch,
dinner every day*

The breakfast omelets draw the morning crowd, and the lunch burgers pull the afternoon business at this no-nonsense spot. There are always weekly specials (meat loaf, German sausage, sirloin tips), and the prices (up to $10.95) are still modest (even though they're almost double what they used to be) for the value. Owners Jim and Carrie Cheatham are proud of their Ray Eyerling paintings and also display the largest Northwest collection of Winchester rifles. Drop in for some peanut-butter pie and coffee just to check it out.

LODGINGS

Black Butte Ranch

*Highway 20, 8 miles west
of Sisters, (503) 595-6211
Mail: PO Box 8000,
Black Butte Ranch,
OR 97759
Moderate; AE, MC, V
Breakfast, lunch, dinner
every day (January-April
closed Mon-Tues)*

With 1,800 acres, this vacation and recreation wonderland remains the darling of Northwest resorts. With a large portion of its business coming from "locals" (well-heeled Oregonians, as opposed to Sunriver's broader clientele from the whole West Coast), Black Butte does a lovely job just by being unassumingly spectacular.

Rimmed by the Three Sisters mountains, scented by a plain of ponderosa pines, and expertly developed by the Brooks Scanlon Company, these rental condos and private homes draw families year-round to swim, ski, fish, golf, bike, boat, ride horses (summer only), and play tennis.

The best way to make a reservation is to state the size of your party and whether or not you want a home (most are quite large and contemporary) or simply a good-sized bed and bath. (In the latter case, the lodge condominiums will suffice, although they are dark and dated, with too much orange Formica and brown furniture.)

The main lodge is a handsome but not overwhelming building that serves as dining headquarters. The two dining rooms at The Lodge Restaurant are tiered so that everyone can appreciate the meadow panorama. Food is straightforward and hearty, and servings are generous.

Looking for a particular place? Check the index at the back of this book for individual restaurants, lodgings, attractions, and more.

BEND

Bend was a quiet, undiscovered high-desert paradise until a push in the 1960s to develop recreation and tourism potential tamed Bachelor Butte into an alpine playground. Then came the golf courses, the airstrip, the bike trails, the river-rafting companies, the hikers, the tennis players, the rock hounds, and the skiers. Bend's popularity and population have been on a steady increase ever since, propelling it in the last three years to serious destination status. You may wonder what all the fuss is about as you approach the predictable main street (Third Street here), but the town's charm, relying heavily on the blinding blue sky and sage-scented air, slowly wins over any visitor with even a moderate affection for the great outdoors. Part of its appeal is due to its proximity to the following.

Mount Bachelor Ski Area (22 miles southwest). Having recently opened three express lifts (Summit, Pine Marten, and Outback Super Express Quad), Mount Bachelor now has 10 lifts feeding skiers onto 3,100 vertical feet of dry and groomed skiing. Even if you don't ski, we recommend you take the Express up to the new restaurant on the hill, **The Skier's Palate**, where they serve excellent lunches of grilled pistachio oysters or a hot sandwich of Dungeness crab and bay shrimp. The 9,000-foot elevation at the summit makes for all-season skiing. High-season amenities include ski school, racing, day care, rentals, an entire Nordic program and trails, and better-than-average ski food at six different lodges. Call (800) 547-6858; inside Oregon, (503) 382-8334 or (503) 382-7888.

The High Desert Museum. Newly expanded, this nonprofit center for natural

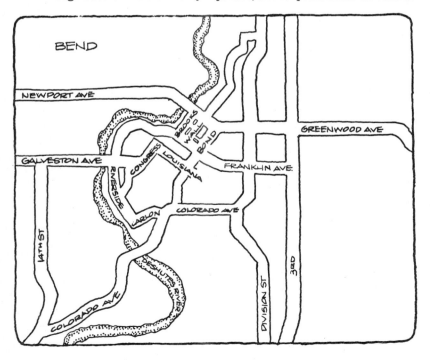

and cultural history located six miles south of Bend on Highway 97 includes live animal presentations on birds of prey, river otters, and porcupines. Fifty acres of natural trails and outdoor exhibits offer replicas of covered wagons, a sheepherder's camp, a settlers' cabin, and an Indian wickiup. Permanent and changing galleries display contemporary and historic artwork. Call (503) 382-4754. (Admission $4.50.)

Pilot Butte (just east of town). This cinder cone with a road to the top is a good first stop, offering a knockout panorama of the city and the mountains beyond.

Lava River Caves (12 miles south on Highway 97). Tours of the lava caves include a mile-long lava tube. As you descend into the dark and surprisingly eerie depths, you'll need a warm sweater. **Lava Lands Visitor Center**, atop a high butte formed by a volcanic fissure, is a lookout point with accompanying geology lessons about the "moonscape" panorama caused by central Oregon's volcanic history. Call (503) 593-2421.

Pine Mountain Observatory, 30 miles southeast of Bend on Highway 20, (503) 382-8331, is the University of Oregon's astronomical research facility. One of its three telescopes is the largest in the Northwest.

Deschutes Historical Museum (corner of NW Idaho and Wall). The museum features regional history and interesting pioneer paraphernalia but keeps limited hours. Call (503) 389-1813.

Cascade Lakes Highway/Century Drive. This 100-mile tour needs several hours and a picnic lunch for full appreciation. Begin in Bend along the Deschutes, using the National Forest Service's booklet "Cascade Lakes Discovery Tour."

Smith Rock State Park. Twenty-two miles north of Bend in Terrebonne, some of the finest rock climbers in the world gather to test their skills on the red-rock cliffs. The climbers' second-favorite hangout is **Rudy's Mexican Restaurant** in Terrebonne.

RESTAURANTS

Geno's Italian Specialties

Head toward Burns on E Highway 20; behind the Food Mart,
(503) 389-3464
2210 E Highway 20, Bend
Moderate; full bar; MC, V; checks ok

★ ★

No stars for the atmosphere, which is about as formal as a high-end Denny's, but this family-style Italian restaurant is the kind of place you'd want two blocks from your house. The prices are reasonable, the servings are large, and the food is beyond satisfying. Geno does almost everything well, but three things in particular are outstanding: veal (either the Parmesan or the Sicilian), ravioli (large meaty pasta pillows), and, believe it or not, the blue-cheese salad dressing. Our lasagne, however, was a bit too cheesy, as was the fettuccine. We can't vouch for the odd feature of barbecued spareribs—they were all gone before we could give 'em a try. Everything washes down well with any selection from the carefully chosen wine list.

Pine Tavern Restaurant

Foot of Oregon downtown at Mirror Pond,
(503) 382-5581
967 NW Brooks Street, Bend
Moderate; full bar; AE, DC, MC, V

Buttonhole three out of four Bend citizens on the street and tell them you're ready for a fancy night out, with good food, service, atmosphere, and a decent value for your dollar. The recommendation time and time again will be the Pine Tavern. Under the fresh ownership of Bert Bender and Joe Cenarrusa, this establishment—and 50 years of history make it truly established—is regaining its reputation for quality. Consider window-shopping at Common Threads across the street while you wait for

Lunch Mon-Sat, dinner every day, brunch Sun

a table (yes, even with reservations).

Request a table by the window in the main dining room. You'll want to take advantage of the unobstructed view of Mirror Pond and, what the heck, marvel at the tree growing through the floor.

The menu runs about $10 to $16.95 for various beef entrees, but a lighter dinner menu offers smaller cuts of steak and petite portions of veal. The prime rib petite cut is ample even for a hungry fellow, but prime rib is the forte of the restaurant, and few can resist the larger cut.

Le Bistro

1 block off Greenwood on Highway 97,
(503) 389-7274
1203 NE Third Street,
Bend
Moderate; full bar;
AE, DC, MC, V
Dinner Tues-Sat

Owner Axel Hoch remains at the helm in the kitchen, and his wife, Sally, handles the front at this French specialty restaurant. Don't be put off by the austere old church facade; inside, the sidewalk-cafe decor warms things up, as does the superlative waitstaff. Yes, it's expensive and pretentious, but it's tough to fault the food. The duck breast with plum sauce begins the meal with a gentle flair. Though Hoch's sauces (nantua, Bearnaise, pepper-cream) are ever-present on the seafood entrees, we prefer the simple preparations of lamb and Chateaubriand. The Dixie-cup-size tower of rice, which topples onto the tablecloth when you try to eat it, is silly.

Don't miss the very attractive lounge downstairs; it's a good place to take your after-dinner coffee, or sample from a light menu.

The Old Bend Blacksmith Shop and Broiler

1 block east off Bond,
(503) 388-1994
211 Greenwood, Bend
Moderate; beer and wine;
MC, V
Dinner Tues-Sat

We had high hopes for chef Steve Block and Le Bistro owner Axel Hoch's 13-table restaurant wedged into a little corner at Greenwood and Tin Pan Alley. It's a wonderfully frenzied atmosphere, with old blacksmith tools from the shop it used to be.

Two years ago, we forgave the negligent service—the food was very good, prices were terrific, and they'd only been open six months. On a recent check, eight of us *still* had to wait for at least 10 minutes before anyone noticed us. Even so, we were ready to overlook the service, again—remembering the tender chicken and steak perfectly sauced and skewered, the tangy house salad dressing, and the cornbread (served with a sweet honey butter). The steaks (and the $9.95 prime rib) and barbecued ribs were as tender as we expected; but the accompanying stir-fried vegetables were not the fresh bounty we were served earlier. The hot bacon salad dressing was not hot, and thick gravy buried the four thin pork chops.

We hope the stumbling blocks will be addressed soon. And we're willing to return—to what could be the coziest and tastiest little dining room for ranch cooking in town—one more time.

Players Grille

*In the city center of
Bend, (503) 382-5859
61 NW Oregon Avenue,
Bend
Moderate; full bar;
MC, V
Lunch Mon-Fri,
dinner Mon-Sat*

It's casual chic at this West Coast–cuisine restaurant. From the neon-lit mahogany bar and black and white tiles to the jazzy Deco intimacy of the back dining room, owners Steve and Liz Rewick have brought trendy to Bend.

Established by El Crab Catcher's former manager (Steve Rewick) and head chef (Howard Friedman), Players specializes in fresh Northwest foods—butter-baked salmon, rosemary-grilled pork chops, a few Cajun preparations, some attractive lunch salads. We agree with the tip to steer clear of the Northwest blueberry chicken but wouldn't have missed the Strawberry Snow specialty drink that we saved for dessert.

Tourists from the Bay Area are immediately at home here, and locals are warming up to the cool, airy decor so different from the pine and prime rib served up everywhere else.

West Side Bakery and Cafe

*Right on Franklin from
Division; on the other
side of Drake Park,
(503) 382-3426
1005½ NW Galveston
Avenue, Bend
Inexpensive; no alcohol;
no credit cards; checks ok
Breakfast, lunch
Wed-Mon*

Locals applaud this wholesome bakery hidden in a shopping mall—and it shows. The place can get crowded in the morning, with everyone dropping by for the famed huevos rancheros, a delicious homemade croissant with scrambled egg and ham, or a blueberry pancake special. For lunch, vegetable, turkey, and pastrami sandwiches are made with inch-thick slices of the West Side's bread. Portions are on the small side, but so are the prices.

Deschutes Brewery & Public House

*Near the corner of Bond
and Greenwood,
(503) 382-9242
1044 NW Bond Street,
Bend
Inexpensive; beer only;
MC, V; local checks only
Lunch, dinner every day*

We want to feel comfortable in Bend's first brew pub but we don't, yet. The place was designed by Portland cityfolk with urbanites in mind: exposed rafters and dark wood wainscoting. The beer is dark too, but it's named after the region: a rich Black Butte Porter, a hoppy Cascade Golden Ale, a robust Bachelor Bitter, and, for non-drinkers, a tasty not-too-sweet *rootbier*. The kitchen's working on creating light gourmet bar food (spicy lamb-vegetable soup, black bean chili, and bratwurst with sauerkraut) that's been attracting lunching professionals from Bend's banking district. Many locals are proud to see Bend on a beer-bottle label; but they can also bring in a sealable bottle and get brew to go.

Tumalo Emporium

*6 miles north of Bend
on Highway 20 W,
(503) 382-2202
64619 Highway 20 W,
Bend
Moderate; full bar;
MC, V, AE, DC*

Finally, a truly "local" eatery; it's a comfortable and friendly bar in a turn-of-the-century building, right on the highway just out of Bend. They keep changing owners, but there's always a warm welcome from the old wood-burning potbelly stove in the foyer as you enter the saloon decor of the 1800s. And while dusty, tired cowboys do frequent the place for a drink and a meal, the am-

Lunch, dinner every day, brunch Sun

bience and menu are well suited to families.

Lunches are variations on a burger, and several sandwiches. Dinners can be anything from liver and onions to halibut, or a pricier steak, pork, or chicken preparation. Every Sunday there's a home-style champagne brunch buffet that's building a popular following.

LODGINGS

Sunriver Lodge

Off Highway 97, 15 miles south of Bend; watch for the signs, (503) 593-1221 Mail: PO Box 3609, Sun River, OR 97707 Expensive; AE, MC, V Breakfast, lunch, dinner every day

More than a resort, Sunriver is an organized community with its own post office and 200 or so full-time residents. Nevertheless, its specialty is big-time escapist vacationing, and this resort has all the facilities to keep families, couples, or groups of friends busy all week long, all year round. Summer months offer golf (two 18-hole courses), tennis (22 courts), rafting, canoeing, fishing, swimming (two pools, seven hot tubs), biking (25 miles of paved trails), and horseback riding. In winter the resort is home base for skiing, both Nordic and alpine, ice-skating, snowmobiling, and indoor racquetball.

Sunriver now sprawls over 3,300 acres, and its own private airstrip does a brisk business. The best way to reserve rooms here is to work through the personnel at the Lodge desk; they manage and rent over 50 percent of the properties and can position you close to your favorite activities. For the best bargain, request one of the large and contemporary homes (these often have luxuries like Jacuzzis, barbecues, and decks) and split expenses with another family. Rates run from $99 to $160 a night depending on the season and size of the home. The rest of the lodging can be as minimal as a bedroom unit—bed, bath, deck, fireplace, color TV—but all units are spacious and modern. Property managers in Sunriver can also rent houses, but make sure you know whether pool and tennis or hot-tub privileges are included in your price (as they are when you go through the Lodge). These managers are: Sunray, (800) 531-1130, Deschutes, (800) 423-5443, Sun Village, (800) 547-8053, Ridgepine, (800) 547-1016, Resort, (800) 544-0300, and Village, (800) 872-2112.

Dining at Sunriver includes decent spicy fare at Cheng's Chinese Restaurant and the popular Mexican menu at spacious Casa de Ricardo. We like to catch the inexpensive and nicely presented breakfast down at The Trout House (you can walk it off on your return to the Lodge), while The Meadows at the Lodge is the much-acclaimed showplace for fine dining. The locals rave about the Friday seafood buffet for $19.95 and the Sunday brunch for $14.95. If cooking in the well-appointed condos and houses is more to your style, the Sunriver Village Mall is headquarters for a good-sized grocery and a few eclectic delis.

Inn at the Seventh Mountain

18577 S Century Drive,
5 miles west of Bend,
(503) 382-8711
Mail: PO Box 1207,
Bend, OR 97709
Expensive; restaurants
moderate; AE, DC,
MC, V

The Inn offers the closest accommodation to Mount Bachelor and is equally popular with families and singles, no doubt due to the vast menu of activities built into the multi-condominium facility. In the winter it has the only ice rink around, one sauna large and hot enough to accommodate a group of about 15 guests, three cloverleaf-shaped, bubbling hot tubs (with a delightfully adult attitude about drinks: they're okay, bring your own thermos-full, but keep the glass plastic), and two moderately heated swimming pools. In the summer the pools are the centerpiece of activity—there's a whole layout complete with water slide and wading pool.

The Inn does a terrific job of social planning. An activities roster for the week gives the rundown on tennis, riding, biking, skating, snowmobiling, skiing, aerobics, Frisbee, golf...you name it.

Lodgings are around the field and the pool. Rooms are beginning to show their age in decor (all that orange and brown) and wear. Soundproofing is minimal, and the Murphy beds are only marginally comfortable. Avoid buildings 18 and 19; they're the least scenic and the most removed from the center. Building 19 burned down recently but has been rebuilt better than before. The Inn offers fabulous off-season rates.

There is plenty of good eating at the resort, if you choose not to use your condo kitchen. The Poppy Seed, a bit spendy, puts on a plentiful and tasty breakfast. Barron's, a deli/hamburger joint, is perfect for those who prefer less formal surroundings. El Crab Catcher, though going through chefs and management changes, remains a local favorite for stepping out. We like the apres-ski Warren Miller films in the lounge (seasonal) and the naughty Hula Pie (a signature dessert from the restaurant's Hawaiian roots: macadamia-nut ice cream, chocolate sauce, and whipped cream on a chocolate crumb crust). The social lounge here serves up casual eats such as hamburgers and nachos.

Mount Bachelor Village

Head toward Mount
Bachelor from Bend
on Century Drive,
(503) 389-5900, toll-free
(800) 547-5204
19717 Mount Bachelor
Drive, Bend, OR 97702
Expensive; AE, MC, V

If you don't want a social chairman, can live without an adjacent dining room, and rarely need a hot-tub soak after 11pm, then Mount Bachelor Village may be your style. What this development has over some of its more famous neighbor resorts is spacious rooms (there are no studios—all accommodations have one-bedroom, one-bedroom/loft, or two-bedroom floorplans). Every unit has a completely furnished kitchen, wood-burning fireplace, and private deck. We like the newer units, where the insulation is better, the color scheme is modern and light, and the soundproofing helps mute the thud of ski boots in the morning. The views aren't particularly breathtaking (some units look out to the busy mountain road). There are 65 units to choose from, with prices starting at $68 a night. Outdoor Jacuzzi, pool, six tennis courts, and laundry facilities round out the amenities.

The Riverhouse

On Highway 97 in Bend,
(503) 389-3111, toll-free
(800) 547-3928 out of
state
3075 N Highway 97,
Bend OR 97701
Moderate; AE, MC, V
Breakfast, lunch,
dinner every day

The Riverhouse has become an institution in Bend for comfortable stays at more reasonable rates than the out-of-town recreation resorts. Amenities are still abundant: a good-sized pool (heated year-round), saunas, whirlpool, exercise room, and indoor Jacuzzi, rooms with river views, walkable shopping, and adjacent restaurants. The Deschutes creates welcome white noise as it rushes over rocks and under the connector bridge. Rooms range from merely utilitarian to fancy suites with spas ($40 to $130).

This is where you'll find Tito's, serving authentic Mexican cuisine, and the Riverhouse Dining Room, respected for its French and continental cuisine (with some tableside preparations). The apres-ski lounge rocks with contemporary bands six nights a week, so avoid adjacent rooms unless you plan to dance all night.

Rock Springs Guest Ranch

On Highway 20, 7 miles
from Bend and 20 miles
from Sisters,
(503) 382-1957
64201 Tyler Road,
Bend, OR 97701
Moderate; DC, MC, V

The emphasis here is very much on family vacations. Counselors take care of the kids in special programs all day, while adults hit the trail, laze in the pool, play tennis, or gobble down hearty meals in the ranch dining room (open only for those staying at the resort). The cabins are quite nice—comfy knotty-pine duplexes with fireplaces and grandmother's furniture. There are only about 23 units, so it's easy to get to know everyone staying at the ranch, particularly since everyone eats together in the lodge. The setting, amid ponderosa pines and junipers alongside a small lake, is secluded and lovely.

The main activity here is horseback riding, with seven wranglers and a stable of 60 horses. Summer season is booked by the week only (starting at $750 per person), which includes accommodations, three meals a day plus beverages and snacks, riding, outdoor games (there's a new outdoor spa and a seasonal swimming pool), and special events. Tennis courts are lit, and there's fishing in the ranch pond. Note special financial arrangements (like free meals and accommodations) for attentive babysitters brought for children under five. You'll have to leave your pets at home.

Entrada Lodge

7 miles from Bend
on Century Drive,
(503) 382-4080
19221 Century Drive,
Bend, OR 97709

Whether you're a weary traveler or just an avid skier looking for a firm mattress, a dependable shower, a clean room, and decent TV reception, you'll get that and more here. The "more" is a covered, outdoor hot tub that cooks all season long, closer proximity to the mountain than town lodging, and a straightforward breakfast menu (your choice of three offerings) that keeps you from having to

Moderate; AE, DC, MC, V

double back into town for eggs when you'd rather be skiing.

Friendly owners Brad and Brett Evert work hard to personalize this 80-room ranch-style Best Western motel. There's hot chocolate and popcorn apres-ski by the office fireplace, a sauna, and pets allowable with some restrictions. The price is thrifty and the location, for those playing at the Mountain, can't be beat. The Everts have opened a new Best Western in town, The Woodstove Inn at 721 NE Third, Bend, OR 97701; (503) 382-1515.

Lara House
Bed and Breakfast

West on Franklin from Highway 97,
(503) 388-4064
640 NW Congress,
Bend, OR 97701
Moderate; MC, V

One of Bend's largest and oldest (1910) homes, Lara House has been renovated from a rundown boarding house to a bright and homey bed and breakfast.

The main room is perfect for small-group socializing—a large fireplace, upright piano, conversation-pit couch, and a sunny adjacent solarium that looks out over the large yard onto the river parkway. Books are everywhere, the lighting is warm, and there's a wonderful community oak table that guests gather around in the morning. Breakfast might feature two kinds of quiche; cream-cheese-filled French toast served with blueberries, strawberries, and whipped cream; homemade bran muffins; whole-grain crescent rolls; Belgian waffles; and freshly ground coffee.

Each of the four guest rooms upstairs has its own shower, vanity sink, cheery wallpaper, and queen-size bed. We like the Cascade and Deschutes rooms best. The place even offers a sauna and hot tub in the basement.

ELK LAKE

LODGINGS

Elk Lake Resort

Century Drive, Elk Lake,
radio phone YP7 3954
Mail: PO Box 789,
Bend, OR 97709
Inexpensive; MC, V

Elk Lake is a small mountain lake about 30 miles west of Bend on the edge of the Three Sisters Wilderness Area. This remote lodge—reached by snow-cat or 10 miles of cross-country skiing in the winter—consists of a dozen self-contained cabins, most with fireplace, kitchen, bathroom, and sleeping quarters for two to eight people. It's nothing grand, but the place is much favored by Bend dwellers (a good recommendation), and the scenery is wonderful. The lodge has a little dining room with standard American grub; reservations required.

Getting a reservation can be almost as tough as getting here, since there's only a radio phone (you'll probably have to inquire by mail) and the place is often booked up to a year in advance. Open Memorial Day through mid-October, Thanksgiving through March.

CULTUS LAKE

LODGINGS

Cultus Lake Resort
*Century Drive, Cultus
Lake, (503) 389-3230
Mail: PO Box 262,
Bend, OR 97709
Moderate; AE, MC, V*

You're well into the mountains, in the Deschutes National Forest 50 miles southwest from Bend, alongside a large lake popular with anglers and boaters. The resort has 23 acceptable cabins, all paneled in wood and some with big windows looking over the lakefront, at good prices ($38–$68). A serviceable restaurant is in the handsome main lodge, and boat rentals are easily managed. Cabins 7, 8, 9, and 10 are the most desirable. Open May to October.

MOUNT BAILEY

Mount Bailey Alpine Ski Tours offers a true backcountry skiing experience, with snow-cats instead of helicopters to take you to the top of this 8,363-foot ancient volcano, and experienced guides who stress safety. Diamond Lake Lodge, (503) 793-3333, headquarters the guide service, offering multiple-day packages including lodging and meals; otherwise, the cost is $85 a day (lunch included). When the snow melts, the operation turns to mountain-bike tours.

CRATER LAKE

Some 6,500 years ago, 15,000-foot Mount Mazama became the Mount St. Helens of its day, blew up, and left behind a deep crater that is now filled with Crater Lake. The area is extraordinary: the impossibly blue lake, the eerie volcanic formations, the vast geological wonderland. The visitor center, at the park headquarters, (503) 594-2211, has been reopened, with a theater, information desk, and a good interpretive exhibit. Visitors to Crater Lake should plan to camp, since the lodge is rather poor; Mazama campground is near the place where rangers give evening talks. Be sure to take the two-hour boat ride from Cleetwood Cove. There are dozens of trails and climbs to magnificent lookouts. In the winter, when the crowds finally thin out, only the south and west entrance roads are kept open.

KLAMATH FALLS

This city of 19,000 people, the largest for 100 miles, is so isolated that it once led a movement to secede from Oregon and California and become the state of Jefferson. Now the residents happily welcome tourists, bird watchers, and sportspersons from both states.

Favell Museum of Western Art is a true Western museum, with arrowheads, Indian artifacts, and the works of more than 200 Western artists; 125 W Main Street, (503) 882-9996.

Klamath County Museum. Exhibits deal with the volcanic geology of the region (an Indian tribe, the Clamitts, was almost wiped out by the eruption of Mount Mazama 6,600 years ago), Indian artifacts from all over Oregon, and artifacts from the Modoc wars; 1451 Main Street, (503) 883-4208.

Baldwin Hotel Museum, in an old (1907) hotel, retains many fixtures of the era; 31 Main Street, opens June 1, (503) 882-2501.

Upper Klamath Lake, 40 miles long, is the largest lake in Oregon; it's fine for fishing and serves as the nesting grounds for many birds, including white pelicans. The Williamson River, which flows into the lake, yields plenty of trout.

RESTAURANTS

Alice's Saddle Rock Cafe
Main and 10th,
(503) 884-1444
1012 Main Street,
Klamath Falls
Moderate; full bar;
MC, V
Breakfast, lunch Sun-Fri,
dinner Wed-Mon

The Saddle Rock, from the outside, appears a consistent part of the time-worn Klamath Falls: a battered facade that says old-main-street cafe all over it. Inside, though, it's up-to-the-minute: brick interior walls adorned with abstract black-and-white artwork. The fare is progressive, too. An excellent choice of fresh pasta dishes, Oregon beef selections, poultry, and special burgers are all served with conscious touches of panache and elegance. The fettuccine alfredo was perfectly cooked, the sauce distinctive and smooth. The hamburgers here are magnificent creations, piled so artistically high they require silverware and resolve to dispatch.

Fiorella's
Corner of Peterson and
Simmer, (503) 882-1878
6139 Simmer Street,
Klamath Falls
Inexpensive; full bar;
MC, V
Dinner Tues-Sat

Residents of Klamath Falls welcome the Northern Italian fare at Fiorella and Renato Durighello's restaurant. On a recent visit we had fine scallopine Marsala, which came with soup, salad, garlic bread, and—best of all—homemade pasta, a rarity around here. Reservations required.

LODGINGS

Thompson's Bed and Breakfast by the Lake
Call ahead for directions,
(503) 882-7938
1420 Wild Plum Court,
Klamath Falls,
OR 97601
Inexpensive; no credit
cards; checks ok

The Thompsons recently moved their successful B&B operation to a better and bigger location and now offer three full bedrooms with king-size beds and private entrances and baths. Sunsets over the Cascade range provide a backdrop to the spectacular view of Upper Klamath Lake. Deer are frequent visitors to the back yard; bring your binoculars for bird watching. Pedal-boats and canoes are available. Owners Mary and Gil Thompson will cook almost anything you'd like for breakfast.

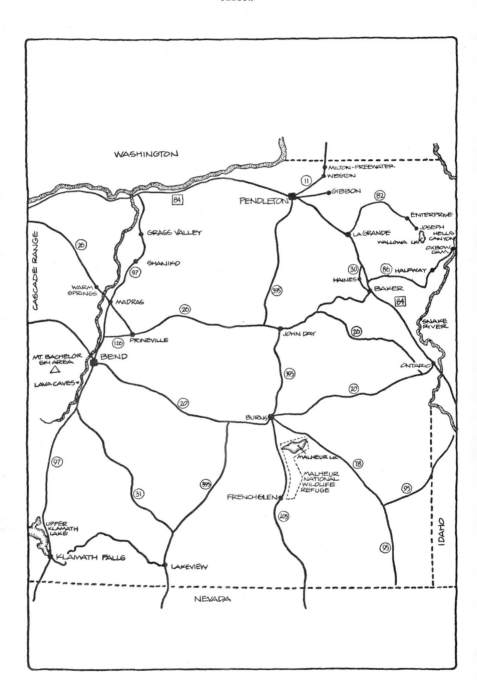

EASTERN OREGON

Two major routes: south mid-state from Grass Valley to Warm Springs, then east to John Day, and southeastward along I-84 from Pendleton to Ontario (with a diversion into the Wallowas), turning in-state again to Burns and Frenchglen.

GRASS VALLEY
RESTAURANTS

Carol's Kitchen
The only restaurant in town, (503) 333-2255
Highway 97,
Grass Valley
Inexpensive; no alcohol; no credit cards; checks ok
Breakfast, lunch every day, dinner Mon–Sat

Wheat and barley farmers, ranchers, and Bend-bound truckers and travelers have one thing in common: an affection for Carol Grout's homemade cinnamon rolls, breads, and pies. Carol and Virgil Grout and their two daughters began this roadside diner nearly 10 years ago—and it's been a favorite Highway 97 stop ever since, with great malted milk shakes, meaty cheeseburgers, and fresh-cut fries. All road trips deserve a stop like this.

SHANIKO
LODGINGS

Shaniko Historic Hotel
Downtown Shaniko, on 4th and "E",
(503) 489-3441
Mail: PO Box 86, Shaniko, OR 97057
Inexpensive; MC, V

For a town that once boasted the Columbia Southern Railway (1900–1911), terrific vitality in shipping wool and gold, 13 saloons—and then died when the railhead moved —this historic hotel restoration in the Oregon high desert is a spark of light and hope that can bring this presence back to life. History buff Jean Farrall bought the wreck in the near-abandoned town in 1985, left his plumbing business in Salem, and rounded up local help to rebuild. The 17 now-cozy rooms are grandmotherly spotless, with good bathrooms (previously, one bathroom served the whole place).

Downstairs, you're never lonely: ranchers amble in to sit and yarn, and they include you too. Mother's Day draws 700 for chicken dinner. Down-home cook Shirley Talentino does great barbecued ribs and a plate-sized breakfast pancake (even if you do have to add powdered cream to your coffee), averring "I'm not a chef—I'm just a cook." The cheery waitresses are ranchers' wives.

WARM SPRINGS
LODGINGS

Kah-Nee-Ta Resort
11 miles north of Warm Springs on Highway 3, (503) 553-1112 or (800) 831-0100 Mail:-PO Box K, Warm Springs, OR 97761 Expensive; AE, DC, MC, V

The Confederated Tribes of Warm Springs Reservation some years ago built this posh resort, complete with a large arrowhead-shaped motel, a vast mineral-springs pool, tepees and cottages for rent, and such amenities as golf, tennis, riding, river rafting, and fancy restaurants. The Indian fry-bread and the bird-in-clay dish (a small hen baked in its own clay pot with wild rice, then broken open with a mallet) are the crowd pleasers, but the results are uninspired.

Even so, Kah-Nee-Ta is a genuinely unusual experience, with excellent service. You might stay in a roomy tepee (the lodge rooms are usually small), for instance, gathering the family around the fire pit in the evening. During the day, you can ride into the desert countryside, splash in the pool, or watch Indian dances.

JOHN DAY

You are in the midst of dry cattle country in an area loaded with history: John Day is just off the old Oregon Trail, and the whole region was full of gold during the Gold Rush (in 1862, $26 million in gold was mined in the neighboring town of Canyon City). The legendary Pony Express used to blaze through John Day, too.

Kam Wah Chung Museum, next to the city park, was the stone-walled home of two Chinese herbal doctors at the turn of the century. A tour makes for an interesting glimpse of the Chinese settlement in the West: opium-stained walls, Chinese shrines, and herbal medicines are on display, as well as a small general store. Open May to October.

John Day Fossil Beds Monument lies 40 to 80 miles west, revealing three distinct geographical features: the banded Painted Hills, extremely ancient fossils, and fascinating geological layers; 420 W Main Street, (503) 575-0721, for maps and brochures.

PENDLETON

In these parts, the name of this town is synonymous with the Wild West. Each September the Pendleton Round-up rolls around—a big event since 1910 that features a dandy rodeo.

Hamley's Saddlery has been selling Western clothing, boots, hats, tack items, and custom-made saddles since 1883. It's a kind of shrine, the L.L. Bean of the West; 30 SE Court Street, (503) 276-2321.

Pendleton Woolen Mills gives tours Monday through Friday, and sells woolen yardage and imperfect blankets at reduced prices; 1307 SE Court Place, (503) 276-6911.

All places in this book are recommended; even "no stars" are worth knowing about.

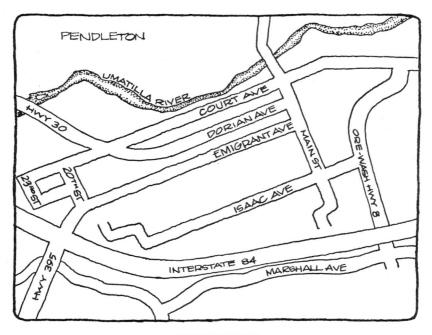

RESTAURANTS

The Skyroom
Take Exit 207 off I-84,
½ mile up Airport Road,
(503) 276-8500
2010 Airport Road,
Pendleton Airport,
Pendleton
Moderate; full bar;
MC, V
Lunch Mon-Fri,
dinner Mon-Sat

Owner Raphael Hoffman has been making noises about moving downtown—but until then, the best food in Pendleton is at the airport. In a restful oasis that overlooks the landing field, the Hoffmans have attractively combined an authentic Indian art store (Ms. Hoffman is a member of the Nez Perce tribe) with a reputable restaurant.

Robert Hoffman, the chef, is not Indian—so don't expect any Native American dishes. The dinner menu runs heavily to well-prepared and well-presented seafood. Steamer clams are generally available, a treat in the deserts of eastern Oregon. An unusual entree is the applewood-smoked prime rib, available on Friday and Saturday nights. Many of the patrons are crazy about it, but others resist such liberties with a standard favorite. There is a good-sized wine list, featuring moderately priced selections.

Cimmiyotti's
Near the corner of Main
and Court, across from
Penney's, (503) 276-4314
137 S Main Street,
Pendleton

A city like Pendleton ought to have a restaurant like this, and here it is: homey, unpretentious, and friendly, with a not-overpowering Western decor. For 30 years it's been going strong, with reasonably priced good steaks, baked potatoes, and salads. There are also a number of Italian

Moderate; full bar;
MC, V
Dinner every day

dishes. There has been some grumbling in recent years about the quality of the salads, but the steaks are still good.

LODGINGS

Indian Hills Motor Inn
Exit 210 off I-84,
(503) 276-6111
304 SE Nye Avenue,
Pendleton
Mail: PO Box 1556,
Pendleton, OR 97801
Moderate; AE, DC,
MC, V

A little to the south of Pendleton is the Red Lion's Indian Hills Motor Inn, the most lavish motel in town. It offers many amenities, including heated pool, lounge, dining room, and coffee shop. There are outsized, gaudy Western bas-reliefs in the reception areas. The view from your balcony over the low mountains and tilled fields of eastern Oregon can be inspiring—more so than the food, which ranges from indifferent to passable. Well-behaved pets okay.

WESTON
RESTAURANTS

Tollgate Mountain Chalet
Highway 204, 16 miles
east of Weston,
(503) 566-2123
Rte 1, Box 80, Weston
Moderate; full bar;
MC, V
Breakfast Sat-Sun; lunch,
dinner every day (except
Mon & Tues in winter)

Walla Walla folks often drive 50 miles south through the lovely, waving wheatfields to this rustic eating place in the Blue Mountain forest. Locals order the chili, a hamburger, a Reuben sandwich, or a reasonable steak; the pies are homemade and different every day. It makes a particularly good spot for breakfast before a day of hiking or touring.

MILTON-FREEWATER
RESTAURANTS

The Oasis
Old Milton-Freewater
Highway and State Line
Road, (503) 938-4776
Rte 1, Box 84,
Milton-Freewater
Inexpensive; full bar;
MC, V
Breakfast, lunch, dinner
Tues-Sun

This isn't a copy of a 1920s Western roadhouse, it's the real thing—and it hasn't ever changed: linoleum floors, lots of chrome. Eat in the bar and eavesdrop on the cowboys swapping stories. New owners Jack and Pat Koch are sticking with the roadhouse atmosphere. While not every dish on the menu is a culinary triumph, the steaks are uniformly reliable and gigantic. Prime rib is good. On Sundays, chicken and dumplings are served family style, all you can eat, for about $6 per person—and a fine meal it is. For breakfast, a platter of biscuits and gravy goes for under two bucks. Students from Walla Walla are fascinated with this place.

LODGINGS

Bar-M Guest Ranch
8 miles east of Gibbon on
the river road,

The Bar-M, 31 miles east of Pendleton and 45 miles south of Walla Walla, is a 2,500-acre working dude ranch operated by the Baker family in the lovely Blue Mountains.

(503) 566-3381
Mail: Rte 1, Box 263,
Adams, OR 97810
Moderate; no credit cards;
checks ok

The main ranch house (eight guest rooms and three baths) dates back to 1864, when it was built as a stage stop; its hand-hewn logs are still in good shape, and the interior is decorated with period pieces. There are also cabins near a brook and waterfall and a small lake.

The ranch takes families (no pets, no children under six) for a one-week-minimum stay (except for day rates in April, May, early June, and September) at about $525 per person per week. Included in the fee are excellent meals (local trout and home-grown vegetables) plus use of the mountain-savvy horses. Youngsters are encouraged to help with chores—mending fences, slopping pigs, or picking vegetables—if they want to. The riding, bird watching, and trout fishing are superb; there's a large warm-water pool; and evenings offer camp-outs, volleyball, and square dancing. Open April through September; many come just for raspberry season in July.

LA GRANDE
RESTAURANTS

10 Depot Street
2 blocks west of Adams
on Depot, (503) 963-8766
10 Depot Street,
La Grande
Moderate; full bar; AE,
MC, V
Dinner Mon-Sat

The cowboy decor of the former Chris's Woodshed has disappeared, and Sandy Sorrels (who also owns the praiseworthy Mamacita's) has complemented the nice old brick building with antique furnishings. We're drawn to the lounge with its beautiful carved-wood back bar. The menu is about what you would expect in a good small-town restaurant: lamb chops, steaks, prime rib, seafood, pasta—all competently prepared. The house salad dressing is a tasty peanut/curry combination. Sour cream apple pie is a popular dessert, but you can get a hot fudge sundae if you like.

Golden Crown Restaurant
Near the corner of Adams
and Elm, (503) 963-5907,
1116 Adams Avenue,
La Grande
Inexpensive; beer
and wine; MC, V
Lunch, dinner every day

It's not hard to find. It's so easy, as a matter of fact—with the vermilion-and-gold sign on the main street—that you might not give this Chinese-American eatery a second glance. Even after you're inside, the vinyl booths give no hint of the menu's treasures. The won ton soup is heaped with freshly wrapped won tons, shrimp, pork, pea pods, mushrooms, and bok choy. The dish called Three Ingredients is a full platter of medium-sized shrimp, shreds of chicken, tender slices of barbecued pork, and an assortment of at least six kinds of vegetables.

Mamacita's
1 block west of Adams on
Depot, (503) 963-6223
110 Depot Street,
La Grande
Inexpensive; beer and

Not only is this the liveliest place in town—on any night—but the Mexican food is fresh and tasty. Assuming that the proof of a good south-of-the-border place is in the salsa, we gave it high marks from the start for the piquancy and fresh chunks of vegetables. We loved the en-

*wine; no credit cards;
checks ok
Lunch Tues-Fri,
dinner Tues-Sun*

chiladas de Acapulco (chicken and cheese) topped with guacamole, sour cream, and a sprinkling of almonds and olives. This pueblo is hopping even on Sunday nights (when the rest of the town is taking a late siesta) with a make-your-own-taco bar. Add to the good food pleasant, helpful service and an adobe-colored wall adorned with bright splotches of Mexicana, and you have our vote for the best meal in La Grande.

LODGINGS

**Stange Manor
Bed and Breakfast**

*Corner of Spring and
Walnut, (503) 963-2400
1612 Walnut,
La Grande, OR 97850
Moderate; AE, MC, V*

La Grande isn't so grand, but this restored timber-baron's house on the hill behind town returns an elegance to this once-booming town. A sweeping staircase leads up to the five bedrooms; all except two have their own baths. Two share a sitting room with stone fireplace. The master suite is, of course, the best—and biggest—room, but even if you opt for the maid's quarters, you won't have to lift a finger. The four hosts graciously accommodate even an on-slaught of unexpected guests (a winter blizzard occasionally closes I-84) with tea in the plush but unpretentious living room. A breakfast of homemade muffins and French toast is served in the dining room.

ENTERPRISE
RESTAURANTS

**A Country Place
on Pete's Pond**

*South of Main; follow the
signs, (503) 426-3642
Montclair Street,
Enterprise, OR 97828
Inexpensive; beer
and wine; MC, V
Breakfast, lunch, dinner
every day (closed in January)*

The best restaurant in Enterprise started out as Marvel and Ford Peterson's awfully good multi-grain sandwich shop: it's still there—behind their house—at the edge of a former livestock watering hole, but now it's a high-beamed country-cute dining room with a behind-the-grain-elevator view of the Wallowas. One evening our steak was exactly rare and the taco salad properly heaping, though a recent unfavorable report on a turkey sandwich makes us wonder if they're more concerned with the kitsch than the kitchen. The marionberry pie is, well, Marvel's.

JOSEPH

This is the fabled land of the Wallowas, ancestral home of Chief Joseph, from which he fled with a band of Nez Perce warriors to his last stand near the Canadian border. Although Chief Joseph's remains are interred far from his beloved "land of the winding water," he saw to it that his father, Old Chief Joseph, would be buried here, in an Indian burial ground on the north shore of Wallowa Lake.

Wallowa Lake State Park, on the edge of the **Wallowa Whitman National Forest** and **Eagle Cap Wilderness**, is perhaps the only state park in the country where locals still lament the fact that there are "never enough people." An Alpenfest with music, dancing, and Bavarian feasts happens every September, but the peak season is still midsummer, when the pristine lake is abuzz with go-carts, sailboats, and windsurfers. In winter the attraction is miles and miles of unpeopled cross-country trails throughout the lovely Wallowa highlands.

Wallowa Lake Tramway takes you by a steep ascent in a four-passenger gondola to the top of 8,200-foot Mount Howard, with spectacular overlooks and two miles of hiking trails. Summer only; (503) 432-5331.

Wallowa County Museum, in town, is housed in the site of a famous frontier bank robbery. Indian and cowpoke relics combine here to tell the tale of this region's Wild West past. Summer only.

Hells Canyon, 35 miles east of Joseph, is the continent's deepest gorge, an awesome trench cut by the Snake River through sheer lava walls. The best view is from Hat Point near Imnaha, though McGraw Lookout is more accessible if you don't have four-wheel drive. Maps of the region's roads and trails, and information on conditions, are available at the Wallowa Valley Ranger District in Joseph, (503) 432-2171.

Hurricane Creek Llamas. You explore the lake-laden Eagle Cap Wilderness with a naturalist, or in your own group, while smiling llamas lug your gear. Hikes vary in length; hearty country meals are included. Depending on the trip, you pay about $90 a day for this unusual adventure (May–September). Call in advance for a brochure or reservation, (503) 432-4455.

Wallowa Alpine Huts. Experienced backcountry ski guides offer three- to six-day powder-bound tours for skiers seeking the best of the Wallowa winterland. You stay in stark tents (with a wood stove and bunks) and dine in a yurt. For more information, call (208) 882-1955.

RESTAURANTS

**Vali's Alpine
Deli and Restaurant**
*Upper Power House Road
at Wallowa Lake State
Park, (503) 432-5691
Joseph
Inexpensive; beer and
wine; no credit cards;
checks ok
Breakfast (doughnuts
only), dinner Tues-Sun
(January to Memorial
Day, Sat-Sun only)*

Don't let its "deli" status mislead; a dinner at Vali's usually requires reservations. The food here is Hungarian-German (and so is the decor), interspersed with a few authentic renditions from other cuisines: on a recent visit a savory shish kabob replaced Sunday's usually exceptional wiener schnitzel. Maggie Vali's homemade doughnuts are local legend, but don't arrive hungry—the morning meal ends there. Sausage and cheese are available to take out for picnics.

LODGINGS

**Chandlers'
Bed, Bread, and Trail Inn**
*End of town at Main and
7th, (503) 432-9765
700 S Main Street, Mail:
PO Box 639, Joseph, OR
97846
Moderate; MC, V*

Cedar shingles, multiangled roof lines, and cushiony wall-to-wall carpets make this bed and breakfast resemble an alpine ski lodge—in the middle of Joseph. A log staircase climbs from the comfortable living room to a loft where five simple bedrooms share 2½ baths, a sitting room, and a workable kitchenette. The substantial breakfast and knowledgeable hosts make this a wonderful stopover for area explorers. No pets, young children, or smoking.

The Horse Ranch

(503) 432-9171
Mail: PO Box 26, Joseph,
OR 97846
Moderate; MC, V

It's officially named The Horse Ranch, but for years it was known only as "Red's," and for locals and regulars this is not likely to change. Red McNulty, the original proprietor, transformed the place from a shelter for transient sheepherders; now, under Cal and Betsy Henry, the place thrives in perfect harmony with its setting: rustic and remote. There are no roads nearby, so one must fly or pack in. Life is basic here: the six cabins scattered along the banks of the Minam River have fireplaces and hot showers, but electricity only for a few hours each evening. Lodge rooms are also available. Meals are huge and farm fresh ("Everything is homemade, 'cause we don't have a choice!"), and happily fed souls return with reports of homemade bread and fresh milk from the Henrys' cow. The real plus here, however, is the attraction of the outdoors. Cal and Betsy's guide service (High Country Outfitters) offers horse-packing trips and Hells Canyon river trips, open May to October.

Wallowa Lake Lodge

Wallowa Lake State Park,
(503) 432-9821
Rte 1, Box 320, Joseph,
OR 97846
Moderate; beer and wine;
MC, V
Breakfast, lunch, dinner
every day

After three years of renovation, this historic 1920s lodge has reopened its doors with a renewed vigor (even the deer are peeking in to see what's abuzz). It's still not perfect, but with new managers at the helm, chef Bruce Malone (formerly a banquet chef at Salishan and a gold medalist in the 1989 Culinary Olympics) behind the line, and the Wallowa Mountains in the back yard, we wager the place will get back on its feet quickly.

Check-in is a bit awkward: you must promise (in writing) not to smoke, eat, or drink alcohol in the rooms. In addition, the rooms are very small (especially the $35 ones). You'll do best if you reserve one of the restored rooms with a lake view; they're darker than the new ones, but furnished with antiques and deep old-fashioned tubs. If you plan to stay longer, the rustic pine cabins on the lake, each with living room, fireplace, and kitchen, allow for a bit more flexibility.

Even if the rooms *were* spacious, we'd spend most of the evening in front of the magnificent stone fireplace in the knotty-pine lobby. A new deck is a splendid addition for summertime barbecues (noon–8pm).

In the dining room, chef Malone claims to be developing a healthy, hearty menu using fresh local ingredients whenever possible. Indigenous ingredients, however, were scarce on one winter's visit, so we chose a huge slab of perfectly rare prime rib and a bowl of oversauced turkey Tetrazzini. For breakfast, the orange hazelnut pancakes with marionberry butter are unmatched. Winters are painfully slow; though we will whisper that the alpine slopes are virtually untouched.

Inspectors for the Best Places *series accept no free meals or accommodations; the book has no sponsors or advertisers.*

HAINES

RESTAURANTS

Haines Steak House
Right in town on
Old Highway 30,
(503) 856-3639
Old Highway 30, Haines
Inexpensive; full bar;
MC, V
Dinner Wed-Mon

If the drive north from Baker through the cattle country of SR 30 doesn't give you a hankering for a hefty slab of beef, the smells from the grill at this Haines institution will. It's local legend for serving the best steaks in Baker County, amid dark surroundings and raw timber walls lined with trophies and bagged game. The salad bar, a Conestoga wagon with a new job, features the usuals, plus baked beans, hearty soup, and dense potato salad. On busy nights, the service may be slow and the waiters confused, but this just gives your appetite time to rev up.

BAKER

Baker's restful city park, old-time main street, and mature shade trees may give it a Midwest flavor, but the backdrop is decidedly Northwest. Located in the valley between the Wallowas and the Elkhorns, Baker makes a good base camp for forays into the nearby mountain gold-rush towns.

The Elkhorn Mountains, west of Baker, contain old mining towns, which you can tour on a 100-mile loop from Baker (some of it on unpaved roads).

Ghost towns. There's a restored narrow-gauge steam train at Sumpter, and the deserted towns of Granite, Bourne, Bonanza, and Whitney are well worth visiting.

Anthony Lakes Ski Area, 20 miles west of North Powder, has good powder snow, a chair lift, and cross-country trails; (503) 856-3277.

RESTAURANTS

The Anthony
1st and Washington,
(503) 523-4475
1926 First Street,
Baker, OR 97814
Moderate; beer and wine;
no credit cards; checks ok
Dinner every day

Restaurateur Anthony Silvers came from his Chocolate Mousse in Portland to open—and run single-handedly—what has become Baker's most unusual restaurant. Busts of General Grant and other classic fellows blend with strange paintings and plaster castings of leaping lions to create an atmosphere that is weirdly eclectic, yet candlelit and intimate.

A fine wine list is the Anthony's greatest coup, with far and away the most extensive selection in Baker. For dinner we found the poached whitefish tender and succulent; the accompanying vegetables were the right degree of underdone. Our harshest criticism concerns the sauces: the sweet sauce over the chicken was a bit assertive for the mild meat, and the butter sauces were too rich.

Wondering about our standards? We rate establishments on value, performance measured against the place's goals, uniqueness, enjoyability, loyalty of clientele, cleanliness, excellence and ambition of the cooking, and professionalism of the service. For an explanation of the star system, see the Introduction.

LODGINGS

Best Western Sunridge Inn
Take the Baker exit off I-5,
(503) 523-6444
1 Sunridge Lane,
Baker, OR 97814
Inexpensive; AE,
DC, MC, V

A sprawling Best Western, it's still the best of the lodgings in town, with 124 comfortable, spacious, air-conditioned rooms and an attractive pine finish. In the hot summer, you'll appreciate the grassy courtyard/pool area. Come winter, move indoors to the 18-foot whirlpool.

HALFWAY

Once just a midway stop between two bustling mining towns, Halfway is now the quiet centerpiece of Pine Valley—stashed between the fruitful southern slopes of the Wallowa Mountains and the steep cliffs of Hells Canyon. The old church in the middle of town is now the headquarters of **Wildflowers of Oregon**, which dries locally picked flowers and sells arrangements internationally, (503) 742-6474.

Hells Canyon, the continent's deepest gorge, begins at the Oxbow Dam, 16 miles east of Halfway. For spectacular views of the Snake River, drive from Oxbow to Joseph (take Highway 86 to Forest Road #39; summers only). Maps of the region's roads and trails are available from the Forest Service, just outside of Halfway, (503) 742-7511.

The folks at **Wallowa Llamas** lead three- to eight-day trips along the edge of Hells Canyon or into the pristine Eagle Cap Wilderness high in the Wallowas, while their friendly, sure-footed beasts lug your gear and plenty of food; for a brochure or information, call (503) 742-4930.

For those who would rather experience the raging river up close, **Hells Canyon Adventures** in Oxbow arranges jet boat tours or float-and-horseback combination excursions leaving from Hells Canyon Dam; call (503) 785-3352.

LODGINGS

Clear Creek Farm
Ask for directions at the
general store, or call
(503) 742-2238
Rte 1, Box 138, Halfway,
OR 97834
Moderate; MC, V

Once you find this somewhat quirky paradise, you'll know why Mary Ann Carr, her mother, and 373 other residents of Halfway have carefully chosen this fertile valley as home. You will be easily welcomed at this bed-and-more-than-breakfast. One wintry night, venison stew awaited our arrival—just in case we hadn't eaten. (We hadn't.)

There are two homey bedrooms in the farmhouse, but during summer, families and small groups bunk up in either of the two board-and-batten cabins. It's delightfully campish, with fully equipped bathrooms in a separate building. There are several small ponds for swimming, a field of lavender, and 500 peach trees. When the snow falls, getting up the driveway can be treacherous, but the cross-country skiing is unbeatable—and all yours.

Billowing Dutch babies, luscious peaches, and fresh-squeezed grapefruit juice await you in the morning. Bring your friends: group rates are cheaper *and* Mary Ann will throw in a wonderful Mexican dinner. Cha cha cha.

ONTARIO

RESTAURANTS

Casa Jaramillo
2 blocks south of Idaho Avenue, (503) 889-9258
157 SE Second Street, Ontario
Inexpensive; full bar; AE, MC, V
Lunch, dinner Tues-Sun

Enter this Mexican spot for a dim, cool respite from the hot eastern Oregon desert. The restaurant is square and unadorned, except for some hanging pinatas and the requisite black velvet painting. John Jaramillo and his friendly family have run this place for over 22 years, turning out authentic Mexican fare that keeps 'em coming back for more. Try the enchiladas rancheros, with fresh crunchy onions and a chile verde sauce that delivers the right amount of punch. Great guacamole.

LODGINGS

Tapadera Motor Inn
Right off Highway 84 in Ontario, (503) 889-8621 or toll-free (800) 525-5333 (outside Oregon)
725 Tapadera Avenue, Ontario, OR 97914
Moderate; AE, DC, MC, V

The finest accommodation in Ontario isn't a Best Western anymore, but it still has all the amenities—swimming pool, sauna, meeting rooms, 100 guest rooms—and now the personality that comes with private ownership. Some suites have waterbeds. The stark cedar/adobe finish works well against the barren landscape.

BURNS

The town of Burns, once the center of impressive cattle kingdoms ruled by legendary figures Pete French and William Hanley, is a welcome oasis in this desolate high-desert country. The land, formed by 10 million years of volcanic activity, was branded on the American consciousness in a few decades by the thousands of Western movies filmed in the area.

Malheur National Wildlife Refuge, 37 miles south on Route 205, is one of the country's major bird refuges—184,000 acres of verdant marshland and lakes. It is an important stop for migrating waterfowl in spring and fall, and the summer breeding grounds for magnificent sandhill cranes (with wing spans approaching 100 inches) and many other birds. Trumpeter swans are permanent residents. A small museum and lots of self-guiding information are available at headquarters; (503) 493-2323.

RESTAURANTS

Pine Room Cafe
On Monroe and Egan, (503) 573-6631
543 W Monroe Street, Burns
Moderate; full bar; MC, V
Dinner Tues-Sat

For more than 30 years the Kinder family has operated this pleasant cafe, and they've built up a faithful clientele. Careful preparation and interesting recipes are the reason: the chicken livers in brandy and wine sauce are different and popular, and the Kinders still refuse to give out the secret ingredients of their German potato-dumpling soup, a local favorite. They also make their own bread and cut their own steaks in the kitchen.

LODGINGS

Best Western Ponderosa
On Highway 20;
look for the big sign,
(503) 573-2047
577 W Monroe, Burns,
OR 97720
Inexpensive; AE, DC,
MC, V

With 52 rooms, this is the preferred place to stay in Burns. It's blessed with a swimming pool to cool you off after a hot day's drive. Pets okay.

FRENCHGLEN

The flooding around Harney Lake kept tourists away from this beautiful little town (population 15) a few years back, but now, happily, the highway is above water and tourists are once again stopping by to spy Steens Mountain, Frenchglen's biggest tourist attraction. It rises gently from the west to an elevation of 9,670 feet, then drops sharply to the Alvord Desert in the east. Geologically, Steens forms the world's largest block fault, created by volcanic lava flows and glacial action.

LODGINGS

Frenchglen Hotel
60 miles south of Burns
on Highway 205,
(503) 493-2825
Mail: General Delivery
Frenchglen, OR 97736
Lodging inexpensive;
restaurant moderate;
MC, V
Breakfast, lunch, dinner
every day

A small, white frame building that dates back to 1916 has eight small, plain bedrooms upstairs with shared baths, renting out for about $30 a night; Room 2 is the largest and nicest. Downstairs are a large screened-in verandah and the dining room. Chef Judy Santillie used to be a ranch cook; her cooking reflects that training, and there's always meat—just good, plain meat—served with potatoes, a vegetable, hot homemade bread, and sometimes beans. You could probably guess dessert: pie —homemade, fruity, and delicious. Those not staying at the hotel can take meals here; dinner has one seating at 6:30 sharp. Closed mid-November through February.

WASHINGTON

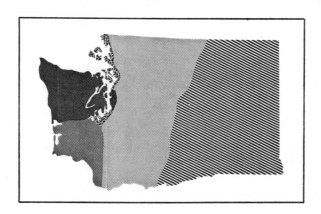

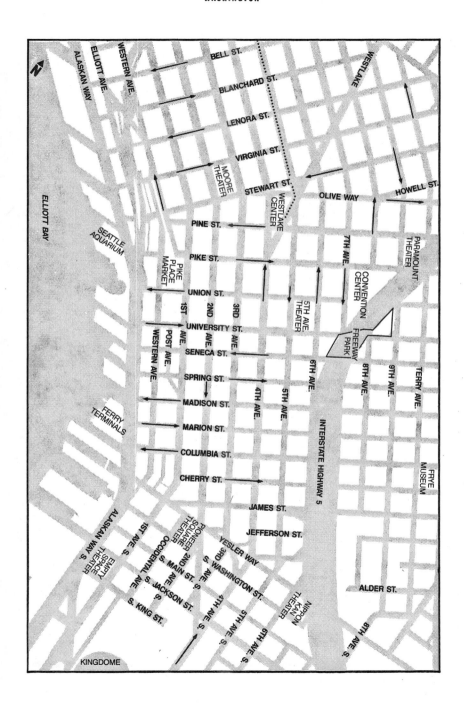

SEATTLE AND ENVIRONS

Including the suburbs: Mill Creek, Edmonds, and Bothell to the north; Woodinville, Redmond, Kirkland, Bellevue, Mercer Island, and Issaquah to the east; Bainbridge Island to the west; Tukwila, Burien, Des Moines, and Kent to the south.

The Emerald City is getting crowded—and discovered. Major new buildings clutter the skyline. The streets buckle under the construction of Metro's bus tunnel. The Convention Center (built literally *over* I-5 in the middle of downtown) opened its doors in 1988. Despite all the upheaval, the city remains a gem with its striking views of Puget Sound and the Olympic Mountains to the west, the Cascades to the east, and Mount Rainier just south. The upside of this rapid growth and international sophistication is outstanding restaurants, thriving cultural organizations, fine sports, and fabulous citywide festivals. The Seattle area supports this abundance because it has a highly educated population dedicated to making it work, a surplus of singles (who like to go out), lots of young families (determined to make it a kids' place), and a climate as temperate in weather as it is tolerant in politics. Add to this one of the largest universities in the West, and you can see why the populace has a striving, bettering cast of mind.

What follows are a few highlights of Seattle's entertainment; for a detailed city guide, we refer you to our companion book, *Seattle Best Places*, or weekly listings in *Seattle Weekly*.

THE ARTS

Music. The Seattle Opera has entered the big leagues in recent years, with productions of often stunning brilliance. The Seattle Symphony, under conductor Gerard Schwarz, has reached a new level of consistency and artistic acclaim; its new music series is particularly notable. Chamber music has become a local passion, with Santa Fe Chamber Music Festival (at UW's Meany Hall) and Seattle Chamber Music Festival (at bucolic Lakeside School) during the summer; Seattle Camerata, Early Music Guild, Northwest Chamber Orchestra, the Ladies Musical Club, and the International Chamber Music Series at Meany Hall fill out the winter and spring seasons.

Theatre. This is this city's strongest cultural card, with a dozen professional theatres (third-largest number in the US) and twice as many small groups. They put on fine productions of first runs (a number have moved on to New York) and classics. The Seattle Repertory Theatre mounts classics and contemporary fare with the highest production values. A Contemporary Theatre excels at modern drama in an intimate space (summer season); The Empty Space, moving to new digs near the Public Market, has a national reputation for new works, crazy comedies, and classics (winter season); Intiman is the place for classics and some more-adventurous works (summer); the Group in the Ethnic Cultural Theatre is Seattle's only theatre with a strong ethnic approach. Pioneer Square Theater launched an agonizingly successful *Angry Housewives*, now Seattle's longest-running play, and also does new works.

Dance. Pacific Northwest Ballet has evolved into a company of national stature; its regular season mixes Balanchine masterworks with new pieces, and the Christmas highlight is a breathtaking realization of *Nutcracker* with sets by Maurice Sendak. Meany's Lively Arts Series and On The Boards present touring companies.

Visual Arts. Seattle Art Museum in Volunteer Park has fine collections in Asian and African art (the downtown branch is scheduled to open in summer 1991); Henry Art Gallery at the UW mounts very thoughtful and challenging shows; the main galleries—it's a very good scene—are found predominantly in Pioneer Square. Traditionally, gallery openings are the first Thursday of every month.

Architecture. Over the past five years Seattle has built a new skyline; the striking new additions are the Washington Mutual Tower (1201 Third Avenue), by Kohn Pederson Fox, and Two Union Square (Sixth and Union), by the NBBJ Group. Pioneer Square, rebuilt after the fire of 1889, has a rare coherence for American "old towns" and makes for a lovely stroll. Pike Place Market is a shrine for architects, in part because no architect had much to do with its jumbled, exuberant vitality. An interesting neighborhood known as Waterfront Place is near the downtown waterfront at First and Seneca.

OTHER THINGS TO DO

Nightlife. There are clubs all over town, but Seattle's music scene is centered around two neighborhoods: Pioneer Square offers every kind of music from jazz to sophisticated rock, and Ballard brings in the blues, as well as traditional and new folk music. The jazz scene is often very good. There are good coffeehouses on Capitol Hill and in the U District; the new music scene is found in the Denny Regrade.

Exhibits. The zoo at Woodland Park is a world leader in naturalistic displays, particularly the uncannily "open" African savannah and the new, exotic Asian elephant forest. The Museum of Flight, at Boeing Field (though it has no formal affiliation with Boeing), is notable for its sophisticated design and impressive collection. Pacific Science Center, with planetarium and revolving displays on all sorts of subjects, graces Seattle Center, that legacy of the 1962 World's Fair; there is a decent aquarium on the central waterfront; and at the Hiram M. Chittenden Locks in Ballard, where the ships are lifted to Lake Washington, salmon climb the ladders on their way to spawn. There are more than 1,000 works of art on public display in the city (due in part to a city ordinance calling for 1 percent of capital improvement funds to be spent on public art). For a free map to these places, call the Seattle Arts Commission, (206) 684-7171.

Parks. Seattle's horticultural climate is among the finest in the world—damp and mild all year—so the parks are spectacular and numerous. The Arboretum, with 5,500 species and gentle pathways amid azaleas, is the loveliest; Discovery Park, with grassy meadows and steep sea cliffs, is the wildest; Green Lake, with it's 2.8-mile running-walking-rollerblading track, is by far the most active. Freeway Park, a flying carpet over Interstate-5 downtown, is the most urban.

Sports. The town has gone football-mad, which means there are hardly any tickets (test your concierge's powers). The UW Huskies, usually contenders, play in one of the land's most beautiful stadiums, with arrival by boat a local custom;

the Seahawks lift the roof off the drab Kingdome. The SuperSonics are playing well again in the bandbox Coliseum; the UW women's basketball team is one of the top 20 teams in the country; the Mariners limp along lovably, playing baseball in the ill-suited Dome. Horseracing at Longacres (one of the oldest and most beautiful tracks on the West Coast) offers a very fast track and good food for late-afternoon, early-evening races (April–October).

Shopping. The downtown area has many of the designer-name stores, plus some excellent, full-line department stores, and a glossy new mall smack in the middle of the downtown congestion, across from Nordstrom's headquarters store. Of the specialty shopping areas, we favor the Pike Place Market (for foodstuffs), Capitol Hill (for clothes and furnishings), the University District (for books), and Pioneer Square (for arts and designer places).

Ferries. The Sound may be too cold for swimming, so the second-best way to enjoy it is to take a round trip on a Washington State Ferry to Bainbridge Island (see listing). The ferry leaves from Colman Dock on the central waterfront (at the foot of Madison).

RESTAURANTS

Cafe Sport
1 block north of Pike Place Market on Western,
(206) 443-6000
2020 Western Avenue, Seattle
Moderate; full bar; AE, DC, MC, V
Breakfast, lunch, dinner every day

With the recent departure of chef Tom Douglas, patrons quietly wondered what would happen here. The transition to chef Diana Isaiou has been ever-so-gentle. Trained under the keen eye of Douglas for two years, and sharing his culinary approach of a consistently fresh blend of New American and Pacific Rim cuisines, Isaiou (who's been writing the menu for a year now) has capably assumed the helm of one of Seattle's most distinctive restaurants.

In spirit, Cafe Sport is two restaurants. First there is the "cafe," where you can eat a casual lunch (better have reservations) or order from the dinner menu at a booth in the bar, noisily populated with the maddeningly fit patrons of the adjoining Seattle Club. Perhaps a third of the regulars order the black bean soup, a cilantro-and-lime–laced version, coarsely pureed, to be sopped up with a chewy boule loaf. Spicy Cajun-style oysters or a hot chicken-breast sandwich—slabs of perfectly grilled poultry served with basil mayonnaise and a mound of shoe-string potatoes, fabulously messy to eat—are similarly popular. Lately, though, the kitchen seems a little bored by these favorites, and they might emerge without their usual luster. Breakfast dishes of omelets and meats and waffles are among the town's best: don't miss the fine, shortcake-like lemon scones.

Then, in the evening, you can enjoy the "restaurant" experience: lights are dimmed, and it all becomes a touch more formal, though far from stuffy. Put yourself in the hands of the waiters, and the kitchen will surprise and delight you: you may find duck sausages lurking among the goat cheese and marinated vegetables on your antipasto plate, a cranberry bun nestled in your bread basket at Christmas. It's sparks of ingenuity—even whimsy—like these that set an exuberant, and at times irreverent, tone for each meal. One recent dish, charred-rare yellowfin tuna with wasabe aioli and tobiko (flying fish roe) was an unexpected meltaway delight—charbroiled on the outside and barely warm inside. The hook-and-line lingcod braised in coconut milk with Thai peanut sauce proved another transcendent treatment of very fresh fish.

You will want to finish with dessert—a big deal here, perhaps because of the cafe's vaguely healthy orientation—of which our favorites are a white and dark chocolate mousse, the city's best silky-thick creme caramel, and buttery-crusted fruit pies. Sport is a fine place to do business, too: in the glassed-in private room, up to 24 diners will be well served and—as ever—well fed.

Fullers

*Between Pike and Union
on 6th, in the Seattle
Sheraton, (206) 447-5544
1400 Sixth Avenue,
Seattle
Expensive; full bar;
AE, DC, MC, V
Lunch Mon-Fri,
dinner Mon-Sat*

Plenty of folks are cynical about Fullers. There's the repeating phenomenon of young women chefs who skyrocket out of the Fullers kitchen and into show-biz chefdom—first Kathy Casey and now Caprial Pence—leading some to wonder if the real talent here isn't in the Sheraton Hotel public relations office. There's the silliness over the art one "dines with" (the restaurant was named for the founder of the Seattle Art Museum, Dr. Richard Fuller; the conceptual focus and decoration being works by famous Northwest artists). And there are those lofty pretensions, from the way the waiters condescend to serve you (and then proudly plunk down the biggest bill you've ever seen), right down to how the vegetables are so purposefully, artfully arranged on your plate that you hate to break it up.

The cynics, however, would do well to reassess. Hoopla notwithstanding, Caprial Pence *is* a star, bringing nothing short of brilliance to her post. Beautiful presentation, aggressive use of fruit in sauces, an Asian accent to the food, and an obvious understanding of subtlety are her hallmarks. Her Scandinavian preparation of tuna and salmon gravlax is given a whisper of Southeast Asia in the sauce of mustard, cardamom, and lime. In one entree, slices of pinkened lamb loin emerge like stepping stones across a pool of pale yellow garlic sauce, enriched with a mound of savory forest mushrooms. In another, breast of duck appears in a dark, savory apple-hazelnut sauce. We ended fishing fresh raspberries out of the evanescent cloud of raspberry souffle, and reveling in its Grand Marnier finish.

Labuznik

*On 1st between Stewart
and Virginia,*

On a recent visit, we went almost hoping to find fault—more for diversion than anything else—but again and again everything that emerged from the kitchen was not

(206) 441-8899
1924 First Avenue,
Seattle
Expensive; full bar;
AE, DC, MC, V
Dinner Tues-Sat

★ ★ ★ ★

only faultless but superb. If consistency is the mark of a fine restaurant, Peter Cipra's hearty Eastern European cuisine certainly qualifies. He's been serving pretty much the same dishes for years, and his devotion to quality ingredients and preparation has attracted a loyal clientele.

In Cipra's native Czechoslovakia, *labuznik* means "lover of good food," and labuzniks will certainly enjoy themselves here. They will find no fault with his roast duck with crisp skin, the superb roast pork, the veal chops with scampi in mustard sauce, or the rack of lamb served with Dijon and garlic. Most entrees are accompanied by Cipra's famous side dishes: bread dumplings, sweet-sour red cabbage, sauerkraut. Some regulars prefer the cafe in front, whose walls open onto the street in fair weather. Here there are light meals at friendlier prices: pastas, steak sandwiches with mustard and green peppercorns, fried cheese, and cold plates. Desserts are rich and glorious.

Cipra's reputation as a taskmaster is legendary. Even so, the waitstaff seem more relaxed these days, although still as professional as ever. A perfectionist, Cipra refuses to serve more than three entree choices per table on the grounds that his kitchen can't properly prepare four. Not to worry—all will satisfy.

Adriatica

Near the corner of Aloha
and Dexter,
(206) 285-5000
1107 Dexter Avenue N,
Seattle
Expensive; full bar;
AE, MC, V
Dinner every day

★ ★ ★

Adriatica is arguably Seattle's most sophisticated Mediterranean restaurant. Chef Nancy Flume commands a kitchen that serves an imaginative selection of foods from Greece, France, Italy, and Yugoslavia. The food is not so much prepared as crafted, in an environment that owner-host Jim Malevitsis has carefully created to promote relaxed appreciation. The crowd is urban and sophisticated, the place a refurbished house perched on a hillside (up a long flight of stairs—no wheelchair access) overlooking the broad expanse of Lake Union.

Most diners start with fried calamari and garlic dip, but don't pass up the taramosalata spread on fresh, warm bread, or the delicate carpaccio—paper-thin raw tenderloin with olive oil and capers. The horiatiki (Greek salad) is a standout among the six salad offerings. The menu includes an unusual grilled duck sausage and a heavenly angel-hair pasta with prawns. Not only does chef Flume procure some of the finest fish in the city, she cooks it to perfection and presents it under inspired sauces (an extraordinary swordfish with red pepper sauce, for example). For dessert try a fine Chocolate Decadence, or a date baklava. It's peasant food brought to the city, polished to perfection with an earthy lustiness all but forgotten in contemporary restaurants.

The wine steward maintains an extensive cellar including more than 20 champagnes and a wine for any budget. The service is as polished as the food, and staff is helpful and knowledgeable without a trace of obsequiousness. One unfortunate feature is the lack of tables for two near the windows. Reservations recommended.

Botticelli Cafe

Corner of 1st and
Stewart, (206) 441-9235
101 Stewart Street,
Seattle
Inexpensive; no alcohol;
MC, V
Breakfast Mon-Fri, lunch
Mon-Sat, dinner Fri-Sat

This very polished, very Italian four-table aperitif bar is a place to linger—over one of Seattle's finest espressos or irresistible panini (toasted Italian sandwiches). If you so much as peek your head in the door, you'll be coaxed in by Angelo Belgrano and expected to stay awhile. The menu is geared toward the mid-afternoon repast: wedges of Sicilian focaccia bread toasted warm with fresh mozzarella, artichoke hearts, Roma tomatoes, and sweet red peppers and drizzled with thyme, oregano, and extra-virgin olive oil. A sprig of basil freshens the superb vegetariano sandwich. The antipasti, which vary daily, might include Gorgonzola smothered with mascarpone and studded with walnuts, or blanched, julienned beets sprinkled with balsamic vinegar and (sometimes too much) olive oil. Expect exceptional quality and freshness; everything, from the prosciutto to the olives, the pate to the pesto, will leave you in a pleasurable delirium. Espresso, Italian mineral waters, and fresh fruit ices are to sip in—if you're in any kind of a hurry, save (the sensational) Botticelli for another day.

Cafe Alexis (Alexis Hotel)

1st and Madison,
(206) 624-3646
1007 First Avenue,
Seattle
Expensive; full bar;
AE, DC, MC, V
Lunch Mon-Fri,
dinner every day

With the opening of 92 Madison (which has replaced Schmick's), the lunch kitchen staff now cooks for two—restaurants, that is. Out one swinging door goes 92 Madison's down-home American food (meat loaf to oyster stew), out the other go Northwest innovations. In the evening, 92 Madison closes its doors to serve banquets only, so that Cafe Alexis remains the showpiece. It's tucked cozily into a space off the lobby that feels relaxed but still retains enough of that Alexis elegance to remind you where you are. Seasonal, inventive treatments of Northwest ingredients are still the focus here, done to a turn by chef Jerry Traunfeld. During the short morel season, for instance, he's likely to pay homage to the delicate fungi with a sumptuous morel souffle; in June the seasonal menu might highlight a salad of grilled trout, smoked salmon, and ginger-mint creme fraiche dressing. We've encountered saddle of rabbit with Black Forest ham and watercress in a nest of crisp noodles and shyly sweet marjoram sauce; mahi mahi sauteed in sesame seeds with pink peppercorns, cucumber sauce, and sorrel pesto; and halibut (just a tad overcooked) with a cream, tarragon, and sweet-cicely sauce. Each was accompanied by a grilled mixture of melon, eggplant, and tomato, and steamed asparagus. If you think it all sounds a little over-

---

All places in this book are recommended; even "no stars" are worth knowing about.

wrought, you're right—but it's all in the name of innovation, and there's scarcely a flaw in execution. Service is usually graceful and correct, but at times has seemed oddly out of sync. Breakfast's now at 92 Madison only.

Chez Shea

Pike Place Market,
(206) 467-9990
Suite 34, Corner Market
Building, Seattle
Expensive; beer and wine;
AE, MC, V
Dinner Tues-Sat

★★★

Chez Shea is the quintessential market restaurant: the freshest ingredients, imaginatively prepared; a cozy, elegant setting; and a real love for the bounty of the region. Half-moon windows look out over Market rooftops to the Sound and the Olympics; candles and subdued lighting provide just enough illumination to keep conversations low and the experience romantic. It's hard to believe a bustling kitchen headed by chef Scott Craig is just behind the bamboo screens.

The four-course prix-fixe meal ($30) often begins with a seafood appetizer—spicy chilled prawns and cucumbers on a bed of daikon radish, for example. Soups are excellent, subtle, nicely balanced: our cream of Walla Walla Sweet onion used a rich meat stock, lots of cream, onions, and Gruyere cheese—a sophisticated version of the old standard. Entree choices might include fresh king salmon with a chive-pumpkinseed pesto, halibut with mango sauce, roast partridge with gooseberries and currants, rack of lamb with a Provencal sauce (which in reality was more of a relish), or beef tenderloin sauced with shallots, onions, cream, and brandy. A delicate green salad cleanses the palate before dessert (a la carte), perhaps tangy lime pie with gingersnap crust or strawberry genoise liberally frosted with buttercream. The wine list, while not long, has an excellent mix of top West Coast and European vintages, carefully chosen by manager Lotta Hashizume.

Dominique's Place

Head east on Madison to
Lake Washington,
(206) 329-6620
1927 43rd Avenue E,
Seattle
Expensive; beer and wine;
AE, DC, MC, V
Lunch Mon-Fri, dinner
every day

★★★

Dominique Place, owner and chef at Dominique's Place, has earned the respect and admiration of Seattle's food community for his hard work and dedication to fine meals at this small Madison Park restaurant with the intimate and homey feel of a provincial French restaurant. Expect top-quality food that does not push the boundaries of honest French kitchen traditions, yet which shows the influence of contemporary food trends, local ingredients, and a subtle imagination.

Four prix-fixe menus as well as an a la carte menu are offered. A tantalizing light meal can be had from the hors d'oeuvres, salad, and soup offerings alone. The pates and terrines vary, but never in quality; the salmon-and-smoked-salmon terrine puts most others to shame with its subtle complexity. The soups taste so authentically French country cooking that you would swear they were flown in that very morning. The menu holds some wonderfully soul-warming dishes such as duck stew, and you'll do equally well ordering fresh fish. A recent salmon fillet with tomato butter sauce and onion confit would meet any exacting Northwesterner's standards for perfectly done salmon—seared on the outside and scarcely a moment past translucent in the center. Desserts are simple, but who could ask for more than an intensely flavored fruit sorbet on a summer evening, looking out from the patio toward Lake Washington?

Dominique's Place falls short of perfection, of course: we have heard complaints of stale bread and inferior ice cream in the crepes, and the coffee should have more soul. It is not the spot for cigar smokers who need a lot of space; but for a quiet meal of good breeding, it hits the mark nearly every time.

The Hunt Club

Madison and Boren, in the Sorrento Hotel, (206) 622-6400 900 Madison Street, Seattle Expensive; full bar; AE, DC, MC, V Breakfast, dinner every day, lunch Mon-Fri, brunch Sun

One of the pleasantest dining rooms in the city, with its burnished mahogany paneling, this restaurant is part of a hotel that keeps changing direction and considering whether to live up to its pretensions. Barbara Figueroa, the chef who came from LA's Spago a couple of years ago, seems to have settled into a comfortable routine, offering the kinds of dishes (roast Oregon rabbit in fruit-and-port sauce, an excellent rack of Ellensburg lamb done with rosemary and mustard) that make the traveling executive feel well fed, as well as the kind of outrageous combinations that make nouvelle cuisine the object of so many ambivalent feelings (fava-bean tart, a wonderful scallop lasagne appetizer, peppery grilled salmon with a too-sweet fruit melange on top).

Figueroa's menu does make excellent use of fresh Northwest ingredients, and mostly in levelheaded ways. We could have eaten a couple of pounds of the smoked (on the premises) salmon with ocean salad (a marinated array of seaweeds) and oyster mayonnaise (laced with oyster nectar and freshly smoked oysters); paper-thin slices of smoked duck on an antipasto plate melts on the tongue. The major problem with this kitchen is its tendency toward overcomplication: entrees occasionally come with so many little bits of vegetables, chunks of bean tart, and exotic mousses that you find yourself wondering what it all is and why it's sharing the same plate. Overall, though, it would be difficult to imagine getting an unsatisfying meal at the Hunt Club.

After dinner, savvy patrons retire to the lobby bar for dessert and coffee (a fine place to go even if you haven't dined at the restaurant, complete with fireplace and cozy sofas). Desserts, while usually fine, are sometimes offered in odd combinations: one recent evening every dessert save one contained chocolate. The exception: a jalapeno gelato.

Il Bistro

Just below Read-All-About-It in Pike Place Market, (206) 682-3049
93A Pike Street, Seattle
Expensive; full bar;
AE, MC, V
Dinner every day

No restaurant in Seattle enjoys as devoted a following as Il Bistro, Peter Lamb and chef Frank Daquila's dimly lit, informal (though expensive) Italian haunt tucked below street level into the elbow of the Market. The appeal is multifold, seeming to center as much on the unselfconsciously sophisticated bistro ambience as on the food: pastas, sautes, salads, unquestionably the best rack of lamb in the city, and a growing reputation for well-prepared seafood. Here you will find Northwest mushrooms—boletes, shiitake, morels, and chanterelles—when they're in season, along with fresh herbs, Italian salad staples like arugula and radicchio, and an extensive wine list featuring many Northwest wines. From this bounty Daquila fashions dishes such as linguine carretiera, tenderloin medallions on roasted peppers, a spicy linguine frutta di mare (clams, mussels, fish, and prawns in a robust, garlicky tomato sauce), veal chops stuffed with fontina cheese and artichoke hearts (they have an outstanding veal supplier). The place has its off nights, and both the waiters and the kitchen seem to lavish their best attentions on regulars (often leaving newcomers bewildered as to what all the fuss over this place is about), but just as often it comes together into an eminently satisfying whole. The place is best late at night (it's where other restaurateurs go when their places have closed) for snacks or a cognac, or wine from Lamb's well-selected list. It's the only Italian restaurant we know of that also prints a Japanese version of its menu.

Le Gourmand

Take the 45th St exit off I-5, head west to the corner of 6th and Market, (206) 784-3463
425 NW Market Street, Seattle
Expensive; beer and wine; MC, V; checks ok
Dinner Wed-Sat

Just a stroll downhill from Woodland Park Zoo, inside an unlikely Ballard storefront, lives the spirit of a small Parisian restaurant. Owners Robin Sanders and Bruce Naftaly have created a calm, intimate dining space, simply appointed with filmy curtains to obscure the traffic, walls of taupe and cream, and a mere dozen or so tables set with fresh linen, candles, and carefully arranged flowers. Indeed, without introduction the passerby would have no reason to suspect that much of what we've come to label as "Northwest cuisine" has been defined in this humble kitchen.

What appears on each evening's prix-fixe menu is tied to whatever seasonal mushroom, blossom, or bottomfish has arrived from carefully chosen local suppliers—generously embellished with Naftaly's forte, sauce. Recent selections included poached salmon in a tart gooseberry-dill sauce; a luscious spray of lamb's-quarters, purslane, lovage, and tender rose petals for a fragrant meal-capper. The waiter is happy to arrange for split portions served as separate courses, so that a meal for two with appetizer, entree, and salad becomes a five-course feast. A divine creme brulee, served in a wide saucer and garnished with chopped hazelnuts and brandied raspberries, nearly gilds the lily.

There are some minor complaints: too many bones in the salmon fillet, a slightly overcooked cut of beef (although we weren't asked how we preferred it), no vegetables unless you order the side plate for $2 extra. Not every meal brings forth the invention Naftaly and Sanders are capable of, but the disposition of the waitstaff has improved, and most of the time an experience at Le Gourmand will be a memorable one.

Le Tastevin

Corner of 1st W and Harrison, (206) 283-0991
19 W Harrison Street, Seattle
Expensive; full bar; AE, DC, MC, V
Lunch Mon-Fri, dinner Mon-Sat

No French restaurant in town can boast as many regulars as Le Tastevin, and the airy, trellised space hidden on lower Queen Anne is large enough to hold many of them at once. For all the volume sales, chefs Jacques Boiroux and Les Goetz maintain an admirable (if not perfect) record of quality, emphasizing slightly lightened versions of traditional French fare. Although you can have the Seattle-standard dishes of grilled fish topped with flavored butters, Le Tastevin is the place to go when you want a kitchen to show its stuff, from a starter of sauteed prawns in creamy, Pernod-spiked sauce to the showcase dessert souffles (much better than the overpromoted chocolate concoctions). We've had stale bread and indifferent salads, but we've also enjoyed a wonderfully textured pheasant pate, meltingly tender sweetbreads with mushrooms, and a classic coulibiac of salmon in buttery puff pastry, lightened by a pomegranate butter sauce.

Not least among Tastevin's long-running attractions is its extraordinary wine cellar, presided over by co-owner Emile Ninaud, it boasts everything from moderate Northwest selections to rare French vintages. There are interesting iced, flavored vodkas to start; at the end of the meal, check out the exquisite cognacs and dessert wines (such as a 50-year-old raisin sherry), many of which are very reasonably priced. We still hear the occasional complaint about off-service here (particularly during the business-suit–packed lunch hour), but the restaurant has tried to overcome this. The barrier imposed by its high dinner prices has been lessened with a lighter, lower-priced pre- and post-theatre menu for the urban crowd.

Nikko

King at 13th, (206) 322-4905
1306 S King St, Seattle
Moderate; full bar; AE, DC, MC, V
Dinner Mon-Sat

If stars for Japanese restaurants were granted solely on the merits of their sushi bars, Nikko would earn the top rating in the city. The sushi bar takes center stage in this not-so-secret hideaway, where congenial owner–sushi chef Shiro Kashiba—a master showman with a knack for putting Westerners at ease—plays to a packed house. If you can't wait for a seat, you have your choice of the dining tables or tatami rooms (one of which holds 40 for a private party), where the sushi tends to be less expertly prepared. Likewise, one must move with care into the conventional menu: single orders of sukiyaki arrive precooked from the kitchen; the menu is too light on vegetables and tofu; and tempura varies from light and lacy to gummy within. Ask for the Japanese menu for more esoteric (and more carefully prepared) items, including snack-size portions of wonderful things like steamed clams with sake, and cold spinach with soy and sesame. Increasingly, servers seem to favor those who display a real knowledge of Japanese cuisine.

Queen City Grill

Corner of Blanchard and 1st, (206) 443-0975
2201 First Avenue, Seattle
Moderate; beer and wine; MC, V
Lunch Mon-Fri, dinner every day

We like this place: you sink into a glossy high-backed booth and disappear from the world to schmooze with friends. Peter Lamb (owner of Il Bistro) has peeled off the veneer of formality to allow a more casual style of eating out. Here we see this invitingly dark bistro in a suitably unprepossessing section of Belltown (if you remember the Queen City Tavern that used to be here, you know what we mean), gussied up into a tres chic little drop-in space with mottled ochre walls, tall booths, and dimly beaming Art Deco wall sconces. Chef Marianne Zdobysz (lured away from Chez Shea) has a way with a grill—specifically New York steak sauteed with a Madeira–green peppercorn sauce; quail in a Kalamata vinaigrette; grilled swordfish; a moist, very flavorful half chicken glazed with a honey/herb concoction. The dishes don't rely on sauces for interest, and everything is presented with zest and a flourish (if, some complain, in meager portions).

Rover's

1½ blocks from the Arboretum, at 28th and Madison, (206) 325-7442
2808 E Madison Street, Seattle
Moderate; beer and wine; AE, DC, MC, V
Dinner Mon-Sat

Rover's has found its place. Located in a small frame house, in a quaint but not yet gentrified neighborhood (Madison Valley), Rover's would seem destined to be a fine neighborhood restaurant and no more. But chef Thierry Rautureau, possessed of flair and training, has created the kind of restaurant people drive across—and sometimes into—town for. The atmosphere is pleasant and serene, with tables spilling out into the courtyard in sunny weather, and service is understated and capable. Dinners —saucy, classically French-inspired treatments of Northwest fare—are served with a generous hand. Recently we've tried halibut bedecked in a sumptuously smoky-sweet morel and bourbon sauce; Alaskan red snapper with mango butter and a seaweed salad; fingers of chicken breast in a rich chevre sauce with slivers of tomato. Rautureau's forte is seafood, and he's adept at finding the best-quality raw materials. Try to come in salmon season, and you may get to sample his exquisite spinach linguine with salmon. If it's raspberry time or if the chanterelles are in, they'll show up in various dishes throughout the menu. Nothing is treated perfunctorily, from the soup (a gorgeous, smooth oyster-salmon bisque flavored with fresh fennel) to the dessert (a glassy, creamy creme brulee). We've yet to hear a complaint. Even the bill will please—unless you've sprung for the $34 five-course menu de degustation. A gem.

Saleh al Lago

On the east side of Green Lake, (206) 522-7943
6804 E Green Lake Way N, Seattle
Expensive; full bar;
AE, DC, MC
Lunch Mon-Fri,
dinner Mon-Sat

The handsome, pink-tinted early-80s decor, with glass brick and neon accents, is already starting to date. But it still glows in the soothing radiance of a Green Lake sunset. And Saleh Joudeh's precise but spirited renditions of Umbrian cuisine are ever fresh and timeless. Joudeh, who won local devotees with Italian-tinged Middle Eastern fare at his Avenue 52 in the University District, now pays full homage to the traditions he learned studying in the medieval city of Perugia. His touch is equally sure with forceful spicings and with delicate cream sauces, which alternate in a menu almost entirely free of the usual southern tomato slatherings; despite its briefness, this is one of the most varied Italian menus in town. Seafood and salad specials can be a bit spotty (except for the calamari, which is said by some to be the best first course in town), but the menu mainstays—pasta dishes and veal medallions in five diverse preparations—have always proven excellent. The tagliatelle in a delicate sauce of champagne, caviar, shallots, and butter and the risotto with sinfully rich mascarpone cheese and smoked duck are especially memorable. Don't miss the signature spinaci alla Perugina (spinach with prosciutto, ham, garlic, and pine nuts), or the noble Grand Marnier cheesecake in pistachio crust when it appears on the rotating dessert list. Service is very attentive but never intrusive, with none of the haughtiness that infects some others in the local Italian restaurant elite. A large bubble window opens the kitchen to view, and no one can resist looking in as they walk by.

Settebello

Olive and Denny,
(206) 323-7772
1525 E Olive Way,
Seattle
Expensive; full bar; AE,
DC, MC, V
Dinner every day

The name, from an Italian card game, means "beautiful seven," but the restaurant exudes an atmosphere not so much of Italy as of high-tech Los Angeles, with a sprinkling of local celebrities to give table-hopping host Luciano Bardinelli a lot of excuses for circling the room. Now there's a celebrity in the kitchen, too: West Seattle–born enfant terrible Scott Carsberg, back in the Northwest after a spin through some of the world's best kitchens (Villa Mozart in Merano, Italy; Le Pavillon in Washington, DC). Aboard just a few weeks at press time, he looks well on his way to success.

At his best, Carsberg is extraordinary. What he offers is the most cutting-edge Italian cuisine—sort of a post nuova cucina—with an absence of butter-and-cream and an infusion of simple, intense, exact flavors. His use of color on the plate matches the perfect piquancy there, so what you get are dishes—a bright purple heap of shredded cabbage atop the freshest, pale red ahi carpaccio; a bowl of profoundly intense yellow tomato soup—which are deeply satisfying. Carsberg's stuff redefines Italian food, infusing its traditional joyful earthiness with style and almost engineer-precise technique. Thus his triumphs already abound: achingly tender lamb fillet, simply served with mushrooms and thin points of asparagus; Angus fillet with black truffle sauce; even an ethereal version of the Italian standard, straw and hay pasta, with baby peas and prosciutto. Carsberg halted Settebello's lunches so he can concentrate on dinners: notably the four-course *menu degustativo*, which benefits from the better part of his passion.

In sum: four-star food. But we'll stay skeptical until Carsberg proves he can maintain his genius in a small kitchen, surround himself with able assistants, ferret out the right food sources, find a way to keep such a menu within the price range of millionaires, and weave a harmony with the front of the house. Fervently, we hope he does. As it is, service is still annoyingly inconsistent and, on recent visits, somewhat grim, especially when Chef Carsberg wreaks havoc with his terrifying perfectionism. Still, Carsberg, temperamental as he is, may be the best chef this city's ever seen. By fall 1989 Luciano will be dividing his time between here and his new restaurant, Stresa, in Kirkland.

Union Bay Cafe

Between University Village and Children's Hospital, off Sand Point Way, (206) 527-8364
3505 NE 45th Street, Seattle
Moderate; beer and wine; AE, MC, V
Dinner Tues-Sun

★ ★ ★

Every neighborhood should be blessed with a cafe like this one in Laurelhurst. It's a blend of local hangout (where the waitress relieves parents of a cranky baby and joins a political debate tableside) and at times superb—serious restaurant. Owner Mark Manley is likely to wander through the two tiny dining rooms, straightening napkins and starched white tablecloths, discussing his carefully chosen, seasonally fluctuating menu.

The kitchen seems to have conquered its old problem with underseasoned sauces—on a recent visit calamari (slightly soggy) was accompanied by an extraordinary aioli, and Manila clams swam in a hot, garlicky broth. Edible flowers top almost everything from the wild green salad to the chocolate mousse. Under the blossoms you may find a crisp-fried soft-shell crab, veal scallops shining through Gorgonzola sauce, or perfectly cooked fresh pasta, all accompanied by bread that's a beautiful compromise between French and healthy cracked wheat. The short but good wine list is very reasonably priced. The inconsistency of the Union Bay's past showed up in only one disappointment on our most recent meal—glutinous strawberry-rhubarb crisp, notably lacking in berries (and this during local strawberry season). But other desserts, such as a buttery-crusted cherry tart and the devastating mocha mousse, provided adequate compensation.

Al Boccalino

On Yesler near Alaskan
Way, (206) 622-7688
1 Yesler Way, Seattle
WA 98104
Moderate; beer and wine;
AE, MC, V
Lunch Mon-Fri,
dinner Mon-Sat

No, it's not the name of that Italian boy down the street who used to date your daughter. Al Boccalino is an extremely promising southern Italian restaurant, at the tag end of Yesler Way in Pioneer Square, which in its first few weeks (as we go to press) has already pulled off some stunning three-star meals. Co-owner Luigi DeNunzio (you'll remember him from Il Terrazzo) has gathered recipes from his native Apulia, the heel of the Italian boot, and with chef Tim Roth produces renditions of these to make your palate sing and your cholesterol level soar into the stratosphere. Trifolato petti de pollo (egg-dipped and tenderly sauteed chicken breast topped with paper-thin slices of prosciutto and Gruyere, then sauced with cognac and truffles) is magnificent, and served, as are all entrees, with a cheesy dish of polenta and fresh vegetables. An entree as simple as sauteed prawns is invested with the fullest flavors of olive oil and garlic. The menu ranges beautifully from salmon to lamb prepared in ways we spaghetti-Northwesterners have never seen in an Italian restaurant before, and includes a long list of daily specials. In short, this is a winner its first month. Even the decor agrees: Chic mottled mustard and raw brick walls, with gleaming dark-wood accents, and a skewed shape to the rooms, which creates the desired atmosphere of intimacy and intrigue.

Ayutthaya

1 block west of Broadway
at Harvard and Pike,
(206) 324-8833
727 E Pike, Seattle
Inexpensive; beer and
wine; AE, MC, V
Lunch, dinner Mon-Sat

With new Thai restaurants opening in almost every neighborhood, Ayutthaya is still hands-down one of the best in town. Everyone raves about "that place on Pine"—but they continually stumble over its name (pronounced *ay-U-te-a*). It also has the nicest atmosphere, at least in terms of contemporary aesthetics. Soft pastel colors and clean, smooth lines create a calming antidote to the fiery food, which is prepared carefully and authentically by the Fuangaromya family (members of which also own Thai Restaurant in lower Queen Anne). Everything is good (with the exception of the too-sweet fried noodles): Naked Bathing Rama, a sweet and crunchy mee krob, exceptionally delicate grilled chicken in coconut milk. Order the special fish of the day, and your waiter will carry the platter out the door and set it afire, filling the street with vast clouds of steam, and then plop the sizzling fish on your table. Local businesspeople are catching on to the best lunch deal in town, so it's best to arrive early (there's not much room to wait). Service is patient and sweet.

Send us your opinions and tips on the report form at the back of this book.

Beeliner Diner

*Across from the Guild
45th movie theater at
45th and Bagley,
(206) 547-6313
2114 N 45th Street,
Seattle
Inexpensive; beer and
wine; no credit cards;
checks ok
Lunch Tues-Sat,
dinner Mon-Sat*

So what if Peter Levy's Beeliner is only a facsimile of a diner? It's a fun spot for those hankering for good old American food. Besides, there isn't a diner around that dishes up meat loaf or macaroni and cheese as good as these, along with flaky-crusted chicken pot pie, charcoal-grilled pork chops, Parker House rolls, roast chicken with mashed potatoes, or the Blue Plate Special. Grab a booth or a counter stool (best for overhearing the hash-slingers bark orders in diner-ese), order a libation off a list marked Cheap White Wine, sink into a creamy slice of coconut cake to finish. It isn't perfect (watch out for tepid soup and dry chops), but it's got personality to burn. There's bound to be a line at the Beeliner Diner, so, as the sign suggests, "Eat it and beat it."

Burk's Cafe

*1 block off Market at
22nd and Ballard,
(206) 782-0091
5411 Ballard Avenue
NW, Seattle
Inexpensive; beer and
wine; MC, V
Lunch, dinner Mon-Sat*

The building, constructed in 1891 as Ballard's first tavern, has been beautifully restored to house the estimable Creole and Cajun cooking of Terry "Burk" Burkhardt. There's both file and okra gumbo, homemade sausage, local crayfish in season, oyster poor boys, and specials that sometimes include fresh catfish (no bargain). Every table has its own crock of pickled okra. All the dinners come, classically, with red beans and rice. The rice is basmati from Texas, an exceptional long-grained variety that, combined with wild rice and onion, is quite flavorful. Finish with a slice of the best pecan pie in town. The cafe can be too crowded for comfort during peak hours, and parking is no fun during lunch.

Cafe Sabika

*Bellevue and E Pine,
(206) 622-3272
315 E Pine Street,
Seattle
Moderate; beer and wine;
MC, V
Lunch Wed-Fri,
dinner Tues-Sat*

The current home of wandering chef John Rios is his homiest to date: a funky—even pleasantly worn—little cafe on back-street Capitol Hill that feels neither farmhouse-quaint (like his Chateau Rios on Lopez Island) nor reverentially elegant (like his Chateau Rios on Roy Street). Finally, he and his wife/partner Gloria have found the perfectly quirky showcase for their own patented brand of charm: John breaks into song as Gloria beams, takes your order, and gives the chef a pat. For all the informality, however, Rios hasn't forgotten his classical roots: escargots, French onion soup, beef Wellington, and snapper in puff pastry with sauce Bearnaise find their way onto even this bistro menu, and you sure weren't prepared for a tab like this in such a neighborly place. We like the less continental departures best: a tenderly braised, garlic-and-Parmesan-breaded appetizer of Sicilian calamari; a refreshing Basque snapper mounded with chunks of fresh sauteed tomato and onion, enlivened with cilantro sprigs. Lately John's been smoking his own meats; the smoked game hen in an apricot brandy sauce and the smoked duck salad are good samplings of his work. For lunch try the subtle fettuccine alfredo with melt-in-your-mouth mussels or the calamari linguine with a tangy, soak-your-bread marinara sauce. For dessert, John's special pear (poached in grenadine, ginger, nutmeg) with a sabayon sauce and topped with chocolate, whipped cream, and a mint sprig steals the show. Personal warmth is the Rioses' magic, and John and Gloria will win your heart.

Campagne

Below 1st Avenue, between Pine and Stewart, at the Inn at the Market, (206) 728-2800 86 Pine Street, Seattle WA 98101 Expensive; full bar; AE, MC, V Lunch Mon-Sat, dinner every day

The original Campagne was charming but flawed; here in its new Market perch the restaurant continues trying to make up its mind whether to be a showcase for Northwest cuisine or a Provencal cafe. This is a marvelous room, with wood floors, Oriental rugs, and views down to the bustle of Pike Place Market. In summer there are tables in the pretty hotel courtyard. Owner Peter Lewis presides over the front and over a highly individualistic wine list (from which you can actually order a good white Burgundy by the glass). We've had a few stunning meals here: a starter of sole-and-salmon sausage, a main course of melting and meaty duck breast marinated with juniper berries, "tuna sandwiches" of eastern sea scallops layered with fresh tuna, the meal topped off with a chocolate chestnut cake and the sunshine of a glass of Muscat de Beaumes de Venise. But the latest version of the menu represents a step backward—in an apparent attempt to recapture the original, Provencal Campagne, the kitchen is now turning out good ingredients (bluefish and free-range chickens) topped with surprisingly bland sauces of sorrel and goat cheese (in the latter instance) or caramelized onions (on a rack of lamb). Lunch has been simplified to a few wonderful sandwiches off the grill (occasionally charred), a beautiful chicken salad, and the day's pasta or fish dish. Desserts, particularly the homemade sorbets and ice creams, are consistently wonderful.

The Canlis Restaurant

Southeast corner of the Aurora Bridge, 2 miles north of downtown, (206) 283-3313 2576 Aurora Avenue N, Seattle Expensive; full bar; AE, DC, MC, V Dinner Mon-Sat

For a town filled with restaurants, Seattle has remarkably few that qualify as institutions. At the top of this short list is Canlis, around for nearly 40 years. It's lasted this long because it delivers exactly what it promises: good food, fine service, and a great view. There's a timeless quality about the place, from the twinkling lights around Lake Union below to the crowd at the piano bar to the kimono-clad waitresses, many of whom are in their third decade here. You won't find the latest in trendy dining at Canlis, but there is no better place for the annual thick steak accompanied by a noble cabernet. There's no shortage of seafood either, including lobster bisque, Canlis' signature sauteed prawns, salmon, or scallops, all superbly prepared. This perfection has its price. The menu is a la carte, and the tariff is among the highest in town. The high prices carry over to the wine list, which is so extensive it has a table of contents. But if you're looking for a perfect evening and price is no object, you can't do better than this.

Chau's Chinese Restaurant
4th and Jackson,
(206) 621-0006
310 Fourth Avenue S,
Seattle
Inexpensive; beer and
wine; MC, V
Lunch Mon-Fri,
dinner every day

Finally—a Chinese restaurant in Seattle that could hold its own in Hong Kong or Taipei—at least for seafood. Chau's gets a big zero for atmosphere, but Yick Chau serves up the best Cantonese seafood this side of the Far East, taking advantage of this region's abundant selection of undersea edibles. Skip the dime-a-dozen items like sweet-and-sour pork and fried rice (these get little or none of the chef's effort) and head straight for the blissful seafood creations: steamed oysters with garlic sauce (huge fresh oysters piled high with chopped garlic and cooked just right, no longer raw but still redolent of the open ocean); heady and flavorful wok-baked Dungeness crab with ginger and green onions; or melt-in-your mouth slices of blanched geoduck. If you order seafood you can bet it was swimming just minutes before. Reports are dismal on the rest of the fare. Try Chau's with a large group: a 10-course seafood banquet can cost as little as $15 per person (in a room that accommodates up to 80 people). Food is served until midnight.

Chinook's
Fisherman's Terminal,
(206) 283-4665
1735 W Thurman,
Seattle
Moderate; full bar;
AE, DC, MC, V
Lunch, dinner every day,
brunch Sat-Sun

It's big, busy, and formulaic, but this time the Anthony's Home Port folks seem to be using the right bait in the Port of Seattle's $13 million renovation of Fisherman's Terminal. The industrial-strength design with very high ceilings, steel countertops, visible beams, and ventilation ducts, matched with an appealing collection of action-packed fishing photos, fits well with the bustle around the working marina. The 125-item menu ranges from broiled to fried seafood, Japanese stir-fries, and big, juicy burgers. We suggest you nab a few things off the regular menu (tempura onion rings and a half-dozen oysters) and the rest from the daily special sheet (Copper River salmon char-grilled with sun-dried tomato basil butter or petrale sole baked with soy sauce and topped with toasted almonds). We have found a few of the charbroiled selections slightly overcooked. For dessert, try a big piece of blackberry cobbler.

The problems are in the staff—often young and forgetful. More than once, the herb-cheese bread was brought to our table just as we were finishing our entrees. Don't overlook the weekend brunch blowouts.

Cutters Bayhouse
1 block north of Pike
Place Market,
(206) 448-4884
2001 Western Avenue,

This stylish restaurant overlooking Elliott Bay on the north edge of the Pike Place Market is jammed morning, noon, afternoon, and night. The hodgepodge menu echoes the interior design, which includes a bar, brasserie, deli, cafe, and restaurant. You can order just about

Seattle
Moderate; full bar;
AE, MC, V
Breakfast Sun, lunch,
dinner every day

anything—Chinese, Hawaiian, Cajun, Italian, salads, pastas, seafood, and more; what's surprising is that most everything is good. We've enjoyed the fresh lingcod with hazelnut sauce served with focaccia (the thick Italian bread that makes the whole restaurant smell like garlic, even at Sunday breakfast) and the bar nibbles that are served until 1am nightly. The bar also has a good selection of wines by the glass. The view is wonderful both outside and in, where the upwardly mobile types congregate after aerobics at the Seattle Club across the street. Service is smilingly accommodating.

El Puerco Lloron

On the Pike Place Market
Hillclimb, (206) 624-0541
1501 Western Avenue,
Seattle
Inexpensive; beer and
wine; AE, MC, V
Lunch, dinner every day

For authenticity of decor and cooking (at cheaper than authentic prices), few Mexican places in Seattle beat "The Crying Pig" on the Pike Place Market Hillclimb. The metal card tables and folding chairs, complete with scars and Cerveza Superior logos, were imported from a cafe in Tijuana. The vivid hues of ordinary Mexico—pink, aqua, yellow—were splashed on the ceiling and walls. And the ersatz fare found in American Mexican restaurants was shunned. Everything here is handmade with fresh ingredients. The masa for the tortillas—from American corn, and therefore yellower—is ground daily. You order from the short menu behind the counter. The prices are astonishingly low, but it's all delicious, especially the fresh chiles rellenos.

Enoteca

4th and Olive,
(206) 624-9108
414 Olive Way, Seattle
Moderate; beer and wine;
AE, MC, V
Lunch, dinner Mon-Sat

Wander down the steps of the Times Square Building to Tom Darden's subterranean wineshop-cum-restaurant. You'll sometimes find winemakers at the bar pouring glasses of their recommendations. Though the restaurant seconds as a wineshop, order the daily WineMaster special ($29.95), a four-course meal complemented by three well-chosen glasses of Northwest wine, and your dinner will be second to none: your entree might be Oregon duck, grilled swordfish, or roasted salmon. One evening we savored a gently smoked grilled Washington rabbit, preceded by a superior truffle and a salad, and followed with a wonderfully smooth loganberry cheesecake. Prices are steep but not unaffordable. Select your wine from the rotating list—or choose a bottle from the shelves and pay only a slight corkage fee. Lunch entrees cost substantially less, although they also tend to be less consistent: we've simultaneously encountered a sublime penne dish with asparagus and a strong but not overpowering Gorgonzola cream sauce, and a shockingly meager Greek salad ($7.50) with mealy tomatoes and scant dressing.
Northwest tapas work well at the wine bar: perhaps

the duck salad with spinach, papaya, walnuts, and raspberry vinaigrette, or the chicken and broccoli dipped in an Oriental soy-based sauce. Service is fast, but perhaps too fast. The desserts finish the evening well.

The Georgian Room (Four Seasons Olympic Hotel)

Between 4th and 5th on University,
(206) 621-1700
411 University Street,
Seattle
Expensive, full bar;
AE, DC, MC, V
Breakfast, dinner Mon-Sat, lunch Mon-Fri,
brunch Sun

★ ★

Befitting the Olympic's cachet as downtown's original and enduring grand hotel, its dining room is as stately as any in town, with massive chandeliers, ample palms, and floral arrangements softening its lofty ceilings and heavy woodwork. The ceremonial mood is moderated by traveling guests relaxing with books and magazines. But the floor crew does its best to restore the tone with solicitous white-glove attention that stops just short of being intrusive. With their flair for the finer touches, however, they overlook some bare basics: a seat and plate covered with bread crumbs, water that doesn't arrive till requested after the wine.

Master sommelier Ken Fasules' wine list is broad and imaginative, with hard-to-find bargains seeded among stiffly priced entries. The menu is what is now becoming mainstream Northwest neo-continental, with seafoods, berries, and wild greens well represented. Presentation is exquisite, from brilliant mosaics of meat and garnish to a delightful corny sculpted apple of an apple torte. Taste for the most part matches the look: an appetizer of softly smoked, wonderfully moist quail haunches with figs; an assemblage of petrale sole fillet, sauteed shrimp, and sea urchin roe on a scallop gateau that is a symphony of marine harmonies. The latter offering was generous, but some diners' complaints of over-dainty portions were confirmed by a skimpy "Sichuan-style" sockeye steak (overly soy-sauced). The little extras do much to atone, however, ranging from perfect grapefruit sorbet as a palate-cleanser to the best Italian-style bread in town, baked on the premises. This is high aspiration even for a grand hotel kitchen, and it's almost fulfilled.

Green Lake Grill

Corner of Densmore and
Green Lake Drive N,
(206) 522-3490
7850 Green Lake Drive
N, Seattle
Expensive; full bar;
AE, MC, V
Lunch, dinner every day

★ ★

Karl Beckley's new Green Lake Grill is actually two places. A casual black-and-white tiled cafe spills out onto a patio; here you choose from a good selection of microbrews and nibble on a salad of chicken, prosciutto, capers and coriander, linguine with sublime duck confit, and outstanding Pagataw pancakes (yearling oysters and fresh corn cooked in egg batter and served with jalapeno whipped cream, salmon caviar). A TV in this room nicely lowers the pretension quotient. In the back is the deep-pockets dining room—white linen, glossy dark wood chairs, muted splatter-chic walls, good art. The menu changes daily, but Beckley's approach to food is straightforward: grilled king salmon with sun-dried tomato and thyme butter, rabbit roasted with red peppers, glazed garlic cloves and dry vermouth, tenderloin of beef with red wine, walnuts and blue cheese butter. Recently, the sauces have not been as flavorful as they could be: we encountered a lackluster morel sauce on the sweetbreads one evening. It's all a la carte; supplement your entree with soup (one of the restaurant's strengths), a seasonal salad, and dessert (not one of the restaurant's strengths). Beckley can be adventurous, but lately he's been working out front, and we'd rather see him behind the line putting together the strong, pure flavors he's quite capable of.

Hien Vuong

On King at 5th,
(206) 624-2611
502 S King Street,
Inexpensive; no alcohol;
no credit cards; no checks
Lunch, dinner Wed-Mon

Simple food has never been so exquisite. The place is nothing much, just a cubbyhole across from Uwajimaya, Seattle's biggest Asian grocery; it's the food that draws, for its freshness and vibrancy of flavors. The beef noodles come in a light but miraculously resonant broth. Papaya with beef jerky combines grated still-green papaya with delicate shreds of spiced, dried beef in a tangy dressing. The shrimp rolls are some of the best in town: very fresh shrimp with romaine, mint, and cilantro wrapped in rice paper, with scallion ends peeking out like little green tails. They come with a rich brown peanut sauce for dipping. All the hot dishes come to your table straight off the stove. You'll feel guilty paying so little for food this good.

Ho Ho

S Weller between 6th &
7th, (206) 382-9671
653 S Weller Street,
Seattle
Moderate; beer and wine;
MC, V; checks ok
Lunch, dinner every day

A bright addition to the International District, Ho Ho proves that some of Seattle's best seafood is to be found in its Chinese restaurants. Ho Ho is a Hong Kong–style place, with a very long menu emphasizing fish and shellfish from in-house tanks. One reviewer was breathless over the lobster, swathed in a broth of fresh shiitake mushrooms and served with spinach. High points also go to the ginger-and-scallion oyster saute, the prawns in lobster sauce, the spicy kung pao shrimp. It's when you stray off the seafood list that things get chancy—seasonings are often way off (too bland, too salty, too sweet), and the mu-shu pork is merely ordinary. Service is friendly or gruff, depending on the night. They do a nice job with private occasions, in a room that holds 30. You can drop in for dinner until 1am weekdays, and 3am weekends.

Il Terrazzo Carmine

Between Jackson and
King, in a courtyard,
(206) 467-7797
411 First Avenue S,
Seattle
Expensive; full bar; AE,
DC, MC, V; no checks

This beautiful, airy room opening onto a terrace (hence the name) overlooking the handsome fountain in Merrill Place is full of contradictions. Country Italian furnishings—flowered drapes and china, terra-cotta tiling, lithographs of vegetable still lifes—bump elbows with such high-tech accoutrements as streamlined Japanese-style light fixtures. The combination might be odd, but it works, and Il Terrazzo has become a natural pre- and post-

Lunch Mon-Fri, dinner
Mon-Sat

theatre gathering spot for the city's urban and urbane, who come for dessert and a latte or just to enjoy the romantic bar.

An appetizer of marinated smoked salmon (Norwegian, strangely enough), though a bit on the salty side, is as delicious as the presentation is beautiful: the salmon, glistening in a perfect olive oil, spreads across the plate like rays emanating from a sun of radicchio, endive, and Bibb lettuce. At the same time, a lackluster plate of calamari arrives chewy and ungarnished. By far the best bets here are the simply grilled, roasted, and sauteed entrees: a recent special, a generous serving of roast duck stuffed with morels and fresh oregano and rosemary, accompanied by succulent roasted vegetables, was exquisitely rich and moist. Though the inconsistencies can be endlessly annoying, they are also what makes it so charming. If you choose carefully and take advantage of an extensive wine list featuring renowned Italian vintages, the food is certainly worth the considerable expense, and the ambience is, as ever, *molto invitante.*

Islabelle Caribbean Catering

Under the University
Bridge on Northlake,
(206) 632-8011
711 NE Northlake Way,
Seattle
Inexpensive; no alcohol;
no credit cards; checks ok
Breakfast, lunch, dinner
Tues-Sat

This shot of sunshine on the north shore of Lake Union is a happy find—exotic, exciting, snazzy, and cheap. Lorenzo Lorenzo is Cuban, but his food is pan-Caribbean in inspiration. He and his wife Crystal eschew frying and fats, favoring instead the light, piquant flavors of lime juice on halibut, salsa and fresh watercress on lean ground beef, lightly grilled chicken. It's all stand-up or take-out only, but there are chairs on the deck if you can't make it to Gas Works Park. The Sopa Sampler ($3.95) gives you a lot to taste: velvety black bean soup with rice, watercress, broiled chicken, salsa, foo foo (doughy little spiced plantain balls), and tortilla chips. This is not fast food; expect to wait 15–20 minutes for your order. Breakfast is mostly baked goods—an espresso muffin, perhaps, or cinnamon rolls—but you can call ahead on the weekend for omelets (try the black bean omelet with salsa and sour cream).

Italia

Between Madison and
Seneca on Western,
(206) 623-1917
1010 Western Avenue
Moderate; beer and wine;
AE, MC, V
Breakfast, lunch, dinner
Mon-Sat

The most upscale cafeteria in Seattle, Italia offers good Italian food in a cavernous urban space that is simultaneously an art gallery and gourmet-food store—bustling by day, lonely at night. There's a dichotomy to the food, too. At lunch it runs to exotic, well-made gourmet pizzas (smoked chicken, pancetta, leek, and chevre), two daily pastas (that don't fare terribly well on the steam table), stuffed Italian sandwiches, and tasty Caesars and other salads. It all seems quite cheap until you realize you've just dropped $10 and served yourself. At dinner, prices go up along with quality on specialties like king salmon with sorrel aioli, or tenderloin medallions with Gorgonzola. They do a great job with breads (the focaccia particularly) and rich desserts. They're also one of the most professional caterers around. Nibble, nosh, and sip at the wine bar until midnight on weekends.

Julia's 14 Carrot Cafe

E Lynn and Eastlake,
(206) 324-1442
2305 Eastlake Avenue E,
Seattle
Moderate; beer and wine;
MC, V
Breakfast every day, lunch
Mon-Sat, dinner Tues-Sat

There are two things you can count on in Seattle: rain and a Sunday-morning line at Julia's. It's warm, steamy, noisy, and plain, serving homemade health-food renditions of dishes pulled from a couple of dozen cuisines—a Greek salad, several pastas—in bountiful portions. Dinner is more consistent, but breakfast is the fabled meal, with big build-your-own omelets, thin, tangy sourdough pancakes, grilled potatoes with scallions and cheese, hefty cinnamon rolls, and Scotch oatmeal, plus exotic inventions like Tahitian Toast: grilled, egg-dipped sourdough bread with sesame butter, served with fresh fruit and yogurt. At the other Julia's in Wallingford (4401 Wallingford, 206-633-1175) there are suggestions of a California nouvelle cuisine influence in the dishes, along with a slightly more upscale ambience and outdoor tables. Both restaurants are clearly overrated—imagination and execution of specials have dropped off; prices keep creeping up, and you practically have to camp out on the doorstep for a breakfast "two-top" (table for two)—but they're as essential to Seattle as water. Plenty of vegetarian choices; no smoking.

Kokeb

12th and Spring,
(206) 322-0485
926 12th Avenue, Seattle
Inexpensive; beer and
wine; AE, DC, MC, V
Dinner every day

It's plain and inexpensive, with a steady clientele of Seattle University students and faculty. Ethiopian food is distinctive and exotic and, because it's eaten with the fingers, appeals to children. Be forewarned, though: nearly all of the entrees are spicy. The base of a meal, literally, is injera, a flat, spongy bread. A round of this on a platter holds an entire party's entree choices, soaks up their sauces, and is eaten to climax the meal. Each entree comes with a choice of two vegetables and a bland homemade cottage cheese called eyeb, a welcome counterpart to the spicy main dishes. Service can be blase, but this food is worth the wait.

Le Petit Cafe

34th Ave NE and NE
55th, north of University
Village, (206) 524-0819
3428 NE 55th Street,
Seattle
Moderate; beer and wine;
MC, V
Dinner Tues-Sun

Algerian chef Ali Chalal is gone, but he's left behind his trademark couscous with lamb sausage—made in-house with fresh spices from Africa—and a cayenne and cumin harissa (an Arabic hot sauce). Chef Angelo Woodman carries on a menu similar to Chalal's, including the mustard-sauced rabbit, Oregon duck with berry sauce, chicken breasts stuffed with ricotta and basil, and some seafood specials—executed not always perfectly but always earnestly. In summer, he also offers lighter selections (marinated calamari served in artichoke hearts with a raspberry vinaigrette, or a variation on the couscous made with seafood instead of lamb); cold soups (perhaps melon accented with papaya); and a number of salads. The front is manned by Bryce Robinson, a *patron* who knows when to ignore the lovers blissfully feeding each other asparagus and when to visit awhile with the party of six. Larger parties (up to 14) can reserve a private room.

Lee Chee Garden

On Elliot between Denny and Mercer,
(206) 281-8838
544 Elliott Avenue W,
Seattle
Moderate; full bar;
AE, MC, V
Lunch, dinner every day

Brothers Andy and Jemmy Ma have divided the growing population of well-heeled Hunan food–fanciers between them. Lee Chee, occupying the windowless former Tiki Hut on an unlikely stretch of Elliott Avenue, is the province of Andy, who works with a safe Hunan, Sichuan, and Mandarin menu (sort of a "greatest hits" of the menu at their former restaurant, Andy and Jemmy's Wok where Jemmy still reigns). Andy's signature dishes are tender shrimp in a rich, gingery black bean garlic sauce and orange beef—strips of flank steak subtly seasoned with citrus. Kung pao chicken (appearing on the menu as "diced chicken sauteed in hot and spicy sauce with peanuts") is also very good. Disappointments center on the sauces, some of which (the oyster sauce, and Chef Andy's Special Sauce) aren't always flavorful enough. Crack service and a high standard of freshness can be expected.

Leroy's Grill

Roosevelt near 64th,
(206) 526-9670
6411 Roosevelt Way NE,
Seattle
Moderate; beer and wine;
MC, V
Dinner Tues-Sun

Four Northwesterners have parlayed the old tavern of the same name into a noteworthy neighborhood restaurant. Vintage bar stools, a handful of sofa-style seats, and 1940s kitchen tablecloths make for a warm, almost misleadingly casual atmosphere—the food is fresh, thoughtfully prepared, and delicious. We can't stop ordering the chicken saltimbocca, chicken livers (sauteed with roasted walnuts, green onions, and Madeira), Cajun prawns with oysters, 40-cloves-of-garlic chicken (for devotees only), and a zesty artichoke-heart-garlic-Parmesan appetizer. Seafood is cooked just right, as are the vegetables that accompany entrees. Service can lag, but these meals and reasonable prices are well worth the wait.

Marrakesh

Just north of Group
Health, 15th Avenue E at
Mercer, (206) 328-4577
605 15th Avenue E,
Seattle
Moderate; full bar;
AE, DC, MC, V
Lunch Tues-Fri,
dinner Tues-Sun

The code of Moroccan hospitality is well preserved at this bit of Fez on 15th, where host Ben H. Alaoui (formerly of the other Moroccan restaurant in town, Mamounia) assures that your meal will begin with the customary finger-washing ceremony and end with the sprinkling of rosewater over your hands. In between you will experience a cuisine—without benefit of utensils. At Marrakesh, $14.50 buys a substantial six-course meal, although the bill creeps substantially higher with wine. Everyone begins with harira Marrakshia, the ubiquitous lentil soup of North Africa and the Middle East, here made with a tomato base. The meal continues through a Moroccan eggplant salad (served too cold on our visit) and a dry and rather uninteresting bastella royale (poultry pie), at which point you choose your entree. The couscous and the honey-prune chicken are lackadaisical versions, so we suggest the braised hare: tender lean Vashon Island rabbit in a rich, warm paprika sauce. Or come with a large group and order the mechoui—Morocco's famous roast lamb. Hosting a group may, in fact, be Marrakesh's best function—the private room is fine for a private party, and the relaxed festivity of the place is great for parties in need of an ice-breaker. Don't plan on whispering sweet nothings, however; the din can really escalate in here, especially on weekends, when the bedizened belly dancer starts to sway.

McCormick & Schmick's
1st and Spring,
(206) 623-5500
1103 First Ave, Seattle
Moderate, full bar; AE,
DC, MC, V; checks ok
Lunch Mon-Fri, dinner
every day

A kind of Tadich's North, this seafood restaurant is an encyclopedia of San Francisco cliches: dark wood paneling, booths, glittering bar, waiters with black bow ties. You'd think they'd been grilling lamb chops and salmon steaks since the turn of the century. Don't smirk—they do it well, if not with perfect consistency. Just remember to keep it simple: order seafood, and stay away from the pasta. Start with roasted garlic and some fresh oysters; then get the fresh fish of the day, usually done in a tasty, uncomplicated sauce. The straightforward work at the grill also includes meat, game, and poultry. At lunch it's too busy for its own good—service adopts a hurry-up attitude, and they make you sit in the hall until your whole party assembles—but dinners are more relaxed, with the bar suppers a nice feature for solo diners. A private room holds up to 25 diners.

Mikado
Jackson and 5th,
(206) 622-5206
514 S Jackson Street,
Seattle
Moderate; full bar;
AE, MC, V
Dinner Mon-Sat

At Seattle's original and largest Japanese restaurant, you can still eat well (or mostly well), but either Mikado's standards have slipped or Seattle's have risen; its food is merely good, no longer surpassing. It is still a very cozy place for one so large, broken up into a warren of distinct, intimate dining settings and styles. You sit at Formica tables and order from any of the menu genres; if you must settle for the main dining room, grab a stuffed-vinyl corner booth. If you're in a large party, reserve a rice-matted, low-seated tatami room; the food perks up in this traditional setting, and a big steaming pot of toban-yaki—meat, fish, shrimp, and vegetables cooked at your table—is a marvelously sociable antidote to winter blahs. If you're solo or in a pair, consider the robata-yaki (grill) or the sushi bar, and compose a meal of the fresh hors d'oeuvres that are Mikado's strongest suit; preparation and service at either of these make for a splendid mealtime show. At our last visit, however, the sushi, while properly fresh, lacked that special grace of presentation and the flourishes—such as the quail eggs on the uni—that set a top sushi bar apart. The salmon steak came slightly dry and smothered in a thick, over-salty teriyaki sauce without mitigating sweetness. Vegetables have arrived tough and cold. Still, service is as quick, warm, and gracious as ever, and the veteran waitresses delight in decoding Japanese cuisine for novices.

Mikado is to be commended for transcending the conventional generic warm-sake-in-a-jug and serving it the way good sake is supposed to be served: cool, in a square box that you'll soon grow accustomed to sipping from.

Nick & Sully

Eastlake and Boston,
(206) 325-8813
2043 Eastlake Avenue E,
Seattle
Moderate; beer and wine;
MC, V
Breakfast, lunch Mon-Fri,
dinner Tues-Sat, brunch
Sat-Sun

Both Nick and Sully are gone, but their legacy has grown from a jewel of a gourmet take-out operation to an Eastlake cafe that gives Julia's (one block north) some stiff competition. You eat in warm, Southwest-feeling quarters (now expanded into the space next door) or out at sun-splashed tables in the courtyard. Chef Pamela Kill (formerly of Cafe Alexis) selects what's freshest in the Market on a given day. Recently, with the addition of a seasonal dinner menu, this has become a place for any mood. Stop by in the morning for good baked items and an espresso; pick up some torta rustica or chicken with jalapeno jelly to take home for dinner; drop in for a light nosh on individual pizzas or grilled eggplant stuffed with Bel Paese cheese, herbs, and peppers, and sprinkled with a warm tomato vinaigrette; or spend the evening feasting on Moroccan chicken braised with eggplant, saffron, cumin, coriander, tomatoes, and onions or on fresh clams, spinach, pancetta, garlic, and Pernod on a bed of pasta. The wine list is well chosen, the desserts elaborate.

1904 Restaurant and Bar

4th and Stewart,
(206) 682-4142
1904 Fourth Avenue,
Seattle
Moderate; full bar;
AE, DC, MC, V
Lunch Mon-Fri, dinner
Mon-Sat

The 1904 is one of downtown's most desirable and consistent lunch places, and one of its most chic evening drop-in spots (serving dinner until midnight). The long, narrow dining room is strikingly modern, with glazed columns, glass bricks, and painted metal. Upstairs in the back is a bar that attracts a lively thirtyish crowd without the stigma of a singles bar. The menu has a European flavor, with Northwest touches in the form of good seafood preparations. The pasta is never a letdown: a recent serving of lemon pepper ravioli with a shrimp, vodka, and red chile sauce was delectable. The bread is fresh and tasty, the fish is usually just right. A sandwich of smoked turkey (from Seattle Super Smoke) was dressed with cranberry chutney and Jarlsberg. Seasonal specials include preparations like salmon with orange, basil, and white wine sauce; prawns in black bean sauce; or blackened halibut with shallot and watercress butter.

Omar Al-Khayam

77th and Aurora,
(206) 782-5295
7617 Aurora Avenue N,
Seattle
Inexpensive; beer and
wine; AE, DC, MC, V
Dinner every day

 ★ ★

Try to overlook the plastic flowers on the tables and the New England calendar scenes on the wall—Omar Al-Khayam is one of the least expensive, most authentic purveyors of Middle Eastern food in town. The menu includes generous shish kabobs (try the very lemony, very garlicky chicken kabob), a sublimely smoky baba ghanouj, and fatoush, a bread salad. Now there are three neighborhood branches: the Greenwood original, Renton, and Hadi's in Georgetown (the last two serve lunch). Banquet facilities in Greenwood hold parties of up to 30.

The Other Place

Union at 1st,
(206) 623-7340
96 Union Street, Seattle
Expensive; full bar;
AE, DC, MC, V
Lunch, dinner Mon-Sat

 ★ ★

Robert Rosellini's other place (now his only place) is stunning: a large, vaguely Art Deco room with booths, blond wood accents, and chandeliers that look like George Lucas–Frank Lloyd Wright collaborations. There's a sweeping view of Elliott Bay, but only if you sit in the bar, or reserve ahead for the one table with a view. For all its visual murmurings about elegance, however, The Other Place is bending over backward to emphasize its Everyman appeal. The lunch list even includes a few $6-ish sandwiches and salads, which are wonderful eaten outside on the breezy view patio.

The Rosellini trademarks still surface, however, the best being his French-inspired treatments of Northwest seafood, and the worst, his inability to hold on to good help. The menu features fish, meat, and pastas (the last available in whole or half portions), with a few lovely innovations, like a superb roast quail dish enriched with port and cream cheese. Still, many are standard combinations, competently executed, but eminently uninspired—even the seafood. It's more the occasion that you find an innovative appetizer such as the grilled prosciutto-wrapped prawns served on a plate prettily accented with a tomato sauce on one half and a basil cream on the other, or an entree of tiny scallops in a silky pool of creme fraiche lightly flavored with fennel and lemon vodka. Desserts have been fine, especially the rich chocolate numbers; and Rosellini's wine collection is still the best in the city, if not the entire region.

Phoenecia

1st and Mercer,
(206) 285-6739
100 Mercer Street,
Seattle
Moderate; beer and wine;
MC, V
Dinner Wed-Sat
(summer), Mon-Sat
(winter)

 ★ ★

Hussein Khazaal, Seattle's star Middle Eastern chef, kept his word. Two years after closing his first Phoenecia in West Seattle—to the anguish of a loyal following—he returned from recipe-hunting in North Africa to open an even better one, this in the back of the Hansen Bakery complex near Seattle Center. It is an elegant little place, done up in cerulean and purple, with billowing ceiling drapes and a pretty garden view from the loft. Unfortunately, the building is scheduled to be torn down sometime in late 1990. So Khazaal is onto another venue, this time possibly in the Pike Place Market, scheduled for opening before the demolition ball swings.

Khazaal still does baba ghanouj, tabouli, and the usual kabobs with a delicacy unusual in Middle Eastern cuisine. And he's added more exotic salads and finger foods, from Egyptian ful moudamas to savory borek pastries to an unusual Syrian lamb version of steak tartare. You can select from the menu, but the real treat is to allow a couple of hours and order one of three grades of mezaa (feast). Choose an entree—anything from couscous or a giant combination kabob to quail, pheasant, scampi, and the famous cut-with-a-spoon Egyptian chicken—and let Hussein do the rest. Two separate rooms are used exclusively for private parties.

Place Pigalle
Pike Place Market,
(206) 624-1756
5 Pike Place, Seattle
Moderate; full bar; MC, V
Lunch, dinner Mon-Sat

It's hard to find a nicer spot to watch the sky change colors at sunset, with a sliver of the moon floating high above the Sound, than in this hidden-away nook in the heart of Pike Place Market. The spiffy bistro boasts breathtaking views of Elliott Bay, windows that open to the breeze, and a thoughtful, inventive menu. Seafood is as fresh as it should be with Pike Place Fish just a staircase away. It shows up in the form of daily specials (salmon with black bean sauce and shiitake mushrooms), seasonal dishes (Alaska sea scallops filled with golden caviar and baked with salmon roe, chives, and nori in a champagne cream sauce), and perennial favorites (calamari Dijonnaise). And we have yet to find a better onion soup than the winy concoction served at "Pig Alley." We used to hear complaints about measly portions, but recent entrees have filled the plate, augmented by a fine assortment of sauteed vegetables. The wine list is outstanding and well priced, and so are the desserts: a not-too-sweet brandied apricot-almond torte served with a pitcher of cream, or a dark chocolate pot de creme. Service ranges from attentive to aloof. You can eat outdoors in summer or perch at the tiny bar with a local ale and lounge the afternoon away.

raison d'etre
1st and Virginia,
(206) 624-4622
113 Virginia Street,
Seattle
Moderate; beer and wine;
MC, V
Breakfast, lunch, dinner
every day

Nowhere in the city are there more skilled espresso artisans than at this cafe, where a broad range of the city's socioeconomic classes mixes agreeably: punk-fashionable youths at one table, three-piece-suited lawyers at another. They are drawn in by the rich aroma of espresso and the superb European-style breakfasts prepared in a tiny kitchen by the entrance—eggs Benedict with perfectly whipped hollandaise; lightly poached eggs on thick slices of sourdough bread; corned beef hash with flavorful homemade ketchup. Brioches are big and buttery, croissants are (usually) fine, and fresh fruits are carefully chosen and artistically displayed (and you pay fancy prices for these elegant preparations). The light lunch menu (offering wonderful salads) flows into dinner via a late-afternoon champagne happy hour, with specials ranging from Oregon duckling with brown rice to bay scallops ceviche to Indonesian chicken satay with jalapeno peppers, coconut-peanut sauce, and kumquats. The raison is nothing if not creative. Servers can be dreamily indifferent—an annoyance to regulars—but still, this is a wonderful spot to begin a day, or to linger when it's past. Light meals are served until midnight.

Ray's Boathouse

60th and Seaview (1 mile west of the Ballard locks), (206) 789-3770
6049 Seaview Avenue NW, Seattle
Expensive; full bar;
AE, DC, MC, V
Lunch, dinner every day

When out-of-towners request seafood-with-a-view, locals try hard to search for an alternative to Ray's—perhaps because it has become as much of a must-visit as the Pike Place Market itself. But it's tough to ignore the self-confident Ray's (which bounced back from a 1987 fire), with its atmospheric pierside ambience, very fresh seafood, casual cafe/bar up a flight, and peerless (and unabashedly romantic) vista of the Sound, the islands, the sunset. Semi-reluctantly, we all add our names to the three-week wait for a Saturday night table.

Concentrate on the simple fresh items that Ray's has proven it can do: grilled rockfish with sun-dried tomato butter; smoked black cod, meltingly broiled; scallop saute. You will find that a superb wine list (beautifully organized by country and varietal, with a page devoted to splits) and the extremely professional service almost lift the whole experience into the realm your final tab reflects—the fish is very capably done, quite good in fact, but perhaps not *this* good. Besides which, the desserts are pedestrian. A private room holds 50 guests.

At press time, Ray's was just about to open a second restaurant, Yarrow Point Grill, in Kirkland.

Salvatore Ristorante Italiano

1 block north of Ravenna Blvd on Roosevelt, (206) 527-9301
6100 Roosevelt Way NE, Seattle
Moderate; beer and wine; MC, V
Lunch Mon-Fri, dinner Mon-Sat

You'll be struck by this northeast neighborhood place of Italian heartiness. A whole wall is painted with a bright mural of a village street scene, peopled with artfully pasted-in photos of crew and friends. Much of the warmth, however, stems from Salvatore himself, who brings his amore for the southern Italian food of Basilicata—one of the country's lesser-known regions—to his north-end landing. The penne puttanesca was a fine example of the region's fondness for red pepper, while the linguine alle cozze with an unusual meld of herbs and rich sweet mussels was spiced with restraint. All in all, you will not be disappointed here. Especially if you're there on an evening when the dessert menu perks up with a tiramisu.

The Santa Fe Cafe

From I-5 take the 65th Street exit, go ¾ mile

The Gibbons brothers from Albuquerque have done an admirable job of transplanting the cuisine of New Mexico's chic-est city intact, blue corn tortillas and all. Their

east, (206) 524-7736
2255 NE 65th Street,
Seattle
Moderate; full bar; MC, V
Lunch Tues-Fri, dinner
every day

★ ★

red chile has the earthy richness, and their green the fresh zing, that are distinctly New Mexican. The sizzle in the green also has perked up as the Santa Fe has pinned down its supplies and grown more confident of its clientele. Start with the artichoke ramekin, a baked spread of artichoke with green chile and kasseri cheese served with garlic toast. The carne adovado, marinated pork in red chile wrapped in a flour tortilla, is a popular dinner, to be savored with an excellent selection of Northwest draft ales or a terrific margarita. The Phinney Ridge branch (5910 Phinney Avenue N, 206-783-9755) also offers a banquet room (seating 24), sidewalk seating, and recently a take-out menu; unless you happen to be in the Phinney Ridge neighborhood, though, the original location is preferred. No smoking at either branch.

Sea Garden

Jackson and 7th,
(206) 623-2100
509 Seventh Avenue S,
Seattle
Moderate; full bar;
AE, MC, V
Lunch, dinner every day

★ ★

The focus in this pastel International District restaurant is mellow, elegant Cantonese fare, the tamely spiced food we all enjoyed before we developed our culinary crush on fiery Sichuan and Hunan food. Fresh seafood just doesn't get much cheaper than this. Steamed crab, excellent geoduck (thinly sliced in a tangy black bean sauce), braised rock cod—it's all here, scrupulously fresh and quite consistent. Such standards as won ton soup and chow mein are infused with new subtleties (everyone agrees that the noodles are first-rate); all is served with fresh vegetables and, if requested, no MSG. The place is filled with Asians (but that's been changing lately), and, after midnight the all-night mah-jongg crowd from the district. Service is up and down.

Takara

Pike Place Market
Hillclimb between
Western and Alaskan
Way, (206) 682-8609
1501 Western Avenue,
Seattle
Moderate; beer and wine;
AE, MC, V
Lunch, dinner Mon-Sat

★ ★

An engaging little place on the Pike Place Market Hillclimb with a broad appeal for Westerners, Takara is a dandy sushi bar, with energetic chef Mimori wielding the cleaver. There is a long list of items such as deep-fried tofu with daikon sauce, moist black cod marinated in sake paste for three days, sauteed geoduck slices, and wonderful soups. As accompaniments come miso soup, ohitashi (spinach greens and sprinkles of dried fish), and oshinko (pickled cabbage). Delicious, traditional—and reasonably priced—dishes of tempura, teriyaki, and a small steak round out the menu. Patio dining is lovely in summer, when Takara is open every day.

Teger's

On 24th E, 6 blocks
south of Highway 520,
(206) 324-3373
2302 24th Avenue E,
Seattle
Moderate; beer and wine;

Montlake residents continue to love this upscale neighborhood place, where the food remains consistently pleasing, elegantly executed by Cordon Bleu–trained Chef Janice Pierce and served by her somewhat whimsical but attentive husband, Gerald. The Pierces go out of their way to meet the individual nutritional needs of each customer. Teger's normally offers some eight appetizers

MC, V
Dinner Tues-Sat

and 10 entrees each night, plus specials: poached salmon, pan-fried oysters, other in-season seafood, petit filet ("the best in town," ventured one fan), and rack of lamb. A complimentary salmon mousse appetizer and a glass of sherry begin the evening. The Pierces take one month off each summer to travel somewhere exotic and pick up a new cuisine (Spain, France, and Italy, most recently). If you have a special request, call ahead. Janice will happily prepare an enticing low-calorie or low-cholesterol selection. Careful, though: once you say you're on a diet, the Pierces will hold you to it—at least on the premises. It's best to make reservations: the place is small (some say cramped) and closed at times for private parties.

Trolleyman Pub
2 blocks west of the
Fremont Bridge on 34th
at Phinney,
(206) 548-8000
3400 Phinney Avenue N,
Seattle
Inexpensive; beer only;
MC, V
Lunch, dinner every day

If taproom manager Pamela Hinkley hadn't been so persistent, Seattle's first brew pub would have been just that: a microbrewery pouring utterly fresh Red Hook beers at the end of a brewer's tour. Hinkley's insistence brought the addition of food. And for beer drinkers who love to linger over an extra-special bitter (ESB) or a golden ale (Ballard Bitter), the black bean chili, sausage lasagne, or Mexican tomatillo casserole is the perfect accompaniment. You can sit at the long, soft-curved wooden bar, nestle in front of the fireplace on an overstuffed couch, or join your friends at one of the long community tables.

The Two Bells Tavern
4th and Bell,
(206) 441-3050
2313 Fourth Avenue,
Seattle
Inexpensive; beer and
wine; no credit cards;
no checks
Lunch, dinner every day,
brunch Sat-Sun

Everybody likes this new-wave, slightly seedy, urban tav-cum-eatery for its engaging blend of artsy atmo and cheap, delicious food. There's always a daily homemade soup or sandwich, a good Caesar, a couple of cold plates, a hot beer-sausage sandwich (two split wieners face-down in sweet hot mustard with Swiss cheese melting over the top), and, of course, the famed burger: a thick hunk of beef and plenty of onions on crusty French bread, with good chunky red-potato salad. Weekend breakfasts offer very un-tavernly things like orange-nutmeg French toast and salsa omelets. There are 25 kinds of beer.

Viet My
Just off 4th near
Washington,
(206) 382-9923
129 Prefontaine Place,
Seattle
Inexpensive; no alcohol;
no credit cards; checks ok
Lunch, dinner Mon-Fri

The name means "Vietnamese-American," in celebration of proprietor Chau Thi Tran's arrival in this hospitable locale, and its clientele is largely non-Vietnamese. But the food is very much the real Vietnamese thing, as authentic, fresh, and inexpensive as that at the slew of Jackson Street spots that serve a largely Vietnamese clientele. Avoid the lunch-hour rush, when Viet My is packed with courthouse types (who even stand to wait) and service slips, despite the addition of a few more tables. At a later lunch (till 3) or dinner, you can dine like a noble at peasant prices (in decidedly non-royal surroundings, however). Even the standard rice-paper rolls (a cleaner, non-fried version of the usual egg rolls) seem tastier at Viet My, and they're sold singly (just 80 cents), a boon for single diners. Soups (especially the spicy chicken and seafood combination), curries, and stir-fries are uniformly good. The star dish, however, is *bo la lot,* beef chunks marinated to an ecstatic succulence and roasted in aromatic leaves; you unpeel the leaf, then roll your own, mu-shu–style, in rice-paper pancakes, with the ubiquitous bean sprouts, cilantro, and fresh basil. After *bo la lot,* no fajita can impress.

A Little Bit of Saigon
12th and S Jackson,
(206) 325-3663
1036B S Jackson Street,
Seattle
Inexpensive; beer and
wine; MC, V
Lunch, dinner every day

The name's a beguiling misnomer. A Little Bit of Saigon, hidden around the back of Asian Plaza, is probably the biggest Vietnamese place in town. It nicely fulfills the first rule of ethnic restaurants: it's a favorite of native eaters, but friendly and accommodating to outsiders. And it hews squarely to the rule that, while Thai food gets trendier and pricier, Vietnamese restaurants remain the cheapest places to eat well. A Little Bit of Saigon's menu is weighted somewhat toward the meat dishes and pho (beef and noodle soups) of North Vietnam, but you can also make a whole meal out of the excellent appetizers (skewers of marinated pork with lemongrass, lemon juice, and garlic, and excellent spring rolls). Sublime pho is the focus of their sister take-out shop next door, Pho 88, 1036A S Jackson Street, (206) 325-0180.

Angkor Thom
Near Washington and
4th, (206) 624-6677
212 Fourth Avenue S,
Seattle
Inexpensive; no alcohol;
no credit cards; checks ok
Lunch, dinner Mon-Sat

"Angkor Thom" means "The Great City" in Khmer and refers to the vast expanse of temples and palaces surrounding the famous Angkor Wat—a site of indescribable national pride for the Khmers of Cambodia. But this Angkor Thom is operated by a (very gracious) Cambodian-Chinese family, and its fare is more mainstream Chinese and Thai than quintessentially Cambodian. As such, it's competently prepared, with no MSG, but with the spicy edges rubbed off and less exhilarating than that in the best Thai and Chinese places. For example, "beef with lemongrass" is a standard stir-fry with green pepper and onions and no discernible lemongrass. For a more characteristic Khmer taste, try the refreshing "Cambodian salad" laced with shrimp paste and peanuts, the deliciously marinated "special Angkor beef," or the mchou kreung ktis firepot soup, chicken and pineapple in a rich coconut and tamarind stock. Or make an emphatic request for special Cambodian preparations, which the Khmer cook can fulfill. The soup firepots—ring-shaped mini-cauldrons around a charcoal fire—are a fun and very authentic presentation, but their contents are rather pricey. Otherwise, prices are reasonable, especially lunch specials. Angkor Thom has also begun to serve breakfasts of continental standards as well as yum bao and hum bao. Here's hoping it comes to trust more Seattle's receptivity to unfamiliar cuisines, dips deeper into the prahok fish paste, and starts really cooking Cambodian.

Bai Tong

Across from Lewis and Clark Theater on S 160th, (206) 241-1122
3423 S 160th Street, Seattle
Inexpensive; beer and wine; MC, V
Lunch, dinner every day

Stashed away near Sea-Tac airport, Bai Tong ("Banana Leaf") is probably the least-known to the general market of Seattle's fast-proliferating Thai restaurants, and certainly the most popular among the local Thai community. (It's attached to a motel owned by a Thai International Airways employee, and for a time existed exclusively to service the employees and friends of the airline company.) You'll see few *farong* (Caucasians), and the loud, singsong chatter in Thai and soft lilting Thai music lend an irresistible air of authenticity. The food is authentic too—maybe almost *too* authentic for some palates. No fooling around with one, two, or three stars; when you order a curry, it simply arrives the way it should be, at a solid four stars. Make a point of asking for the fragrant and succulent marinated chicken in aromatic leaf, which isn't on the menu but is always available. Desserts are served in true Thai style from a stack of plastic-cartoned confections by the register. Service can be erratic; we started with a waitress who was gracious as only the Thai can be and wound up with another who was grim and inattentive. Don't *sawasdee* unless you're ready for a full-tilt Thai conversation.

The Chile Pepper

50th and University Way NE, (206) 526-5004
5000 University Way NE, Seattle
Inexpensive; beer and wine; no credit cards; checks ok
Lunch, dinner Mon-Sat

Hidden behind the inauspicious exterior and the fast-foodish-sounding name is one of Seattle's most distinctive Mexican restaurants. The Chile Pepper serves authentic regional cuisine of mountainous Guanajuato, home state of proprietor Rodolfo and his chef and mother Catalina Gonzales. The chicken mole poblano is neither the Oaxacan chocolate nor the bland peanut sauce found elsewhere, but a rich, redolent infusion of tomatillo, sesame, almonds, cinnamon, cloves, laurel, and diverse other spices. The puerco en adobo is an equally complex balance of fiery, sweet, and tangy flavors, topped by that signature cinnamon. Their chiles rellenos are usually the best in town—piquant deep-red dried chiles anchos lightly battered and cleanly fried, with sweet, sour, and spicy accents in the usual cheese filling—but a recent sample was not up to their usual standard. And service seems to be sliding. We hope success hasn't gone to their heads, because we love the low-key atmosphere. Fresh limeade (no American lemons here, thank you) and, at long last, beer and wine cool the fire.

Copacabana

Pike Place Market,
(206) 622-6359
1520½ Pike Place,
Seattle
Moderate; beer and wine;
AE, DC, MC, V
Lunch every day,
dinner Mon-Sat

Seattle is home to two Bolivian restaurants—both the Copacabana. Neither recall the authenticity of Ramon Palaez's original Pike Place Market dive—the one with the counter that tilted so much that servers had to jam forks beneath the plates to keep them upright—but the Market branch comes closer, with a splendid sun deck for viewing Elliott Bay and the human condition on Pike Place. The family recipes are still used: the spicy shrimp soup; saltenas, juicy meat-and-raisin stuffed pastries; huminta, a piquant corn pie topped with cheeses; poached halibut with sauteed onion and tomato in a mild saffron sauce. Like the Spanish, Bolivians seem to cook everything to death, and everything here is pricier than you'd expect—but not too bad. The second outpost, on the upper level of the Broadway Market, (206) 323-7554, though quite good, seems shiny and strategized, with a long list of snacks for strolling grazers and nods to Mexican and Chilean cuisines in addition to Bolivian.

Gravity Bar

Below the Inn at the
Market between Stewart
and Pine, off 1st,
(206) 443-9694
86 Pine Street, Seattle
Inexpensive; no alcohol;
no credit cards; checks ok
Breakfast, lunch, dinner
every day (closes at 6pm)

Unless glowing neon and wheatgrass juice are already part of your daily routine, you'll probably feel as though you're walking into a private Plutonian party as you enter this electric-hip juice bar. Don't let it stop you: this is good, vegetarian, body-mind-soul food—thick fingers of Russian rye bread covered with smoky mozzarella and sun-dried tomatoes; open-faced pine-nut, pesto, and chevre sandwiches; a bowl of brown rice, tofu, and steamed vegetables in a lemon-tahini dressing; miso soup with buckwheat noodles—things like that. Wash it all down with a shot of the slime-colored wheatgrass potion and a chaser of carrot-pineapple juice. Service is ridiculously slow. A second location (on Broadway between Harrison and Republic) stays open until midnight on weekends (but watch out for the after-movie rush); (206) 325-7186.

The Green Village

On King between 7th and
8th, (206) 624-3634
721 S King Street,
Seattle
Moderate; beer and wine;
MC, V
Lunch, dinner every day

Once there was an ineffable thrill of discovery about the Green Village: a cheaply appointed International District walk-up, where mysterious machinery below shook the floor and Joby Lu cooked the tastiest Chinese fare in town. But fire ravaged those quarters, and success enabled the Lu clan to occupy the elegant, pink-toned ground-floor quarters of the old Quong Tuck Company up King Street. The reborn Green Village is still a very pleasant place to dine, with excellent cheery service and due respect given to both the Mandarin and Sichuan traditions it incorporates. But whether because Joby is less active in the kitchen or because the food no longer brazenly outclasses its setting, the thrill has faded some. Shredded chicken and mu-shu pork are now just good, not breathtaking. The signature, finely chopped "eggplant Sichuan-style," seems to come with less fire and in a little bigger pool of oil each time.

House of Hong

8th S and Jackson,
(206) 622-7997
409 Eighth Avenue S,
Seattle
Moderate; full bar;
AE, DC, MC, V
Lunch, dinner every day

If you drive down Eighth Avenue S on a Sunday morning a few minutes before 11am, you're sure to notice, just off Jackson, a throng of Chinese families three generations strong, milling about in their Sunday best. No, this is not some storefront church discharging the faithful after the morning's services. These are food worshipers, waiting for the doors to open on the International District's best dim sum. No other restaurant in the area prepares these Cantonese teahouse delicacies with such finesse. Shrimp balls, shumai, and pork ribs are refined in flavor and texture; the fried dumplings contain a wonderfully gingery pork filling; the duck feet are the best in town; and all are wheeled to your table piping hot (though by midafternoon both the selection and the temperature begin to diminish a bit).

House of Hong, with its dusty-pink decor and court-yardlike layout, serves dependable dinners, with seafood carrying the banner: prawns in lobster sauce are ambrosial, and steamed black cod in ginger oil is a special delight. Others praise the order-ahead banquets (served in a private room), the earthy qualities of the home-style dishes (salted fish and fried rice), and the customer parking lot—no small plus in this crowded district.

Jake O'Shaughnessey's

1st and Mercer, north
side of Seattle Center,
(206) 285-1897
100 Mercer Street, Seattle
Moderate; full bar;
AE, DC, MC, V
Dinner every day

The building is set for demolition in August of 1990, and owner Tim Firnstahl is negotiating (at press time) a new spot to house this popular steak and seafood joint that launched him and former partner Mick McHugh into restaurateur superstardom. We're confident the new venue will be just as busy.

The formula remains: there's the young (albeit over-drilled) help, the high quality of food and drink, and the reasonable prices (a tab perhaps two-thirds of what you'd pay at similar downtown spots). The dining room retains its noisy, saloonlike atmosphere (sedate, however, compared with the boisterous bar) and continues to feature the reputation-building aged beef and baked russets, but is turning increasingly in the direction of fish—some dozen variants on our last visit. We sampled an order of fresh halibut with lime-ginger butter on the side, and shark with red pepper–Parmesan butter. Both come with a pile of crisp-cooked vegetables and a choice of three okay salads. There are flaws, certainly—fish may be overcooked, the sauteed artichoke hearts are a spiny disappointment, and the quality-control people cruising the

Looking for a particular place? Check the index at the back of this book for individual restaurants, lodgings, attractions, and more.

floor may leave you feeling supervised. But Jake's, more than any other restaurant in Seattle, goes a long way toward convincing us that even a formula restaurant can have a soul.

Kells
Between Stewart and
Virginia on Post Alley,
(206) 728-1916
1916 Post Alley, Seattle
Moderate; full bar;
MC, V
Lunch, dinner Mon-Sat

This Irish pub–style restaurant in Post Alley fits perfectly into the rich ethnic mix of Pike Place Market. The food is straightforward, but often surprisingly good: meat pies, leg of lamb, a warming bowl of coddle, broiled fish, and roasted chicken—hearty, hot, and accompanied by particularly good soda bread. They get a little fancier with their specials. We had some wonderful sole stuffed with a crab mousse and garnished with pretty vegetables. The friendly staff is Irish to the core. Drop by for a pint of ale in the cozy bar; there's live Irish music Wednesday through Saturday nights.

La Rive Gauche
On 2nd between
Blanchard and Bell,
(206) 441-8121
2214 Second Avenue,
Seattle
Moderate; full bar;
AE, MC, V
Lunch Mon-Fri,
dinner Mon-Sat

Here's one we like more for what it is than for what it does. Jean-Paul and Nina Kissel have re-created a drop-in-casual Left Bank bistro in Belltown (open late night), with a menu starring the simple neighborhood food of France: a plate of simply steamed mussels in cream; couscous; a beautiful, complex cassoulet; Paris' ubiquitous steak and frites. It can be fine (more often at dinner than at lunch), and the linger-awhile mood that prevails with Kissel at the helm and neighborhood regulars at the bar sipping chardonnay is irresistible. Execution is frequently off, though, and the diner might run into stingy portions or a fatty steak. Still, the tasty bouillabaisse; the salad with Jarlsberg, bacon, and potatoes; and the Armagnac-flavored, raisin-studded ice cream all provide toothsome reminders of how good the peasant-born aliments of France can be.

Lao Charearn
Off Washington, between
3rd and 4th,
(206) 223-9456
121 Prefontaine Place S,
Seattle
Inexpensive; beer; no
credit cards; no checks
Lunch Mon-Fri,
dinner Mon-Sat

If the menu reminds you of the last Thai restaurant you stopped in, don't worry; you're not experiencing culinary flashback. The differences between Lao Charearn's spring rolls, "phud thai lao," lard narr, and curries and the same dishes at your usual Thai spot are slight to indistinguishable. Which doesn't mean this isn't an authentic Lao restaurant, simply that the cultural and historic ties between Laos and Thailand are many and deep. But the familiar dishes are prepared well and reliably here, the service is friendly, and, most notable, the prices are lower than those at most Thai restaurants. The curries are unexceptional, but the soups are excellent: the usual shrimp hot-and-sour (toom yum goong) and chicken-coconut (toom kah gai), plus hearty concoctions of vegetables, pork, and seafood, and vegetables and meatballs in Chinese-style clear broths. The phud phet neua, beef with chile, green beans, and sweet basil, and other stir-fries are also recommended. And of course there's Thai Singha beer to wash it all down. Lao Charearn's location is an apt metaphor for Lao's geopolitical situation: a Vietnamese restaurant on one side, and the Thai Video Store on the other.

Leschi Lakecafe
Alder and Lakeside S,
(206) 328-2233
102 Lakeside Avenue S,
Seattle
Moderate; full bar;
AE, DC, MC, V
Lunch, dinner every day

The place simply tries too hard. You are besieged with information about the historic site, the sources of seafood, exactly how the tea is brewed, and on and on. Despite the overload, the staff is less than helpful when you ask a question they are not programmed for, and service can be shaky even with all the drilling. The result is a place that ends up making you nervous and a little embarrassed for all its effort to produce passable food. The seafood is good, if they get the orders right, and the beer selection in the bar is extensive. Best to come for some fish 'n' chips, sit outside (it's very pretty), and stay away when the crowds arrive, by boat and BMW.

Lofurno's
1 mile south of the
Ballard Bridge on 15th
W, (206) 283-7980
2060 15th Avenue W,
Seattle
Moderate; full bar;
AE, MC, V
Dinner every day

It's easy to drive by this place on 15th Avenue West, but once you're inside it's tough to leave. Lofurno's is an unassuming, intimate neighborhood Italian restaurant with a jazz piano, high-backed booths, and a dying breed of staff (veteran waiters and bartenders pulled from a better time and place—say, Chicago, 1948). Phil Lofurno is a restaurateur's restaurateur, and his food lives up to the atmosphere. The pasta is heavy on the garlic (to the delight of most of the diners); the thick, flavorful marinara sauce is a welcome antidote to the light Northern Italian fare all over town; and the house salad is loaded with Gorgonzola. There's a long list of veal preparations, including one rolled in raisins and pine nuts with a mushroom-and-Marsala cream sauce.

The Maddox Grill
Take 185th Street exit
from Highway 99, head
west 1 mile,
(206) 542-4766
638 NW Richmond
Beach Road, Seattle
Moderate; full bar;
MC, V
Lunch Mon-Sat,
dinner every day

Browny's in Richmond Beach, named for original owner Michael "Browny" Brown, was succeeded in mid-1989 by The Maddox Grill, named for new owner Rick Maddox. The restaurant still stands alone in the parking lot of a North Seattle mini-shopping center. Inside, wooden latticework creates an airy, almost gazebolike environment. Fresh fish, respectfully prepared, and friendly, attentive service continue to be the restaurant's strong suits, although recent visits show signs of inconsistency. We found the marlin steaks cooked exactly right: grilled just long enough to leave them moist but not underdone, and gently seasoned by mesquite charcoal. A pineapple chutney, properly restrained to avoid overpowering the delicate marlin, added interest. Less successful were the calamari (rubbery from overcooking) and the tiger shrimp (upstaged by an aggressive though tasty black bean sauce). The New England–style clam chowder, a long-time favorite at Browny's, was a shade watery. The wine list, moderate in price and depth, naturally favors whites. Doodlers and kids will like the paper tablecloths and crayons.

Maximilien-in-the-Market
Pike Place Market,
(206) 682-7270
81-A Pike Place Market,
Seattle
Moderate; full bar;
AE, DC, MC, V
Breakfast, lunch, dinner
Mon-Sat, brunch Sun

Francois and Julia Kissel's French market cafe in the Main Arcade is a splendid place—full of noble antiques and blessed with a view of Elliott Bay—with fare that has been increasingly inconsistent. In addition to croissants, espresso, and so on, breakfasts include a souffle and homemade sage sausage. At lunch, you can get anything from country pate with cornichons to dilled meatballs with nutmeg sauce, but we suggest you keep it simple and order the fish and chips or a Maximilien burger with grilled onions on French bread. Even the dinners, which range from grilled sweetbreads in mustard-caper sauce to a halibut and red snapper soup, have recently proved to be less appealing: one evening we encountered a disappointing sole amandine and an unremarkable salmon and shrimp salad. Until there are drastic changes in the kitchen, we recommend you meet upstairs in the bar, nibble on steamed mussels, and finish off the evening with bread pudding, topped with Francois's incomparable caramel sauce—desserts are a consistent strong point at Maximilien's. The bar is available for private parties up to 30.

McCormick's Fish House & Bar
4th and Columbia,
(206) 682-3900
722 Fourth Avenue,
Seattle
Moderate; full bar;
AE, DC, MC, V
Lunch Mon-Fri,
dinner every day

This may be the best of the downtown fish houses (not that that's saying much), and it certainly is the most popular. Lunch is noisy and frenetic, the bar jams up with City Hall–types after 5pm, and even dinners feel crowded —particularly during the tourist season. Make reservations. The formula here is simple: the heavy-on-seafood menu, printed daily, offers several types of fish prepared in largely simple ways (grilled with a flavored butter, sauteed with another butter, baked more elaborately). Preparation can be uneven—we've had tough and lukewarm tuna aided only slightly by its Madeira and rosemary butter—but you can usually rely on decent cooking and generous portions. Oysters are fine, salads pedestrian, the wine list carefully chosen and overpriced, the beautifully fresh sourdough bread always a treat. We'd enjoyed a run of good service until a recent evening, when our lingering party was evicted from a table to make room for a larger group. (The next day's elaborate apology and make-up gift certificate provided some mollification.)

Mediterranean Kitchen
On the corner of Queen
Anne and Roy, northwest
of Seattle Center,
(206) 285-6713

This is the most garlicky kitchen in town. But there are other distinctions, notably the presence of owner-chef Kamal Aboul Hosn, a Lebanese. He serves fare from the entire Mediterranean basin and even has an Afghan chicken burger. His zahrah (cauliflower florets with a light

4 W Roy Street, Seattle
Inexpensive; beer and
wine; AE, MC, V

tahini dressing) are the best in town; we also appreciate his North African couscous (with carrots, potatoes, onions, and a spoon-tender lamb shank braised in a to-mato-based sauce) and a Lebanese farmer's dish of broiled chicken wings and rice in—naturally—garlic sauce. Enormous quantities (even with the appetizers) at very low prices have earned this place institution status (the couscous lasted us through two more lunches). This is the place to go with an appetite; you'll actually be turned away at the door if all you want is soup or appetizers.

Metropolitan Grill
2nd and Marion,
(206) 624-3287
818 Second Avenue,
Seattle
Moderate; full bar; AE,
DC, MC, V; checks OK
Lunch Mon-Fri, dinner
every day

This handsome haunt in the heart of the financial district does a booming business among stockbrokers and Asian tourists. The soul of the restaurant is its steaks, and you'd do well to stick to them, since they really do live up to the hoopla. Pastas and appetizers are less well executed, but a growing list of large, appealing salads (and terrific clam chowder) presents a good alternative to beef for the lunch crowd. There's a lot of table-hopping going on here, which puts the poker-faced waiters in even nastier spirits. Financiers like to use the Met's private room (holds 34) as a dependable venue for private dinners.

Pho Hoa
Columbian Way exit off
I-5 to Rainier Avenue,
(206) 723-1508
4406 Rainier Avenue S,
Seattle
Inexpensive, no alcohol;
no credit cards; no checks
Breakfast, lunch, dinner
every day

We're not usually in the business of saluting chain restaurants, but this one has two mitigating qualifications and one compelling one: it's a very small chain, based in the Vietnamese-American heartland of Orange County; it's such a heartening reuse of an old Kentucky Fried Chicken shack; and it serves the best bowl of pho in Seattle. Pho (pronounced like the French *feu*) is the ubiquitous breakfast, lunch, and anytime quick meal of Vietnam, a soup of rice noodles, scallions, and beef in a clear broth that, like a good bagel, is one of the irreducible perfect food forms. Pho Hoa, like a good Saigon soup stand, serves only pho, in 15 different forms (from rare steak to tendon to beef balls). But it's the broth that figuratively as well as literally carries the pho, and Pho Hoa's is bracingly rich and fragrant with a mysterious infusion of spices. Bowl sizes vary from ample to enormous, all ridiculously cheap. On the side is the full complement of garnishes—lime, fresh herbs, chiles, and bean sprouts —to finish your pho to taste. And though alcohol's lacking here, as in most Vietnamese restaurants, fresh-squeezed orange juice, soy milk, and super-concentrated Vietnamese coffee more than fill its place.

The Pink Door
Pike Place Market,
(206) 443-3241
1919 Post Alley, Seattle
Moderate; full bar; MC, V

It feels awfully clandestine: you enter through a pink door (there isn't any sign) in the alley and descend a flight of stairs. The idea is exemplary: an inexpensive trattoria with cheap wine, reasonably good pasta, and a sort of built-in cachet. At lunch, the large room grows noisy

Lunch, dinner Tues-Sat

around a burbling fountain, and the service becomes forgetful. To be safe, stick with the pasta selections—especially the fettuccine with clam sauce or the spinach fettuccine with salmon and cream. In warm weather, owner Jacki Roberts opens a splendid outdoor cafe on the roof with a pleasant view of Elliott Bay. At night, when the pace slows, the tables are lit by candlelight, the service becomes more attentive, and you can dine—prix-fixe—on four courses that always end with a salad. The quality of cooking is still uneven, but certain dishes—a full-bodied cioppino, a wonderful bubbling lasagne, a Gorgonzola soup we'll never forget—can shine. The decor is overflowing with silly Italian kitsch, but it's cheerful. Later you can order nibbles in the bar and watch the entertainment (sometimes cabaret).

Restaurant Shilla
Denny Way and 8th, across from Denny Park, (206) 623-9996 2300 Eighth Avenue, Seattle Moderate; full bar; AE, DC, MC, V Lunch Mon-Fri, dinner every day

We've received lots of mixed reports on this converted oversized motel coffeeshop which now holds its own as a Japanese/Korean restaurant. Lunches are easy on the purse ($5–$7) and include nabeyaki udon (a steaming cast-iron kettle full of fat noodles in a vegetable and shiitake mushroom broth) and makanouchi bento (a Japanese sampler of sashimi, tempura, steamed vegetables, and rice). We advise to avoid the sushi and order the Korean national dish, bul ko ki, and you can cook it yourself—sliced beef, chicken, ribs, squid, or even seldom-ordered organ meats (this is true Korean)—at a table fitted with a hibachi barbecue. Seven kinds of kim chee are made on the premises. At dinner it's all a little pricier than you'd find in the International District, but the Korean fare, at least, is worth it.

Salute
Corner of 35th NE and NE 55th, just north of University Village, (206) 527-8600 3410 NE 55th Street, Seattle Moderate; beer and wine; MC, V Dinner Tues-Sun

Breathless crowds keep returning to this convivial Italian neighborhood joint for the reasonably priced meals, the warmth of Raffaele Calise's hostmanship, and the best pizza this side of Naples (on those nights when the kitchen slows down to bake the dough enough). Rabid popularity, alas, almost spoiled it—regulars are sometimes annoyed with the long wait to eat and the "move 'em out" urgency in the waiters' attitude. Recent reports, however, indicate that the food is now keeping pace with the crowd: the pastas have been coming out al dente, and the sauces are more correct than in the past. Many items are still not inspired, but we'll vouch for the antipasto misto (thin slices of Japanese eggplant lightly fried, a peppery frittata wedge, tender bay scallops with roasted peppers), a terrific spaghetti marinara, and a plate of cold squid simply dressed with lemon, oil, and garlic. Exuberant charm just oozes out of this place—right down to the

---

The facts in this edition were correct at press time, but places close, chefs depart, hours change. It's best to call ahead.

Italian accent of the waiter who's never been to Italy. A new deli, Salute da Portare, at 7500 35th Avenue NE, (206) 522-8580, services Wedgwood with fresh pasta, sauces, and pizza (take-out only).

Testa Rossa
At Broadway E and E Olive (2nd floor),
(206) 328-0878
210 Broadway E, Seattle
Inexpensive; beer and wine; AE, MC, V;
checks ok
Lunch Mon-Sat,
dinner every day

The main draw at this sparkling, bright Broadway eatery is stuffed pizza—the closest analogy we can draw being four and twenty blackbirds baked in a pie. These rich pies ooze all manner of fabulous treats: San Remo sun-dried tomatoes, roasted eggplant and red peppers, fennel sausage, pine nuts, Montrachet cheese, pesto, artichoke hearts. All this bounty is laced together with milky, top-quality domestic mozzarella and reggianito cheese from Argentina, and then bathed in a rich tomato sauce. The crust, its taste alive with yeast, delivers flavor as well as texture. The basic stuffed pizza easily serves three, especially if those three have nibbled through the wait with focaccia or pumate spread, a pleasing mix of sun-dried tomatoes, ricotta, cream cheese, and garlic. The smokeless atmosphere buzzes cheerfully. Testa Rossa is open until 1am on Friday and Saturday, and until midnight the rest of the week.

Tlaquepaque
Seneca and Post Alley,
(206) 467-8226
1122 Post Alley, Seattle
Moderate; full bar;
AE, DC, MC, V
Lunch Mon-Sat,
dinner every day

Don't come here if you're looking for quiet conversation: Tlaquepaque is about as quiet as a Mexican plaza on *Cinco de Mayo.* Mariachi music, crowds of chatty patrons, and the occasional whoops and hollers that ensue when some poor soul orders a tequila popper blend into a general festive cacophony. In spite of all the fuss, however, the food is pretty authentic, running to the fancier meats and seafoods of Mexico's Gulf Coast. A hearty pollo laredo topped with melted cheese and served with fresh vegetables, fabulous mesquite-broiled fajitas, and cabrito (milk-fed baby goat) defy the usual Cal-Mex lineup of burritos and such (which aren't on the menu but are available on request). The colorful, rough-walled space in the Cornerstone sector of Post Alley is the perfect home for all this noisiness (you can rent the upstairs level for a festive gathering of 75), and it's packed during happy hour. A little deli across the alley sells their tortillas and salsas plus tasty breakfast and lunch tidbits to go.

LODGINGS

Four Seasons Olympic Hotel
5th and University,
(206) 621-1700, toll-free
(800) 223-8772
411 University Street,
Seattle, WA 98101

Quiet elegance and gracious service make this hotel Seattle's class act. The Olympic has been a Seattle landmark since the 1920s, and now it is refurbished in a style befitting its earlier grandeur. The rooms (450 on 11 floors) are softly lit and tastefully furnished in period reproductions; they're not always as luxurious as you might expect, but their simplicity is refreshing. The finishing

Expensive; AE, DC, MC, V

touches are exacting: valet parking, 24-hour full room service, a stocked bar, chocolates on your pillow, complimentary shoeshines, and a terrycloth robe for each guest. A massage in the hotel's health club—where you can swim against the backdrop of the city skyline—will complete your stay. A team of well-informed concierges offers uncommonly good service; indeed, the staff exhibits just the right blend of unobtrusiveness and thorough care.

The Olympic is further distinguished by its grand public rooms: armchairs, potted plants, marble galore, tapestries, wood paneling. You can lounge amid the swaying palms in the skylit Garden Court, taking afternoon tea with Devonshire cream and scones, finger sandwiches, and sweets, if you wish. The showcase dining room, the Georgian Room, is a handsome space; downstairs is the livelier Shuckers, an oyster bar with excellent mixed drinks. There are several elegant meeting rooms (the ornate Spanish Ballroom for large affairs), and the retail spaces off the lobby offer the best boutique shopping in town. Room prices are steep, especially when there are few views, but this is Seattle's one venerable, world-class contender, and the service (and location) cannot be bested.

Alexis Hotel

1st and Madison,
(206) 624-4844, toll-free
(800) 426-7033
1007 First Avenue,
Seattle, WA 98104
Expensive; AE, DC, MC, V

Few cities can boast a hotel as elegant as the Alexis—a gem carved out of a lovely turn-of-the-century building in a stylish section of downtown near the waterfront. It's small (54 rooms), full of tasteful touches (televisions concealed in armoires, complimentary sherry upon arrival), and decorated with the suave modernity of Michael Graves' postmodern colors. You'll be pampered here, with Jacuzzis and real-wood fireplaces in some of the suites, a steam room that can be reserved just for you, nicely insulated walls between rooms to ensure privacy, and a concierge at the ready. Other amenities include complimentary continental breakfasts, a morning newspaper of your choice, shoeshines, a guest membership to the Seattle Club (eight blocks north), and a range of cuisine options from elegant Northwest dinners (Cafe Alexis) to all-American breakfasts (92 Madison). No convention facilities: the Alexis favors well-heeled travelers on the Stanford Court–Pierre circuit who prefer quiet poshness. It is a hotel where the front-desk people always know your name and will solve any problem (they're especially helpful with advice about the city).

However, the Alexis is still not a hotel of world-class performance. The staff is very young and lacks the air (and polished skill) of seasoned help. Lately, we've gotten reports of understocked rooms and loud air conditioner noise. And there are no views. We suggest booking a room that faces the inner courtyard; rooms facing First Avenue can be noisy. Or book next door in the jointly managed Arlington Suites—spaces geared to longer stays, with views, kitchens, and full Alexis maid and room service. They're also less expensive.

Inn at the Market
1st and Pine,
(206) 443-3600, toll-free
(800) 446-4484
86 Pine Street, Seattle,
WA 98101
Expensive; AE, DC,
MC, V

It's become one of the finest places to stay in the city, largely because of the location. You are right in the famous Pike Place Market, looking out over its rooftops to the lovely bay beyond. The hotel is small—65 rooms—so service can approximate that of a country inn; and you won't feel oppressed by conventioneers (there's just one meeting room). The architecture is quite good (by the local firm of Ibsen Nelsen), with oversized rooms, bay windows that let even some of the side rooms enjoy big views, and a configuration that is a modern version of a medieval inn built around a central courtyard. Opening off the courtyard are smart shops, a sumptuous spa, the elegant Campagne Restaurant (see review), and the eccentric Gravity Bar.

The hotel struggled in its first years, but now its management is under the Alexis folks. With no in-house kitchen, room service is a problem (although you may order from the Gravity Bar or from the nearby du jour), and there is no complimentary breakfast, but there are great places to discover right out the door, especially in the morning when it all resembles a bustling Parisian market. A hotel in America's finest public market is a marvel.

Sorrento Hotel
9th and Madison,
(206) 622-6400, toll-free
(800) 426-1265
900 Madison Street,
Seattle, WA 98104
Expensive; AE, DC,
MC, V

When the Sorrento opened in 1909—in time for the Alaska-Yukon-Pacific Exposition—it commanded a bluff overlooking the young city and Puget Sound. For years thereafter, it was the most elegant hotel in the city— Renaissance architecture modeled after a castle in Sorrento, with Honduras mahogany in the lobby and a famous dining room on the top floor. The place faded badly, and the view was lost as the city grew up around the hotel. Then, in 1981, it was fixed up and reopened. It's a real beauty. The mahogany lobby is now a fireside lounge that is a fine place for talking or afternoon tea. The rooms (76 of them) are decorated in muted, tasteful coziness with a slight Oriental accent. We recommend the 08 series of suites, in the corners. Suites on the top floor make elegant quarters for special meetings or parties—the showstopper being the $700 penthouse, with its grand piano, six-person hot tub on the deck, view of the bay, and multiple rooms all steeped in luxury. The location, up the hill five blocks from the heart of downtown, may

Would you like to order a copy of Best Places *for a friend? There's an order form at the back of this book.*

be inconvenient, but it's somewhat quieter. The recently remodeled main restaurant, The Hunt Club, boasts a fine menu and food more worthy of its lustrous new setting (see review).

Westin Hotel

Between Stewart and Virginia on 5th, (206) 728-1000, toll-free (800) 228-3000 1900 Fifth Avenue, Seattle, WA 98101 Expensive; AE, DC, MC, V

Westin, a major international chain, is headquartered in Seattle, so this flagship hotel has quite a few extras. The twin cylindrical towers may be called corncobs by the natives, but they afford spacious rooms with superb views, particularly above the 20th floor (this is the only remaining hotel in town with unobstructed Puget Sound views). Convention facilities, spread over several floors of meeting rooms, are quite complete. There is a large pool, along with an exercise room and a licensed masseuse. On the top floors are some ritzy, glitzy suites. The location, near shopping and the monorail station, is excellent. Trader Vic's is still here (one of the better ones in the chain), as well as a posh restaurant, The Palm Court. For more casual dining, try the good (though overpriced) Market Cafe, and perhaps later a drink at Fitzgerald's, the long, dark cocktail bar.

Beech Tree Manor

Lee Street and Queen Anne, (206) 281-7037 1405 Queen Anne Avenue N, Seattle, WA 98109 Inexpensive; AE, DC, MC, V

Virginia Lucero has taken this 1904 mansion on Queen Anne Hill and transformed it, with floral prints and original artwork, into a stunning bed and breakfast. The decor, though rich and detailed, is neither fussy nor foreign; it simply hits the mark. The extras in this four-bedroom, three-bath inn include all-cotton sheets and pillowcases, extra-large towels, a back porch with wicker furniture, an antique lace and linen shop, and a small patio for summer reading or breakfasting. Concierge services are provided, and the manor is available for receptions and seminars. Pets and children okay. Smoking is restricted.

Gaslight Inn

15th and Howell, (206) 325-3654 1727 15th Avenue, Seattle, WA 98122 Moderate; AE, MC, V

Praised by repeat guests and bed-and-breakfast owners alike, the Gaslight is one of the loveliest, most reasonably priced, and friendliest bed and breakfasts in town. Trevor Logan and Steve Bennett have polished the turn-of-the-century mansion into an eight-guestroom jewel: six with private baths, all decorated in distinct styles—some contemporary, some antique. Outside are three decks, a large heated swimming pool, and a shady arbor. No pets or kids under 12. Smoking is okay.

Holiday Inn Crowne Plaza

6th and Seneca, (206) 464-1980, toll-free (800) 521-2762 Sixth and Seneca, Seattle, WA 98104

This hotel bends over backward for the repeat and corporate visitor. The striking top-floor rooms, which are comfortable and very clean, receive (at a slightly higher price) a lot of individual attention: free papers, a lounge, and their own concierge desk. Guests on lower floors stay in spacious but rather bland rooms and must venture to

Expensive; AE, DC, MC, V

the 32nd floor to use the concierge services. The lobby is elegant and comfortable, the staff attentive and accommodating. In addition to the pleasant Parkside Cafe, there's the pricier Parkside Restaurant (open for dinner only). Conference rooms and parking (for a fee) are available. The location is ideal—right downtown, near the freeway, and two blocks from the convention center.

Mayflower Park Hotel
4th and Olive,
(206) 623-8700, toll-free
(800) 426-5100
405 Olive Way, Seattle,
WA 98101
Expensive; AE, DC,
MC, V

A handsome 1927 hotel, located right in the heart of the downtown shopping district. The coolly elegant lobby opens onto Oliver's Lounge on one side and Clipper's, one of the prettiest breakfast places in town, on the other. Rooms are small, bearing charming reminders of the hotel's past: lovely Oriental brass and antique appointments; large, deep tubs; thick walls that trap noise. Modern intrusions are for both better and worse: double-paned windows in all rooms keep out traffic noise, but the new furnishings in many of the rooms are undistinguished. Rooms in the 15 series are slightly bigger and have corner views; aim for one on a higher floor or you may find yourself facing a brick wall. The 21 series mini-suites are brand new and are distinguished by their French provincial decor. For $10 more, you're a guest member at an athletic club four blocks away. The mezzanine is now a direct link into splashy Westlake Mall.

Meany Tower Hotel
45th and Brooklyn,
University District,
(206) 634-2000
4507 Brooklyn Avenue
NE, Seattle, WA 98105
Moderate; AE, DC,
MC, V

Old-timers might not recognize their favorite U District hotel, formerly the University Tower. The distinguished 1930s design remains, but inside there are double-paned windows and air conditioning, and the whole place—lobby and rooms—is quite cloyingly turned out in shades of peach. Each room has a bay window with a good view, and those on the south side are sunny. The bathrooms sparkle. Doubles run around $85. You're one block from shopping on "The Ave" and two blocks from the University of Washington campus. The hotel's restaurant, The Meany Grill, is prettified with brass and deep green, but the food isn't much. The bar boasts a big-screen TV for sports fans.

Roberta's
16th E near Prospect,
(206) 329-3326
1147 16th Avenue E,
Seattle, WA 98112
Moderate; AE, DC,
MC, V

Roberta is the gracious, somewhat loquacious lady of this Capitol Hill house, a few blocks from Volunteer Park, the Seattle Art Museum, and the funky Broadway district. Inside it's lovely: refinished floors gleam throughout; there are a comfortable blue couch, an old upright piano, and a large oval dining table with country-style chairs. Of the four rooms, the one in peach tones with an antique desk, bay window, love seat, and queen-size brass bed is our favorite. Early risers will enjoy the Madrona Room with its morning sun and private bath; others would want the Plum Room with its queen bed and cozy loft. Three rooms share two baths (note the ceramic sinks). In the morning, Roberta puts out a smashing full breakfast (no meat, though), maybe homemade cinnamon rolls or grainy raisin bread with blackberry jam. No children. No smoking.

Salisbury House
*Corner of Aloha and
16th, (206) 328-8682
750 16th Avenue E,
Seattle, WA 98112
Moderate; AE, MC, V*

A welcoming porch wraps around this big, bright Capitol Hill home—an exquisite hostelry neighboring Volunteer Park. Glossy maple floors and lofty beamed ceilings lend a sophisticated air to the guest library (with a chess table and a wood-burning stove) and the living room. Up the wide staircase and past the second-level sun porch are four guest rooms (one with twin beds) that share two large baths. Our favorite is the Rose Room with its bay window and walk-in closet; if you can stand this much purple, the Lavender Room comes in second. Breakfast is taken in the dining room or on the sunny terrace. Classy, dignified, and devoid of children (under 12) and pets.

**Seattle Airport
Hilton Hotel**
*Take 188th Street exit off
I-5, head north 1½ miles
on Pacific Highway S,
(206) 244-4800, toll-free
(800) HILTONS
17620 Pacific Highway
S, Seattle, WA 98188
Expensive; AE, DC,
MC, V*

This streamlined building miraculously manages to create a resort atmosphere on a busy airport hotel strip. Plush rooms (at posh prices) circle a large, landscaped courtyard with outdoor pool and indoor Jacuzzi. There's an exercise room, and meeting and party rooms are available. A versatile menu offers continental cuisine.

**Seattle Sheraton Hotel
and Towers**
*6th and Pike,
(206) 621-9000, toll-free
(800) 325-3535
1400 Sixth Avenue,
Seattle, WA 98101
Expensive; AE, DC,
MC, V*

Seattle's Sheraton is an 840-room tower that rises over the new Convention Center. The Sheraton aims at the convention business, so the rooms are smallish and standard, and the emphasis is on the meeting rooms, VIP floors upstairs, and the restaurants. Banner's restaurant offers mainstream continental fare, plus an authentic Japanese breakfast and a 27-foot-long dessert spread; Gooey's is the disco; and Fullers, adorned with outstanding Northwest paintings, is perhaps the city's finest restaurant (see review). The overall architecture is bland and confusing, but a notable corporate art collection focusing on Northwest artists helps pep up the public spaces.

Service is quite efficient. Convention facilities are complete, and the kitchen staff can handle the most complex assignments. Snootier business travelers will want to head for the upper four "VIP" floors, where a hotel-within-a-hotel offers its own lobby and considerably more amenities in the rooms (which are the same size as the economy ones). The top floor features a health club and a private lounge with a knockout city panorama. You pay for parking.

Stouffer Madison Hotel

6th and Madison,
(206) 583-0300, toll-free
(800) 468-3571
515 Madison Street,
Seattle, WA 98104
Expensive; AE, DC,
MC, V

This large hotel at the southeast edge of downtown successfully conveys a sense of warmth and intimacy inside. The lobby, dressed in signature greens and peaches, is tasteful and uncluttered; upstairs hallways are softly lighted; and the rooms sport elegant marble countertops, coffered ceilings, and wood cabinetry. Extras include feather pillows, oversized towels, coffee, and morning papers. The pricey new "Club Floors," 25 and 26, offer exclusive check-in privileges, their own concierge services, hors d'oeuvres and continental breakfast at "Club Lounge," a library, and the best views (although views from most rooms are quite good). Comfortable conference facilities, parking (for a fee), free in-town transportation, and concierge on duty round out the offerings. The big-deal dining room, Prego, is consistently disappointing; other eating options here are standard.

WestCoast Camlin Hotel

9th and Olive,
(206) 682-0100, toll-free
(800) 426-0670
1619 Ninth Avenue,
Seattle, WA 98101
Moderate; AE, DC,
MC, V

This 1926 grande dame of Seattle has been remodeled and made soundproof with double-paned windows. (The elevator and the ventilation system, however, both hark back to an earlier era.) Though there are no conference facilities, the Camlin appeals to the business traveler (the large rooms have small sitting/work areas), and it's a good buy for the money. Rooms are decorated with sophistication, featuring spacious closets and spotless bathrooms; those ending in the number 10 have windows on three sides. Avoid the cabanas (they're small and dreary) and the room service (it's quite slow). There's free parking, and rooftop dining in the Cloud Room. The downtown location is closer to the retail district and Convention Center than to offices.

WestCoast Roosevelt Hotel

7th and Pine,
(206) 621-1200, toll-free
(800) 426-0670
1531 Seventh Avenue,
Seattle, WA 98101
Moderate; AE, DC,
MC, V

Gone is the grand skylit lobby that so distinguished the Roosevelt when it first threw open its doors in 1929; new owners who reopened the Roosevelt in 1987 deemed that space better suited to Von's Restaurant. The new lobby is low-ceilinged and cramped, but elsewhere the WestCoast installation has somewhat preserved the Roosevelt's Art Deco sensibilities, with a touch of Southwest warmth. The hotel's 20 stories have been reconfigured for the contemporary traveler (allowing much more comfort in its present 150 rooms than was available in its original 234), but standard rooms are still almost humorously small. Deluxes are a better choice, with adjoining sitting areas; the 13 superior-class rooms each boast a Jacuzzi, a separate sitting area, and a perspective northwest toward Puget Sound. Prices are good—$77 to $97 for a double—especially with the hotel's proximity to the convention center and the shopping district—but the service could use some polish.

The College Inn Guest House

40th and University Way,
(206) 633-4441
*4000 University Way
NE, Seattle, WA 98105
Inexpensive; AE, DC,
MC, V*

Burgundy carpets, window seats, antiques, and pastel comforters create a cozy, if somewhat spartan, atmosphere in this hospitable inn designed along the lines of a European pension. Housed in a renovated 1909 Tudor building that is on the National Register of Historic Places, it's in the heart of the lively U District, with a cafe and rathskeller pub below. (Late-night noise travels quite handily into west-side rooms.) Each room has a sink but no toilet, TV, radio, or phone. (For the musically inclined, there's an upright piano in room 305.) Tiled bathrooms are at the end of each hall, and a guest living room is tucked away on the fourth floor. A generous continental breakfast is included—a good deal at these budget prices.

Edgewater Inn

*Pier 67 at Wall and
Alaskan Way,*
(206) 728-7000, toll-free
(800) 624-0670
*2411 Alaskan Way,
Seattle, WA 98121
Expensive; AE, DC,
MC, V*

Alas—you can't fish from the famous west windows of this waterfront institution anymore. New ownership, which took over in 1988, has spiffed up the place quite a bit (and didn't want any fishy rooms). The lobby and rooms have a rustic tone, with bleached oak and overstuffed chairs. It's like an urban motel (parking is free), but with a popular little piano bar and a serviceable restaurant. Waterside rooms are quietest, with the best views and $135 price tags.

Seattle Marriott at Sea-Tac

*Off Pacific Highway S on
176th,* (206) 241-2000,
*toll free (800) 228-9290
3201 S 176th Street,
Seattle, WA 98188
Expensive; AE, DC,
MC, V*

Another megamotel, but on a human scale. The Alaska motif makes the lobby feel warm, albeit somewhat cluttered. Rooms are standard but suites are spacious. A pool and courtyard area are part of an enormous covered atrium; there are also two Jacuzzis, a sauna, and a well-equipped exercise room. Disco bar, too (open until 2am).

Villa Heidelberg

*Corner of 45th SW and
Erskine Way,*
(206) 938-3658
*4845 45th Avenue SW,
Seattle, WA 98116
Moderate; no credit cards;
checks ok*

Leaded-glass windows, beamed ceilings, Puget Sound views, and a wraparound covered porch distinguish this 1909 minimansion in West Seattle, built and named by a German immigrant. The three guest rooms (double $45, kings $55) share a bathroom; another bath is in the works. The newest room has French doors leading to a sunny deck. Owners John and Barb Thompson serve a breakfast of popovers and fruit, waffles, or French toast. Look for extras like a bouquet of roses on the table, grown in their own beautifully landscaped garden.

The Williams House

Galer and 4th N,
(206) 285-0810
*1505 Fourth Avenue N,
Seattle, WA 98109*

In its 90-year history, this south-slope Queen Anne residence has also done stints as a gentlemen's boarding house and as an emergency medical clinic for the 1962 Seattle World's Fair. Doug and Sue Williams and their

Moderate; AE, DC, MC, V

daughter Danielle manage it as a quiet, five-guestroom (four with views) bed and breakfast. The enclosed south sun porch is a nice meeting spot. Brass beds, original fixtures, fireplaces, ornate Italian tile, and oak floors hearken back to the home's Edwardian past. You will get a full breakfast; but don't expect the Williamses to be of the usual school of chatty bed-and-breakfast owners— they'll leave you alone.

GREATER SEATTLE: MILL CREEK
RESTAURANTS

Imperial Garden
Exit 183 off I-5 in the Mill Creek Gardens Mall, (206) 742-2288
16300 Mill Creek Blvd, Mill Creek
Moderate; full bar; AE, DC, MC, V
Lunch Mon-Fri, dinner every day, brunch Sun

For the full aesthetic Chinese dining experience, this new restaurant in the planned community of Mill Creek cannot be bested. Architecturally, it's a contemporary spectacle, employing terraced levels and a lot of glass so that every diner has a view of the stunningly composed Asian garden outside. It's elegant—on that point nobody will argue—and a wonderful place for a private party (a room holds 60). The real bone of contention here is the food, over which even Cantonese experts will disagree. One Hong Kong native pronounces Imperial Garden's food to be as close to the Hong Kong standard as one can find in the state, praising especially the steamed salmon with garlic and black bean sauce. Another encountered dullness of preparation in some dishes, poor ingredients in others. Portions are tiny and delicate, and the menu is startlingly eclectic: you'll find a sushi bar, Cointreau-marinated pork chops, and European pastries here. It would be a pleasure to see a space this sleek and lovely narrow into a showcase for the oft-overlooked (and recently underappreciated) Cantonese style—sauces light and benign, cooking exact and restrained. On the basis of some, but still not all, of the dishes we've sampled here, we expect it to mature in that direction.

GREATER SEATTLE: EDMONDS

The area thought of as Edmonds is really just a small village in a much larger area. Funky stores, wide sidewalks, and waterfront views encourage evening strolls through town. The ferry departs to Kingston; for information call (206) 464-6400.

Edmonds bills itself as the City of Celebrations. Most popular are the **Edmonds Art Festival** (third weekend in June) and **A Taste of Edmonds** (third weekend in August).

Brackett's Landing Beach Park, just north of the ferry terminal, has a jetty and an offshore underwater marine-life park that draws lots of scuba divers. **Edmonds Historic Walk** was prepared by the Centennial Committee and offers a look at old Edmonds. Stop by the Chamber of Commerce (120 Fifth Street N) for a free map of the walk.

RESTAURANTS

Chanterelle Specialty Foods

*Up from the ferry
terminal on Main,*
(206) 774-0650
316 Main Street,
Edmonds
*Inexpensive; beer and
wine; MC, V*
*Breakfast, lunch Tues-Sun,
dinner Tues-Sat*

Edmonds is fortunate to have this cafe/deli/bakery shop. Here is gourmet take-out at only slightly higher than grocery-store deli prices and with vastly higher quality. As we entered, our eyes were treated to an array of salads (tabouli, Nicoise, seafood, hummus). Meats, including beef and turkey breast, are roasted on the premises, and there's a fabulous seafood sausage. A variety of entrees to go are prepared fresh daily, and there's an overwhelming choice of desserts. Don't miss the German sourdough rye that sits on top of the dessert counter. Condiments and beverages line the outer walls. There are also seven butcher-block tables for in-store dining. The place is very popular with joggers, bicyclists, and browsers, so it can be chaotic.

Evergreen Restaurant

*North of Aurora Village
near the corner of 236th,*
(206) 771-8874
23628 Highway 99,
Edmonds
*Moderate; full bar;
MC, V*
*Lunch Mon-Fri, dinner
every day*

This place is much nicer once you're inside; white tablecloths and overdressed waiters add an air of formality. The prices and the vast menu reassure you that this is a Chinese restaurant. The food tells you this is a good Chinese restaurant. Most dishes are of the hot and spicy variety, and your waiter will be disappointed if asked to turn down the heat. The won ton soup is bright orange and surprisingly good. Another favorite is the hot-and-sour soup, with an abundance of pork, bean curd, mushrooms, and bamboo shoots. Seafood is treated with respect; the Mongolian beef can be too salty. Lunch is a real bargain. A banquet room is available for private parties.

brusseau's

*Near the corner of 5th
and Dayton,*
(206) 774-4166
117 Fifth Avenue S,
Edmonds
*Moderate; beer and wine;
MC, V*
*Breakfast, lunch, dinner
every day, brunch Sun*

Jerilyn Brusseau is Edmonds' own culinary ambassador to the world and has become a star on the TV talk show circuit. Maybe because these activities require so much of her time away from the popular cafe-bakery, or possibly because she has spoiled us with her high standards, quality control has slipped lately. On a recent visit, two of the three salads (turkey and marinated vegetable) were quite bland; the third, a pasta salad, was average. The vegetable soup was pale and flavorless. On the other hand, the French toast (more like a gigantic slice of bread pudding) was the same wonderful creation as in years past. When the kitchen's on, you can still get a thick and hearty vegetable soup and well-stocked clam chowder. Even with the occasional blunders, people enjoy this pleasant neighborhood cafe. Overall, the food is good and the baked goods better (though they're sometimes sold out early). Jerilyn is also expanding her catering business.

Love a good bargain? Then you'll really like Seattle Cheap Eats, *a compendium of 230 terrific bargain eateries in and around Seattle, brought to you by the same folks who bring you the* Best Places *series.*

LODGINGS

Pinkham's Pillow
Corner of Dayton and
3rd, (206) 774-3406
202 Third Avenue S,
Edmonds, WA 98020
Moderate; MC, V

This clean, ageless home is right in the heart of downtown Edmonds, two blocks from the waterfront, with views of Puget Sound. Don't worry about the name: Pinkham's Pillow does lean toward lace and ruffles, heart-shaped rugs and antique-style furnishings, but still remains comfortable and uncluttered, with an overriding sense of organization and welcome. Each of the five guest rooms —Melissa, Shannon, Lacey, Joy, and Adria, named after the owners' daughters—has a private bath; Lacey is handicapped-accessible. Prices are $45 to $68 and include a full breakfast.

Edmonds Harbor Inn
Dayton and Edmonds
Way, (206) 771-5021
130 W Dayton,
Edmonds, WA 98020
Moderate; AE, DC, MC, V

Strategically located near the ferry and train terminals, this is one of Edmonds' most attractive hotels: large rooms, oak furnishings, continental breakfast, valet services, and access to a nearby athletic club. Get directions —the place is a little difficult to find in the gray sea of new office and shopping developments, but it's worth looking for.

GREATER SEATTLE: BOTHELL

The town stands at the north end of Lake Washington, on the way into open country. **Bothell Landing** is a pleasant park, and from here you can take a 9.5-mile hike, bike ride, or roller-skating tour along the Sammamish River, stopping part of the way at the Ste. Michelle winery for a picnic; food and wine can be purchased at the winery (see Woodinville).

RESTAURANTS

Gerard's Relais de Lyon
Just inside Bothell city
limits, north of Seattle,
(206) 485-7600
17121 Bothell Way NE,
Bothell
Expensive; full bar; DC,
MC, V
Dinner every day

One way to delight a Francophile is to send him or her to Gerard's. Eating here is to return the senses to France, in a country inn appointed with crisp linen, Wedgwood china, leaded glass, and fresh flowers. Gerard takes a full menu of prime ingredients and makes it sing in fragrant and succulent harmony: salmon in sorrel sauce, duck breast in ginger and honey, filet of beef in green, pink, and black peppercorn sauce—it's all here, the essence of classic French cooking. The lamb tournedos were a perfect taste match with their light stone-ground mustard sauce, as was the boneless saddle of rabbit (stuffed with a pate de foie gras and baked in pastry) with its creamy port wine–shallot sauce. To be able to achieve this balance takes a chef with a true gift and a saucier with brilliance. We wish we could have sampled more.

The preceding courses were equally outstanding: a warm salmon mousse enclosing crayfish tails, covered with a dreamy mushroom sauce; a superb seafood consomme with mussels and lobster; a large, light salad of several greens. Let the wine steward offer a suggestion—there's a good selection of notable French and American vintage varietals. The service was knowledgeable but could have been more attentive. Private rooms are available, as is an attractive outdoor dining area.

Big Doug's Better Burgers
Corner of 180th and Bothell-Everett Highway, (206) 486-0755 18001 Bothell-Everett Highway SE, Bothell Inexpensive; no alcohol; MC, V Lunch, dinner Tues-Sat

You know you're onto a respectable burger when a restaurant goes to the trouble of making its own burger buns. Big Doug says they go through as many as 500 of these homemade white, wheat, and French buns a day when they're busy. The menu is old-fashioned, reliable American, with big juicy burgers and Darigold Deluxe ice cream being the standouts.

GREATER SEATTLE: WOODINVILLE

Woodinville, another town in the boom belt, shows some signs of growing pains, but the outlying countryside is grand, particularly heading out toward Duvall.

Molbak's is a vast nursery and greenhouse operation, so extensive that it ranks as a tourist attraction. 13625 NE 175th, (206) 483-5000.

Chateau Ste. Michelle is the state's largest and best-known winery. It is located on a former estate graced by manicured lawns, trout ponds, and experimental vineyards (the grapes for the wine come from eastern Washington). The tour of the winemaking complex, ending in a tasting room, is well worth taking, especially during the fall crush (September and October). 1411 NE 145th, (206) 488-1133.

Located across the street from Ste. Michelle in the former Havilland Winery, **Columbia Winery** is the state's oldest premium-wine company, originally established as a hobby by some University of Washington academics. The tasting room is open seven days a week from 10am to 5pm. 14030 NE 145th, (206) 488-2776.

RESTAURANTS

Armadillo Barbecue
Take Woodinville exit from 522E, on the main drag, (206) 481-1417 13109 NE 175th Street, Woodinville Inexpensive; beer and wine; AE, MC, V Lunch, dinner every day

The words scrawled on the windows of "222 Pork Avenue" announce Cement Soup and Lizard Gizzards, but inside you'll find neither—simply tasty barbecued pork ribs, short ribs, chicken, and all the right sides (molasses-y beans; dense, unsweet corn bread; extra "killer haut sauce" for 25 cents). It's a regular West Texas barbecue joint plopped down in west Woodinville and bearing the marks of someone's engaging, slightly perverse sense of humor. And the barbecue is very good—sort of Northwest meets the Deep South—in which the first bite reveals nuances of teriyaki deepened with alder smoke and a tang of hot sauce. The meat is tender and beautifully smoked, but they're too skimpy with the sauce. Great beer and wine selection.

Newman's

131st and 177th Place,
(206) 485-9372
13120 NE 177th Place,
Woodinville
Moderate; beer and wine;
AE, MC, V
Dinner Tues-Sat

A game restaurant is a brave endeavor and a pleasant discovery, particularly in rural Woodinville. Dennis Newman (trained at the Culinary Institute of America) specializes in meats from quail to venison, antelope, bison, and elk, sauteed or grilled in their own juices and bathed in sauces of their own reduction. We had an excellent cold smoked duck salad with a raspberry vinaigrette, but quibbles cropped up as the meal progressed: caribou pate with an overpoweringly sweet plum sauce, poor bread, uninspired boar. Newman is committed to quality suppliers, so the ingredients will be good, if erratic in supply. Be prepared for strong flavors. To cater to broader tastes, Newman has added a decent selection of Italian fare.

GREATER SEATTLE: REDMOND

Redmond is the land of explosive suburban growth: the pretty countryside is being gobbled up by condo projects and strip malls. Still, the drive northward along the Sammamish River Valley—or better yet, canoeing the river or biking the trail—is wonderfully pastoral.

Marymoor County Park offers vast stretches of play and picnic space, plus frequent gatherings for jazz and fairs. The Velodrome is the region's leading facility for bike racing. Highway 520 and W Lake Sammamish Parkway, (206) 885-2553.

RESTAURANTS

Kikuya

Off the Redmond-
Kirkland Highway on
161st NE,
(206) 881-8771
8105 161st Avenue NE,
Redmond
Moderate; beer and wine;
MC, V
Lunch, dinner Tues-Sat

Stuck in the back of an undistinguished shopping center in Redmond is this small, family-run, informal Japanese restaurant that just keeps getting better. No kimonos or tatami rooms here—the draw is the excellent sushi bar run by sushi chef Hiroaki Ito. It's the kind of place where you order the good, honest, simple things—spicy yakisoba (which you can see the chef cooking), gyoza, donburi—and always count on a good tempura. Kikuya is a favorite with local Japanese, and there's frequently a line at the door. When you walk in, the staff welcomes you with a bow, just like in Japan.

LODGINGS

Cedarym

Just off NE 8th at 240th
NE, (206) 868-4159
1011 240th Avenue NE,
Redmond, WA 98053
Inexpensive; MC, V

We wish this magnificent bed and breakfast had more than two rooms. It's a brand-new Colonial, situated amid gorgeously cultivated grounds with a wide lawn, an arbor, and a dandy spa-in-a-gazebo, surrounded by bursting rhodies and roses and a ring of tall cedars. Inside, Mary Ellen and Walt Brown have re-created a Colonial homestead, right down to the gleaming pine plank floors, hand-forged lift latches, and the enormous brick cooking hearth (which Mary Ellen really uses) in the family room. The Tulip and Anchor rooms feature big, comfortable beds, TVs, sitting areas overlooking the grounds, and a shared bath. The Browns make uncommonly cordial hosts.

GREATER SEATTLE: KIRKLAND

Marina Park anchors the waterfront parklands, easily reached from the shopping core. Historic boats are moored in the marina, and duck-feeding is quite up to kids' standards.

RESTAURANTS

Cafe Juanita

116th exit off 405, west to 97th, take a right, 1½ blocks to 120th Place,
(206) 823-1505
9702 NE 120th Place,
Kirkland
Moderate; full bar; MC, V
Dinner every day

Owner Peter Dow threads his way happily among tables of pasta eaters in this charming restaurant, presenting a bottle of his own 1988 Cavattapi sauvignon blanc or recently his Nebbiolo (he makes them both on the premises). The place that once was booked up months in advance and accepted no credit cards is now a little more accessible to the modern diner: now they suggest booking just a week and a half ahead for a weekend table. Weekdays are much more accessible.

A recent appetizer, puttanesca—a mix of capers, sun-dried tomatoes, green and black olives, Parmesan, onions, and spaghettini—was a delight. So was the moist Dijon chicken breast with artichoke hearts, olives, and red peppers, but the lasagne marchese was rich yet bland with its mix of veal sausage, chicken liver, spinach lasagne, and bechamel sauce. Likewise, the pollo ai pistacchi (chicken breasts covered with a pistachio-filled cream sauce) overwhelmed even the most hardy of our party with its richness. The wine list comprises one of the best selections of inexpensive Italian wines we've seen locally.

Kirkland Roaster & Ale House

Lake Washington Blvd and Central Way,
(206) 827-4400
111 Central Way,
Kirkland
Moderate; full bar; AE, DC, MC, V
Lunch, dinner every day

We can't help it, we like this place. Tim Firnstahl brings sizzling spit-roasted meats to Kirkland, in a space Kirkland can't possibly resist: next to a winery (Covey Run) on one side and a brewery (Hale's Ales) on the other. The gimmicks start right inside the door: a stagey bar, appropriately packed; a couple of bustling dining rooms with copper-top tables; glistening meats hotly roasting on the enormous vertical spit; views of Moss Bay out the window. You should stay with the ham, chicken, or lamb, which are usually very good, served with scalloped corn and seasonal vegetables. The clam chowder is thick and good. Some of the other dishes don't work at all: the three-meat hash appears as doctored chili; we've had horrid, leaden desserts. But an achingly tender slab of roast lamb, allowed to wallow in nothing but its own juices, can quickly make up for the rest.

LODGINGS

Shumway Mansion

Near NE 116th on 99th Place NE,
(206) 823-2303
11410 99th Place NE,

When the owners of Shumway Mansion heard that developers wanted to demolish the historic 1910 building to make room for condos, they hauled the four-story house to a safe location three miles up the road. Now it's a gracious bed and breakfast with an equal emphasis on

Kirkland, WA 98033
Moderate; MC, V

seminars and receptions. Of the 23 rooms, seven are guest rooms furnished with antiques and private baths. The wicker-filled public rooms feature glimpses of Kirkland's Juanita Bay (just a short walk away). The full breakfast is served on white tablecloths. The Columbia Bay Athletic Club (available for guest use) is across the street; downtown Seattle is 20 minutes away. Children over 12 only. No pets. Smoking is restricted.

Woodmark Hotel
Kirkland exit off 520,
north on Lake
Washington Blvd, NE
to Carillon Point,
(206) 822-3700
1200 Carillon Point,
Kirkland, WA 98033
Expensive; AE, MC, V

(unrated)

Just as we went to press this splashy new hotel opened on the eastern shore of Lake Washington. At a glance, it resembles any new office building. But closer inspection reveals the soft touches of a fine hotel: 100 plush rooms (most with mountain or lake views) with fully stocked mini-bars, VCRs (with complimentary movies available at the front desk), baths equipped with a *second* TV, terrycloth robes, and oversized towels, and service (from laundry to valet) to match. A full breakfast is included in the price of the room, and, if you get late-night cravings, the refrigerator is yours to raid. Doubtful you'll be hungry: next door are two new restaurants which bring their Seattle reputations to the Eastside: Ray's Yarrow Point Grill and Luciano (Settebello) Bardinelli's Ristorante Stresa.

GREATER SEATTLE: BELLEVUE

Until the floating bridges came, Bellevue was a sleepy, rural outpost where people built summer homes. Now it is an explosively growing "second city" with a downtown office-building boom to rival Seattle's and a core of high-tech firms that have earned it the nickname Silicon Valley North.

Bellevue Square, NE Eighth and Bellevue Way NE, is a large, enclosed mall jammed with shops, some quite good. Inside it is the **Bellevue Art Museum**, devoted to regional and national shows, with an emphasis on the decorative arts.

Main Street, starting at 108th Avenue SE downtown, is a boutiquey bit of "old" Bellevue, with peek-a-boo views of Meydenbauer Bay.

Kelsey Creek Park, in the region where Bellevue Way meets I-90, is part of an ancient marshy slough; duck ponds, a baby animal farm, an old log cabin, and a Japanese tea garden highlight your nature walk.

Andre's Gourmet Cuisine
Between 148th NE and
140th NE on NE 20th,
(206) 747-6551
14125 NE 20th Street,
Bellevue
Moderate; beer and wine;
MC, V
Lunch Mon-Fri, dinner
Mon-Sat

Andre Nguyen, a young Vietnamese-born chef who earned his stripes at Fullers, Daniel's Broiler, and The Lakeside, has brought inexpensive, innovative Franco-Vietnamese cuisine to Bellevue's strip-mall never-never land. The menu is about equally divided between Vietnamese and European selections, so order once from the East and once from the West. Vietnamese entrees include lovely, peppery grilled shrimp, ground beef wrapped in lemon grass, and fabulous pork meatballs fragrant with garlic—all resting on a bed of rice noodles that were a good foil for the strong flavors, although they were a bit

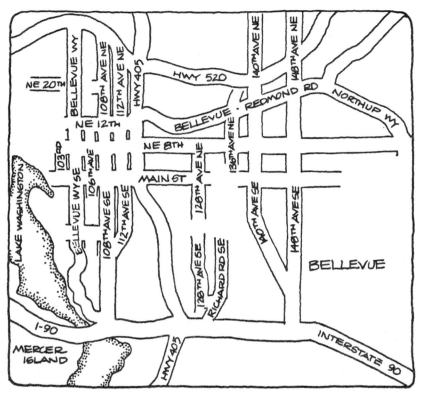

dry. From the European side of the menu we chose the veal with wild mushrooms, which came with a piccata/ cream sauce and escalloped potatoes—well prepared and subtly flavored. At times Andre's cuisine borders on routine—on the evening we were there, every plate sprouted carrots, cucumbers, and lettuce. We suspect Andre knows better, and we'll return, because what Andre does well, he does wonderfully.

Bravo
108th and Northup,
(206) 827-8585
10733 Northup Way,
Bellevue
Moderate; full bar;
AE, MC, V
Lunch Mon-Fri, dinner
every day

The brightest star from the Pagliacci people (Trattoria Pagliacci, Pizzeria Pagliacci) is Bravo, home of—among other things—the best lunch in Bellevue. The pizza comes from a wood-fired oven, which makes for a very crisp crust, and the toppings would be at home in any trendy spot. The pasta is cooked firm, with good fresh sauces. A few fresh seafood and veal selections round out the menu. The restaurant sprawls into many rooms, including two large banquet rooms, and the help sometimes seems to have gotten lost in the maze, but you will eat well at good prices in this happy marriage of West Coast cuisine and Italian cooking. A piano bar is in full swing Wednesday through Saturday nights.

Fountain Court Off Main
Just off Main in old Bellevue, (206) 451-0426 22 103rd NE, Bellevue Expensive; full bar; AE, DC, MC, V Lunch Mon-Fri, dinner Mon-Sat

The menu in this quietly inviting haven in old Bellevue comfortably mingles French country and Northwest cooking. Portions are ample and sauces rich, and a lot of care is taken with the presentations. Appetizers lean toward oysters, mussels, and other seafood platters. Mussels in prawn sauce are tender and sweet; less successful are the oysters Bienville, so overwhelmed with bread crumbs, mushrooms, butter, and cheese as to obliterate any hint of oyster. Our roast duck was too tough, but the sole paupiettes, stuffed with shrimp, were near-perfect. Service is superb, prices are fair, and the eclectic wine list is pricey but yields up some gems. Accommodations are available for private parties.

RESTAURANTS

Landau's
Between 4th and 8th in the Koll Center, (206) 646-6644 500 108th Avenue NE, Bellevue Expensive; full bar; AE, DC, MC, V Lunch Mon-Fri, dinner Mon-Sat

Until now, Bellevue has (curiously) lacked a budget-busting showpiece of a restaurant. Introducing Landau's: all polished granite, enormous flower arrangements, plush carpeting, and satiny upholstery. The place exudes professionalism, with a dignified staff and rapt attention to detail. Complimentary bite-size hors d'oeuvres begin the meal; little cookies and chocolates end it. Food is artfully arranged on oversized plates, a piano tinkles softly in the background, the service is prompt and polished.

Happily, all this attention to setting isn't a screen to mask mediocre food. The owners have crafted a menu for broad appeal, with classic continental dishes tweaked for the 1990s palate—changed every three to six months to reflect availability of fresh ingredients. Choices for June included warm duck breast salad with a piquant red plum vinaigrette, tossed colorfully with purple cabbage and redleaf lettuce. The gravlax with mustard dill sauce was superb and the portion generous. A lovely tart lime ice cleansed our palates for the entrees: a classic French peppercorn steak (perfectly pink, as requested) and a flaky salmon fillet with crisp skin resting in an onion–red pepper sauce. Accompaniments were equally tasty: lightly deep-fried potato puffs, garlicky saffron gnocchi, snappily fresh green beans. The dessert menu is sinfully tempting, and weak spirits may succumb to the satellite—a ball of vanilla ice cream enclosed in sponge cake which was flamed in brandy and sauced with dark chocolate.

Landau's is expensive, but its interesting, four-course prix-fixe menu is reasonable ($25), and for a wear-the-glad-rags special occasion, this elegant restaurant would be an excellent choice—even for the budget-conscious. Private parties (8–50) are grand.

Marian's

*Corner of NE 8th and
108th, (206) 451-7474
777 108th Avenue NE,
Bellevue
Moderate; full bar;
AE, DC, MC, V
Breakfast, lunch Mon-Fri,
dinner Mon-Fri*

Marian's suffers from an identity crisis. It's got the setting (the glittering, neo–Art Deco ground level of Security Pacific Plaza) and the setup (a deli take-out bar in front, with the business-lunch or formal dinner restaurant in back, spilling out onto a pretty patio)—but the whole operation, from food to annoyingly hesitating service, is shot through with such naive hopefulness and self-consciousness that the diner can't help but feel insecure. It would be a shame if this new regime with chef Patrick Faye at the helm repeated the errors of the old, but it looks as if it might: too-timid executions of promising dishes; fine-tuning errors of the most elementary nature (overcooked pasta, a dish wherein fresh sole is overwhelmed by the aggressive flavor of smoked salmon). There's so much promise here—bravo for any restaurant that features more than one fresh raspberry dessert at the height of raspberry season!—and we've seen glimmers of real talent in the kitchen. Marian's just needs to loosen up and let a little exuberance out.

Olympic

*NE 8th and 112th NE,
(206) 455-9305
1200 112th Avenue NE,
Bellevue
Moderate; full bar;
AE, MC, V
Lunch, dinner every day*

Some of the best Korean food in the Seattle area is in a non-descript office complex in Bellevue. There's a whole page of untranslated Korean-only entrees and if you ask what they are the waitress will just shake her head and say: "too hot" or "not cooked" or "too strange." Well, you don't need to *read* Korean to order the yuk hui (raw strips of beef marinated in vinegar and graced with pine nuts, apples, and pears) or the Korean barbecued beef (grilled beef that's been marinated in soy sauce, sugar, and wine). Traditionally, you grill your own, which here you can do in the small barbecue room in back. Adventuresome eaters who do find themselves randomly ordering off the Korean-only page may find themselves faced with a hearty soup of beef, tripe, and tubular animal innards.

Wang's Garden

*Bel-Red Road and 140th
NE, (206) 641-6011
1644 140th Avenue NE,
Bellevue
Moderate; full bar;
AE, DC, MC, V
Lunch Mon-Sat, dinner
every day*

The newer, elegant brother of Wang's Chinese Kitchen, also in Bellevue, boasts plush American/Chinese decor and the personage of C. C. Wang himself (from Lotus East in Seattle and renowned East Coast restaurants) in the kitchen. Our reviewers report that when Wang does the cooking, you can expect an exquisite meal; the others in the cooking crew often fall short of that standard. Service is better here than at the sibling restaurant, and the surroundings are more high-ticket. The menu has a few pretensions as well, with about half of the items getting the designation "imperial." Try the Hunan pork with hot pepper sauce, the minced chicken with pine nuts, or a 30-minute Peking duck. A large banquet room holds up to 70.

Pogacha

3 blocks south of the intersection of 106th NE and NE 8th in the Bellevue Plaza,
(206) 455-5670
119 106th Avenue NE, Bellevue
Inexpensive; beer and wine; AE, DC, MC, V
Lunch Mon-Fri, dinner Mon-Sat

Pogacha, a sauceless Croatian relative of Italian pizza, is the specialty of the house in this odd, sterile Bellevue strip-mall space. The light, crisp—but chewy on the inside—disks are baked in the centerpiece brick oven and topped with any of a half-dozen combinations, including mushrooms, pesto, salami, red onions, basil, tomatoes, and various cheeses. It's really good pizza. There are also some generously sauced pastas; hearty peasant soups and good salads; and buttery pastries by the score. A terrific wine-by-the-glass program is an unexpected delight.

LODGINGS

The Bellevue Hilton

Main and 112th NE,
(206) 455-3330, toll-free
(800) BEL-HILT
100 112th Avenue NE, Bellevue, WA 98004
Expensive; AE, DC, MC, V

With every amenity in the book, the Bellevue Hilton is the best bet on the Eastside's Hotel Row. Rooms are tastefully done in soft, warm colors; extras include use of a nearby health and racquet club, free transportation around Bellevue, 24-hour security and room service, cable TV in every room, and three restaurants. Meeting rooms recently have been renovated. Doubles run from $91 to $99; parlor suites, at $225, have sitting rooms, wet bars, and large dining tables.

Bellevue Holiday Inn

112th and Main,
(206) 455-5240
11211 Main Street, Bellevue, WA 98004
Moderate; AE, DC, MC, V

This understated two-story motel neither stimulates nor overloads the senses; many regular visitors to Bellevue won't stay anywhere else. The units are arranged campus-style around a well-manicured lawn and heated pool. The fancy dining room, Jonah's, is better than most.

Hyatt Regency at Bellevue Place

NE 8th and Bellevue Way, (206) 462-1234, toll-free (800) 233-1234
900 Bellevue Way, Bellevue, WA 98004
Expensive; AE, DC, MC, V

Bellevue Square developer Kemper Freeman's latest splash in Bellevue is the sprawling retail-office-restaurant-hotel-health-club complex called Bellevue Place. Hyatt Regency operates the 382-room hotel (at 24 stories, the highest in Bellevue), which offers all the extras: two pricier "Regency Club" floors, two big ballrooms and several satellite conference rooms, an adjoining health club (for a fee), and a classy restaurant called Eques. This slightly formal, nonetheless warm and pleasing restaurant dispels the presumption that hotel dining is bound to be disappointing. The kitchen scores high on every dish—starting with a delicious salmon tartare and a satiny butter lettuce salad right through to the swordfish and black cod (grilled with a choice of three sauces—we tried them all and recommend the ginger soy butter sauce). Dessert (a hazelnut souffle with cappuccino sauce) was no less a delight. There are also a lounge and some less formal eateries and shops which occupy the dramatic glass-walled Wintergarden atrium. The hotel has views, a lot of them, best on the south side and above the seventh floor.

MERCER ISLAND

RESTAURANTS

Subito
*Due to the I-90
construction, call for
directions, (206) 232-9009
2448 76th Avenue SE,
Mercer Island
Moderate; beer and wine;
AE, MC, V
Lunch Mon-Sat,
dinner every day*

After about a year, the elements of Mercer Island's favorite new restaurant have begun to settle in. Chef Eric Napoleone has found the establishment's niche and re-written the menu to reflect more—but not strictly—Italian selections. The place won the hearts of islanders early on, and the enthusiasm is now beginning to wane a bit. It's favored at lunch for a chewy, cheesy pizza (it was provolone, mozzarella, and Parmesan on our visit). Dinners can be inconsistent. One evening we had a delightful seafood linguine alfredo, but the veal al Sarto (topped with artichoke hearts, capers, and prosciutto) was inexplicably (and disastrously) paired with rotelle in a tomato sauce laden with yet more prosciutto (served separately, they would have been fine). The cool, contemporary dining space beams with enthusiastic (though untutored) servers, big, colorful paintings, and a truly extraordinary wine list. A small private room in back works nicely for a party of 14.

GREATER SEATTLE: ISSAQUAH

The town retains a bit of its coal-mining character even though it's now a typical suburban village. It makes a nice stop if you're heading up I-90 to the mountains.

Gilman Village, Gilman Boulevard at Juniper Street, assembles about a dozen old farmhouses, bungalows, and farm buildings into a small shopping complex: boutiques, crafts places, and eateries. A nifty idea.

Issaquah State Salmon Hatchery is open every day; here's where those to-be-tasty salmon start their lives. 125 Sunset Way, (206) 392-3180.

Boehm's Candies, located in what appears to be a Swiss chalet on Gilman Boulevard, makes and dips almost every one of their chocolates by hand. You can tour the factory, but you'll need to call ahead: (206) 392-6652.

RESTAURANTS

Mandarin Garden
*Exit 17 off I-90, right to
Front and Sunset,
(206) 392-9476
40 E Sunset Way,
Issaquah
Inexpensive; beer and
wine; MC, V
Lunch Tues-Fri,
dinner Tues-Sun*

This Issaquah restaurant has the distinction of producing spiciness where promised—a rarity among Chinese restaurants in the area, and all the more admirable since the chef and owner, Andy Wang, is a native of Shanghai. The decor is simple and lightly festive, and the food (Sichuan, Hunan, and Mandarin) is a close match—colorful and uncomplicated. Praiseworthy dishes include melt-in-your-mouth kung pao chicken and variations on bean curd. Two private rooms (one holding up to 50 guests) are available for banquets. Peking duck can be ordered a day in advance.

LODGINGS

The Wildflower

Take exit 17 from I-90, head left, then right onto Issaquah-Fall City Road for 2 miles,
(206) 392-1196
25237 SE Issaquah-Fall City Road, Issaquah, WA 98027
Inexpensive; no credit cards; checks ok

Laureita Caldwell has decorated the four guest rooms of her log-house bed and breakfast in floral themes native to Issaquah: the Strawberry Room, the Fern Room, the Daisy Room, the Rose Room. The last boasts the classiest decor (although it shares a bath with Daisy): all rooms have raw-pine walls, charming window seats (great for reading), and handmade quilts. Downstairs there's a cozy common room where guests can relax by the wood stove. All this and breakfast too for $45.

The massive cabin sits quite impressively in the lonesome woods just north of Issaquah—a terrific base camp for travelers torn between the mountains and the metropolis.

GREATER SEATTLE: BAINBRIDGE ISLAND

Captain Vancouver stopped here in 1792 to cut tall trees for masts, and the island has been a major logging port several times since. Now it is a quiet, semi-rural retreat favored by commuters, novelists, and people seeking simpler lives. It makes a pleasant tour, by car or bike, during which you can see Victorian homes, handsome modern edifices, and enviable waterfront estates. **Bloedel Reserve** is 150 acres of lush tranquil gardens, woods, meadows, and ponds. Plants from all over the world make the grounds interesting at any time of the year. Reservations are required and limited. Open Wednesday–Sunday; (206) 842-7631.

Fay Bainbridge State Park, on the northeast corner of the island, is noted for its fine beach and stunning view back toward Seattle's skyline.

The wooded and waterfront trails in **Fort Ward State Park**, on the south end of the island, make for a nice afternoon stroll (good picnic spots, too). Also on the south end of the island at Lynwood Center is the **Four Swallows**, a comfortable pub with local brews and light nibbles; 4569 Lynwood Center Road, (206) 842-3397.

A simpler trip is to ride over on the ferry from downtown Seattle, sans car, and then walk a few blocks to the town of Winslow, take in the shops, have coffee and pastry at **Pegasus Espresso House** at the foot of Madison Avenue South, and then float back to Seattle.

RESTAURANTS

Little Italy West

On the corner of Winslow Way and Madison,
(206) 842-0517
104 Madison Avenue N, Bainbridge Island
Inexpensive; beer and wine; no credit cards; checks ok
Dinner every day

This tiny trattoria in an eyesore of a building puts out the best Italian food on Bainbridge Island: light, thin-crusted pizza with pesto and sun-dried tomatoes (or cappocolla and anchovy, or several other combinations); fat calzones bursting with cheese; a dozen or so pastas, including vegetarian manicotti with walnuts and sun-dried tomatoes; or a fabulous pesto pollo. They don't stray far from the classics, but entrees such as the chicken or veal saltimbocca work well in this island eatery. It's all cleverly seasoned with a light but sure hand, and meant to be savored with the house wine, a delightful Nebbiolo, or to be ordered to-go. With portions this big, you hardly have room for dessert.

Streamliner Diner

Winslow Way and Bejune, (206) 842-8595
397 Winslow Way, Bainbridge Island
Inexpensive; beer and wine; MC, V
Breakfast every day, lunch Mon-Fri

For eight years, nothing could be finer at the island's favorite diner. The windows are invitingly steamy, promising home-cooked food in a companionable setting. Breakfasts include incomparable buttermilk waffles with real maple syrup; huge, inventive omelets; nutritious homemade granola; and potatoes deluxe—the famed spiced potatoes, stir-fried with vegetables and topped with Cheddar cheese. Lunches are natural homemade soups, salads, quiches, and sandwiches. Recently, locals have been griping over the slowly rising prices at their favorite weekday hangout and now avoid the place on weekends, when off-islanders stand in the inevitable line for a hearty breakfast at the Diner. There's no smoking inside, but smokers are welcome on the small deck outside.

LODGINGS

The Bombay House

4 miles south of the ferry, just off W Blakely Avenue, (206) 842-3926
8490 Beck Road NE, Bainbridge Island, WA 98110
Moderate; AE, MC, V

★ ★

Located near a beachside park, the Bombay House has a hearty dose of the country-hideaway mood that's so much of the bed-and-breakfast mystique. It's a sprawling turn-of-the-century house, with a widow's walk, set in a lavish flower garden with a rough-cedar gazebo overlooking scenic Rich Passage. The large living room has a huge fireplace, and all five bedrooms are done up in country antiques (three have private baths). The vast second-floor captain's suite has a wood-burning parlor stove and a claw-footed tub. New innkeepers Roger Kanchuk and Bunny Cameron are friendly hosts; their breakfast includes homemade muffins and breads and fresh fruits. Children by prior arrangement. Smoking restricted.

Beach Cottage B&B

4 miles from the ferry off Eagle Harbor Drive,
(206) 842-6081
5831 Ward Avenue NE, Bainbridge Island, WA 98110
Moderate; no credit cards; checks ok

Right across Eagle Harbor from the ferry-stop town of Winslow is this charming, flower-bedecked four-cottage setup, each with a queen-size bed, kitchen (stocked with breakfast fixings), logs for the fireplace, and stereo. Two are right on the beach, and the other two boast views of Eagle Harbor and its marina (the brand-new two-bedroom on the hill even views Seattle and Mount Rainier on clear days). Each goes for $75 for two people ($95 for four people). Smoking is allowed (pets and children aren't), and if you want to go to sea, there's a rowboat.

GREATER SEATTLE: TUKWILA

LODGINGS

Doubletree Inn and Plaza

Take the Southcenter exit off I-5 (exit #153 northbound, #154-B southbound),
(206) 246-8220, toll-free

The Doubletree, fixed between I-5 and the Southcenter shopping mall, is two hotels. The Plaza has handsome luxury suites ($110 to $136) with refrigerators, TVs (you pay per cable movie), and small wet bars. Southeast-facing rooms have views of Mount Rainier. There's a Jacuzzi

(800) 528-0444
16500 Southcenter Pkwy,
Tukwila, WA 98188
Expensive; AE, DC,
MC, V

and a sauna at the Plaza. The pool is across the street in a secluded courtyard at the Doubletree Inn, the more plebeian sibling. Here, the woody, Northwest lobby is nice, but the rooms ($79 to $92) are average; avoid the north-facing ones, which hum with the sounds of I-5 and offer views of the Frederick & Nelson department store. Service is quite friendly.

GREATER SEATTLE: BURIEN
RESTAURANTS

Filiberto's
Off Highway 518,
(206) 248-1944
14401 Des Moines Way
S, Burien
Moderate; full bar; AE,
DC, MC, V
Lunch, dinner Tues-Sun

Filiberto's is the most authentic of the local Italian restaurants, and, on a good day, one of the best. The look is cheery and trattoria-perfect, with even the dishwashing section in back finished in imported tile. Service can be erratic or excellent, but the food seems to have gotten more consistent, with good attention to the basics. The long menu emphasizes Roman and other midregion preparations of pasta, veal, poultry, and rabbit, right down to the real stracciatella alla romana (egg-drop soup)—and it's not too salty, as it often is in Rome. Three special treats: the huge, very well-priced selection of Italian wines in a take-your-pick glass case (here's where you'll find that unforgettable label with the forgotten name), and a bocce court out back.

Satsuma
Off 148th on Ambaum,
(206) 242-1747
14301 Ambaum Way
SW, Burien
Moderate; beer and wine;
MC, V
Lunch Mon, Wed, Fri;
dinner Wed-Mon

Plain as a box on the outside, this tranquil Burien hideaway has captured the interest of the local Japanese, who come to enjoy the cooking of Tak Suetsugu, formerly of the Mikado. The tempura is light as air, the sushi merely creditable. For a twist, try the Washington roll, with smoked salmon, tamagoyaki, cucumber, and strips of Washington apple. The black cod kasuzuke, marinated in sake lees and broiled, is a velvety ambrosia. Tatami rooms are available, including one that holds 20—great for a private function. Service is gracious.

GREATER SEATTLE: DES MOINES
RESTAURANTS

Le Bonaparte
S 216th and Marine
View, (206) 878-4412
21630 Marine View
Drive, Des Moines
Expensive; full bar;
AE, DC, MC, V

By mining the territory between traditional French and nouvelle cuisines, this restaurant-in-a-house draws diners from the entire region to the waterfront community of Des Moines, south of the airport. Plan to make an evening of it. Not all of owner-chef Jacques Mason's creations are successful, but he normally has up to four kinds of game birds (squab, duck, quail, pheasant), which he

*Lunch Mon-Fri, dinner
every day, brunch Sun*

prepares in good sauces. Veal dishes have been exemplary. There are some surprising touches, such as the halibut with a light cream fennel sauce, which, oddly enough, accentuates the halibut's own flavor. The chocolate Marie Antoinette gateau made without flour continues to wow even convicted chocoholics. It's especially lovely in summer, when you can eat on the verandah in the shade of venerable old fruit trees. On Sundays, a five-course brunch (with everything from omelets and fruit to pheasant and escargots) literally packs the house—tables are quite close together. Chef Mason puts together imaginative customized menus for private groups of up to 60.

**D'Andrea
(Des Moines Marina Inn)**
*Just west of Marine View
Drive at 223rd and 7th,
(206) 824-7083
22308 Seventh Avenue S,
Des Moines
Moderate; full bar; AE,
DC, MC, V
Lunch Mon-Fri, dinner
every day*

★

A solid white-linen Italian spot in the South End, D'Andrea's features upscale pastas in large portions, well-prepared seafood and veal dishes, chicken, a steak or two, but no pizza. They do an excellent Caesar salad, and good, herby steamed clams. For lunch, a sausage-pepper-onion sandwich—the street-food classic from Little Italy—is transformed into an open-faced knife-and-fork banquet. Some deck seating is provided, but any view of Puget Sound has been pretty effectively blocked by other buildings. Good bar. A private room holds 20.

GREATER SEATTLE: KENT
RESTAURANTS

Cave Man Kitchens
*W Valley Highway at the
James intersection,
(206) 854-1210
807 W Valley Highway,
Kent
Inexpensive; no alcohol;
MC, V
Lunch, dinner every day*

The late Dick Donley was a tinkerer with both machines and food. He spent years experimenting with methods of smoking ribs, chicken, turkey, sausage, and salmon over alder and (when available) apple wood. What he finally achieved was outstanding—especially the moist smoked turkey. Donley's six children carry on after him, and nothing has changed. There is no inside seating, but during warm weather you can eat outside on picnic tables and go across the street to the neighborhood store for beer. Most people take out, loading up on the smoked goods and adding accompaniments such as beans, potato salad, coleslaw, and a terrific bread pudding with butterscotch-whiskey sauce.

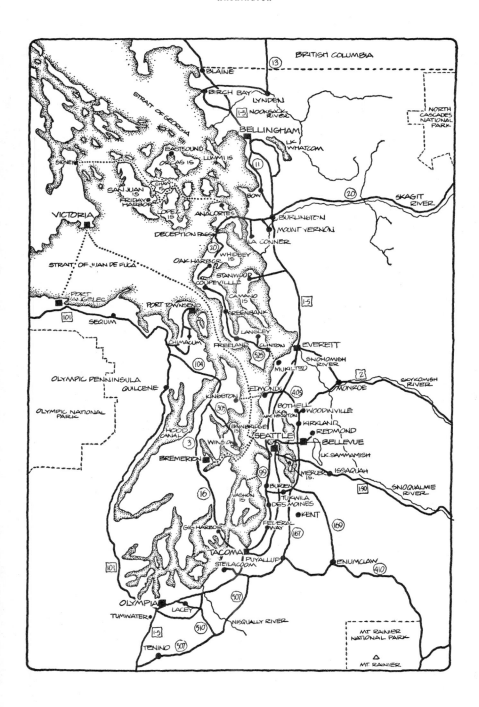

PUGET SOUND

North to south along the I-5 corridor, including side trips to the islands.

BLAINE

Blaine is, well, plain. Not exactly the kind of spot you're likely to make a travel destination unless you have some other reason for visiting this little community snugged up against the border. The flower-bright gardens and the lawns at the border-crossing park around the International Peace Arch are quite lovely, so if you want to picnic en route to or from British Columbia, this is a good, if sometimes crowded, place.

LODGINGS

Inn at Semiahmoo
Take exit 270 off I-5, travel west, watch for signs, (206) 371-2000 9565 Semiahmoo Parkway, Blaine, Mail: PO Box 790, Blaine, WA 98230-0790 Expensive; AE, DC, MC, V

Semiahmoo Spit is a stunning site for a resort, with beachward views of the sea and the San Juans from many of the buildings. It sports lots of amenities: a 300-slip marina convenient to the inn; a house cruise vessel on which you can book excursions through the San Juans or scenic fishing trips; a thoroughly outfitted athletic club (swimming pool, racquetball, squash, tennis, aerobics, weight lifting, tanning, massage, sauna, and Jacuzzi); an endless stretch of beach. Three restaurants (Stars, the Northwest gourmet dining room, plus two more-casual spots) provide the necessary range of culinary alternatives. The golf course, designed by Arnold Palmer, has a very resorty character: not much rough terrain, which accelerates the play. And the place is still spanking new, having just opened its doors in spring of '87.

So why isn't it the best resort in the West? Lots of little things, which leave us feeling vaguely as though Semiahmoo is more glorified motel than luxury resort. If anything, the Inn is more a convention destination and less a tourist attraction. The adjacent convention center, where revamped cannery buildings make top-notch meeting arenas, is really Semiahmoo's greatest strength: it's a nice place to do business. But vacationers might well be disappointed by the mediocre food in the restaurants and by the mindless cliches of decor (a books-bought-by-the-linear-foot library; a fireplace that is left dark and cold on a dark and cold day). Rooms, while sporting all the right postmodern colors, don't integrate them into a harmonious scheme. Systems noises have been far too audible through the walls. Views, though splendid from the bayside rooms, are nonexistent in others (request a second-floor room). Food in the lounge is overpriced and no better than average.

BIRCH BAY

It's just the place for 1950s teenage nostalgia. The crescent-shaped beach draws throngs of kids—cruising the strip, go-carting, hanging out in the arcade (open Memorial Day through Labor Day). Frankie and Annette are all that's missing. There's a state park for camping and lots of sandy beach to wiggle between your toes. Off-season can be very off.

LODGINGS

Jacobs Landing Rentals
Take exit 270 off I-5,
head west for 5 miles
follow signs,
(206) 371-7633
7824 Birch Bay Drive,
Birch Bay, WA 98230
Moderate; AE, MC, V

This is the best of the condo developments, right in the "middle of town," across the main street from the beach. Units are set at angles among the beautifully maintained grounds—affording some of them better water views than others. Suites (1-, 2-, and 3-bedroom units) are modern and deluxe, with fireplaces, kitchens, and washers and dryers. There are outdoor tennis courts, an indoor heated pool, a Jacuzzi, and racquetball courts to keep everyone busy.

LYNDEN

This picture-perfect, neat and tidy community sports immaculate yards and colorful gardens lining the shady avenue into downtown, which has adopted a Dutch theme (slightly overdone) in tribute to a community of early inhabitants. Be sure to visit the charming and informative **Pioneer Museum** full of local memorabilia and antique buggies and motorcars.

RESTAURANTS

Hollandia
In the Dutch Village
at Guide Meridian and
Front, (206) 354-4133
655 Front Street, Lynden
Inexpensive; beer and
wine; MC, V
Lunch Mon-Sat,
dinner Tues-Sat

Riding on the tails of bigger Dutchified establishments is a slightly more tasteful and quiet bistro that offers a selection of authentic fare imported from The Netherlands. It's located just off the base of the windmill in the center of town. Chef Dini Mollink works competently on what is, to the American palate, rather heavy cuisine. A safe choice is, believe it or not, the Toeristenmenu: Groentesoep (Dutch meatball soup—firm, tasty meatballs in a luscious homemade broth with bits of vegetable), Schnitzel Hollandia (chicken breast in a just-crunchy light breading), and little almond tarts for dessert. A less filling selection would be the Koninginnesoep met crackers (the Queen's cream soup, a rich chicken soup served with fresh raisin bread and thin slices of Gouda cheese). A small spice cookie accompanies your after-dinner coffee—a nice touch.

LODGINGS

Le Cocq House Bed and Breakfast
Exit 256 off I-5, head north on Route 539 for 12 miles, (206) 354-3032 719 West Edson Street, Lynden, WA 98264 Moderate; MC, V

Mary Le Cocq, the town's best-loved civic matriarch, once lived here; now Bonnie and Bob Sunday warmly welcome guests to select from four large, comfortably furnished rooms—with a maximum of two rooms occupied per night to maintain the quiet calm a bed and breakfast implies. One room is wheelchair-accessible. Guests have their own cozy den, where they may nestle in front of a fire with their morning coffee or afternoon tea. Breakfasts reflect the bounty of nearby dairy and berry farms; the Dutch baby is a favorite.

Dutch Village Inn
Front and Guide Meridian, (206) 354-4440 655 Front Street, Lynden, WA 98264 Moderate; MC, V; checks ok

One might question an inn located in a windmill in a Dutch-theme village. This particular inn, however, provides six authentically designed, tastefully furnished, and luxuriously appointed rooms to please all but the most jaded of travelers. Not surprisingly, the rooms are named for the Dutch provinces; Friesland Kamer, the room named for the northernmost, occupies the top of the windmill. Views are lovely, but interrupted rhythmically as the giant blades of the windmill pass by (turning, fully lit, until 10pm). There are special touches in all the rooms—two have extra beds fitted into curtained alcoves in true Dutch fashion, and several have two-person tubs. Breakfast is served from the full menu of the cafe, just off the lobby and along the village "canal."

FERNDALE

Hovander Homestead Park is a county-run working farm where kids can pat the animals, prowl the barn, or have a picnic along the Nooksack River. The centerpiece is the farmhouse, built in 1903 by a retired Swedish architect, Holand Hovander, with many gables set off by scalloped trim. 5299 Neilsen Road, south of Ferndale off Hovander Road, (206) 384-3444. Call ahead for hours.

BELLINGHAM

Four earlier towns compose the present city, situated on three rivers that flow into a broad bay (the mishmash grid of streets stems from this origin). Only recently has the downtown architecture been rediscovered: the town is full of fine old houses, distinguished newer architecture at Western Washington University, stately streets, and lovely parks. It's also the most "Californian" of Washington's cities, with a lingering dash of counterculture at the university and its environs. Currently, an economic boom promises to bring change and economic expansion to Whatcom County, this "Fourth Corner" of the continental US.

Whatcom Museum of History and Art, a massive Romanesque building, dates from 1892 and was used as a city hall until 1940. It has been beautifully restored, and the exhibits are imaginatively mounted: Eskimo and Northwest Coast Indian

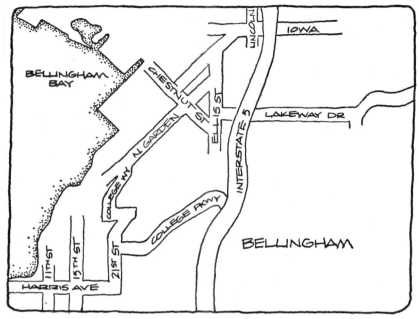

artifacts, pioneer photographs, logging lore. Sometimes the rotunda hosts concerts. 121 Prospect Street, (206) 676-6981.

Old homes. For some of the best touring of turn-of-the-century mansions, check out Utter Street, between Madison and Monroe; West Holly Street, from Broadway to C Street; Eldridge Avenue; and North Garden Street, from Myrtle to Champion. Also worth a visit, in the south end of town, are the homes on Knox Avenue from 12th to 17th and on Mill Street near 15th; the Roland G. Gamwell House (1890) at 16th and Douglas; and the Craftsman-style Roeder Home on Sunset Drive, open to the public.

Big Rock Garden Nursery has a vast array of azaleas, rhododendrons, and Japanese maples set back in the woods on a wonderful site. 2900 Sylvan, near Lake Whatcom, (206) 734-4167.

Old Town, around West Holly and Commercial streets, hosts antique and junk shops and some interesting eateries.

Fairhaven. A short-lived railroad boom from 1889 to 1893 created this burg, which went into a decline until a California investor bought a lot of the old buildings in the 1970s. Now it's a district of Bellingham. In 1988 **The Marketplace**, the central figure among the old attractive buildings, was reopened after restoration, with many interesting shops and restaurants inhabiting its stately interior. The district is rich with diversion: craft galleries, coffeehouses (**Tony's Coffees and Teas** roasts their own beans and supplies much of Bellingham), an excellent bookstore, two intimate art-film houses, and a hopping evening scene make this the place for Bellingham bohemia. As of October, 1989, it is also scheduled to be the southern terminus of the **Alaska Marine Highway System** (formerly located in Seattle), offering weekly sailings for passengers and vehicles to and from Southeast Alaska along the Inside Passage; (800) 642-0066.

Western Washington University, on Sehome Hill south of downtown, is a fine expression of the spirit of Northwest architecture: warm materials, formal echoes of European styles, respect for context and the natural backdrop. Notable are the Ridgeway Dormitory complex by Bassetti and Morse, with its extraordinary sensitivity to terrain; the Social Sciences Building, by Ibsen Nelsen & Associates, with its elaborate concrete structural patterns; Mathes and Nash Hall by Henry Kelin, with a curvilinear echo of Aalto; and the Central Quadrangle, with its feeling of a Danish town square and sculpture by Noguchi (sculpture throughout the campus is of high international order).

Lake Whatcom Railway, at the south end of Lake Whatcom, makes summer weekend runs through lake, creek, and canyon scenery, using an old Northern Pacific steam engine; (206) 595-2218.

Mount Baker Vineyards is an attractive, cedar-sided, skylit facility specializing in rather exotic wines. Rare varietal offerings such as Muller-Thurgau and Madeleine Angevine accompany somewhat less exotic blushes and blends. This far-north vineyard, a fine stop on a day trip to Mount Baker, is located 11 miles east of Bellingham on the Mount Baker Highway; (206) 592-2300.

Teams from all over the world participate in the annual **Ski to Sea race**, a six-sport relay on Memorial Day weekend that begins at Mount Baker ski resort and ends in Fairhaven at Marine Park.

RESTAURANTS

Il Fiasco

Across from the parkade,
at Commercial and Holly,
(206) 676-9136
1309 Commercial Street,
Bellingham
Moderate; full bar;
MC, V
Lunch Mon-Fri,
dinner every day

★ ★ ★

Il Fiasco (Italian for "the flask") has built a dedicated clientele who come often because the welcome is warm and sincere, the staff friendly and knowledgeable, the decor sophisticated and comfortable, and the menu interesting and ambitious. Many of the selections can be ordered as either appetizer- or entree-sized portions—a relief when you're stymied by indecision—and you're warmly encouraged to make up a dinner of individual appetizer selections if that's what suits. A particularly appealing choice is the antipasti assortito. The chef's selection of seven or eight appetizers might include Anaheim peppers stuffed with mozzarella and pork in a tomato/mint salsa; fresh crab ravioli with brown butter and pecorino; melon wrapped in prosciutto; chicken tortellini in a sun-dried tomato sauce; marinated goat cheese on a garlic crouton. We often select the unusual lasagne di carnevale alla napoletana: layers and layers of lamb, polenta, fresh sage and fontina cheese, tomatoes and spinach—a complex and satisfying dish. Even the simple soups, though, show real talent. The wine list is predominantly Italian, recently broadened by domestic special offerings. Many selections are under $20, and all are available by the glass for those who would like to sample.

La Belle Rose

In the Harbor Center
Building, along the
waterfront,
(206) 647-0833
1801 Roeder Avenue,

In an inconspicuous courtyard corner of Harbor Center is a six-table country-French restaurant with a limited selection—primarily seafood—and a condensed list of beverages. Tres petit, yes, and also tres bon: French cuisine big on flavor and presented with dignity but no fanfare. In allegiance to its harborside location, La Belle

Bellingham
Moderate; wine;
MC, V
Lunch Fri,
dinner Tues-Sat

★ ★

Rose selects (and prepares) seafood with obvious care. A recent saumon en sauce verte arrived delectably moist, accompanied by a mild vinaigrette brimming with plump capers. While meat dishes are scarce, they reflect the skill of Toulouse-trained Mariette Wood. On a cool winter's evening, try the choucroute alsacienne (two large, spicy sausages, a slice of smoky pork, and a generous serving of delicious just-crisp sauerkraut with a boiled potato and, of course, Dijon mustard). For a perfect little hideaway for a romantic tete-a-tete, there's nothing else like it in Bellingham, although a little more attention to detail from the kitchen (eliminating the packaged butter cubes, and fine-tuning the desserts) would be welcome here. Given the menu, we'd like to see a few more whites on the wine list.

M'sieur
Corner of Railroad and
Champion,
(206) 671-7955
130 E Champion Street,
Bellingham
Expensive; beer and wine;
AE, MC, V
Lunch Tues-Fri,
dinner Tues-Sat

★ ★

In step with the times, owner-chef Daniel Ripley over 10 years has established reliable sources for marvelously fresh local products: clams, shrimp, oysters, chicken. On this foundation, the menu offers a variety of selections and preparations. You'll find the sophistication of the kitchen will quell the small irritations of uncomfortable seating and the unfortunate acoustics that make intimate conversation difficult.

We appreciate utterly fresh oysters served on the half shell—with a simple red wine vinegar with shallots. The veal cognac pate remains irresistible. Apparently simple soups, often vegetable purees, are rich in complexity, and a rather straightforward salad wins our respect for its variety of crisp, fresh greens, even in the dead of winter, and its distinctive vinaigrette dressing. High recommendations are awarded to the plump, just-right shrimp and clams in the shell in wonderfully fragrant bouillabaisse-style broth. The lunch selection is dominated by creative salads: shoyu pasta, or chicken, avocado, and orange salad with honey poppyseed dressing.

The wine list (short-shrifted in reds) has a good selection of Northwest, California, and European whites. The list contains a cryptic note to ask about the Meursaults and Montrachets. You ought to. We enjoyed a lovely Meursault for a very reasonable price. Well, for a Meursault, at least.

Pacific Cafe
Off Holly on Commercial,
(206) 647-0800
100 N Commercial,
Bellingham
Moderate; beer and wine;
AE, MC, V

White walls, rice-paper screens, and warm wooden shutters create a serene, tasteful atmosphere. This spot is snuggled into the historic Mount Baker Theatre building in the heart of downtown Bellingham. The menu reflects a bit of owner Robert Fong's Asian influence (via Hawaii). Rib steak with oyster/plum sauce, an appetizer of char sui (Cantonese barbecued pork loin), and teriyaki chicken (not the ubiquitous fast-food version) all grace the menu. Recently both the Alaska spot prawns in black bean garlic

*Lunch Tues-Fri, dinner
Tues-Sat, brunch Sun*

sauce and the Punjabi shrimp curry showed careful attention to selection and preparation, but the sauces displayed a certain timidity in spicing. Portions are generous, and the accompanying Thai jasmine rice pilaf is a nice touch. Desserts are luscious; save room. A lingering lunch here is a treat—savoring a perfectly prepared rack of lamb or a flavorful bowl of borscht and culminating with a cafe latte accompanied by a dreamy chocolate eclair. The wine list offers a better selection of whites than reds, with the Northwest well represented, and there are some interesting though expensive white Burgundies.

Around the Corner Cafe
*Holly and Railroad,
(206) 733-8996
133 E Holly, Bellingham
Inexpensive; no alcohol;
no credit cards; checks ok
Breakfast, lunch Mon-Fri*

Denise Ranney and her two helpers get the place rolling early in the morning, baking all their own pastries and desserts (except the whole-wheat cinnamon rolls) and concocting their daily specials. "Morning pick-me-ups" include our favorite all-in-one muffins (bacon, egg, and Cheddar baked into a muffin), pocket breakfasts (biscuit-like pastry stuffed with Cheddar and ham, bacon, or sausage), and the old standby biscuits and gravy. No fried eggs here, though a funky little quichelike omelet with optional salsa satisfies egg-eaters. For lunch the meat pies are faves; but the daily special (lemon herbed chicken, lasagne, or the very popular meat loaf and mashed potatoes) is always a substantial meal, including two salads and a hot roll ($3.95). Denise will make you feel right at home, remembering your face, name, and occupation on your second visit. You'll remember the blueberry muffins!

The Bagelry
*Railroad near Champion,
(206) 676-5288
1319 Railroad Avenue,
Bellingham
Inexpensive; no alcohol;
no credit cards; local
checks only
Breakfast, lunch every day*

Expatriate East Coasters will delight in the dense crusty New York–style bagels, six or seven kinds of which are offered hot from the ovens daily. The pumpernickel is especially good, with onion running a close second. The tasty bialys here look more like large bagels without a hole and make an addictive base for a sandwich. Try the tender and moist smoked Virginia ham. The bagel sandwiches are double, open-faced and piled with freshly made spreads and salads—the chopped chicken liver is delightful, and the scallion and veggie spreads are very good too. The large breakfast omelets are quite reasonable, most under $3 (try the pesto-filled for $4.25). Dharma juices are fresh and flavorful, and the cooler holds a lot of other drinks as well.

Cobblestone Kitchen
*Behind Great Stuff on
11th in Fairhaven,
(206) 671-0442
1308B 11th Street,
Bellingham
Inexpensive; beer and
wine; AE, MC, V*

It's set up as half cafeteria, half sit-down dining, so diners aren't quite sure what to do; but don't be shy. Help yourself from the array of fresh hot soups (four to choose from), intriguing salads, interesting entrees, and wonderful baked goodies. Have a seat (out on the walk, in the dining room, or in the old double-decker bus parked outside), and your harried waitress will be with you shortly

Lunch, dinner Mon-Sat, brunch Sun

Eleni's

The Lakeway Drive exit off I-5, directly across from Fred Meyer, (206) 676-5555 1046 Lakeway Center, Bellingham Inexpensive; beer and wine; MC, V Lunch, dinner Mon-Sat

The Mona Lisa Italian Deli

The Lakeway exit off I-5, 200 yards east of Fred Meyer, (206) 734-4646 1310 Lakeway Drive, Bellingham Inexpensive; no alcohol; no credit cards; checks ok Lunch, dinner Mon-Sat

Pepper Sisters

Near the corner of Garden and Holly, (206) 671-3414 1222A Garden Street, Bellingham Inexpensive; beer and wine; MC, V Dinner Tues-Sat

to take your beverage order. There are a select wine list, local juices, and espresso to choose from, and if you've room, luscious homemade desserts.

In Greece, hospitality is taken seriously, and Eleni's brings that tradition to this Formica-and-plastic setting sandwiched between the supermarket and Radio Shack. Eleni spoils with open arms and warm-hearted food. The dolmathes—tender grape leaves wrapped around a moist, flavorful filling in a shimmering egg-lemon sauce alive with fresh juice—are remarkably good. Eleni's Greek salad is a feast of sturdy feta, tomatoes, olives, peppers, onions, cucumbers, and crisp lettuce in tangy Greek vinaigrette. For those with an insatiable appetite—or for the indecisive—a sure bet is the Greek platter for two, a generous sampling of moussaka, pastitsio, dolmathes, pork souvlaki, spanakopita, and tyropita. A word of caution for those who prefer their red wine at room temperature: your demestika will come ice-cold unless you request it otherwise.

Only a few tables in a tiny storefront amid a neon strip, this unpretentious little deli is one of the few sources of true Italian prosciutto in the Northwest (via Canada). The selection is modest, but the quality is very good (especially the sausages in links or bulk). The pasta dishes are authentic, and many of the dishes, whether lasagne, cannelloni, or pizza, share a particularly tasty tomato sauce thick with lusty herbs. Take home a sandwich or a pizza (you bake). For dessert, the cannoli are utterly fresh, crisp, and only moderately sweet. Pity there's no vino rosso to wash down all this hearty Italian bounty.

For a quick trip to Santa Fe, head to the Pepper Sisters. The cafe has made the best of a tiny, out-of-the-way location—even so, you're there for the food. The kitchen handcrafts the carne adovada, a pork stew simmered in chile sauce served with beans and posole (hominy)—similar to, but more picante than, their pork and posole stew. A favorite is the individual-size Southwest Pizza—a cornmeal crust with tomatillo sauce, topped with fresh-roasted chiles, cherry tomatoes, mushrooms, pine nuts, and cheese ($6.50; $7.50 with chorizo—and worth the extra). A tasty departure from the Mexican version is the pork burrito—a whole-wheat or flour tortilla rolled with chiles and pork and topped with green chile sauce. We'd like to see the chips and salsa ($1.50) served free while you wait for your entree. Billowy sopapillas with honey are a delightfully sweet ending.

Seoul Garden

Behind the Mount Baker
Theatre in downtown
Bellingham,
(206) 671-3083
121 Unity Street,
Bellingham
Inexpensive; beer and
wine; AE, MC, V
Lunch Mon-Fri,
dinner Mon-Sat

Koto music and Korean top-40 hits alternate in this boxy restaurant with all the charm of a dry cleaner's. Korean food is more—and less—than a hybridized Japanese cuisine. The influences are clear, yet certain things are quite dissimilar—an utter indifference as to presentation, for one. No careful Zen arrangements of sushi here; everything is plopped hastily onto the plastic dishes. On the other hand, portions are generous. Our combination sushi ($6.90) included an excellent tako (octopus), toro (salmon), ebi (prawn), and several types of maki. The uninformative menu makes careful interrogation of the waitperson necessary.

Begin with miso shiro, the familiar miso broth cloudy with bean paste, tasty but served in a clunky plastic bowl. The classic Korean kim chee, a spicy-hot, vinegary preparation of pickled cabbage, is homemade and is quite a popular side dish. The bul go kee, thinly sliced barbecued beef in a rich, garlicky sauce, is particularly good. Hot and spicy prawns prove to be seven large prawns with a rather predictable mix of vegetables. We were disappointed to find the tempura-like batter had turned utterly soggy in the fiery sauce. The beer list is more ambitious than the wine list—running the gamut from Tiger and Tsingtao to Anchor Steam and Watney's. If you're careful and persistent, you can enjoy an authentic and memorable meal here.

Colophon Cafe

11th near Harris in
Fairhaven,
(206) 647-0092
1210 11th Street,
Bellingham
Inexpensive; no alcohol;
no credit cards; checks ok
Lunch, dinner every day

Distributed between two levels of the best bookstore in town (Village Books), Colophon Cafe is an eatery full of hearty—but not necessarily healthy—persuasions. The food here can be playful—a peanut-butter jambon (on a French roll, of course), or a Reese's sandwich (PB&J with chocolate chips). The soups are good: the "crowded chowder" brims with fresh seafood and comes with several kinds of cheese and wholesome bread. The African peanut soup—popular enough for a permanent place on the menu, in vegetarian and nonvegetarian versions—is chunky with fresh tomatoes, grainy with peanuts, and sparkling with gingerroot. Robust fare to fortify you for that third volume of Proust. A new addition opens onto a cobblestone walkway and grassy area. The Colophon encourages patrons to tarry over their lattes, as is evidenced by a bevy of devotees who meet friends for a lively discussion or snuggle down alone with a good book.

LODGINGS

Schnauzer Crossing

Take exit 253 off I-5,
travel 3.2 miles on
Lakeway Drive, turn left,
(206) 733-0055
4421 Lakeway Drive,

Three miles out of Bellingham, Schnauzer Crossing looks out over Lake Whatcom just below. The main floor is given over to the guests, and consists of a spacious and unusually attractive sitting room, large enough to entertain in (which you are welcome to do), a kitchen (from which will emerge Donna McAllister's creative and ex-

Bellingham, WA 98226
Expensive; MC, V

travagant breakfast), sunny decks, and two guest rooms. The smaller room has a view of the lake, an interesting library, a spacious closet, and its own bathroom. The larger suite is heavenly: an oversized bedroom with a huge bed, a fireplace, overstuffed chairs, and a smaller sitting room (kids can be housed here) looking out over lush greenery and small garden "rooms." A cleverly placed desk provides business travelers with a serene work space. The large and well-appointed bathroom is outstanding, with a big double-headed shower, a skylit Jacuzzi, and loads of thick, raspberry-colored towels.

Tennis on a private court is offered, as are the outdoor hot tub and the use of a canoe or an El Toro sailboat, and joggers and walkers alike will find lots to keep them busy. Donna and Vermont McAllister are warm, friendly people who genuinely enjoy their guests but are never intrusive. Breakfast is often served on the deck overlooking the lake. The schnauzers are dandy but little in evidence.

The Castle
Bed and Breakfast
Corner of 15th and Knox,
(206) 676-0974
1103 15th Street,
Bellingham, WA 98225
Moderate; MC, V

★

Painted an improbable, unmistakable mauve, this ornate house perches high on a hill above Bellingham's Fairhaven District. Inside, nearly every window affords far-reaching views over the bay, if you can take your eyes off the furniture long enough to notice them. The place is full—in the Victorian sense—of antiques. Not just ordinary things, but writhing ebony eagles (that one's a letter holder), clawed tables, wax busts, and lifesize statuary of several persuasions. What isn't carved is beaded, fringed, knobbed, or at least draped with something that is. The walls (and ceilings) are covered with lush floral Victorian papers. One bathroom is very large and similarly adorned. In a word, the decor is authentic.

Glo and Harvey Harriman, the owners, sold their thriving antique business and are enjoying semi-retirement in their castle guest home. The healthful breakfast is served in style, candlelit, at a long formal table looking out on the iris garden. A stay here is a slightly eccentric experience, perfect for those with a sense of humor, not to mention adventure, looking for a comfortable and interesting getaway. Straight across the bay sits the Harrimans' second guest home, Seagoat, a simpler, comfortable waterfront retreat facing Lummi Island.

DeCann House
West on Holly, which
turns into Eldridge,
(206) 734-9172
2610 Eldridge Avenue,
Bellingham, WA 98225

Within this neighborhood of historic homes overlooking Squalicum Harbor Marina, Bellingham Bay, and the San Juan Islands, you'll find a rather unpretentious Victorian bed and breakfast that warmly welcomes visitors to a quiet and comfortable haven. Amid family heirlooms, you may test your skills at the ornate pool table in the front

Moderate; no credit cards;
checks ok

parlor or the interesting collection of wooden mazes in the sitting room. Barbara and Van Hudson provide a log in which you can pass along your impressions and special tips to fellow travelers—a nice touch. They also maintain an extensive current library of travel-related materials, apprising guests of the many opportunities available locally. A complete breakfast, beautifully served, assures a cheery start to the day.

North Garden Inn
Maple and N Garden,
(206) 671-7828
1014 N Garden Street,
Bellingham, WA 98225
Moderate; MC, V

It's really something. This Victorian house (on the National Register of Historic Places) boasts over two dozen rooms plus seven baths, the result of additions early in the century. Only 10 are rented as guest rooms (6 in winter); some have lovely views over Bellingham Bay and the islands. Five full baths are shared. All the rooms are attractive, clean, and with a bit more character than usual—due partly to the antique house, partly to the influence of the energetic and talented hosts. Barbara and Frank DeFreytas are both musical—two grand pianos in performance condition are available to guests, and musical or dramatic evenings occur here just as they probably did at the turn of the century.

In the morning, Barbara is quite likely to grind the wheat for your muffins, and certainly the coffee will be freshly ground. A buffet breakfast here has that wholesome Bellingham flavor; if there aren't too many guests, even the juice will be squeezed that morning.

LUMMI ISLAND

Technically it's one of the San Juan Islands, but this pastoral island is set apart enough from its cousins that it's often forgotten. A small ferry (not state-run) makes the five-minute crossing at least once an hour from Gooseberry Point. Lummi is an ideal day trip for bike riding (especially the island's northern loop), and the **Village Point Restaurant** is a great biker's stop for a piece of pie; (206) 758-2565.

LODGINGS

The Willows
3½ miles from ferry;
call for directions,
(206) 758-2620
2579 West Shore Drive,
Lummi Island, WA 98262
Moderate; beer and wine;
MC, V
Dinner Sat

Run as a resort since 1920, the old Taft family house stands on a bluff, 100 feet above the (accessible) beach, offering a sweeping view of the San Juan and Gulf Islands, active with ship and boat traffic of all sorts. There are four rooms in the main building, and a newly remodeled cottage makes a stunning hideout for incurable romantics. Our favorite room, "Sunset," though smaller than others, reminds us of an enveloping cloud, so inviting are the billowing oh-so-white duvet and crisply starched pillowcases and sheets.

Hostess Victoria Taft Flynn quietly delivers a beautiful tray with coffee and a loaf of hot Irish soda bread first thing in the morning—to get you going and tide you over until you emerge for her superb breakfast (we missed two ferries, lingering over the many special courses of that breakfast). But it's the Saturday night dinner that has won such a following among locals. Guests gather on the porch or in the sitting room for sherry and appetizers, soaking in the expansive view to the strains of a harpist and a classical guitarist. As the sun dips to the horizon, Gary Flynn invites all to the dining room and announces the meal: soup (say, a carrot and orange puree), pasta (fresh spinach fettuccine with scallops and shrimp), salad (a visual and textural extravaganza, including radicchio, arugula, several types of flower blossoms, and lettuces, dressed in a tangy homemade raspberry vinaigrette), entree (Moroccan chicken, mildly spiced, with figs, dried apricots, and black olives), followed by a choice from the dessert trolley (a strawberry meringue torte with mounds of airy whipped cream or a dense chocolate walnut tart). All of this is accompanied by an appropriate and often daring selection of wines. Gary possesses both a sensitive palate and a wonderful cellar. The wines he carefully chooses for each meal are often from the smaller vintners, never available in much quantity and long since gone from your local wine merchant's shelves. Gary is happy to take them from his collection, serve them to his guests, and discuss them with enthusiasm. In civilized fashion, after dinner the guests repair to the sitting room for port. Then, for the lucky few, it's off to their rooms; the less fortunate are off to the ferry and a satisfied drive home.

West Shore Farm
From the ferry, head north on Nugent for 3 miles, (206) 758-2600
2781 West Shore Drive, Lummi Island, WA 98262
Moderate; MC, V

Hop the Lummi Island ferry for a peaceful stay at West Shore Farm; Carl and Polly Hanson will pick you up at the dock if you like. Their handbuilt octagonal house tucks into a slope overlooking the north tip of the island and the Strait of Georgia. Accommodations on the lower level have sweeping views and ground-floor entrances. Readers will appreciate the plethora of interesting books and magazines, comfortable seating, and individual reading lights above the beds. The two guest rooms each have (not en suite but handy) a cedar-paneled and thoughtfully appointed bath.

A substantial breakfast is served at the big round table in the Hansons' inviting quarters; lunch and dinner are available on request. Sleep late, walk the secluded beach, laze on the deck, relax in the sauna.

CHUCKANUT DRIVE

This famous stretch of road between Bellingham and Bow used to be part of the Pacific Highway; now it is one of the prettiest drives in the state, curving along the mountainlike hills and looking out over the water and the San Juans. Unfortunately, if you're in the driver's seat you'll have to keep your eyes on the road and wait for turnoffs for the view; the road is narrow and winding. Take the Chuckanut Drive exit off I-5 heading north, or follow 12th Street south in Bellingham.

Teddy Bear Cove is a nudist beach, and a pretty one at that, on a secluded shore along Chuckanut Drive just south of the Bellingham city limit. No signs; watch for the crowd of cars.

Larrabee State Park, seven miles south of Bellingham, was Washington's first state park. Beautiful sandstone sculpture along the beaches and cliffs provides a backdrop for exploration of the abundant sea life.

The Blau Oyster Company sells not only excellent Samish Bay oysters and clams but an array of other seafoods as well. Call ahead 24 hours (Monday–Thursday) and get a discount on all orders. Go east at the Bow–Edison Road, then right on Bayview Edison Road, and follow the signs to the shucking sheds; 919 North Beach Road, Bow (206) 766-6171.

BOW

RESTAURANTS

The Oyster Bar
Exit 250 off I-5,
(206) 766-6185
240 Chuckanut Drive, Bow
Expensive; beer and wine;
MC, V
Dinner every day

High above quiet Samish Bay, the Oyster Bar has experienced many changes over its 70-odd years. In the 1920s, this was a humble roadside stand, serving oysters—mostly Pacifics introduced by Japanese immigrants—that were hand-carried up a steep trail from the Rockpoint Oyster Company on the beach below. Today this small, 12-table establishment caters mostly to upscale types. Over the last two years we have heard tales of uneven quality and overly effete presentations—failings that were traceable, perhaps, to owner Guy Colbert experimenting with a roster of guest chefs. So we were heartened to discover on a recent visit that the Oyster Bar has recovered its footing. With chef Dennis Hansen (formerly of San Francisco's Chez Michelle) in the kitchen, we were offered a plate of delicate crab cakes, followed by a most aromatic and light-tasting salmon en croute. A shelled, steamed Australian lobster was bedded on pasta and flavored with a delayed-action lime beurre blanc sauce. The tendency of chefs to oversalt food here has disappeared; we found the seasonings to be imaginative and complementary—and the size of the portions increased.

Desserts are exceptional, particularly the strawberry mousse and the thick but not debilitating mórt au chocolat, several layers of chocolate genoise and chocolate mousse sealed in a chocolate ganache. The daunting wine list offers some better bargains than it used to. Service is attentive and democratic (a party of high-school prom-goers next door received as much care as we did), if a bit formal and rehearsed. Small children are not permitted in the restaurant; cigarettes are.

Oyster Creek Inn

About a half-hour's drive
south of Bellingham on
Chuckanut Drive,
(206) 766-6179
190 Chuckanut Drive, Bow
Moderate; beer and wine;
MC, V
Lunch, dinner every day

Tucked into the woods, this peaceful place is green and cool in summer, pleasantly cozy in winter. Walls are covered with nautical charts, tables are widely spaced, and the prevailing mood is calm. A casual downstairs bar area that overlooks a small, busy creek is a good spot for appetizers, a beer, or dessert and coffee. The bar is frequented by an amiable mix of fishermen in jeans and cool guys in business suits. Raw yearling Samish oysters are excellent here, as are steamed mussels in fresh basil cream. Most of the food is simple, fresh, and well prepared (read *classic*). The baked oyster medley comes to the table on the mandatory rock-salt base, and includes oysters topped with cream cheese and shrimp, some with spinach and slivers of onion in a tangy hollandaise, and others with a spicy vegetable and bacon topping. Broiled prawns are big Alaskan beauties, split and grilled in their jackets with a lovely garlicky lemon sauce. Geoduck is a unique item, sauteed and served with hazelnut butter. The beer and wine list is exclusively Northwestern.

The Rhododendron Cafe

At the Bow-Edison
junction, (206) 766-6667
553 Chuckanut Drive, Bow
Moderate; beer and wine;
MC, V
Lunch Fri-Sat, dinner
Wed-Sun, brunch Sun

The modest printed menu gives little hint of what is in store for the adventurous eater at the Rhododendron. Six to ten daily specials appear on the board: generally a couple of seafood dishes, a stew, something with meat, and a pasta, but the specifics change constantly. The idea, something like cuisine spontanee, is to make use of the freshest available ingredients, combining them in new ways so that neither the kitchen nor the clientele gets bored. In practice it can make for some unevenness, especially when the house is packed, and recent reports of laziness in the kitchen are a big yellow flag.

Still, basics are very good: the oysters and clams always fresh and well prepared, the steaks among the best in the area. A staple of the regular menu is the snapper esmeralda, marinated, baked on sliced potatoes, and then topped with a toasted nut sauce. Salads are outstanding: always crisp, with nicely varied greens and inventive dressings. Soup might be chicken almond—rich stock with cream, shreds of chicken, and lashings of grated toasted almonds—or a fragrant vegetable broth chunky with mussels. Broiled halibut or mahi mahi is often treated with marvelous, simple, buttery herb sauce. Desserts are homemade and locally famous; ice creams, pies, and a silky pot de creme are all outstanding. The beer and wine list reflects regional bests, with some fine imports as well; but the coffee is surprisingly average. Service, though usually adequate, can get shaky when the place fills up. No smoking.

LODGINGS

Alice Bay B&B
*Just right of the map
billboard at the base of
Samish Island, at the end
of Scott Road,
(206) 766-6396
982 Scott Road, Bow,
WA 98232
Moderate; no credit cards;
checks ok*

Overlooking the eelgrass beds and clamming flats of Samish Bay, on the southeast side of Samish Island, rests this small, quiet B&B. There's only one guest room, but it has a private entrance and its own bath. The attractive, uncluttered room has a thick, comfortable futon bed; this, the quiet, and the fresh air make you sleep very soundly. Guests have access to a private beach, wonderful for solitary rambling, and the hot tub is a pleasure at night. A heron rookery adjoins the property, and you might see several hundred of these glorious creatures fishing in the small bay. Nonsmokers only.

Every morning Julie Rousseau fixes a fine continental breakfast of excellent homemade scones, coffee cake, or muffins, with fresh fruit and first-rate freshly ground coffee accompanying. If the tides are right, the Rousseaus will harvest the excellent local clams and oysters from the beach, serving them steamed or on the half shell; obviously, nothing could be fresher.

BURLINGTON

RESTAURANTS

El Gitano
*Across from the
Memorial Park at
E Fairhaven,
(206) 755-9010
624 E Fairhaven,
Burlington
Inexpensive; beer
and wine; MC, V
Lunch, dinner every day*

El Gitano started out as a Mexican/Hungarian restaurant, logically enough: founding owners John and Angie Bosver are of, respectively, Hungarian and Mexican origin. However, due to a thriving Latino community and not much interest in Hungarian food, the Bosvers decided to serve exclusively Mexican food. Now nephew Adrian Ivarra is carrying on that tradition, using locally procured vegetables and meats to make hot homemade salsas and some of the most sumptuous nachos we've seen. Highly variable—but when it's good, it's marvelous.

ANACORTES

RESTAURANTS

La Petite
*34th and Commercial,
(206) 293-4644
3401 Commercial
Avenue, Anacortes
Moderate; full bar;
AE, DC, MC, V
Breakfast every day,
dinner Tues-Sun*

La Petite, hidden in the Islands Motel, is the brightest spot in Anacortes' generally humdrum eating offerings. The food is predominantly French-inspired with a few Dutch touches, reflecting the heritage of the Hulscher family, the long-time owners. The limited menu changes regularly and seasonally; some favorites are chicken breast with garlic sauce atop freshly made Parmesan pasta; pork tenderloin in mustard sauce; and fresh sole stuffed with shrimp, blanketed with a tart lemon and wine cream sauce. And then there are the extras: wine-laced cream of mushroom soup; delicious, crackling-crusted dinner-size bread loaves baked fresh; desserts heavy on chocolate. The fixed-price Dutch breakfast is intended primarily for motel guests, but makes a treat for outsiders as well.

LODGINGS

Channel House
Oakes and Dakota,
(206) 293-9382
2902 Oakes Avenue,
Anacortes, WA 98221
Moderate; MC, V

Just a mile and a half from the ferry dock, Dennis and Pat McIntyre's Channel House is a 1902 Victorian home designed by an Italian count. There are four antique-filled rooms in the main house, two with private baths, all with grand views of Puget Sound. A new cottage contains two suite-style units, complete with fireplaces and private whirlpool baths; the Victorian Rose room has its own deck and is especially nice. There is a large hot tub out back—great for weary travelers—and the McIntyres serve cozy breakfasts before a roaring fire on chilly days. Freshly baked cookies and Irish Cream coffee await guests returning from dinner.

SAN JUAN ISLANDS

There are 743 at low tide and 428 at high tide; 172 have names; 60 are populated; and only 4 have major ferry service. The San Juan Islands are varied, remote, and breathtakingly beautiful. They are also located in the rain shadow of the Olympics, and most receive half the rainfall of Seattle. Great! But, as expected, the sparsely populated islands are rather overrun in the summer months, and getting a ferry out of Anacortes can be a long, dull three-hour-and-up wait. Bring a good book—or park the car and board with a bike. The lineup for accommodations can be even more troublesome: reserve early.

The four main islands—Lopez, Shaw, Orcas, and San Juan— have lodgings and eateries and some beautiful parks. Lopez, Orcas, and San Juan are discussed below; Shaw has little on it other than the world's only ferry landing run by nuns (they also have a certified dairy—three cows—and a campground with eight sites).

SAN JUAN ISLANDS: LOPEZ

Lopez Island, flat and shaped like a jigsaw-puzzle piece, is a sleepy, rural place, famous for its friendly locals (they always wave) and its cozy coves and full pastures. It has the easiest bicycling in the islands: a 30-mile circuit suitable for the whole family to ride in a day. You can camp at **Odlin County Park** (80 acres) or **Spencer Spit State Park** (130 acres), both on the north side. Odlin has many nooks and crannies, and grassy sites set among Douglas firs, shrubs, and clover. Spencer Spit has around 30 conventional campsites, and more primitive sites on the hillside. Both parks have water, toilets, and fire pits. **Agate County Park**, at the southwest tip of the island, has a pleasant, rocky beach for the tired cyclist. A great place for a sunset.

Lopez Village is basic, but has a few spots worth knowing about, such as **Holly B's Bakery**, with celebrated fresh bread and pastries and coffee to wash them down (open June through September); and **Jeanna's Seafood Gallery**, a fresh-fish market that also serves the goods cleanly fried for lunch and dinner. Both are located in the Lopez Plaza.

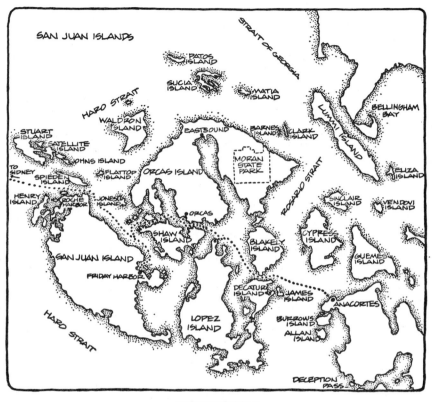

San Juan Islands map

RESTAURANTS

Bay Cafe
*Across from the post
office in Lopez,
(206) 468-3700
Main Street,
Lopez Village
Inexpensive; beer
and wine; MC, V
Lunch, dinner Wed-Sun,
brunch Sun*

Without sacrificing any of its cheerful, personal appeal, new owner and chef Bob Wood has expanded the Bay Cafe to occupy the whole of this former storefront space in "downtown Lopez." Entertaining a full house of both tourists and Lopezians most nights, the restaurant seems only to be increasing in popularity.

Specializing in ethnic dishes, Bob changes the menu monthly to include such innovative preparations as Dungeness crab enchiladas, pork tenderloin with Indonesian-style peanut sauce, at least one continental entree (such as London broil), and at least one vegetarian dish (perhaps red and black bean quesadillas, or a curry of the day). On weekends, a single regional cuisine is explored, with locals reporting preferences for his Thai and Indonesian specialties. One Mediterranean spree started with delicious chilled garlic soup and a colorful Greek salad, and included splendid entree choices of lemon chicken, Fisherman's Stew (a sherry-flavored cioppino), and marinated lamb with vegetables. The vegetarian moussaka was the only disappointment, being somewhat bland and overrun with cinnamon. For dessert we sampled a refreshing raspberry sorbet and passed on a luscious-looking chocolate fudge cake. Prices are reasonable: if we were lucky enough to live nearby we'd be regulars too.

Gail's
Lopez Village,
(206) 468-2150
Moderate; beer and wine;
MC, V
Breakfast, lunch, dinner
every day (dinner Fri-Sat
only in winter)

Gail's covers a lot of ground: as restaurant, delicatessen, and catering service. It's a local standby that also attracts droves of bicyclists and weekend motorists. Soups, entrees (different every day), and decadent desserts are all homemade, and a complete wine and beer list is available. Deli sandwiches and burgers are basic but satisfying, while the daily lunch offerings of quiches, vegetable pastries, and chowders vary in quality. Still, Gail's is best on a summer's eve, when you can sit on the deck, quaff a beer, and finish off a bowl of Lopez mussels. At peak mealtime hours Gail's can get quite hectic, which is reflected in the service.

LODGINGS

Inn at Swift's Bay
Head 1 mile south of
ferry to Port Stanley
Road, left 1 more mile,
(206) 468-3636
Port Stanley Road,
Mail: Rte 2, Box 3402,
Lopez Island, WA 98261
Moderate; MC, V

With their remarkable knack for knowing how to prepare and care for guests without ever appearing intrusive, Robert Herrmann and Christopher Brandmeir have turned this former summer home into the most appealing accommodation on Lopez Island. Choose from two large and comfortable bedrooms with shared bath, or two luxurious suites: one with a magnificent view of the fir-encircled yard, the other a highly successful renovation of the attic, featuring an antique sleigh bed and several rectangular skylights ($95). There's also a secluded, outdoor hot tub which can be scheduled for private sittings (towels, robes, and slippers provided). There's a first-class selection of recorded music and movies on tape for evening entertainment.

Expect to be pampered. Christopher is an excellent breakfast chef and serves the morning meal in the bright dining room.

MacKaye Harbor Inn
12 miles south of the
ferry landing on
MacKaye Harbor Road,
(206) 468-2253
Mail: Rte 1, Box 1940,
Lopez Island, WA 98261
Moderate; beer and wine;
MC, V
Dinner Tues-Sun (summer),
Sat only (winter)

Bicyclists call it paradise, after their sweaty trek from the ferry to this little harbor. The tall house sits above a sandy, shell-strewn beach, perfect for sunset strolls or pushing off to explore the scenic waterways—which makes the crowd at the inn sometimes seem like a kayaking mini-convention. For nature-lovers not of the paddling persuasion, there's plenty of bird and other wildlife to enjoy on land, as well. Inside, the five rooms have been done up a bit sparsely but tastefully, with a second-story deck for lounging and sunset-ogling. An extra treat is the best dinner on Lopez, served six days a week in summer, Saturdays only in the off-season, in the elegant, sunny mauve-

and-oak dining room. Nonguests are welcome, but space is limited. Fresh local seafood is the specialty, prepared and served with some flair. Breakfasts are full and filling.

Marean's
Blue Fjord Cabins
Elliott Road at Jasper
Cove, (206) 468-2749
Mail: Rte 1, Box 1450,
Lopez Island, WA 98261
Moderate; no credit cards;
checks ok

Lopez is the most secluded and tranquil of the three islands with tourist offerings, and Blue Fjord Cabins is the most secluded and tranquil getaway on Lopez. The three log cabins are tucked away up an unmarked dirt road, each concealed from the others by thick .woods. They're of modern chalet design, clean and airy, with full kitchens. Rates are a deal: $55 a night with a two-night minimum (three nights in July and August). A fourth cabin, "Sugarbush," is more a home than a cabin, with 1,300 square feet, loft, fireplace, full kitchen, limited view of the water, and sleeping accommodations for six; $95 for a couple, $10 per extra body. Doing nothing never had such a congenial setting.

SAN JUAN ISLANDS: ORCAS

It was named by a Spanish explorer for the Viceroy of Mexico Don Juan Vicente de Guemes Pacheco y Padilla Orcasitas y Aguayo, Conde de Revilla Gigedo, but let's just call it Orcas for short. Orcas is the hilliest of the four big San Juans, boasting Mount Constitution, from whose old stone lookout tower you can see Vancouver, Mount Rainier, and everything in between. You can drive to the top, but the trail through 4,800-acre **Moran State Park** is prettier. Moran has one lake for freshwater swimming, three more for fishing and boating, and nice campsites, but you must write at least two weeks ahead for reservations: Moran, Star Route Box 22, Eastsound, WA 98245.

RESTAURANTS

Bilbo's Festivo
Northbeach Road and A
Street, (206) 376-4728
A Street, Eastsound
Inexpensive; full bar;
AE, MC, V
Lunch Thurs-Sat, dinner
Tues-Sun, brunch Sun

Orcas Islanders, and off-island fans who keep coming back, speak of this cozy little place with reverence. Its decor and setting—mud walls, Mexican tiles, arched windows, big fireplace, handmade wooden benches, spinning fans, in a small house with a flowered courtyard—are charming, and the Navajo and Chimayo weavings on the walls are indeed from New Mexico. The fare is a combination of Mexican, Spanish, and New Mexican influences with improvisation on the themes of enchiladas, burritos, and chiles rellenos. Distinctively seasoned but only moderately fiery. Nightly specials grilled over mesquite might be carne asada (lime-marinated sirloin strips served with Spanish rice, refried beans, and flour tortillas), or pollo en naranjas (chicken marinated in orange sauce served with new potatoes, fresh asparagus, and salad). Lunch includes ceviche salad (raw fish or seafood marinated for 24 hours in lime juice) and a wide array of soups, salads, and grilled white fish. Full selection of Mexican beers, plus liquors. Get a margarita. No lunches, and variable dinners in winter.

Christina's

North Beach Road and
Horseshoe Highway,
(206) 376-4904
Horseshoe Highway,
Eastsound
Moderate; full bar;
AE, DC, MC, V
Dinner every day
(summer), Thurs-Mon
(winter), brunch Sun

Meals at Christina's vary from superb to merely quite good—a result not of sloppiness but rather of continual experimentation within the neo-continental/new Northwest genres. This means that Christina's doesn't grow boring with repeated visits. The decor is a nice balance of elegance and natural-wood simplicity; try for one of the small tables on the enclosed porch, where the view of sunset over East Sound makes lingering even easier, or if weather permits, a seat on the new rooftop terrace. Christina's works hard to land the best seafood and other fresh local ingredients. It does (and never overdoes) fish and meats with impeccable care: a grilled chicken breast stuffed with pancetta, eggplant, and peppers; a lamb chop with juniper aioli; *fresh* oysters from Crescent Beach Farm. The salmon dishes are reportedly the best around. The changing dessert selections tend toward the irresistible—top-flight cappuccino cheesecake and delicate ice cream puffs in loganberry sauce on last trial. Christina's wisely eschews scattering its attention on lunch, but it serves a fine Sunday brunch. Closed annually from January 1st through Valentine's Day.

Deer Harbor Lodge and Inn

Follow signs to
Deer Harbor,
(206) 376-4110
Mail: PO Box 142,
Deer Harbor, WA 98243
Moderate; beer and wine;
AE, MC, V
Dinner every day
(weekends only in winter)

This expansive, rustic dining room with a large view deck is a cozy, soothing place despite its size, done up nicely in dark blue prints and natural wood. Pam and Craig Carpenter have rescued the inn from its long career as a poultry farm-cum-restaurant (featuring fried chicken) and made it home to the island's best seafood, with generous portions and a strong emphasis on fresh, local ingredients. About a dozen entrees, including beef, chicken, and a staple vegetarian fettuccine, are outlined on the blackboard at the door and varied according to what's in season. Soups and salads arrive in large serving bowls, allowing each diner to partake according to capacity with a minimum of fuss. Fresh homemade bread comes with them. Not only the wine list but the beer list is thoughtfully conceived, with novelties like German wheat beer. Dessert may be homemade ice cream.

The Deer Harbor was the first resort on Orcas, and happily, the Carpenters have seen fit to open a two-story log-cabin bed and breakfast, with eight rooms, two decks, and a breakfast that arrives in a picnic basket outside your door. No smoking at all.

Cafe Olga

Near Moran State Park
at Olga Junction,
(206) 376-4408
Olga Junction, Olga
Inexpensive; beer and
wine; MC, V
Lunch every day

Olga is the name of the hamlet, not the owner. Marcy Lund runs a cozy, inexpensive country kitchen in one corner of the Orcas Island Artworks, a sprawling cooperative crafts gallery in a picturesque renovated strawberry-packing barn. The cooking, usually good, may suffer on Lund's days off. The food is wholesome, international home-style: Greek salad, cheese-spinach manicotti, blackberry pie and other fruit cobblers according to season, fresh-baked cinnamon rolls and pastries, and daily specials. Espresso or chilled applemint cooler wash it all down nicely and make Cafe Olga a favorite local rest station on chilly and sweaty days alike, from brunch to early supper.

La Famiglia

A Street and North Beach Road, Orcas Island, (206) 376-2335
A Street, Eastsound
Inexpensive; full bar;
AE, MC, V
Lunch Mon-Sat,
dinner every day
(Mon-Sat in winter)

Here's a mainstream Italian lunch and dinner spot that seems to have achieved the consistency to match its pleasant, sunny decor, friendly service, and reasonable prices, as witnessed by the many discriminating locals who've become regulars. The emphasis is on fresh pasta, calzone, and other hearty family fare befitting the name; try the chunks of veal sauteed in butter, wine, and lemon, nestled nicely alongside pasta and vegetables.

LODGINGS

Beach Haven Resort

9 miles from the ferry at President Channel, (206) 376-2288
Mail: Rte 1, Box 12, Eastsound, WA 98245
Moderate; no credit cards; checks ok

The sign as you exit on the dirt road reads "Leaving Beach Haven. Entering the world." Cute, but appropriate, especially after the seven-day minimum summer stay. The cabins, shielded by tall trees, are of the genuine log variety, with Franklin stoves. The accommodations range through various grades of rustic to modern apartments and one "Spectacular Beachcomber" four-bedroom house. Everything faces on the long pebble beach, canoes and rowboats are ready if you feel energetic, and the air of tranquillity is palpable enough to chew.

Rosario Resort

Horseshoe Highway, east side of Orcas Island, (206) 376-2222
Mail: Eastsound, WA 98245
Expensive; AE, DC, MC, V

Rosario, the region's premier large resort, has had its share of financial and operational problems. The centerpiece of the complex is a spectacular one, worth a sightseeing stop: the lavish old mansion of shipbuilding tycoon Robert Moran, decked out with memorabilia and an awesome pipe organ still frequently played. You can't stay in the Moran Mansion, however, and the "villas" and "haciendas" (hotel units) up the hill are rather less exciting, with some reports of spotty maintenance. But the view over Cascade Bay is lovely from every point. And the common facilities—bayside pool, tennis, marina, and a full spa in the mansion basement (whose architecture lends an elegant, antique touch to aerobics or hot-tubbing)—are excellent. They also tend to be underused, which should leave you plenty of room while everyone else tours the island. The food, in the gracious Orcas Room, is still mainstream resort.

Turtleback Farm Inn

10 minutes from the ferry, on Crow Valley Road, (206) 376-4914
Mail: Rte 1, Box 650,

The Turtleback is inland, but still scenically located amidst tall trees, rolling pastures, and private ponds. In 1984 it was just another dilapidated farmhouse, used to store hay. Bill and Susan Fletcher have redone it entirely and added a wing, but have kept the country flavor

Eastsound, WA 98245
Moderate; MC, V

with natural wood, wide floor planks, private claw-footed tubs for six of the seven rooms, and excellent antiques. They live in a separate house past the pond, so you won't suffer the B&B horror of feeling you're imposing on Aunt Irma and Uncle Ralph. A glass of sherry tops the evening. Their breakfasts, which may be taken in the well-appointed dining room or on the sunny deck, are the most praised on the island. Besides the usual bacon and eggs, they may include fresh yogurt, crepes with lingonberry sauce, and an example of the ultimate B&B staple that reportedly won the San Juan granola contest.

Doe Bay Village Resort
4 miles east of Olga,
(206) 376-2291
Mail: Star Route 86,
Olga, WA 98279
Inexpensive; AE, MC, V
Breakfast, dinner every
day (summer), breakfast
weekends (winter)

Doe Bay offers not only the cheapest but some of the most peaceful and scenic lodgings on Orcas. The old boat landing on a pretty bay at the island's west end sprouted a ramshackle cluster of cabins that became a resort, then an artist's colony, then the still-much-talked-about Polarity Institute. Lately returned to resort use, the "village" retains some countercultural ambience, but also draws plenty of families driven by noise or overfilling from Moran State Park. Yoga and Tai Chi workshops take the place of water polo, and bathing suits are optional at the bathhouse, where the giant wood-fired sauna and three outdoor tubs (two hot, one cold) overlooking an inlet are a joyous discovery, especially in winter (the resort's open year-round). Accommodations range from campsites to hostel berths to inexpensive cabins with worn or minimal furnishings to better-appointed cottages at moderate prices. There are communal kitchen facilities, a new cafe serving scrumptious, wholesome breakfasts and healthful dinners, kayak trips to a nearby wildlife refuge, and a general store (they'll open it up for you in winter) full of whole-wheat pasta, tofu, and natural body-care products. Retreat facilities are now available, and, for folks just passing through, the hot tubs are open to nonguests at a $5 charge.

Kangaroo House
North Beach Road,
(206) 376-2175
Mail: PO Box 334,
Eastsound, WA 98245
Moderate; MC, V

The location of this bed and breakfast, just past the Orcas airport, isn't scenic, but it's convenient to Eastsound and North Beach. And it's a pleasant, attractive old bungalow, done up in period fashion with good antiques and classic wallpaper. The five rooms are a tad on the small side but well appointed. And the big front porch and rear deck suit lounging in the sun any time of day. New owners Jan and Mike Russillo have added a bit of their personality to the furnishings and have been busy upgrading the place (new mattresses, wallpaper, gardens) since they took over in 1988. The namesake kangaroo that "Cap" Ferris brought here in 1953 is no longer resident.

North Beach Inn

1½ miles west of the airport at North Beach,
(206) 376-2660
Mail: PO Box 80,
Eastsound, WA 98245
Moderate; no credit cards;
checks ok

The Gibson family home, once but no longer the main dining lodge, is a movie-set dream of a turn-of-the-century summer camp. It's high-gabled and surrounded by tall trees; the beach-fronting porch, lined with massive log pillars, will inspire you to put up your feet and start into a very long novel. The 12 little cottages up the rocky beach are nearly buried in blackberries, and worn down to the funky side of rustic. (The spiffier Columbia, Shamrock, and Fraser are available for a price.) But the splendid view and ambience may distract you entirely from the vintage linoleum. The sense of history here is no illusion: the Gibson family has presided over the North Beach Inn since 1932. Pets okay.

Orcas Hotel

Orcas Ferry Landing,
(206) 376-4300
Mail: PO Box 155,
Orcas, WA 98280
Moderate; AE, MC, V
Breakfast, lunch, dinner
every day

Renovated and reopened just a few years ago, this Victorian hostelry is an indispensable addition to the local scene. Sited scenically and conveniently, it perches grandly above the Orcas dock; its deck is the perfect place to wait out a tardy ferry. Proprietor Barbara Jamieson, scion of a notable Virgin Islands hotel family, brings a bed-and-breakfast level of gracious solicitude to this larger 12-room inn and has gathered an equally cheerful, accommodating staff. The rooms are clean, simple, and full of the appropriate period furnishings. Ten rooms share showers down the hall, three of which have half-baths, and at press time two new, larger rooms with private balconies and whirlpool tubs were opening. The kitchen has a new chef who has expanded the menu of fresh seafood dishes. Good, inexpensive soup and sandwiches are served for lunch in the dining room and bar, the latter a convivial local meeting ground.

Outlook Inn

Eastsound,
(206) 376-2581
Mail: PO Box 210,
Eastsound, WA 98245
Moderate; AE, MC, V

Built as a cabin in 1938, this dwelling has had a long history, expanding slowly into a 30-room white clapboard inn (including a 10-room motelish annex) and restaurant. The current tenants have labored with nostalgic zeal to restore it to its original homey ambience. They've antiqued the rooms to hearken back to Grandpa Walton's salad days; the atmosphere is cheery and the motifs relentlessly floral. The inn (as one might guess by its punningly meditative name) was once staffed by members of the Louis Foundation dedicated to upholding the principles of guru Louis Gither. Professional reasons have severed that tie, though new age literature is available at the desk.

The newest addition to Outlook is chef Antony Vincenza Carbone, who is infusing the homespun menu with creative soups, sauces, and ethnic entrees. The menu changes daily, and focuses on fresh seafood, meat, and poultry. The restaurant has a family feel—it's a good place to bring kids.

SAN JUAN ISLANDS: SAN JUAN

San Juan Island is the biggest in the archipelago, and it sports the biggest town, Friday Harbor. The sites of the **American and English camps** are remnants of the famous Pig War of 1859–72, so called because the sole casualty was a pig. The English had the nicer camp; American Camp looks like a desert and is occupied only by rabbits. If you want to do some camping yourself, there's **San Juan County Park**, (206) 378-2992, a dozen often-crowded acres on Smallpox Bay, and **Lakedale Campground**, (206) 378-2350. The best **diving** in the whole archipelago can be had here at **Henry Island**, across from **Snug Harbor Marina Resort**; (206) 378-4762. **Anacortes Dive**, 2502 Commercial Avenue in Anacortes, is the nearest outfitter; (206) 293-2070.

One interesting stop is the nation's first official **whale-watching park**. Pods of orca and minke whales swim regularly by Lime Kiln Point on the western shore of San Juan; here you can spot them (best in late spring, summer, and fall) and the interpreter can answer your questions. West Side Road, six miles from Friday Harbor. There's also **The Whale Museum** downtown, the only museum in the US dedicated to the study of the natural history of cetaceans; 62 First Street N, (206) 378-4710.

Jazz Festival. Throngs of people infest the streets of Friday Harbor for three days of dixieland jazz, mid- to late July; for information, call (206) 378-5509.

RESTAURANTS

Cafe Bissett
1st and West,
(206) 378-3109
170 West Street, Friday Harbor
Moderate; beer and wine;
MC, V
Dinner Thurs-Mon
(every day July-Sept)

Walter Bissett, who formerly operated an acclaimed bed and breakfast (Rally House), worked a small wonder in a bistro-sized sidestreet site, serving dinners of precision and remarkable flavor here: crisp duck in a green peppercorn and brandy sauce, smoked chicken with black-eyed peas, rack of lamb. From its beginning, Cafe Bissett announced a change from the usual island style (or stylelessness)—the furnishings elegant and harmonious, the linen white, the music Edith Piaf. Service was meticulous and polished, but not intimidating.

Now under new ownership, the high standards may be flagging. The decor is still subdued, but the service, while accommodating, is spotty. To start, the music flips indecisively from classical to disco to reggae. Our meal began favorably with fish soup St. Tropez, a delicate combination of salmon and orange topped with roasted red pepper puree, and delicious, crisp French rolls hot from the oven. But after that, the quality faltered. When "salmon wrapped in grape leaves with lemon butter" arrived, it appeared to be a dish of yellow soup with a morsel of salmon on the side. Aside from the portion being disconcertingly stingy (even for nouvelle cuisine), the fish had lost its distinct flavor, and the fresh greens and new potatoes on the side were drenched in oil. The vegetable puree, however, was simple and sweet. Cornish Hen Aioli arrived in a strange, dark broth with limp strands of vegetables; the aioli, which our waiter almost forgot to bring, had only the faintest hint of garlic. The Cafe

Seafood Stew, which turned out to be cioppino, was the popular choice of the evening (perhaps due to its relatively low price and generous servings, though shells can be deceptive). There's every indication that the new owners are resting on someone else's laurels.

Duck Soup Inn

4½ miles north of Friday Harbor on Roche Harbor Road, (206) 378-4878
3090 Roche Harbor Road, Friday Harbor
Expensive; beer and wine; no credit cards; checks ok
Dinner Wed-Sun (closed in winter)

No kitchen in the San Juans is more ambitious than that of Joan Jernigan. The Duck Soup Inn is a pretty, barnlike building by a pond; the cooking is more or less Mediterranean, with a short list of entrees that changes day to day, with an increasing emphasis on fresh local fish. Specialties include local Westcott Bay oysters, plump and tender; Dominican chicken baked in a piquant rum sauce; and mussels prepared with tomato and wine. Squid, sauteed in butter and olive oil and tossed in a sauce of fresh tomatoes and parsley, is simple and delicious. Duck Soup has a fine list of aperitifs and a good, well-priced wine list drawing on Northwest, California, and a few European vintners. Service can be testy at times.

Springtree Eating Establishment and Farm

Under the elm on Spring, (206) 378-4848
Spring Street, Friday Harbor
Moderate; beer and wine; MC, V
Breakfast, lunch, dinner every day

Springtree claims to be "perfecting the fine art of candlelight." This certainly seems true; the waitresses continually rearrange the votives on the tables to keep them from singeing the fresh wildflower bouquets. No problem, however, because everything else is perfect. Now in its second year, Springtree has the culinary expertise of both French-born chef Mark Bilski and newcomer from Colorado Jodi Calhoun. Using produce, herbs, and flowers grown organically at Springtree's very own farm, Bilski and Calhoun serve up a varied menu ranging from arugula stuffed chicken breasts to Island cod florinada (fresh citrus and garden mint sauce over freshly caught cod) to New York steak with sweet pepper salsa. The generous entrees include a crisp green salad, soup or seafood chowder, seasonal vegetables, and basmati rice or potatoes. Meal-sized salads, pastas, and burgers are also available, and the desserts are heavenly.

The homey decor might be described as "contemporary Victorian": white walls, large plate-glass windows, lots of plants, touches of chintz, a china-filled antique hutch, books, and other smaller props. Even the waitresses, who were dressed in floral prints, enhanced the visual effect. (Patio dining available.) The management is clearly dedicated to service, and over the pleasant din of conversation and laughter, we heard more than one party effusively thanking their waitperson for making their evening such an enjoyable one.

Winston's

1 block off Harrison on Nichols, (206) 378-5093
95 Nichols Street,

The menu at this handsome, English-toned restaurant in an old Friday Harbor home strays well beyond the usual fare into eclectic Oriental preparations, still done with admirable consistency. Meats and poultry are featured:

Friday Harbor
Moderate; beer and wine;
MC, V
Dinner Wed-Sat
(daily in summer)

pepper steak with pinot noir wine sauce, duck breast in plum sauce, Asian rib steak. The Sichuan chicken in tangerine sauce doesn't stint on the peppers or the fruity sweetness. An excellent meat-free cannelloni, redolent of herbs, and spicy Sichuan cashew and other vegetarian dishes ensure something for every diet. Salads, an extensive wine list, and the delicious fresh-baked breads and desserts show the same attention to detail. When the place is busy, service can be forgetful.

LODGINGS

Duffy House

Take Argyle Road south
from town to Pear Point
Road, (206) 378-5604
760 Pear Point Road,
Friday Harbor,
WA 98250
Moderate; MC, V

Duffy House bed and breakfast displays an architectural style (Tudor) that's rare in the islands, in a splendid, isolated site above Griffin Bay with a view of the Olympics. A secluded beach and nearby gardens, woods, and orchard offer plenty of room for contemplation. The large farmhouse, with leaded glass and much mahogany, is attractive enough to merit its setting, and plenty roomy for five guest parties. Get ready for a tasty breakfast of quiche, fresh fruit, coffee cake, and muffins. There is also a small beachside cabin that sleeps four for rent in the summer, with its own hot tub.

Hotel de Haro

Roche Harbor, San Juan
Island, (206) 378-2155
Mail: PO Box 4001,
Roche Harbor, WA 98250
Expensive; MC, V

Remember that old Patrick McGoohan TV show *The Prisoner*? When you walk out of the stately old ivy-clad Hotel de Haro at Roche Harbor and gaze out at the trellised, cobblestoned waterfront and yacht-dotted bay, you will—it's a ringer for The Village, the show's setting. The resort evolved from the company town that John McMillin built a century ago for his lime mill, once the largest west of the Mississippi. The hotel attracted such notables as Teddy Roosevelt. It has seen some renovation since his time, but one visitor remarked that the rooms "seem to have been glued together with repeated applications of wallpaper." Still, the 103-year-old hotel has a terrific view, and if it's too quaint for you, you can try the cottages or the new suburban-style condos. The hotel rooms with private baths (only four) have the best views.

Except for the addition of a clothing store above the grocery, you'll barely notice the recent change of ownership—and Vern and Mary Howard (long-time islanders) plan to keep it that way. There's plenty to do at Roche Harbor. A sign with multiple arrows reads "Airport, Mausoleum, Swimming Pool, Tennis, Snack Bar," and there's moorage for 200 boats, a seaplane dock for Lake Union Air from Seattle, a chapel, a grocery, swell gardens, a yacht-side restaurant, and regular entertainment in the lounge. The restaurant serves mediocre food, at odd hours, but everyone looks forward to their seafood brunch (Sundays, June through September). Come evening, the safest course is to drink here and eat elsewhere.

Lonesome Cove Resort

*Take Roche Harbor Road
9 miles north to
Lonesome Cove Road,
(206) 378-4477
5810 Lonesome Cove
Road, Friday Harbor,
WA 98250
Moderate; MC, V*

Back in 1945, Roy and Neva Durhack sailed their 35-foot yacht here from the Hawaiian Islands. They were getting ready to sail it around the world, but once they saw Lonesome Cove, their wanderlust subsided. Now, under newer management, the resort remains a pretty spot. The six immaculate little cabins set among trees at the water's edge, the manicured lawns, and the domesticated deer that wander the 75-acre woods make the place a favorite for honeymooners—fully 30 percent of Lonesome Cove's guests are newlyweds. The sunsets are spectacular, and there's a fine view of nearby Speiden Island. Cabins start at $75 a day.

Olympic Lights

*Take Argyle Road out of
Friday Harbor to Cattle
Point Road,
(206) 378-3186
4531-A Cattle Point
Road, Friday Harbor,
WA 98250
Moderate; no credit cards;
checks ok*

As you approach this isolated bed and breakfast, you may recall the movie *Days of Heaven*: the tall Victorian farmhouse sits lonely as a lighthouse in a sea of open meadow. The renovated interior is more modern, and quite elegant: four upstairs rooms, all with queen beds, done up in bright whites and soft pastels and furnished with antiques. The downstairs room, however, is the only one with a private bath. You must remove your shoes to tread the off-white pile carpet. All the rooms are lavishly bathed in sunlight, reflecting it in a fashion that's heavenly. The panorama of Olympic Mountains and Strait of Juan de Fuca from the south rooms adds to the effect. The proprietors, Christian and Lea Andrade, are San Francisco refugees who came to San Juan's empty south tip seeking a more calming, contemplative milieu. They also have three cats who roam downstairs. No smoking inside.

Blair House
Bed and Breakfast Inn

*4 blocks up Spring to
Blair, (206) 378-5907
345 Blair Avenue, Friday
Harbor, WA 98250
Moderate; AE, MC, V*

Believe it or not, Blair House is a country retreat—four blocks from the ferry (which is very convenient if you happen to arrive late). Owners Jane Benson and Jeff Zander have tastefully decorated their early-1900s home in pastels, floral prints, and antique furnishings, without overdoing the frou-frou, so just about anyone can feel comfortable here. Most of the six rooms have their own baths; the one-bedroom cottage is fully equipped. A bountiful morning buffet featuring assorted home-baked coffee cakes, fresh fruit, and other delights is included, and on sunny days breakfast may be taken to the attractive poolside patio. Since the salt water is too cold for leisurely swimming, the heated pool is a definite attraction. You share the parlor, equipped with a VCR (tape rentals nearby), as well as a huge, old-fashioned wraparound verandah. The owners are both attentive and businesslike, striking the perfect balance between warm hospitality and invisibility.

If you've found a place that you think is a Best Place, send in the report form at the back of this book. If you're unhappy with one of the places, please let us know why. We depend on reader input.

Moon & Sixpence Bed & Breakfast

3 miles from the ferry dock on Beaverton Valley Road, (206) 378-4138
3021 Beaverton Valley Road, Friday Harbor, WA 98250
Moderate; no credit cards; checks ok

Moon & Sixpence is a classic country B&B with an artsy flourish (witness the nod to Somerset Maugham in the name). The big, sunny farmhouse in the middle of San Juan Island is done up brightly but tastefully in a gamut of folk arts, from family heirlooms and Pennsylvania Dutch to Eskimo prints and Navajo rugs. A one-bedroom cabin is a new addition to the grounds. Hostess Evelyn Tuller is more than glad to give a tour of her weaving studio out back, and maybe even show you a flip or two of the shuttle. Breakfast is a more-than-substantial continental meal, and the bread is freshly baked. The farm pond is a dandy spot for picnics, barbecues, or just counting the clouds.

San Juan Inn

A half block from the ferry (206) 378-2070
50 Spring Street
Mail: PO Box 776,
Friday Harbor,
WA 98250
Moderate; MC, V

Formerly the San Juan Hotel, this nicely restored little place near the ferry has 10 antique-filled guest rooms with a tidy, old-fashioned feeling. Joan and Norm Schwinge serve continental breakfast in the parlor, a cozy room with an 1870 marble-top buffet, an old parlor stove with isinglass doors, and a complete view of Friday Harbor. The resident cat, Abigail, entertains.

Tucker House

1½ blocks from the ferry (206) 378-2783
260 B Street, Friday Harbor, WA 98250
Moderate; MC, V

On a quiet street a few blocks from downtown Friday Harbor and the ferry dock, this B&B offers a total of six rooms: three pleasant-but-plain rooms in the somewhat-cramped main house and three more elegant cottage-type quarters in back (two with space for four, one with a kitchen, all with private baths and fireplaces). Each opens onto a peaceful enclosed yard, deck, and hot tub—a nice chance to get away from it all without driving halfway across the island. Breakfast is served in the solarium.

Westwinds Bed & Breakfast

2 miles from Lime Kiln Whale Watch Park, (206) 378-5283
4909-H Hannah Highlands Road, Friday Harbor, WA 98250
Expensive; MC, V

Westwinds commands what may easily be the most magnificent view on all of the San Juan Islands. Unfortunately, too few people will have the opportunity to enjoy the 10 acres of mountainside abundant with deer and quail. This private paradise remains a one-bedroom facility, even though the property has recently been doubled in size. Owners Chris Durbin and Gayle Rollins have built an extraordinary glass-and-wood home that uses the setting to optimal advantage: look from your cathedral-ceilinged bedroom, private bath, patio, living room, or virtually any seat in the house, and you're likely to feel in possession of a large part of the world (or at least the Strait of Juan de Fuca and the Olympic Mountains). Breakfast is almost as majestic.

Although Chris and Gayle live at Westwinds, the entire facility is at your disposal, and privacy is never an issue. In spring the hillside is covered with a rainbow of wildflowers. Particularly popular with honeymoon couples, this bed and breakfast is to be enjoyed whatever the occasion, whatever the season. Be sure to reserve well in advance.

**Wharfside
Bed & Breakfast**
*On the K Dock in Friday Harbor, (206) 378-5661
Mail: PO Box 1212,
Friday Harbor, WA 98250
Moderate; No credit cards; checks ok*

If nothing lulls you to sleep like the gentle lap of the waves, the Wharfside's the B&B for you. It's this region's first realization of the European tradition of floating inns. Two guest rooms have been installed on the 60-foot sailboat *Jacquelyn*, both very nicely finished with full amenities and that compact precision that only living on a boat can inspire. The fore cabin has a double bed and sleeping berths for kids or extras. When the weather's good, you can breakfast on deck and watch the local fishermen gather their nets. And what other B&B can you hire for a sail around the islands?

LA CONNER

La Conner was founded in 1867 by John Conner, a trading-post operator, who named the town after his wife L(ouisa) A. Conner. The little fishing and farming community grew to be a major stop on the water-based trade routes until the railroads moved inland, leaving La Conner a literal backwater. Attracted by its pastoral beauty, artists such as Mark Tobey, Morris Graves, and Guy Anderson lived here, and the Skagit landscapes they painted became a well-known body of Northwest work. Today, La Conner has become a popular tourist stop. Its main street runs alongside the Swinomish Slough, and many of its picturesque buildings have wooden decks from which you can enjoy the sleepy channel. Little courtyards and benches are dotted throughout the town. On sunny weekends the town is mobbed with daytrippers, but so far it has avoided becoming a spoiled Carmel. Weekdays offer a

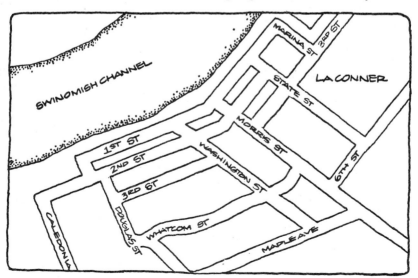

quieter visit. Clothing, crafts, book, and "country" gift stores make for enjoyable browsing: **Chez La Zoom, Skagit Bay Books, Palace Market Interiors, The Town Clothier, Nasty Jack's Antiques, Go Outside, Janet Houston Gallery,** and **The Cheese & Wine Shoppe** are good places to start.

Tillinghast Seed Co., at the entrance of town, is the oldest operating retail and mail-order seed store in the Northwest (since 1885); it has (of course) a wide variety of seeds, a wonderful nursery featuring the best plant varieties for western Washington, a florist shop, and a general store. (206) 466-3329.

Gaches Mansion, on Second Street overlooking the main drag, is a wonderful example of American Victorian architecture, with a widow's walk that looks out on the entire Skagit Valley. It is filled with period furnishings, and a small museum of Northwest art occupies the second floor. Open weekends. (206) 466-4288.

Sea King Products, across the bridge, on the Swinomish Indian reservation, sells smoked, fresh, and canned salmon (April to November); 950 Moorage, (206) 466-4016. Next door is the **Longhouse Restaurant,** open year-round under the new management, with a splendid seafood buffet the last Friday of each month; (206) 466-4444.

The **La Conner Tavern** is a classic Northwest joint, a good place to hang out over a beer or a basket of shrimp. Come as you are and enjoy the outdoor deck.

RESTAURANTS

The Black Swan

1st and Washington,
(206) 466-3040
505 S First Street,
La Conner
Inexpensive; beer and
wine; MC, V
Dinner Thurs-Tues

The Black Swan inspires cultish devotion among a far-flung following, who think nothing of making a pilgrimage to La Conner for a ceremonial meal. Founder and chef Martin Hahn, a seminal innovator in the new Northwest cuisine, has achieved a distinctive marriage of diverse Mediterranean styles and the freshest possible Northwest ingredients, including many gathered from the fertile Skagit Valley wilds.

Unfortunately, the Swan isn't soaring quite as high as in its glory days. It's obvious there is someone with talent in the kitchen, but at the same time a certain laziness is evident: the chilled borscht could have been much better had it been made with stock instead of water. The fresh basil used in the pesto was great, but the pasta was overcooked. Yet the red king salmon, marinated in herbes de Provence, was cooked to perfection.

At press time, owner Hahn had returned from a three-year stint as a new father and will be back in the kitchen full-time. We know the potential is here for a terrific meal, and we hope that with his able hands and the return of the bistro-style menu, the Swan will once again soar. Stay tuned.

Barkley's of La Conner

2nd and Washington,
(206) 446-4261
205 Washington,
La Conner
Moderate; full bar;
AE, MC, V

The menu at Michael Hood's country-French-tinged place (adjoining the La Conner Country Inn) emphasizes pastas and fresh seafood—baby bay scallops, local mussels, and the specialty, barbecued salmon—and is generally considered "the second-best dinner house in La Conner," although the gap is getting smaller. One source favors its smoky beef pizza (flavorful beef with a chile verde

*Lunch Mon-Sat, dinner
every day, brunch Sun*

sauce, tomatoes, Monterey jack cheese, and sour cream). Our tortellini primavera, with baby mushrooms, red and green peppers, crisp pea pods, purple onions, and artichoke hearts in a garlicky butter sauce, was tasty and interesting. You can also order from the lunch and dinner menus downstairs in the pub (or from the new after-5pm pub menu, with half-orders of most dinner entrees), where lots of nooks and crannies make a cozy, convivial hangout for the whole melange of natives: local gaffers, starving artists, and cauliflower farmers. There are Thomas Kemper and Grant's Ale on tap, and Barkley's can pull a mean espresso.

Calico Cupboard

*End of the line on 1st,
(206) 466-4451
720 S First Street,
La Conner
Inexpensive; beer and
wine; no credit cards;
checks ok
Breakfast, lunch every day*

It's awfully cute—Laura Ashley meets Laura Ingalls Wilder—but the bakery is the reason to go, turning out excellent carrot muffins, pecan tarts, shortbread, raspberry bars, currant scones, apple danish, and much more. Our advice for avoiding the weekend crowds is to buy your goodies from the take-out counter of the bakery and then find a sunny bench by the water. Waffle-and-omelet breakfasts here are enormous and generally overrated (dry hash browns, plain eggs) except for the excellent baking-powder biscuits, slathered with good raspberry jam. Lunches run to sandwiches on homemade bread, salads, and terrific soups.

LODGINGS

The Heron in La Conner

*On the edge of town,
(206) 466-4626
117 Maple Street,
Mail: PO Box 716,
La Conner, WA 98257
Moderate; MC, V*

This is about as sparkling new as it gets in high-character La Conner, and from the road you might mistake the structure for a Victorian-style condo project. We predict, however, that once it settles into its space it will become one of the prettiest hostelries in the new section of town. Eleven rooms are done in jewelry-box fashion; we like those that show a little individuality, like the Writer's Room (#35), with a writing desk and an old claw-footed tub, or the View Suite with its gas fireplace and view of Mount Baker. All rooms have private baths and TVs. There's also a bridal suite with a two-person Jacuzzi. Downstairs is an elegant living room with wing chairs and lush carpeting, along with a formal dining room in which you can eat your continental breakfast. Out back you may barbecue in the stone fire pit or unwind in the sun or the hot tub.

La Conner Country Inn

*2nd and Morris,
(206) 466-3101
107 Second Street,
La Conner,
Mail: PO Box 573,
La Conner, WA 98257*

It's a hospitable guest house in the center of town. Each of the 28 spacious rooms has a gas fireplace and a modern bath, beds are either brass or country pine, and second-floor rooms have cathedral ceilings. Pretty French windows are fitted with European-style wood shutters to keep out too-early morning light (though they don't keep out the noise of passing traffic). Guests enjoy a complimen-

Moderate; AE, DC, MC, V

tary continental breakfast of cinnamon rolls, juice, and coffee, served in the library, where an enormous field-stone fireplace and comfortable furniture tempt you to curl up with a book and lounge the day away. It's a little more like a small hotel than the rest of the hostelries in town.

Rainbow Inn

1/2 mile east of town, (206) 466-4578
1075 Chilberg Road,
La Conner,
Mail: PO Box 1600,
La Conner, WA 98257
Moderate; AE, MC, V

On Chilberg Road on the way into La Conner sits an elegant turn-of-the-century farmhouse, the Rainbow Inn, amidst acres of Skagit Valley flatlands. From the eight guest rooms you get sweeping views of the region you came to see: lush pastures, Mount Baker, the Olympics. Inside is pretty too: most of the furnishings are American country-pine, consistent with the farmhouse, and some of the baths have claw-footed tubs. Downstairs are plenty of lingering zones, from the parlor with its wood-burning ceramic fireplace to the hot tub on the back deck. New owners Marilyn Lee, Ray Degler, and Tori Furnish are eager to make your stay a pleasant one. A full breakfast (homemade pastries, omelets, fruit) is served on the newly enclosed front porch. Cookies and tea are available all day, and wine is served in the evening.

White Swan Guest House

6 miles southeast of
La Conner, (206) 445-6805
Mail: 1388 Moore Road,
Mount Vernon,
WA 98273
Moderate; MC, V

When Peter Goldfarb made his exodus from the Big Apple a few springs ago, he stumbled upon a blossoming Skagit Valley, and was so taken by it that he found an old Victorian farmhouse and put his renovation and design background to work. Walk into the house today and you'll think you've entered your grandmother's place: Peter has tossed handmade quilts on the beds, has installed lace curtains around the windows, and often has cookies in the oven. There are three wallpapered guest rooms with an odd assortment of antiques (two with queen beds, one with a king); they share two baths down the hall. Pamper yourself with a soak in the large claw-footed tub, or curl up on the pink sofa in front of the wood stove. Peter serves a light but filling breakfast of freshly baked scones or muffins, fruit from his garden, and coffee. Out back there's a bird sanctuary of sorts: Peter's cottage tenants care for injured eagles, hawks, and other wild birds.

Downey House

3½ miles southeast of
La Conner, (206) 466-3207
1880 Chilberg Road,
La Conner, WA 98257
Moderate; MC, V

Just three miles out of La Conner, Downey House has perfect access to the tulip fields in spring. (No matter when you're reading this, reserve now for tulip season.) It's a lovely, neat, tidy place with five guest rooms (three with baths) and Victorian appointments. Jim and Kay Frey have lived in the house for 25 years and love to welcome guests: there's a hot tub out back, and in the evenings they serve guests warm blackberry pie with ice cream. The full breakfast may include sourdough pancakes, omelets, fruit-topped crepes, or, for lighter eaters, yogurt and granola.

Katy's Inn

3rd and Washington,
(206) 466-3366
Mail: PO Box 304,
La Conner, WA 98257
Moderate; no credit cards;
checks ok

Built a century ago as the home of a sea captain, Katy's has all the warmth and charm a B&B should have, with guest rooms that look like the one you grew up in. All four are furnished with pretty iron beds and handmade quilts (one has an antique iron crib in the corner), and all open onto a balcony overlooking the Swinomish Channel. Two baths are shared, but only one has a shower. Dale and Vivian Rancourt live in a separate wing and are good about letting guests do their own thing. Breakfast is big—fresh fruits, juice, cereal, muffins, quick breads, and a hot dish such as quiche—and served in the dining room or outside in the sunshine. The coffee pot is always on in the kitchen, and there are cookies for snacking. A big old wood-burning stove takes the edge off nippy days.

MOUNT VERNON

Take one part traditional stores catering to local farming and the area's timber industry, add a little shopping-mall mania and fast-food frenzy, and top it off with a few counterculture shops—there you have Mount Vernon.

West of Mount Vernon, the lush farmlands of the Skagit Valley reach out to Puget Sound. Spring is the best season to come here: the valley is a center for commercial growing of daffodils (March 15–April 15), tulips (April 1–May 10), and irises (May 15–June 15). The pastoral countryside is flat and ideal for bicyclists, except for the traffic gridlock that can occur on the small farm lanes during any of the festivals.

There seems to be a festival almost every month here, celebrating the area's bounty. The biggest is, of course, the **Tulip Festival** in early April. But February is Swan Month, June—Strawberry Month, September—Apple Month, and October—Redleaf Month. For information and maps, call the Chamber of Commerce, (206) 428-8547.

Little Mountain Park has a terrific picnic spot atop the mountain, plus a knockout vista of the entire valley. **Washington Cheese** offers tours of its facility during normal business hours Monday through Saturday; (206) 424-3510.

RESTAURANTS

The Longfellow Cafe

In the historic Granary
Building, (206) 336-3684
120-B First Street,
Mount Vernon
Moderate; beer and
wine; MC, V
Lunch Mon-Sat,
dinner Tues-Sat

The Longfellow Cafe is a culinary bargain and *not* the place to arrive late! Daily specials such as the grilled salmon with apple beurre blanc and the sole stuffed with shrimp often get erased from the blackboard before the end of the evening. The seafood is flown in fresh from Hawaii or bought locally in small quantities. Sandwich bread and dinner rolls are baked on the premises. Skagit Valley suppliers of anything and everything are used whenever available. Preparation is solid, and creative without going crazy. Try the marinated flank steak or the Alaska spot prawns if your favorite special is already gone. The menu changes seasonally. An excellent selection of wines available by the glass, including vintage port, and a nice variety of beers. There is nothing formal here

...no pretense, just good (and occasionally sensational) food cooked by chef/owner Peter Barnard. The knowledgeable staff enjoy talking about the food and its preparation. Even more, they are proud of what they serve, and the quality shows.

Wildflowers

3 minutes east of I-5 from the College Way exit, (206) 424-9724 2001 E College Way, Mount Vernon Moderate; full bar; MC, V Lunch, dinner Wed-Mon

Not far north of Seattle sits a small Victorian house in a tiny green garden. Inside, there's David Day, a fine chef with lots of talent—tapped and untapped. Mostly that's because no one asks for better, and partly because what he already does, he does well. Our snapper fillet was broiled and then draped with a ribbon of green mayonnaise. The pork tenderloin was dressed in a blue cheese sauce and topped with an apple fan. Day's partner, Michele Kjosen, tempts guests by parading freshly baked goods past their tables. The golden rhubarb pie was delicious. Service can be attentive to the point of obsession. This pair needs a little more confidence and a lot more stretching of their abilities. They are considering opening for lunch and are available for catering and private parties. We have high hopes for the day when chef Day is able to cut loose from his second career as a gallery owner and run the restaurant full-time.

Cafe Europa

In old downtown Mount Vernon, (206) 336-3933 516 S First Street, Mount Vernon Inexpensive; beer and wine; no credit cards; checks ok Lunch, dinner Mon-Fri

★

Begging and bribery will not help. Kari and Ken Vonnegut will not sell any of the French and wheat bread they bake daily, until the restaurant closes. It's Mount Vernon's favorite lunch spot, and they often need every slice. The sandwich fillings are as good as their bread. Marinated lemon chicken is charbroiled to perfection and served with sticky rice, a good salad, and of course the aforementioned bread. At the busiest of times we've encountered mediocre soups (a flavorless clam chowder and a thin mushroom), but those evenings tend to be the exception. At dinner, the addition of some pasta dishes (especially the clam or primavera) is appreciated. Save room for homemade dessert and espresso. You order at the counter (and may need to pick through the silverware), but the ambience is pleasant.

La Tienda

Over the West Side bridge in west Mount Vernon, (206) 336-2304 602 W Division, Mount Vernon Inexpensive; beer and wine; no credit cards; local checks only Lunch every day, dinner Mon-Sat, brunch Sun

Mercifully, what you see (black velvet paintings and chipped tile floor) is not what you get. Inside this tacky storefront cafe is some great Mexican food. The quesadilla verde is covered with chunks of meat and loaded with cheese. Possibly the best cheese enchilada north of LA is here. The salsa is fresh and very mild. Ask for the hot stuff. Portions are large and prices are cheap. Service is fast and friendly.

STANWOOD

Stanwood is a sleepy little farm center with a Scandinavian heritage, a Midwestern air, and one good reason for a few minutes' sightseeing. Years ago, local daughter Martha Anderson started working at *rosemaling*, traditional Norwegian "flower painting," and teaching it to her fellow Stanwoodians. Now they've embellished many everyday businesses with charming rosemaled signs—not for tourist show as in Leavenworth, but out of an authentic impulse to express their heritage and make Main Street pretty.

Pilchuck School. Founded in 1971 by glass artist Dale Chihuly and Seattle art patrons John Hauberg and Anne Gould Hauberg, Pilchuck is an internationally renowned glass art school. Students live and study on this campus, situated in the midst of a country tree farm. An open house twice each summer gives folks a chance to see craftspeople at work; call first for times and directions. Summer: (206) 445-3111; winter: (206) 621-8422.

CAMANO ISLAND
LODGINGS

Wilcox House
1 mile west of Stanwood off Smith Road,
(206) 629-4746
1462 Larkspur Lane,
Camano Island,
WA 98292
Moderate; no credit cards;
checks ok

The clapboard house looks like a remodeled Victorian with its turrets and wraparound porch, but it was built just a few years ago. Out of 60 windows you get fine views of Skagit Bay, and in clear weather you can see Mount Baker from the meadowlike lawn. Four guest rooms are decorated with antiques and brass and iron beds. Only one has a private bath. The Captain's Room that adjoins the turret is a wonderfully sunny spot to read. The morning's meal, which might be an omelet of local wild mushrooms, muffins, fruit, juice, and coffee, is served in a cozy breakfast nook. No smoking.

EVERETT

Enormous population and economic growth are forcing this sleeping bear to wake up and plant some roses. Progress is slow, but at least it is moving. Hanging flower baskets now decorate the main boulevard downtown, the waterfront is being cleaned up, and the city is experiencing new pride.

The **Everett Giants** are an exciting Class A minor-league affiliate of the San Francisco Giants. Games are played outdoors, tickets are cheap, and the ballpark food isn't bad. Call (206) 258-3673 for tickets and information.

The **Boeing 747/767 plant**, in south Everett on Highway 526, offers free 90-minute tours of the world's largest plant (measured in volume). No children under 10; (206) 342-4801.

Heritage Flour Mills boasts Washington's largest stone grinding mill. Tours of the mill, located at 2925 Chestnut, and the adjacent country store are regularly scheduled Monday through Saturday; for tour times, call (206) 258-1582.

Marina Village is a small but pleasant shopping center/restaurant complex on Port Gardner Bay. A ferry shuttle service runs from mid-July to September to Jetty Island, for beachcombing and bird watching; schedules vary with the tide.

Everett Chamber of Commerce provides maps of walking and driving tours, as well as a current schedule of events. Call (206) 252-5181 for information.

RESTAURANTS

Panivino

*Across the street from
Pay Less on Evergreen
Way, (206) 353-4635
6309 Evergreen Way,
Everett
Moderate; full bar;
AE, MC, V
Lunch Mon-Fri,
dinner Mon-Sat*

★ ★

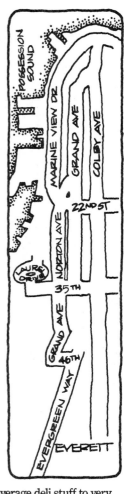

Bread and wine (panivino) may be the staples of life, but at this whitewashed restaurant oddly placed in a mini-strip mall, owners Kathleen and Wenceslao Aguirre celebrate good food with an eclectic creativity. First off, a buddha (carved by Wenceslao) greets you at the door. Loaves of French bread become unusual sandwiches, such as the Pan Bagnet, filled with provolone, tomatoes, artichoke hearts, roasted red peppers, cucumbers, and capers, moist with a basil vinaigrette. Salads are simple—Gorgonzola and walnut, perhaps. Mexican overtones are found in the Panivino sandwich —mashed black beans and sauteed flank steak, broiled with Swiss cheese and salsa. That said, the pasta is what many people return for—with sauces as simple as garlic and mushroom or as sophisticated as walnuts, capers, and tomatoes sauteed in a tarragon olive oil. What this restaurant lacks in consistency, it makes up for in imagination.

The Sisters

*8 blocks west of
Broadway, in the Everett
Public Market,
(206) 252-0480
2804 Grand Street,
Everett
Inexpensive; beer and
wine; MC, V
Breakfast, lunch Mon-Fri*

This place is as popular as it is funky. Soups such as mulligatawny, gazpacho, or just plain old beef barley can be outstanding. Salads are also consumer-friendly. Sandwiches range from average deli stuff to very healthful concoctions, including a vegetarian burger made with chopped cashews and sunflower seeds. Among the usual morning fare are some delights—the blueberry or pecan hotcakes, granola with yogurt and blueberry sauce, or scrambled eggs with bacon, onion, cottage cheese (or cheese of choice), sprouts, and salsa, wrapped in flour tortillas. Fresh-squeezed lemonade and strawberry lemonade are available year-round. A slice of blackberry pie weighs 10.5 ounces.

Love a good bargain? Then you'll really like Seattle Cheap Eats, *a compendium of 230 terrific bargain eateries in and around Seattle, brought to you by the same folks who bring you the* Best Places *series.*

LODGINGS

Marina Village Inn
Take exit I-5 onto Pacific, turn right on W Marine View Drive to waterfront,
(206) 259-4040
1728 W Marine View Drive, Everett, WA 98201
Expensive; AE, DC, MC, V

Waterfront accommodations are a surprising rarity on Puget Sound, making this 15-room inn on Port Gardner Bay all the more attractive. It offers all the sophistication of a big-city hotel without the parking problems and convention crowds, and is therefore becoming increasingly popular with corporate executives. Best to book rooms a month or more in advance.

Rooms here are very contemporary and stylish (we've actually picked up decorating tips), featuring oak chests of drawers, tasteful art and lamps, refrigerators, handcrafted ceramic sinks, color satellite TVs, extension phones in the bathrooms, and trouser presses; some rooms have notably comfy couches and easy chairs. Four of the rooms have Jacuzzis; the executive suite is equipped with a marvelous telescope for gazing out over the water through an enormous bay window. Be sure to book a room on the harbor side; sea lions might be lollygagging in the sun on the nearby jetty. A new addition (not open at press time) features 11 rooms, all with harbor views and Jacuzzis.

The only visible drawback here is the lack of room service. There is no restaurant, although the surrounding Marina Village offers more than enough dining alternatives and some good browsing.

MUKILTEO

Unfortunately, Mukilteo is probably best known for the traffic congestion caused by the Whidbey Island Ferry. There are, however, a small state park and a historic lighthouse worth seeing. You can also stroll along the waterfront and fish off the docks.

RESTAURANTS

Charles at Smugglers Cove
2 blocks west of the intersection of Highways 525 and 526,
(206) 347-2700
8310 53rd Avenue W, Mukilteo
Moderate; full bar; MC, V
Lunch Mon-Fri, dinner Mon-Sat

It's Mukilteo magic: the spell begins as you leave your car and approach the mansion (formerly a speakeasy) that is now the home of artist/chef Claude Faure (formerly of Chez Claude). With partner Janet Kingma, he has created one of the most romantic sites in the Northwest. We started with what is arguably the best French onion soup anywhere. You might need a knife for the butter; you certainly won't need one for the incredibly tender calamari, simply prepared with lemon and capers, or the fork-tender duck medallions with a port/Madeira sauce enhancing, not covering, the entree. The rack of lamb was perfection. We chose a delicate yet flavorful passion-fruit cake for dessert.

A walk through the grounds was a perfect finish to a magic evening. Charles is closed on Sundays but is available for weddings and receptions. Service still has some bugs to work out, but that's to be expected with a place so new.

WHIDBEY ISLAND

With the recent Supreme Court declaration of New York's Long Island as a peninsula, Captain Whidbey's namesake landfall now qualifies as the longest island in the US. Besides that distinction, Whidbey boasts pretty villages, viewpoint parks, sandy beaches, and some lovely farmland. It makes for a particularly nice family-outing day, during which you can combine browsing, varied sightseeing, and sun.

WHIDBEY ISLAND: CLINTON
LODGINGS

Home by the Sea
6 miles north of Clinton
on Useless Bay,
(206) 221-2964
2388 E Sunlight Beach
Road, Clinton, WA 98236
Expensive; MC, V

Home by the Sea captures a relaxed beachhouse mood better than most other B&Bs on the island, situated as it is right on the driftwood-strewn beach of Useless Bay. The main house, a modern split-level with two upstairs suites, features a hot tub on the deck right outside the door. Other alternatives are a Nordic cottage on the shores of Lone Lake, a Swiss chalet in the woods (for two adults only), the Chanterelle Cottage nearby, and a lovely Cape Cod cottage just up the street from Home central. All cottages come with full kitchens, fireplaces, and basket breakfasts and require a two-night minimum stay.

WHIDBEY ISLAND: LANGLEY

Sized just right, perched on a bluff over the beach, the nicest town on Whidbey evinces small-town virtues. The arts and crafts festival takes place over the Fourth of July weekend, the Island County Fair in mid-August. The residents like to attend movies at the **Clyde Theatre**, drink pitchers of ale at the **Dog House Tavern**, and swap stories with Josh Hauser at **Moonraker Books**. Islandesign Interiors and **Virginia's Antiques** are among the best shops for home furnishings; the **Star Store** and **Annie Steffen's** provide great upscale general mercantile and woven wearables, respectively.

RESTAURANTS

Cafe Langley
At the south end of town,
(206) 221-3090
113 First Street, Langley
Moderate; beer and wine;
MC, V
Lunch, dinner every day

Right now Langley is having cravings for Middle Eastern fare. It doesn't take much to make big news in this small town, but this very new cafe owned by Shant and Arshavir Garibyan is creating local hunger for lamb kebobs (with meat sliced from a freshly roasted leg), red lentil or spinach yogurt soups, and hummus and baba ghanouj wiped up with chewy warm pita bread. When it's busy, it's really busy: locals and sailboarders sometimes order to go to help alleviate the increasing number of diners. Considerate, yes, but it doesn't always work. The Garibyan brothers have been known to drive take-out patrons down to the marina—"we didn't want it to be cold by the time they ate it."

Star Bistro

*Above the Star Store on
1st, (206) 221-2627
201½ First Street,
Langley
Moderate; full bar;
AE, MC, V
Lunch, dinner every day,
brunch Sun*

Art Deco is not exactly what you'd expect to find in Langley, but nibbling Penn Cove mussels during late afternoon on a sunsplashed deck is a favorite pastime at this somewhat trendy black, white, and red bistro. Carol Hurless and Joe Leger opened this eatery, on the second floor of the Star Store, in May 1988. Ever since, diners return for generous servings of good (though predictably yuppie) food: Caesar salads; a burger with onions, peppers, bacon, and cheese; and a shrimp and scallop linguine with a tangy sauce of mustard, mushroom, tomato, cream, and sherry. When the place gets hopping (usually hot summer days), the Bistro gets erratic in quality and service.

Dog House Backdoor Restaurant

*Corner of 1st and
Anthes, (206) 321-9996
230 First Street, Langley
Inexpensive; beer and
wine; no credit cards;
checks ok
Lunch, dinner every day*

Somewhat dumpy, this is Langley's only honest-to-goodness waterfront eatery (tavern with pool table in the front), and the view of Saratoga Passage makes it well worth a stop, especially for a burger. They're big half-pounders here, juicy and lean. Tough to fathom why the Dog House stoops to lackluster American cheese slices for such a formidable quality burger on a fresh bun. Still, even the locals say this is the best burger on the island. The ghivetch, a hearty vegetarian soup topped with a thick layer of melted jack cheese, is a good alternative to red meat. Steer clear of the nachos, made with tasteless tortilla chips, and the pork and slaw sandwich, which doesn't deliver the shredded pork the menu promises but tough little cubes of pork in a slaw blended with barbecue sauce.

LODGINGS

Inn at Langley

*At the edge of town at
400 1st, (206) 221-3033
Mail: PO Box 835,
Langley, WA 98260
Expensive; beer and wine;
MC, V
Continental breakfast
Mon-Wed, dinner Fri-Sat
(reservation only)*

Paul and Pam Schell's first private venture since Paul left Cornerstone Development (Alexis in Seattle) is one of Whidbey's finest. Architect Alan Grainger designed the building in a marriage of three themes: Frank Lloyd Wright's style, Northwest ruggedness, and Pacific Rim tranquillity. For the most part, it works—fabulously. Inside this rough-hewn, cedar-shingled building (whose size is disguised by the clever design) are 24 rooms finely decorated with an eye for pleasing detail: quiet shades of tan and gray, simple Asian furnishings, trimmings of three different woods, and a quarry-tiled bathroom (in a brown hue reminiscent of beach stones) with hooks made from alder twigs, and a hand-held shower. Adjacent is a Jacuzzi from which you can watch the movement of Saratoga Passage and the flicker of your fireplace through the opaque shoji-style sliding screen. All this opens onto a private deck with cushioned bench seats overlooking Saratoga Passage. Every room's a winner, though we prefer the upper-level rooms; others are approached by a dark concrete stairwell. With all this elegance, the Inn takes business seriously. The conference room (equipped with up-to-the-minute business needs) has the expansive view of the Passage that the dining room (above the parking lot) lacks. Meals can be arranged.

In a country-style kitchen, Chef Steve Nogal (formerly of McCormick's Fish House) serves an ample five-course dinner at 7pm ($24.95). If there's space, opt to join other guests at the large center table where conversation can be lively and service is slightly more attentive. On a recent visit an appetizer of fresh mozzarella on a spicy paste of olives, garlic, and anchovies was followed by a rich, flavorful, and generous bowl of potato and leek soup. The entree was a choice of two fishes: lightly cooked rockfish stuffed with crab, topped with a Bearnaise sauce; or ling cod with a variation on a Thai peanut sauce that tasted too much of Sunny Jim's. Next came a salad of fresh greens with a raspberry vinaigrette. A bowl of island raspberries and cream finished the meal. Reservations are required, and don't be late: dinner starts in the lobby with a glass of sherry and a tour of the wine cellar. Help yourself to the continental breakfast (complimentary to guests) spread in the dining room from 8am to 10am.

Country Cottage
5 blocks up the hill from downtown on 6th,
(206) 221-8709
215 Sixth Street, Langley,
WA 98260
Expensive; MC, V

Californian couple Trudy and Whitey Martin recently took over this tasteful B&B and immediately began adding to its already lovely appearance. They've converted an outbuilding into two large suites, added on to the deck, and spruced up the landscaping with a pretty flower garden. The two rooms in the main house have en suite toilets (behind standing screens, if that bothers you). Coffee and juice arrive at your door in the morning, and an hour later a full breakfast is served in the sunny solarium. Downtown Langley is just a hop and a skip away.

Log Castle
1½ miles west of Langley on Saratoga,
(206) 321-5483
3273 E Saratoga Road,
Langley, WA 98260
Moderate; MC, V

This is the house that Jack built—literally—and whenever he's home from his job as state senator, Jack Metcalf builds on it some more, to his wife Norma's newest designs. As a result the beachside castle has a slightly unfinished air about it—which shouldn't in the slightest detract from what can be a distinctly unusual experience. Every log tells a story (ask Norma about the log-end floor entrance, the branded-log table, the hollow-log sink), and the place can feel quite cozy on a winter evening. The loft bedroom looks over the public living room; two rooms on the other side of the house are built into a turret and feature remarkable views. Each room has its own bath. Breakfast usually includes Norma's homemade bread. Do engage the Metcalfs in conversation—apart from their obvious design skills, these two possess a genuine gift for the art of hospitality.

Saratoga Inn

Brooks Hill and S Coles,
(206) 221-7526
4850 S Coles Road,
Langley, WA 98260
Expensive; no credit cards;
checks ok

★ ★

More like a country inn than a B&B, the shingled, five-bedroom beauty is fairly unusual for its kind: it was built for the purpose. It's lovely, with handsome, restrained decorations in the rooms (note the quilts, many made by your host, Debbie Jones) and sophisticated (not cutesy) country decor in the guests' own living room downstairs. The Willow Room ($85) with a bent-willow bed and rocker and wood stove, is our favorite. Queen Anne's Lace Room, gazing out to Camano Head, has the best view. The grounds, with 25 acres, much of it in woods and the rest attentively gardened, make for excellent walks. Even winters are a pleasure here: holly, fir, and juniper fill the inn, and gingerbread and cider have been known to be served. Breakfast (with wild berries picked on the property), served on trays, can be taken wherever you wish. No smoking or children.

Whidbey Inn

On the waterfront main
drag, 1st Street,
(206) 221-7115
106 First Street, Langley
Mail: PO Box 156,
Langley, WA 98260
Expensive; AE, MC, V

★ ★

Formerly the Whidbey House, Shannon and Richard Francisco's B&B clings to Langley's bluff and offers six sparkling guest rooms that look out onto the grand sweep of beach and bay below. The three downstairs rooms ($80-$85) are country-Victorian dreams of furnishing; three top-floor suites ($110-$120) capitalize best on the view and have fireplaces. One of these has a walkway to an atmospheric gazebo on stilts outside. Look one way, out to sea, and you feel wonderfully isolated; turn the other way into town, and you have an old-fashioned sense of small-town belonging. A simple and filling breakfast-in-a-basket is served in your room.

The Franciscos have bought an old Victorian house just down the road and plan to open it as a restaurant by fall 1989.

Lone Lake Cottage & Breakfast

5½ miles from the
Clinton ferry, off
Highway 525 on S
Bayview, (206) 321-5325
5206 S Bayview Road,
Langley, WA 98260
Expensive; MC, V

★

Delores and Ward Meeks have poured heart and soul into their lakefront B&B—which is a considerable amount. Out back, Delores tends the raspberries that will yield jam for your breakfast toast; she's also a semiprofessional potter, wedding-cake baker, and bird lover (check out their large outdoor aviary). Ward putters around doing things like designing and building a beamed-ceiling sternwheeler ("The guests would rather tour the lake at 5mph than 30mph") and building beautiful guest cottages. The result is a charming, eclectic, somewhat kitschy accommodation: a definitive break from the all-too-familiar country chic. Two private cottages, both with great views of tiny Lone Lake, are decked out with fine Oriental furnishings and are joined now by a third unit, the aforementioned sternwheeler, moored right outside. Each goes for $85. The Garden Cottage has two bedrooms, a fireplace, and a large kitchen, but we prefer the newer, one-bedroom Terrace Cottage, built right over the workshop with a slightly better view. The *Whidbey Queen* is small, but the novelty of sleeping above the paddlewheel and cooking in the tiny "galley" makes it an appealing choice. And where else can you take your room for a spin around the lake?

WHIDBEY ISLAND: FREELAND

Just a serviceable little town, but it does have the one good bakery on the island, an essential spot for picnic supplies: **The Island Bakery**. The seven-grain breads are very good. Main Street, (206) 321-6282.

LODGINGS

Cliff House
Take Bush Point Road to Windmill, (206) 321-1566
5440 Windmill Road, Freeland, WA 98249
Expensive; no credit cards; checks ok

Seattle architect Arne Bystrom designed this dramatic house, which makes an extraordinary getaway. The home on a cliff above Admiralty Strait is full of light from lofty windows, centering on a 30-foot-high atrium (open to the weather) and a sunken fireplace. For $225 a night you have use of the entire house, with two large loft bedroom suites and a kitchen for cooking your meals ($325 with two couples). The house is strikingly decorated with an interesting arrangment of oriental rugs, modern art and Indian baskets, and is set amid 13 acres of woods with hammocks, bench chairs, and a platform deck built high on the cliff with a hot tub. Also on the property, the elfish, one-bedroom Sea Cliff Cottage has its own bath, kitchenette, and porch and goes for $125 a night. Peggy Moore sets the country kitchen table (in both houses) with a continental breakfast.

WHIDBEY ISLAND: GREENBANK

LODGINGS

Guest House Bed & Breakfast Cottages
1 mile south of Greenbank off Highway 525 on E Christenson, (206) 678-3115
835 E Christenson Road, Greenbank, WA 98253
Expensive; AE, MC, V

We love this place, partly for all its alternatives. You can stay in the $75 Wildflower Suite farmhouse (closest to the swimming pool and hot tub), a pricier log-cabin cottage ($97.50), the one-bedroom carriage house ($110), or the new Pine Cottage ($150). All have kitchens, baths, and VCRs; all but the Wildflower have Jacuzzis. But our favorite—everybody's favorite—is the $189-a-night lodge cabin. Full of antiques but built in 1979, the lodge combines the old (a wood stove next to the breakfast nook, a hammock and picnic tables outside by the pond) with the new (two-person Jacuzzi, microwave, remote control TV, dishwasher) to a most appealing effect. Perched at the edge of a lovely pond and ringed by green trees, the two-story home features a broad deck and views of the Cascades and the Sound from the loft bedroom. Breakfast makings are left in the fully equipped kitchens. You're just a mile away from an outpost of Chateau Ste. Michelle, where they grow the loganberries to make Whidbey's Liqueur.

WHIDBEY ISLAND: COUPEVILLE

This old town dates back to the 1850s, when farming commenced on the fertile isle. A fort was built in 1855 after some Indian scares, and part of it, the Alexander Blockhouse on Front Street, is open for touring. Coupeville's main street has souvenir-oriented stores and a few antique shops. Three miles south of town is **Fort Casey**, a decommissioned fort with splendid gun mounts, beaches, and commanding bluffs. The Keystone ferry, connecting Whidbey to Port Townsend, leaves from Admiralty Head, just south.

LODGINGS

Captain Whidbey Inn

Off Madrona on W Captain Whidbey Inn Road, (206) 678-4097 2072 W Captain Whidbey Inn Road, Coupeville, WA 98239 Moderate; full bar; AE, DC, MC, V Breakfast, lunch, dinner every day

The old inn, dating back to 1907 and built from madrona logs, nestles picturesquely in the woods overlooking Penn Cove. The lodge has 13 upstairs rooms with two shared bathrooms; there are four sparsely furnished cottages with fireplaces and baths and two with separate bedrooms, plus 13 lagoon rooms—the best choices—with private baths and verandahs. The public rooms—a dining room and deck (when the weather's warm), a cozy bar, a well-stocked library, a folksy fireplace room—are quite attractive. With previous arrangements Innkeeper Captain John Colby Stone will take you for a cruise on his private sloop.

Lorren Garlich is no longer cooking; apprentice Emery Budahazi has the reins. The menu hasn't changed much except that it's been trimmed down to about six items per night. The food still has its inconsistencies; so stick with the simpler preparations such as the fresh Penn Cove mussels steamed in white wine and herbs (how could you go wrong when you can almost see where they came from?), or the seafood fettuccine. Desserts are magnificent, particularly the rich gateau mousseline served with a raspberry sauce on one side and a cream sauce on the other.

Colonel Crockett Farm

Follow signs to Fort Casey off Highway 20, (206) 678-3711 1012 S Fort Casey Road, Coupeville, WA 98239 Moderate; MC, V

A few years ago, while on sabbatical in Yorkshire, Bob and Beulah Whitlow grew enamored of the English institution of bed and breakfast; so enamored, in fact, that when they returned they sold their Seattle home on Queen Anne Hill and remodeled a dilapidated homestead just south of Fort Casey. Five guest rooms have their own baths; our favorites are the Crockett Room, the biggest, with a Victorian claw-footed tub in the bath and a canopy bed, and the white-and-lavender Davis Room that opens off the smart oak-paneled English library. Breakfast is taken downstairs at individual tables in the dining room; however, we've heard recent reports of an overbearing Christian atmosphere complete with morning prayer. The grounds feature plenty of vintage pines and chestnuts, a grand old gnarled holly tree, and even a Sierra red-wood—along with sweeping views of the water. It's a grand place for cat fanciers: the Whitlows have five felines (all outside). New addition: an English Bulldog named Punch.

The Victorian
6th and N Main,
(206) 678-5305
602 N Main Street,
Coupeville, WA 98239
Expensive; MC, V

New owner Dolores Fresh went right to work on this National Historic Register Victorian home, laying carpeting, bringing in family photos and mementos, adding a bath, and generally warming the place up. There are two large guest rooms in the main house; an adjacent cottage has its own kitchen and bath. All have queen beds and lots of lacy charm. A full breakfast is included. Kids okay in the cottage.

WHIDBEY ISLAND: OAK HARBOR

Dutch settlers have now been overtaken by the Navy, which operates a big air base for tactical electronic warfare squadrons here. A tulip show in late April and the Holland Garden (500 Avenue W and 30th Northwest) commemorate the Dutch heritage, but for the most part the town is engulfed in growth and retired military folk. The name comes from the Garry oaks in the area.

Deception Pass. The beautiful, treacherous gorge has a lovely, if usually crowded, state park with 2,300 acres of prime camping land, forests, and beach. **Strom's Shrimp/Fountain and Grill,** just north of the pass, sells fresh seafood and shrimp for your cookout. They also grill up a mean oyster burger to go; (206) 293-2531.

LODGINGS

Auld Holland Inn
8 miles south of
Deception Pass on State
Road 20, (206) 675-2288
5681 State Road 20, Oak
Harbor, WA 98277
Moderate; full bar;
AE, DC, MC, V
Dinner Mon-Sat (Sun in
summer)

A half mile north of Oak Harbor, this newish motel is just fine, if a shade close to the highway. Some upper-story rooms have antiques, and there's a tennis court, a hot tub, and a pool. Prices are good.

The adjacent restaurant, Rasteel Franssen, has quite a regal, European feel about it and a solid reputation among locals. There's a big gas fireplace, tapestry-upholstered dining chairs, and heavy wooden beams throughout. Appetizers here are best, especially pate maison and herring with capers and onion. Seventy-eight-year-old chef Jean Paul Combettes has a creative way with seafood (even if it's sometimes oversauced); be sure to ask what's fresh. Combettes' chowder has won numerous awards.

VASHON ISLAND

Faintly countercultural, this bucolic isle is a short ferry ride away from Seattle (take the Fauntleroy ferry) or Tacoma. It's a wonderful place to explore by bicycle, although the first long hill up from the ferry dock is a killer. Few beaches are open to the public.

Unlike Bainbridge, its northern neighbor, Vashon Island employs many of its own in island-based companies that market their goods both locally and nationally; many of these offer tours: **K-2 Skis, Inc.**, (206) 463-3631; **Stewart Brothers Coffee**, Island Highway, (206) 463-3932; **Wax Orchards**, with its preserves, fruit syrups, and apple cider, on 131st SW, north of 232nd, (206) 463-9735; **Maury Island Farms**, with berries and preserves, at 99th and 204th on Island Highway, (206) 463-9659; **Island Spring, Inc.**, with locally made tofu, (206) 463-9848. Or you can make one stop at **The Country Store and Farm**, an old-fashioned general store that stocks most of the island-made products, along with natural-fiber apparel, housewares, sundries, dried herbs, and gardening supplies; on Island Highway south of Vashon town, (206) 463-3655.

RESTAURANTS

Sound Food Restaurant
2 miles south of the ferry on Island Highway,
(206) 463-3565
20246 99th Avenue,
Vashon Island
Moderate; beer and wine;
AE, MC, V
Breakfast Mon-Fri;
lunch, dinner every day;
brunch Sat-Sun

It's a delightfully mellow place, an airy room with wood floors, fresh flowers, and, in summer, pretty wisteria overhanging the windows. The restaurant started out as a hangout for the island's artsy population, but lately mainlanders have been coming over, drawn by the honest cooking and excellent ingredients.

Indeed, there were urban expatriates all over the place on a recent visit, giving the cheerfully rustic, raw-beamed place the feeling of a bustling downtown cafe at lunchtime. The rush resulted in interminably long waits for waiter, water, and menus—but you'd have to be pretty mean of spirit to let anything annoy you in laid-back land.

Weekend brunches are especially popular: potato pancakes, crepes, French toast, whole-wheat waffles, blintzes with fresh fruit toppings, omelets—perhaps with asparagus and ham, and topped with Mornay sauce. Lunches offer healthful soups, salads, and sandwiches made from Sound Food's own bread. Five dinner specials are offered daily: a steak special is standard, while the other four may include bay scallops poached with sherry and baked with leeks in a light cream sauce, avocado-and-crab-stuffed chicken breasts, a garden-vegetable linguine, or spicy Mexican meatballs. An incredible array of fresh-baked goods—seven-grain bread, sprouted-wheat bread, cinnamon rolls, cheese danishes, muffins, cookies (try the snickerdoodles), wonderful pies—is offered for consumption on the spot or to take home. Live a little—do both. Good espresso, too.

LODGINGS

The Shepherd's Loft
Corner of 63rd and
232nd SW on Maury
Island, (206) 463-2544
Mail: Rte 3, Box 289,
Vashon, WA 98070
Moderate; no credit cards;
checks ok

This guest cottage high on Maury Island (which is really attached to Vashon) will accommodate two for $55 and up to four for $60. Kids are welcome. Hosts David and Mary Cooper don't do breakfast, but you can cook your own in the complete kitchen. Wander outside; there really are sheep.

PUYALLUP

At the head of the fertile Puyallup Valley, this frontier farm town serves as a major gateway to Mount Rainier. While much of the bulb, rhubarb, and berry farmland continues to be cultivated, a great part of it has been malled and auto-row-ravaged around the edges. Avoid the fast-food strip to the south and head east up the valley to Sumner, White River, Orting, Wilkinson, and Carbonado.

Ezra Meeker Mansion is the finest original pioneer mansion left in Washington. Its builder and first occupant, Ezra Meeker, came west in an oxcart in 1852, introduced hops to the Puyallup Valley, and later became known as the "hops king of the world." The lavish Italianate house (built 1890) is complete with fireplaces, carved cherrywood staircases, and ornate brass doorknobs. The 17-room Meeker mansion now stands beautifully restored in the rear parking lot of a Main Street furniture store; 321 E Pioneer, (206) 848-1770. Open Wednesday through Sunday, 1 to 5pm, March through mid-December.

Puyallup is big on old-time seasonal celebrations, and it's home to two of the biggest in the Northwest: the **Daffodil Festival and Parade** in early April and **Western Washington Fair**, better known as the Puyallup Fair, in September. Beginning the Friday after Labor Day, over one million people "do the Puyallup." One of the nation's biggest fairs; call (206) 845-1771.

Puyallup Downtown Farmers' Market is held every Saturday starting at 9am, June through September, at Pioneer Park.

RESTAURANTS

Balsano's
Between Pioneer and E Main, (206) 845-4222
127 15th SE, Puyallup
Moderate; full bar;
MC, V

You wouldn't expect to find decent Italian food in an ex-drive-in on the outskirts of Puyallup. Neither would you expect to step over boxes of produce on your way in the door. Here's the unexpected: learn the chef's Northern Italian ways by eating a dish of tender chicken and artichokes (native to Sicily), or try a homemade Sicilian sausage of coarsely chopped pork and fennel seeds. A colorful combination is the fettuccine of fresh vegetables and tasty little round *ceci* (garbanzo beans). Lunches are very reasonable, and there are special suggestions at all meals for children. Pinch some anise from a bowl by the cashier to freshen your mouth after eating.

TACOMA

Mention Tacoma and most people will think of an odoriferous lumber-mill town—a place to drive around as quickly as possible. Bad reputations are hard to shake, but Tacoma's doing a commendable job. This city, sided by Commencement Bay and the Tacoma Narrows, and backed by Mount Rainier, provides everyone—residents and visitors alike—with spectacular views. Stately homes and cobblestone streets abound in the north end, and students still fill the turreted chateau of Stadium High School. Old City Hall, with its Renaissance clock and bell tower, Romanesque First Presbyterian Church, the rococo Pythian Lodge, and the one-of-a-kind copper-domed Union Depot, now being restored, are history and architecture buffs' delights.

Pantages Center (901 Broadway), the restored 1,100-seat Pantages Theatre, originally designed in 1918 by B. Marcus Priteca, is the center for dance, music,

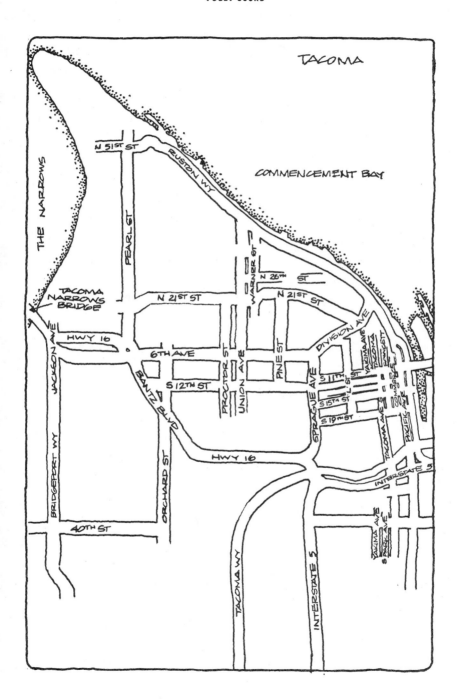

and stage presentations; (206) 591-5894. **Tacoma Actors Guild** (1323 S Yakima) is Tacoma's thriving young professional theatre, offering an ambitious and successful blend of American classics and Northwest premieres, (206) 272-2145.

Tacoma Art Museum (12th at Pacific) is housed in a former downtown bank. This small museum has paintings by Renoir, Degas, and Pissarro, as well as a collection of contemporary American prints, (206) 272-4258. **State Historical Museum** (315 N Stadium Way) has some valuable Native American artifacts, including canoes, baskets, and masks from British Columbia and Puget Sound. Early Tacoma memorabilia include arresting photographs, (206) 593-2830.

The **University of Puget Sound** in the north end and **Pacific Lutheran University** in the south not only are major educational institutions but also provide a variety of cultural programs and art events open to the public.

OTHER THINGS TO DO

Point Defiance Park is situated at the west side of Tacoma; its 500 acres of untouched forest jut out into Puget Sound. Combined with its many other attractions, this park is one of the most dramatically sited and creatively planned city parks in the country. The five-mile drive and hiking trails open up now and then for sweeping views of the water, Vashon Island, Gig Harbor, and the Olympic Mountains beyond. There are rose, rhododendron, Japanese, and Northwest native gardens, a railroad village with a working steam engine, a reconstruction of Fort Nisqually (originally built in 1833), a museum, a swimming beach, and the much-acclaimed zoo/aquarium. Being able to watch the almost continuous play of seals, sea lions, and the white Beluga whale from an underwater vantage point is a rare treat, (206) 591-5337. **Wright Park** at Division and I streets is a serene, in-city park with many trees, a duck-filled lake, and a beautifully maintained, fragrant conservatory, built of glass and steel in 1890.

The **Tacoma Dome**, the world's largest wooden dome, is the site of many entertainment and trade shows as well as a sports center. The dazzling neon sculpture by Stephen Antonakos provides a dramatic backdrop for events such as the **Tacoma Stars** indoor soccer games, championship ice-skating competitions, and many other regional activities. Ticket information (206) 272-6817.

Fans who like their baseball played outdoors in a first-class ballpark arrive in enthusiastic droves at **Cheney Stadium** to watch the **Tacoma Tigers**, the farm team of the Oakland A's, (206) 752-7707.

Fishing/boating: with the waters of South Puget Sound lapping at virtually half of Tacoma's city limits, it is to be expected that many Tacomans and visitors choose to spend their leisure time afloat or on the dock. There are two fishing piers jutting out from Ruston Way, and public launches and boat rentals at Point Defiance.

RESTAURANTS

C.I. Shenanigan's

Take the City Center exit off I-5 and follow it onto Ruston Way,
(206) 752-8811
3017 Ruston Way, Tacoma
Moderate; full bar;
AE, DC, MC, V
Lunch, dinner every day,
brunch Sun

With the increasing number of diners looking for both good food and great views, the many restaurants bordering scenic Commencement Bay are booming. C.I. Shenanigan's is one of the best of the formula restaurants, and in good weather even a sardine can't wiggle in without a reservation. The classy bar specializes in oysters on the half-shell, which, with fried artichoke hearts, fresh, peelable shrimp, and a bottle of dry white wine, make a perfect way to while away a sunny afternoon on the deck. Seafood dominates both the lunch and dinner menus: even the steaks may come sauced with crab, dill, and scallions. While there are plenty of fancier seafood dishes, our favorite, particularly when we have dry-land guests, is the Seafood Feast. Served for two, it will feed several more and includes broiled lobster, grilled salmon, halibut, crab, prawns, oysters, and clams. Those with really gargantuan appetites can finish with mud cake—a mile-high creation (well, almost) of ice cream, cookies, fudge, whipped cream, and nuts. Subtle it is not. Good it is.

Fujiya

*Between Broadway and
Market on Court C,
near the Sheraton Hotel,
(206) 627-5319
1125 Court C, Tacoma
Moderate; beer and wine;
AE, MC, V
Lunch Mon-Fri,
dinner Mon-Sat*

Although there are no tatami rooms and the menu is more limited than those of many of Seattle and Vancouver's Japanese restaurants, owner–sushi chef Masahiro Endo is matching their quality. The Fujiya continues to be one of downtown Tacoma's more distinguished and popular eating spots, particularly for lunch. It does not take reservations, so come early if you want to be seated right away. The Japanese concern for color, texture, and composition is apparent in Endo's presentation of sea-briny fresh sashimi and sushi. Another top choice here is gyoza, a Japanese rendition of the familiar Chinese pot-sticker, only smaller and made with a thinner dough. Gyoza come both fried and steamed, but the texture and flavor of the savory pork filling are more apparent when steamed. The real test of a Japanese kitchen is the tempura: here the seafood and vegetables are done to just the right golden-crisp stage.

Lessie's Southern Kitchen

*6th and Division,
(206) 627-4282
1416 Sixth Avenue, Tacoma
Inexpensive; no alcohol;
no credit cards; checks ok
Breakfast, lunch, dinner
Mon-Sat (closes at 7pm)*

Oh God, it's good! If you're prepared to forgo your calorie counting for one meal, there is no better place to abandon restraint than this comfortable cafe on the busy five-way corner. The thin, light corncakes alone are worth it. It's a place for those with a hankering for smothered pork chops, liver and onions, and catfish. Or, perhaps, crusty fried chicken and barbecued ribs. Lessie, who hails from southern Alabama, dishes these all up with helpings of yams, greens, grits and black-eyed peas, and finishes the meal with the likes of bread pudding or sweet potato pie. Butterfish with eggs, home fries, and biscuits, and of course a side order of corncakes, can start your day—or finish it, but what better way to go?

Rose Room

*Take the City Center exit
off I-5; between 13th and
15thon Broadway,
(206) 572-3200
1320 Broadway Plaza,
Tacoma
Expensive; full bar;
AE, DC, MC, V*

The elegant image of the Rose Room on the 26th floor of the Sheraton Tacoma Hotel (muted Art Deco roses on the walls, subdued lighting, fresh roses on every table) is well complemented by the efforts of its staff: the attentive waiters really appear to know their kitchen. There is a diverse menu, with food well prepared and well presented. The seafood dishes, such as lobster linguine, are standouts, and of special note is a salad of wild greens mixed with smoked pheasant and air-cured pancetta. If

*Lunch, dinner every day,
brunch Sat-Sun*

you are looking for a special brunch, this is the place. We particularly like the adjacent bar, where judges, lawyers, and faculty from UPS law school often gather to relax and talk.

Stanley and Seaforts Steak, Chop, and Fish House
*Take the Tacoma Dome
exit off I-5, left to Pacific
and south to the top of
the hill, (206) 473-7300
115 E 34th Street,
Tacoma
Moderate; full bar;
AE, MC, V
Lunch Mon-Fri,
dinner every day*

You can see it, but it may be tough to get to this hilltop location overlooking the city and Commencement Bay. As with Cutters Bayhouse in Seattle and Morgan's Lakeplace in Bellevue (under the same ownership), the view is outstanding, and the menu contains a number of good choices. The standouts are still the seafood dishes, such as the roasted prawns with garlic and the albacore tuna or swordfish grilled over mesquite. Try a fresh berry sherbet or a piece of Key lime pie for dessert. The spacious bar features a comprehensive and distinctive selection of Scotch whiskies.

Antique Sandwich Shop
*Corner of 51st and N
Pearl, (206) 752-4069
5102 N Pearl, Tacoma
Inexpensive; no alcohol;
no credit cards; checks ok
Breakfast, lunch, dinner
every day*

A visit here is a little like returning to a storybook grandma's house. Plastic bears filled with honey adorn the shared tables; a roomy couch usually has several students curled up on it studying and eating; and everyone just generally has a good time here. On the way to Point Defiance Park, it's also a favorite luncheon gathering place for the diaper set and their accompanying parents. Toys abound on a carpet-covered platform, which doubles as a stage when the folk or classical music concerts begin. Peanut butter and jelly sandwiches with bananas and fresh-fruit milk shakes share the menu with big-people food such as hearty homemade soups, quiches, and a variety of other tasty sandwiches. The clam chowder is still, hands-down, the best in town. There is excellent coffee from your choice of beans, and the tea is correctly brewed in your own china teapot. Tuesday is open-mike night, when locals drop in to perform.

Bimbo's
*15th and Pacific,
(206) 383-5800
1516 Pacific Avenue,
Tacoma
Inexpensive; full bar;
AE, MC, V
Lunch, dinner every day*

Three generations of good-food lovers can't be wrong. Since 1921, Tacomans have been flocking to this lower-Pacific Avenue Italian restaurant, where little has changed either architecturally or gastronomically. Praise be! The area around, though, is being upgraded now, spurred on by the restoration of the Union Depot across the street. Forget the environs; slide into your booth and you will immediately have a plate of fresh vegetables topped with crisp scallions plopped on your table, along with crunchy French bread and icy-cold butter. Members of the original owners' family are still cooking their native Tuscan recipes, with emphasis on quality of raw materials and simple preparation. The rabbit saute and the various

Would you like to order a copy of Best Places *for a friend? There's an order form at the back of this book.*

veal dishes are excellent. The homemade ravioli and the pasta with clams are both show-offs—the accompanying sauces, sopped up with bread, provide the impetus for repeated visits.

Engine House #9

6th and Pine,
(206) 272-3435
611 N Pine Street, Tacoma
Inexpensive; beer and
wine; no credit cards;
checks ok
Lunch, dinner every day

For connoisseurs of taverns, this former firehouse, complete with hoses, ladders, and a dalmatian near the entry, is a definite winner. It offers close to 50 brands of quality draft beer and ale, including the rare Xingu from the jungles of Brazil. Try one of the three types of cask-conditioned beers—still fermenting and changing daily. An eatery it is, too. The eclectic daily specials spice up the standard but good pizza and sandwich offerings; Thai salad with marinated beef, calamari in a wine-and-caper sauce, or a bowl of fennel soup. For those who need a cause as an excuse to eat oysters, every April enthusiastic oyster-eaters line up to slurp down an unlimited supply of extra-small Hood Canal oysters at a fund-raising contest for the local children's hospital. A limited menu is served until midnight.

Harbor Lights

Take the City Center exit
and follow it onto Ruston,
(206) 752-8600
2761 Ruston Way, Tacoma
Moderate; full bar;
AE, DC, MC, V
Lunch Mon-Sat,
dinner every day

Tacoma's pioneer Ruston Way waterfront restaurant still packs them in. Nothing trendy here. Decor is circa 1950, with glass floats, a stuffed marlin, and a giant lobster. The main concession to progress is a new, glassed-in sun deck. Up-to-the-minute it may not be, but that doesn't seem to bother the seafood fans who regularly crowd into the noisy dining room to consume buckets of steamed clams and plates of Columbia River smelt in season. The halibut and chips are the best around, as are the crisp hash browns. Reservations are becoming essential.

Katie Downs

Take the City Center exit
off I-5, follow it onto
Ruston, (206) 756-0771
3211 Ruston Way, Tacoma
Moderate; beer and wine;
MC, V
Lunch, dinner every day

This attractively designed tavern and restaurant rates two superlatives—it has probably the most memorable pizza to be found in the Puget Sound region, and, built above Commencement Bay, it's way up there in the view ratings.

Place your order at the food counter for one of the hand-rolled Philadelphia-style pizzas. We are particularly fond of the Number 10 super combination, paved with shrimp and topped with fresh tomato. Do get an order of fresh steamer clams to tide you over as you wait for your pizza. Watch the ever-changing activity on the waterfront, with sea lions, hydrofoil fire boats, freighters, and sailboats all vying for attention. The fish and chips, made with either red snapper, halibut, or prawns in a slightly sweet beer batter, is also a good choice. One caution: don't expect a quiet, restful dinner, particularly on weekends. This place is noisy, boisterous, and fun.

Inspectors for the Best Places *series accept no free meals or accommodations; the book has no sponsors or advertisers.*

The Lobster Shop

Off Dash Point Road,
(206) 927-1515
6912 Soundview Drive
NE, Dash Point, Tacoma
Moderate; beer and wine;
AE, DC, MC, V
Dinner every day

The original Lobster Shop, situated out on Dash Point, is a welcome change from the increasing number of pricey, slick eateries blossoming along the local waterfront. This sea-weathered restaurant, tucked away next to a small public beach, is one where we particularly like to spend a blustery winter or fall evening. In comfortable and intimate surroundings you can eat a grilled salmon the like of which you've seldom tasted. No wonder those who crave simply prepared, fresh seafood flock here. The owners have never bothered to put in a bar, but there is a good selection of wines.

A larger version of the Lobster Shop has a distinctly different flavor—and not half the personality: 4013 Ruston Way, Tacoma, (206) 759-2165.

Prosito

6th at Proctor,
(206) 752-0676
3829 Sixth Avenue, Tacoma
Moderate; full bar;
AE, MC, V
Lunch Mon-Sat,
dinner every day

No blarney is needed to coax people to return after they have once eaten at this Irish-run Italian restaurant. Sarah McCrory and Jim Horrigan have taken a rather unlikely looking restaurant, spruced things up decidedly, put together a simple but well-conceived menu, and begun to cook. Appetizers include fritto misto, mushrooms stuffed with basil sauce, and deep-fried artichokes—the latter approaching those originating in Rome's Jewish quarter. Lasagne, featured on weekends, is a combination of pasta, super-rich meat sauce, and cheese, melded into one irresistible glob of flavor. A credible cioppino and clams in wine are also good choices. McCrory makes the bread and pies on the premises.

Top-quality jazz is available here nightly, and on Sunday afternoons the first sets are for nonsmokers, with children welcomed. A place to acquaint your progeny with good pasta and good jazz at the same sitting.

Tokyo Bento

In the Green Firs
Shopping Center,
(206) 564-3399
3830 Bridgeport Way,
Tacoma
Moderate; beer and wine;
MC, V
Lunch Mon-Fri,
dinner Mon-Sat

With the trend toward lower cholesterol, every neighborhood should have a good sushi bar. Diminutive in size and number of menu items, but bold in decor and strong in flavors, the Tokyo Bento offers Tacoma's west side a shopping-center surprise. For a traditional Japanese meal for two, order both the sushi plate of impeccably fresh raw fish and a grilled dish, such as chicken teriyaki or yaki sakana (a marinated fish). For a lunch on the run, try the ubiquitous noodle dishes or the donburi—a large bowl of rice topped with vegetables, meat, or seafood as your palate dictates. The staff is extremely helpful to those unfamiliar with Japanese food. Be careful, though; they tend to bring all the dishes at the same time unless asked not to.

Towry's Le Snack

Corner of 4th and
Tacoma, (206) 272-5937
322 Tacoma Avenue

This tiny place near Wright Park is a pleasant surprise. Invigorating dishes line the menu. At breakfast is a Hangtown fry omelet, filled with plump oysters, or peasant potato pies with bacon, mushrooms, and Swiss cheese.

South, Tacoma
Inexpensive; beer and
wine; MC, V
Breakfast, lunch Tues-Fri,
brunch Sat-Sun

The fennel sausage served with grilled new potatoes, colorful peppers, and onions is exceptionally good. At lunch you'll encounter unusual soups, salads, and hot entrees such as Hungarian noodles or grilled oysters on a bed of pasta.

Towry's is opening a dinner house, the Key Eatery, on the Key Peninsula sometime in 1989. Plans are to feature Northwest bounty, including Minterbrook oysters, freshly picked from down the road: 9013 Key Peninsula Highway N, Lake Bay, (206) 884-4403.

Yen Ching

Across from Picway Shoes
and the Sears outlet,
(206) 582-3400
8765 S Tacoma Way,
Tacoma
Moderate; full bar;
AE, MC, V
Lunch, dinner every day

The jolly, life-size Buddha greeting you at the entrance sets the tone for this restaurant, where eating is a happy experience. The combination of first-rate food and handsome decor makes it popular with couples, who only give up hand-holding when the first dish arrives. A favorite appetizer is the Cold Seafood Delight, with its scallops, tiny shrimp, and chunks of chicken breast punctuated by thin slivers of celery, all glistening in a white wine sauce. There is a good range of other standard dishes, but, in deference to the Western palate, nothing too exotic. The sauces here are excellent—even on the more incendiary selections, the differing and unique flavors shine through. The twice-cooked pork, with its slices of meat contrasted with crunchy cabbage and bamboo shoots, is a good dinner choice, or the smoky tea duck, with its complexity of seasonings. As in many Chinese restaurants, the luncheon specials are not too special; order from the regular menu. One caution: on weekends, if you don't have reservations, you may be seated in the less-than-satisfactory bar.

Thai Garden

Corner of 11th and L,
(206) 627-2590
1202 S 11th Street, Tacoma
Moderate; no alcohol;
AE, MC, V
Lunch Mon-Fri,
dinner Mon-Sat

The spiced beef with curry and coconut milk and the shrimp over deep-fried beancake are two good introductions to the recent wave of incendiary food from Thailand. This small, unadorned restaurant offers a whole range of unusual Thai dishes (with Chinese and Indian overtones), starting with light and spicy spring rolls and ending with coconut ice cream to extinguish the fire.

Ya Shu Yuen

Between Park and
Yakima on 38th,
(206) 473-1180
757 South 38th Street,
Tacoma
Inexpensive; beer and
wine; MC, V
Lunch, dinner Tues-Sun

Through the thicket of plastic strawberry vines and red-tasseled lamps lies the small family-run restaurant that almost all Tacoma fans of Chinese food have on their list of favorites. They come for the spring rolls, with their delicate casings and stuffing of crunchy vegetables; for the chicken with a piquant plum sauce; or the almost-crisp dry-braised beef. The menu is limited, but what this place has it does well, although occasionally the dishes are oilier than they should be.

Looking for a particular place? Check the index at the back of this book for individual restaurants, hotels, B&Bs, parks, and more.

LODGINGS

Sheraton Tacoma Hotel
Exit 135 off I-5,
between 13th and 15th
on Broadway,
(206) 572-3200
1320 Broadway Plaza,
Tacoma, WA 98402
Expensive; AE, DC, MC, V

The Sheraton Tacoma Hotel, with its elegant decor, 319 rooms, and two restaurants, has filled a real need in Tacoma. Adjacent to the massive Bicentennial Pavilion, it's most suitable for conventions. Most rooms look out over Commencement Bay or have a view of Mount Rainier. The more expensive concierge rooms on the 24th and 25th floors include a continental breakfast and early-evening hors d'oeuvres. Guests can eat either at the Wintergarden, attractively situated off the mezzanine balcony, or on top of the hotel in the scenic Rose Room (see review). The Music Room on the side of the lobby offers a restful place for afternoon tea or drinks, and Elliott's bar offers a plentiful array of appetizers to placate the after-work customers.

Keenan House
Exit 132 off I-5, corner
of 26th and N Warner,
(206) 752-0702
2610 N Warner Street,
Tacoma, WA 98407
Moderate; no credit cards;
checks ok

There are two Keenan bed-and-breakfast houses located in the historic district of Tacoma near the University of Puget Sound. The original spacious Victorian home is furnished with antiques, and the newly acquired Tudor home around the corner is decorated tastefully with country furnishings. This brings the capacity of the two houses to eight rooms, but only one room has a private bath. Lenore Keenan serves a full breakfast with fresh fruit and croissants. Children are welcome.

GIG HARBOR

By land and water, weekend vacationers flock to the small fishing community of Gig Harbor. It's still homeport for an active commercial fishing fleet, and the good anchorage and various moorage docks also attract a parade of pleasure craft. There are many interesting shops and galleries for browsing, and when the clouds break, Mount Rainier holds court for all. There's an annual arts festival in mid-July.

Nearby, **Kopachuck State Park** is a popular destination, as are **Penrose Point and RFK state parks** on the Key Peninsula, all with numerous beaches for clam digging (Purdy Spit and Maple Hollow Park are the most accessible spots). At **Minter Creek State Hatchery** the public can watch the various developmental stages of over four million coho salmon.

Performance Circle, resident theatre group, mounts seven enjoyable productions from July to March, with summer shows staged outside in the meadow at Celebrations, 9916 Peacock Hill Avenue NW. Theatergoers bring picnics and blankets, watching the shows beneath the stars. It's turning into a wonderful small-town custom. Celebrations is now open for meals. Their brunch is especially abundant, (206) 851-7529.

Wondering about our standards? We rate establishments on value, performance measured against the place's goals, uniqueness, enjoyability, loyalty of clientele, cleanliness, excellence and ambition of the cooking, and professionalism of the service. For an explanation of the star system, see the Introduction.

RESTAURANTS

Tides Tavern

*At the intersection of
Harborview and
Soundview,
(206) 858-3982
2925 Harborview Drive,
Gig Harbor
Inexpensive; beer and
wine; MC, V
Lunch, dinner every day*

This historic waterfront tavern retains the flavor of its colorful past, which began with Teddy Roosevelt's signature on a homestead certificate in 1904. A loud, happy place—everybody's there. When the sun is out, you have to scramble for a table on the deck, but wherever you sit you will enjoy the hearty sandwiches, burgers, and pizzas. The shrimp salad is a local favorite. A word of warning: the Tides has strict age-identification procedures and children are not allowed, even on the deck. In the evenings, the crowd becomes younger and, if possible, even louder. Live music most weekends; boat and float-plane moorage available.

W.B. Scotts

*Corner of Harborview and
Pioneer, (206) 858-6163
3108 Harborview Drive,
Gig Harbor
Moderate; full bar;
AE, DC, MC, V
Breakfast, lunch, dinner
every day, brunch Sun*

Other local restaurants may have better views, but right in the heart of Gig Harbor is the best eatery in town. It's small and attractive, with a varied menu and consistently good quality and service. Even before the emphasis on low-calorie/low-cholesterol meals, W.B.'s specialized in seafood and chicken dishes. At lunch, nibble on the hot seafood salad. For dinner, we opt for the blackened salmon, halibut crusted with walnuts, or chicken stir-fry with a zingy, sesame-ginger-cashew sauce. Red meat, though downplayed here, shows up as a choice top sirloin pepper steak. A piano bar brings in the after-dinner crowd.

LODGINGS

The Pillars

*Take the first Gig Harbor
exit off Highway 16,
(206) 851-6644
6606 Soundview Drive,
Gig Harbor, WA 98335
Expensive; MC, V*

From the windows of this landmark Gig Harbor house overlooking Puget Sound you can see Colvos Passage, Vashon Island, and Mount Rainier. It's a newly opened guest house with all three guest rooms beautifully decorated, large private baths, and separate reading areas furnished with writing desks and telephones. An added bonus is the covered, heated swimming pool and Jacuzzi.

The breakfasts feature home-baked breads and muffins. No smoking. Children okay if you call ahead; no pets.

STEILACOOM

Once an Indian village and later Washington Territory's first incorporated city (1854), today Steilacoom is a quiet village of old trees and houses, with no vestige of its heyday, when a trolley line ran from Bair's drugstore to Tacoma. October's **Apple Squeeze Festival** and mid-summer's **Salmon Bake**, with canoe and kayak races, are popular drawing cards.

The **Steilacoom Tribal Museum** is located in the turn-of-the-century church overlooking the South Sound islands and the entire Olympic Mountain range. Ferries run to Anderson Island, with restricted runs to McNeil Island (a former state penitentiary).

RESTAURANTS

E.R. Rogers
*Corner of Commercial
and Willes, off Steilacoom
Blvd, (206) 582-0280
1702 Commercial Street,
Steilacoom
Moderate; full bar;
MC, V
Dinner every day,
brunch Sun*

View restaurants on Puget Sound are not novelties, but views like this one are still exceptional, particularly when seen from a restored Queen Anne–style home built almost 100 years ago. The halibut baked in parchment paper is noteworthy, but the Steilacoom special prime rib, first roasted, then sliced and quickly seared, is still tops. You can't beat the huge Sunday buffet brunch, with its large selection of seafood: oysters on the half-shell, cold poached salmon and flavorful smoked salmon, cracked crab, pickled herring, steamed clams, and fettuccine with shrimp. There is a beautiful upstairs bar, with a widow's-walk deck just wide enough for one row of tables. Fresh flowers appear in unexpected places, and chamber music plays softly in the background.

**Bair Drug and
Hardware Store**
*Lafayette and Willes,
(206) 588-9668
1617 Lafayette Street,
Steilacoom
Inexpensive; beer
and wine; MC, V
Lunch every day,
breakfast Sat-Sun*

Side orders of nostalgia are presented gratis when you step into Bair's. Except for the customers, little has changed since it was built—in 1895. Products your grandparents might have used—cigars, washtubs, perfume, and apple peelers—are still on display. Old post office boxes mask the bakery, which turns out pies and pastries such as flaky apple dumplings; the potbelly stove warms customers in the winter. Best of all, there is a 1906 soda fountain, where you can still get a sarsaparilla, a Green River, or a real ice-cream soda.

OLYMPIA

All Olympia is divided into three parts: Crown, Gown, and Town.

Crown. A focus of interest for most visitors is the Washington State government, its centerpiece the classic dome of the Legislative Building. Replete with bronze and imported marble, the striking Romanesque structure, recently redecorated, houses the offices of the governor and other state executives. The state Senate and House of Representatives meet here in annual winter sessions. Their debates can be critiqued from visitors' galleries. The Capitol itself is open daily, and hourly tours are offered from 10am to 3pm, (206) 586-TOUR.

Just opposite rises the pillared **Temple of Justice**, seat of the state supreme court. To the west is the red brick Governor's Mansion. Though architects scorn it, Olympians love it, as was discovered a few years ago when someone proposed tearing it down. It's open to visitors on Wednesday afternoons from 1 to 2:45pm, (206) 586-TOUR.

Handsomest of the newer state buildings is Paul Thiry's squarish **State Library**, directly behind the Legislative Building. Open to the public during business hours, it boasts a unique abstract mural by Washington's best-known painter, the late Mark Tobey. In its Washington Room are artifacts from the state's early history and a collection of books by Washington authors. Around its upper walls a mural by Kenneth Callahan—one of the best of this artist's works—details events in the state's history.

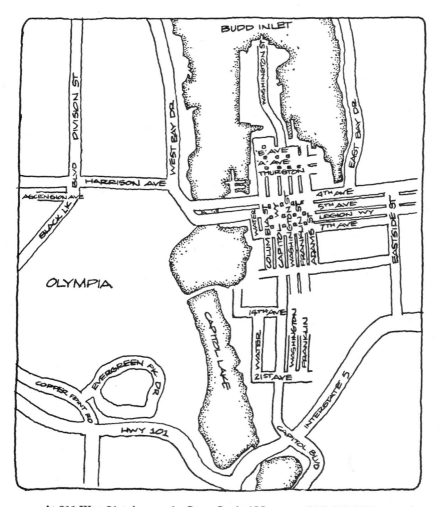

At 211 West 21st Avenue the **State Capitol Museum**, (206) 753-2580, occupies the former mansion of banker Clarence Lord. Its permanent exhibit includes an outstanding collection of western Washington Indian baskets. Periodic shows involving Northwest history and Northwest artists' work are held here. Closed Mondays.

Downtown on Seventh Avenue between Washington and Franklin streets is the recently restored **Old Capitol**, whose pointed towers and high-arched windows suggest a late-medieval chateau. Currently occupied by the superintendent of public instruction, this architectural fantasy fronts **Sylvester Park**, a green town square designed in traditional New England style.

Gown is a triad of colleges: **The Evergreen State College**, west of Olympia on Cooper Point; **St. Martin's**, a Benedictine monastery and college in adjacent

Lacey; and **South Sound Community College**, just across the freeway in Aberdeen. Though TESC is relatively new, its innovative educational policies have already won national praise. It offers a regular schedule of plays and movies, as well as special events like its annual **February Tribute to Japan**. Its library and swimming pool are open to the public, (206) 866-6000, ext. 6220.

Free concerts are regularly held in St. Martin's at Abbey Church. Over the years the monks have assembled an unusual store of regional art, called the **Martin of Tours Collection**, beginning with paintings of turn-of-the-century Olympia executed by Joseph Carpenter and including works by such 20th-century Northwest greats as Tobey, Callahan, Guy Anderson, and Paul Horiuchi. Tours of the collection can be arranged through its curator, Abbot Gerald, (206) 438-4204.

Town is another triad: Olympia, Lacey, and Tumwater, each proud of its separate identity. Historic heart of the whole area is **Tumwater Falls**, where the Deschutes River flows into Capitol Lake and ultimately to the sea. This was the site of the first American settlement on Puget Sound. Established here today is the chief local industry, the Tumwater Division of the **Pabst Brewing Company**—formerly the Olympia Brewing Company—which offers daily tours of its plant.

The area's finest nature preserve lies well outside the city limits. This is the relatively unspoiled **Nisqually Delta**—outlet of a river starting at a Mount Rainier glacier and entering the Sound just north of Olympia. Take Exit 115 off I-5 and follow the signs to the headquarters of the **Nisqually National Wildlife Refuge**. From here, a five-mile hiking trail follows an old dike around the delta, alive with bird life, both resident and migratory. Just south, a rookery of great blue herons occupies the treetops.

In Olympia proper, the recent opening of the **Washington Center for the Performing Arts** (on Washington Street between Fifth Avenue and Legion Way) has brought new life to the downtown area. In the same block is the **Marianne Partlow Gallery**, a leading outlet for contemporary painting and sculpture. Across Fifth Avenue, the **Capitol Theatre**, a onetime movie house, provides a showcase for the offerings of the Olympia Film Society, as well as locally produced plays and musicals. Toward the harbor, at the corner of North Capitol Way and West Thurston Street, is the lively **Olympia Farmers Market**. Open 10am–3pm, except in winter, it's filled with South Sound produce, flowers, and crafts.

Wholly different in character is **West Fourth Avenue**, between Columbia and Water streets, a hangout for students and ex-students, artists and would-be artists, gays, lesbians, and counterculture members. At the corner of Water Street is **Childhood's End**, a gallery for arts and crafts, and across from it is **Percival Landing**, where the city has created a new waterfront park. A boardwalk extends from the moored craft of the Olympia Yacht Club to the mainland and continues on out to the working port. Here you can climb a tall viewing tower to survey the whole of Olympia's harbor, from the snowy Olympic Mountains to the north all the way back to the Capitol Dome.

RESTAURANTS

Carnegie's
7th and Franklin,
(206) 357-5550
302 E Seventh Avenue,
Olympia
Moderate; full bar;

Andrew Carnegie might be a bit taken aback were he to know that the sturdy old Olympia library bearing his name has been converted to a restaurant—but its book-lined interior walls provide agreeable surroundings for lunch or dinner. At lunch, the place is a buzzing hive of yuppies and state workers. At dinner it's quieter, with the cheerful fireplace from its library days making the room particularly pleasant on chilly winter evenings. The

AE, DC, MC, V
Lunch, dinner Mon-Sat

menu is the same throughout the day and includes a good selection of sandwiches, soups, and salads; steak, veal, and prime rib; and a variety of seafood entrees. Carnegie's is particularly well known for its Cajun cooking. A recent successful daily special—Bayou Chicken—featured sauteed chicken and Cajun-cured ham tossed with fettuccine. Prime rib is available Cajun-style, served with a piquant orange sauce. Though the wine list is quite comprehensive, we were surprised to note the absence of any Burgundies or pinot noirs in a house where so much attention is paid to the careful preparation of beef.

Fleur de Lys
1 block east of Plum,
(206) 754-6208
901 E Legion Way,
Olympia
Moderate; beer and wine;
MC, V
Lunch Tues-Fri,
dinner Thurs-Sat

Owner-chef Jim Jones seems to cook just for the joy of it at this small, unpretentious country-style restaurant, which despite its simplicity offers some highly sophisticated traditional cuisine. Salmon is a favorite here, prepared in a variety of ways—with dill sauce, for instance, or en croute, topped with crab. The menu at dinner is a bit more elaborate than at lunch, and also a bit more expensive—duck a l'orange, for instance, replaces chicken a l'orange. Two of the chef's star dinner turns are beef Wellington and Grand Marnier souffle. A less elaborate finale is crepes suzette, of which co-owner Mary Jones says, "If I have too many on order, I have to have one myself." Special care has been taken with the wine list, which includes a selection of dessert vintages. Though some of his customers would like to see Jones vary his menu a bit more, others are quite content. "As good as anything in Europe, bar none," claims one enthusiastic fan.

Gardner's Seafood and Pasta
Drive north on Capitol
Way to Thurston,
(206) 786-8466
111 W Thurston Street,
Olympia
Moderate; beer and wine;
AE, MC, V
Dinner every day

Seafood lovers are loyal fans of Gardner's. Here the geoduck—that mighty superclam that has given its name to The Evergreen State College's sports teams—is prepared as well as anywhere in Olympia. A true Puget Sound specialty is an appetizer of a dozen Olympia oysters, each the size of a quarter, served on the half-shell ($6.50). Interesting soups include rock shrimp with dill; a variety of pastas come with or without seafood. A Dungeness crab casserole is sauteed with bacon, green onions, mushrooms, Chablis, and cream and topped with mozzarella and Cheddar. The wine list is a bit startling because of the chef's candid judgment calls. Of one sparkling vintage from France he confides, "pretty dry for a cheapie." Connoisseurs of ice cream won't want to miss Gardner's homemade product, which comes in ever-changing flavors—Kahlua chocolate chip, for example, served with whipped cream and a slice of kiwi fruit.

La Petite Maison
1 block south of the
intersection of Division

Ever since its opening as a restaurant, this small converted 1890s farmhouse has been a quietly elegant refuge for people interested in imaginative cooking. Among its

and Harrison,
(206) 943-8812
2005 Ascension Avenue
NW, Olympia
Moderate; beer and wine;
MC, V
Lunch Mon-Fri,
dinner Tues-Sat

especially memorable appetizers is a plate of small steamer clams, fresh from Kamilche Point near Shelton, prepared with herbs—about the best thing being done in Olympia with this particular shellfish. Entree specialties can include roast leg of lamb marinated in herbs and black pepper, or fresh Alaska halibut baked in parchment. The chef is fond of original recipes, like crisp roast duckling served with wild blackberry sauce. Attention is paid to the appearance of the food as well as to its taste: a recent carrot soup was little less than a work of art, a deep, orange puree with a carrot slice floating like an exotic flower in its center. Service is quietly formal, and classical music accompanies dinner. The wine list includes such carefully chosen vintages as Knudsen Erath's Oregon pinot noir, and among the desserts is an Italian torte prepared with Grand Marnier. In spring or summer, it's pleasant to eat on the glassed-in porch—though the view of over-trafficked Division Street is anything but inspiring, the outdoor atmosphere is enjoyable.

Seven Gables
¾ mile north of the 4th
Avenue bridge,
(206) 352-2349
1205 W Bay Drive,
Olympia
Moderate; full bar;
AE, MC, D
Dinner Tues-Sat,
brunch Sun

Each year Sally Parke and Kevan Saunders manage to further improve the already lovely gardens surrounding this striking old Carpenter Gothic pile, built by Olympia's turn-of-the-century mayor, George B. Lane, to take full advantage of a spectacular Mount Rainier view. They vary their menu as well. An interesting dish is Indienne crab and prawns, arranged on a scallop shell with vegetables and fresh strawberries. Like other entrees, it's preceded by soup and salad. One of the restaurant's unchanging standards is Chicken Southern Blue, a variant of chicken cordon bleu, stuffed with ham and Swiss cheese and baked in sherry. Among appetizers are smoked salmon and Brie, and the Greek pastry spanakopita. Wines include vintages from France, Italy, Germany, Spain, and Australia. Offered also is an intercontinental list of beer and ale, ranging from Guinness Stout to Tusker (from Kenya). Fresh flowers from the garden adorn each table, and the owners have gone to great lengths to maintain a homelike atmosphere. It's a very pleasant place for a quiet, companionable dinner, and at Sunday brunch (where offerings include seafood crepes as well as—alas—Eggs Benedict Arnold) you can enjoy daytime views of Mayor Lane's mountain and the owners' garden with your meal.

Arnold's
4 blocks north of
the Capitol, in the
Aladdin Motor Inn
(206) 754-9409
900 S Capitol Way,
Olympia

Chef Arnold Ball, who gave his name to this restaurant, has long since departed, but his influence lingers in its wide-ranging menu. Unusual specialties such as frogs' legs appear together with more conventional offerings, like seafood fettuccine and fresh Pioneer oysters. There's a variety of steaks and chops, including a tenderloin

Moderate; full bar;
AE, DC, MC, V
Breakfast every day,
lunch, dinner Mon-Sat

topped with crab legs and artichokes, as well as fresh baby-beef liver sauteed with bacon.

Careful thought has brightened the decor and done much to improve a basically unattractive site: the sand-blasted interior windows echoing the red foliage on the Japanese plums outside were designed by Olympia's Mansion Glass. Service is somewhat more formal than in most Olympia restaurants. Arnold's is a place where you'd be happy to take your grandmother, but it's also a popular rendezvous for downtown businesspeople. Good martinis are concocted in the adjacent bar, long a gathering place for Republicans (and even an occasional Democrat, during legislative sessions).

Ben Moore's
4th and Columbia,
(206) 357-7527
112 W Fourth Avenue,
Olympia
Moderate; full bar;
AE, MC, V
Breakfast, lunch, dinner
Mon-Sat

Don't be put off by the modest entrance to this historic establishment. In the post–World War II era, it was a favorite hangout for politicians and journalists, and its exterior has changed little since then. Inside, though, something new has been added, in the person of owner-chef Mike Murphy, who has spruced up the dining room and put his own distinctive stamp on the menu. A thick steak served with prawns and fettuccine is a memorable staple here. Murphy's seafood dishes, like fresh grilled rainbow trout or oysters—served al pesto, grilled, carbonara, or tempura—are specialties. His sauces are so rich and flavorful you won't want to leave any on your plate. He prepares interesting soups such as turkey tomato. Murphy's prices are quite reasonable, and he often features live entertainment, but it's his skill as a chef that draws patrons here.

Bristol House
Off Evergreen Park Drive,
(206) 352-9494
2401 Bristol Court SW,
Olympia
Moderate; full bar;
MC, V
Breakfast Sun-Fri, lunch
Mon-Fri, dinner Tues-Sat

Adolph Schmidt, a member of the large and active family that founded the Olympia brewery, owns and serves as chef at this cheerful, small restaurant in the rapidly developing professional office area south of the Thurston County courthouse. His menu is eclectic, featuring a limited number of standard dishes, such as chicken Dijon, fettuccine alfredo, and steak in various forms, all well prepared. Our chicken curry with mushrooms was cooked just right and served in a meltingly flavorful sauce. At lunch there's a selection of seafood salads and a variety of sandwiches—crab au gratin, for example. Beers are not limited to Olympia, and there's a conservative wine list. Overseeing all with an appropriately no-nonsense mien is a gold-framed portrait of an unidentified Schmidt ancestor, who looks as though he would tolerate no inefficiency in this enterprise.

Wondering about our standards? We rate establishments on value, performance measured against the place's goals, uniqueness, enjoyability, loyalty of clientele, cleanliness, excellence and ambition of the cooking, and professionalism of the service. For an explanation of the star system, see the Introduction.

Budd Bay Cafe

Between A and B on
Columbia, (206) 357-6963
525 N Columbia Street,
Olympia
Moderate; full bar;
AE, DC, MC, V
Lunch Mon-Sat, dinner
every day, brunch Sun

Olympia has long needed a waterfront restaurant with an outdoor deck overlooking Budd Inlet. Now it has one, and it's a smash hit. The Budd Bay Cafe has been designed so each table can take maximum advantage of the sunset view, and it's full from afternoon well into the late evening. Don't look for haute cuisine here—the menu (steaks, salads, pastas, and seafood) is designed for boaters and their friends. There are salmonburgers and oysterburgers, and sandwiches with nautical names like Intrepid. Most dishes are available in less costly, lighter versions, which the average landlubber will find sufficient. There's a long list of specialty beers. The bar is pleasant and lively. Indeed, in its short span of existence, this place has become such a scene that you wonder what people were doing before it opened.

Chattery Down

Across from the Capitol
Theatre, (206) 352-9301
209 Fifth Avenue,
Olympia
Moderate; beer and wine;
AE, MC, V
Breakfast Mon-Sat, lunch
Mon-Fri, dinner Tues-Sat

Entrepreneur Ann Buck's buoyant personality sets the tone at this small dining room, an annex to Buck's Fifth Avenue, her gift shop next door. Continental breakfast is offered Monday through Friday—Saturday's full breakfast features brioche French toast and smoked trout. A variety of teas are offered in the afternoon, with high tea Wednesdays and Saturdays featuring Cornish pasties. For lunch there are homemade breads, soups, and salads. Many patrons prefer Friday, when the specialty is always an oyster dish—Angels on Horseback, scalloped oysters, oyster stew, or chowder.

Until recently Chattery Down has been taken over each evening by chef Mark Lougheed, who served dinner in the same space under the name Mark's After Five. At this writing Lougheed intends to move to his own restaurant across Fifth Avenue. Ann Buck plans to serve dinner and to open a wine and hors d'oeuvres bar (mostly for patrons of the nearby Capitol Theatre and Washington Center for the Performing Arts), offering after-theatre wines and desserts.

Crackers

Corner of 4th and
Adams, (206) 352-1900
317 E Fourth Avenue,
Olympia
Moderate; full bar;
AE, DC, MC, V
Breakfast, lunch, dinner
every day

"Yeah, we went through San Francisco without any brakes. . . ." That's the kind of offhand comment you can expect to hear at Crackers, where the clientele is young and trendy, the menu full of jokes that would make a high-schooler cringe, and the portions very large indeed. The menu is long and unchanging throughout the day; on weekends it's the late-night place in town. Salmon is served poached, broiled, or smoked. There's a variety of interesting salads, among which the Cobb is especially good. Chicken dishes are prominently featured. Teenagers particularly applaud Crackers' Clacker, a breast of chicken wrapped around cream cheese, shrimp, and olives. Less successful, in our view, is the chicken Dijon ("You mustard heard of this one," says the menu). There are steaks, omelets, pastas, and a mixed bag of sandwiches with funny names (Maui Wowie Burger). Service is casual but cheerful, with occasional indifference to significant details (our French bread arrived stone-cold). There's a good selection of beers and an acceptable wine list; the restaurant likes to promote mysterious novelty drinks such as the Bear Hug, built around a shot of Tuaca.

Migel's

Exit 102 off I-5, watch for signs, (206) 352-1575
4611 Tumwater Valley Drive SE, Tumwater
Moderate; full bar; AE, DC, MC, V
Lunch Mon-Sat, dinner every day, brunch Sun

With the name of the saint misspelled for the benefit of the gringo clientele, and with prints by the likes of van Gogh scattered about freely, you'd never suppose you were back in Guadalajara. Nevertheless, prices are reasonable, and the food is good: a chicken-based enchilada suisa served piping hot, is appropriately mellow. Margaritas are large and glacial, and come in several flavors. Migel's is located next to the Tumwater Valley golf course; the view from the dining room is pleasant, and the place is popular with sportsmen.

The Spar

1 block east of Capitol Boulevard, (206) 357-6444
114 E Fourth Avenue, Olympia
Inexpensive; full bar; AE, MC, V
Breakfast, lunch, dinner every day

A highly positive review in *The New York Times* has brought new customers to this survival of traditional Olympia, which may pretty much represent what Easterners think the real West should be. But to the local regulars it's the same old reliable Spar, with its J-shaped counter, around which assemble the same utterly classless crowd of students, attorneys, businesspeople, artists, seamen, tourists, and leisured retirees. All know they can depend on the food, which is wholesome American and very reasonably priced. The Spar's robust milk shakes, thick turkey sandwiches, and homemade bread pudding are locally celebrated, as is its water, which comes from its own artesian well. Some days there's a remarkable dinner special—Willapa Bay oysters, say, or fresh halibut or salmon, served with salad ($6.95). Owners Alan and Maylene McWain are proud that, with a glass of Washington wine, a good Northwest dinner can be had here for under $10. For many, though, the best time to come is breakfast, when the political talk can flow hot and heavy, and waitress Genia Sutter—latest in a long line of feisty Spar servers—seldom fails to brighten the drabbest mornings with her unforgettable double entendres. "What's the Spar?" a well-known 3rd Congressional District politician asked an aide not long ago. "That's why you don't do better in Thurston County," the aide reproved him.

Tug's Restaurant and Bar

Off Harrison at the end of West Bay Drive, (206) 352-2261
2100 West Bay Drive, Olympia
Moderate; full bar; AE, MC, V

Here at the West Bay Marina is a new waterfront restaurant that doesn't depend solely on its view to attract customers. Tug's specializes in carefully prepared seafood. Halibut cooked with sour cream and dill sauce is available in season, as are razor clams, pan-fried in butter. King salmon is offered in several forms: cold, smoked, or broiled, and served with a butter and Scotch whisky sauce. Other items include rack of Ellensburg lamb

Lunch Mon-Sat, dinner every day, brunch Sun

served in a red-wine sauce and an Oriental salad that mixes slices of duckling with Chinese noodles. A dessert tray features tortes from Wagner's Bakery. Though in general the cooking here can't be faulted, an artichoke we had recently, stuffed with scallops and bay shrimp, seemed a bit underdone. The ceiling at Tug's is low, and the noise level, consequently, is high when the place is crowded—as it usually is.

Urban Onion

1 block east of Capitol Way at the corner of Legion and Washington, (206) 943-9242
117 E Legion Way, Olympia
Inexpensive; beer and wine; AE, MC, V
Breakfast, lunch, dinner Mon-Sat

Those who see sprouts as mattress stuffing may have reservations about this cheerful, laid-back place, which features them in many of its sandwiches and salads. Others will love it. The menu includes lots of pasta and Mexican-inspired dishes, open-faced sandwiches, good soups (the lentil is noteworthy), specialty burgers made from grain-fed beef, and drinks from herb tea and espresso to carrot juice. There are unusual vegetarian dishes like gado gado—sauteed vegetables in an Indonesian sauce of tahini, peanut butter, and spices. For breakfast you can order standard omelets or huevos rancheros. At this writing, Urban Onion plans to expand to include the view of Sylvester Park, through the great arched windows of the onetime Olympian Hotel.

Wagner's European Bakery

Near the corner of Capitol and Union, (206) 357-7268
1013 S Capitol Way, Olympia
Moderate; no alcohol; no credit cards; checks ok
Continental breakfast, lunch Mon-Sat

Almost as *echt deutsch* as an opera by that other well-known Wagner is the formidable collection of pastries regularly produced by Rudy Wagner's bakery, which effortlessly fabricates stuff like Black Forest tortes, apricot squares, apple-almond rolls, cherry-cheese pockets, raspberry mousse tortes, carrot cakes, triple-chocolate squares, pig's ears, cream horns, several species of doughnut, lemon puffs, blueberry muffins, Danish pastries, and all kinds of fresh-baked bread. It's *Gotterdammerung* for the weight-watchers. An attached deli, featuring light breakfast and lunch, is a popular stop for coffee breaks. A bargain lunchtime special is the Baker's Feast: a sandwich containing ham, roast beef, turkey, and two kinds of cheese, with soup, salad, and dessert—all for $3.95. German-born Wagner, chief baker as well as owner, gets new ideas on trips back to Europe. "Lately I've been going out and having breakfast before showing up at work," he mused in an interview not long ago. "Otherwise I eat five or six pastries, eat some more, then just keep on eating."

LODGINGS

Harbinger Inn

1 mile north of State Street, (206) 754-0389
1136 E Bay Drive,

Occupying a restored historic house, this B&B offers Edwardian furnishings, a fine outlook over Olympia Harbor and the distant Olympic Mountains, and four choice guest rooms (two with view, two without). Nicest is the two-room suite on the view side, with its own bath (all

Olympia, WA 98506
Moderate; AE, MC, V

other rooms share); but rooms on the back side are farther from the street and therefore a bit more tranquil. A light breakfast of fresh fruit and home-baked pastry is served. The whole place is pleasant and well maintained, with a bright garden in front to welcome you and a view that'll make you want to stay.

Puget View Guesthouse
Take exit 111 from I-5
toward the Nisqually
Delta, (206) 459-1676
7924 61st Avenue NE,
Olympia, WA 98506
Moderate; MC, V

Old Puget Sound survives in the lovely setting of this small two-bedroom guest cottage, detached from the home of Dick and Barbara Yunker, and available only as a single unit. Located north of Olympia in a deep forest above the Nisqually Delta, it's set on a high bluff overlooking Anderson Island. Lilacs, magnolia, and rhododendron bloom in its well-tended garden, where a flourishing fig tree suggests a slightly warmer microclimate (bandit raccoons sometimes steal the figs). "Continental plus" breakfasts of fruit, pastries, and coffee are served. Kids are welcome.

There's lots to do in the area: just adjacent is densely wooded Tolmie State Park, with hiking trails and picnic grounds. Boat rentals are nearby, as is an overnight anchorage for visitors arriving by water. And the owners offer summertime outboard excursions to nearby islands (there are still deserted beaches in this remote area) for a fireside cookout, returning home by dark—a classic Puget Sound adventure.

Westwater Inn
Take exit 104 from I-5,
(206) 943-4000
2300 Evergreen Park
Drive, Olympia, WA
98502
Moderate; AE, DC, MC, V
Lunch Mon-Thurs, dinner
every day, brunch Sun

Few urban hotels around Puget Sound take such striking advantage of the Northwest's natural beauty as this one, dramatically perched on a high hill above Capitol Lake, with such greenery in view, and the Capitol Dome—illuminated at night—rising to the north. There are fairly large rooms ($64 for a double overlooking the lake), a heated outdoor pool, and an entertainment lounge presenting live music Tuesday through Saturday nights. It's a short drive to the center of town, the Capitol grouping, or the shops of Capitol Mall. The Thurston County Courthouse and county administrative buildings lie within walking distance. Some rooms can be noisy, so it's advisable to choose one on the water side, although these cost more.

Meals are served in a coffee shop and at Ceazan's, a restaurant with as scenic an outlook as any in town and offering a number of tables well suited for intimate talks. Meals are surprisingly inexpensive (one recent lunchtime special featured asparagus soup and a roast beef sandwich for $3.95). In the opinion of some, the quality of the cuisine doesn't always measure up to the fast and at-

---

If you've found a place that you think is a Best Place, send in the report form at the back of this book. If you're unhappy with one of the places, please let us know why. We depend on reader input.

tentive service. Nevertheless, for sheer quantity, it would be hard to beat Ceazan's lavish Sunday brunch, which at $8.50 per person ($6.95 for seniors) is one of the best restaurant bargains in town.

TENINO

RESTAURANTS

Alice's Restaurant
Call for directions,
(206) 264-2887
19248 Johnson Creek
Road, Tenino
Moderate; beer and wine;
MC, V
Dinner Wed-Sun

Urbanized city folk may be a bit undone as they plunge recklessly through the Skookumchuck Valley outback in search of Alice's, one of the last of the old-style rural farmhouse restaurants. Once they arrive, though, they'll delight in its picturesque setting, about as remote from daily I-5 traffic snarls as you can get in western Washington. As on any good farm, there's plenty to eat. Alice's offers a six-course dinner served family-style, the all-inclusive price determined by the price of the entree. The hearty meal begins with vegetable hors d'oeuvres and a thick peanut soup accompanied by small loaves of fresh-baked bread. This is followed by a salad with hot bacon dressing, a rainbow trout served with fresh fruit, and the chosen entree. For dessert there's a choice between apple crisp or upside-down cake, both very nice.

Entrees might range from steak and spare ribs to oysters, but the most distinctive items are wild game, which might include breast of pheasant or quail, buffalo stew, or venison chops—the latter an expensive dish we found more rewarding in anticipation than in consumption. Be forewarned: Alice's only seats people with reservations.

Alice's is operated in conjunction with the Johnson Creek Winery, and you're invited next door to sample a few of its wines before dinner.

YELM

RESTAURANTS

Arnold's Country Inn
Across from the
Thriftway Shopping
Center, (206) 458-3977
717 Yelm Avenue E, Yelm
Moderate; full bar;
AE, MC, V
Breakfast Sat-Sun, lunch,
dinner Tues-Sun

Long known as one of Olympia's most accomplished chefs, Arnold Ball has established his latest restaurant just outside Yelm on the road leading from the state capital to Northwest Trek (see Eatonville) and Mount Rainier. Though it's called a country inn—and you can order such traditional country staples as pork chops with applesauce or veal with country gravy—the cuisine here is far more cosmopolitan than such a name might suggest. Appetizers include mushrooms stuffed with crabmeat, and entrees include sweetbreads in a port wine sauce. Try one of Arnold's specialties as a main course—like fresh chicken raspberry, sauteed with raspberry brandy and chicken broth. A daily special might be beef tips Malayan, served in a rice ring. Meat dishes are available in lighter versions at lower prices. Arnold's delectable rolls are baked on the premises, as are his fine pies.

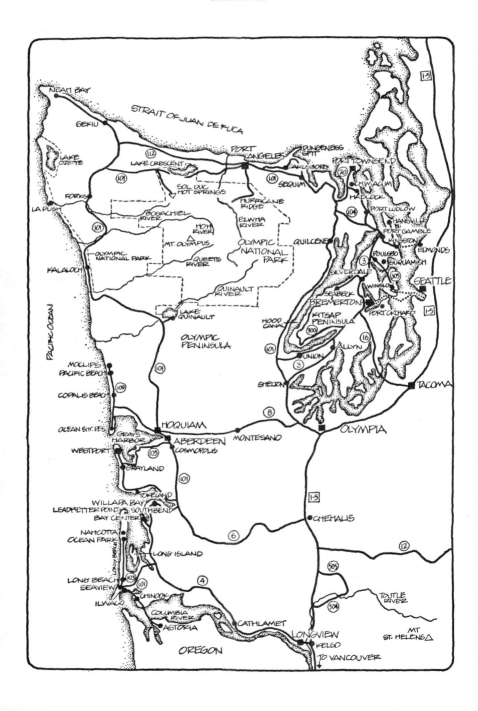

OLYMPIC PENINSULA

▲

The Kitsap Peninsula north to the Hood Canal Bridge,
then west along the Juan de Fuca shore of the Olympic Peninsula,
and southward along the Pacific coast to Ocean Shores.

BREMERTON

Bremerton, as even many residents will admit, can seem a pretty dismal place. Its first reason for existing is its huge US Naval Shipyard, and the Trident nuclear submarine base, across the Kitsap Peninsula in Bangor, is now bringing a frenetic boom to the entire area. Bremerton sometimes seems built of tough sailors' taverns at the center and endless roadside sprawl at the edges. The town has found a new tourist identity since it lost its ace, the battleship *USS Missouri*—the *USS Nimitz* will most likely be moored here until the Everett Naval Base is complete. Some lesser old warships are still here to be seen from outside the shipyard fences. The **Bremerton Naval Museum**, half a block from the ferry terminal, tells of shipbuilding history back to bowsprit-and-sail days; (206) 479-7447. It's an hour trip via ferry to Seattle; a foot ferry (walk-on only) cuts the trip to 35 minutes, but at press time it was temporarily suspended; (206) 464-6400.

RESTAURANTS

Boat Shed
East side of Manette
Bridge, on the water,
(206) 377-2600
101 Shore Drive,
Bremerton
Inexpensive; full bar; MC, V
Lunch Mon-Sat, dinner
every day

A mile from the ferry landing is this nautical place, not far from the road but perched grandly out over the water. The food runs to seafood, sandwiches, and salads; you wait in a long line (lunch only) to look at the menu (during which you should commission one member of your party to grab a table on the deck), but the line moves fast and the hearty food is worth it. Try the Skipjack Sandwich, with three kinds of cheese, chopped olives, and red onions in hot pita bread. The nachos, perhaps the most generously bedecked in the region, are also the *best* in the region.

PORT ORCHARD

Fifteen minutes by car from Bremerton, a wander through this charming port makes for a fine afternoon jaunt. **Olde Central Antique Mall** on Bay Street is full of pottery, stained glass, and handcraft shops, as well as antiques and restaurants.

ALLYN

RESTAURANTS

Bellagamba's
*On Lakeland Drive; look
for signs, (206) 275-2871
Lakeland Village
Golf Course, Allyn
Moderate; full bar; MC, V
Lunch, dinner Tues-Sun*

Here's a place you'd never just stumble upon. Tucked into the little Hood Canal town of Allyn, this romantic downstairs restaurant has its roots in the original Bellagamba's in Shelton but is a new place altogether—the best-kept secret among the canal's sophisticated set of summer dwellers. It's a charming sliver of a space, with an intimate loft and a serene outlook onto a pond and a lake beyond. The menu includes a few each of fish, pasta, beef, and chicken entrees, but, Gentle Diner, choose wisely: you are in the heart of shellfish country. On a recent visit our oysters Bellagamba (a rendition of oysters Rockefeller) were impeccably fresh and covered with a bubbling cheese-and-wine sauce; our steamed mussels had surely been plucked off the beach that morning. With dinners come big baked spuds, wild rice, or fettuccine; a basket of warm, yeasty bread; pedestrian shrimp-and-lettuce salads with excellent homemade dressings; and side plates of stir-fried zucchini. The wine list (and their willingness to uncork any white to try by the glass) impressed us; the heavy lumpia appetizer did not. Have dessert.

UNION

RESTAURANTS

Victoria's
*¼ mile west of
Alderbrook Inn on
Highway 106,
(206) 898-4400
E 6790 Highway 106,
Union
Moderate; full bar; MC, V
Breakfast Sat-Sun,
lunch, dinner every day*

Inside a large A-frame adorned with wooden beams and log-style walls, this dining room makes up in charm for any misgivings we may have about the food. An open fireplace sets off a view of Hood Canal beyond; outside is a beautiful garden-terrace with a stream running alongside—quite idyllic. Its culinary aspirations, however, while high, do not quite measure up to the setting. The local seafood is the safest bet, and often the freshest: the trout amandine sauteed in Amaretto and almonds was competently prepared. The waitress's recommendation, lasagne with five cheeses, did not live up to our expectations (though perhaps our culinary expectations were too high for this remote town on the elbow of the Hood Canal).

LODGINGS

Alderbrook Inn
*At the north end of
Union on Highway 106,
(206) 898-2200
E 7101 Highway 106,*

Although its history dates back to 1913, this all-purpose resort has been thoroughly modernized. The lawn by the beach gives a fine view of the boaters on Hood Canal—the inn, in fact, has its own dock, should you wish to get there on your yacht—but the buildings feel somewhat

Union, WA 98592
Expensive; AE, DC, MC, V

claustrophobic. Plaza units dwarf a courtyard that could be pleasant, and the motel units are ordinary. A far better bet are the waterfront two-bedroom cottages that go for about $110. Other guest rooms run from $72 for a double to $130 for a suite. Children under 12 can stay free. On hand are a restaurant that offers banquet facilities and a lounge, pool, Jacuzzi, and nearby tennis courts and golf.

SHELTON
RESTAURANTS

Cafe Luna
In the Mercantile Mall,
(206) 427-8709
Third and Railroad,
Shelton
Moderate; beer and wine;
no credit cards; checks ok
Dinner Tues-Sat

It's apartheid on the plate at Cafe Luna in downtown Shelton, where the day's special, pasta alla vongole, is a plate of plain buttered fettuccine on which sit, expectantly, nine clams in their steamed-open shells. Grated Romano is offered—apart from that, no sauce at all. Still, this pretty little gray-green Art Deco restaurant with its silvery fingernail new moons hanging from ceiling and glued to walls is an oasis in this tough lumber town. Evening pastas are a few dollars more and include salad.

Pricing is topsy-turvy throughout, with house wine (good Chianti classico) at $2.50 a glass (high for this town), yet a perfect chocolate mousse, generously filling a tulip glass and prettily topped with a flying spiral of orange peel, costing only $2.

SEABECK
LODGINGS

Willcox House
8 miles south of Seabeck
at 2390 Tekiu Road,
(206) 830-4492
Mail: 2390 Tekiu Road,
Bremerton, WA 98312
Expensive: MC, V

The Hood Canal. To some, it's the home of the Trident submarine; to others it's a boater's playground, an oyster lover's feast, and a fisherman's find. In early 1989, Philip and Cecilia Hughes opened the first inn on the 242-mile-long shoreline of the Hood Canal. Their expansive canal-front home (once a retreat center accommodating up to 40 people at a time) is now an elegant refuge for a maximum of eight. The four bedrooms (all with their own baths, one with a double Jacuzzi) are impressive. Hope for a stormy night and reserve the master bedroom with stone fireplace ($130). After one of Cecilia's satisfying breakfasts, the rest of the day (and the house and the undeveloped waterfront) is yours. That is, until hors d'oeuvres in the evening. It's a half-hour drive from the Bremerton ferry, or set your own sails and tie up at their dock.

Looking for a particular place? Check the index at the back of this book for individual restaurants, lodgings, attractions, and more.

SILVERDALE
RESTAURANTS

Yacht Club Broiler
From 305 take Silverdale exit, first right into town, then left on Bayshore,
(206) 698-1601
9226 Bayshore Drive, Silverdale
Moderate; full bar; MC, V
Lunch, dinner every day, brunch Sun

The owners of Bremerton's Boat Shed are stretching themselves—to Silverdale. Their new restaurant, with a view of Dyes Inlet, is all polished in (yawn) brass and oak, but the gently cooked seafood will waken any tired Kitsap County tastebuds. Daily specials include prawns, scallops, salmon in a black-bean sauce, or lamb-and-Brie sandwiches (try one with an order of their criss-cross fries). The menu offers a selection of pastas, chicken, and fish in all preparations from broiled to blackened. There's a reason the salmon is the most popular item on the menu: it's undercooked just enough and broiled with garlic and herb butter.

LODGINGS

Silverdale on the Bay Resort Hotel
Silverdale Way and Bucklin Hill Road,
(206) 698-1000
3073 Bucklin Hill Road, Silverdale, WA 98383
Moderate; full bar; AE, DC, MC, V
Breakfast, lunch, dinner every day

It's a Best Western in name only, operated by crack veteran hotelier Sam Standard. Inside, tasteful design highlights serene views over Dyes Inlet. Each view room has a private balcony, remote-control TV, and clock radio; mini-suites are the best ($145). Extras establish it as the resort it aspires to be; an indoor lap pool with sliding glass doors that open onto a large brick sun deck (where you can sip cool drinks all afternoon if you'd like), a sauna, weight room, pool tables, video game room, boat dock, and convention facilities.

But the Mariner Restaurant is an even bigger surprise for this military town booming with new malls, with white-linen–appointed tables, professional service, and expertly prepared dinners that aren't too pricey. Executive chef Frank Goff has taken over the reins from Pierre Bitterer, and he's obviously striving to keep up the quality. Young, well-trained hands toss the Caesar salads at tableside and light the flambes—showy food that sometimes misses the mark, but it's good here. Seafood—such as the heartbreakingly sweet scallops sauteed with artichoke hearts—is their specialty.

POULSBO

This attractive small community that hugs a fine harbor wears its Scandinavian heritage on its sleeve. Somehow, the heavy dose of heritage comes across in good taste and with good cheer. Recent reconstruction of the main street in town is now complete.

Sluys Bakery is surely a diabolical initiative by the League of Scandinavian Dentists (if there is such a thing). Inside you'll find sweets galore, (*too* sweet, some say) in manifestations that can barely be imagined. As well as the Nordic goodies, Sluys bakes bread that is estimably healthful. A local specialty, Poulsbo Bread, has national distribution; there are various Scandinavian loaves; 18924 Front Street NE, (206) 779-2798.

At the end of a pier on Fjord Drive in the Liberty Bay Marina is **Marie's Wild & Woolly**, selling quality yarns. It's the only shop of its kind that we know of with a knitting-deck looking out on the marina; (206) 779-3222.

Lemolo Custom Meats is particularly well known for its curing and smoking of hams, bacon, jerky, and salmon; it also offers a full range of locally raised meat. 17166 Lemolo Shore Drive, 1½ miles out of Poulsbo towards Seattle, (206) 779-2447.

RESTAURANTS

Larry's Best BBQ

At the south end of Poulsbo on Old Silverdale Highway,
(206) 697-BEST
19559 Viking Way,
Poulsbo
Inexpensive; beer only; no credit cards; checks ok

Yee haw! Inside an old strip mall it's the board-and-batten Old West, complete with a cow skull, a snakeskin, and a leather halter on the walls. A sombrero shades the water cooler. Barbecue is its beat: pork, ham, beef, turkey, chicken—and "smoked out" beans. You order by the pound (on or off the bone), and a quarter-pound of deboned pork ($3.50) including a whole-wheat roll and a "sidewinder" is plenty for one hungry vaquero; but even the hottest sauce will not scare off the gringos.

LODGINGS

Manor Farm Inn

4 miles south of Hood Canal Bridge on Big Valley Road,
(206) 779-4628
26069 Big Valley Road NE, Poulsbo, WA 98370
Expensive; MC, V
Breakfast, dinner every day

A lavish retreat in the middle of nowhere, Manor Farm is a working farm with horses, sheep, dairy cows, chickens, and a trout pond—a beguiling mix of the raw and the cultivated that succeeds in spoiling even the city-bred. Englishman Robin Hughes, a former veterinarian, and his wife, Jill, a Los Angeles native, are the proprietors; these expansive hosts run a superlative accommodation and pour heart and soul into the food—sometimes successfully.

There are eight bright, airy guest rooms and one two-room cottage with vaulted ceilings, furnished with French country pine antiques, fresh flowers, down comforters, and Robin's own watercolors. Two rooms have fireplaces; most have private baths. A central hot tub bubbles outside; other activities are mostly unhurried variations on the long walk around the acres of rolling farmland. At this writing, serenity remains the essence of the place, although the Hugheses are finalizing plans to transform the garage into a conference center/sportsmen's club and the acreage next door into a spa facility with its own accommodations. Our advice is to visit before the place is overrun, and book early—for this dose of rural quiet, people often must book six months in advance.

Breakfast happens twice at the Manor Farm: first with a tray of hot scones and orange juice left at your door, next (for non-guests as well) at 9:30 with fresh fruit, oatmeal folded with whipped cream, eggs from the farm chickens, and rashers of bacon. Ample but too simple for the $10 prix fixe. Dinner is even more of an event: a one-seating (6:30) affair that begins with sherry and canapes in the lovely drawing room and a lengthy discourse on the particulars of the five-course meal (weekends only). You proceed to the dining room, into which Robin will emerge from time to time to sit down for a chat at your table or to invite you back to his kitchen, where he loves to perform. His efforts are earnest though sometimes inconsistent, not unlike dining at the home of close friends; therefore occasional gaffes like gummy fettuccine sauce or overdone chicken are forgivable. The entree might be a sauteed chicken breast fragrant with rosemary, or perhaps grilled red snapper with usually wonderful vegetable side dishes like peas with mint or carrots with ginger. The finish is dessert, cheese, port, coffee, and Robin's own chocolates—a proper finale for what aspires to be a proper English meal. Set price is between $15 and $29 per person (depending on number of courses served), wine and service not included.

SUQUAMISH

In Suquamish on the Port Madison Indian Reservation (follow the signs past Agate Pass), the **Suquamish Museum** in the Tribal Center is devoted to studying and displaying Puget Sound Salish Indian culture; (206) 598-3311. **Chief Sealth's grave** can be found nearby, on the grounds of St. Peter's Catholic Mission Church. Twin dugout canoes rest on a log frame over the stone, which reads, "The firm friend of the whites, and for him the city of Seattle was named."

RESTAURANTS

Karsten's
Head west on 305 across
Bainbridge, take first
right after Agate Pass
Bridge toward Suquamish,
(206) 598-3080
18490 NE Suquamish
Way, Suquamish
Moderate; no alcohol;
MC, V
Breakfast, lunch, dinner
every day

Suquamish has boasted some funky come-and-gone diners in the past, but Karsten's represents the first known attempt at first-class dining in a new shopping area, built by Karsten Solheim (a former golf club manufacturer who spent childhood summers on the shores of Suquamish). Just outside this small Indian village is this casual restaurant (unobtrusive golfer motifs on the wallpaper) that borders on elegant (complete with tablecloths). The menu presents seafood, most of it fresh, and a number of steaks. We sampled the moist and well-prepared pan-fried Alaskan halibut and two beef tenderloin medallions sauteed with a perigordine sauce. Lunch is light, with soup, salad, and sandwich fare.

PORT GAMBLE

Built in the mid-19th century by the Pope & Talbot timber people, who traveled here by clipper ship from Maine, this is the essence of the company town. Everything is company-owned and -maintained, and the dozen or so Victorian houses are beauties and in splendid repair. The town, which was modeled on a New England village, also boasts a lovely church, a vital and well-stocked company store, and a historical museum—down the steps and in back of the store—that is a gem. An ideal presentation of a community's society and industrial heritage, it was designed by Alec James, who designed the displays for the Provincial Museum in Victoria. The lumber mill, incidentally, is still in operation and proves to be an interesting sight. Unfortunately, a grand hotel that sat on a splendid bluff overlooking the water was razed in the 1960s; the hotel's splendid lobby is re-created in the museum. For more information, call Pope & Talbot at (206) 297-3341.

HANSVILLE
LODGINGS

The Last Resort
*Call for directions,
(206) 638-2358
2546 NE Twin Spits
Road, Hansville,
WA 98340
Moderate; no credit cards;
checks ok*

It's a minimal resort, of the sort popular in the 1940s: a few small cabins, a beach, a pool. Each of the five cabins has two tiny bedrooms, a kitchenette, and a view of the beach; they are fixed up, in the mom-and-pop style of yore, with cowboy oil paintings, cast-iron pots and pans, and a wood stove to keep the rooms warm. A newer duplex has slightly bigger rooms and equally good views, and there is still the three-bedroom house for large parties (a deal at $68 for four). There's blessed little to do: hike the long beach, lie around the pool, cook, read, doze.

QUILCENE
RESTAURANTS

Loggers Landing
*At the south end of town
on Highway 101,
(206) 765-3161
30281 Highway 101 S,
Quilcene
Inexpensive; beer
and wine; MC, V
Breakfast, lunch, dinner
every day*

It's easy to be thrown off by this modest building and its cement floors. From behind the counter comes a clam chowder fragrant with large pieces of tender bivalve, snippets of bacon, inch-square cubes of potato, and secret seasoning. Or join the forest workers, who use this place as their mess hall, for the $7.95 logger's breakfast: OJ, a hefty 8-ounce steak, hash browns, three eggs, toast, and coffee refills. The place is perpetually packed with locals, and the service is no-nonsense friendly.

The Timber House
*About ½ mile south of
Quilcene on Highway
101, (206) 765-3339
Highway 101 S, Quilcene
Moderate; full bar; MC, V
Lunch, dinner Wed-Mon*

★

The Timber House, a charming place, resembles nothing so much as a large and rough-hewn hunting lodge. Although the menu is not without more pretentious items, the local seafood is the thing to go for. Quilcene oysters come from right down the road, and there's much from the waters around the Sound. Sauteed Dungeness crab is a winner, as are the scallops Timber House, sauteed with mushrooms and onions and bathed in a Mornay sauce. Even the deep-fried selections that make up the Captain's Plate are nicely done and not over-battered.

Love a good bargain? Then you'll really like Seattle Cheap Eats, *a compendium of 230 terrific bargain eateries in and around Seattle, brought to you by the same folks who bring you the* Best Places *series.*

PORT LUDLOW
LODGINGS

The Resort at Port Ludlow
6 miles north of Hood Canal Bridge on the west side, (206) 437-2222 9483 Oak Bay Road, Port Ludlow, WA 98365 Expensive; AE, DC, MC, V

While you're dining at the Harbormaster Restaurant, imagine the same view enjoyed by old Cyrus Walker—Pope & Talbot's legendary 1880s sawmill manager. His "biggest damn cabin on the Sound," actually a splendid Victorian manse, once occupied this site with its eye-filling Olympic peaks, teardrop bay, and rolling, timber-covered hills. Now 148 units, indoor and outdoor pools, a marina, seven tennis courts, a championship golf course, hiking and cycling trails, and a hidden waterfall fill the 1,500 developed acres.

All of the individually decorated suites have fireplaces, kitchens, and private decks; many include views of the water. The suites with loft are grand, but other buildings boast outlooks just as lovely onto the green countryside. Designed as a family resort, Port Ludlow also hosts a good number of conventions; these usually prove to be the kiss of death for a romantic weekend, but here a feeling of spaciousness acts as a serene buffer. In the Harbormaster, Northwest salmon and Dungeness crab are our dinner recommendations. Lunches are nothing much, but the breakfast fried potatoes and seafood omelets are treats.

CHIMACUM
RESTAURANTS

The Chimacum Cafe
9 miles south of Port Townsend, (206) 732-4631 4900 Rhododendron Drive, Chimacum Inexpensive; no alcohol; MC, V Breakfast, lunch, dinner every day

Sunny atmosphere, spotless facilities, and cheerful help have created a fiercely loyal, mostly local, clientele who'll argue with anyone who denies this place serves the best food for the price on the peninsula. Draws are the succulent homemade pies and farm-style meals, including special Sunday chicken dinners with gravy made the old-fashioned way. Friday clam chowder is a knockout. This is truly an institution worth seeking out, between the Hood Canal Bridge and Port Townsend.

HADLOCK
RESTAURANTS

The Ajax Cafe
2 blocks south of Hadlock; watch for signs, (206) 385-3450 271 Water Street,

This comfortable, funky old place has suffered inconsistency of late. Unavailability of some of the menu's best items, such as the salmon and mussels—in fact, most of the seafood selections on one occasion—and excruciatingly slow service can cause no small amount of impatience.

Lower Hadlock
Moderate; beer and wine;
MC, V
Dinner every day

★

But the help readily and cheerfully admits to pokiness, and when the food does arrive, it's usually fine. Portions are invariably huge. There's still a long wait for a table on weekends. Sunsets reflected in the water are tranquil and lovely.

PORT TOWNSEND

Riding high until the 1890s, the city fell flat when the Union Pacific failed to hook up the town with its transcontinental rail system. Lucky city, for people's energies aimed in other directions, and dozens of Victorian houses and commercial structures were spared. Though the area's economy is still fragile, these buildings are the pride of the region and a reason in themselves for a visit.

Architecture. The town's charm can be quickly taken in on a walking tour of Water Street, an agreeable stretch of ornate old brick-and-stone buildings mostly erected about the same time Seattle's Pioneer Square was being rebuilt from the fire of 1889 (and in some cases by the same architects). Pick up an auto/bike/walking tour map from the Visitors' Center at 2437 E Sims Way, (206) 385-2722, to check out the town's mansions. Notable are the Daniel Logan House (Taylor and Lawrence), with an iron roof crest; Bartlett House (end of Polk Street on the bluff), with its famous mansard roof, and Starrett House (Adams and Clay), with 1890 Stick-style architecture (see review). Buildings open for public tours are the Jefferson County Courthouse (Washington and Jefferson), with its clock tower and fantasy-castle appearance; City Hall (Water and Madison), with a fine museum, jail, restored Victorian hearse, and every imaginable whatnot; Rothschild House (Jefferson and Taylor), with an antique rose garden and period rooms with breathtaking views; and the Commanding Officer's House at Fort Worden.

Chetzemoka Park, in the northeast corner of town, has a charming gazebo, picnic tables, tall firs, and a grassy slope down to the beach; you can also gobble up blackberries here during the fall.

Events. Old homes are toured the first weekend in May and the third weekend in September—always worth doing. **The Rhododendron Festival** in May, with a parade and crowning of the queen, is the oldest festival in town. The **Centrum Summer Arts Festival,** (206) 385-3102, one of the most successful cultural pro-

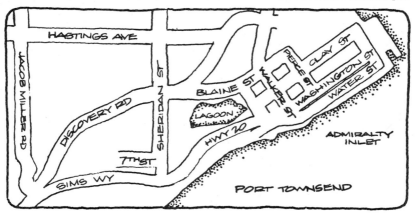

grams in the state, with dance, fiddle tunes, chamber music, a writers' conference, jazz, and theatre performances, runs at Fort Worden June to September. The **Wooden Boat Festival**, (206) 385-3628), first weekend in September, is a charming bit of creative anachronism.

Wandering. On Water Street you'll find colorful shops. **Earthworks** and **Baltic Art Gallery** both deal in ceramic and graphic arts; **Captain's Gallery** has an amazing selection of pricey kaleidoscopes. **Imprint Book Store** is a superior bookshop, well stocked with classics, best sellers, and a great selection of contemporary verse. The best ice cream cone can be had at **Elevated Ice Cream**; the best pastry at **Bread & Roses Bakery**; and the best antique selection at **Port Townsend Antique Mall** (820 Washington), where 26 antique merchants have convened under one roof. For a nip with the natives, head for **Russell's Back Alley Tavern** for live music and local color, or the historic **Town Tavern**, recently taken over by new owners. Finally, check out the retail revitalization of Uptown at **Aldrich's** (940 Lawrence), an authentic 1890s general store come to life with an upscale twist.

RESTAURANTS

Fountain Cafe

At the Port Townsend
fountain steps,
(206) 385-1364
920 Washington Street,
Port Townsend
Moderate; beer and wine;
MC, V
Lunch, dinner every day

Locals are proud to bring their out-of-town guests here. And they'll line up several-deep in the cozy storefront dining room to inspect quirky local art on the walls and wait for a table. Chances are they've come for the oysters, on the menu in a variety of preparations, including pan-fried, or one of the fresh-pasta-and-shellfish dishes. Things can get spicy—our prawns diablo with black squid-ink linguine was downright satanic—and young, confident chef Michael Maxwell has a penchant for pepper. But the wine list is good. And you'd have to be loony not to try the loganberry fool for dessert. Service is courteous even with patrons queued in front.

Shanghai Restaurant

At the north end of town,
(206) 385-4810
Point Hudson,
Port Townsend
Inexpensive; beer and
wine; MC, V
Lunch, dinner every day

The oddest—and in many ways a very pleasant—facet of dining at the Shanghai is the dissonant juxtaposition of wonderfully sophisticated Chinese food with funky, roadhouse decor. There is only one downside to the Shanghai: Point Hudson's RV park obscuring what could be a splendid view of Mount Baker. The rest is the upside—all 93 Hunan and Sichuan selections. Each dish is impeccably prepared and presented with consistently excellent texture and flavor—Chinese food that could hold its own in Vancouver, BC.

Particularly enchanting are the Shanghai's mu-shu pork, which offers a sweet and cool counterpoint to hotter dishes like asparagus beef or kung pao shrimp. The Shanghai cabbage—hottest and spiciest item on the menu—is indispensable. The array of curry dishes and seafood, fowl, beef, pork, and vegetable entrees guarantees something for everybody, and prices are low enough for customers to order twice the number of dishes they might order elsewhere.

The Landfall

The very last building on the north end of Water Street, (206) 385-5814 412 Water Street, Port Townsend Moderate; beer and wine; no credit cards; local checks ok Breakfast, lunch every day, dinner Wed-Sun

This funky neighborhood standby, with its octagonal boathouse-style add-on and a wood stove for warming up Point Hudson winters, is frequented for its burgers and fish and chips. But the nicely seasoned cod and tender grilled salmon, accompanied by flavorful brown rice on the side, are also highly respectable. So are the prices. The menu features some Mexican selections. With a typical Port Townsend touch, the restrooms are out back.

The Lido

Downtown next to J.C. Penney, (206) 385-7111 925 Water Street, Port Townsend Moderate; full bar; AE, DC, MC, V Lunch, dinner

Smack-dab downtown in an old, exposed-brick building, this shoreside spot seems to encourage leisurely dining and conversations. Rudy Valiani's proprietorship, as well as his accommodating service, continues to attract both tourists and locals (lots of business suits), but the place still has its gastronomic ups and downs. Sandwiches and seafood specials are usually trustworthy—check out the seafood crepes—except for a rather dried-out quiche. Wednesdays, Italian specials dominate the menu. Ask for a table on the mezzanine and watch the ferries, or check the bar downstairs for periodic low-key entertainment.

Upstairs—way upstairs—is the convenient Lido Inn, a hideaway in the middle of everything. Three rooms and one suite with a kitchenette, old-world overstuffed furnishings, and water views are the attractions.

Salal Cafe

Near the corner of Quincy and Water, (206) 385-6532 634 Water Street, Port Townsend Moderate; beer and wine; MC, V Breakfast every day, lunch Mon-Sat, dinner Fri-Sat

Breakfasts are justly famous here, with a couple of morning newspapers circulating and locals trading stories back in the solarium. The omelets are legendary—we like the avocado with homemade salsa and the spinach and feta cheese—and cheese blintzes, oyster scrambles, and tofu dishes are satisfying. By popular demand, a small dinner menu is now served Fridays and Saturdays; Sundays it's breakfast all day.

LODGINGS

The James House

Corner of Washington and Harrison, (206) 385-1238 1238 Washington Street, Port Townsend, WA 98368 Moderate; MC, V

The Bogarts are back! After a six-year hiatus, Lowell and Barbara Bogart repurchased one of the finest Victorian houses in Port Townsend. The James House of 1889—which claims to be the Northwest's first B&B—is arguably one of the most pleasant places to stay in the entire state. And the Bogarts are still trying to improve it. All 12 rooms are beautifully furnished in antiques, and the units in the front of the house have the best views out across the water. Not all rooms have private baths, but the shared facilities are spacious and well equipped. The main floor has two sumptuous adjoining parlors, each with a fireplace and plenty of stimulating reading material. Guests can look forward to a delicious continental breakfast of fresh fruit and scones, either at the formal dining room's big table or in the charming kitchen with its antique cookstove.

F.W. Hastings House Old Consulate Inn

At the intersection of Washington and Walker on the bluff,
(206) 385-6753
313 Walker Street,
Port Townsend, WA 98368
Moderate; MC, V

One of the most photographed Victorians in these parts, the Hastings House is also one of the most comfortable and nonstuffy, with its wrap-around porch and Sound views. Finishing touches are being made after a long remodeling by owners Rob and Joanna Jackson, in possession since autumn 1987, and all but one of the eight charmingly decorated rooms have their own private baths or half-baths. The third-floor Tower Suite, with a sweeping bay view and dripping with lace, is a honeymooners' dream; in the parlors, furnishings are comfortable and whimsical. Mammoth breakfasts—over which Joanna will be delighted to wittily recount the inn's history—are made with only natural ingredients.

Heritage House

Corner of Washington and Pierce,
(206) 385-6800
305 Pierce Street,
Port Townsend,
WA 98368
Moderate; MC, V

An immaculate yard welcomes visitors to this hillcrest Victorian B&B. The sprightly variety of refinished antiques matches guest rooms with names like Lilac, Peach Blossom, and Morning Glory; three of the six rooms have private baths. Relax in the evenings on the porch swing. Children over eight are permitted, but pets are not. Views over the North Sound and the business district come close to rivaling those of Heritage's venerable neighbor, the James House.

Arcadia Country Inn

Turn off Highway 20 onto Jacob Miller Road; look for signs,
(206) 385-5245
1891 S Jacob Miller Road, Port Townsend, WA 98368
Moderate; MC, V

World-renowned jugglers The Flying Karamazov Brothers own this handsome 1908 country estate (formerly speakeasy, brothel, and roadhouse) on 7 lush acres just outside of town. The show-owners have spared no expense to revamp the huge barn—their practice arena—and they occupy the inn periodically when they're not on tour. Though the guest rooms have been reduced to five, all have private baths and antiques, and family-style continental breakfasts are included. There's a hot tub out back.

CLOSED

Fort Worden

1 mile north of Port Townsend,
(206) 385-4730
Mail: PO Box 574, Fort Worden State Park Conference Center, Port Townsend, WA 98368
Moderate; no credit cards; checks ok

Fort Worden was one of three artillery posts constructed at the turn of the century to guard the entrances of Puget Sound. The troops have since marched away, and the massive gun mounts on the bluff have been stripped of their iron, but the beautifully situated fort has become a state park, a conference center, the site of the splendid Centrum arts festival, and an unusual place to stay.

Twenty-four former officers' quarters, nobly proportioned structures dating back to 1904, front the old parade ground. These homes, including a few duplexes slightly off the parade ground, have been furnished with period reproductions and made into decent lodgings. They are wonderfully spacious, each has a complete kitchen, and the bargain rates range from $51 for one bedroom to $133 for a house with 10 twin beds. Reservations should be made well in advance (the office recommends a year to the day).

There are many attractions at the fort, which is open all year. A picturesque lighthouse adjoins the primitive beach; the hill and parade ground where scenes for the film *An Officer and a Gentleman* were shot inspire some great imagining. The adventuresome find the maze of empty bunkers an endless source of delight, and the summer festival lends an enlightened note to it all.

Lizzie's

Near the corner of Lawrence and Pierce in the historic district, (206) 385-4168 731 Pierce Street, Port Townsend, WA 98368 Moderate; MC, V

Interior and exterior improvements at this model of Victorian excess continue under owners Patti and Bill Wickline. Breakfast in the farm kitchen can turn into a friendly kaffeeklatsch, and a bubble bath in the tub of the spacious, sunlit corner bathroom is a Victorian treat. (The Wicklines have their own line of soaps, lotions, and very sudsy bubble bath.) Two parlors, once frequented by the former boardinghouse tenants, seem to have been plucked from the past. There are views from about half of the eight bedrooms, and flowered decor.

Palace Hotel

Near the corner of Water and Tyler, (206) 385-0773 1004 Water Street, Port Townsend, WA 98368 Moderate; AE, MC, V

Right downtown, this 1889 Romanesque building places visitors in the midst of Port Townsend's most interesting shopping and gawking district. Shops, eateries, and rare examples of Victorian seaport architecture are everywhere. Check-in's a little confusing—you stop in Tibbles Gallery at 1010 Water Street. The owners have added rooms (now a total of 15) and spruced things up while retaining the antique, ex-bordello ambience. Rates, from $47 to $79 (for Madame Marie's room, with kitchenette), are within most budgets. Warning: long flights of stairs, though handsome reminders of another era, are a challenge to the infirm or impatient guest.

Starrett House Inn

Corner of Clay and Adams, (206) 385-3205 744 Clay Street, Port Townsend, WA 98368 Moderate; MC, V

The most opulent Victorian in Port Townsend, this 1889 multigabled Queen Anne hybrid appears to have thrived under the ownership of Edel and Bob Sokol. The spiral stairway, octagonal tower, and "scandalous" ceiling fresco (the Four Seasons, complete with unclad winter maiden) are visually stunning. All rooms are antique-furnished and have high ceilings and lovely decorating touches. But all in all, it's not as impressive as it sounds, and not everyone feels comfortable here. The color scheme may throw the artistically inclined for a loop. The Drawing Room (with a fake fireplace) opens to fabulous views of the Sound and Mount Baker; while the less expensive, brick Carriage Room (billed as being on the main floor) feels more like a basement room, with old carriage doors and a sleigh bed. Breakfasts, served in stately Victorian splendor, are a chocoholic's dream and a dieter's nightmare.

Ravenscroft Inn
Corner of Quincy and Clay on the bluff, (206) 385-2784 533 Quincy Street, Port Townsend, WA 98368 Moderate; MC, V

It's set apart from other Port Townsend bed and breakfasts by virtue of its vintage: it was built in 1987. The Ravenscroft affords all the comforts of modernity—to the visitor weary of Port Townsend's unremitting Victorianism, Ravenscroft offers draft-free rooms, firm beds, pristine decor, unlimited hot water, and a working fireplace in every room. Three of the second-story rooms open onto a long verandah. A breakfast specialty is orange French toast, part of a three-course breakfast prepared in a capacious open kitchen.

DISCOVERY BAY
RESTAURANTS

Fat Smitty's
Discovery Bay 17 miles west of Hood Canal Bridge on Highway 101, (206) 385-4099 7980 Highway 101, Port Townsend Inexpensive; beer and wine; no credit cards; checks ok Breakfast, lunch, dinner every day

The giant chainsaw-carved wooden hamburger out front is so obvious that we've passed by this place on our way to Neah Bay for years. Our mistake. It's been serving meaty burgers and simple fare for about five years now. Try the gargantuan Fat Smitty burger ($3.75); it's truly obese. Accompanying orders of fries are just 25 cents extra. The tender, non-greasy fish sandwich is also a winner. Though there's a choice of 30 or so bottled beers, you'd better choose judiciously—Smitty enforces a sensible two-beer limit. The pies are homemade and much-requested.

SEQUIM

Until about 16 years ago, Sequim (pronounced *skwim*) was one of Washington's best-kept secrets. The town sits smack in the middle of the "rain shadow" cast by the Olympic Mountains: cacti grow wild here, the sun shines, glaciated mountains border New England–style saltwater coves, and the fishing's just fine. Now Sequim's been discovered and is growing. Farms have become subdivisions and golf courses sprout in former grain fields. Retirees form the bulk of the new population, and their influence colors Sequim's transformation from a quiet cultural community into a semi-suburban town. Mitsubishi International has been laying the groundwork for the establishment of a huge new resort.

Cedarbrook Herb Farm (mid-March to Christmas, 10am to 5pm daily) has a vast range of herb plants, scented geraniums, and fresh-cut herbs. The owners have cultivated many unusual items, such as salad burnet and elephant garlic. Good gift shop. 986 Sequim Avenue S, (206) 683-7733.

Olympic Game Farm breeds endangered species and raises a line of beasts for Hollywood; a nice drive-through. Five miles south of Sequim in Dungeness, (206) 683-4295.

Dungeness Spit, six miles northwest, is a national wildlife refuge for birds (though duck hunting is allowed in season) and the longest sand spit in the country

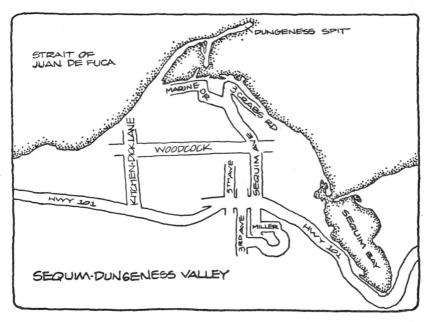

(a favorite spot for horseback riders during the off-season). The driftwood displays are extraordinary and the winds are often good for kite flying. Call (206) 683-5847 for camping information.

Two wineries are in the vicinity: **Lost Mountain Winery** offers tours and tastings by appointment, 730 Lost Mountain Road, (206) 683-5229; **Neuharth Winery** is open daily for tours in summer, winter hours vary, 148 Still Road, (206) 683-9652.

RESTAURANTS

Eclipse Cafe
Near the Landmark
Mall, (206) 683-2760
144 S Fifth Avenue,
Sequim
Inexpensive; no alcohol;
no credit cards; checks ok
Breakfast, lunch Sat-Tues

It's not a pork-chop-eggs-over-easy cafe, but it looks like it. Inside, surprises await. First is the warm welcome from the couple who own the restaurant: Lay Yin, the tiny, dark-haired, enthusiastic Cambodian cook, and her subdued, white-bearded, tall husband, Tom Wells, the restaurant's cook and odd hand. When Tom, an experimental physicist, retired from the National Bureau of Standards, he and Yin opened her long-dreamed-of restaurant in Sequim. They're usually open for breakfast and lunch, and occasionally for weekend dinners for groups of 10 to 15 by reservation only— unless Lay Yin's back bothers her (signs appear: "Sorry, closed today. Yin hurt her back"), or when the couple travels to view Tom's passion and the cafe's namesake, total solar eclipses.

In addition to the interesting owners, the other delight is the food. The simple breakfast and lunch menus change very little. Mornings, expect crisp-fried spring rolls and *con oc* (a flour pancake filled with bacon and green onion), dipped in a mixture of fish sauce, homemade hot pepper sauce, and hoisin sauce, and perhaps a sample of the day's lunch special, with Sumatran coffee or tea. For lunch they serve the breakfast foods plus a daily special (including some vegetarian entrees), soup, kim chee, and perhaps Hong Kong fried ice cream for dessert.

The Oak Table

1 block south of Highway 101, (206) 683-2179
Third and Bell, Sequim
Inexpensive; no alcohol; no credit cards; checks ok
Breakfast every day, lunch Mon-Fri

On weekends, the waiting area of this changeless country cottage is packed with people cheerfully anticipating breakfasts of huge omelets, fresh-fruit crepes, or legendary, gigantic, puffy apple pancakes. They're never disappointed. Service is friendly and efficient—the coffee keeps coming—and the cream is the real thing. Lunches are lighter, with quiches, sandwiches, and seafood salads. It's noisy and boisterous and chatty. Espresso is served all day.

Casoni's

1½ miles west of Sequim on Highway 101 at Carlsborg Junction, (206) 683-2415
104 Hooker Road, Sequim
Moderate; full bar; AE, DC, MC, V
Dinner every day in summer, Wed-Sun rest of year

The popularity of Casoni's sparkling-clean Italian restaurant is undeniable. Perhaps it is the lingering memory of the fresh pasta served alongside the veal Marsala, or perhaps it's the gray-haired warmth of Mamma Casoni herself which keeps diners returning for more. The meltingly tender calamari and the very fresh salads with homemade dressing are enough to bring us back, though we're still wary of the overpowering sauces, which sometimes are too much for Mamma's delicate noodles. The delectable desserts, such as the peanut-butter chocolate-chip cheesecake, are another arena in which Mamma goes too far. We were just too full to bear it this time.

Scarborough Fayre

On the main street going east, before the stoplight, (206) 683-7861
126-128 E Washington Street, Sequim
Inexpensive; no alcohol; no credit cards; checks ok
Lunch, tea Mon-Sat, breakfast buffet Sun

Behind a Tudor storefront in the Old Sequim Marketplace on a busy stretch of highway, you'll find a charming spot featuring English food—homemade sausage rolls, steak and kidney pie, Cornish pasties—as well as quiche and such bakery goodies as fresh breads and pastries. The little back tearoom is pleasant for tea, crumpets, and talk, and you can buy British imports and other stuff to take home: jams and jellies, shortbread, plus gourmet coffees and teas, mugs, and coffee grinders.

Three Crabs

Turn north from Highway 101 onto Sequim Avenue, head 5 miles toward the beach, (206) 683-4264
101 Three Crabs Road, Sequim
Moderate; full bar; MC, V
Lunch, dinner every day

For some unexplainable reason, a trip to Dungeness Spit in not complete without a stop at Three Crabs. The Dungeness crab is one of the major culinary delights of the Northwest, and this modest place right on the beach is the place where many pay tribute to the sweet, flavorful creature. Unfortunately, the reputation here way outclasses the reality. A dated overfondness for deep-fried (okay, so it's fresh) seafood—not even the salmon escapes breading—and lack of regard for the food's presentation (limp, tired dyed-apple-ring garnishes) leave us in puzzlement at its ceaseless rave reviews and weekend hordes. Order the whole, crack-it-yourself Dungeness crab when it's in season (October to April), and try for a table overlooking the bay. Pies are baked on the premises.

LODGINGS

Groveland Cottage

From Sequim, follow signs toward the Three Crabs, (206) 683-3565 1673 Sequim Dungeness Way, Dungeness, WA 98382 Moderate; no credit cards; checks ok

It's oh-so-comfortable Sequim: the kind of place you walk into with sandy shoes (and it's a good thing, since Simone Nichol's place is only a spit away from the Dungeness), plus plenty of views and fair weather that's almost a guarantee. This 90-year-old building has four simple rooms upstairs and, well, it comes with the territory, a crafty gift shop below. The place fills up in the summer—more for its location than anything else, but receiving the newspaper and coffee in your room before Simone serves her four-course breakfast isn't so bad either.

Juan de Fuca Cottages

7 miles north of Sequim, (206) 683-4433 561 Marine Drive, Sequim, WA 98382 Moderate; no credit cards; checks ok

You can't go wrong at any of these five charming and comfortable cabins: four overlook Dungeness Spit, the fifth overlooks the Olympics. Each is equipped with kitchen utensils, a television, a clock radio, and reading material; outside is the spit, begging for beach walks and clam hunts. Two-night minimum stay on weekends.

PORT ANGELES

Hardly a tourist trap, the town offers a fine, broad harbor, and one interesting architectural artifact, the Clallam County Museum. Built in the Georgian style in 1914 as the county courthouse, the building makes a strong, distinctive statement (except for an incongruous, ultramodern added-on wing). Its collections tell a low-key story of the local history and industry. Lincoln and Fourth, (206) 452-7831.

Port Angeles is the jumping-off point to both Victoria (via the privately owned Blackball ferry; (206) 457-4491) and to the north (and most popular) end of **Olympic National Park**. The park fills the interior of the peninsula. The often-inclement weather ensures a low human population and large numbers of elk, deer, bear, and (on the highest crags) mountain goats. Follow the signs to the visitors' center, (206) 452-4501 ext. 230, and stop in for an orientation to the area. Then drive 17 miles along winding precipices to an expansive view that few mountains with twice the altitude can offer (the Olympics only make the 6,000–8,000-foot range). **Hurricane Ridge**, with restrooms and snack facilities, sits among spectacular vistas. The best time to see wildflowers is after mid-July; in winter there is good cross-country skiing and a poma-only downhill area (weekends only). It is always wise to check current road and weather conditions by calling a 24-hour recorded message, (206) 452-9235, before you set out.

If you prefer the low road to the high, for a more relaxing form of recreation you'll find the Elvira natural hot springs in the backcountry west of Port Angeles. Call the visitors' center for hiking and camping information, (206) 452-4501.

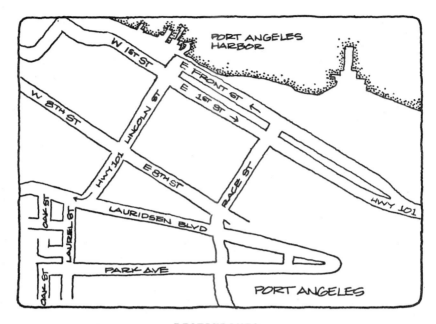

RESTAURANTS

C'est Si Bon

4 miles east of Port Angeles on Highway 101, (206) 452-8888 2300 Highway 101 E, Port Angeles Expensive; full bar; AE, DC, MC, V Dinner Tues-Sun

Situated in a modern structure right off Highway 101, this renowned French restaurant is the creation of Norbert and Michele Juhasz, French emigres who arrived here via Southern California. The room itself is remarkably pleasant, with dramatic paintings, tables set with crisp linens and gleaming silverware, and large windows for viewing the rose garden and the Olympic Mountains beyond—a fit setting for the most sophisticated food on the peninsula, even if the staff can be overwhelmed by Saturday-night crowds.

The menu features a small selection of classical favorites, usually augmented by daily specials. Most nights you have a choice of four of Michele's tried-and-true appetizers—escargots au Pernod, oysters in beurre blanc, onion soup, or fruits de mer au gratin. Entrees might be salmon, coquilles St. Jacques, roast duck, tournedos royal (topped with crabmeat and a shallot sauce), and prawns with garlic and tomato; specials may include a delectable salmon in parchment, fresh halibut with lemon sauce, or a succulent veal Normande, prepared with apples and calvados. Desserts don't range far from familiar favorites, but the velvety chocolate mousse would be hard to improve.

First Street Haven

*1st and Laurel, next
to the Toggery,
(206) 457-0352
107 E First Street,
Port Angeles
Inexpensive; no alcohol;
no credit cards; checks ok
Breakfast, lunch Mon-Sat;
brunch Sun*

It's just a skinny slot of a restaurant, easily missed among the storefronts if you're not paying attention, but it's the best place in Port Angeles for informal breakfasts and lunches. Fresh salads with homemade dressings, hearty sandwiches, and quiche constitute the menu, with pleasing arrangements of fresh fruit on the side. We've heard great things about the chili and fajitas. Expertly made espresso and their own coffee blend are fine jump-starters, especially with a fresh blueberry muffin. Prices are reasonable, service friendly and attentive.

The Greenery

*Behind the Country Aire,
(206) 457-4112
117-B E First Street,
Port Angeles
Moderate; full bar; MC, V
Lunch, dinner every day
(closed Sundays in winter)*

They don't serve breakfast anymore, but it's still one of the most consistent lunch spots in town. Pastas (exceptional fettuccine), homemade soups, and very fresh fish are lunchtime favorites. Dinner brings Caesar salads prepared at tableside; the cioppino is still highly regarded, as is the homemade seafood bisque. Great service. We've never heard a discouraging word about the Greenery.

The Coffee House Restaurant and Gallery

*1st and Lincoln,
(206) 452-1459
118 E First Street,
Port Angeles
Inexpensive; no alcohol;
no credit cards; checks ok
Breakfast, lunch, dinner
every day in summer
(closed Sundays in winter)*

Port Angeles' countercultural minority calls this urban place home: the bulletin board lists all the alternative events that the newspaper skips, and the menu lists adventurous vegetarian fare and electric espresso drinks (which most peninsula restaurants skip). There's some form of entertainment—music or poetry readings—here every Friday night and some Saturdays. We like their original sandwiches (try the Mediterranean), the sweet-potato biscuits, and newer inventions, including the vegetable cream-cheese turnover and the homemade fresh fruit pockets. Hang out with a cup of caffeine and a sweet, sumptuous truffle or two.

LODGINGS

Lake Crescent Lodge

*20 miles west of Port
Angeles on Highway 101,
(206) 928-3211
Mail: HC 62, Box 11,
Port Angeles, WA 98362
Inexpensive; AE, DC,
MC, V*

Some places never change, and in the case of Lake Crescent Lodge, it's a good thing. The lodgings are comfortable and well worn, but well kept up. The main lodge has a grand verandah overlooking the placid, enormous, mountain-girt lake, and the cabins have nice porches. The service is just fine: eager college kids having a nice summer (the lodge is closed from mid-November through April). Fishing (for a fighting *crescenti* trout, found only in this lake), hiking, evening nature programs, and boating are the main activities. The food is merely adequate, but the bar is above average.

We recommend staying in the motel rooms or in one of the four cabins that have fireplaces; the main lodge is, as they say, rustic—a euphemism that means, among other things, the bathroom is down the hall.

All places in this book are recommended; even "no stars" are worth knowing about.

The Tudor Inn
11th and Oak,
(206) 452-3138
1108 S Oak Street, Port
Angeles, WA 98362
Moderate; MC, V

A completely restored Tudor-style bed and breakfast is located 12 blocks from the ferry terminal in Port Angeles. Owners Jane and Jerry Glass have decorated the five-guestroom inn with antiques from their own collection, crisp linens, and a well-stocked library. The best room has its own bath and wonderful views of both the Strait of Juan de Fuca and the Olympics. Breakfast is usually English traditional (bacon, eggs, muffins, fresh fruit juice, and coffee), although Mrs. Glass will surprise her guests occasionally with treats such as sourdough pancakes. Other pluses include transportation to and from the ferry dock and airport (with advance notice), afternoon tea, winter ski packages, and hosts who really know what they're doing.

SOL DUC HOTSPRINGS

LODGINGS

Sol Duc Hotsprings Resort
12 miles off Highway
101, between Port
Angeles and Forks,
(206) 327-3583
Mail: PO Box 2169, Port
Angeles, WA 98362
Moderate; MC, V
Breakfast, lunch, dinner
every day

"The place sure looks better than it did last time I was there—in 1966," said one native Washingtonian. In the heart of the rain forest, this 1910 family resort has re-opened after the completion of road construction in spring 1988. Don't get us wrong: it's still the old Sol Duc, but with a paint job, bathrooms in each of the 32 minimal cabins (some with kitchens, some without), and three re-tiled hot sulfur pools (98 to 104 degrees). There is also a freshwater pool. The area offers plenty of hiking and fishing.

Families still flock around the outdoor burger stand, but now, with chef Lony Ritter (the Lido—remember?) behind the line, the dining room is a refuge from the fast food around the pool. After a stint in the Virgin Islands, Ritter's back among the firs, dipping into the Northwest's bounty (with the same heavy hands we knew in Port Townsend): Dungeness crab with fresh mushrooms, grapes, green onions, and Stilton cheese, for example.

Camping facilities and RV hookups are also available, and you don't have to stay in the resort to use the hot springs ($3.75 a day). Open mid-May to mid-October.

SEKIU

Right about here you begin to think you really are getting away from it all: the road's getting small and snaky, and the coast has enough primitive ruggedness to make it seem uninhabitable. The little towns stay alive on lumbering and fishing. The season for salmon is April through October.

If you've found a place that you think is a Best Place, send in the report form at the back of this book. If you're unhappy with one of the places, please let us know why. We depend on reader input.

LODGINGS

Van Riper's Resort
Corner of Front and Rice
on the main street,
(206) 963-2334
Mail: PO Box 246,
Sekiu, WA 98281
Inexpensive; MC, V

The only waterfront hotel in Sekiu, Van Riper's is family-owned and -operated, friendly, low-key, and comfortable. The protected moorage of Clallam Bay draws picturesque fishing boats, so views from 6 of the 11 rooms are great. The best room is the Penthouse Suite: it sleeps seven, has a complete kitchen and three walls of windows, and goes for just $59. Other rooms are smaller and cheaper, some with thin walls.

NEAH BAY

The little town of Neah Bay, located on the Makah Indian Reservation, was the site of an 18th-century Spanish settlement. It offers some fine fishing (charters are available and fishing permits may be obtained from the tribal council), but it is most famous for its museum and research center, housing some of the finest artifacts from the magnificent archaeological dig nearby at **Lake Ozette**. The Makah Indian fishing village there was obliterated suddenly by a mudslide over 500 years ago. The clay soil sealed the contents of the houses, retarding the decay of a wealth of wooden and woven items. Discovered in 1970, the village has yielded some 55,000 artifacts. Unfortunately the dig was closed in 1981 as a result of budget cuts, but signs still direct you to the three-mile hike to the lake (20 miles from Neah Bay).

The Makah Cultural and Research Center displays photomurals from pictures taken by Edward S. Curtis in the early 1900s, dioramas, a life-size replica of the longhouse that was the center of village life, and whaling, sealing, and fishing canoes. The seasonal displays reveal the pattern of life in the village, and artifacts include seal harpoons, clubs, nets, hooks, baskets, and barbs. A cedar carving of a whale fin inlaid with 700 sea-otter teeth is one of the most prized possessions. (206) 645-2711.

Cape Flattery, the northwesternmost point of mainland America, is supposedly the most perfect "land's end" in the United States, with the longest unbroken expanse of water before it. It can be reached by a short trail that leads to a viewpoint of Tatoosh Island.

Point of Arches, south of Neah Bay, is reached by a hike of about two miles. The beaches are lovely, and the offshore rocks make a grand display of foam and tide pools.

Hobuck Ocean Beach Park offers pleasant camping facilities. It is located three miles south of Neah Bay. (206) 645-2422.

FORKS

LODGINGS

Manitou Lodge
Call for directions,
(206) 374-6295
Mail: PO Box 600, Forks,
WA 98331
Inexpensive; AE, MC, V

The very remote and stunning Manitou Lodge (formerly the River Run fishing lodge) is recently reopened and refurbished for Olympic Peninsula adventurers of all kinds. This four-bedroom log structure seems better suited to being a bed and breakfast than to being a fishing lodge (though you may want to dip your rod into the fish-abundant Soleduck and Bogachiel rivers). The centerpiece of the structure is a spacious two-story main room with a 30-foot fireplace (with a wood stove insert) and lots of cozy nooks you can settle into with one of the hundreds of books available. Owner Ray Antil often prepares Belgian waffles with fresh strawberries for breakfast. This faraway lodge is perfect for small seminars and workshops.

Miller Tree Inn
5th and E Division,
Forks, (206) 374-6806
Mail: PO Box 953,
Forks, WA 98331
Inexpensive; MC, V

A large, attractive house, Miller Tree Inn was one of the original homesteads in Forks. Conveniently located a few blocks east of Highway 101, it's popular with hikers and fisherfolk. The six rooms are attractive, if a bit small, with comfortable furnishings. Two have private baths. Breakfast is served in the big farmhouse kitchen. The atmosphere is relaxed and friendly—smokers, kids, and well-behaved pets are welcome. At $45 a couple (summer rate) the price is at least as good as the motel down the road.

LA PUSH

The town is a Quileute Indian village noted for its rugged seascape, fine kite-flying, salmon charter boats, and Indian fishing by canoe. Offshore stacks of rocks give the coastline its haunting appeal. One of the finest beach walks in the world is the 16-mile stretch south from Third Beach to the Hoh River Road; trailheads to the beaches are along the highway coming into La Push. Be sure to stop in at the ranger station in nearby Mora to get a backcountry use permit and tide tables; (206) 374-5460. It's easy to get stranded on the beaches if you're not careful.

LODGINGS

La Push
Ocean Park Resort
La Push Road, La Push,
(206) 374-5267
Mail: PO Box 67,
La Push, WA 98350
Moderate; MC, V

The remodel is a long, slow process, but we like what we've seen thus far. If you want cleanliness, request one of the remodeled cabins (so far 33, 34, 39–41). Most of the front row of cabins have new queen-size mattresses and new ovens and refrigerators (good thing, since there's no restaurant in La Push). Those in front are, not surprisingly, the better ones: each has its own well-stocked fireplace (numbers 36 and 37 have huge stone fireplaces), fully equipped kitchen, bath, and beautiful ocean view. The townhouses remind us of cheap apartments (we've been told they're scheduled for a remodel). The motel units on the top floor have nice views but thin walls; all have balconies overlooking the beach.

The campers' cabins, about as rustic as you can find on the coast, are small A-frame structures with wood stoves and toilets; you lug your wood from the woodshed and shower in the communal washroom. Showers have been installed in only two of the eight camper cabins (in the back row). For drinking and cooking, bring your own water (if you're bothered by the sulfur smell of the local stuff) or purchase bottled water in the convenience store across the street. The beach, the main reason for going to La Push, is beautiful, and just beyond the driftwood logs.

KALALOCH

The attraction here is the beach, wide and wild, with bleached white logs crazily pitched on the slate gray sand. The road from the Hoh River to Kalaloch hugs the coast and offers magnificent vistas if the weather isn't too foggy. A good way to learn about the area is to take one of the guided walks and talks conducted out of the ranger station; summer only, (206) 962-2283. You can see whales offshore during fall and spring.

Rain forests. These shaggy regions lie along the Bogachiel, Hoh, Queets, and Quinault rivers, all within easy drives from Kalaloch. The Hoh, 25 miles north, has a nice visitors' center, (206) 374-6925, and many moss-hung trails leading into the mountains. There are self-guided nature hikes, lots of wildlife to spy, and some of the most amazing greenery you're likely to see anywhere. Some of the world's largest Douglas fir, Sitka spruce, and red cedar are in the area, reachable by trails of varying difficulty. You can get details in the Hoh ranger station. Rainfall in these parts reaches 140 inches annually.

LODGINGS

Kalaloch Lodge
Highway 101, Kalaloch,
(206) 962-2271
Mail: HC-80, Box 1100,
Forks, WA 98331
Moderate; AE, MC, V

Note that Kalaloch is quite impossible to get into on short notice during the summer: long stays may require reservations half a year in advance. The attractions are obvious: a wonderful beach, cabins dotted around the bluff, a wide variety of accommodations (the lodge, cabins, duplex units, and a modern motel). Recent negotiations with the American Recreation Association indicate a turnover of this family-owned resort by mid-March 1990; however, unfavorable reports of their changes at Lake Quinault Lodge leave us uneasy about their newest acquisition.

The rooms in the lodge, which allows no cooking, are quite good—bright, clean, and quiet—and rooms 1, 6, 7, and 8 have ocean views at prices of around $60. Sea Crest House is the modern motel, set amid wind-bent trees; rooms 407 to 409 have nice glass doors that open onto decks with ocean views, while suites 401, 405, 406, and 410 have fireplaces and more space (the tab runs about $80). The old cabins can be rather tacky and hard to keep warm; the 21 new log cabins are a bit expensive, but they have nice facilities (except for the annoying practice of not providing eating utensils in the kitchenettes). Six duplexes on the bluff all feature ocean views, for $80 a night. Two-day minimum stays on weekends; pets allowed in cabins only.

The mediocre food in the dining room rarely matches the splendid ocean view. The kitchen gets fresh Quinault salmon as well as fresh local oysters; after that, it turns to steaks, awful chowder, and plain home cooking. Everything tastes fine, however, after a day of salt air and a few belts in the lounge while you admire the Pacific sunset. The waitstaff is surprisingly calm—even when the electricity goes out.

LAKE QUINAULT

The lake, dammed by a glacial moraine, is carved into a lovely valley in the Olympic Range. The coast-hugging highway comes inland to the lake at this point, affording the traveler the easiest penetration to the mountains. You are near a mossy rain forest, the fishing for trout and salmon is memorable, and the ranger station can provide tips on hiking or nature study.

Big Acre is a grove of enormous old-growth trees, an easy hike from the lodge. **Enchanted Valley** is a 10-mile hike into the fabulous old forests, with a 1930s log chalet at the end of the trail.

LODGINGS

Lake Quinault Lodge
*S Shore Road, Lake Quinault, (206) 288-2571
Mail: PO Box 7, Quinault, WA 98575
Expensive; MC, V*

A massive cedar-shingled structure, the lodge was built in 1926 in a gentle arc around the sweeping lawns that descend to the lake. The public rooms are done like Grandma's sun porch in wicker and antiques, with the clumsy addition of video games by the lodge's new owner, the American Recreation Association. There's a big fireplace in the lobby, the dining room overlooks the lawns, and the rustic bar is lively at night. You can stay in the main building, where there are nice (small) rooms, but only half of them with a view of the lake; all have private baths and go for about $75. The newer adjoining wing has balconies and queen-size beds in each unit, but the decor is tacky, including plasticky fireplaces; they run $90. Summer reservations take about two months' advance notice.

Amenities consist of a sauna, an indoor heated pool, a Jacuzzi, a game room, canoes and rowboats for touring the lake, and well-maintained trails for hiking or running. Reports are varied on food in the dining room, but we found it unconscionably bland. Stick with simpler items—waffles for breakfast, seafood for dinner—and brown-bag it when you can. There are often too many conventioneers around (mainly in the winter months), drawn by the spa-like features of the resort, but somehow the old place manages to exude some of the quiet elegance of its past.

MOCLIPS

LODGINGS

Ocean Crest Resort
18 miles north of Ocean Shores, (206) 276-4465 Highway 109, Moclips, WA 98562 Moderate; AE, MC, V

Nestled in a magnificent stand of spruce on a bluff high above one of the nicest stretches of beach on the Olympic Peninsula, the Ocean Crest has always offered rooms with memorable views. Now there's a handsome new wing featuring modern units done up in smart cedar paneling, with fireplaces. The ocean views from these rooms are even better.

A handsome new recreation center is just across the road, with a swimming pool, sauna, Jacuzzi, weight rooms, tanning beds, and massages. They'll sell you a vinyl swimsuit if you forgot to bring yours.

The original resort building has been refurbished as well, but it still isn't as spiffy. Some kitchens are available, however, and an annex a quarter-mile down the road offers two apartments with complete kitchens, porches, and two bedrooms each ($78 for two, $4.50 per child). Maids are hard-pressed to trek the extra distance and have been known to come by only on request.

Access to the beach is along a winding walkway through a lovely wooded ravine. The rickety old stairways have been replaced with sturdy ones.

Even on a drizzly day, there's no view on the Northwest coast outside of Cannon Beach that can rival the panorama from the dining room at the Ocean Crest. For many, the best news here is that the Ocean Crest's food is now consistently excellent, with prompt and friendly service. There's a new sense of attention to detail. With a bottomless cup of rich coffee, a plate of scrambled eggs, hash browns, muffins and preserves, breakfasts are outstanding. The lunch and dinner menus feature fresh, expertly cooked seafood. One floor above, there's a cozy bar, furnished with Northwest Coast Indian artifacts and offering the same view.

PACIFIC BEACH

LODGINGS

Sandpiper
Route 109, 1½ miles south of Pacific Beach, (206) 276-4580 Mail: PO Box A, Pacific Beach, WA 98571 Moderate; MC, V

Here's the place to vacation with four other couples, or to bring the kids, the grandparents, and the family dog. The resort consists of two four-story complexes containing large, fully equipped suites—usually a sitting room with a dining area and a fireplace, a compact kitchen, a small porch, and a bedroom and bath. There are splendid views of the beach if you can get beyond the ugly play area in the foreground. Penthouse units have an extra bedroom and cathedral ceilings. We prefer the rooms in the northern complex, since they are a tad larger. There are also five cottages, and one-room studios are available. The Pacific Select management has recently upgraded the place with new paint, carpets, and linoleum. They've remodeled the former owner's suite (with Jacuzzi) and made it available to a maximum of six for $150.

The resort fits in very well with the landscape: wood-clad structures tucked into the cliff and pines, with rock gardens on the terraced walls down to the beach. No pool, no television, no restaurant, no in-room telephones; they even removed the game machines. A resort that has the good sense not to try to compete with the Pacific surf knows what it's doing. Prices cover a full range too: from $49 to $85 for most doubles (with two suites which sleep six for $140–$150). Minimum stays are imposed on weekends, and reservations usually take months to get. The lack of daily maid service makes this feel like your own home at the shore indeed.

COPALIS BEACH

LODGINGS

Iron Springs Resort
*Route 109, 3 miles north
of Copalis Beach
(206) 276-4230
Mail: PO Box 207,
Copalis Beach,
WA 98535
Moderate; AE, MC, V*

Friendly owners maintain this complex of cabins along a well-forested bluff, overlooking a beautiful stretch of beach. Some cabins are quite old and spacious—and amiably dowdy: light bulbs can be dim, and the sun can beat its way through the roof in the summer. Decor is mid-century chartreuse and orange, but each cottage has its own fireplace. Other cabins are newer, with vast view patios (number 8) and beautiful corner windows (number 14). Number 6 is the only one with no view; newer (and quite spiffy) are those numbered 22 to 25. The beach is especially fine here, with a river meeting its destiny with the surf just south of the resort. The heated pool is covered for year-round use, and Olive Little's famous clam chowder and cinnamon rolls are still available. As a family place, where nobody's kids and pets seem to bother other people, Iron Springs is at its best. It's also a great clamming spot. Three-day minimum stays are imposed in the summer, two-day minimum stays on weekends after Labor Day.

OCEAN SHORES

As the big, silly gate to the city might indicate, Ocean Shores would like to become Atlantic City West. Big-time gambling has not yet been approved by the legislature, so the town has to make do with casino-style gambling most Saturday nights at the Ocean Shores Inn right by the main beach.

A good way to avoid downtown altogether is to reserve one of the private beach houses that owners occasionally put up for rent. Most are located a few miles away from the hotels, are on the beach, and boast fireplaces, kitchens, room for six to eight, and individualized decor. The homes rent for $85 to $200 a night, with a two-night minimum on weekends. Winter rates are lower, and there are weekly rates, too. Reservations need to be made weeks in advance; toll-free (800) 562-8612, or (206) 289-2430 outside the state. The same numbers can also take motel reservations. For charter fishing arrangements, call (206) 289-3391.

LODGINGS

The Grey Gull
In town on Ocean Shores Blvd, (206) 289-3381
Mail: PO Box 1417,
Ocean Shores, WA 98569
Expensive; AE, DC, MC, V

This condominium-resort looks like a ski lodge (a rather odd style here on the beach), with jagged angles, handsome cladding, and a front door to strain the mightiest triceps. There are 35 condominium units, facing the ocean at a broad stretch of the beach, each outfitted with a balcony, fireplace, kitchen, and attractive furnishings. The resort has a pool, a sauna, and a spa.

You are right on the beach, the main plus, and the lodge has been built with an eye for good Northwest architecture. Prices for the suites get fairly steep, but there are smaller rooms, and you can save money by doing your own cooking in the complete kitchens.

SOUTHWEST WASHINGTON

*A clockwise route: southward on the southern half of I-5,
west along the Columbia River, north along the Long Beach Peninsula
and the south coast, and eastward again at Grays Harbor.*

CHEHALIS

RESTAURANTS

Mary McCrank's
*Jackson Highway, 4 miles
south of Chehalis,
(206) 748-3662
2923 Jackson Highway,
Chehalis
Inexpensive; beer and
wine; MC, V
Lunch Tues-Sat,
dinner Tues-Sun*

Take a break from I-5: this dinner house, in business since
1935, is one of the nicest stops you can make along the
freeway corridor. The restaurant occupies a large home,
with fireplaces in some of the dining rooms, windows
overlooking the garden and lawns and stream, and armchairs scattered around the comfy rooms. The food is all
homemade and prices are very low.

Owners Ralph and Linda Peel have preserved the
recipes and the "Grandma's house" ambience created by
the late Mary McCrank. Dinner starts with breads, jams,
and a tray of oustanding homemade relishes. Dinner offerings include fried chicken, chicken with dumplings,
pork chops, steaks, and other country fixings. Grilled
chicken livers and onions are a local favorite. A glorious
pie comes for dessert: never turn down the sour-cream
raisin if it's offered. Your girth may widen, but your wallet
will only be out about $10 per person.

St. Helen's Inn
*Exit 77, 3 blocks off
Main on Market,
(206) 748-1486
441 Market Blvd,
Chehalis,
Inexpensive; full bar;
AE, MC, V
Breakfast, lunch, dinner
every day*

It's easy to find: the tallest building in Chehalis, once the
town's premier hotel. After a brief closure, it's now a
family-oriented restaurant with some intriguing touches:
French fare such as filet mignon and coquilles St. Jacques
right beside down-home entrees like chicken-fried steak
and liver and onions. And if that's not enough contrast,
there's also an official *Diet Center* menu with low-fat, low-
salt, low-cal meals. But wait, there's more: huge breakfasts
served all day, top-40 rock and roll on the weekends, banquet facilities for up to 100 folks, and catering. Phew!
What more could Chehalis want?

*The facts in this edition were correct at press time, but places close, chefs depart, hours change.
It's best to call ahead.*

LONGVIEW

Longview may seem to be nothing but a lumber-exporting town, but it has the unusual distinction of having been a totally planned community, ever since R.A. Long appeared in 1918 and hired Kansas City planners to make a town for his sawmill workers. **Lake Sacajawea Park**, a lovely stretch of green alongside a necklace of ponds, is the best evidence of this design. The town also is the jumping-off point for southwest Washington's biggest natural draw, Mount St. Helens.

RESTAURANTS

Henri's
*3 miles west of downtown
on Ocean Beach,
(206) 425-7970
4545 Ocean Beach
Highway, Longview
Moderate; full bar;
AE, MC, V
Lunch Mon-Fri,
dinner Mon-Sat*

The Longview big shots all come here for lunch, when the large place can be fun and reliable; at dinner, when the pretension level rises and the number of customers dips, things can be rather lonely and the food not really worth the money. Still, the steaks are perfectly good, you can have some nice seafood bisques, and the rack of lamb with Bearnaise is quite tasty. There is a fancy wine room, into which guests are escorted by owner Henry Paul, who learned how to do this kind of thing years ago at Seattle's Golden Lion. Service and decor are only passable.

LODGINGS

Monticello Hotel
*Larch and 17th,
(206) 425-9900
1405 17th Avenue,
Longview, WA 98632
Inexpensive; AE, MC, V*

It fronts Civic Center Park with an impressive facade of brick and terra-cotta, obviously the heart of town. But the 1923 edifice has suffered a loss of confidence over the years: now the hotel rooms are rented out as senior housing and offices, and the public rooms are showing their age. However, four new executive suites have recently opened in the old hotel, and you can stay in a motel-like wing to one side, where the rooms are perfectly standard but the cost is low (around $40 for a double). The dining room, still spiffy, is quite the place to be seen in Longview, particularly for lunch and breakfast. In short, it's rather fun, and there are no better places to stay in this area of plug-ordinary motels.

MOUNT ST. HELENS

The US Forest Service's new wood-and-glass visitors' center—3029 Spirit Lake Highway, Castle Rock, (206) 274-6644, (206) 274-4038 for recorded weather and view outlook—is beautifully situated in a stand of timber in the Gifford Pinchot National Forest near Silver Lake. On clear days the view of the mountain is stunning, either with the naked eye or through one of the center's telescopes. Exhibits include a walk-through volcano, hundreds of historic and current photos, and geological and anthropological surveys. There is also a network of trails, some of which accommodate wheelchairs. To get there, take Exit 49 from I-5 and travel five miles east on Highway 504. A better view is from the north, the side on which the blast carved out a crater two miles across and half a mile deep. From I-5, turn east on Route 12 and follow the signs to Mossyrock; five miles farther east is Hopkins Hill viewpoint, overlooking Riffe Lake and aimed right into the gaping crater. You can get a closer peek at the crater by climbing one of the two trails on the south face of the mountain. Climbers must pre-register with the Forest Service in Amboy: for information call (206) 247-5473 or (206) 247-5800.

Ape Cave. Don't let the name deceive you—there ain't no apes. Named after a spelunking expedition called the "Cave Apes," the cave is the longest continuous lava-tube cave in the Americas (over two miles). Spelunkers, bring your lanterns, warm jackets (the cave is a chilly 42 degrees), and sturdy boots. To get there, take Forest Road 90 out of Cougar (seven miles); branch left onto Forest Road 83; two miles later turn left onto Road 8303; another mile and you're at the cave's parking area.

VANCOUVER

Vancouver, long known as the bedroom community of Portland, is coming into its own with the advent of new industry. Among the modest tourist attractions is the Northwest's oldest apple tree (in Old Apple Tree Park, east of I-5 on Columbia Way). Locals claim that it was planted in 1829 by a member of the Hudson's Bay Company.

Fort Vancouver was the major settlement of the Hudson's Bay Company from the 1820s to the 1860s, when it passed to the Americans. The stockade wall and some of the buildings have been reconstructed, and the visitors' center has a decent museum; 1501 E Evergreen Boulevard, (206) 696-7655. On your way to Officers' Row, you'll pass the active military post, Vancouver Barracks. The Heritage Trust of Clark County gives walking tours of the restored officers' quarters nearby; (206) 699-2359.

Clark County Historical Museum reconstructs pioneer stores and businesses; 1511 Main Street at 16th, (206) 695-4681. **Covington House** is the oldest log house (1846) in the state; 4201 Main Street, (206) 695-6750.

Ridgefield Wildlife Refuge, three miles west of I-5 exit 14, has nature trails leading to the bird refuge on the lowlands of the Columbia; (206) 887-3883.

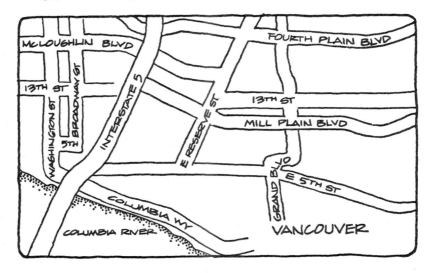

RESTAURANTS

Grant House

Follow the signs from
Fort Vancouver Way,
(206) 696-9699
1101 Officers' Row,
Vancouver, WA 98661
Expensive; full bar;
AE, DC, MC, V
Lunch Mon-Fri, dinner
Mon-Sat, brunch Sun

The Grant House is festively beflagged to set it apart from all the other former officers' quarters in a soldierly row at Fort Vancouver. Platters of food are works of art, with finely diced tomato and feathers of anise decorating your homemade pate. Elegance reigns, coupled with warmth from pale yellow wooden walls, snow-white moldings, candle-glow, and maitre d'hotel Seaberg Einarsson himself, captured by Vancouver's restoration committee from Columbia Gorge Hotel to set up this showplace in November 1988.

His native Iceland shows in the hors d'oeuvres platter of smoked fish and in ravioli stuffed with lobster and salmon, sauced with basil and cream. Flames from the waiters' stand announce the making of the best hot salad dressing in the West (for wilted spinach), boasting slices of smoked duck, brandy, Worcestershire sauce, mustard, oil, and wine vinegar. A scoop of raspberry sorbet refreshes your palate before your Columbia River sturgeon covered with crisply toasted pine nuts, or the medallions of beef lounging in two sorts of sauce. Chauvinistic wine lovers strike gold: the list of 250 is extensively Northwest.

Clever temptation: waiter brings four desserts on a silver tray to your elbow, just as you're saying, "Thanks, no." Don't miss crackly-top creme brulee, and then take your liqueurs upstairs before the blazing fire, where quartermaster Ulysses S. Grant (based here in 1852) doubtless lingered with a glass of aged port.

Pinot Ganache

Corner of Washington
and Evergreen,
(206) 695-7786
1004 Washington Street
Moderate; beer and wine;
AE, MC, V
Lunch, dinner Mon-Sat

Passersby are bound to see ecstatic expressions as diners taste the salmon and spinach dill mousse: this handsome modernistic bistro sits uncurtained on a corner of what's not the chic-est part of the world—downtown Vancouver. There are moments (say, on a rainy night) when you'd welcome a warming curtain between you, the strolling public, and the flashing neon Lucky Beer sign in the distance.

That mousse, by the way, is superb. An alternative hors d'oeuvre, the chicken satay, beats that served in many a Thai restaurant in the Northwest—plump and moist, its peanut sauce stingingly spicy.

The great thing about this sterile restaurant with high ceilings and black simulated-marble tables is that it's open late. Although the kitchen closes at 9pm, you can get any light dish from 11:30am to 11pm. A good Paris concept—rare in Vancouver—and it's a good thing, because the dinners don't stand up to the starters. One dinner consisted of a plate of grilled shark with a Brie sauce (disappointingly chill) accompanied by pasta in alfredo sauce *plus* ramrod-stiff green beans (whisked past a steamer) topped with a memorable Pernod cream sauce.

Though there were too many sauces, each one stood on its own. The after-movie crowd drops in for any of the made-on-the-spot cakes, plus coffee or wine from an excellently varied list.

Who-Song and Larry's Cantina
Take the Kamas exit off I-5, go east 1 mile, turn right at light,
(206) 695-1198
111 E Columbia Way, Vancouver
Moderate; full bar;
AE, DC, MC, V
Lunch, dinner every day

If you wondered, wandering around downtown Vancouver, where all the *people* were, this is the place. The entire basketball team is packing in enchiladas by your side, families are rounding the large buffet with dedicated zeal, there's lots of chat to make you feel part of a large, homey party. Jolly menu patter is a bit of a delusion: Larry's actually back East, in his 80s, and his Mexican partner Who-Song is no longer living—the place is yet another link in the vast El Torito chain. Mexican buffet ($4.95) is no great shakes (tired taco shells, etc.), but there are great margaritas and swift service (free corn chips and salsa before you draw a breath). A jolly little cantina away from the hubbub lets you nibble nachos with your Corona and watch the grain boats force the Vancouver-Portland bridge to open up.

LODGINGS

Red Lion Inn at the Quay
Under the I-5 bridge on the Columbia River,
(206) 694-8341, toll-free (800) 547-8010
100 Columbia Street, Vancouver, WA 98660
Expensive; AE, DC, MC, V
Breakfast, lunch, dinner every day

You'll know you're in a hotel dining room, but the food at the Quay is not half bad. It's wisest to opt for seafood: the ambitious menu offers more than a dozen sorts, including Willapa oysters, razor clams, Oregon scallops, halibut, haddock, snapper, and sole, all cooked to your specifications. Most tables offer handsome views of the Columbia and the Oregon shore. All the rooms have just been remodeled to the Red Lion standard. Be sure to request a room overlooking the river.

CATHLAMET

Cathlamet, seat of Wahkiakum County, is an old-style river town, tied almost as closely to the Columbia as Mark Twain's Hannibal was to the Mississippi. Although hunting is good in this area, fishing is everyone's recreation—in season, for trout, salmon, and steelhead, all year round for the Columbia's mammoth, caviar-bearing sturgeon. Nearby **Puget Island**, reachable by bridge, is flat dairyland, ideal for cycling; a tiny ferry can take you from there directly across to Oregon. Wahkiakum County is the sort of place where nostalgia buffs discover round barns and covered bridges, and it's refreshingly free of late-20th-century schlock. You can camp right on the river beach at **Skamokawa Vista Park** (say *ska-MOCK-away*).

LODGINGS

Our Place
Take Welcome Slough Road off Highway 409,
(206) 849-4328
305 N Welcome Slough

A net shack (but cozy and refurbished) on the shore of picturesque Puget Island has been polished into a comfortable, rustic bed and breakfast. Owners ElRose and Everett Groves live in the fisherman's house next door. Perfect for families or couples seeking privacy, there's

Road, Cathlamet,
WA 98612
Inexpensive; no credit
cards; checks ok

a fully equipped kitchen, bath, wood stove, double bed on the main floor, three-person loft above, and a stretch of beach outside for long, meditative tromps. The house is stocked with plenty of games and surrounded by lots of greenery.

CHINOOK

Fort Columbia, on Scarborough hill near the fishing hamlet of Chinook, displays spacious old frame buildings, once officers' quarters and barracks dating to 1889, that have become part of a state historical park. An interpretive center has exhibits on local history. Open daily from June to September, and at varying hours during the rest of the year; (206) 777-8221.

RESTAURANTS

The Sanctuary
Highway 101 and Hazel,
(206) 777-8380
Hazel Street, Chinook
Moderate; full bar;
AE, MC, V
Dinner Wed-Sun, every
day in summer

A high-vaulted Methodist church (with pews intact) in tiny Chinook has been renovated into this dinner house, where good food is presented with lots of small-town earnestness. Svenska Kottbuller (Swedish meatballs) is the house specialty, but Italian dishes are well represented in the form of Provimi veal preparations, and out-of-towners head straight for fresh local seafood (which, however, tends to be overcooked). The wine list is fairly priced and more extensive than you might expect; desserts are homemade and wonderful, particularly the chocolate rum cake.

ILWACO

LODGINGS

The Inn at Ilwaco
Off 4th on Williams,
(206) 642-8686
120 Williams Street NE
Mail: PO Box 922,
Ilwaco, WA 98624-0922
Moderate; MC, V

Located atop a quiet dead-end street overlooking the town of Ilwaco, this new bed and breakfast is housed in the old Ilwaco Presbyterian Church. The Sunday school has been converted into nine guest rooms (seven with private baths), all very new yet rich with a sense of history and grace: plush bedding, lacy curtains, original wood floors, some even with window seats. There's a room with two twins, ideal for the kids. In the large public room, guests take their ample continental breakfast, read the morning papers on comfortable furnishings, or tickle the ivories. Innkeepers John and Jo Thorson provide first-rate hospitality and great conversation (if you're feeling talkative).

The old church has been converted into a performing arts center; if you're lucky, the Peninsula Players will be providing the entertainment.

Would you like to order a copy of Best Places *for a friend? There's an order form at the back of this book.*

LONG BEACH PENINSULA

The slender finger of land dividing Willapa Bay from the Pacific is famous for its association with explorers Lewis and Clark; for its gentle climate, freer of fog than the shoreline farther north; for its rich sea life, its rhododendrons, its wintering trumpeter swans, and its exhibition kite flying; and, above all, for its food, which probably cannot be equaled in any coastal town north of California.

Lewis and Clark Interpretive Center is part of Fort Canby State Park; it contains exhibits depicting Lewis and Clark's voyages and other regional history. Also in the park is the North Jetty, two miles of mighty boulders marking the mouth of the Columbia and serving as a fishing pier. High above stands North Head Light, a sturdy white structure beloved of photographers for its handsome contours and cliff-top placement. Fort Canby State Park, (206) 642-3029.

Ilwaco is the sport-fishing hub of the lower Columbia River. Local salmon are sought during the summer season; in August, tuna charters venture much farther out (if the fish are running).

Seaview visitors will find a pleasant community of lovely, funky old houses, sporting touches of Carpenter Gothic.

Long Beach, the town, offers Marsh's campy Free Museum ("Have you seen a shrunken head? We have one") and a number of carnival attractions. Cottage Bakery and Delicatessen has fresh bread produced on the premises, the Bookvendor is the best place to seek out literature on the area, and Milton York produces some of the best chocolate candy and ice cream in the world—or at least in the state. **Clark's Nursery** is widely known for its fields of rhododendrons, and annually, on the weekend after Mother's Day, holds a special sale of the plants that draws visitors from miles away.

Oysterville sports the most distinctive row of old shoreside houses.

Long Island, a wildlife refuge in Willapa Bay, harbors one of the last old-growth cedar forests, There are oysters to pick and a few superb camping sites on the island, though it can only be reached by boat. Information about the island and a boat ramp are available near the southeastern corner of the island, just off Highway 101.

Leadbetter Point State Park, on the very tip of the peninsula, is a vast preserve where migratory birds flock twice a year and mushrooms abound in the fall.

SEAVIEW

RESTAURANTS

The Shoalwater Restaurant
*Pacific Highway 103 and
N 45th, (206) 642-4142
In the Shelburne Inn,
Seaview
Moderate; full bar;
AE, DC, Mc, V
Lunch Tues-Thurs, dinner
every day, brunch Sun
(shorter winter hours)*

 ★ ★ ★

A meal at the Shoalwater (formerly the Shelburne) is a superb way to appreciate the fruits of Northwest cuisine. Chef Cheri Walker, sous-chef Francis Schafer, and owners Ann and Tony Kischner (late of Seattle's Other Place) are the creators who carry it off—usually very skillfully. Kischner's wine list—in which he takes a true enologist's interest, and about which you should consult with him if he's on hand—is splendid, representing good imports and local labels.

The great strength here is fresh seafood. Fishermen bring their catches of halibut and cod right to the kitchen door; caviar (at $12 per serving) comes from Columbia River sturgeon. The menu changes every six weeks to remain seasonal. In winter you may get an entree of Oregon quail in raspberry sauce, and in fall pan-fried cod in orange, lime, and cranberry sauce. Lunch items run to innovative, reasonably priced salads and sandwiches; desserts and pastries, in the hands of master pastry chef Ann Kischner, are peerless.

You sip good wine in the cozy dining room, enjoying the old-fashioned ambience and clear-tasting, well-seasoned seafood. It is that way most of the time.

The Heron and Beaver Pub
Pacific Highway 103 and N 45th, (206) 642-4142
In the Shelburne Inn, Seaview
Inexpensive; full bar; AE, DC, MC, V
Lunch, dinner every day

It's the kind of place you can put your feet up—well, if there were space. This attractive pub with fine dark woodwork and stained glass windows makes it possible to get light meals—pasta, pate, sandwiches, soup, and, oh, try the cheese fondue—all prepared under the discriminating supervision of the Shoalwater's Tony Kischner. A fine wine list is available, as well as a wide assortment of beers. You may not be able to fit enough food for two on the small table tops—and your conversation may spill over onto the next table. All entrees are also available for take-out.

LODGINGS

The Shelburne Inn
Pacific Highway 103 and N 45th, (206) 642-2442
Mail: PO Box 250, Seaview, WA 98644
Expensive; AE, MC, V

The Shelburne Inn is "historic," which is the source of both its strengths and its weaknesses. As a place to stay, it won't suit everyone. It's not on the beach, and it's right across the street from a well-lit supermarket; but it was here first—90 years ago—and over the past few years its management has been working hard to mitigate the shortcomings of its invaded location: etched roadside windows, an herb and flower garden out front, private west-facing decks, and baths in most of the rooms (only five share facilities now).

Even so, guests should choose their rooms judiciously: those on the highway side can be noisy, and those on the third floor heat up in summer. Request a new room (numbers 13–17 were added in 1986) on the west side. These lavish rooms are all bright and cheerful, with antiques, homemade quilts on queen-size beds, and private baths. They're also pricey. Downstairs, the cozy public room is beautifully appointed, with a wood stove, antique organ, and overstuffed couch, but it may be too cramped for relaxed lingering.

Prices ($69–$97 double, $129 for the suite) are up a bit but still include the best breakfast on the coast. Try David Campiche's pan-fried trout or his divine oyster omelet—fragrant with garlic and topped with marinara sauce.

Sou'wester Lodge
1½ blocks southwest of Seaview's traffic light,
(206) 642-2542
Beach Access Road (28th Place), Seaview,
WA 98644
Inexpensive; MC, V

Those who appreciate good conversation, a sense of humor, and rambling lodgings on the beach will return again and again to Leonard and Miriam Atkins' simple, old-fashioned resort. It's of the type that flourished around Puget Sound in the first half of the century. The 1892 main structure was originally built as a summer home for US Senator Henry Winslow Corbett, of the well-known Portland family. The lodge and cabins were full on our first visit, so the Atkinses booked us into Harry's trailer—part of TCH! TCH! (Trailer Classic Hodgepodge). We've returned often—and always request TCH! TCH! ($28–$63). Not everyone chooses the trailers, though; the rooms in the lodge, some with kitchens, feel like home. And all the cabins are fully equipped.

The Atkinses are as much a draw as is the unspoiled beach itself. Originally from South Africa, they came to Long Beach by way of Israel and Chicago; the view from the lodge's balcony—across quiet, grassy dunes to the sea—is enough to keep them here forever. Interesting periodicals like *Foreign Affairs* adorn their living room; they sometimes hold chamber music concerts there.

No food is served; Leonard has deemed the Sou'wester Seaview's official outpost of the "B & (MYOD)B club"—Bed & (Make Your Own Damn) Breakfast.

LONG BEACH
RESTAURANTS

My Mom's Pie Kitchen
Pacific Highway and 12th S, (206) 642-2342
Pacific Highway 103,
Long Beach
Inexpensive; no alcohol;
MC, V
Lunch Tues-Sun

Jeanne McLaughlin moved from the small blue cottage where she once created her magic pies into a grounded mobile home next door. Though a step backward aesthetically, the move marked a step forward in terms of convenience for her growing clientele—and her pies are worthy as ever. Among her specialties: banana whipped cream, chocolate almond, pecan, sour-cream raisin, and fresh raspberry. Her increased space permits her to serve a few other items, such as clam chowder, a shrimp salad, and a Dungeness crab quiche (seasonal) of which she is especially proud.

OCEAN PARK
LODGINGS

Klipsan Beach Cottages
Highway 103, 2 miles south of Ocean Park,
(206) 665-4888
Mail: Route 1, Box 359,

In an area justly known for its fine marine views and spectacular Maytime rhododendrons, it's remarkable that so few lodgings have bothered with landscaping. This cozy operation, a row of eight small, separate, well-maintained older cottages, is an exception; it stands facing the ocean in a parklike setting of pine trees and clipped lawns. Since

Ocean Park, WA 98640
Moderate; MC, V

these are individually owned condominiums, interior decoration schemes can vary widely, but all of the units have fully equipped kitchens and bed linens. The charges range from $48 for a one-bedroom cottage to $72 for three bedrooms. All cottages have broad decks with outlooks over the grass to the sea. They all feature fireplaces, for which wood is furnished. Guests may bring their children, but no pets.

NAHCOTTA

RESTAURANTS

The Ark
On the old Nahcotta
Dock, on the jetty,
(206) 665-4133
273 Sandridge Road,
Nahcotta
Expensive; full bar;
AE, MC, V
Seasonal hours

Outside your window, across empty Willapa Bay, lies uninhabited Long Island, where you can hunt the great elk, but only with bow and arrow. The Ark, located at the oyster dock in remote Nahcotta, is operated by Jimella Lucas and Nanci Main, whose cooking once drew high praise from food critic James Beard. Recently, the restaurant's reputation for very fresh regional seafood, expertly prepared, seems to be riding more on past performance than on present culinary exactitude.

We've seen what Main and Lucas can do: sturgeon swathed in an orange-bacon marmalade; salmon prepared with a sauce of Champagne and Chambord and influenced with wild flowers and blackberries; halibut served with a corn-jalapeno relish; and—in a marriage of two of the chefs' passions—whole garlic cloves dipped in chocolate. Lately, the preparations have been less inspired. We've encountered an overpriced petrale sole steamed with a bland salmon and scallop mousse and too-long-refrigerated salads. For dessert, Main's exceptional baked goods and regional delicacies include cranberry Grand Marnier mousse, Amaretto balls, and bread pudding with blackberries. House wines are well chosen.

Local residents graze in the bar, where a fine, less expensive, light fare is offered, with such items as French onion soup and grilled oysters. Service is often a problem at The Ark, and nobody seems to be making much of an effort to change it.

BAY CENTER

RESTAURANTS

Blue Heron Inn
1 mile west of Highway
101, 12 miles southwest
of South Bend,
(206) 875-9990
Water Street, Bay Center
Inexpensive; beer and

The one-mile detour to the fishing village of Bay Center on pristine Willapa Bay is worth your while for the scenery alone—all the better if you're hungry, particularly if it's breakfast time. The Blue Heron Inn is a genuine roadside attraction, with oyster omelets and tasty fish and chips, checkered oilcloth on the tables, and Elvis on

wine; checks ok
Breakfast, lunch, dinner
every day

the jukebox. The cooler near the cash register offers fresh oysters and crab to go, plus smoked and pickled salmon. Unfortunately, when 10 of the 18 chairs in the tiny cafe are occupied by utterly unrepentant smokers, the ambience suffers. On the whole, however, this is a cozy place with a nice staff and nice prices.

SOUTH BEND

The sleepy Pacific County seat perches picturesquely on the low bluffs that ring the inside curve of the north arm of Willapa Bay. The outsized **county courthouse** two blocks south of US 101 atop Quality Hill rules over the town like a medieval castle.

RESTAURANTS

Boondocks
Highway 101, downtown
South Bend,
(206) 875-5155
1015 W Robert Bush
Drive, South Bend
Moderate; full bar;
MC, V
Breakfast, lunch, dinner
every day

★

South Bend, the historic county seat of Pacific County, bills itself as "The Oyster Capital of the World." That's a classic bit of boosterism, but the oysters *are* world-class, and this pretty little town is coming out of its shell. Boondocks is right on the waterfront, with an outdoor deck and a fine view, not to mention pan-fried fresh Willapa Bay oysters and razor clams. The delicious Hangtown fry is a crowd-pleaser at breakfast, and the dinner menu now features combination plates and blackened prime rib.

TOKELAND

Set on the long peninsula reaching into northern Willapa Bay, this crabbing community named after 19th-century Chief Toke is the loneliest part of the southwest coast, where the omnipresent tackiness of contemporary resort life is least apparent.

Its most notable building is the **Tokeland Hotel** (Kindred Avenue and Hotel Road), a chaste, century-old structure that's currently trembling on the edge of genteel collapse. Closed for the past three years, the former hotel is now just a tourist attraction.

GRAYLAND

RESTAURANTS

The Dunes
Right off Highway 105 at
the sign of the giant
geoduck, (206) 267-1441
783 Dunes Road,
Grayland
Moderate; beer and wine;
MC, V

Follow the bumpy gravel road a quarter of a mile down to the dunes. You will discover a funky kind of place that's as comfortable as an old windbreaker: a beachcomber's hideaway, eclectically decorated with shells, ship models, stained glass, and blooming begonias. Here you can work up an appetite by taking a brisk walk on the beach and wander in with sand in your shoes.

John and LaRene Morrison have been setting a bounteous table for 25 years. Things have slipped slightly of

Breakfast, lunch, dinner every day (winter hours vary)

late, with LaRene no longer doing all the cooking, but the main dining room is always warm and wonderful, with a fireplace in the middle and linen-draped oak tables. Families are everywhere, especially on Sunday mornings, dressed in their Sunday best or their Eddie Bauer gear.

The restaurant offers a front-row seat on the ocean just beyond the dunes, and you won't find fresher seafood—clams, salmon, crab, oysters. The chowder is a purist's delight, with large chunks of succulent razor clams in a rich cream broth. Each entree is served with flawlessly cooked fresh vegetables and puffy homemade rolls.

WESTPORT

For a small coastal town that regularly endures the flood tide of tourists out to catch The Big One, the city of Westport remains surprisingly friendly and scenic. The short salmon-fishing season has changed charter boat marketing, so many now feature whale-watching cruises as well.

Most visitors rise early and join the almost comically hasty 6am exodus from the breakwater to cross the dreaded bar and head for the open sea. Breakfast cafes are open by 5am, some much earlier (especially those down by the docks). **Charters:** Rates vary little from company to company. Some of the best charters include Cachalot, (206) 268-0323; Gull, (800) 562-0175 or (206) 268-9186; Deep Sea, (800) 562-0151 or (206) 268-9300; Westport, (800) 562-0157 or (206) 268-9120; Islander, (800) 562-0147 or (206) 268-9166; Ocean, (800) 562-0105 or (206) 268-9144; Travis, (206) 268-9140. (Toll-free numbers are in operation only during the season.) Things quiet down until the 3:30pm return of the fleets. You can explore the town during this lull, or head for the expansive beaches—open for driving, surfing, jogging, clamming, or picnicking—along the coast from Grayland to Westport.

RESTAURANTS

Constantin's
*½ block from the dock, (206) 268-0550
320 E Dock Street, Westport
Moderate; beer and wine; MC, V
Dinner Wed-Mon (call for winter hours)*

Constantin "Dino" Kontogonis, who came to Westport in 1987 "to get away from Seattle," is a Greek with a gift for cooking. Beware only of calories—and garlic. From behind the plastic grapes emerges some chewy, fresh pita bread, which bears no resemblance to the cardboardy stuff that's inexplicably popular today. Dino gives you a lot of good food for your money; dinners include soup or salad, sauteed fresh vegetables, and rice pilaf, pasta, or potatoes. The moussaka casserole (eggplant layered with ground beef, tomatoes, and Parmesan) is delicious. Likewise the leg of lamb. You're only a stone's throw from the Westport docks, so there's fresh seafood too. A joint venture with the wine shop next door provides Constantin's with an inexhaustible wine list and over three dozen varieties of beer. Alas, perhaps Westport isn't ready for Dino: at press time his fabulous tabouli was pulled from the menu due to lack of demand.

All places in this book are recommended; even "no stars" are worth knowing about.

Arthur's

Westhaven and Cove,
(206) 268-9292
2681 Westhaven Drive,
Westport
Moderate; beer and wine;
MC, V
Lunch, dinner Tues-Sun

Arthur Lawrence, former chef at the landmark Islander (now under new owners after 28 years) across the street, operates this cheery spot that offers good seafood, steaks, prime rib, and pasta. You can rationalize dessert by vowing to climb the viewing tower opposite the cafe. It offers a panorama of the Grays Harbor channel.

LODGINGS

Glenacres Inn

1 block north of the
stoplight at 222 N
Montesano,
(206) 268-9391
Mail: PO Box 1246,
Westport, WA 98595
Moderate; MC, V

Turn-of-the-century entrepreneur Minnie Armstrong ran a horse 'n' buggy service from the docks of Westport to her bed and breakfast, long before B&Bs became the latest thing in charming accommodations. Now it's back in service with a hot tub, no less—a gabled gem with lots of lodging alternatives. In addition to the five plush bedrooms (all with private baths), there are three simpler "deck" rooms and four cottages on the property, ranging from the two-bedroom Chickadee ($65–$80) to the Rainbird, which sleeps twelve ($100–$160). Rooms numbered 2 and 4 feature bay windows; room 6 has a view of the wooded back yard and the bay beyond. Breakfast is continental.

The Chateau Westport

W Hancock and S Surf,
(206) 268-9101
Mail: PO Box 349,
Westport, WA 98595
Moderate; AE, DC,
MC, V

This is considered the fanciest hotel lodging in Westport—and now the former Canterbury Westport has a name to match. Prices range up from $55; pool and hot tub are available. Studio units have fireplaces and can be rented alone (with a queen-size hideabed) or in conjunction with adjoining bedrooms to form a suite. It's not the quietest place, and the service can be moody, but the ocean views are magnificent and those from the third and fourth floors are best.

COSMOPOLIS

LODGINGS

Cooney Mansion

Follow C Street to 5th,
(206) 533-0602
802 E Fifth Street,
Cosmopolis, WA 98537
Moderate; MC, V

They built 'em big. This enormous 1908 manse housed timber tycoon Neil Cooney, his servants, and his out-of-town guests for many years. There's a very masculine feel to the place (Cooney was a bachelor): spruce wainscoting in the living room, large windows with dark wooden frames, heavy furniture throughout. There are five rooms, with private baths. A clubby feel prevails: from the deck on the second floor you can sit and watch golfers on the public course next door, and you see tennis courts as you head up the driveway (they are part of Mill Creek Park but are available for guests' use). In the morning, owner George Barker prepares a full breakfast, including eggs Benedict or perhaps the Cooney omelet, with shrimp, sugar peas, mushrooms, peppers, onions, and havarti.

ABERDEEN/HOQUIAM

On a slow rebound from the forest products recession, these old Siamese-twin lumber towns have an interesting history, plus some fine homes overlooking the harbor.

Hoquiam's Castle gives tours of the 20-room mansion, built for a prominent lumberman in 1897; 515 Chenault Avenue, Hoquiam, (206) 533-2005.

Polson Park is a fine house by Arthur Loveless, with a rose garden; 1611 Riverside Avenue, Hoquiam, (206) 533-5862.

A half-million Arctic-bound shorebirds migrate from as far south as Argentina and congregate at **Bowerman Basin** each spring from about mid-April through the first week of May. There are trails through the marsh (located just beyond the Hoquiam airport), but be sure to wear boots. For more information and peak migratory days, call the Grays Harbor National Wildlife Refuge, (206) 753-9467.

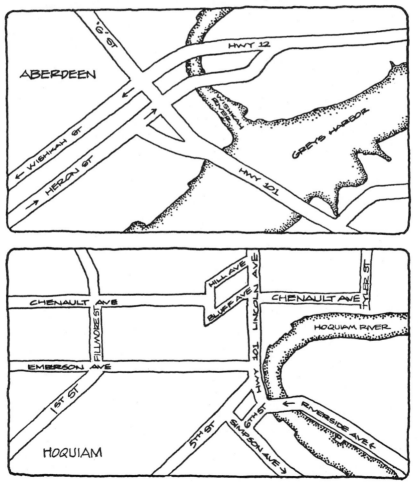

RESTAURANTS

Misty's

*On Heron, 1 block west
of Broadway,*
(206) 533-0956
116 W Heron Street,
Aberdeen
Moderate; beer and wine;
AE, MC, V
Lunch, dinner Mon-Sat

"Miss T" is Tracy Walthall, an exuberant perfectionist who uses exclamation points like croutons. A local girl who became an ace bartender, she is now the most innovative, hard-working chef you'll find on the loop between Long Beach and Port Townsend. In 1984, she bought a tavern with a leaky roof and no kitchen and transformed it into a stylish, pink and gray hole-in-the-wall with big ambitions. She grows her own herbs and has been known to swoon over a bag of chanterelles fresh from the forest. Misty's offers intriguing soups, wonderful salads, stir-fry specials, pasta punctuated with pesto and tender bits of chicken. Our baked halibut was rolled in crushed walnuts, Parmesan cheese, and garlic, and presented on a bed of pasta, with fruit, sauteed vegetables, and edible flowers spilling out of an oyster shell. Tracy has been heavily influenced by The Ark at Nahcotta, but she devours cookbooks and never stops experimenting with sauces.

There's a solid selection of Northwest wines by the glass, but the big draw here is the beer. There are more than 48 bottled brands from around the world, plus five Northwest microbrews on tap. The desserts are decadent—truffles and cheesecakes—and there's a new, industrial-strength espresso machine in the corner. Catering available.

Billy's Bar and Grill

Corner of Heron and G,
(206) 533-7144
322 E Heron Street,
Aberdeen
Inexpensive; full bar;
AE, DC, MC, V
Lunch, dinner every day

This historic pub features a handsome antique bar and the original ornate ceiling. The best little whorehouse in town used to be right across the street, and the walls at Billy's sport some original artwork that recalls Aberdeen's bawdy past. The place is named after the infamous Billy Gohl, who terrorized the Aberdeen waterfront in 1907. Billy shanghaied sailors and robbed loggers, consigning their bodies to the murky Wishkah River through a trapdoor in a saloon only a block away from the present-day Billy's—where today you get a square-deal meal and an honest drink without much damage to your pocketbook. The thick "gourmet" burgers and ranch fries are popular. The service is excellent.

Bridges

First and G,
(206) 532-6563
112 N G Street,
Aberdeen
Moderate; full bar;
AE, DC, MC, V
*Breakfast, lunch, dinner
every day*

This is the best full-service restaurant in town. Born to a restaurant family, Sonny Bridges started out with a corner cafe and kept expanding his horizons, both in space and in taste. A recent extensive remodel produced an airy, pastel restaurant with casual class. The diverse menu features fresh seafood, including razor clams and salmon, plus prime rib and pasta. Bridges is bolder now, offering some tasty Cajun-style specials. The bar is first-class, with Northwest wines, beers, and espresso drinks. The staff, as always, is extraordinarily professional. We're almost ready to hand Bridges a second star, if only the menu were more imaginative.

The Levee Street
7th and Levee,
(206) 532-1959
709 Levee Street,
Hoquiam
Moderate; full bar;
MC, V
Dinner Tues-Sat

Roy Ann Taylor spent 12 years as a cook at a logging camp, where her grub played a key role in morale and productivity. You won't find flapjacks and chicken-fried steak at her lovely little spot overlooking the tugboats and swooping seagulls on the Hoquiam River, but the crab-stuffed cod is delicious, the salmon fresh from the docks, and the prime rib beautifully cooked. Roy Ann is a conscientious woman with good instincts, and she is getting more adventuresome.

LODGINGS

Lytle House Bed &
Breakfast
Head west on Emerson,
turn right on Grant, go 3
blocks, (206) 533-2320
509 Chenault, Hoquiam,
WA 98550
Moderate; no credit cards;
checks ok

In 1900, when Robert Lytle built what was to become Hoquiam's big architectural landmark, Hoquiam's Castle, his brother Joseph erected a smaller version next door. This has become Lytle House, Jim and Elsie Reynolds' bed and breakfast showplace, decorated throughout with Victorian embellishments. There's a carousel horse in the parlor, but otherwise the room feels too formal to hunker down in a big chair and read. Having just two guest rooms allows Jim and Elsie to really get to know their guests—something these hospitable hosts love—but guests can choose whether or not to get to know each other, as there are more than enough living rooms for all. Guests share the upstairs bathroom (sans shower) but are free to shower downstairs, which is fortunate, considering only a trickle of hot water comes out of the upstairs claw-footed tub. Jim's breakfasts are ample: pancakes, scrambled eggs, sausage, fresh fruit, orange juice, and coffee. For all this, $40 a couple is a bargain.

MONTESANO

RESTAURANTS

Savory Faire
Take Montesano exit
off Highway 12,
(206) 249-3701
135 S Main Street,
Montesano
Inexpensive; no alcohol;
MC, V
Breakfast, lunch Mon-Sat

This is a charming place a block away from the handsome and historic Grays Harbor County Courthouse (whose murals have been freshly restored). The restaurant grew out of Candi Bachtell's popular cooking classes at Montesano's ambitious Community School. A superb baker, Bachtell is a stickler for freshness and presentation. Breakfasts are wonderful: omelets, country-fried potatoes, and homemade breads. At lunchtime, she can elevate a French dip sandwich into a veritable event. Visiting Savory Faire is like being in a country kitchen. Customers crane their necks to admire the food at the next table as they peruse the menu and sniff the aromas from Candi's ovens.

Fresh-baked breads, rolls and cakes, pasta, and specialty coffees are available for take-out.

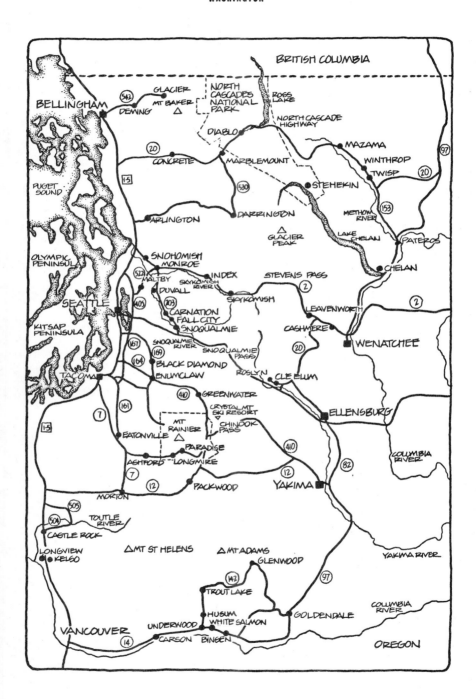

WASHINGTON CASCADES

Easterly crossings, starting in the north from Deming to Mount Baker, then Concrete to the Methow Valley along the North Cascades Highway. Farther south, the "Cascade Loop": eastward from Snohomish to Cashmere on Route 2, south to Cle Elum, westward again on I-90, then north through dairy country to Duvall. Then two Mount Rainier approaches—Maple Valley to Chinook Pass; Eatonville to Ashford—followed by a southward route through the heart of the Cascades and a short easterly jog along the Columbia River.

DEMING

RESTAURANTS

Deming Tavern
Off Mount Baker Highway at Deming and 1st, (206) 592-5282
5031 Deming Road, Deming
Moderate; beer and wine; no credit cards; checks ok
Lunch, dinner every day

★

In operation since 1922, this is one of the few real steak houses left hereabouts. It's not a fancy place, but everyone (a mix of loggers, suburbanites, and Bellingham city slickers) comes for the steak. You can get a tender, well-aged 6-ounce tenderloin for $7.95, a 16-ouncer for $13.25. The ultimate challenge here: you can have a 72-ounce steak, with a baked potato and spaghetti, for *free*—provided you can eat the whole thing in half an hour. If you can't, it's $36.95. So far, everyone has paid up. Ten beers on tap.

Carol's Coffee Cup
1½ miles east of Deming at Mount Baker Highway, (206) 592-5641
5415 Mount Baker Highway, Deming
Inexpensive; no alcohol; MC, V
Breakfast, lunch, dinner every day

Carol's is a local institution: a pleasant little cafe/hamburger joint/bakery, long a favorite with loggers, skiers, and hikers. The hamburgers are fine, but the big cinnamon rolls and homemade pies are best. Be prepared for a long wait on summer weekends and during the height of the Komo Kulshan (Mount Baker) ski season.

LODGINGS

The Logs
18 miles east of Deming on Mount Baker Highway, (206) 599-2711
9002 Mount Baker Highway, Deming,

Be sure to bring your fishing rod, berry bucket, and mulled wine to this foothill retreat: in July the streams run clear and the trout begin to bite, in September the bushes are laden with blueberries, and in winter no place could be cozier. Five log cabins (built by owner Rod Ohlsen) and a pool are hidden in dense stands of alder and fir at the confluence of the Nooksack River and Can-

WA 98244
Moderate; no credit cards;
checks ok

yon Creek. Cabins are spare and the twin beds are bunks, but the necessities are there: a large fireplace (built from river cobbles and slabs of Nooksack stone) complete with firewood; a couple of small bedrooms; a large, fully equipped kitchen. Instead of TV, you'll have entertaining visits from deer, grouse, foxes, raccoons, and eagles. Cabins sleep up to 10; pets are okay.

GLACIER
RESTAURANTS

Innisfree
31 miles east of
Bellingham on Mount
Baker Highway,
(206) 599-2373
9383 Mount Baker
Highway, Glacier
Moderate; beer and wine;
MC, V
Dinner Thurs-Mon
(summer); variable
in winter

★ ★

Discriminating taste buds lure folks from Seattle and Vancouver to Fred and Lynn Berman's special treatment and food at Innisfree. The Bermans are organic farmers, and they opened the restaurant as a reliable outlet for their produce. Over the years they've honed their cooking skills to the point of excellence. The menu is simple (only four entrees per night—a vegetarian dish, meat or poultry, a fresh local fish, a Northwest seafood) but intriguing. This cuisine is pure, ever-changing Northwest eclectic: Nooksack Valley fowl, beef, and veal; halibut with strawberry butter. Our butternut apple soup was delicate, the bread was fresh and warm, and the finisher, tart local blueberries with the Bermans' homemade kefir (from a culture they brought back from Norway) was exceptionally flavorful. The Bermans were adding on a bit at press time, expanding their kitchen and wine cellar and creating a sitting/waiting area where diners can have their appetizers while they wait for that intimate table. Drop by for a big bowl of soup and all the freshly baked bread you can eat ($4.50) or stay for the surprising, healthful meal. It's probably not a place for everyone (the food is unsalted; no smoking is allowed), but for a getaway evening in Washington's own North Woods, you can't do better.

Graham's
In the middle of town on
Mount Baker Highway,
(206) 599-2833
9989 Mount Baker
Highway, Glacier
Moderate; full bar;
AE, MC, V
Breakfast, lunch Sat-Sun,
dinner Fri-Sun
(breakfast, lunch, dinner
every day July-Aug)

For 17 years, Graham's has been a marvelous place to stop on the way into the Cascades for food, drink, rollicking company, and oddball entertainment. Gary Graham is constantly renovating this, revamping that, brainstorming a new party idea, inventing a new toy. (Latest addition: a patio out front for sunset and traffic watching). One staff member is Pat, a robot built by Gary, who resembles R2-D2 but has the annoying habit of relieving himself on a carefully selected customer's leg (fortunately, he's temporarily out of commission).

When Graham's cook left last year Gary decided, What the heck, let's do something different. Thus the "hot tub" was born: an old bathtub, converted into a barbecue, positioned out back in the beer garden. The cook-it-yourself idea was such a hit that even after a new grill man was hired the hot tub remained as a dining option. Choose from steaks, half-chickens, or burgers to flip yourself and dress up as you like (try the famous Gableburger sauce, named for Clark Gable, who once filmed parts of *Call of the Wild* right here). Inside, the menu includes seafood, salads, pasta, and deli items to go. Create your own sundae at the self-serve dessert bar. Food is only okay, but then food really isn't the main attraction—especially when you're the cook.

MOUNT BAKER

Mount Baker, 56 miles east of Bellingham, has downhill slopes but is best as a cross-country skiing destination. It's open daily from mid-November through December; Friday, Saturday, and Sunday and some select "holiday weeks" during the remaining (longest in the state) season. The mountain never lacks for snow, and runs are predominantly intermediate, with bowls, meadows, and trails. Call (206) 734-6771.

Hiking in the area is extensive and beautiful, especially in the late summer when the foliage is turning, the wild blueberries are ripe, and the days are hot and dry. The end of the road (which in winter doubles as the Mount Baker ski resort) is a jump-off point for some easy day hikes and spectacular views of both Mount Baker and the most photographed mountain in the world, the geographically eccentric **Mount Shuksan**. For trail and weather conditions call the Glacier Ranger Station, (206) 599-2714.

CONCRETE
LODGINGS

Cascade Mountain Inn
5 miles west of Concrete, off Highway 20,
(206) 826-4333
3840 Pioneer Lane, Concrete, WA 98237
Moderate; MC, V

Here's one of the few bed and breakfasts that began life as inns, not as residences. Ingrid and Gerhard Meyer celebrated their retirement by building this spacious log inn on 10 acres in the Upper Skagit Valley, near where hundreds of bald eagles gather in the winter. There are six guest rooms, each named after a different country; piles of down gently pillow you to sleep in the German room. Breakfast is served in a cozy dining room or on the patio with its calming views of the North Cascades. The Meyers will pack you a picnic before your jaunt into the surrounding countryside, if you'd like.

MARBLEMOUNT

Eagle watching. Hundreds of bald eagles perch along the Skagit River from December 1 through March 1. The best area to view these scavengers is along Route 20 between Rockport and Marblemount (bring your binoculars). The adventuresome may want to canoe downriver from Marblemount to Rockport (an easy eight miles); the river appears tame but can be deceptively swift. For more information call the National Park Service, (206) 877-4590.

RESTAURANTS

Mountain Song Restaurant
In the middle of town,
Milepost 106, Highway
20, (206) 873-2461
Moderate; beer and wine;
MC, V
Breakfast, lunch, dinner
every day; variable
in winter

The old Mountain Song sings a different tune these days, and some patrons are put off by its new serve-your-own-damn-self remodel. However, even with absentee service this restaurant makes for a nourishing stop along the North Cascades Highway. Homemade breads and organically grown vegetables become big sandwiches; soups, salads, and quiches round out the menu. For dessert, try a slice of fresh berry pie. Northwest microbreweries and vintners are well represented. The feeling is rustic and faintly countercultural, with a wood stove and hanging plants inside, a pleasant, tree-ringed garden outside.

DIABLO

Since the only road access to Ross Lake is south from Hope, BC, the best way to get to the southern end of the lake—save by a 3½-mile hike—is on the Seattle City Light tugboat from Diablo. Here Seattle City Light built an outpost for crews building and servicing the dams on the river. The tugboat leaves twice daily (8am and 3:30pm) and the ride is a few bucks round trip.

Worth visiting are the dams themselves, built by a visionary engineer named James Delmage Ross. **Skagit Tours** offer 3½ hour journeys through the Skagit Project, including an informative slide presentation, a ride up an antique incline railway to Diablo Dam, then a boat ride along the gorge of the Skagit to Ross Dam, a construction of daring engineering in its day. Afterward there is a lavish chicken dinner back in Diablo. Six miles down the road in Newhalem are inspirational walks to the grave of Ross and to Ladder Creek Falls, with plantings gathered from around the world. Tours are arranged through Seattle City Light, 1015 Third Avenue, Seattle, 98104, (206) 684-3030; summer only.

MAZAMA

LODGINGS

Mazama Country Inn
14 miles west
of Winthrop,
(509) 996-2681,
toll-free (800) 843-7951
Mail: PO Box 223,
Mazama, WA 98833
Moderate; MC, V
Breakfast, lunch, dinner
every day

With a view of the North Cascades from nearly every window, this spacious 6,000-square-foot lodge makes a splendid year-round destination (especially for horseback riding and cross-country skiing), with 10 good-sized rooms of wood construction with freestanding cedar beams. Some of the guest rooms have lofts that can be a bit stuffy in the summer, but each has a private bath, thick comforters on the beds, and futonlike pads that can be rolled out for extra guests.

Prices are reasonable, and many winter packages include three meals. Although the kitchen works at serving big, family-style meals, our latest visit provided more show than go. Pasta remains the best choice for dinner. Meals for nonguests require reservations.

The original inn, a converted farmhouse, lacks the

charm of the new one. The extra rooms there (that share two baths) are used only during busy periods. Families might want to try one of the two cabins that sleep up to eight.

WINTHROP

Stroll through this Western-motif town and stop in at the **Shafer Museum**, housed in pioneer Guy Waring's 1897 log cabin on the hill behind the main street. Exhibits tell of the area's early history and include old cars, a stagecoach, and horse-drawn vehicles. It is said that Waring's Harvard classmate Owen Wister came to visit in the 1880s and found some of the material for *The Virginian* here.

Winthrop's rendezvous with destiny appears to be drawing near, as Early Winters' downhill ski resort faces its last challenge from opponents. Meanwhile, there is plenty for the outdoor enthusiast to do here. The valley offers fine white-water rafting, spectacular hiking in the North Cascades, horseback riding, mountain biking, fishing, and cross-country or helicopter skiing (North Cascade Heli-Skiing, Mazama, 509-996-2148).

The Methow Valley Touring Association is keeping the valley's excellent cross-country ski trails groomed and available to visitors. Write to the association at PO Box 146, Winthrop, WA 98862, or phone Central Reservations (below) for ski conditions.

Methow Valley Central Reservations is a booking service for the whole valley—Mazama to Pateros—as well as a good source of information on things to see and do and on current ski conditions. Write PO Box 505, Winthrop, WA 98862, or call (509) 996-2148. For road and pass conditions, call (509) 976-ROAD or (206) 434-ROAD.

Hut-to-Hut Skiing offers miles of cross-country ski trails connecting with three spartan huts in the Rendezvous Hills. Each hut bunks up to eight people and comes equipped with a wood stove and a propane stove. Open for day skiers—a warm, dry lunch stop. For Rendezvous Huts information, call the Central Reservations office listed above.

RESTAURANTS

Duck Brand Cantina and Hotel
On the main street,
(509) 996-2192
248 Riverside Avenue,
Winthrop
Inexpensive; beer and wine; AE, MC, V
Breakfast, lunch, dinner every day

Despite its slightly seedy exterior and its slipping reputation, this cantina remains the best place in Winthrop to get a hearty lunch or dinner. Built to replicate a frontier-style hotel, Duck Brand is a local favorite for good meals at good prices. The menu ranges from bulging burritos to fettuccine to sprout-laden sandwiches on whole-grain breads. The smooth homemade salsa has plenty of zip. Try a wedge of fudgy brownie or a three-inch-thick slice of fabulous berry pie. The American-style breakfasts, shared by hotel guests, feature giant whole-wheat cinnamon rolls and other good homemade breads.

Upstairs, the Duck Brand Hotel has six homey, sparsely furnished rooms, but the price is right (starting at $43 for two).

Looking for a particular place? Check the index at the back of this book for individual restaurants, lodgings, attractions, and more.

LODGINGS

Sun Mountain Lodge
*9 miles south of
Winthrop on Patterson
Lake Road,
(509) 996-2211
Mail: PO Box 1000,
Winthrop, WA 98862
Expensive; full bar;
AE, DC, MC, V
Breakfast, lunch, dinner
every day*

If you haven't been to Sun Mountain Lodge for a while, you're going to be surprised at the $13 million remodeling taking place. When the lodge reopens (December 1989), you can stay in greater comfort and style than it has ever offered before.

Ask for one of the new rooms. They are dressed in natural colors, from the hand-painted bedspreads to the bent-willow headboards. Each new room has a fireplace and a view of the spectacular Methow Valley. In winter, over 50 miles of pristine cross-country trails make this a haven for Nordic skiers. The Meadowlark Loop is long and lively, with fabulous views. Expert instructors are available for skiers of any level. There's downhill skiing available 30 miles away at Loop Loop.

In summer there are guided nature hikes through the wilderness, brisk trail-ride breakfasts, and outfitter pack trips available. If you want to stay close to the massive log lodge, there are a heated pool, a hot tub, and tennis courts (new), and there's a golf course down the road near Winthrop.

The updated restaurant now offers a great table to every guest, whether a warm spot by the massive stone fireplace or a sweeping view of the valley by the windows. Chef Jack Hanes, formerly of Salishan Lodge, has brought a Southwest influence and a welcome upgrade to the food.

When the European-based Haub family completes all four phases of the remodel in 1992, we expect a truly premier getaway. During temporary closures due to construction, the cabins at the Patterson Lake Resort are a good alternative.

The Farmhouse Inn
*709 Highway 20,
(509) 996-2191
Mail: PO Box 118,
Winthrop, WA 98862
Moderate; AE, MC, V*

A restored farmhouse, this bed and breakfast a quarter mile outside Winthrop has lots of charm but not enough floor space to spread around its six rooms. You're best off with Number 6, a two-bedroom suite with private bath; or Numbers 1 and 2, with private baths and queen-size beds. The others are too small (about as big as the bed), and they share baths. The beds are soft. There's a hot tub and very limited cable TV. You register at the Duck Brand Hotel in town, but a continental breakfast is served here.

METHOW
RESTAURANTS

Methow Cafe
*The only business in
Methow, (509) 923-2228
Highway 153, Methow*

In summer, river rafters pile into the cozy Methow Cafe; in winter, the locals and cross-country skiers keep the doors open. The food is the same year-round—hearty fare with names like the Steelheader Breakfast (two eggs, two

Inexpensive; beer and wine; no credit cards; checks ok

oversized buttermilk pancakes, and thick strips of bacon from nearby smokehouse Wenatchee Pack) and the McFarland Creek Sandwich (grilled ham and turkey with Monterey jack and Cheddar cheeses). Nothing fussy, nothing gourmet.

Owners Pat and Kristy Luft keep the menu true to small-town tastes and the conversation lively. Visit awhile and they'll talk about the beavers that felled a dozen poplars on a nearby creek, or the best trails for skiing or hiking on this particular day.

TWISP

RESTAURANTS

Twisp Pastries and Savories
Off Highway 20 in the heart of Twisp,
(509) 997-2464
128 N Glover Street, Twisp
Inexpensive; beer and wine; no credit cards; checks ok
Breakfast, lunch, dinner Tues-Sat, brunch Sun

Any meal you take at this classy cafe on Twisp's main street—breakfast of a filled pastry and espresso, a midday country picnic packed with a freshly baked mushroom strudel, or a dinner of linguine topped with homemade Italian sausage marinara—is certain to bring you back. Leslie Myrick has joined Sylvia Martinez as co-owner, and together they are turning out creamy scones, coffee cakes, flavorful breads, and savory pastries from around the world. The daily savory special is back, the pirogi are wonderful, and table service is now offered. The adjoining Confluence Gallery adds a nice touch.

PATEROS

LODGINGS

Amy's Manor
5 miles north of Pateros,
(509) 923-2334
Mail: PO Box 441, Pateros, WA 98846
Moderate; MC, V

Orchardists Barb and Rodney Nickell opened their enchanting four-bedroom home as a B&B a few years ago to keep it in the family. Built in 1928, the manor is dramatically situated at the foot of the Cascades overlooking the Methow River, and the rooms are country-quaint, with patchwork quilts tossed over rocking chairs and comfortable beds. The 170-acre estate has a small farm where chickens and rabbits wander freely. The Nickells serve a continental-plus breakfast (something easy but filling, says Barb) such as fresh fruit and waffles.

The French House
Heading north on Highway 97, take a left after the Methow River bridge, then a right onto Warren, (509) 923-2626
206 W Warren, Pateros
Mail: PO Box 595,

Formerly Lake Pateros Bed and Breakfast, this pretty colonial manse was built in 1922 for a retired naval officer and his wife. Now it's a B&B with two sunny rooms that share one full bathroom. And everybody leaves talking about Bob and Charlene Knoop's breakfast: fresh fruit, homemade fruit breads, and an exotic egg dish such as a garden omelet, asparagus strata, or basil frittata. The

All places in this book are recommended; even "no stars" are worth knowing about.

Pateros, WA 98846
Moderate; MC, V

Knoops and their two young sons are genuinely interested in their guests' travels and can steer you to the Columbia River beaches or the best cross-country tracks.

SNOHOMISH

This small town, formerly an active lumber town, now bills itself as the "Antique Capital of the Northwest." It certainly has plenty of antique shops filling the downtown historic district; the **Star Center Mall** is the largest, with 150 antique dealers from all over the area. Open every day; 829 Second Street, (206) 568-2131.

In addition to antiquing, get a lift in a **hot air balloon** at Harvey Field, (206) 568-3025, which also offers scenic flights, (206) 259-2944, and skydiving opportunities, (206) 568-5960.

RESTAURANTS

Peking Duck
In old downtown
Snohomish,
(206) 568-7634
1208 Second Avenue,
Snohomish
Inexpensive; beer and
wine; MC, V
Lunch, dinner daily

Can you possibly eat Chinese food in a flannel-shirt town? The answer is an unqualified yes. Under the gaudy yellow sign, in a strip shopping mall, with the standard decor (red and black lacquer with vinyl overtones), is an unexpected Oriental gem. There's nothing exotic here—just lots of people chowing down on heaping plates of cheap food made from fresh ingredients. The sweet-and-sour sauce doesn't get any raves, but the Sichuan-type dishes (hot, hotter, and hottest) do. Try the terrific ginger-onion chicken, or the garlic-onion prawns, or scallops—not on the menu, but ask for them. In fact, you'll do best if you don't order from the menu.

Cabbage Patch
Near the corner of Second
and A, (206) 568-9091
111 Avenue A, Snohomish
Moderate; full bar;
AE, MC, V
Lunch, dinner every day

Ask anyone in town where to eat, and you'll be pointed in this direction. Unfortunately, so is everyone else. In true Snohomish style, this eatery presents a unique hybrid of decor—Victorian meets early bordello. A menu printed on newsprint details some of this community's lesser-known bits of history. Their chocolate–peanut butter pie alone is worth a visit, and the soup isn't bad either, provided you like beef in your cabbage patch soup. Less thrilling are the seafood saute and the heavy cream sauces that suffocate the fettuccine dishes. It's all very charming and it's all very busy. Service can be forgetful when the place is full, especially at lunch. There are three modest bed-and-breakfast rooms next door.

LODGINGS

Noris House
2 blocks north of central
shopping area on a major
thoroughfare,
(206) 568-3825
312 Avenue D,

There's a gracious, tranquil atmosphere about this classic Edwardian bed and breakfast, even though it's on the main drag into Snohomish's historic shopping district. It's gaining quite a reputation for breakfasts, served in an elegant mission-style dining room. Large, oven-baked Dutch babies (puffy pancakes smothered with stewed cin-

Snohomish, WA 98290
Moderate; MC, V

namon apples) and homemade scrapple are typical fare. Owners Thom Ris and Lee Nokleby join guests for breakfast to fill them in on the area.

There are three spacious rooms available, with a capacity for four guests (and a limit of two couples) at one time. One room has a working fireplace and its own balcony. A big bathroom, with an enormous claw-footed tub and a quaint writing desk that holds hand towels, is shared. No smoking.

MONROE
RESTAURANTS

Ixtapa
Main and Lewis,
(206) 794-8484
118 E Main Street,
Monroe
Inexpensive; full bar;
AE, MC, V
Lunch, dinner every day

Ixtapa is a nice find on an otherwise sleepy main street in Anytown, USA. The richly spiced shredded beef, with its hints of cloves and cumin, is a big hit at Ixtapa. Chorizo here is upstaged by that shredded beef and the chile verde. Chiles rellenos are not as light and fluffy as they should be, but the sizzling fajitas—chicken or beef—come with a good array of condiments.

Be prepared to wait in line, but don't despair—the service is fast, particularly if you're willing to sit at the counter. The owners have opened another branch of the restaurant in Snohomish, at 515 Second Street; (206) 568-4522.

INDEX
RESTAURANTS

Bush House Country Inn
1 mile north of Highway
2 in Index,
(206) 793-2312
300 Fifth Street, Index
Inexpensive; full bar;
AE, MC, V
Breakfast, lunch Mon-Sat,
dinner every day,
brunch Sun

First established during the mining boom of 1898, the inn has operated on and off (and up and down) over the years. In 1988, new owners Tom Dufault, Dan Harmon, David Marshall, and Patte Ross began upgrading the place and at press time were about two-thirds of the way through.

The restaurant has a nice country charm, with a big stone fireplace in the middle. The menu has been revamped to feature fresh fish, aged beef, Washington fryers, and fresh fruits and vegetables. The portions are generous (the main-course salad was enough to feed the proverbial army). Recently we sampled the fresh vegetable and dip appetizer, the New York steak, and a pecan-encrusted pork loin special, all quite good. So was the fresh-from-the-oven blackberry cobbler. Sunday brunch has become quite popular and includes fresh fruits, waffles, old-time favorites like biscuits with gravy, assorted meats, omelets made to order, and a nice assortment of home-baked pastries and rolls. Friendly service.

The 11 rooms are still small, clean, and unmemorable, the view alpine. There are only two shared baths, but the third-floor suite (which sleeps six) has its own bath. It's all very country—especially the plumbing. The price is fair ($35; $65 for the suite).

SKYKOMISH

RESTAURANTS

Molly Gibson's Restaurant and Lounge
Right next to the only stop sign in town,
(206) 677-2345
Hotel Skykomish, Fifth and Railroad Avenue, Skykomish
Inexpensive; full bar;
DC, MC, V

Molly Gibson's is what you'd expect in a little town that's evolved from loggers' town to bustling railroad stop to skiers' base: good, basic American food at affordable prices. The hotel itself is showing its age (it opened in 1904). The 23 rooms aren't much, with shared bathrooms on each floor, dormitory style ($25). Since it is a former railroad hotel, it is close to the tracks; the trains do rumble through your sleep.

LEAVENWORTH

A railroad-yard-and-sawmill town that lost its industry, Leavenworth decided 30 years ago to recast itself in the Bavarian style, with tourism as its primary industry. Apparently, it was successful enough that other Northwest communities have tried to emulate this town, which has the advantage of a stunning alpine setting in the Cascade Mountains that supports its resemblance to a little town in the Alps. There are several popular festivals: the Autumn Leaf Festival the last weekend in September and the first weekend in October, the Lighting Festival the first two Saturdays in December, and the Mai Fest the second weekend in May.

Shopping. We recommend browsers head to The Clock Shop, with an impressive display of new and antique clocks, 721 Front Street; the Blue Heron, for original artwork and limited edition prints, 905 Commercial Street; Village Books, for an excellent collection of books about the Northwest, books by Northwest authors, and cookbooks, 215 Ninth Street; and Hoelgaard's Danish Bakery, for Danish pastries, cakes, and cookies, 731 Front Street.

Other attractions include **Homefires Bakery,** where visitors can see the German-style wood-fired oven (the nine-grain bread is a favorite, but don't pass up the dark German rye) and during fair weather can sit at the picnic table on the lawn and have cinnamon rolls and coffee; 13013 Bayne Road (off Icicle Road).

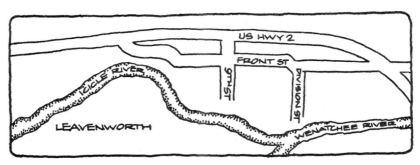

Outdoor activities include river rafting on the Wenatchee; fishing and hiking at Icicle Creek; touring the national fish hatchery on Icicle Creek to watch the Chinook salmon run (June and July) and spawn (August and September), 12790 Fish Hatchery Road (off Icicle Road), (509) 548-7641; golfing at the scenic 18-hole Leavenworth Golf Club, (509) 548-7267; skiing at Stevens Pass, (206) 973-2441, or Mission Ridge, (509) 663-6543; fabulous cross-country skiing around the area, at the golf course or at the Leavenworth Nordic Center, (509) 548-7864; horseback riding at Eagle Creek Ranch, (509) 548-7798; sleigh rides behind Belgian draft horses at Red-Tail Canyon Farm, (509) 548-4512; walking along the river on a new city center trail system which leads via wheelchair-accessible ramps to Blackbird Island; and mountain biking with rentals available at Icicle Bicycle at the Leavenworth Nordic Center, (509) 548-4566.

Scottish Lakes Snomad Camps, eight miles into the backcountry west of Leavenworth, is a cluster of primitive plywood cabins at the edge of the Alpine Lakes Wilderness Area. It's most popular for backcountry skiers, but open (and less expensive) for hikers come summer. You can ski up the eight miles or be carted up in a snowmobile and ski down the 3,800-foot drop; PO Box 312, Leavenworth, WA 98826; (509) 548-7330, reservations only.

RESTAURANTS

Gustav's Onion Dome Tavern
On Highway 2 at the west end of town,
(509) 548-4509
617 Highway 2,
Leavenworth
Inexpensive; beer and wine; MC, V
Lunch, dinner every day

Popular with the outdoors crowd, Gustav's recently expanded and remodeled both the exterior and interior and moved the patio to the roof. In fair weather you can sit under colorful umbrellas, taking in the panorama and enjoying beers and a burger. For a change from Leavenworth's ubiquitous German fare, Gustav's offers homemade fries and onion rings with its burgers and a good selection of imported beers. Because it's a tavern, you must be 21 to patronize Gustav's.

Reiner's Gasthaus
Across from the gazebo,
(509) 548-5111
829 Front Street,
Leavenworth
Inexpensive, beer and wine; AE, MC, V
Lunch, dinner every day

For the quintessential Bavarian culinary experience in Leavenworth, Reiner's is the place. The menu offers Austrian and Hungarian specialties as well. The smoked Bavarian-style farmer's sausage with sauerkraut and German rye bread is a safe selection for the uninitiated. More adventuresome eaters can try the homemade dumplings (boiled liver, egg, and bread) served with melted cheese for lunch; or the schnitzel topped with paprika sauce or the Hungarian goulash for dinner.

Seating is European-style (which means tables are sometimes shared); service is prompt and knowledgeable. Because it's located on the second floor at the back of the buildings on Front Street, the views of the town from the restaurant are slim (although a tiny balcony seats a few patrons in good weather). There's a wide selection of imported wines and beers. Have dessert somewhere else.

Terrace Bistro
On the corner of 8th and the alley between Commercial and Front,

There's *one* wiener schnitzel on the menu, but for the most part this second-floor eatery leaves the German food alone. Favorites from the menu are chicken Jerusalem (chicken breasts grilled with bread crumbs, parsley, basil,

(509) 548-4193
200 Eighth Street,
Leavenworth
Moderate; full bar;
MC, V
Lunch, dinner every day

and Parmesan cheese, with artichoke sauce) and tortellini with shrimp. The medallions of pork tenderloin sauteed in a brandied cream sauce were rich and tender, although they were served with too-soft vegetables and rice. As the name implies, there's a terrace for fair-weather dining. The meal is unhurried and it's easy to linger over coffee and dessert; the dessert tray ranges from German chocolate cake to mocha cream torte to cheesecakes, most made on the premises. Service is attentive and hospitable. The extensive wine list includes many imported wines and champagnes. Reservations recommended.

LODGINGS

Mountain Home Lodge

Mountain Home Road off
Duncan and Highway 2,
(509) 548-7077
Mail: PO Box 687,
Leavenworth, WA 98826
Expensive; AE, MC, V

In the winter, a heated snow-cat will pick you up from the parking lot at Duncan Orchard Fruit Stand, just east of Leavenworth. That's the only way to this peaceful and secluded lodge. (In the summer, Mountain Home is accessible over three miles of dirt road, appropriately labeled primitive.) Miles of tracked cross-country ski trails leave from the back door; you can snowshoe and sled, and there's a 1,700-foot toboggan run. Cross-country ski rentals are available at the lodge. There's a Jacuzzi on the deck overlooking a broad meadow and the mountains across the valley. Summer activities include hiking, horseshoe pitching, badminton, swimming, and tennis.

This is a serene adult haven—kids and pets are outlawed—and the big stone fireplace creates a slow, romantic ambience. Although the walls are double-thick, noise travels from bedroom to bedroom, so it is fortunate everyone goes to bed early and rises early and quietly. Hearty country meals are included in the price during the winter and are available at an additional cost in the summer. Weekend reservations should be made a full year ahead for the winter, three to four months for the rest of the year.

Run of the River

1 mile east of Highway 2,
(509) 548-7171
9308 E Leavenworth
Road
Mail: PO Box 448,
Leavenworth, WA 98826
Moderate; AE, MC, V

Built on the bank of the Icicle River, this log-construction bed and breakfast boasts such solitude and comfort that you may want to spend the entire day on the deck, reading or watching the wildlife in the refuge across the river. Hosts Monty and Karen Turner recently added three rooms, each with private bath and one with a Jacuzzi. The rooms facing the river have commanding views of the mountains. Some rooms have their own wood stoves, decks, and cozy loft sitting areas; all are furnished in country pine. Hearty breakfasts such as yogurt and fruit, juice, eggs, French toast, and baked apples are served. There's a Jacuzzi on the deck near the river. This is an excellent quiet and relaxing getaway for adults. No smoking whatsoever.

Haus Lorelei Inn

2 blocks off Commercial on Division,
(509) 548-5726
347 Division Street,
Leavenworth, WA 98826
Moderate; no credit cards;
checks ok

Here's a rarity: a bed and breakfast that not only welcomes kids but is run by four of them (and their mom). The two-acre site surrounded by towering pines and flanking the Icicle River is only two blocks from Leavenworth's main street and provides many activities for the younger guests. Hostess Elisabeth Saunders and her children, Bettina, Billy, Kelly, and Mike, offer six bedrooms furnished in comfortable European tradition, four with private baths. Each of the rooms affords gorgeous views of the Cascades; at night you can hear the river rushing over the boulders. During the summer months, guests eat on the screened sun porch and may use the private tennis court. There's a hot tub, and a short walk away there's a sandy swimming beach.

River Chalet

4½ miles west of Leavenworth off Highway 2, (509) 663-7676
Mail: 1131 Monroe Street, Wenatchee, WA 98801
Expensive; no credit cards;
checks ok

Equally suited to large group meetings and intimate trysts, this brand-new contemporary guest house on the Seattle side of Leavenworth gives the visitor a real feel for the Northwest. It's right on the Wenatchee River, and large windows look out over mountains. Three bedrooms sleep 12 comfortably (but slumber parties of 22 sleeping-baggers have occurred); wood stoves keep you warm. Outside there's a hot tub.

It's an ideal vacation spot for groups of couples especially: in winter there's ample skiing all around, and a large kitchen makes gourmet collaborations a pleasure. Cost is $200 for four. Catering can be arranged on request.

Haus Rohrbach Pension

About 1 mile off Ski Hill Drive, (509) 548-7024
12882 Ranger Road,
Leavenworth, WA 98826
Moderate; AE, MC, V

It's a true European pension, with alpine architecture, bathrooms down the hall, friendly hosts, and breakfast included with the room. They were set back by a fire in January 1989, but were reopening at press time after a brief closure to repair the roof and replace damaged belongings.

The lodge is tucked into the base of Tumwater Mountain, so it has a terrific view over the valley farmland back toward town. Most of the rooms open onto small, flower-decked balconies with this view, and breakfast is served on a large deck with the same majestic vista. Six of the 10 rooms have private baths. The rooms are small, the walls are thin (though the lodge is small and quiet), and you sleep on very firm platform beds. Breakfasts are delicious and ample. Bring the kids—there's a sled hill out back and an ice-cream parlor in the basement.

CASHMERE

If you're not in a Bavarian mood, this little orchard town gives cross-mountain travelers an alternative to stopping in Leavenworth. The main street has put up Western storefronts; the town's bordered by river and railroad.

Chelan County Historical Museum and Pioneer Village has an extensive collection of Indian artifacts and archaeological material; the adjoining pioneer village features 19 old buildings, carefully restored and equipped, in a nostalgic grouping; 600 Cottage Avenue, (509) 782-3230.

Aplets and Cotlets. These confections, made with local fruit and walnuts from an old Armenian recipe, have been produced for decades; you can tour the plant (weekdays January through April, daily May through December) and consume a few samples; 117 Mission Street, (509) 782-2191.

RESTAURANTS

The Pewter Pot
*Downtown Cashmere in
the business district,
(509) 782-2036
124½ Cottage Avenue,
Cashmere
Moderate; beer and wine;
MC, V
Lunch Tues-Sat, dinner
Tues-Sat, brunch Sun*

Here you can get early American food such as apple-country chicken topped with owner Kristi Biornstad's own apple-cider sauce, Plymouth turkey dinner, and New England boiled dinner. Desserts are tasty. Although her restaurant's short on atmosphere, Biornstad tries hard to serve dishes that reflect the area, using local ingredients. Try one of the daily specials or the Sunday buffet.

CLE ELUM

Easy access brings travelers from the freeway to Cle Elum, a former coal-mining town now undergoing a modest rediscovery.

Cle Elum Bakery is a longtime local institution doing as much business these days with travelers as with locals. From one of the last brick-hearth ovens in the Northwest come delicious torchetti, cinnamon rolls, and great old-fashioned cake doughnuts. Closed Sundays. First and Peoh, (509) 674-2233.

Cle Elum Historical Telephone Museum. Open Memorial Day to Labor Day only, this museum displays the area's original phone system, which was operating well into the 1960s. First and Wright, (509) 674-5702.

RESTAURANTS

**Mama Vallone's
Steak House & Inn**
*On the main drag at the
west end of town,
(509) 674-5174
302 W First Street,
Cle Elum
Moderate; full bar;
AE, DC, MC, V
Dinner Tues-Sun,
brunch Sun*

Talk to the regulars and they'll tell you about the warm welcomes, great steaks, and good homemade pasta at Mama Vallone's. It's definitely the best Cle Elum has to offer, but it never seems to live up to its rumored reputation. Or maybe we just ordered the wrong things. Our chicken breast in marinara sauce was fine, but the pork scalloppine, a special the day of our visit, was disappointingly underseasoned. One of the big deals is bagna cauda, a "hot bath" of garlic, anchovy, olive oil, and butter into which you dip strips of steak, chicken breast, or your favorite seafood. Or simply order steak, the tastiest version of which tosses Sicilian-spiced steak slices over homemade fettucine. The real winner in a recent meal was the soup—a bean-rich pasta e fagioli, brought to the table in a tureen and topped with Parmesan (a bottomless cup with bread goes for $6.50—a meal in itself). Wines are only okay; service (you're cared for by several members of the staff) is exceptional.

Upstairs there are three bedrooms with private baths, decorated with antique reproductions, that rent for $55 a night.

LODGINGS

The Moore House

Adjacent to Iron Horse State Park at 526 Marie Avenue, (509) 674-5939 Mail: PO Box 2861, South Cle Elum, WA 98943 Moderate; AE, MC, V

It's a winner. Named for owners Connie and Monty Moore, who lovingly restored the structure, this bed and breakfast was originally built in 1913 to house transient employees of the Chicago, Milwaukee, St. Paul & Pacific Railroad. Now on the National Historic Register, the bunkhouse with 10 guest rooms is light and airy, and pleasantly furnished with reproduction antiques. Four of the rooms have their own baths; the others share two and a half immaculately clean baths. Throughout the house the railroad motif is evident: rooms are named for men who actually stayed in the house decades ago, and railroad memorabilia—vintage photographs, model trains, schedules, and other artifacts—are displayed in the hallways and the public rooms. A newly added caboose in the side yard is fully equipped with bath, fridge, queen bed, and private sundeck. At least two more cabooses are scheduled to take up residence soon. Included in the reasonable price (rooms range from $39 to $89) is an ample breakfast, and should you feel the spirit, there's an outdoor hot tub that the Moores will rev up for your use.

Hidden Valley Guest Ranch

Off Highway 970 at Milepost 8, Hidden Valley Road, (509) 674-5990 Mail: HC 61, Box 2060, Cle Elum, WA 98922 Moderate; MC, V

With the return of owners Bruce and Matt Coe in 1987, a little pride of ownership has come back to the state's oldest dude ranch. The 11 cabins are still quite rustic and thin of wall, but miles of wildflower-lined trails, horseback riding, nearby trout fishing, a pool, a hot tub, and splendid cross-country terrain help to redeem the quarters. Cabins and rooms come with full kitchens and baths, and go for $49 per person, including food provisions for all meals.

ROSLYN

Roslyn is now just a sleepy reminder of its rough-and-tough days as a thriving coal-mining town, but vestiges remain to make it an interesting detour while driving across the Cascades.

City folk have converted some of the modest turn-of-the-century homes to weekend places, and the former mortuary is now a video store and movie theater, but the main intersection still offers a cross-section of the town's character: the historic NWI building (which once housed the company store) occupies one corner, while the old brick bank across the way still operates behind the original brass bars and oak counters.

An old stone tavern, inexplicably called **The Brick**, has a water-fed brass spittoon running the length of the bar; (509) 649-2643. Down the road, behind the town's junkyard, you'll find **Carek's Market**, one of the state's better purveyors of fine meats and sausages. Notable are the Polish sausage, the pepperoni, and the jerky; 4 South A Street, (509) 649-2333.

RESTAURANTS

Roslyn Cafe
2nd and Pennsylvania,
(509) 649-2763
28 Pennsylvania Avenue,
Roslyn
Inexpensive; full bar; no
credit cards; checks ok
Breakfast Sat-Sun; lunch,
dinner Tues-Sun

Here's the kind of funky eatery that every picturesque, slightly chic town like Roslyn should have. It's an old building with high ceilings, a short bar that is now a counter, neon in the window, hard chairs, a juke box with original 78s—full of a sense of different types belonging. You can get burgers—really good ones with blue cheese or spinach and onions on them—but why, when you can have tenderloin tips with Bearnaise, grilled halibut with dill sauce, Chinese pepper steak, or a great Philadelphia steak sandwich (which one of us ordered on a recent visit and the rest of us coveted). Dessert is a hard choice from among several candidates, but you can't go wrong with the chocolate cream pie or the pineapple upside-down cake. Breakfast is also exceptional (but it begins at 11am): bacon and eggs, blueberry shortstacks, homemade fried potatoes, gooey cinnamon rolls, and huevos rancheros.

Village Pizza
Main and Pennsylvania,
(509) 649-2992
6 Pennsylvania Avenue,
Roslyn
Inexpensive; beer and
wine; no credit cards;
checks ok
Dinner every day

You've found the local hangout, run by a real character, Nan Harris. She's traveled the world, pausing only occasionally to run small businesses in places that suit her. Lucky for Roslyn, she's put down at least temporary roots in this little restaurant, where her urban literary passions (she'll have copies of the *New York Review of Books* and *Architectural Digest* arrayed on the tables) are well in evidence.

She makes good pizza, some bordering on *delizioso* (the pungent fresh garlic pizza is out of this world). She also serves sandwiches and bagels in the summer. Everyone is here—gangs of wild children with their bicycles piled outside, longhairs, local ranchers, yuppies—peacefully coexisting, which is perhaps the biggest tribute to Nan and her pizza. Across the street from The Brick.

SNOQUALMIE

In this lovely country, the dairyland folds into the mountains, and you begin to understand why the Cascades have that name.

Snoqualmie Falls. The spring thaws and the fall rains turn these 268-foot falls into a thundering spectacle. There is an observation deck; better is to take a picnic down the one-mile trail to the base of the falls.

Puget Sound Railway is a volunteer-operated steam-locomotive-drive train that runs from May through September, Saturdays and Sundays, up to Snoqualmie Falls gorge. There's also a good railroad museum. Snoqualmie Depot, (206) 888-3030.

Snoqualmie Pass, the historic, low-lying transmountain route of the Indians, is a good starting point for hikes. In winter, three ski areas offer the closest downhill and cross-country skiing for Seattle ski buffs.

Snoqualmie Winery is a splendid stop on the way through the Cascades, with tours, tastings, and a marvelous view; 1000 Winery Road, (206) 888-4000.

LODGINGS

The Salish
Exit 27 off I-90, follow signs to Snoqualmie Falls, (206) 888-2556
37807 SE Fall City Road, Snoqualmie
Expensive; full bar; AE, DC, MC, V
Breakfast, lunch Mon-Sat, dinner every day, brunch Sun

Until recently, the draw has always been the spectacular Snoqualmie Falls. And for the moment, they still are the main pull, but the new owners (who run Oregon's famed resort, Salishan) have built—and rebuilt—a lodge that is quickly becoming as much of a draw as the falls themselves. Each room is designed in a tempered country motif: light, clean-lined wooden furnishings, pillowed window seats (or balconies in some), flagstone fireplaces (and a woodbox full of split wood and kindling), and a cedar armoire. The details are covered here: TV and champagne cleverly concealed, bathrobes, telephone sockets and even an emoryboard in the bathrooms. Jacuzzis are separated from the bedroom with a swinging window to invite the full effect of fire. Still, it's tough to book a room with a great view. There are only 8 (out of 91) with a view of the falls; most have views of the upper river (and the power plant). The rooftop open-ceiling hot tub is another nice feature. In tourist season, there's a constant flow of waterfall watchers around the rest of the grounds (from the informal flagstone entryway to the intimate library complete with a chess table). For the most part, the inn hosts honeymooners, second-honeymooners, and small business conferences (there are two banquet rooms downstairs). It's a good getaway, but there's not much to do in the area besides falls-gazing.

One dinner began fabulously with a refreshing chilled cucumber soup served in an iced terrine, and a wild smoked duck and wilted spinach salad. Neither a savory veal with wild mushrooms and a Marsala sauce nor the highly touted steak Salish (two small, overcooked rounds smothered in lobster, forest mushrooms, and a bland creamy chardonnay sauce) could stand up to the starters. You can eat too much, since each course is punctuated with another—salmon pate compliments of the chef, raspberry rhubarb sorbet compliments of the sous-chef, truffles compliments of the dessert chef. The wine list is almost legendary.

The notorious brunch lives on, but it continues to leave us (and numerous others) full but dissatisfied from the watery poached eggs, underdone bacon, bland breaded trout, frozen-packaged–style hash browns, and, yes, the world's best oatmeal. The knowledgeable servers are, at times, forgetful. During high season, reservations for dinner are almost as tough to get as those for brunch.

The Old Honey Farm Country Inn

Exit 27 off I-90, Old Highway North Bend and 384th, (206) 888-9399 8910 384th Avenue SE, Snoqualmie, WA 98065 Moderate; full bar; MC, V Breakfast, lunch, dinner every day

The B&B rooms in Con and Mary Jean Potter's farmhouse are still available, but the big news is the lovely 10-guestroom country inn next door. Brand-new in April '89, the rooms are airy and cheerful, all with big windows opening to the pastoral Snoqualmie Valley. The upstairs suites and the downstairs rooms have Jacuzzis and fireplaces and are handicapped-accessible. The large lobby has a stone fireplace, and just down the hall is a full country-style dining room—breakfast, lunch, and dinner for everyone—with an adjoining deck facing Mount Si. No pets.

FALL CITY

RESTAURANTS

The Herbfarm

3 miles off I-90 from Exit 22, (206) 784-2222 32804 Issaquah-Fall City Road, Fall City Moderate; wine only; MC, V Lunch Fri-Sun (late April-Dec)

The Herbfarm has successfully grown a first-class lunch restaurant, a trustworthy little haven of gourmandise in rural Fall City. Chef Ron Zimmerman transforms the fresh and the offbeat from the farm's surplus yield into six-course herbal feasts that attract the luncheon crowd from Seattle (30 minutes away) like bees to honey.

The menu changes with each new herb. A summer menu might include sweet cicely biscuits with edible-flower butter, stuffed zucchini blossoms with tomatoes and thyme-flower sauce, Copper River salmon with lemon verbena and tuberous begonia sauce, a sorbet of lavender and violets, rack medallions of spring lamb with morel mushrooms and caraway, accompanied by potatoes with savory and carrots with cumin, salad with roasted hazelnut vinaigrette, rose geranium ice cream, and sauce of fruit-scented sage.

Each meal is served to no more than 24 people and is prepared and served with such care and love that the whole experience can be quite inspirational—and educational. In fact, it's much more of a seminar than a luncheon. Guests can tour the farm and then watch the chef in action in the open kitchen as he shares his techniques and answers questions. You will take several new discoveries home with you and find yourself reaching again for snips of herbs you haven't used in years. Reservations can take months, though a new reservation policy allows for six seats available a week in advance (call at 1pm sharp on Friday).

CARNATION

Twenty-five miles northeast of Seattle is the home of the **Carnation Research Farm,** where self-guided tours let you glimpse several stages in the pasteurizing process. Kids love it; (206) 788-1511. Closed Sunday and during the winter.

At **King County McDonald Memorial Park,** meandering trails and an old-fashioned suspension bridge across the Tolt River provide a great family picnic setting; Fall City Road and NE 40th Street.

Biking. The Cascade Bicycle Club sponsors rides all over the region. The Carnation–North Bend ride leaves from McDonald–Tolt River Park and winds its way up to Snoqualmie Falls, the Herbfarm in Fall City, and George's Bakery in North Bend. Free to anyone who wants to ride. Call (206) 522-BIKE for a recorded message updated weekly.

Remlinger Farms. The sky's the limit for your favorite fruits and vegetables at this U-pick farm. The Strawberry Festival in mid-June starts off the season. Throughout the summer you can choose from the best in raspberries, apples, corn, and grapes. And don't forget the pumpkins in October. The kids, young and old alike, love tromping through the fields in search of the perfect jack-o'-lantern-to-be. Call (206) 333-4135 or (206) 451-8740 for more information.

RESTAURANTS

The Original Brown Bag Restaurant and Bakery
On the main drag,
(206) 333-6100
4366 Tolt Avenue
(Highway 203), Carnation
Inexpensive; no credit
cards; checks ok
Breakfast, lunch Tues-Sat,
brunch Sun

Back in the family of the original owners, The Brown Bag still fills Carnation's air with the sweet fragrance of fresh cinnamon rolls and breads. The historic 1913 building (recently spruced up with a coat of paint and wallpaper) holds only 10 tables (plus six outdoors for the overflow), and gets pretty packed on weekends. Alex and Allison Awasthi serve up wholesome and hearty soups and sandwiches to the teeming mobs.

MALTBY

RESTAURANTS

Maltby Cafe
From Highway 405, go
4½ miles east on Monroe
Highway 522, turn left at
the light, 206 483-3123
8809 212th Street SE
(Maltby Road), Maltby
Inexpensive; beer and
wine; MC, V
Breakfast, lunch every day

Four women have taught the old Maltby schoolhouse cafeteria a new lesson: how to cook. It's now a tough-to-find country cafe, contemporary in design but not overly trendy. Unhurried breakfasts feature delicious, fluffy, rich omelets (the sauces and sausages in the Italian omelet were not too tangy or spicy), good new potatoes (although we would have waited an extra minute to have them piping hot), and buttermilk biscuits. The giant cinnamon rolls are so legendary that the cafe often runs out. Don't feel compelled to stick with the breakfast standards when you see Swedish pancakes filled with fresh fruit, oatmeal with raisins, or prime-rib omelets on the menu. The orange juice is indeed fresh-squeezed, but comes in a shot-sized glass. Go early. If you do miss breakfast, you can take a seat at one of the nine counter stools for a quick Reuben sandwich (they cook their own corned beef) and local beer for lunch.

Wondering about our standards? We rate establishments on value, performance measured against the place's goals, uniqueness, enjoyability, loyalty of clientele, cleanliness, excellence and ambition of the cooking, and professionalism of the service. For an explanation of the star system, see the Introduction.

DUVALL

RESTAURANTS

The Silver Spoon
Corner of Stella and
Main, (206) 788-8997
6 Main Street, Duvall
Inexpensive; no alcohol;
no credit cards; checks ok
Breakfast, lunch every day

After numerous incarnations, Donna Beeson's Silver Spoon has been resettled on Duvall's main street for over two years now. The tiny restaurant, bright with pine booths, is the kind of place where local artists hang out while their art hangs on the walls. Breakfast, baked treats, welcome espresso, sandwiches, soups, and salads sum it up. The lunch special could be pasta, tofu lasagne, or vegetarian enchiladas. Soups are particularly delicious, with homemade, clean-tasting stock; salads wear honest dressings that are a welcome antidote to fancy fruit vinegars. We found the burgers to be so-so and surprisingly greasy (possibly because Beeson likes cooking vegetarian). Mostly, we're glad the pretty drive to Duvall yields such rich rewards.

BLACK DIAMOND

Black Diamond Bakery boasts the last wood-fired brick oven in the area. The bread that comes out of it is excellent: 26 different kinds, including raisin, cinnamon, sour rye, potato, seven-grain, honey-wheat, and garlic French. They offer doughnuts and cookies too, but it's the bread that people line up for. To get there, take the Maple Valley exit from I-405; at Black Diamond turn right at the big white Old Town sign; at the next stop sign veer left; the bakery is on the right. **32805 Railroad Avenue,** (206) 886-2741; closed Monday.

ENUMCLAW

RESTAURANTS

Baumgartner's
East end of town
on Highway 410,
(206) 825-1067
1008 E Roosevelt,
Enumclaw
Inexpensive; beer and
wine; MC, V
Lunch every day

Stop here to collect picnic supplies for a trip to Mount Rainier, or stop on your way back for an early supper. It's a full delicatessen with a range of European sausages and cheeses, imported beers and some wines, lots of large glass jars filled with coffee beans, teas, and spices, and even hand-dipped ice cream and Boehm's chocolates. The friendly staff make up delectable sandwich combinations on fresh bread and croissants. Try the croissant with turkey, bacon, sprouts, and a special apricot sauce, or a poor-boy roll with hot beer sausage and Swiss cheese. The freshly baked desserts have made a name for themselves; especially the chocolate espresso cheesecake and the raspberry tarts filled with a heavenly white chocolate-almond mousse.

Would you like to order a copy of Best Places *for a friend? There's an order form at the back of this book.*

GREENWATER
RESTAURANTS

Naches Tavern
North side of the highway, (206) 663-2267
Highway 410, Greenwater
Inexpensive; beer and wine; no credit cards; no checks
Lunch, dinner every day

Now *this* is the way to do a country tavern. The fireplace is as long as a wall and roars all winter long to warm the Crystal Mountain apres-ski crowd. The food is bountiful, homemade, and modestly priced—deep-fried mushrooms, chili, burgers, pizza, four-scoop milk shakes. There's a countrified jukebox, pool tables, a lending library (take a book, leave a book) of yellowing paperbacks, and furniture so comfortable that the stuffing is coming out. It's not pretty: Big Don, the "chef," wouldn't want it pretty, but he's a gracious host and a no-nonsense barkeep. The group assembled is a peaceable mix of skiers, hunters, loggers, and locals—depends on the season. Bring your own good company, play a little cribbage, stroke the roving house pets, nod off in front of the hearth.

CRYSTAL MOUNTAIN

The ski resort is the best in the state, with runs for beginners and experts, plus fine cross-country touring; (206) 663-2265. Less well known and less used are the summer facilities. You can ride the chair lift and catch a grand view of Mount Rainier and other peaks; rent condominiums with full kitchens, balconies, or other facilities from Crystal Mountain Reservations, (206) 663-2558 or (800) 852-1444; play tennis; and go horseback riding from Crystal Mountain Corral, (206) 663-2589. Other than that, there's just a grocery store, sports shop, and Rafters, the new bar-and-buffet restaurant atop Crystal's lodge. In summer, the Summit House offers weekend dinners. Off Highway 410 just west of Chinook Pass.

EATONVILLE

Northwest Trek is a "zoo" where animals roam free while people tour the 600-acre grounds in small, open-air trams. The five-mile tour passes by a large collection of native wildlife, with all kinds of Northwest beasts from caribou to mink. The buffalo herd steals the show. The whole tour is impressive for kids ($3.50) and adults ($5.75) alike; you can also combine visits with breakfast at the in-park food service concession, the Fir Bough. Group rates available. Open daily February through October, weekends only the rest of the year. Seventeen miles south of Puyallup on Route 161, (206)832-6116.

LODGINGS

Old Mill House Bed and Breakfast
Highway 161 to south end of town, turn east to 116 Oak Street,

A 1920s mill baron's mansion, complete with dance floor and prohibition-era bar, is now a B&B. Cathy and Mike Gallagher have delightfully re-created the excess of the period: the enormous mauve, gray, and ice green Isadora Duncan Suite resonates with the free spirit of this

(206) 832-6506
Mail: PO Box 543,
Eatonville, WA 98328
Moderate; MC, V

dancer—private his-and-hers dressing rooms, a prettily tiled bath with both a tub and a shower (the latter with seven shower heads), and a king-size bed. The three other rooms share a bath and have equal character (Will Rogers, Bessie Smith, and F. Scott Fitzgerald). The Fitzgerald room comes with an ongoing novel penned by guests (reportedly *full* of cliffhangers). Call ahead; mystery weekends ($150 per person) can be popular here.

ASHFORD

Wellspring is a privately operated, judiciously situated hot tub/sauna/massage center, where the tub is nestled in a sylvan glade surrounded by evergreens. Perfect after a day on Mount Rainier. Two and a quarter miles east of Ashford on Kernahan Road. Call ahead to schedule a massage, (206) 569-2514.

RESTAURANTS

Wild Berry Restaurant

4 miles east of Ashford,
(206) 569-2628
37720 Highway 706 E,
Ashford
Inexpensive; beer and
wine; MC, V
Lunch, dinner every day,
breakfast every day (July-
Aug), Sat-Sun (Sept-June)

Decorated in self-proclaimed "mountain yuppie" style, this place a mile from the Nisqually entrance to Mount Rainier National Park is the perfect spot for hearty mountain fare—and lots of it—that tastes surprisingly good. Chicken crepes, big pizzas, rainbow trout, huge sandwiches, and excellent homemade wild blackberry pie; absolutely no grease. The seasonal breakfast skips the fried eggs in favor of quiche, yogurt, and granola. Everything (beer and wine too) is available for take-out.

There's a log cabin for rent (sleeps up to eight) across the way, equipped with full kitchen facilities, claw-footed tub, and wood stove. Perfect for cross-country skiing groups.

LODGINGS

Alexander's Country Inn

4 miles east of Ashford
on Highway 706,
(206) 569-2300;
toll-free (800) 654-7615
37515 Star Rte 706 East,
Ashford, WA 98304
Moderate; beer and wine;
MC, V
Lunch, dinner every day
(weekends only in winter)

This quaint country inn has gained such a following that it now rivals the mountain itself as the best reason to visit Ashford. First opened in 1912 by lumberman Alexander Mesler as a hotel, the building lay dormant for a time after the Depression shut down operations. Now it's owned by Gerald Harnish and Bernadette Ronan, who have lovingly restored the rambling inn to much of its early grandeur. The result is a hideaway reminiscent of a bygone era.

Our small room contained an exquisite antique wardrobe, and the bed wore a hand-quilted coverlet. Tieback curtains, tiny-floral-print wallpaper, a stained glass lamp—it could've been Grandma's guest room. Best is the Tower Room: a suite in the turret of the manor. A large wheelchair-accessible suite has been added on the second floor—very private, with its own deck. Most of the bathrooms are shared, but they're large, modern, and immaculate. Indeed, this blending of old and new is the real genius here; it feels turn-of-the-century, but the comforts such as carpeted rooms and an indoor Jacuzzi are pure 1980s. Breakfast, included in the room cost, is juice, fruit, muffins, and omelets or French toast.

The dining room, open to guests and nonguests alike, is your best bet in these parts for a fine meal. And with the new chef behind the line the food is finally matching the once-high prices. The artichoke soup is exquisite in texture and taste. Our fresh trout—caught out back in the holding pond, pan-fried quickly, and then filleted at the table—were perfect; the chicken fettuccine was flavorful. Accompaniments were lightly buttered new potatoes and sauteed zucchini; dessert was a delectable homemade berry pie. At press time, a brick patio, ideal for summer dining, was being completed.

Ashford Mansion
Off Highway 706 at
30715 Mt. Tahoma
Canyon Road,
(206) 569-2739
Mail: Box G, Ashford,
WA 98304
Moderate; MC, V

★

The town founders, the Ashfords, built this large white English-style house in 1903 on an open hillside. Seventy-five years later, Jan Green decided to open it as a bed and breakfast. It's now on the National Register of Historic Places. There's a lovely porch that wraps around the house—complete with a porch swing for balmy summer evenings. Spend cooler evenings inside beside the fireplace, or tickling tunes on the grand piano.

There are four rooms, all on the second floor. A couple have sinks, but they all share the two baths down the hall. Our favorite, the Van Dyke Room, offers a Franklin fireplace, a canopy bed, an old claw-footed bathtub, and a private verandah looking out on Ashford Creek.

MOUNT RAINIER

The majestic mountain is the abiding symbol of natural grandeur in the Northwest and one of the most awesome mountains in the world. Its cone rises 14,410 feet above sea level, thousands of feet higher than the other peaks in the Cascade range. The best way to appreciate the mountain is to explore its flanks: 300 miles of backcountry and nature trails lead to ancient forests, dozens of massive glaciers, waterfalls, and alpine meadows, lush with wildflowers during its short summer. Chinook and Cayuse passes are closed in the winter; you can take only the loop trip or the road to Sunrise between late May and October. The road from Longmire to Paradise remains open during daylight winter hours. It is advisable to carry tire chains and a shovel during winter, and it is always wise to check current road and weather conditions by calling a 24-hour recorded message, (206) 569-2343.

Visitor information centers are reachable by phone through the communications center at (206) 569-2211. They are located at Longmire (ext. 237) and Paradise (ext. 277); both are open year-round. Centers at Ohanapecosh (ext. 238) and Sunrise (ext. 244) are open summer only. Hiker information centers (open daily during summer at Longmire and White River; ext. 275) dispense more detailed information for backpackers. Obligatory backcountry use permits for overnight stays can be obtained from any of the ranger stations.

Climbing the mountain. There are two ways to do it: with **Rainier Moun-**

taineering, the concessionaire guide service, or in your own party. Unless you are qualified to do it on your own—and this is a big, difficult, and dangerous mountain on which many people have been killed—you must climb with the guide service. Call Paradise (206) 569-2227 in the summer; Tacoma (206) 627-6242 in the winter. If you plan to climb with your own party, you must register at one of the ranger stations in Mount Rainier National Park, (206) 569-2211. They will make sure you have adequate experience and the proper equipment, and will inform you of route and avalanche conditions, and weather forecast. You also must check in with them when you get back down. Generally, the best time to climb the mountain is from late June through early September.

Longmire. A few miles inside the southwestern border of the park, the little village of Longmire has a simple inn—still closed for renovations at press time; call (206) 569-2275 for updated information—a small wildlife museum with plant and stuffed-animal displays, a hiker information center, and a cross-country skiing rental outlet. It is also the only place that sells gas in the park.

Paradise. At 5,400 feet, Paradise is the most popular destination point on the mountain. On the way to this paved parking lot and visitors' center, you'll catch wonderful views of Narada Falls and Nisqually Glacier. The visitors' center, housed in a flying-saucer-like building, has a standard cafeteria and gift shop, extensive nature exhibits and films, and a superb view of the mountain from its observation deck. Depending on the season, you can picnic (our advice is to bring your own) among the wildflowers, explore some of the trails (the rangers offer guided walks), let the kids slide on inner tubes in the snow-play area, try a little cross-country skiing, or even take a guided snowshoe tromp.

Sunrise. Open only during the summer months, the visitor center at Sunrise (6,400 feet) is the closest you can drive to the peak. The old lodge here has no overnight accommodations, but it does offer a snack bar and exhibits about the mountain. Dozens of trails lead from here, such as the short one leading to a magnificent viewpoint of Emmons Glacier Canyon.

LODGINGS

Paradise Inn
Highway 706, Paradise,
(206) 569-2291,
(206) 569-2275
Mail: PO Box 108 Star
Rte, Ashford, WA 98304
Moderate; full bar; MC, V
Breakfast, lunch, dinner
every day

The hotel at Paradise, just above the visitors' center, is a massive, old-fashioned lodge, full of exposed beams, log furniture, and American Indian rugs. Unlike the modest inn at Longmire, the Paradise Inn has 125 rooms, a comfortable full-service dining room, a small, smoky bar, and a lobby with two big stone fireplaces. The greatest advantage to staying here, however, is the proximity to the summit; the rooms are nothing grand, the bathrooms can be antiquated, and the expensive meals in the restaurant tend toward routine beef and frozen seafood dishes. Open late May to October only.

MOUNT ADAMS

Mount Adams and its surrounding area are a natural splendor largely overlooked by visitors from Portland and Seattle, who seldom venture in from the Gorge. Besides climbing to the summit of the 12,276-foot mountain—greater in displaced mass than any of the five major volcanic peaks in the Northwest—hikers and skiers can explore miles of wilderness trails in the Mount Adams Wilderness Area and the Gifford Pinchot National Forest. You can even arrange a **dogsled** excursion through Wilderness Freighters Guide Service, (503) 761-7428.

Volcanic activity long ago left the area honeycombed with caves and lava tubes, including the **Ice Caves** near Trout Lake with stalactites and stalagmites formed by dripping ice. To the southwest of Trout Lake is the **Big Lava Bed**, a 12,500-acre lava field filled with cracks, crevasses, rock piles, and unusual lava formations. Contact the Mount Adams Ranger Station in Trout Lake, (509) 395-2501, to register for ascents and for information on area activities.

In the warm months, Klickitat County is a land of abundance: morel mushrooms in the Simcoe Mountains (April–June), wildflowers in the Bird Creek Meadows (part of Track D, the only area of the Yakima Indian Reservation open to the public) in late July, and wild huckleberries—reputedly the best in the state—in and around the Indian Heaven Wilderness (mid-August to mid-September).

TROUT LAKE

LODGINGS

Mio Amore Pensione
Just off Highway 141, take a sharp right onto Little Mountain Road, (509) 395-2264
Mail: PO Box 208, Trout Lake, WA 98650
Moderate; MC, V

It looks like the International Embassy of Trout Lake from the road with all those flags in the front yard, but they're actually part of the welcome mat: proprietors Tom and Jill Westbrook fly the country flags of their guests during their stays. The restored 1904 farmhouse sits alongside Trout Lake Creek, with Mount Adams looming up over the cow pasture on the other side. The inside is decorated with memorabilia collected from spots around the world. Our only quibble is that everything here is a little *too* precious. Bedrooms are small, but the Venus Room is the most spacious—and the priciest—with a private bath and a two-seat sitting room with a view of Mount Adams. The converted stone icehouse in the corner of the yard sleeps four; it's a bit rustic, but it's private and cozy, with a fire stoked in the wood stove to keep your teeth from clacking.

Breakfast includes a bountiful array of Jill's award-winning baked goods, with a hot dish such as French toast soaked in Grand Marnier. Tom, a trained chef, will prepare a Northern Italian dinner—perhaps a loin cut of pork with garlic and rosemary, painted with a Marsala demi-glaze, or roast rabbit with garlic and herbs—for $20 extra (including appetizer, dessert, coffee, and wine). You don't need to be a guest to sample these savories, but you do need a reservation.

GLENWOOD

LODGINGS

Flying L Ranch
Off the Trout Lake-Glenwood Road on Flying

Their brochure just doesn't do this place justice. For 40-odd years the Lloyd family has owned and operated the 160-acre Flying L Ranch, which they opened to guests

*L Lane, (509) 364-3488
25 Flying L Lane,
Glenwood, WA 98619
Moderate; MC, V*

in 1960. The current host, Darvel Lloyd, is well known in these parts for his active involvement in establishing hiking trails and other outdoor activities.

The pace here is relaxed. You'll feel quite comfortable putting on some classical music and curling up with an old issue of *National Geographic* by the lava fireplace in the main lodge's spacious living room. The bedrooms, named after Old West notables or old cowhands, are nothing fancy—but we love 'em that way. Those in the main lodge offer the authenticity of the original ranch, complete with shared baths (the Charles Russell and the George Fletcher have fireplaces); those in the adjacent guest house are less charming but have the Mount Adams view. A two-room cabin back in the woods offers the most privacy.

As you dive into your huckleberry pancakes in the cookhouse at breakfast (included with a night's stay), Darvel offers a long list of ways to spend the day. Close-by options include bicycling the backroads around Glenwood, bird watching at Conboy Lake National Wildlife Refuge, or skiing the three miles of groomed trails on the ranch property. The Flying L also lines up a calendar of workshops and special events: a recent schedule offered a wildflower weekend, a watercolor painting workshop, and an intimate concert by the Philadelphia String Quartet. For lunch and dinner you'll have to bring your own food to prepare in one of the two well-equipped, wood-heated kitchens (though you cook on an electric range). And if you bring your own horse, the Flying L will provide a corral and a tack room.

COLUMBIA RIVER GORGE (WASHINGTON SIDE)

When windsurfing took off, the town of Hood River was poised to go along for the ride. The folks on the Washington side of the Gorge, though, had no grand tourism plan, and they stuck to logging and milling. This is why, a local waitress explains, crossing the Hood River–White Salmon bridge is "like going back 20 years." But while the protected waters across the Columbia make Hood River an ideal spot for beginning windsurfers, the wind "really pulls" on the Washington side. Here the hottest boardheads circumvent rocky shores and industrial areas to surf off points in the road like **Swell City** and **Doug's Beach**. To find them, follow the streams of vans and wagons piled high with boards and masts, or tune in to radio station KMCQ 104 for the local wind report, delivered by "Bingen" Bart live every morning.

CARSON
LODGINGS

**Carson Hot Mineral
Springs Resort**
*On Windriver Highway,
2 miles from the*

Carson Hot Springs, on Windriver Road outside of Stevenson, is a serene, eccentric resort reminiscent of (and open since) the days when the sickly "took the waters" to improve their health. Current bathhouse talk

Highway 14 and Carson junction, (509) 427-8292
Mail: PO Box 370, Carson, WA 98610
Inexpensive; MC, V

ranges from rheumatism and arthritis to the day's wind-surfing feats on the Gorge. The 1897 resort consists of two charming white clapboard structures—one, the nine-room hotel and restaurant; the other, the hot mineral baths—and 13 very basic cabins. The newly added Hot Tub Suite is available at an additional cost. There's nothing pretentious or elegant here ("well-worn" may be more like it), but we do recommend the hot mineral bath ($5), after which you're swathed in towels and blankets for a short rest. Massages ($12 per half-hour) available to complete the bliss, but reserve these well in advance.

Don't expect as healthy a treatment from the restaurant; it serves standard soups, salads, steaks, and some seafood—mostly fried.

HUSUM

Orchard Hill Inn
2 miles up Oak Ridge Road out of Husum, Milepost 2,
(509) 493-3024
199 Oak Ridge Road, White Salmon, WA 98672
Moderate; MC, V

You're asked to leave your shoes by the doormat (and they might even get a shine) at this B&B on 13 acres that revels in its setting, overlooking pear and apple orchards and the White Salmon River valley. The inn's three bedrooms, decorated with family antiques, offer refreshing respite from the wallpaper mania that has overtaken so many B&Bs. Two bathrooms—one with a whirlpool bath—are shared. The bunkhouse out back has its own bath and sleeps eight. A full sideboard breakfast includes homemade breads, huckleberry bran muffins, baked apples, eggs, and local produce. The barn has been partially converted into a beer garden for guests. Children are welcome at Orchard Hill and have a place of their own in a two-story tree house in front; hosts James and Pamela Tindall will even supply parents with a list of local babysitters. There's pitch-and-chip golf on the premises, and a full nine-hole course at nearby Husum Hills.

BINGEN
RESTAURANTS

Fidel's
1 mile east of Hood River Bridge (toll bridge) on Highway 14 in downtown Bingen, (509) 493-1017
120 E Stuben Street, Bingen
Inexpensive, full bar; MC, V
Lunch, dinner every day

Fidel's is a signal of the change beginning in Bingen. This Mexican restaurant seems transplanted straight from California; in fact, Fidel and Martha Montanez and their family recipes recently arrived from San Diego. Lively Mexican music sets the mood. Enormous margaritas go with the warm chips that arrive at the table with a disappointing salsa. The menu is surprisingly varied, offering carne asada, a chili verde, a chili colorado, and machaca (a shredded beef omelette). Portions are generous; a plate of chorizo con huevos (mild) with rice and beans is big enough for two. The chile relleno is encased in a thick layer of egg whites, so that it resembles a big pillow on your plate bathed in a delicious spicy sauce. Tables and chairs are big and comfortable, service is friendly and efficient. It's a place that everybody loves.

LODGINGS

The Grand Old House

*⁹⁄₁₀ mile east of
Hood River Bridge (toll
bridge) on Highway 14,
(509) 493-2838
Mail: PO Box 667,
Bingen, WA 98605
Moderate; MC, V*

"Any place that's dry enough for rattlesnakes is dry enough for my wife." That's how Greg de Bruler and his wife Cyndy chose to settle in Bingen, where rattlesnakes are rare but beautiful sunny weather—even when it's raining in Portland and Hood River—is not. The FOR SALE sign in the front yard has been there awhile and, given the right offer, they might actually part with the place. Still, the Grand Old House deserves its star, providing comfortable room and board for the growing influx of tourists to the Columbia River Gorge for windsurfing, hiking, and rafting in the summer; skiing in the winter; and wine-tasting all year round. The 130-year-old house—built by the first white settler in the area—resembles a big boarding house, with seven large bedrooms and updated (shared) bathrooms.

A corner room upstairs has a hulking four-poster bed with mirrors above. The full-service restaurant downstairs (open to the public from mid-April through December) features a fine breakfast for guests and a dinner menu with chicken, steak, seafood, and other items. There's a hot tub (often out of commission) and an outdoor shower out back, and the de Brulers will arrange sailboard rental and lessons. Just a couple of blocks away is the Mont Elise Winery, and several others—Mount Hood, Charles Hooper, and Three Rivers—are within 15 minutes' drive. The de Brulers are ideal B&B hosts—knowledgeable, helpful, but not intrusive.

GOLDENDALE

Maryhill Museum, a stately Palladian mansion, perches rather obtrusively upon the barren Columbia River benchlands. Constructed in 1917 by the eccentric Sam Hill, son-in-law of railroad tycoon James J. Hill, Maryhill began as the European-inspired dream home for Hill and his wife Mary, but became instead what it is today: a fine art museum. With one of the largest collections of Rodin sculptures in the world, three floors of classic French and American paintings and glass work, unique exhibitions such as chess sets and Romanian folk textiles, and splendid Northwest tribal art, the museum makes for quite an interesting visit. A cafe serves espresso, pastries, and sandwiches; peacocks roam the lovely landscaped grounds. Highway 14, 13 miles south of Goldendale, (509) 773-3733. Up the road is another of Sam Hill's bizarre creations: a not-quite-lifesize replica of Stonehenge, built to honor World War I veterans.

Goldendale Observatory, on a hill overlooking town (20 minutes north of Goldendale on US 97), was a popular spot when Halley's comet dropped in. Through high-power telescopes you get incredible celestial views through unpolluted skies. Open daily and some evenings, call ahead on weekends; (509) 773-3141.

LODGINGS

Three Creeks Lodge

18 miles north of the Columbia River on Highway 97,
(509) 773-4026
2120 Highway 97,
Goldendale, WA 98620
Moderate; AE, MC, V
Breakfast, lunch Mon-Sat,
dinner every day,
brunch Sunday

Changes in ownership have taken their toll on the Three Creeks Lodge, set down to meet no obvious demand in the Simcoe Mountains on the Satus Pass Road to Yakima. It is a collection of vaulted-ceiling cedar chalets, some with wood-burning fireplaces and private spas, scattered throughout the backwoods wilderness. You fish in summer and go on sleigh rides in winter: the place capitalizes on the romance of seclusion. Yet the fourplex creekhouses, with plywood siding, have an unfinished feel, and thin walls between units make televisions a bother.

The dining room in the main lodge makes splendid use of its situation at the confluence of three creeks, with glass and cedar walls that seem to bring the trees inside. But the beauty of the place ends here. One Saturday evening, inexperienced servers brought us halibut in a thick cheese sauce when we ordered it simply broiled, and suggested "chalomine" tea (but brought us, as we had hoped, chamomile). The desserts claim to be made fresh daily, but there weren't any left—because they were "baked on Monday." A later lunch produced a decent plate of pork cutlets. Word is they're getting a new chef, but until then stay in a chalet with a kitchen.

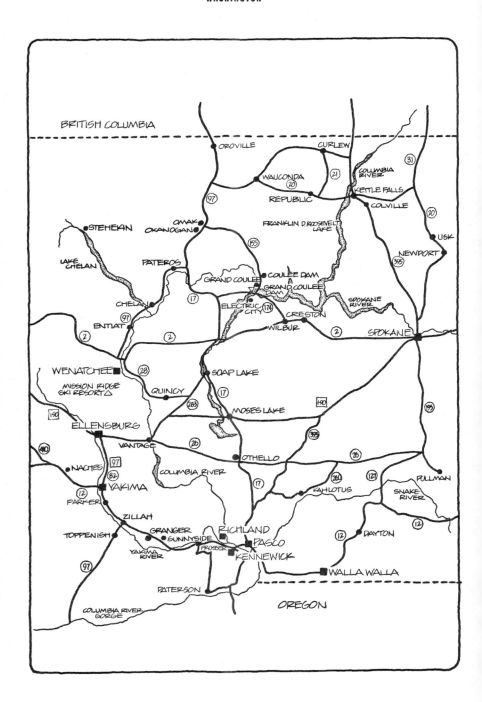

EASTERN WASHINGTON

*An eastward route along I-90, Ellensburg to Spokane,
then a northwesterly arc through the northeast corner of the state
to the Okanogan and Colville national forests. The Wenatchee loop begins
in Okanogan and continues clockwise through Grand Coulee, Soap Lake,
and north again to Wenatchee and Chelan (and Stehekin, accessible from Chelan).
Finally, an eastward drive along the bottom of the state—Yakima to Pullman.*

ELLENSBURG

If you get away from the tourist ghetto by the freeway, as you should, this college-and-cowboy town projects a pleasant ease. Its famous Labor Day rodeo, now in its sixth decade, draws many for its slice-of-life view of rural America.

Architecture. Ellensburg has more than its share of interesting buildings. The downtown area was rebuilt after a devastating fire in 1889. Among the handsome structures still standing are the Davidson Building, on the corner of Pearl and Fourth, and the Masonic Temple, with its intriguing asymmetrical facade. Off on the fringes of town, at Third and Wenas, is a prime example of the Great American Train Station, built late in the last century for the Northern Pacific. Art Deco is represented by the Liberty Theater, at Fifth and Pine, and by the Valley Cafe, whose interior is prime. For modern architecture, turn to the campus of Central Washington University, which displays Fred Bassetti's library and dormitory compound and Kirk/Wallace/McKinley's fine-arts complex. Close to the campus along Ninth Street are tree-lined blocks of attractive turn-of-the-century homes.

Arts. Sarah Spurgeon Gallery in the fine-arts complex at Central presents regional and national exhibits in all media. Monday–Friday, 8am–5pm, October–May. On 14th Street, (509) 963-2665. Summer Theatre, a joint university-community-funded summer stock season, is performed by the Laughing Horse Company, a hodgepodge of students, pro, and semi-pro actors. Plays are staged in another architectural gem: the new Tower Theater on the Central campus, (509) 963-1766. Community Art Gallery, 408½ North Pearl, (509) 925-2670, has nice quarters in an old building, displays good contemporary art, and sells local crafts; open noon to 5pm Tuesday–Saturday.

Olmstead Place, four miles east of town on Squaw Creek Trail Road (off I-90), is a cottonwood log cabin from an 1875 cattle ranch now coming back to life; tours Thursday–Monday, 8am to 5pm, (509) 925-1943.

Yakima River. There are scenic canoe and raft trips to be made through the deep gorges, and the river is one of the finest trout streams in the country; Highway

---

Looking for a particular place? Check the index at the back of this book for individual restaurants, hotels, B&Bs, parks, and more.

821, south of town, follows the gorge. Information about floats and river trips: (509) 925-3137.

Mills Saddle 'n Togs, Fourth and Main, (509) 962-2312, has been outfitting riders and cowboy types for as long as anyone can remember.

RESTAURANTS

The Valley Cafe
Near the corner of
3rd and Main,
(509) 925-3050
103 W Third, Ellensburg
Moderate; beer and wine;
AE, DC, MC, V
Breakfast, lunch, dinner
every day

This 1930s-built bistro, with mahogany booths and back bar, would be an oasis anywhere—but is especially so in cow country. People traveling on business to Ellensburg arrange to arrive around lunchtime just to eat at this airy Art Deco spot. Salads are the choice at lunch. Freshly grated Parmesan, walnuts, and a tangy vinaigrette top the colorful shrimp pasta salad. For breakfast you'll find variations on Mexican huevos, adaptations of the crepe, and an all-American breakfast saute that happily marries hash browns, broccoli, onions, mushrooms, tomatoes, scrambled eggs, and cheese.

Italian concoctions and fresh seafood compose most of the dinner menu: tortellini and chicken saute, coho salmon grilled in herb butter, and cheese-filled tortes. The Valley clearly stays away from anything that resembles red meat. There's a choice list of Washington wines, and there are some bracing espresso drinks. If you want a leisurely look at Ellensburg, this is the place to go. Service, though it favors regulars, has on recent visits been quite efficient.

VANTAGE

Situated on a splendid stretch of the Columbia, Vantage has nothing much in the way of food, but the view from the parking lot of the A&W surpasses that from any root-beer stand known to us.

Ginkgo Petrified Forest State Park has an interpretive center—daily during summer, 10am to 6pm; the rest of the year, by appointment only; (509) 856-2700—that takes you back to the age of dinosaurs; then you can go prospecting for your own finds. It's a lovely spot for a picnic, by the way.

GEORGE

The naturally terraced amphitheater looking west over the Columbia Gorge at **Champs de Brionne Winery** offers a spectacular summer evening setting for musical performances and attracts thousands of people, with big-name performers such as Bob Dylan, Tracy Chapman, Robert Cray, and The Judds; (509) 785-6685. You can bring a picnic, but any liquor must be purchased on the premises. Arrive early, the one country road leading to George is not fit for crowds of this kind.

MOSES LAKE

It's the RV capital of the state, with many campers and boaters attracted by the fishing and hunting around the lakes. The anglers come for trout and perch. You can rent a boat, then motor out to a sandy island in Potholes Reservoir for a picnic or camping.

OTHELLO

RESTAURANTS

Freddie's
2 blocks north of the Old
Hotel on 1st,
(509) 488-2704
67 First Street, Othello
Moderate; full bar;
AE, MC, V
Lunch, dinner every day

★

Freddie's son, Don Eng, now runs the restaurant his father started about 35 years ago. The chef is a Southern California refugee, and brings with him a working knowledge of three cuisines: American, Cantonese, and Mexican. The regular Chinese dishes are still solid, and the Cantonese specials can be quite good.

SPOKANE

The friendly city by Spokane Falls is far more attractive to visit than is generally recognized. It is full of old buildings of note, marvelous parks, and splendid vistas, and the compact downtown is most pleasant for strolling. The city has a sense of maturity about it that's rare for the Northwest, in part because the gold rush of the 1880s brought it wealth and first families a decade or so before such growth came to western Washington cities. Railroads also arrived in the 1880s, making Spokane the major railroad city in the West for a time and consolidating the economy. Fine homes and parks were built—and as Spokane settled into its long afternoon of slow growth, these early manifestations of wealth were not swept away by suburbanization.

    Architecture. The three blocks on West Riverside Avenue between Jefferson and Lincoln contain a wealth of handsome structures in the City Beautiful mode—doubtless the loveliest three blocks in any Northwestern city. **The Spokane Club,** West 1002 Riverside, is a fine example of the work done by Kirtland Cutter, who rebuilt most of the city after the fire of 1889; the **Spokesman-Review Building,** West 999 Riverside, is everybody's idea of what a newspaper building should look like, especially one that is the seat of power for the dominant Cowles family. The **Spokane County Courthouse,** north of the river on West Broadway, is a fairy-tale French

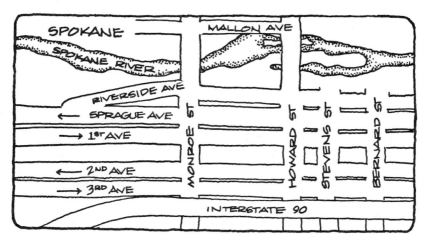

chateau, a Loire Valley clone built in 1895 by Willis A. Ritchie. **City Hall,** on Spokane Falls Boulevard, occupies an old Montgomery Ward building, now elaborately restored in an award-winning blend of the profoundly practical and the aesthetic to full Art Deco elegance. Inside, it is a treasure of art, local and otherwise.

Old homes. Tour Overbluff Drive to see the small palaces of the upper crust, and Cliff Drive or Sumner Avenue on South Hill to view some splendid older homes. Browne's Addition, west of downtown, is full of late-Victorian homes, one of which, **Campbell House,** is part of Cheney Cowles Memorial Museum. A copper king's palace, **Patsy Clark's,** has been restored as a restaurant (see listing).

Parks. Riverfront Park is the pleasant green heart of the old city. Developed out of old railroad yards by Expo '74, the park is now an airy place full of meandering paved paths, with entertainments ranging from ice skating to an IMAX theater. The 1909 carousel is a local landmark, hand-carved by master builder Charles Looff. The music is too loud for children under about four (and most adults), but older kids love a chance to grab the brass ring for a free ride. **Manito Park,** at Grand Blvd and 18th, has a splendidly splashable duck pond and various formal borders and theme gardens: a rose garden, a Japanese garden, a small conservatory. **Finch Arboretum** (west of downtown Spokane), a pleasant picnic site, hosts a modest but attractive collection of trees and shrubs among ravines and a stream. **Bowl and Pitcher** rock formation (located in **Riverside State Park**) is just past the Downriver Golf Course; the park is an ideal place to hike, picnic, or ride a mountain bike. For a panoramic vista of Spokane, visit **Cliff Park** at 13th and Grove.

Culture. Conductor Bruce Ferden has been working with the **Spokane Symphony,** and programs, including a pops series, are lively and innovative. An annual free Labor Day concert in Comstock Park draws thousands of picnicking spectators. Under artistic director Christopher Aponte, the **Spokane Ballet** has improved dramatically and has moved from the Opera House to the more intimate Metropolitan Performing Arts Center. The **Spokane Civic Theatre,** 1020 North Howard, offers a mixed bag of semiprofessional performances each season; the **Interplayers Ensemble Theatre,** 174 South Howard, is a young professional theatre with a full season. Riverfront Park often hosts concerts of jazz, bluegrass, and popular music during the summer; call (509) 456-5512 for information.

Museums. The **Museum of Native American Cultures,** 200 East Cataldo, (509) 326-4550, contains one of the most comprehensive collections of Indian artifacts and archives in the country, housed in an interesting tepee-shaped building. Nearby is **Crosby Library,** on the Gonzaga University campus, 502 East Boone, the crooner's gift to his alma mater, with lots of gold records, an Oscar, and other memorabilia; Bing grew up in the house a block away at 508 East Sharp. **Cheney Cowles Museum** displays pioneer relics, a variety of art in its small gallery, and one of the fine old mansions from Spokane's mining era; 2316 West First Avenue, (509) 456-3931.

Sports. Golf is very good here. Indian Canyon, (509) 747-5353, and Hangman Valley, (509) 448-1212, two of the most beautiful public courses in the nation, have recently attracted a number of professional tournaments; others are Esmeralda, (509) 487-6291, Downriver, (509) 327-5269, The Fairways at West Terrace, (509) 747-8418, Sundance, (509) 466-4040, and Liberty Lake, (509) 255-6233. Spokane's parks and hilly roads offer great **bicycle riding** for serious riders, mountain-bike fans, and family tourists. **Runners** will find themselves in good company; Spokane's annual Bloomsday Run, held during the lilac season on the first Sunday in May, is the second-largest road run in the country, drawing nearly 65,000 runners. The good **ski areas** nearby are: 49 Degrees North, 58 miles north of Spokane on Flowery Trail Road, (509) 935-6649, a good place for beginners; Mount Spokane, 31 miles north on Highway 206, (509) 238-6281, with fair facilities and some challenging runs; and Schweitzer Mountain Resort in Sandpoint, Idaho, (208) 263-9555, with excellent facilities for family skiing. Mount Spokane also has 17 kilometers of groomed cross-country ski trails; a SnoPark pass is required. Trails are also groomed on the city's public golf courses when there's sufficient snow. **Horse races** run in the evening from May through October at Playfair Racecourse, (509) 534-0505. The more popular dog races are run daily year-round at Coeur d'Alene Greyhound Park in Post Falls, Idaho, (208) 773-0545.

RESTAURANTS

Milford's Fish House and Oyster Bar
Corner of Broadway and Monroe, (509) 326-7251
719 N Monroe Street, Spokane
Moderate; full bar;
AE, MC, V
Dinner every day

★★

Spokane's oldest fish house offers simple decor—exposed brick, red-and-white checkered tablecloths, a few green plants—and good food at reasonable prices. Check the fresh list, updated daily, for best bets, and don't hesitate to ask the waiter for recommendations. Fresh salmon, baked or poached, is available in season, and the halibut is always a winner. Service can be slow, especially in the trendy Oyster Bar. Reservations are a must unless you don't mind a wait.

Moreland's
2 blocks north of River-side on Main at Howard, (509) 747-9830
216 Howard Street, (skywalk level), Spokane
Moderate; full bar;
AE, MC, V
Lunch Mon-Sat, dinner Tues-Sat

★★

As you enter the historic Bennett Block building, your nose leads you up the stairs to Moreland's. The new furnishings still feature oak, exposed brick, brass, and lacy doilies, the design of which has been repeated in the etched windows. Cafeteria-style lunches feature a consistently good soup or casserole option, and picnic specials offer combinations of fruits, cheeses, salmon pate, and breads. Premium wines are available by the glass, and the selection constitutes a revolving tour of the Northwest. Dinner at Moreland's is always a treat; the specials based on lamb or pork are a welcome sight-and-savory in this steak town. The excellent mustard-marinated rack of lamb is deservedly a local favorite.

Auntie's Bookstore and Cafe
In the middle of town, between Washington and Bernard, (509) 838-0206
313 Riverside Avenue, Spokane
Inexpensive; no alcohol; MC, V
Breakfast, dinner Mon-Sat, lunch every day

★

This cheerful cafe-in-a-bookstore makes a great place to settle with a cup of coffee and a good read. It's so casual, in fact, that many lingerers have fallen prey to the vigilant meter maid. Soups, salads, pasta, and dessert are all made daily from scratch. The thick and hearty lentil soup is the obvious favorite. On a chilly day, try the melted cheese and mushroom sandwich, spiced with a mild salsa. Breakfasts consist of muffins, cinnamon rolls, or bagels, and coffee.

Clinkerdagger's
Just off Monroe in the Flour Mill, (509) 328-5965
621 W Mallon Avenue, Spokane

Located in the Flour Mill, Clinkerdagger's offers consistently good food of the chicken and steak variety, basic but well handled. When fresh seafood is available, there might be four or five specials featuring fish and lobster. Presentation is attractive. Even with reservations, expect

Moderate; full bar;
AE, MC, V
Lunch Mon-Sat, dinner
every day

a lengthy wait in the bar. In the spring, when the Spokane River is rushing, the views from the window tables are exciting.

Lindaman's Gourmet-to-Go, Inc.

South on Stevens to
Grand, (509) 838-3000
1235 S Grand Avenue,
Spokane
Moderate; beer and wine;
MC, V
Breakfast, lunch, dinner
Mon-Sat

Native palates think Marilee Lindaman may be doing the most innovative cooking of anyone in Spokane—even though she boldly serves dinner on paper plates. The menu changes daily, although you might encounter some regulars such as chiles rellenos, smoked salmon lasagne, or salmon en croute (layered with wild rice, asparagus, ricotta, and dill sauce in a cottage-cheese pastry). The cafe, housed in a former grocery store, is without pretense. Breakfast is simple: fresh muffins and scones and good, strong coffee served in real mugs. Take-out is as popular here as eating in.

Niko's Greek & Middle Eastern Restaurant

2 blocks off Sprague,
(509) 928-9590
321 S Dishman-Mika
Road, Spokane
Inexpensive; beer and
wine; AE, MC, V
Lunch Mon-Fri, dinner
every day

Niko's is deservedly popular locally for traditional Greek food, much of which is homemade in this modest taverna-style restaurant. Lamb is especially well treated here, and the garlicky, smooth hummus can be ordered as an entree with a plate of vegetables or pita. The Greek salads have plenty of salty, strong feta and Greek olives; the baklava is loaded with honey and nuts between layers of phyllo. There's also a chocolava. Thursday is belly-dancing night; Sunday is a five-course Moroccan dinner (reservations are recommended) featuring rack of lamb or marinated kabobs of chicken, lamb, or beef, or half-chicken with oregano and lemon. Niko II is located at W 720 Sprague Avenue, (509) 624-7444.

The Onion

On Riverside at Burnard,
(509) 747-3852
302 W Riverside Avenue,
Spokane
Inexpensive; full bar;
AE, DC, MC, V
Lunch, dinner every day

The magnificent old bar is a relic of the days when the building that houses this eatery, The St. Regis, was a fine hotel. Some of the furnishings—the pressed-tin ceiling, the wood dividers—are also from the original hotel. The Onion set the standard in Spokane for gourmet hamburgers, and they're still local classics. The beer selection would be outstanding anywhere; fruit daiquiris are a specialty. (The huckleberry daiquiris—and the other huckleberry offerings such as huckleberries over cheese-cake—are seasonal favorites.) A young, informal crowd dominates on most nights, especially on Monday nights during NFL football season; the service can be slow, exceeded only by the wait for a table.

Patsy Clark's

15 blocks west of
downtown,
(509) 838-8300
2208 W Second Avenue,
Spokane

Patrick F. Clark, "Patsy" to his friends, arrived in America in 1870 at the age of 20, and by the time he was 40 he was a millionaire many times over, thanks to the success of Montana's Anaconda Mine. Naturally anxious to display his success, he instructed architect Kirt-

Expensive; full bar;
AE, DC, MC, V
Dinner every day,
brunch Sun

land Cutter to build him the finest mansion he could conceive—never mind the cost. Cutter, a man who had considerable experience creating luxury, did his best for Patsy. Marble was shipped in from Italy, wood carvings and clocks from England, a mural from France, and a spectacular stained-glass window (with more than 4,000 pieces) standing 14 feet tall from Tiffany's of New York. It all went into what is, brick for brick, one of the finest mansions in the Northwest.

While most entrees are well handled and presented attractively, the kitchen has been cutting corners with the quality of produce and fish it chooses. We suggest you go on a special occasion—when elegant atmosphere and fine service are important—and order the New Zealand lamb marinated 24 hours in a red-wine marinade.

Since the restaurant doubles as one of Spokane's more intriguing tourist sights, you should find some excuse to go by, even if it's only for a drink (the wine list is one of the best in the area). The bar, located in the mansion's original wood-paneled dining room (where hand-carved faces edge the beamed ceiling), is relaxing and luxurious. Drinks on the second-story verandah can be pleasant on a summer evening. Sunday brunch requires reservations.

Thai Cafe

Sprague at Washington,
(509) 838-4783
410 W Sprague Avenue,
Spokane
Inexpensive; beer and
wine; no credit cards,
checks ok
Lunch Mon-Fri, dinner
Mon-Sat

You won't just stumble into this ethnic oasis in the eastern Washington desert. Its location off the beaten track of the downtown skywalk system keeps this Thai restaurant exclusive to those in the know. A waft of curry greets patrons at the door; and you'll find curry seasonings, along with coconut milk and peanuts, in most of the entrees. If you ask, the cooks will spice the dishes to the degree of hotness you want; but be aware that "medium" is hot by the standards of most American palates. We've yet to be disappointed with any of the 12 chicken selections. If you can't decide, try the Praramrlongsong chicken and fresh spinach with peanut sauce. And don't miss the Thai desserts—black rice pudding over ice cream or warm bananas in coconut milk.

Azar's

Take the Hamilton Street
exit off I-90,
(509) 487-0132
3818 N Nevada, Spokane
Inexpensive; no credit
cards; checks ok
Breakfast, lunch every
day, dinner Mon-Sat

The chrome doesn't shine at this Lebanese eatery, but those who seek out ethnic food know that more effort is put into Azar's food than into its sanitation. Close your eyes—and you won't be disappointed. Everything is fresh; if you can't decide, try the gyros, which, although it's unusual because it's made with beef and lamb, is especially tasty. Breakfasts are basic; lunches and dinners feature more interesting fare.

Coyote Cafe

Corner of 3rd and Wall,
(509) 747-8800

The walls of this Mexican place are covered with offbeat art, and the service is prompt and relentlessly cheerful. If you want to be in and out in 20 minutes, that's no prob-

700 W Third Avenue,
Spokane
Inexpensive; beer and
wine; MC, V
Lunch, dinner every day

lem. Food includes standard south-of-the-border fare—tacos and burritos, refried beans and fajitas—all of which are enhanced by the large, icy margaritas. The menu is reasonably priced.

Europa Pizzeria Restaurant

North side of the railroad
trestle downtown,
(509) 455-4051
125 S Wall Street,
Spokane
Inexpensive; beer and
wine; no credit cards;
local checks ok
Lunch, dinner Tues-Sat

Exposed brick walls and bare wood give this place a certain Old World charm, and the relaxed atmosphere attracts well-tempered students from the adjacent colleges. The food fits collegiate needs well: Yugoslavian pizza and pita roll-ups. The large calzones can be overwhelming, especially as a midday meal. Dinners often feature Slavic fare such as stuffed cabbage. The service is cheerful, advice reliable, and pace relaxed enough for you to feel entirely comfortable settling in with a beer and a book.

Howard Street Cafe

Near the corner of
Spokane Falls Blvd and
Howard, across from
Riverfront Park,
(509) 624-6003
221 N Howard Street,
Spokane
Moderate; beer and wine;
MC, V
Lunch, dinner Mon-Sat

Healthful eating is uppermost in the minds of owners Sheila Collins and Nina Lyman, who use few cream sauces in their foods, preferring to season with fresh herbs, wine, and olive oil. However, the decor—a converted downtown coffee shop—falls short as a backdrop for the interesting food. If you're looking for ambience, take your meal a half-block to Riverfront Park for a picnic. The cafeteria-style eatery touts an interesting selection of pasta salads for lunch. The spicy Sichuan pasta is good and served with an order of the focaccia, a heavy bread with herbs and cheese.

LODGINGS

Fotheringham House

On W 2nd at Hemlock,
(509) 838-4363
2128 W Second Avenue,
Spokane, WA 99204
Moderate; AE, MC, V

In 1891 an early mayor of Spokane showed remarkable foresight by building what was going to become one of Spokane's most charming hostelries, next to the mansion that was going to become one of its favorite special-occasion restaurants—Patsy Clark's. In historic Browne's Addition, one of the oldest residential districts in town, Fotheringham House is a well-preserved classic in the Victorian style, with hand-carved woodwork, tin ceilings, and an open, carved staircase. By the fireplace in the main room, guests are treated to an afternoon glass of wine. Three guest rooms feature big, comfortable beds and period furniture. The Pink Room is enchanting in winter, warm and snug, with a fetching view of snowy trees. The host, Sue Holter, fixes whole-wheat croissants as part of an expanded continental breakfast.

Cavanaugh's Inn at the Park

Off Division,
(509) 326-8000
303 W North River
Drive, Spokane, WA
99201

This hotel on the bank of the river across from Riverfront Park has 266 rooms, many with southern views of downtown Spokane (and a few of the hydropower weir). The spacious lobby is the center of the main building, and all seven stories of rooms open out to it; it can be noisy, so specify a quiet corner room or perhaps one in

Moderate; AE, DC, MC, V

the new wing at the east end of the hotel, away from the lobby and busy Washington Street. The attractive restaurant overlooks the river, but the food is perfunctory.

Sheraton Spokane Hotel

In the River Park Center, (509) 455-9600 322 N Spokane Falls Court, Spokane, WA 99220 Moderate; AE, DC, MC, V

Right on the riverfront next to the Convention Center and the Opera House, this large hotel occupies an ideal location for visitors to downtown Spokane. The main shopping district and Riverfront Park are within an easy walk. This 15-year-old hotel is beginning to show signs of old age, but the rooms are airy and pleasant, many with attractive river views, and the corner rooms are spacious indeed. The bathrooms are large and very clean. The pool is enclosed in a greenhouse atrium—very cozy in the winter. The staff is courteous and helpful, the rates surprisingly modest.

Waverly Place

Take the Division Street exit off I-90 and head north to Waverly Place, (509) 328-1856 709 W Waverly Place, Spokane Moderate; MC, V

Across the street from what was once a racetrack, Waverly Place retains the elegance of the Victorian era. The track is now Corbin Park, a lovely oval with a couple of tennis courts, a tree canopy, and plenty of places to walk. Guests at this bed and breakfast can sit on the broad porch overlooking the park and sip lemonade. There are three guest rooms: The Skinner Suite (named for the man who built the house, Harry J. Skinner), decorated in a country motif with a brass bed, a breakfast table, and a private bath; Anna's Room, with a window seat overlooking the park; and the Garden Room, (the last two share a bath). Fresh fruit, Swedish pancakes with huckleberry sauce, sausage, and coffee are a sample of the breakfast fare.

West Coast Ridpath Hotel

In the heart of downtown, (509) 838-2711 515 W Sprague Avenue, Spokane, WA 99204 Moderate; AE, DC, MC, V Lunch Mon-Fri, dinner Mon-Sat, brunch Sun

The rooms are pleasant and spacious, and those in the tower overlook the city. The downtown location is as convenient as they come. At press time the hotel was undergoing a major renovation, due to be completed by fall 1989. This place is popular with conventioneers and tourists, and some of the public areas can be crowded, but the mood here is always convivial.

The rooftop restaurant, Ankeny's, boasts a grand view of Spokane. At night, when all is glittering and reflected repeatedly by the smoked glass and mirrors of the interior decor, the effect can be dazzling, glitzy, or just plain bewildering. The food is somewhat predictable, although the Sunday brunch continually surprises us. The bar really hops on weekends, despite some fairly dubious live music.

Wondering about our standards? We rate establishments on value, performance measured against the place's goals, uniqueness, enjoyability, loyalty of clientele, cleanliness, excellence and ambition of the cooking, and professionalism of the service. For an explanation of the star system, see the Introduction.

NEWPORT

RESTAURANTS

**Fay's Lounge
and Steak House**

*On the Idaho side of the
Pend Oreille Bridge,
(208) 437-3926
402 N Idaho Avenue,
Oldtown, Idaho
Inexpensive; full bar;
MC, V
Lunch, dinner Mon-Sat*

Technically, Fay's is on the wrong side of the tracks for this book. We decided to make an exception. The eatery is located in Oldtown, Idaho, a community separated from Newport, Washington, by the railroad tracks that serve as the state line. The original owner, Sharon McEvers, and her daughters Debbie and Kristina are running this traditional meat-and-potatoes restaurant after a 3½-year hiatus. Tender, perfectly cooked steak is the staple here, sided with—what else—salad and baked potato. Atmosphere is bland. But you won't find any better along the Washington-Idaho border north of Spokane.

COLVILLE

The Colville River Valley has tiny farming communities, but outdoor recreation—fishing and cross-country skiing, primarily—is beginning to draw many to the pristine area.

Hale's Ales is a microbrewery in the raw, but owner Michael Hale generally welcomes visitors after 5pm, when the day's brewing work is done. Call ahead. There are wall taps for the brews: Hale's pale ale, bitter, and porter, Moss Bay ale, and seasonal specialties. They also retail by the keg. 410 North Washington, (509) 684-6503.

RESTAURANTS

The Roadhouse

*½ mile south of Colville
on Highway 395,
(509) 684-3021
Moderate; full bar;
AE, MC, V
Lunch Tues-Fri,
dinner Tues-Sat*

A few things have changed around John and Sarah Lee Pilley's wonderful restaurant—namely, John's gone. But don't worry, he's not forgotten, just off in Spokane with a good job and hunting up investors for the projected Spokane branch of The Roadhouse. In the meantime, Sarah Lee has the lonely helm.

The Pilleys lovingly restored the century-old farmhouse which sits on a grassy knoll overlooking the valley. Inside, Sarah Lee serves enormous amounts of delightful, carefully prepared Southern cuisine. It's fixed-price ($12.50 for adults, $4.50 for kids under 13) with two seatings on Friday and Saturday (5:30pm and 7:30pm), one on Tuesday through Thursday (6:30pm). You need reservations.

With this much food, we remain astonished that it's consistently good. Dinner begins with a hot loaf of bread and soup (perhaps split pea, or clam chowder on Fridays), then salad with a delicious blue cheese or home-style ranch dressing (which the Pilleys make themselves and market locally). Fresh, hot cornbread comes with the salad. For the main course you might select from heaping platters of fried chicken, seafood fettuccine, and prime rib—as much of each as you desire. Then the accompaniments: eggplant Parmesan, glazed carrots, Southern green beans, steamed cabbage, parsleyed new potatoes. Fruit follows, then dessert: chocolate torte or hot pecan pie. A new lounge upstairs allows folks to linger longer. You will waddle out contentedly, wishing you'd grown up in the South.

CURLEW

RESTAURANTS

The Riverside Restaurant and Lounge
On the main drag,
(509) 779-4813
813 River Street, Curlew
Moderate; full bar;
MC, V
Dinner Wed-Sun

Curlew's downtown cafe has gained quite a reputation among backcountry hikers and mountain climbers. The setting is pleasant, comfortable, and funky: wooden tables and chairs and a wooden bar, all of them looking more or less handmade.

The dining room has a large wood stove. There's a lovely view of the river, the produce is fresh, and the food is fairly simple but always good: fresh prawns in homemade beer batter or all-American thick sirloins, accompanied by steamed vegetables.

WAUCONDA

RESTAURANTS

The Wauconda Cafe, General Store and Post Office
The only thing in town,
(509) 486-4010
2432 Highway 20,
Wauconda
Inexpensive; beer
and wine; V
Breakfast, lunch, dinner
every day

If you want atmosphere, here it is in this small general-store-cum-gas-station-cum-post-office-cum-restaurant. A lunch counter with a few booths is squeezed between the general store and the dining room. It's a popular hangout for the local folk, both rancher-types and counter-culturalists. The view is out across the rolling meadows so typical of the Okanogan Highlands, with a few weatherbeaten barns enhancing the horizon and wildflowers in the spring.

New owner Bruce Johnson has changed the menu a bit, but the food remains homemade and simple: tasty burgers, milk shakes, sandwiches, and homemade soups for lunch; sauteed prawns, prime rib, big salads for dinner. Breakfast wasn't up to snuff on a recent visit.

OROVILLE

RESTAURANTS

Don Ernesto's
Main and Central,
(509) 476-2339
Main Street, Oroville
Inexpensive; full bar;

The hand-colored and -embellished menus give you an idea of the extra care taken at this oasis of good Mexican food, now located in the old Orada Theater. They still serve a long menu of tacos, enchiladas, burritos, and so forth, plus tamales, menudo, and chile verde, all well

AE, DC, MC, V
Lunch, dinner every day

prepared. The decor is better than it used to be, and they now have some appealing extras: fried ice cream, swimming-pool-sized margaritas, and live music Friday and Saturday nights.

LODGINGS

Sun Cove Resort
11 miles southwest of Oroville, (509) 476-2223
Mail: Rte 2, Box 1294, Oroville, WA 98844
Moderate; MC, V

For 18 years John and Marge Donoghue have run this cozy lakefront hideaway that's both comfortable and away from it all. Reasonably priced cabins are squeaky clean and fully stocked with kitchen utensils (even soap for the dishes), bedding, and linens. Ten of these rustic cabins sleep four each comfortably. There are also two- and three-bedroom cottages for families of six or eight; a one-week minimum stay is required.

You'll undoubtedly want to stay longer, though. There's excellent rainbow trout fishing in two-mile-long Wannacut Lake, swimming in a heated pool, kayaking, canoeing, sailing, horseback riding, a game and toy center for youngsters, even a small library and a tanning center. The family that runs the store and snack bar makes scrumptious pies. If there's a drawback, it's the dusty, narrow drive in to the resort—but that's a small price to pay for such seclusion.

OMAK

The famous—and controversial—Suicide Race is the climax of the Omak Stampede the second weekend each August. At the end of each of the four rodeos that take place over the three-day weekend, a torrent of horses and riders pours down a steep embankment, across the Okanogan River, and into the arena. No one's ever been killed during the races since the race started in 1933, but plenty of horses have broken their legs.

Indian tribes from all over the Pacific Northwest gather here during the Stampede to celebrate their heritage. A tepee Indian village is constructed, and traditional games and dances are performed.

RESTAURANTS

Breadline Cafe
Ash and 1st,
(509) 826-5836
102 S Ash Street, Omak
Inexpensive; beer and wine; MC, V
Breakfast, lunch Mon-Sat, dinner Fri

New age gourmet fare is alive and well here in the heart of steak and Stampede country. The big, informal, cheerfully cluttered eatery, in the back of a craftsy mini-mall, serves home-style breakfasts and creative lunches with daily specials. You watch the whole-grain bread come out of the oven as your hearty sandwich or salad is prepared. Their newest salad, Washington's Best, combines lettuce, smoked salmon, tomato, and cucumber in a unique cranberry dressing (especially tasty), served with a hot whole-grain roll. Dinner is a treat, with live music (ranging from Celtic folk to r&b) and entrees such as fresh pasta, crepes, and bouillabaisse. The Hungarian walnut crepe with chocolate espresso sauce finishes you off.

OKANOGAN

LODGINGS

U and I Motel
*Off Highway 97 on old
97,* (509) 422-2920
*838 Second Avenue N,
Okanogan
Mail: PO Box 549,
Okanogan, WA 98840
Inexpensive; MC, V*

The name suits this family-run place's folksiness. It's not much to look at from its front on the old back road between Okanogan and Omak, but a closer look uncovers a more-than-usually pleasant little nook for hiding away from it all. The two-room cabinettes are less than spacious, but they're clean and cozily done up in rustic paneling. They are a deal at $30, as are one-roomers with a double bed for $24. Best of all, the whole back yard of the motel is a grassy lawn and flower garden fronting on the tranquil Okanogan. Grab a deck chair, cast a fishing line, and watch the river flow. Pets okay.

COULEE DAM

LODGINGS

Coulee House Motel
Birch and Roosevelt,
(509) 633-1101
*110 Roosevelt Avenue,
Coulee Dam, WA 99116
Moderate; AE, DC,
MC, V*

With a great view of the dam, this motel has decent amenities—pool, sauna, and refrigerators in some of the large, clean rooms, to name a few. At night you can sit on the tiny lanai outside your room and watch the new animated laser-light show (summers only) over the dam as the water cascades past.

GRAND COULEE

Grand, yes—this is a wonderful area from which to appreciate the outsized dimensions of the landscape and the geological forces that made it. The Columbia, as it slices through central Washington, has an eerie power: the water rushes by in silky strength through enormous chasms. The river, the second-largest in volume in the nation, traverses a valley of staggering scale; in prehistoric times glacier-fed water created a river with the largest flow of water ever known.

Grand Coulee Dam is one of the largest structures on the earth—tall as a 46-story building, with a spillway twice the height of Niagara, and a length as great as a dozen city blocks. The dam, completed in 1941, was originally intended more to irrigate the desert than to produce electricity; so much power was generated, however, that the dam became a magnet for the nation's aluminum industry. The north-face extension (completed in 1975) was designed by Marcel Breuer, a great practitioner of the International Style, and the heroic scale of the concrete is quite magnificent. There are daily guided and self-guided tours of the dam: 8:30am–10pm (summer); 9am–5pm (winter); (509) 633-9265.

Eccentric inventor Emil Gehrke amassed an oddly compelling **windmill collection** at North Dam Park on Highway 155 between Electric City and Grand Coulee. Four hardhats tilted sideways catch the wind, cups and saucers twirl around a central teapot—it's whimsical and fascinating.

Houseboating. Until two years ago, Lake Roosevelt was untapped by the RV-on-pontoons fleet. Now there are 30 houseboats available to explore the 150-mile-long lake, and most book up early for the summer months. The sun's almost guaranteed, and all you need to bring is food, bed linens, and your bathing suit; boats are moored at Kelly Ferry Marina, 14 miles north of Wilbur, (800) 648-LAKE.

CRESTON

RESTAURANTS

Deb's Cafe
Highway 2, in the middle of town, (509) 636-3345
600 Watson, Creston
Inexpensive; full bar; MC, V
Breakfast, lunch, dinner every day

The glory days of Deb Cobenhaver, a world-champion rodeo rider back in the mid-1950s, are kept in a kind of time capsule here. Outside, there is a wooden porch, like a stage-set saloon; inside, the place is strewn with trophies, photos, and saddles. Cowboy-hatted men and women shoot pool in the bar or line up at the lunch counter.

The main cafe opens early for its hearty breakfasts with homemade cinnamon rolls; at lunch there are a few decent sandwiches, served with home-cut fries; dinner is steaks—natch—and on Saturday nights they grill your steak out back. There's also an all-you-can-eat barbecued rib special with salad bar and great Western music.

SOAP LAKE

Early settlers named the lake for its unusually high alkali content, which gives the water a soapy feel.

Dry Falls, off Route 17 north of town, is the place where the torrential Columbia once crashed over falls three miles wide and 400 feet high; an interpretive center (Wednesday–Sunday, 10–6, summer) explains the local geology, which has been equated with surface features of Mars. From this lookout, you can also see **Sun Lakes**, which are actually puddles left behind by the ancient Columbia. It's RV territory, but the waters are prime spots for swimming and fishing; (509) 632-5583.

RESTAURANTS

Don's
Corner of Main and Canna, (509) 246-1217
14 Canna Street, Soap Lake
Moderate; full bar; no credit cards; checks ok
Lunch Mon-Fri, dinner every day

Here's the most popular steak-and-seafood eatery in the region, where man-sized meals are served in a dark, slightly seamy interior. Authentic Greek cuisine, served Mondays and Fridays only (until the food is gone), is worth stopping in for: owner Marina Romary is quite a character, and she and her family have made the Greek theme serve as the center for the Greek Festival held in town every summer.

QUINCY

LODGINGS

Crescent Bar Resort
Route 28, 7 miles west of Quincy, (509) 787-1304

Great for families, this is a collection of Mediterranean-style condo units surrounding a big swimming pool and Jacuzzi; other amenities include a flat 9-hole golf course,

Mail: 864 Crescent Bar Road #22, Quincy, WA 98848
Expensive; MC, V

four tennis courts, water-skiing on the Columbia River, and boating (public boat launch available). Units start at $75 for a studio unit with living room, kitchenette, bathroom, and bedroom divided by an accordion door. Perhaps the biggest advantages are the smallness of the resort (with less than half the units around the pool), and the splendid setting beneath the brooding basalt cliffs of the river.

You can get all meals in the undistinguished restaurant. The resort is very hot in the summer, but the heat is dry and invigorating.

WENATCHEE

You're in the heart of apple country, with an Apple Blossom Festival the first part of May.

Ohme Gardens, three miles north on Route 97, is a 600-foot-high promontory transformed into an Edenic retreat, with a fastidiously created natural alpine ecosystem patterned after high mountain country. Splendid views of the valley and the Columbia River, (509) 662-5785.

Mission Ridge, 13 miles southwest on Squilchuck Road, offers some of the best powder snow in the region, served by four chair lifts (cross-country skiing too), (509) 663-7631. In May, the Ridge-to-River Pentathlon is an impressive sporting event.

Rocky Reach Dam, six miles north on Route 97, offers a beautiful picnic and playground area (locals marry on the well-kept grounds), plus a fish-viewing room. Inside the dam are two large galleries devoted to the history of the region.

RESTAURANTS

John Horan House Restaurant
South on Easy Street to Horan, (509) 663-0018
2 Horan Road, Wenatchee
Moderate; full bar; MC, V
Dinner Tues-Sat

You'll have to scout a bit to find this delightful restaurant, set in the cozy riverbank house built in 1896 by Mike Horan, Wenatchee's self-made "Apple King." His son John's furnishings are the ones you see, down to the decor in the living room and the antique velvet hats in the closet upstairs—sort of a museum of family memorabilia. The sense of history is unforced and irresistible, almost as if the Apple King himself had invited you over for dinner.

This is also where you'll find the finest dinner in the area, under the careful direction of Mark Lanfear and Ken Shores. They are forever experimenting, and the dinner-only menu is brief, changing every season. Reports are consistently good. Try the crisp salad with vinaigrette dressing, grilled salmon in a light vermouth and caper sauce, chicken with Brazil nuts, and heavenly hot sourdough rolls. A cold barbecued pork tenderloin, a recipe developed by the duo, gets applause throughout the region. Berries with homemade vanilla ice cream and an indulgent chocolate-pecan brownie are two of the many desserts; the wine list includes mostly the pick of the regionals. After dinner, you can stroll the attractive little lawn and herb garden.

New Orleans Kitchen

Just before the East
Wenatchee bridge on
Mission at ferry,
(509) 663-3167
928 S Mission Street,
Wenatchee
Moderate; beer and wine;
no credit cards; checks ok
Dinner Wed-Sat

Lots of flavor here—and it's not all in the food. You can select Creole, Cajun, or classic French eats from the extensive menu offered in this ramshackle restaurant in Wenatchee's south end. Oysters Bienville is a good choice for a starter, although the blackened prime rib comes with its own spicy "bones" as an appetizer. Catfish and specials like crab-stuffed quail are prepared with equal expertise. For dessert, Fudge, Fudge, Fudge (chocolate spoon cake with layers of fudge poured onto vanilla ice cream, whipped cream, and pecans) is unbelievable.

Jim Swickard, the seasoned restaurant owner-manager-waiter-cook, wants to keep things small and intimate, as though you were at his place for dinner. It's a get-to-know-your-neighbor atmosphere, and if Swickard doesn't pour the wine fast enough, he doesn't mind if you do it yourself. Reservations are a good idea.

Steven's at Mission Square

1 block off Wenatchee at
2nd and Mission,
(509) 663-6573
218 N Mission Street,
Wenatchee
Moderate; full bar;
AE, MC, V
Lunch Mon-Fri,
dinner every day

Steven's is a handsome place where Wenatchee's premier chef Steve Gordon serves Northwest cuisine with a few international excursions. The split-level dining room is elegant in a trendy sort of way, with potted plants; full-length mirrors reflect the well-dressed clientele. Pasta and seafood dishes are served here with pride and a flourish, from fettuccine with asparagus and prosciutto to apricot-honey-mustard chicken with sweet basil on a bed of spinach, pecans, and Bermuda onions. We've had best luck with the specials (East Coast scallops sauteed with red and green bell peppers, artichoke hearts, and scallions, in a tomato sauce). Bread is freshly baked and warm, and desserts are first-rate, especially rich triangles of chocolate-peanut-butter ice cream pie or chocolate hazelnut cheesecake.

The Windmill

1½ blocks west of Miller,
on the main drag,
(509) 663-3478
1501 N Wenatchee
Avenue, Wenatchee
Moderate; beer and wine;
AE, MC, V
Dinner Tues-Sat
(summer Mon-Sat)

A constantly changing number on a blackboard keeps track of the number of steaks sold at this great steakhouse. On our last visit it was 171,000. That's not the number of steaks sold since The Windmill opened 69 years ago, that's since January 1982, when Pat and Linda Jackson took over as owners, and we haven't heard of even one that wasn't terrific.

Waitresses here don't come and go—they stay and stay, sporting pins that proudly declare the number of years they've served. The meals, too, are time-tested and classic. You arrive and, usually, face a short, sociable wait (which does wonders for your appetite, so don't be put off by it). They start you off with breadsticks and a relish tray, a lettuce salad, and a bottle of wine. There are seafood and pork chops, but don't be a fool—order the steak! You'll get a hunk of aged, high-quality beef, unblemished by tenderizers, cut when you order it, just the way you like (with an emphasis on trimming fat), and accompanied by fries or a baked potato. Ritual dictates that you finish with a piece of one of the magnificent pies, baked fresh daily.

With a sigh, you'll realize you've just glimpsed a perfect specimen of what may be this country's equivalent of an Italian trattoria or a French country cafe: a US prime steak house.

El Abuelo

Chehalis and Mission,
(509) 662-7331
601 S Mission Street,
Wenatchee
Inexpensive; full bar;
MC, V
Lunch, dinner every day

Amigos, you're never a stranger at El Abuelo. Jose Garcia, his family, and friends are serving their native Mexican dishes in a festive, crowded atmosphere of camaraderie—always with a word of Spanish mixed into the conversation. In fact, some of the waiters speak very little English, and that causes some good-natured confusion.

This has quickly become one of the most popular spots to eat in the area. The combination dinners, served on 13-inch plates, are heaped high with rice and beans on the side. Try the pork enchiladas with verde (tomatillo) sauce or chorizo huevos (eggs with spicy Mexican sausage). Both are served with an authentic Mexican coleslaw.

There are large margaritas and pina coladas, as well as a good range of Mexican beers. You might have to wait to be seated, but it won't be for naught. Service is quick and as warm as the chunky salsa.

LODGINGS

The Chieftain

Half a block from the
corner of 9th,
(509) 663-8141,
toll-free (800) 572-4456
1005 N Wenatchee
Avenue, Wenatchee,
WA 98801
Moderate; AE,
DC, MC, V

The motels all line up along Wenatchee Avenue, but this one stands out for its dependable quality year after year (since 1928). It's popular with the locals, who come for executive lunches, brunches after church on Sunday, or the famous prime rib in the evening. Guests will note that rooms are larger than those of the Chieftain's cousins down the pike. Ask for rooms in the newer wing, the "executive rooms," and you'll be surprised what spacious quarters you've got for about $40. There's a swimming pool, a hot tub, and a helicopter pad (which doubles as a basketball court). You can bring your pet with advance notice.

West Coast Wenatchee Center Hotel

Wenatchee and 2nd,
(509) 662-1234
201 N Wenatchee
Avenue, Wenatchee,
WA 98801
Moderate; AE, MC, V

The newest hotel has a new name, and it's the nicest one on the strip, with its view of the city and the Columbia River. It's elegant, but not overdone for this city. The nine-story hotel has three floors designated nonsmoking, with a total of 14 large moderately priced rooms. A restaurant on the top floor is open for breakfast, lunch, and dinner, and the city's convention center is next door, connected by a sky bridge. The outdoor pool is great under the hot Wenatchee sun. Also available are an indoor pool, a Jacuzzi, and a weight room.

Send us your opinions and tips on the report form at the back of this book.

CHELAN

This resort area is blessed with the springtime perfume of apple blossoms, a 55-mile lake thrusting like a fjord into tall mountains, 300 days a year of sunshine, and good skiing, hunting, fishing, hiking, and sailing. It's been trying to live up to its touristic potential since C.C. Campbell built his hotel here in 1901, but with mixed success so far. Now that time-share condos are springing up near the golf course and B&Bs are blooming near the cross-country trails, the amenities are improving. No one need improve the scenery.

Lake Chelan. The top attraction is the cruise up the lake on an old-fashioned tour boat, *The Lady of the Lake*. The lake is never more than two miles wide (it's also one of the deepest in the world), so you have a sense of slicing right into the Cascades. At Stehekin, the head of the lake, you can check out craft shops, take a bus tour, eat a barbecue lunch, and get back on board for the return voyage. The tour boat departs Chelan at 8:30am daily in summer, three or four days a week off-season, and returns in the late afternoon; rates are $19 per person round-trip; kids six to eleven years are half price. No reservations needed. More info: The Lake Chelan Boat Company, (509) 682-2224. Or you can fly up to Stehekin, tour the valley, and be back the same day: Chelan Airways, (509) 682-5555.

Chelan Butte Lookout, nine miles west of Chelan, provides a view of the lake, the Columbia, and the orchard-blanketed countryside.

Sports. Echo Valley, northeast of Chelan, offers rope tows and a poma lift on gentle slopes; Lake Chelan Golf Course, (509) 682-5421 for tee times, is an attractive, sporting course near town; fishing for steelhead, rainbow, cutthroats, and Chinooks is very good, with remote, smaller lakes particularly desirable.

One thousand feet above Lake Chelan sits **Bear Mountain Ranch,** a 5,000-acre estate which recently opened its gates (and 50 kilometers of tracked and skating trails) to cross-country skiers. There's a warming hut with picnic tables and ski videos, and the snow-covered wheatfields provide gentle slopes for beginning tele-markers. Bigger plans are in the works, but for now you just go here to ski. Open for two weeks at Christmas, and weekends December through mid-March; (509) 682-5444.

Nostalgia. St. Andrew's Church, downtown Chelan, is a log edifice, reputedly designed by Stanford White in 1898, still in service; from the Chelan Museum (Woodin Avenue, 1–4pm in summer) you can learn about other restored houses nearby, such as the old Lucas Homestead.

RESTAURANTS

River Park Dining
By the log church near the old bridge,
(509) 682-5626
114 E Woodin, Chelan
Inexpensive; beer and wine; MC, V
Breakfast, lunch every day, dinner Mon-Sat
(closed Sundays in winter)

This hideaway just up the street from Campbell's Lodge had the misfortune of burning to the ground in the fall of '88, but at press time it's set to reopen. They'll still be serving their famous hearty lunches (the veggie sandwich is a meal of avocado, cream cheese, sprouts, tomato, and almonds; the baked potatoes, notably the mushroom-and-cheese-filled baker, will still be enormous), and there'll be a much broader dinner menu, including such things as glazed salmon and grilled chicken. Breakfasts include Belgian waffles and frittatas. It's not all vegetarian fare, but it's all healthy and tasty.

LODGINGS

Campbell's Lodge

*On the lake at 104 W Woodin, (509) 682-2561
Mail: PO Box 278, Chelan, WA 98816
Expensive; AE, DC, MC, V
Breakfast, lunch, dinner every day*

Chelan's venerable resort, whose history goes back to 1901 and includes the recent absorption of its rival to the north, Cannon's, continues to be the most popular place for visitors, with its prime lakeside properties and 120 rooms, many with kitchenettes. Among the facilities you'll find three heated pools and an outdoor Jacuzzi, a sandy beach, and moorage, should you arrive by boat. A new convention center is able to service up to 250 people.

The most dependable restaurant at the lake is here: Campbell House Cafe. The menu changes frequently, but you can usually start the day with pumpkin-apple bread (and fresh strawberries in season), stop in for a spicy Cajun chicken sandwich lunch, or dine upstairs on informal Italian fare like richly flavored cioppino or garlicky prawns and pasta. Reservations here, as at the lodge, are not always easy to get.

Mary Kay's Romantic Whaley Mansion

*2 blocks east of the Highway 97 and Woodin Intersection at 415 Third, (509) 682-5735
Mail: Rte 1, Box 693, Chelan, WA 98816
Expensive; AE, DC, MC, V*

Mary Kay offers a romantic return to the Victorian Age in this historic Chelan home, built in 1911. Overstuffed beds, lace and ruffles, handmade French wallpapers, Belgian velvets, and lots of pink create a paradise for those who like that kind of stuff.

Each of the 11 rooms has a private bath attached, and you can ask for a room with a view of the lake. Our brunch (included in the cost of a room) featured raspberry ice garnished with fresh raspberries marinated in Chambord, topped with Chantilly cream; brioche; eggs Florentine with Italian sausage; and strawberry mousse in baked meringue shells. Mary Kay caters to every want (she's even been known to purchase a negligee for a forgetful honeymooner). A good-bye hug and a hand-dipped chocolate seem to be part of the stay. *The Whaley Mansion High-Cholesterol Happy-Heart-Attack Cookbook* is due out soon.

Darnell's Resort Motel

*Off Manson Highway, (509) 682-2015
Mail: PO Box 506, Chelan, WA 98816
Expensive; AE, MC, V*

Situated right on the shore of the lake, this is a resort especially suited to families. Bedroom suites are large and attractive and all have views. At press time all were being refurbished. Lots of amenities are included with the price of the room: putting green, heated swimming pool, sauna, hot tub, exercise room, shuffleboard, volley ball, badminton, tennis, barbecues, bicycles, rowboats, and canoes. Down the road from Campbell's and the center of town, Darnell's is removed from the hurly-burly that overtakes the town in season.

Love a good bargain? Then you'll really like Seattle Cheap Eats, *a compendium of 230 terrific bargain eateries in and around Seattle, brought to you by the same folks who bring you the* Best Places *series.*

STEHEKIN

A passage to Stehekin, a little community at the head of Lake Chelan, is like traveling to another world, where there is no telephone service. This jumping-off point for exploring the rugged and remote North Cascades National Park can be reached only by a four-hour *Lady of the Lake* boat trip (daily in summer, less frequently in winter), (509) 682-2224; by Chelan Airways float plane, (509) 682-5555; by hiking (write Chelan Ranger District, PO Box 189, Chelan, WA 98816); or by private boat. The boat and the plane will take you to Stehekin from the town of Chelan.. For a shorter boat ride, catch the *Lady* uplake at Field's Point.

Exploring the area is the prime reason for coming here. There are several day hikes, including a lovely one along the lakeshore and another along a stream through the Buckner Orchard, and many more splendid backcountry trails for the serious backpacker. In winter there are some fine touring opportunities for cross-country skiers or snowshoe enthusiasts, although the town pretty much shuts down then. The ranger station at Chelan (open year-round), (509) 682-2576, is an excellent source of information for these activities. A shuttle bus provides transportation from Stehekin to trailheads, campgrounds, fishing holes, and scenic areas, mid-May to mid-October. There are also bicycle, boat, and car rentals at the North Cascades Lodge.

Stehekin Valley Range. The Courtney family picks you up at Stehekin in an old bus and takes you to the farthest end of the valley for seclusion and hearty family-style meals at their ranch. Open in the summer months, their rustic tent-cabins offer a place to bunk and just the basics (a kerosene lamp, showers in the main building) at a decent price ($44 per night per person), plus the food that the whole valley raves about. **Cascade Corrals**, also run by the family, arranges horseback rides and mountain pack trips; (509) 682-4677 or write Stehekin Valley Ranch, Box 36, Stehekin, WA 98852.

If Robbie Breeze Courtney doesn't meet you at the landing, hike or bike up Valley Road for chewy whole-grain breads, cinnamony bearclaws, and soul-satisfying chocolate mousse at the new **Stehekin Pastry Company**. Riding on the tail of the famed Honey Bear Bakery (now in Seattle), this spot is a local favorite for sweet desserts and rich conversation.

LODGINGS

Silver Bay Inn

Take the Lady of the Lake *to Stehekin,*
(509) 682-2212
Mail: PO Box 43,
Stehekin, WA 98852
Moderate; no credit cards;
checks ok

The Silver Bay Inn, located where the Stehekin River flows into Lake Chelan, is a wonderful retreat for those who want to explore the Stehekin Valley. Friendly Kathy and Randall Dinwiddie welcome their guests to this passive-solar home with hikes and stories only the locals know. At breakfast you may find fresh fruit with Devonshire cream, along with an apple pancake, or scrambled eggs with cashews, or orange French toast with blueberries. And if you're there at the right time, Kathy might share a piece of warm blueberry cake with a scoop of Randall's homemade ice cream in the evening while you relax on the deck.

The setting is spectacular: 700 feet of waterfront with a broad green lawn rolling down to the lake. The main house has a master suite (with a two-night minimum to ensure you'll take time to enjoy yourself) decorated in antiques, with a separate sitting room, two view decks, a soaking tub, and a faraway view. Two separate lakeside cabins are remarkably convenient (dishwasher, microwave, all linens) and sleep six. Bicycles and the family car are available.

North Cascades Lodge
Boat landing, Stehekin,
(509) 682-4711
Mail: PO Box 1779,
Chelan, WA 98816
Moderate; MC, V
Breakfast, lunch, dinner
every day (May-Oct)

A rustic resort with a range of accommodations: choose the lodge itself (the larger rooms are much better) or a housekeeping cabin. Suites in simple A-frames or cottages are available for larger parties and are booked early in the season. A hot tub is now available for lodge guests.

The lodge, overlooking the lake, tends to be swarming with tourists who arrive for lunch each day when the *Lady of the Lake* steams up to the dock and sandwiches are mass-produced in the restaurant. Breakfasts and dinners are more relaxed. In the evening there is a varied salad bar, freshly baked bread, steaks, chicken, and seafood. A longtime favorite, the Veggie Potato, filled with vegetables and topped with cheese, sour cream, and mushrooms, is still on the menu. The chef will also prepare your catch if you've been lucky fishing in the local waters. Supplies, which must come from Chelan, are sometimes short.

NACHES

LODGINGS

Whistlin' Jack Lodge
40 miles west of Yakima
on Highway 410,
(509) 658-2433
18936 Highway 410,
Naches, WA 98937
Moderate; AE, MC, V

Nestled in the pines on the Naches River, this rustic lodge at the base of Mount Rainier is named for the marmots that inhabit the rocks in the area. Nearby Chinook Pass is closed almost seven months of the year, but lodge patrons are used to driving the winding road from Yakima. Ideal for all manner of outdoor activity, from hiking and fishing to alpine and cross-country skiing, this 17-unit mountain hideaway has all the comforts of home and then some. Some cottages have hot tubs, and kitchenettes are available in some units. All have river views. The restaurant is not such a bad deal. Its specialty is a 12-inch pan-fried trout. A good family spot.

YAKIMA WINE COUNTRY

The Yakima Valley is a few years away from the boom and fun of California's Napa and Sonoma valleys, but compared to the California industry, it has more space to grow and lustier panoramas to fill the eye. Its burgeoning wine industry has unique restaurants and lodgings to support tourist demand. Also, the price is right. Fine winemakers have made their homes in the valley, and the region's soil has proven ideal for raising premium varietals. You'll find chardonnay, white riesling, chenin blanc, gewurztraminer, merlot, an interesting Limberger or two, and cabernet sauvignon among the bottlings being offered for tasting and/or sale. Several wineries have gift shops. The last week of April is when the barrels are tapped and the tasting gets serious.

Between Yakima and the Tri-Cities are several first-rate wineries; most offer tours and tastings. The Yakima Valley Wine Growers Association (PO Box 39, Grandview, WA 98930) produces a handy brochure, available throughout the region, that lists all the wineries with tasting-room hours and easy-to-follow maps. Don't hesitate to seek out the smaller, out-of-the-way wineries. **Staton Hills**, 71 Gangl Road, Wapato, (509) 877-2112, attractive building, view of Union Gap, picnic grounds. **Bonair Winery**, Zillah, (509) 829-6027, a small, friendly, family-run winery. **Hyatt Vineyards Winery**, Zillah, (509) 829-6333, new, by appointment only. **Zillah Oakes Winery**, Zillah, (509) 829-6990, mostly whites, faces Highway I-82. **Covey Run**, Zillah, (509) 829-6235, very popular, with a sweeping view. **Horizon's Edge**, Zillah, (509) 829-6401, great view from the tasting room. **Cascade Crest Estates**, Sunnyside, (509) 839-WINE, one of the region's newest. **Stewart Vineyards**, Granger, (509) 854-1882, located atop Cherry Hill Road. **Tucker Cellars**, Sunnyside, (509) 837-8701, a family winery and produce stand just off I-82. **Chateau Ste. Michelle**, W Fifth and Avenue B, Grandview, (509) 882-3928, a bit of Washington wine history. **Chinook Wines**, Prosser, (509) 786-2725, a charming, intimate setting with dry whites a specialty. **Hinzerling Vineyards**, 1520 Sheridan, Prosser, (509) 786-2163, rich, red wines. **The Hogue Cellars**, Prosser, (509) 786-4449, an enthusiastic family selling whites. **Yakima River Winery**, Prosser, (509) 786-2805, riverside view, one of the pioneers in the region. **Blackwood Canyon**, Benton City, (509) 588-6249, a winery on rolling hills. **Kiona Vineyards Winery**, Benton City, (509) 588-6716, personable, enthusiastic owners, picnic patio. **Oakwood Cellars**, Benton City, (509) 588-5332, at the foot of Red Mountain. **Columbia Crest Winery**, Paterson, (509) 875-2061, an extensively landscaped and impressive winery, worth the half-hour detour south of Prosser.

Picnics. Grassy vistas and picnic tables can be found at most of the wineries. The **Matterhorn Deli and Sausage Shop** is tops for picnic provisions, 1313 North 16th Avenue (at freeway), (509) 248-1600.

YAKIMA

Irrigation (first tried by the Indians and missionaries here in the 1850s) has made this desert bloom with grapes, apples, mint, and hops. The town also blooms with small conventions.

Front Street Historical District includes a 22-car train that houses shops and restaurants, and the renovated Pacific Fruit Exchange Building, which holds a local farmers' market.

The Greenway Bike Path winds along the Yakima River for 4.6 miles. Start out in Sherman Park on Nob Hill and go to the Selah Gap. Along the way, look for bald eagles and blue herons, or pick out a fishing hole; (509) 453-8280.

The Wine Cellar is a fine place to sample local vintages and orient yourself for a more extended foray into the wine country. Lenore Lambert, the owner, is a good source for local lore. Food products sold. 5 North Front Street, (509) 248-3590.

Interurban Trolley. A restored 1906 trolley provides summer-evening and weekend rides around Yakima. Call (509) 575-1700 for schedules.

Horse racing. Yakima Meadows has live races, November through mid-December; races are beamed by satellite from Seattle's Longacres on weekends,

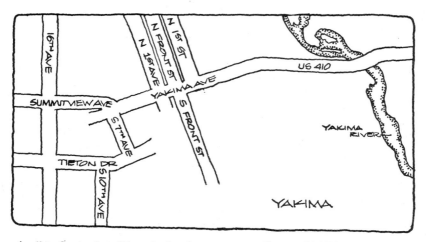

April to September. It's a dandy place to see small-town, Old West racing. 1301 South 10th, (509) 248-3920.

Yakima Valley Museum has handsome pioneer pieces, plus a collection from Yakima's most famous native son, Justice William O. Douglas. 2105 Tieton Drive, (509) 248-0747. Open Wednesday–Sunday.

RESTAURANTS

Gasperetti's Restaurant

6 blocks south of the N Front Street exit off I-82,
(509) 248-0628
1013 N First Street,
Yakima
Moderate; full bar;
AE, MC, V
Dinner Tues-Sat

Almost a quarter century after its beginning, John Gasperetti's Northern Italian restaurant continues to be one of the most innovative establishments in the region. You feel comfortable here in this intimate, leisurely, and friendly place—even if it's your first visit. Originally a family-style restaurant, the place still offers spaghetti with meat sauce and ravioli with meatballs on the left side of the menu, but the daily fresh sheet on the right side displays the real skill of chef Brad Patterson.

The restaurant, too, is double-sided. Those in the know head to the room on the right; first-time patrons may find themselves shunted to the more austere left-hand room. Either way, you'll find pastas made fresh daily with seasonal sauces—light tomato cream, fresh pesto, rabbit with Chianti. You might want to split an appetizer of roasted garlic and Idaho chevre, or the ravioli in lemon butter sauce—the latter is not on the menu, but locals know that its utter simplicity won't fill you up before you sample the entrees. Fresh fish is brought from Seattle several times a week; you may find salmon lightly sauteed and finished with lemon, capers, and cream. This same light touch extends to meat dishes such as Provimi veal with Marsala sauce or pan-fried filet mignon with a Gorgonzola-pecan sauce. And save room for dessert—fresh berries in season; praline cheesecake; something chocolaty; or the pick of a dessert cart with delicacies ranging from light to ultra-rich. The wine list offers excellent bottlings of Washington wines, including many hard-to-find reds. Service is informed, attentive, and unobtrusive. Parking can be a problem on busy N Front Street.

Birchfield Manor

Take exit 34 off Highway 24, head east 2 miles, then south on Birchfield, (509) 452-1960
2018 Birchfield Road, Yakima
Expensive; wine only; AE, MC, V
Dinner Fri-Sun

All in all, Birchfield Manor offers elegant French country dining. When you arrive for your appointed seating, owners Wil and Sandy Masset greet you at the door and show you to your table in the large living room of this antique-filled historic home. Meals here are preceded by their reputation, which is taken *very* seriously. Young children are not welcome, lest they disturb others' enjoyment of the evening. The prix-fixe menu ($25, not including wine) combines the best of local ingredients with Wil's European training as a chef, to produce an ambitious, imaginative meal. If only the ambience were more pleasing. It's the kind of place that deserves candles. Instead, the bad lighting produces a gloomy effect. That said, Birchfield Manor is one of a kind in central Washington, and therefore worth visiting when you're in the mood for a formal evening.

We started with a delicate chicken-liver and brandy pate. Next, a salad with the house special vinaigrette dressing (which can be purchased, bottled, at the Manor). Of the four entrees, we selected the double breast of chicken Florentine and the bouillabaisse; the latter was small, but everything one visitor from Marseilles intended. Washington wines are featured, and the courses—dutifully explained by a friendly waitperson—are both individualistic and complementary to each other.

The Massets have moved across the road to allow for five B&B rooms upstairs ($65–$75 with baths). In contrast to the dark color scheme of the restaurant, bright colors and continental appointments fill each bedroom. An outdoor pool and hot tub are for guest use only.

The Greystone Restaurant

Corner of Front and Yakima, (509) 248-9801
5 N Front Street, Yakima
Moderate; full bar; AE, MC, V
Dinner Tues-Sun

Here, amid turn-of-the-century decor in the historic Lund building, Yakima's young professionals relax and dine. Owners Gayla Games-Hopkins and Nancy Beveridge-Camper took over in 1983, and have developed a menu drawing on family recipes and new creations by chef Steven Woods. Seasonal entrees are thoughtfully chosen and carefully prepared: excellent veal in caper cream sauce, pork tenderloin in a port and green peppercorn sauce, Yakima-apple-and-sausage-stuffed breast of chicken in a brandy cream sauce. Daily specials emphasize fresh seafood. A cafe menu of rotating daily specials (tamales, chicken, and phyllo with jalapeno peppers) and the appetizers from the larger menu make a fine, light supper or late snack in the comfortable lounge. The staff is friendly and helpful. A well-chosen wine list emphasizes regional vintages, with some fine selections from California and Europe, as well as several good wines by the glass.

Desserts are all homemade and change with the seasons—shortcake with fresh rhubarb sauce, local cheeses, and fresh fruits. The piano bar swings.

Ichiban
11th and Tieton,
(509) 248-2585
1107 Tieton Drive,
Yakima
Moderate; full bar;
MC, V
Dinner Tues-Sat

Joe and Susan Sugimoto's authentic Japanese restaurant continues to be a central Washington treat. The restaurant's low-key interior resembles neighborhood eateries in Japan, and the menu is varied. The sushi selection is small but excellent (fresh ingredients come over from Seattle), and the tempura coating is light and crisp. Nebemono (single-pot items) are a specialty, and the menu offers a variety of sukiyaki, donburi, curry dishes (as hot as you wish), and assorted udon. A short drive from downtown Yakima, but worth the extra mile or two.

The Brewery Pub
Head west on Yakima,
turn right on Front,
(509) 575-2922
25½ N Front Street,
Yakima
Inexpensive; beer; MC, V
Lunch, dinner Mon-Sat

Bert Grant is one of the creators of the Northwest's boom in microbreweries, which is bringing back full-flavored, fresh, locally made ales. This cozy establishment (especially popular on weekends) alongside his brewery is fitted out with oak paneling and a dart board, and serves up a British pub menu to accompany his ales. (Only Grant's ales are served.) Homemade soups and Mexican food occasionally appear at lunch. On a given day, you might find the rich, black Russian Imperial Stout or novelties such as the cask-conditioned Scottish Ale and the Yakima Hard Cider. A local wine is available for non-beer-drinkers. A good place to meet friendly Yakima residents.

Santiago's
Close to the intersection
of 1st and Yakima,
(509) 453-1644
111 E Yakima Avenue,
Yakima
Inexpensive; full bar;
MC, V
Lunch, dinner every day

The high ceiling, huge murals, and Southwestern art are festive—if the effect is somewhat over-designed. Still, the price of the Mexican offerings is right, and the taste quite good. The chalupas and the tacos Santiago (with beef, guacamole, and two kinds of cheese) are especially popular. Steak picado (their version of fajitas) was on the menu long before the sizzling sirloin strips became chic at every other Mexican restaurant. Daily specials appear at lunch, and dinner could take the form of smoked salmon fettuccine or Cajun fish. Owners Jar and Debra Arcand are especially proud of their all-Washington list of wines, every one of them available by the glass.

Haleaina
Corner of N 16th and
Highway 12,
(509) 248-1965
1406 N 16th Avenue,
Yakima
Moderate; full bar;
AE, MC, V

On the edge of manmade Lake Aspen, in a business park complex, Haleaina ("restaurant" in Hawaiian) presents a menu inspired by Polynesian and Asian cuisines. A buffet is now served at lunch and dinner. The menu lists such standbys as almond chicken and teriyaki niku (marinated beef on skewers) but also tries its hand at classical presentations like mahi mahi baked in parch-

Lunch Mon-Fri, dinner Mon-Sun, brunch Sun

ment paper or broiled lamb chops. But it's the ample portions of Polynesian food that keep people coming back. A very different Yakima dining experience, especially at night, when lights reflect off the water.

Track 29 Dining Company
About 1 mile off I-82 on Yakima, (509) 457-2929
1 W Yakima Avenue, Yakima
Moderate; full bar; AE, MC, V
Lunch, dinner every day

Straightforward steak and barbecued chicken dinners, and burgers and sandwiches for lunch—but the railroad-car atmosphere is fun. Set in Yakima's Old Town in the midst of a tourist center called Yesterday's Village and Farmers' Market, this restaurant consists of two 1928 cozy dining cars and the Night Train lounge—which needs an old stand-up bar to accurately relive the Great Northern's Empire Builder days. Entertainment some nights, and an eager, young staff to serve.

LODGINGS

The Tudor Guest House
32nd and Tieton,
(509) 452-8112
3111 Tieton Drive,
Yakima, WA 98902
Moderate; MC, V

This stately Tudor mansion was built in 1929 by a prominent Yakima philanthropist, whose standards of quality are evident throughout the house. Oriental carpets cover hardwood floors, leaded-glass windows look out onto the gardens and grounds, and graceful archways lead into many of the rooms. Each room is tastefully decorated with beautifully restored antiques. The five guest rooms ($45–$60 for a double), all on the second floor, share two spacious bathrooms. The mansion is peaceful and sedate, and so tends to attract mature customers. The home has two working fireplaces, one in a guest room, the other a back-to-back affair in the large living room/morning room, where an ample breakfast is served. Summer use of the formal garden and lawn is encouraged.

Rio Mirada Motor Inn
Exit 33 off I-82,
(509) 457-4444
1603 Terrace Heights Drive, Yakima, WA 98901
Moderate; AE, DC, MC, V

Just off the I-82 freeway, and right next to the shimmering Yakima River, this Best Western motel doesn't look like much from the road. A peek inside reveals 96 attractive rooms, each with a small balcony and a view of the river ($41–$51). Most rooms have tiny refrigerators and a few have kitchenettes. For exercise there's an outdoor heated pool, an indoor exercise room with a Jacuzzi, and a recently expanded 4.6-mile path along the riverbank. Although the place is showing a bit of wear, its convenience and views are worth the stay. The staff could use some orientation about the sights and events in the Yakima area.

PARKER

RESTAURANTS

Maria's Cafe
About 4 miles out of Union Gap,

For 10 years Denver-born Maria Layman has been holding forth at this simple, whitewashed roadhouse on the edge of the Yakima Indian Reservation, 10 minutes from

(509) 877-6322
Highway 97, Parker
Inexpensive; no alcohol;
no credit cards; checks ok
Lunch, dinner Mon-Sat
(closes at 7pm)

downtown Yakima. She learned the cooking trade from her Mexican parents and at church suppers. If you appreciate 1940s decor, Formica tabletops, and a true Mexican menu, this is the place. You can savor tender, bite-sized Mexicana steak and the hottest salsa in Yakima County. The prices, like the doorways, are low, but the atmosphere and food is warm and filling. Quaff a beer in Yakima, for it's the only thing Maria's lacks.

TOPPENISH

Yakima Nation Cultural Center, located on ancestral grounds, houses an Indian museum and reference library, plus a gift shop, a Native American restaurant, a commercial movie/performing arts theater, and the 76-foot-tall Winter Lodge, for conventions and banquets. Open every day (closed January–February). On Fort Road off Highway 97, Toppenish, (509) 865-2800.

Fort Simcoe was built in 1856, and its Gothic Revival officers' quarters still stand in desolate grandeur; 28 miles west of Toppenish on Route 220.

ZILLAH
RESTAURANTS

El Ranchito
Exit 54 off I-82, follow
the signs, (509) 829-5880
1319 E First Avenue,
Zillah
Inexpensive; no alcohol;
no credit cards; checks ok
Breakfast, lunch, dinner
every day

Here in hops- and fruit-growing country, where many Mexican-Americans live, is a jolly tortilla factory-cum-cafeteria that makes a perfect midday stop. You eat in the large dining area or, during the summer, on the cool patio shaded by flowering plants. After lunch you can browse in the store for Mexican pottery or hard-to-find Mexican peppers, spices, canned goods, very fresh tortilla chips, and even south-of-the-border medicines.

The authentic food is ordered a la carte. The creamy burritos, tasty nachos, and especially the barbacoa, a mild, slow-barbecued mound of mushy beef served in a tortilla shell or a burrito, are generous and recommended. There is a Mexican bakery on the premises, but no cerveza.

GRANGER
LODGINGS

Rinehold Cannery
Homestead
½ mile east of Gurley
Road and Yakima Valley
Highway intersection,
(509) 854-2508
530 Gurley Road, Route
1, Box 1117, Granger,

Friendly and unpretentious, Floyd Rinehold's early 1900s homestead is a large farmhouse surrounded by orchards, vineyards, fields, and farm animals. Local produce was once processed in the adjacent building that is now home of Eaton Hill Winery (scheduled to produce its first bottling in June 1989). Gary and Arlene Rogers manage the B&B for the owners; their relaxed graciousness suits the setting. Two guest rooms and a single bathroom occupy the second floor and share a wonderful sitting room with

WA 98932
Moderate; MC, V

an expansive view of the countryside; the Rogerses provide glasses and a corkscrew so you can sip your latest discovery. The home is furnished in "user-friendly" antiques and pictures carefully chosen by Arlene at garage sales over the years. Arlene prepares a huge country breakfast before you head out for a day of touring local wineries, several of which are within 15 minutes of the inn.

SUNNYSIDE
RESTAURANTS

Extra Special Pantry
In the mini-mall,
downtown Sunnyside,
(509) 837-5875
214 S Sixth Street,
Sunnyside
Inexpensive; beer and
wine; no credit cards;
checks ok
Lunch Mon-Sat

This open-area gem serves healthy lunches, prepared in bright Scandinavian-type surroundings somewhat hidden in Sunnyside's mini-mall. Engaging Anne and Bill Flower make their guests feel pampered. The hot casserole and tossed salad is the most robust meal, while sandwiches on cracked-wheat bread with local Gouda cheese are a popular choice. The pineapple cake—like its carrot sister—was moist, rich, and generous-sized.

GRANDVIEW
RESTAURANTS

Dykstra House Restaurant
Exit 73 off I-82; 1½
miles on Wine Country
Road, (509) 882-2082
114 Birch Avenue,
Grandview
Moderate; beer and wine;
AE, MC, V
Lunch Mon-Fri,
dinner Sat

Who can resist a restaurant that features bread made from hand-ground whole wheat grown in the Horse Heaven Hills? Rich desserts and a few choice Washington state wines complement this mansion's simple menu. If you go with an open mind, you won't be disappointed. Chef Judy Nagle plans meals according to her impulses, so the menu changes daily. The tasty bean soup is thick with mysterious ingredients. Proprietor Linda Williams takes the time to make visitors feel at home in the graystone 1914 home of Grandview's former mayor and in the town at large. The present mayor and his council members (and other local groups) often reserve the upstairs for meetings or parties. Reservations are required for Saturday dinner, at which time there is a choice of two entrees only. A screened front porch is used for summer meals.

PROSSER
RESTAURANTS

The Blue Goose
Exit 80 off I-82,
(509) 786-1774
306 Seventh Street,

Wine-country visitors will get a fast start with chef Ed Sebens' hearty breakfasts. An early-bird dinner menu (4pm–6pm) and special Sunday dishes such as breaded veal and teriyaki chicken help make this off-the-beaten-

Prosser
Inexpensive; beer and
wine; AE, MC, V
Breakfast, lunch, dinner
every day

path restaurant a treat; the generous servings of pasta can be a bit oversauced. Washington wines are featured, and the waitpersons have been given special training about the nuances of local wineries. The current expansion might be a little distracting—and premature.

LODGINGS

Harvest House B&B
Exit 80 off I-82, near the
corner of E 6th and
Meade, (509) 786-1622
1204 Meade Avenue,
PO Box 388, Prosser,
WA 99350
Inexpensive; AE

Accommodating a need spawned by the increasing influx of wine tourists, Ken and Nita Speaks have revived this old two-story downtown hotel. Reluctant to displace any of the longtime tenants, they've capably combined apartments (in a separate wing) with a simple, homey B&B. Nita's cooking and baking talents provide breakfasts in the commodious upstairs parlor. The dominating presence of a sturdy brick fireplace and rosewood stairway and trim helps make the setting memorable. A cafeteria just opened next door.

TRI-CITIES WINE COUNTRY

Columbia Valley is the largest vineyard appellation (geographic designation) in Washington State, stretching from Quincy in the north to Paterson in the south, with its hub in the Tri-Cities. Call ahead for tours and tastings. **Seth Ryan Winery**, 681 South 40th Street, Richland, (509) 375-0486, one of the area's newest. **Bookwalter Winery**, 2708 Commercial Avenue, Pasco, (509) 547-8571, a small facility already attracting attention (open weekends only or by appointment). **Gordon Brothers Cellars**, 531 Levey Road, Pasco, (509) 547-6224, nice view of the Snake River. **Preston Wine Cellar**, 502 East Vineyard Drive, Pasco, (509) 545-1990, has a charming park. **Quarry Lake**, 2520 Commercial Avenue, Pasco, (509) 547-7307, don't be put off by the industrial park location. **Columbia Crest Winery**, Highway 221, Paterson, (509) 875-2061, Chateau Ste. Michelle's $25 million third winery, well worth visiting. **Mercer Ranch Vineyards**, 17 miles west of Paterson on Alderdale, (509) 894-4741, good red wines off the beaten track. **Fox Estate**, 1549 SW Road 26, Mattawa, (509) 932-4132, tours and tastings by appointment only. **F.W. Langguth**, 2340 Winery Road, Mattawa, (509) 932-4943, the state's most up-to-date facility, with extensive tours by appointment only. **Champs de Brionne**, 98 Road "W" NW, Quincy, (509) 785-6685, magnificent view of the Columbia River, worth the detour. **Hunter Hill Vineyards**, 2752 West McMannaman Road, Othello, (509) 346-2607, near a wildlife refuge in the heart of Eastern Washington.

TRI-CITIES: RICHLAND

Richland was once a secret city, hidden away while the workers on the atomic bomb project did their thing in the 1940s; now "the Atomic City" is the largest of the Tri-Cities. However, as nuclear reactors close and the controversy over hazardous waste continues, civic leaders are working hard on industrial diversification.

Hanford Science Center tells a bit of the saga of atomic energy; the energy displays are quite instructive. 825 Jadwin Avenue, (509) 376-6374.

Howard Amen Park, along the bank of the Columbia, makes a very nice spot for picnics, tennis, golf, jogging, or just ambling.

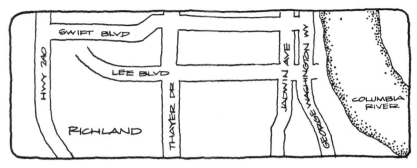

RESTAURANTS

The Emerald of Siam
William and Jadwin,
(509) 946-9328
1314 Jadwin Avenue,
Richland
Inexpensive; beer and
wine; MC, V
Lunch Mon-Fri,
dinner Mon-Sat

One of the most authentic Thai restaurants in the North-west is improbably located in a converted drugstore in a Richland shopping center. Floor space has been con-siderably expanded in the last year, and the place now includes a cultural center for visiting school groups and a display of Thai handicrafts for sale. Thai-born Ravadi Quinn and her family have created something of the feel of a small restaurant in Southeast Asia, and they are serv-ing delicious native recipes. The curries, satays, and noodles all get high marks. Thai salad, a favorite in Asia, is a good bet. Weekday buffet lunches are popular. Family members run a smaller branch in Kennewick, located just behind the Columbia Center Shopping Mall at 8300 Gage Blvd, (509) 783-6214.

Giacci's
Corner of George
Washington and Lee,
(509) 946-4855
94 Lee Boulevard,
Richland
Inexpensive; beer and
wine; no credit cards;
checks ok
Lunch Mon-Sat,
dinner Fri-Sat

Good salads and Italian sandwiches are the weekday lunch offerings at this attractive deli/restaurant in Rich-land. Owner Bev Giacci returned to her home town after several years of running a restaurant in upstate New York. Dinner is served Friday and Saturday nights. It's all Italian fare: fettuccine, cannelloni, and such. Outdoor tables in summer.

Gaslight Restaurant and Bar
At the first main
intersection on George
Washington,
(509) 946-1900
99 Lee Boulevard,
Richland
Inexpensive; full bar;
MC, V
Lunch, dinner every day

The Gaslight was here long before Shakey's and Pizza Hut, and for a long time it was the only place to get piz-za in Richland. Although it looks like just another dive tavern on the outside, it has evolved into a more stylish place, and it's still where everybody goes to get a good pizza. Try the pepperoni and jalapeno. There's the usual excess of period brass lamp fixtures and Gay Nineties mirrors, but there are also cozy booths and an outdoor deck that overlooks the Columbia River.

LODGINGS

Hanford House Thunderbird

Take the Richland Exit off I-84 to George Washington,
(509) 946-7611
802 George Washington Way, Richland, WA 99352
Moderate; AE, DC, MC, V

Since this is a prime Richland social center, you'll notice a great deal of pro-nuclear activity, but do not be dissuaded: this is *the* place to stay in the Tri-Cities, with large rooms overlooking an attractive courtyard and a dandy pool for lazing in the broiling sun. What used to be the Columbia rushing by is now Lake Wallula, transformed by the construction of McNary Dam. Best rooms are those in the section overlooking the lake (odd-numbered rooms 169–187 and 269–287); otherwise, to avoid the parking lot, ask for a room facing onto the courtyard (the even numbers). The lounge is pleasant; the popular dining room serves standard Red Lion fare.

TRI-CITIES: PASCO

This was the first of the Tri-Cities, a railroad town started in 1884.

Columbia Basin Community College, near the airport, puts on shows and lectures; the Performing Arts Building (design: Brooks/Hensley/Creager) is a splendid, virtually windowless building in the Brutalist mode.

LODGINGS

Red Lion Inn

Take the 20th Street exit off Highway 395,
(509) 547-0701

The large, sprawling motel (281 rooms) in half-timbered style has several notable attractions. There is a nice outdoor pool, surrounded by the rooms; the 18-hole municipal golf course is right alongside, making the motel appear

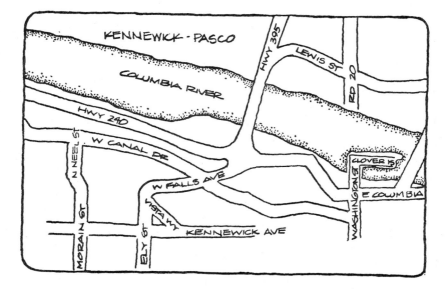

2525 N 20th Street,
Pasco, WA 99301
Moderate; AE, DC,
MC, V

to be set in a park, even though it's right on the freeway; and it's exceptionally convenient to the Tri-Cities airport and Columbia Basin Community College. Local residents like the dining room for "dressy" occasions such as birthdays and anniversaries.

TRI-CITIES: KENNEWICK

RESTAURANTS

The Blue Moon
Almost a block from
Washington,
(509) 582-6598
21 W Canal Drive,
Kennewick
Expensive; wine only;
MC, V
Dinner Fri-Sat

Considering the economic problems in the Tri-Cities, opening this first-class restaurant in 1987 was a real gamble, but so far it's a success. Owners Linda, Dale, and Dean Shepard opened the Blue Moon as an adjunct to their catering business. Diners enjoy a seven-course meal at one seating (7pm) in quiet and attractive surroundings, Fridays and Saturdays only (private parties of 10 or more can book Tuesday–Thursday). You get a prix-fixe ($25) menu with choice of entree. The lobster bisque is full-flavored, rich, and spicy. After a good Caesar salad, a tasty cabernet sorbet cleanses the palate. Entree selections include Cajun blackened catfish, tournedos Blue Moon, sauteed pork Dijon, and breast of chicken Grand Marnier. The wine list is composed entirely of local bottlings. Reservations are essential. A gem.

Flamingo Beach Club
1 mile east of Columbia
Center, (509) 735-3434
6321 W Canal Drive,
Kennewick
Moderate; full bar;
MC, V
Lunch, dinner every day

New owners Mike Skidmore and Mark Jones have expanded the hours and the menu of this Florida-style cafe. Dinner items include chicken, seafood, and steaks served in the pretty pastel dining room. The Flamingo Beach Club is located beside a large water-slide park, and summer customers can watch the activity. There is also outside dining, weather permitting.

LODGINGS

Clover Island Inn
Columbia Drive
and Washington,
(509) 586-0541
435 Clover Island,
Kennewick, WA 99336
Inexpensive; AE, DC,
MC, V

It's actually on an island, and thus offers wonderful river views from many of its 156 rooms. Otherwise, there's not much to distinguish it from its Thunderbird and Holiday Inn cousins, except for inexpensive rates. Avoid dining here.

KAHLOTUS

RESTAURANTS

Tom's Inn-Digestion
(aka Tom's Place)
In Kahlotus, 45 miles
north of Pasco on
Highway 395,

It's easy to find the Inn-Digestion; however, on a recent visit we learned that no one in town knows the name of its street. It is generally thought that no one has ever gotten around to naming it. Besides, tiny, remote Kahlotus, population 250, has only one commercial establish-

(509) 282-3324
Kahlotus
Inexpensive; beer and
wine; no credit cards;
local checks only
Breakfast, lunch, dinner
every day

ment. On one side, groceries are sold, and on the other, beer, wine, and very good hamburgers are served. Breakfasts are popular. Owner Tom Keene is something of a pack rat, and an amazing collection of curious items hang from the ceiling. While the general ambience is barnyard/outhouse, there are probably artifacts to interest more sedate scholars.

WALLA WALLA

The valley of the Walla Walla is an important historical area: Lewis and Clark came by in 1805, fur trappers set up a fort in 1818, and in 1836 Marcus Whitman built a medical mission west of the present town, where he and his wife, Narcissa, were murdered by Indians in the famous massacare of 1847. The town itself was founded in 1858 and has grown into a pleasant vale with fecund wheatlands all around and a pretty private college anchoring the city.

Whitman Mission, seven miles west, off Highway 12, sketches out the story of the mission and massacre; there aren't any historic buildings, but the simple outline of the mission in the ground is strangely affecting.

Fort Walla Walla Museum, in Fort Walla Walla Park on the west edge of town, has a collection of old buildings and pioneer artifacts. Call (509) 525-7703 for tour hours; open summer only.

Whitman College. The lovely campus is worth a stroll, and Memorial Building, an 1899 Romanesque Revival structure, is worth admiring for architecture; tours: (509) 527-5176. The campus puts on lots of plays, some in the wonderfully funky Harper Joy Theatre, a wooden playhouse; Penrose Library has a strong collection of Northwest materials; and there are some summer workshops.

Old houses. Kirkman House Museum, listed on the National Historic Register, is a fine period home museum; 214 North Colville Street, (509) 529-4373. Mature

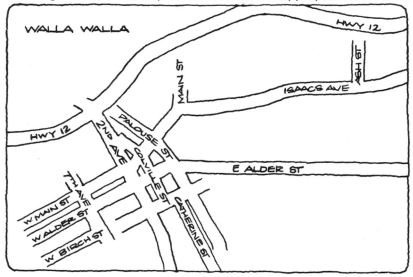

trees and colonial styles lend a New England feeling to Catherine Street, South Palouse Street, and West Birch Street. Pioneer Park on East Alder Street is a good example of the urban park style of 80 years ago, and was designed by the Olmsted Brothers, the landscape architects who created New York City's Central Park and Seattle's Lake Washington Boulevard.

Onions. Walla Walla Sweets are splendid, truly sweet onions, great for sandwiches; here you can get the "number ones," with thin skins. For information on the onion festival, call the Chamber of Commerce, (509) 525-0850.

Local food products. Ascolano's, a specialty food store located in the restored Northern Pacific Depot, 416 North Second, has almost all of the Walla Walla Valley wines, and at reasonable prices. It also stocks some fine and unusual local grocery selections, such as barley mustard from Dayton and jars of pickled peppers, asparagus, and cherries from the Robison Ranch processors.

Wines. Grapes grow here too, and consequently wineries have sprouted throughout the region. **L'Ecole No. 41,** Lowden, (509) 525-0940; **Leonetti Cellars,** Walla Walla, (509) 525-1428; **Waterbrook Winery,** Lowden, (509) 522-1918, which also bottles for the new **Seven Hills Winery,** (509) 529-3331; **Biscuit Ridge,** (509) 529-4986, with a Waitsburg address but actually located just outside the village of Dixie.

RESTAURANTS

Merchants Ltd.

Take the 2nd Street exit off Highway 12, turn left on Main, (509) 525-0900
21 E Main Street,
Walla Walla
Moderate; beer and wine;
MC, V
Breakfast, lunch Mon-Sat,
dinner Wed-Sat,
brunch Sun

★★

Charles and Norma Austin created this New York–style deli and sidewalk cafe; it's a cluttered place, with tempting culinary merchandise piled ceiling-high on broad shelves, a deli counter loaded with breads, cheeses, sausages, salads, caviar, and such, and a glass-fronted bakery from which enticing smells waft into the rooms. You can get great coffee, deli items (adequate), and sensational French pastries. The homemade soups are deservedly popular. There are tables inside, or you might sit out front, at sidewalk tables, and watch Walla Walla go by.

Upstairs is a more sedate dining room, where the food is quite good. Lunch is served here buffet-style Tuesday through Friday, and there is a Sunday brunch. Thursday night is Mexican/Southwestern dinner night, and Friday and Saturday nights feature standard buffet dinners, usually with prime rib. Wednesday nights feature spaghetti in the deli—quite good. Excellent wine list.

Rees Mansion

2 blocks south of Main,
(509) 529-7845
260 E Birch Street,
Walla Walla
Moderate; full bar;
MC, V
Lunch, dinner Tues-Sat

★

This beautiful Georgian colonial has been a landmark in Walla Walla since it was built early in the 20th century. The grandeur of the old house is still evident, although some of the recent restoration seems a bit gaudy and contrived. Owners Adrian Phipps and Jack Laughery originally opened the mansion as a bed and breakfast, and there are still two rooms for rent upstairs, but their recent concern has been the restaurant.

After a shaky start, the dining room has benefited from the arrival of chef Michael McCann. The menu is still somewhat limited, but recent reports on the quality of the food are good. Prime rib is a weekend standby, and some fine seafood dishes surface during the week. Service is well intentioned but sometimes clumsy.

The bar is a delight. It's friendly and attractive, reminiscent of some of the wonderful small hotels in London.

The Whitman Inn

Take the 2nd Street exit from Highway 12,
(509) 529-7276
107 N Second Street,
Walla Walla
Moderate; full bar;
AE, DC, MC, V
Breakfast, lunch, dinner every day

We're getting quite used to changes at the Whitman. At this moment it's undergoing yet another transformation. Former chef Ken Beck, who introduced some fine innovations, has left the area. At press time the menu was drastically changed, and the new chef yet to be named. There is now an entire menu category devoted to "Country Cooking," with such items as meat loaf, and liver and onions. These are well prepared and quite inexpensive ($5.95–$6.95).

The once-dreary rooms in this old "symbol of civic pride" have finally been redecorated. They are light and attractive and offer, if nothing else, a comfortable stay. New heat pumps have been installed, improving air conditioning that is a necessity in the summer.

The Ice-burg Drive-In

Corner of W Birch and 9th, (509) 529-1793
616 W Birch Street,
Walla Walla
Inexpensive; no alcohol;
no credit cards; checks ok
Lunch, dinner every day

Some say the hamburgers served at this back-street drive-in are the best in the nation, but let's just say they're strong contenders for the title in the Pacific Northwest. Owner Alan Jones is dedicated to using strictly fresh ingredients, and each burger is grilled to order. The price for the basic burger is $1.14. Terrific French fries and thick milk shakes (some made of seasonal fruits) are accompaniments. The ice cream sodas, unfortunately, are the weak point here: soda purists complain that they're made with soft ice cream.

You can eat at a wooden picnic table or take your meal to one of Walla Walla's pretty parks. Order by phone to avoid a long wait in the car line.

Jacobi's Cafe

Take the Second Street exit from Highway 12 to the old Burlington Northern Depot,
(509) 525-2677
416 N Second Street,
Walla Walla
Inexpensive; beer and wine; AE, MC, V
Lunch, dinner every day

In a town with many beautiful old buildings, it is surprising that there isn't more interest in historic preservation and restoration; thus Jacobi's, in the former Northern Pacific Depot, is a welcome addition. Although this isn't the spot for a quiet dinner (old railroad stations seem to echo from their hardwood floors to their ceilings), the food is quite good. Restaurant owner Bill Pancake provides deli-type salads and some hot dishes, predominantly pizza. Desserts are attractive and flavorful. Local wines are featured.

Pastime Cafe

Half a block east of the courthouse,
(509) 525-0873
215 W Main Street,

Very little has changed since this Walla Walla institution opened in 1927, except that the current nostalgia craze for diners has made it even more popular than before. It is still run by some of the original owners, the Fazzari family, which pleases Walla Walla's large Italian popula-

Walla Walla
Inexpensive; full bar; no
credit cards; checks ok
Breakfast, lunch, dinner
Mon-Sat

tion. They come for the homemade pasta and the best lasagne in town and don't seem to mind that everything's just a touch underseasoned. Experienced patrons skip the vegetables—usually pale canned peas. It's strictly a 1930s atmosphere, complete with card room.

LODGINGS

Pony Soldier Motor Inn
2nd Avenue exit off
Highway 12,
(509) 529-4360
325 E Main Street,
Walla Walla, WA 99362
Moderate; AE, DC,
MC, V

It's just another motel, but proximity to Whitman College makes it very popular. When there's an event at the college, book early. There's a pleasant swimming-pool courtyard, and continental breakfast is included in the room price. A fitness room containing Jacuzzis, saunas, and such has been added. You can bring your poodle, but more proletarian dogs (particularly those with long hair) are not welcome.

DAYTON

RESTAURANTS

Patit Creek Restaurant
On Highway 12, at north
end of town,
(509) 382-2625
725 E Dayton Avenue,
Dayton
Moderate; beer and wine;
MC, V
Lunch Tues-Fri,
dinner Tues-Sat

Bruce and Heather Hiebert have achieved the seemingly impossible: they've turned a small rural cafe into an excellent regional restaurant. Serving good food to the locals (both conservative farmers and more liberal college types) has been an experience—at times frustrating and educational—but the effort has paid off. There is now a steady and very appreciative clientele who don't mind driving long distances to eat superbly roasted meat at Patit Creek. The menu has been expanded to feature more regional dishes and four different seasonal menus. Appetizers are notable, particularly the smoked salmon cheesecake (non-sweet) and the chevre-stuffed dates wrapped in bacon and broiled. Bruce uses only the freshest ingredients. In the spring, fresh morel mushrooms are offered in a different entree each night. A little later in the season, he'll wander into the hills in search of extraordinarily sweet wild onions to use in some of his sauces. The pork chop with a sauce of walnuts, dried currants, and cream is popular, as is the steak in green peppercorn sauce.

The wine list is short but carefully chosen, including some of the fine Walla Walla Valley wines as well as relatively inexpensive French selections. Heather's homemade pies and desserts provide a proper conclusion to such delightful fare, especially her gooseberry pie. Reservations are crucial on weekends—and make them for an early hour or you may miss out on some of the specials.

PULLMAN

Pullman's population swells in the fall with Washington State University students, while the permanent residents are a mix of wheat farmers and university faculty. The largest of the Palouse towns, Pullman retains some of its cowpoke image but covets an international reputation as a university town. The central business district consists mostly of one main street crowded with shops and some restaurants. There is abundant free parking just off the main street. Browsers might visit the **Nica Gallery** for an excellent representation of Eastern Washington artists, 125 NE Olson; **Bruised Books**, for used books that sometimes include hard-to-find first editions, 105 North Grand; **The Combine**, for pastries, espresso, ice cream, and teas and herbs, 215 East Main; and the **Sport Shack**, 460 East Main, for an amazing array of fishing lures.

Washington State University. The campus is expanding constantly, and one of the newest buildings is a science center, Fulmer Hall, near the center of campus. The Fine Arts Center is a showcase with a spacious gallery which attracts notable artists' exhibits. Martin Stadium, home of the WSU Cougar football team, can now hold Pac 10 Conference–sized crowds; the baseball team plays on the new Bailey Field near Beasley Performing Arts Coliseum, which houses both the basketball team and frequent rock concerts. Visitors might want to drop by Ferdinands, located in Troy Hall and open weekdays only, which offers ice cream and milk shakes, and Cougar Gold cheese, made from milk and cream from WSU's own dairy herd, (509) 335-4014.

Kamiak Butte, 13 miles north on Route 27, offers a good place for a picnic and nice overlooks of the rolling wheat country.

Steptoe Butte. About 30 miles north of Pullman on Highway 195, this geologic leftover towers above the Palouse and affords an impressive view of the Palouse or great stargazing.

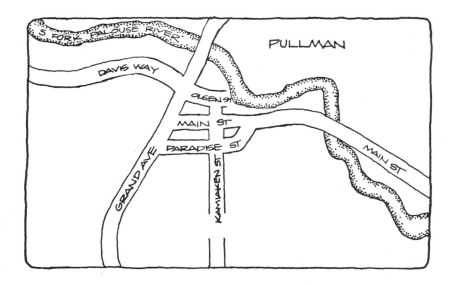

RESTAURANTS

The Seasons

On the hill about half a block off Grand,
(509) 334-1410
215 SE Paradise Street,
Pullman
Moderate; beer and wine;
AE, DC, MC, V
Dinner Tues-Sun

No doubt Pullman's finest dining experience. This elegant eatery occupies an old house, recently expanded, atop a flower-covered cliff. A winding wooden staircase leads diners to the front door. The interesting menu changes often, and dinner is presented in a proper and elegant fashion; chicken and seafood are good choices. Salad dressings are made on the premises and salads are served with scrumptious homemade breads such as whole-wheat with cornmeal, poppyseeds, and sesame seeds. Sauces for the chicken and the salmon were well flavored and distinctive, vegetables were crisp, and the rice was done to perfection. A chocolate mint mousse from the dessert tray was a wonderful finish.

Swilly's

1 block east of Grand,
(509) 334-3395
200 NE Kamiaken Street,
Pullman
Moderate; beer and wine;
AE, MC, V
Lunch, dinner Mon-Sat

This eatery is located in what in the 1920s was Pullman's railroad depot. It flanks the Palouse River and sports a small outdoor cafe in good weather. Across the street is one of the 20 artesian wells, drilled between 1890 and 1909, that were the deciding factor in locating a state college in Pullman. Inside, the warmth of the hardwood floors, the exposed brick walls, and the rich smell of espresso invite lingering. Works by area artists, all for sale, decorate the walls. The eatery boasts fresh local ingredients, right down to cream from a nearby dairy and bread from a local bakery. Diners will find a separate calzone menu (billed as "the freshest and finest in the Palouse"), and on the regular menu there are entrees such as fettuccine with Italian blue cheese, sweet pine nuts, and a cream sauce; smoked salmon fettuccine; or balsamic tortellini. For lunch, a tarragon chicken sandwich with walnuts, celery, green onions, parsley, and tomato on a sourdough roll was served with apples and potato chips. Swilly's has a modest selection of imported beers and a wine list with a good representation of Washington wines. Plan to spend enough time to enjoy a second cup of caffe latte.

Hilltop Steakhouse

Less than a mile before town on Highway 195 coming from Spokane,
(509) 334-2555
Colfax Highway,
Pullman
Moderate; full bar; AE, DC, MC, V
Lunch Mon-Fri, dinner every day, brunch Sun

This motel and restaurant has probably the best steaks in Pullman, family-style chicken dinners Sunday afternoons, Sunday brunch, and a wonderful view of the university and surrounding hills. The food is consistently good, albeit fairly standard, fare.

If you've found a place that you think is a Best Place, send in the report form at the back of this book. If you're unhappy with one of the places, please let us know why. We depend on reader input.

LODGINGS

Paradise Creek Quality Inn
A quarter mile east of the WSU campus near the junction of Highway 270 and Johnson,
(509) 332-0500
1050 SE Johnson Avenue, Pullman, WA 99163
Moderate; AE, DC, MC, V

Just far enough off Route 270 to afford guests quiet nights away from traffic noises, this motel is also within easy walking distance of the WSU campus. It's situated over the meandering creek for which it's named.

BRITISH COLUMBIA

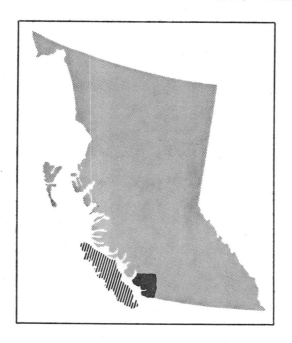

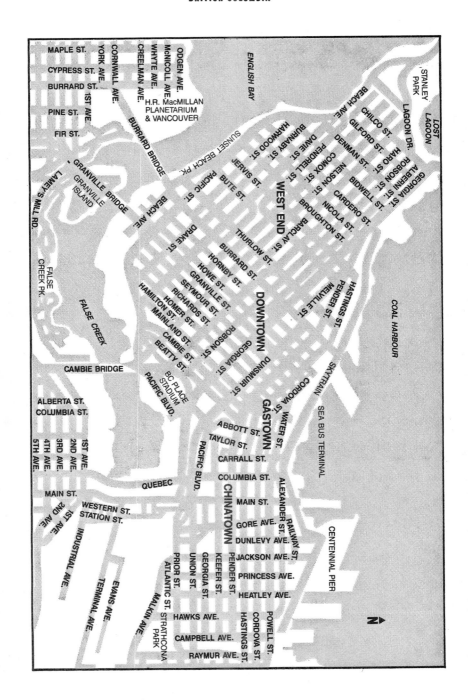

VANCOUVER AND ENVIRONS

Including the suburbs: West Vancouver; North Vancouver; and Surrey, Richmond, and Ladner to the south.

For the past hundred years, Vancouver's fortunes have ebbed and flowed with the price of lumber. The good news is that, at the end of the 1980s, worldwide demand for wood pulp hit a record high, and the city has risen, wobbling slightly, on the crest of one of its intermittent booms.

Dropping unemployment and stable interest rates attracted 55,000 new residents to the city in 1988, many of them from Asia. Vancouver has long touted itself as Canada's gateway to the Pacific Rim. But only when Hong Kong billionaire Li Ka-shing scooped up the old EXPO site, two hundred acres of prime development land, did the realization sink in that the city was also becoming the Pacific Rim's gateway to Canada. Vancouver has always accepted the waves of immigrants that have broken on its shores. Indeed, the city seems living proof that a benign environment will produce an easygoing disposition. Despite a stiffening of the work ethic of late, this is still a place of leisure and relaxed enjoyment, where the office population thins out noticeably on Friday afternoons.

Glance away from the opulence of the shops as you saunter along Robson and you will see why; at the end of that side street lap the peaceful waters of Burrard Inlet. Beyond, the mountains on the north shore glitter in snowy majesty for half the year. Vancouver, residents are fond of saying, is one of the few cities in the world where you can go skiing and sailing on the same day. How remarkable, then, that it should also be one of the few where, sitting outside a Neapolitan cafe, you can eavesdrop on an impassioned argument in Hungarian and see graffiti in Khmer.

More than any other city in the Northwest, Vancouver marches to a different drummer. The rest of Canada, on the other side of the Rockies, is as remote as Mexico. Seattle, just a couple of hours' drive down I-5, is definitely another country, despite the shared heritage of fishing and tall trees. Vancouver's chameleon identity is that of home to the children of the dispossessed, whether they be Scottish Highlanders or Hmong tribespeople. To the sculptors and the screenwriters, the dancers, jugglers, retired war correspondents, and exiled aristocrats, to the drifters and dreamers who have settled here in such disproportionate numbers, this is as close to the Promised Land as it's possible to get.

THE ARTS

Visual Arts. Francis Rattenbury's elegant old courthouse has been born again as the Vancouver Art Gallery, which holds more than 20 major exhibitions a year and whose permanent collection includes works by Goya, Gainsborough, and Picasso; 750 Hornby, (604) 682-4668. Many of the city's commercial galleries are located on the dozen blocks just south of the Granville Bridge, and Granville Island, site of the Emily Carr College of Art and Design, has a number of potteries and craft studios. The avant-garde is most often found on the east side of the city, at spaces such as Grunt Gallery, 209 E Sixth, (604) 875-9516, and Pitt International Galleries, 36 Powell Street, (604) 681-6740.

Music. After a bumpy patch in 1988, the Vancouver Symphony Orchestra is back on the tracks, thanks to vigorous fund-raising by the musicians and their supporters and injections of government cash. The main season starts in October at the Orpheum, an old vaudeville theatre (884 Granville). The Vancouver Opera Association puts on four productions a year at the Queen Elizabeth Theatre (630 Hamilton): the program is a balance of popular and experimental; a coproduction of *Tosca* with the Los Angeles Music Center Opera is slated for the 1990–91 season. The city also has choirs, quartets, and ensembles of varying musical hues, from medieval to electronic. For information about any musical event, call Ticketmaster (604) 280-4444.

Theatre. The Vancouver Playhouse is heading away from recycled Broadway hits, American musicals, and thrillers, and entering the world of contemporary theatre; in the Vancouver Playhouse at Hamilton and Dunsmuir, (604) 872-6622. The Arts Club is a commercial operation with three theatre locations and, usually, less production panache than the Playhouse; Granville Island, (604) 687-1644. Contemporary theatre in Vancouver is largely centered in the VECC—Vancouver East Cultural Center, 1895 Venables Street, (604) 254-9578.

Architecture. Much of Vancouver's outstanding architecture, often overshadowed by the powerful scenery around it, is the work of one of the major names in international design, Arthur Erickson. Downtown you can see his waffle-textured MacMillan Bloedel tower on West Georgia; Erickson's Law Courts at Robson and Howe are a tour-de-force demonstration of how landscaping can make a large complex almost disappear from view. EXPO's brief flowering of the steel-pipe high-tech style doesn't seem to have had much of a lasting impact on Vancouver except in the number of rapid transit stations, but other new additions (the crystalline condominium addition on English Bay, and the Burrard Street corridor, for instance) have been lauded. Finally, for earlier history—and a sense of how the other one percent lived—go out to Shaughnessy Heights, a subdivision created by Canadian Pacific in 1907 to be the most exclusive residential district in the city.

OTHER THINGS TO DO

Parks and Gardens. The city is blessed with a perfect climate—very similar to Britain's—for flowers and greenery. Take a walk through the quiet forest in the heart of Stanley Park, which is rimmed by swimming beaches, tennis courts, a rose garden, and an extraordinary aquarium. At Queen Elizabeth Park, dramatic winding paths, sunken gardens, and waterfalls skirt the Bloedel Conservatory. The University of British Columbia campus boasts three superb gardens—the Botanical Garden, Mitobe Memorial Gardens, and Totem Park—along with a top-drawer Sunday-tea setting at Cecil Green Park House, 6251 Cecil Green Park Road, (604) 228-6289. The new Chinese Classical Garden within Dr. Sun Yat-Sen Park (E Pender and Carrall streets) is a spectacular model of the Oriental garden complex. Built more than planted, with pavilions and water-walkways, it's the only example in North America of this fabulous garden tradition.

Shopping. Vancouver has always been bursting with storefronts. Robson Street

Wondering about our standards? We rate establishments on value, performance measured against the place's goals, uniqueness, enjoyability, loyalty of clientele, cleanliness, excellence and ambition of the cooking, and professionalism of the service. For an explanation of the star system, see the Introduction.

has a pleasant, European feel with few high rises, colorful awnings, and a proliferation of delicatessens, boutiques, and restaurants. Downtown is full of outstanding shops. In poor weather, head underground for the Pacific Center and Vancouver Center malls, with shops like Eatons, The Bay, Birks, Woodward's, and Marks & Spencer. At Granville Island Public Market on the south shore of False Creek, you can get everything from just-caught salmon to packages of fresh herbs to fine unpasteurized lager (at the Granville Brewery) to a wonderful array of fresh produce in late summer. Gastown is a restored 1890s precinct, once touristy, now anchored by some very good shops of more use to locals. Book Alley, the 300 and 400 blocks of West Pender, has bookstores specializing in everything from cookbooks to radical politics to science fiction.

Nightlife. On a warm summer night, the music spilling out from Vancouver's clubs and bars will range from down-and-dirty R&B at the suitably raunchy Yale Hotel, 1300 Granville, (604) 681-9253, and the sprung-floored Commodore Ballroom, 870 Granville, (604) 681-7838; through local bands at the Town Pump, 66 Water, (604) 683-6695; and disco thump at Richard's on Richards, the yuppie meat market, 1036 Richards, (604) 687-6794; to swing at the Hot Jazz Society, 2120 Main Street, (604) 873-4131. The Railway Club at 579 Dunsmuir, (604) 681-1625, has a remarkably varied membership and presents consistently good music, whether jazz or rock. Top names perform at BC Place Stadium, 777 Pacific Blvd S, (604) 669-2300. To find out who's playing where, pick up a copy of the *Georgia Straight* or Thursday's *Vancouver Sun.* Jazz fiends can call the Jazz Hotline, (604) 682-0706.

Sports. The Vancouver 86ers, the local soccer team, have a devoted following which cheered them all the way to the 1988 Canadian championship; 1126 Douglas, in Burnaby; (604) 299-0086. Visiting baseball enthusiasts should try to catch a Vancouver Canadians game at the Nat Bailey Stadium, a venue of which many locals have fond memories; Queen Elizabeth Park, (604) 872-5232. Hockey buffs look forward to the Vancouver Canucks' 20th year with the NHL. A number of new, promising names on the roster suggests the Canucks may just be next year's up-and-coming team; (604) 254-5141. But most Vancouverites would rather play than watch. Golf, sailing, hefting weights, exploring the local creeks and inlets by any kind of boat you can name—the city has first-rate facilities for these activities and many more. For information, contact Sport, BC at 1367 W Broadway, (604) 737-3000.

Ethnic Vancouver. The oldest and biggest of Vancouver's ethnic communities is Chinatown, and it's still growing. The 200 block of East Pender is the main market area; to get started, try Yuen Fong for teas or the Dollar Market for barbecued pork or duck. Italian commercial and cultural life thrives in the distinctive neighborhood around Commercial Drive, east of downtown. A second, less discovered Italian district is on Little Italy's northern border—the 2300 to 2500 blocks of East Hastings. Vancouver's 60,000 East Indian immigrants have established their own shopping area called the Punjabi Market in south Vancouver at 49th and Main streets, where you can bargain for spices, chutney, and sweets. Vancouver's longest-established group of ethnic inhabitants, the Greeks, live and shop west of the intersection of MacDonald and West Broadway.

RESTAURANTS

Bishop's
Corner of Yew and 4th,
(604) 738-2025
2183 W Fourth Avenue,
Vancouver
Expensive; full bar;

Six years in business and Bishop's is still Vancouver's most highly regarded restaurant. The fashionable dining crowd may flirt with the newer places, but in the end it is to Bishop's that they remain faithful. The reason for this lies less with the food (which is excellent) than with their devo-

AE, DC, MC, V
Lunch Mon-Fri, dinner
every day

tion to owner John Bishop himself, whom many consider to be a personal friend. A man who truly understands the art of hospitality, Bishop treats all his customers, whether they are first-time visitors or twice-a-week regulars, to a welcome that is gracious and sincerely warm. In this he is assisted by the most professionally polished young restaurant staff in the city.

The restaurant itself maintains its refined, sophisticated look without the usual pretensions. If there is a decorator theme here at all, it is in the bright and bold Jack Shadbolt paintings present on the walls and echoed on the menu covers and labels of the house wines. The rest—pale gray walls, crisp white linen, and simple white china—is kept understated to enhance the visual impact of the food in much the way a plain frame and matting set off a painting.

Bishop calls his cuisine "contemporary home cooking"—not classical French nor American nouvelle, but a style that borrows the best ideas from these and many others. Lately he has moved away from experimentation with Oriental crossover or BC regionally inspired dishes and settled down to the slightly more hearty fare preferred by his customers. Everything, though, bears the Bishop trademark of light, subtly complex flavors and bright, graphic color. A typical dinner begins with a basket of homemade braided curry bread; fragile, thin toasts threaded onto a bamboo skewer; or a small plate of tidbits such as grilled marinated eggplant and mushrooms, courtesy of the chef. Then it's on to the appetizers—which might include a delicate, savory potage like the squash and apple soup with sage, or a more robust roasted eggplant bisque; fresh Dungeness crab cakes; steamed clams in a black bean sauce; or a cool, fresh mozzarella and tomato salad.

Pastas exhibit Bishop's more adventurous side. Among our favorites is a spicy linguine with grilled calamari and sweet and hot chiles and a sumptuous fettuccine with smoked trout and caviar. Entrees are an uncomplicated listing: eggplant Parmesan, a couple of fish-of-the-day selections, and several meat-based dishes. You can't go wrong with any of them. We always enjoy the lamb—tender chops enhanced with fresh herbs and accompanied with a colorful arrangement of squash, yellow beans, and sliced beets. On our last visit, a daily special of beef tenderloin slices with a horseradish creme fraiche proved a sublime inspiration.

Desserts are not to be missed. The papaya flan in

Wondering about our standards? We rate establishments on value, performance measured against the place's goals, uniqueness, enjoyability, loyalty of clientele, cleanliness, excellence and ambition of the cooking, and professionalism of the service. For an explanation of the star system, see the Introduction.

a macadamia crust is heavenly, as is the famous Death by Chocolate, easily the most talked-about dessert in Vancouver. It's a rich slab of chocolate pate that wouldn't by itself be extraordinary, if not for Bishop's own Peckinpah-style presentation, which must be seen to be believed.

Le Crocodile

Corner of Robson and Thurlow, (604) 669-4298 818 Thurlow Street, Vancouver Moderate; full bar; AE, MC, V Lunch Mon-Fri, dinner Mon-Sat

The best French food in the city can be found at Le Crocodile. Forget your preconceptions of heavy, overly sauced, overly fussed-over food. We are talking about honest regional French cooking—country-style ingredients cooked with elegance and presented with flair.

Chef-owner Michel Jacob named the bistro-style restaurant after his favorite restaurant in his hometown of Strasbourg, and there are many clues to his Franco-Germanic culinary heritage on the menu: an Alsatian onion tart, almost jammy with its rich concentration of onions; a perfect round of warm goat cheese nestling in a bed of greens; braised red cabbage and bacon-fried potatoes served alongside the entrees, and an authentic tarte Tatin served for dessert.

Entrees are hearty, richly flavored, and tastefully presented. Meats are mostly grilled or lightly pan-sauteed, augmented with light sauces redolent of fresh herbs, flavored mustards, or wine. We've had excellent grilled calf liver with spinach butter, roast leg of lamb in a mint and orange sauce, and garlicky baked mussels—all uncomplicated but exquisite-tasting dishes. A recent meal featured succulent breast of duck in a port sauce—crisp-skinned, tender within—and a fine preparation of sweetbreads in a pink peppercorn sauce. The best desserts are the traditional ones: a tangy lemon tart, soothing creme brulee, and of course the aforementioned tarte Tatin.

The restaurant, being small, has an attractive, cozy atmosphere; but the tables, particularly in the middle of the restaurant, are pushed close together, and conversation is unlikely to escape the ears of your neighbor.

Tojo's

Broadway and Willow, (604) 872-8050 777 W Broadway, Vancouver Moderate; full bar; AE, MC, V Dinner Mon-Sat

Tojo Hidekazu is the heart of Tojo's, just as he was the soul of Jinya (the little restaurant that was a mecca for Vancouver sushi lovers until it closed in 1987). Some devotees were faithful enough to follow Tojo to the Soft Rock Cafe, where he briefly mass-produced sushi for the Cajun-chicken-strips crowd. But most waited for the ultimate—Tojo's own restaurant—and they have not been disappointed.

A few blocks west of the Jinya (currently reopened with the same owner and a new chef), up one story in a flashy new green glass building, Tojo's is a pleasantly

Looking for a particular place? Check the index at the back of this book for individual restaurants, lodgings, attractions, and more.

spacious restaurant, with a view out to the mountains, plenty of table seating, and six tatami rooms. The sushi bar is bigger than his throne at Jinya's too. It seats ten instead of four, which still isn't big enough for his devoted patrons, but ten people is the most Tojo likes to tend at one time. A brilliant sushi chef, endlessly innovative, surgically precise and committed to fresh ingredients, Tojo has one other important quality: he genuinely likes feeding people. Show an interest in the food, and if the restaurant isn't frantically busy, you will be offered a bit of this and that from the kitchen, or perhaps "newest Tojo sushi"—an inside-out roll with asparagus, scallops, wasabe, and Japanese mayonnaise on the inside and smoked salmon on the outside. Getting to be a regular is not difficult, and it's highly recommended.

Tojo's hot kitchen is mostly out in the open. Japanese menu standards such as tempura and teriyaki are always reliable and daily specials usually superb. There's a list of seasonal offerings: pine mushroom soup in October and November; wonderfully satisfying deep-fried tofu covered with seasonal stir-fried vegetables from October to May; cherry blossoms with scallops in April and May; and homemade egg tofu in the summer. Make sushi-bar reservations if you want to be sure of watching Tojo's small plump hands turn rice and fish into masterpieces as casually perfect as a Japanese tea ceremony bowl.

Angelica

Corner of W 4th and Trafalgar, (604) 737-2611 2611 W Fourth Avenue, Vancouver Moderate; full bar; AE, MC, V Lunch Tues-Fri, dinner every day, brunch Sat-Sun

Angelica is Mark Potovsky's new place. In his move from the former Cherrystone Cove to a more upbeat Gastown location, something has been lost, but a lot more has been gained. The new restaurant attempts to be a little bit of LA in Kitsilano. The atmosphere is cooler, more sophisticated. Fan-pleated white drapery adorns the windows, ceramic fish and geometric pastels add an arty touch, and over all is cast a predominant hue of blue neon. (The lighting does nothing to enhance the color of the food or the color of your skin.) Then there is the view; the outlook from the Cherrystone's windows had a sort of wrong-side-of-the-tracks romanticism to it. At Angelica, you are treated to the sight of the spandex set across the street at Ron Zalco's Fitness Emporium doing jumping-jacks. With nothing to shield the lower half of the windows, diners sitting next to them almost have the feeling that they are sitting out on the sidewalk. The general feeling of chilliness is not improved by frequent blasts of cold air from an unprotected front door.

But if coziness has been lost, Potovsky and his cooking are just as good as ever. Here is a young chef who shows real determination, impressive energy, and the bravery to continue to be innovative when there must be a lot of pressure to settle into the tried-and-true. If the new digs allow him the elbow room to experiment and keep on improving, then that's okay with us.

Everything served at Angelica is made on the premises, from the house bread with its hint of curry to the desserts. The menu changes daily according to what Potovsky has found in the market. Some favorites from the Cherrystone menu remain: salmon tartare with miso garlic toasts and mahi mahi in black and white sesame seeds continue to rank among our favorites. And there are many new items. We liked the well-balanced flavors of a smoked duck and veal sausage with balsamic poached onions (mild, yet spicy) and a delicate tuna tempura appetizer, wrapped in nori and finished with Osaka mustard greens, ginger, soy sauce, and scallions. A dish of quail, filled with veal and chanterelles and finished with a cabernet glace de viande, was a winning combination. So were the local prawns, grilled and finished with mirin, ginger, lime, cilantro, and red chiles. Chances are that, when you go, Potovsky will have a whole new menu full of exciting ideas. Desserts are wonderful and should be indulged in—no matter how guilty the hardbodies across the street are making you feel.

Caffe de Medici

*Between Burrard and
Thurlow, (604) 669-9322
1025 Robson Street,
Vancouver
Moderate; full bar;
AE, DC, MC, V
Lunch Mon-Fri, dinner
every day*

The most beautiful Italian restaurant in Vancouver features some of the most patrician decor: high molded ceilings, serene portraits of members of the 15th-century Medici clan, chairs and drapery in Renaissance green against the crisp white of the table linen, and walls the color of zabaglione. Waiters have the polish of kindly diplomats; no matter which one is assigned to your table, they all seem to look after you. Businesslike by day, romantic by night—the mood changes, but the quality of the Northern Italian food does not.

The antipasto is beautifully presented here: a bright collage of marinated eggplant, artichoke hearts, peppers, olives, squid, and Italian cold meats. The bresaola della Valtellina (air-dried beef, thinly sliced and marinated in olive oil, lemon, and pepper) is well worth trying. Pasta dishes are flat-out magnifico—a slightly chewy plateful of tortellini alla panna comes so rich with cheese you'll never order any of the others: cannelloni with spinach, ricotta, and meat sauce; trenette with a robust pesto; or the house fettuccine (sauteed with prosciutto, chicken breast, and peas in cream). Although it's mostly a Florentine restaurant (with a knockout version of beefsteak marinated in red wine and olive oil), we've also sampled a Venetian-style fish soup, brimming over with fresh fish and shellfish, and a Roman-style rack of lamb baked with mint, mustard, and Martini & Rossi sauce. For dessert, stick with the zabaglione alla Medici, a concoction of egg yolks whipped with Marsala, brandy, and sugar into a heady, aromatic froth.

Chartwell

*Corner of W Georgia and
Howe, (604) 689-9333
791 W Georgia Street,
Vancouver
Expensive; full bar;
AE, DC, MC, V
Lunch Mon-Fri, dinner
every day*

Chartwell, named after the famous abode of Sir Winston Churchill, could be a setting right out of "Masterpiece Theatre" with its darkwood-paneled walls, leather and brocade chairs, stiff white napery, and large paintings that give the illusion of tapestry wall hangings. There is definitely an upper-class English men's club atmosphere here, so it is no surprise when at lunch time the waiter rolls out a huge copper-domed baron de boeuf. Fortunately, this is where the hotel-stuffy predictability ends. The service, under the watchful eye of manager Angelo Cecconi, is attentive and efficient, yet very unselfconscious; the cuisine, though grand, is spiced with the unconventional. Chef Kerry Sear, one of the new breed of culinary Wunderkinder, is one of Canada's best and most inventive chefs; unfortunately, at press time he was on his way to Toronto. It was he who introduced Vancouver's suspicious palates to such new experiences as flying-fish roe and sea asparagus, and it is his cooking to which we would have given four stars. Now that he's leaving and Wolfgang von Weiser (from the Four Seasons in Toronto) is stepping in, what will happen six months down the road remains to be seen.

In the past, Sear elevated us to new sensual heights with his humble pumpkin soup, presented in a tall clear glass and topped with a mound of nutmeg-flavored milk foamed in a cappuccino machine. A fillet of salmon lightly fried in a skillet is served alongside a phyllo strudel of curried banana. A simple roast chicken is layered under the skin with herbs to infuse the meat with verdant, aromatic flavors.

A smoker is part of the kitchen equipment, and the resulting dishes, such as the cinnamon-smoked duck and wood-smoked yellow snapper with grilled fennel, are among the best choices on the menu. The smoked-salmon-and-caviar-cake appetizer is not to be missed. We hope chef von Weiser continues Sear's art of blending the salmon and caviar with cream and layering it between paper-thin buckwheat crepes. Wrapped in seaweed and strewn with caviar, it is as dazzling as a jewel box.

For the diet-conscious, Chartwell marks several selections among the daily specials as low in cholesterol, sodium, and fat. They help you feel less guilty about ordering dessert, which at Chartwell is a must: pastry chef Kurt Ebert and his staff are the best in the business. Among their most seductive creations are individual tea-saucer-sized apple and pear tarts with a vanilla cream sauce and an elegant pouf of hot Grand Marnier souffle. Port and Stilton are offered after dinner—a civility that Sir Winston surely would have approved of.

---

*The facts in this edition were correct at press time, but places close, chefs depart, hours change.
It's best to call ahead.*

Gerard's (Le Meridien Hotel)

Corner of Burrard and Robson, (604) 682-5511
845 Burrard Street, Vancouver
Expensive; full bar; AE, DC, MC, V
Dinner Mon-Sat

Le Meridien Hotel is noted for taking traditional European concepts of hospitality seriously. So, too, Gerard's restaurant takes seriously the standards of French haute cuisine. In the dining room, maitre de Francisco Nieto and his troupe of tuxedoed, French-accented young waiters glide smoothly to and fro against a plush background of beige fabric walls, handsome oil paintings, cabinets displaying antique china, mirrors, and lush floral arrangements.

Young French chef Olivier Chaleil presides in the kitchen, composing gourmet extravaganzas. Appetizers include escargots braised in white wine, thinly sliced smoked duck breast with peppered goose liver, and a dish described as a symphony of caviars and smoked fish. On a recent visit we ordered asparagus and were presented with a fragile diamond-shaped section of flaky pastry with pencil-thin asparagus rotating outward from beneath it like spokes on a wheel. The mushroom soup, a luxurious bit of business, was loaded with shiitake and morel mushrooms, the latter stuffed with chicken mousse.

Ponderously expensive entrees are served with a flourish. The Duckling in Two Acts, for example, appears first as the breast in a cider-vinegar sauce and second as a leg *confit* served with a small tossed salad and duck cracklings—an idea that could work better if only the two "acts" were not split by such a long intermission. The ubiquitous sauteed salmon achieves star status on a smooth pool of port and red wine butter sauce. It is all classical-French-modern, but the high proportion of seafood dishes, such as the Sea Medley of lobster, sole, scallops, and prawns, hints at an infatuation with the cuisine of Brittany. If you can't make up your mind, Chaleil will provide a "degustation surprise" menu of five courses for $49.

A chocolate mousse, served in triangular slabs and sprinkled with fresh mint, looked like chicken liver pate and had a lackluster flavor. The wine list, though, is excellent, and surprisingly complete for a province that has difficulty assembling good lists. On the way out, pinch a chocolate truffle from the tray on the sideboard—they're delicious.

Kirin Mandarin Restaurant

Between Thurlow and Bute on Alberni,
(604) 682-8833
1166 Alberni Street, Vancouver
Moderate; full bar; AE, MC, V
Lunch, dinner every day

The best of Vancouver's new upscale Chinese restaurants, the Kirin has a confidently postmodern decor with rose-colored tablecloths, slate green walls, and black lacquer trim. The live seafood tanks are set into the walls like an aquarium in a luxurious private home. There's valet parking, service is attentive, and prices are moderate. Its Alberni Street location and its trilingual menu—Chinese, English, and Japanese—announce its intention to win the Japanese tourist trade. Accordingly, the atmosphere can be stuffy and the staff too obsequious for comfort. The Kirin specializes in Shanghai, Sichuan, and Beijing food, with a few Cantonese specialties such as scallops steamed in the shell with black bean sauce. Live lobsters and crabs can be ordered in 11 different preparations, including cream and butter sauce, brown bean sauce, Sichuan hot and spicy, and as sashimi with wasabe and soy sauce. Dessert is sublime: red bean pie—actually a thin crepe, folded into a rectangle around a sweet-bean-sauce filling, then fried. Yes, sublime.

Le Gavroche

Across from the Westin Hotel, (604) 685-3924
1616 Alberni Street, Vancouver
Expensive; full bar; AE, DC, MC, V
Lunch Mon-Fri, dinner Mon-Sat

★ ★ ★

Going to Le Gavroche for dinner is like stepping into the past: in this pretty French restaurant in an old Vancouver house, a woman dining with a man gets a menu without prices; Caesar salad is prepared with ceremony at tableside; and waiters still give excellent, unobtrusive service. Luckily for the cholesterol count of its customers, the food at Le Gavroche is much more modern. Cream and butter are used sparingly. A long, luxurious meal (punctuated by small surprises like the tiny puff-pastry savory that appears once the serious business of ordering is over, and the scoop of palate-clearing sherbet) doesn't necessarily mean a day of remorse to follow.

Le Gavroche is for wine lovers. Owner Jean-Luc Bertrand is especially fond of Bordeaux and hunts out little-known finds; waiters can be counted on for good recommendations. The large menu features the usual fish, meat, and game dishes, usually not as interesting as the many daily specials. Try steamed mussels served with a saffron, white wine, and cream sauce; homemade rabbit pate with quince puree; or salmon fillet with dill and cucumber. Specials on one recent visit included a scallops and escargots appetizer, in portions approaching nouvelle cuisine, but perfectly prepared, and a moist, tender smoked pheasant breast resting on an intensely flavorful puree of celeriac, shallots, and wine with a light truffle sauce.

Raintree

Corner of Alberni and Cardero, (604) 688-5570
1630 Alberni Street, Vancouver
Moderate; full bar; AE, MC, V
Lunch Mon-Fri, dinner every day, brunch Sun

★ ★ ★

The Raintree bills itself as a Northwest Coast restaurant. You can hardly fail to miss this concept, inasmuch as it is cheerfully and enthusiastically explained by your waiter, reiterated on the menu, and fully explained once more on cards supplied to you at the end of the meal. Enough already. It's a good idea to focus on fresh local ingredients, but on our last visit we were served local oysters so inferior to the available imports that they shouldn't have been on the menu at all. On the whole, though, we think this place has great potential.

Chef Rebecca Dawson offers an interesting combination of sophisticated innovation and honest heartiness. There are many wonderful entrees: the wild spring salmon wrapped in savoy cabbage and napped with sweet pepper-sorrel cream is a melt-in-your-mouth luxury; the Washington rack of lamb in a crust of mustard and herbs with garlic zinfandel sauce is savory and succulent; the risotto with local shiitake and oyster mushrooms could make a name for itself in Italy. Vegetables are served on a communal platter. Desserts include such old-fashioned treasures as Okanagan apple pie with Cheddar cheese or fireweed-honey ice cream or chocolate bread pudding. The wine list echoes the Northwest Coast theme, with wines from BC, Washington, and Oregon, as well as California, and—what a blessing—a really good selection of decent wines by the glass and even by the half glass.

It's a pretty place, decorated with a serene sophistication and, provided you are seated facing the right way, a spectacular view of the North Shore skyline. Sit facing inward, however, and you are subjected to a blinding fluorescent strobe light from the kitchen as the waiters zoom in and out through the saloon-style doors.

Szechuan Chongqing Restaurant
*Corner of Victoria
and Broadway,
(604) 254-7434
2495 Victoria Drive,
Vancouver
Inexpensive; full bar;
AE, MC, V
Lunch, dinner every day*

Since our last review, the owners have been doing some interior decorating. The outside of the building still resembles a shoebox, but inside, new furniture, lamps, and wall coverings have considerably brightened up the place. The food is still the best Sichuan fare in the city. With Mrs. Wong managing the front and Mr. Wong ruling the kitchen, you can count on the quality of the food to remain consistent. The Wongs, originally from Chongqing, feature Northern Chinese cuisine on their menu: rich brown sauces, heavy on the garlic; lots of explosive red peppers; and wheat (not rice) as the principal starch. Our favorite dish on a rainy Saturday afternoon was a big bowl of #168 Deluxe Tan Tan noodles—a noodle soup in a rich peanutty broth accented with red chiles, green onions, and crushed peanuts. True Sichuan penicillin. The #56 Chongqing Chicken is tender morsels in a hot and garlicky brown sauce served on a bed of crisp deep-fried spinach. And then there's #88. . . . The seafood specials, visible in long tanks by the front door, are reliably good, and the hot-pot dishes—strips of meat and vegetables to cook at your own table in a pot of blistering hot broth— are fun for groups. Order a sliced roll (one easily feeds two) to mop up all the sauces.

If we have a complaint about the Chongqing, it is that the owners have not yet learned how to handle their ever-increasing popularity. You must make a reservation now, particularly on Sunday evenings, when large family groups converge unannounced on the restaurant and claim every seat in sight.

Looking for a particular place? Check the index at the back of this book for individual restaurants, hotels, B&Bs, parks, and more.

Umberto's Fish House

*Near the corner of Pacific
and Hornby,*
(604) 687-6621
1376 Hornby Street,
Vancouver
Expensive; full bar;
AE, DC, MC, V
Dinner Tues-Sat

Vancouver is a city that should have outstanding seafood restaurants but doesn't. The number of really good ones can be counted on the fingers of one hand, and, oddly enough, the best of these is an Italian version. Umberto's Fish House (formerly La Cantina) radiates a sunny, Mediterranean atmosphere with its tiled floor, colorful throw cushions, open service kitchen, and jars of antipasto and cans of olive oil shelved along the walls for decoration. Except for a couple of salads—and the desserts, of course—the place is seriously dedicated to things that swim and variations thereof. There are excellent pastas: cannelloni filled with crab meat and spinach; baked noodles with layers of mixed seafood; and fusilli in ginger and shrimp sauce. Entrees include grilled tuna with wasabe-lime butter; a melt-in-your-mouth dish of pan-fried skate wings in black butter sauce; and a Dungeness crab dish in which the meat is removed from the crab, mixed with spinach, nutmeg, and bechamel sauce, gratineed with Parmesan, and set under the grill—heaven! Umberto's cioppino, bursting with fresh shellfish and chunks of fish, may well be the best dish on the menu. The wine list contains—for obvious reasons—only white wines, except for a selection of ports. In summer there is a small patio for dining alfresco—near where the fish is grilled over apple wood.

Vassilis Taverna

*Near MacDonald
and Broadway,*
(604) 733-3231
2884 W Broadway,
Vancouver
Moderate; full bar;
AE, DC, MC, V
Lunch Mon-Fri,
dinner every day

Some restaurants seem to live in a blessed steady state, defying the edict that all things either improve or decline but cannot stay the same. Since 1977, Vassilis has been consistently perfect—a family-run, moderately priced restaurant doing outstanding ethnic cooking. In summer, the restaurant's front opens onto the sidewalk. Inside, the decor is catalogue Greek, right down to the paper place mats with their maps of the Greek islands. The menu has just enough originality, just enough comforting traditionalism.

Start with a huge plate of calamari—the region's best—or the saganaki, Greek kefalotiri cheese fried in oil and sprinkled with lemon juice. The house specialty is perfectly juicy kotopoulo: chicken pounded flat, seasoned simply with lemon juice, garlic, and oregano, and then barbecued. Simple, but impossible to replicate on a backyard hibachi. The lamb fricassee, in a casserole of artichoke hearts and broad beans, is falling-off-the-bone tender. The Greek salad is a sufficient meal in itself if you side it with a succulent pile of quick-fried baby smelts to eat like French fries. Bouzouki music fills the background. Try to fit in one last treat: a honey-sweet piece of homemade baklava or Georgia Demiris' navarino, a lighter almond/custard/syrup creation that is truly luscious. Then be on your way—little money spent, but much enriched.

The William Tell

In the Georgian Court Hotel, across from BC Place Stadium,
(604) 688-3504
765 Beatty Street,
Vancouver
Expensive; full bar;
AE, DC, MC, V
Lunch Mon-Fri, dinner every day, brunch Sunday

The William Tell is one of Vancouver's finest tributes to old-world dining elegance; owner Erwin Doebeli is the consummate restaurateur. All evening Doebeli seems to be here, there, and everywhere, greeting arrivals at the door with enthusiasm, dispensing bread from a large wicker tray like one of the busboys, or whipping up a mean cafe diablo with a flamboyance that alone makes the expensive tab bearable.

It's a luxurious setting; tables are resplendent with fine china, sparkling crystal, and gleaming silver. Although some diners find it a little too dim in the evening, there's no restaurant more special at lunchtime, when the light streams in through windows embellished with stained-glass Swiss coats of arms.

New chef Lars Jorgensen, formerly of the Mandarin Hotel and a member of Team Canada (which competes for international culinary awards), maintains the tradition of French perfectionism while adding his own style to the menu. Among the appetizers there is Swiss-style air-dried beef or British Columbia–style smoked salmon. We liked the fresh pan-fried foie gras (thin, rich slices of duck pate served warm on a bed of greens), but found the soup of the day to be insipid and disappointing. A better choice would have been the duck consomme baked under puff pastry—sometimes a 15-minute wait, but worth it. An entree of sweetbreads in a rich morel sauce was satisfyingly tender and pungent with the earthy essence of mushrooms. A broiled New York steak came with a sauce deepened with herbs and marrow. A dish of sliced duck breast "with caramelized apples" was cooked to pink perfection and carefully served with a small, warm duck salad on the side, but we could find only two small apple slivers. As a rule, the desserts prepared in the kitchen, such as an amazingly good coconut ice cream, far surpass those on the pastry cart. The wine cellar is one of this restaurant's most rewarding features; ask to see the "reserved wine menu" for a listing of its most special contents.

Accord

27th and Main,
(604) 876-6110
4298 Main Street,
Vancouver
Moderate; wine and beer;
MC, V
Dinner every day
(open until 2am)

A particularly good entry among the host of new Chinese restaurants that have set up far from the high rents of Chinatown, the Accord is as bashful as the Yuen Dung but less expensive. Behind those impenetrable white venetian blinds, it serves excellent Cantonese seafood—try the live shrimp, when available, steamed in the shell and brought to the table with a spicy soy-based dipping sauce, or the beef tenderloin teppan with peppercorn sauce (essentially pepper steak with a Chinese accent). The menu includes a handful of Chiu Chow specialties, the food of most of Southeast Asia's Chinese immigrants. Open until 2am weekdays, 3am on weekends—perfect for those evenings when the '50s come back and the only thing that will do at midnight is Chinese food.

Alma Street Cafe

Broadway and Alma,
(604) 222-2244
2505 Alma Street,
Vancouver
Moderate; full bar;
AE, MC, V
Breakfast, lunch, dinner
every day, brunch Sat-Sun

An original neighborhood sort of place with a lively atmosphere, Alma Street manages quite successfully to offer something for everyone. It's open all day; the food is imaginative, reasonably priced, and homemade. From 7:30am on weekdays and during the popular weekend brunches, a central table billows with fresh breakfast buns and baked goods, and you can choose from among honest breakfast fare like omelets, hot cereal, or cinnamon-scented whole-wheat waffles with fresh fruit toppings. The black bean and tortilla soup and chicken in stone-ground mustard sauce are tops in the afternoon. For the vegetarian, there are several choices, including some inventive tofu selections. Live jazz Wednesday to Saturday, from 8pm.

Ashiana

Near 35th and Victoria,
(604) 321-5620
5076 Victoria Drive,
Vancouver
Moderate; full bar;
AE, MC, V
Lunch Tues-Sun,
dinner every day

Not a restaurant that worries about either decor or service, the Ashiana continues to thrive because it makes some of the best Indian food to be found in this international city. Fluent in many of the country's cuisines, it specializes in exotic tandoori dishes and the curried food of the Mughlai-Punjabi. Neighborhood Indian families frequent the place at lunch, but at night and weekends it's the domain of many adventurous Anglos.

Outside there's a spiffy new awning, but inside you'll find the same eccentric plaster job and no-frills decor as in years past. Concentrate on the bread, a draw in itself, accented with coriander and baked in the tandoor. For appetizers, try either the cheese pakoras—little squares of paneer cheese dipped in a thin chickpea batter and deep-fried until they puff up, or samosas—triangular pastries stuffed with spicy potatoes and peas or ground lamb and served with a sweet/spicy condiment that tastes like a cross between barbecue sauce and raspberry jam. Don't let the famous tandoori chicken here blind you to other finds, such as the lamb in a voluptuous mild and creamy yogurt sauce with ground nuts, or the herb-rich lamb curry. Intensely sweet Indian fudgelike candies and pastries can be purchased at the sweetmeat bar to take home.

The Avenue Grill

Corner of West Blvd
(Arbutus) and W 41st,
(604) 266-8183
2114 W 41st Avenue,
Vancouver
Moderate; full bar;
AE, MC, V

The only thing recognizable about the old Avenue Grill these days is the original '40s Art Deco neon sign above the front door. Two years ago Jim Ayers took the dowager in hand and rejuvenated her into a California girl. Everything fits the Califoria bistro formula: pastel peach-and-mint decor; glass blocks; a palm tree named "Larry"; whirling ceiling fans; modern art on the walls; and a light,

Breakfast, lunch, dinner
Mon-Sat, brunch Sun

trendy menu with nouveau California-French-Asian-Italian influences.

Very popular with the neighborhood Kerrisdale crowd, and a fun place to be when The Grill puts on its two-week-long culinary festivals (garlic, hot pepper, lover's). The most imaginative food is offered during these theme weeks, but there are some excellent items on the regular menu as well. The pecan-breaded breast of chicken with Pommery mustard sauce, for instance—the tangy sauce giving a pleasant kick to the moist pan-fried chicken. The calf liver with apples, onions, and calvados, and the meat loaf are tasty variations on familiar themes. But who's the guy in the kitchen that insists on garnishing even the spiciest dishes with a strawberry rosette? Dessert is a pleasure and so is brunch. We've heard reports about rude waiters.

Bandi's

Between Beach and
Pacific on Howe,
(604) 685-3391
1427 Howe Street,
Vancouver
Moderate; full bar;
AE, MC, V
Lunch Mon-Fri,
dinner every day

This is the sort of place we would like to see at Whistler. After a cold day on the ski slopes, nothing would be more comforting than a warm bellyful of the robust country food of Hungary. At Bandi's, chef-owner Bandi Rinkhy produces authentic cuisine, with maitre d' and co-owner Kader Karaa's sense of humor providing the dash of paprika. The peasant bread (deep-fried and puffy) comes with a side dish of raw (not roasted) garlic; goulash soup is presented in a little kettle set over a portable flame; and the paraszt sonka (smoked farmer's ham with fresh horseradish and green onions) is served in large, hearty portions. Uborkasalata (cucumber with sour cream dressing) may be the only concession to a timid palate. Remarkably enough, on our last visit, Bandi's was out of cabbage rolls—which is something akin to a Scandinavian restaurant being out of herring. Desserts consist mostly of rich, sweet crepes.

Bridges Seafood Restaurant

Across from the Granville
Island Market,
(604) 687-4400
1696 Duranleau Street,
Granville Island,
Vancouver
Moderate; full bar;
AE, MC, V
Lunch, dinner every day,
brunch Sun

On a warm, sunny afternoon or a sultry summer evening, the most popular grazing spot in the city is on Bridges' outdoor deck. If the fare here were downright bad, it wouldn't matter much; the star of the show is not food but downtown Vancouver, its glittering towers making an irresistible light show across the waters of False Creek. The Burrard and Granville bridges dominate the view (hence the name), and fresh yields from the Granville Island Market just across the street dominate the menu.

There are four places to eat here: the deck; the pub for drinks and appetizers; the bistro for light informal meals; and the upstairs dining room, where more ambitious offerings (mahi mahi with jicama-grapefruit relish, or grilled partridge with polenta and blackcurrant tea sauce) make up the menu.

Bruno's Restaurant

41st and Granville,
(604) 266-3210
5701 Granville Street,
Vancouver
Moderate; full bar;
AE, MC, V
Lunch Mon-Fri,
dinner Mon-Sat

Bruno Born, who made his reputation at The Chef and The Carpenter and Mama Gold's, now has a place of his own at one of Vancouver's busiest intersections. Even so, it is definitely a neighborhood restaurant—a long, narrow, comfortably upholstered, tables-slightly-too-close-together sort of place, extremely popular with the local Kerrisdale residents. Watch for the blackboard at the entrance listing the daily specials as well as wines available by the glass, and don't miss Born's rich-tasting baked rabbit if it's available. Once you're seated, the waiter will bring you a tiny dish of salmon mousse and another of herb butter, to enjoy with a selection of house breads while you peruse the menu. The menu items are conservative but masterfully prepared. Best are the fresh veal kidneys Dijon, sauteed in a mustard cream sauce and dotted with green and pink peppercorns; a rustic chicken with caramelized garlic; and a satisfying pork tenderloin with an apple stuffing, placed on a brandy sauce and sprinkled with roasted pecans.

Chez Thierry

Toward Stanley Park on
Robson between Bidwell
and Cardero,
(604) 688-0919
1674 Robson Street,
Vancouver
Moderate; full bar;
AE, DC, MC, V
Dinner every day

The quintessential neighborhood restaurant—small and warmed by the sunny good nature of owner Thierry Damilano, a transplanted Frenchman who rolls out the red carpet for regulars and grants newcomers a more reserved but polite welcome. (In his spare time, Damilano coaches the Canadian windsurfing team.) Don't visit Chez Thierry looking for the cutting edge in food. Chef Francois Launay leaves experimentation to the nouveaux chefs and instead prepares simple, traditionally based meals without a lot of ornamentation. The house pate is good but not outstanding; try a watercress and smoked salmon salad instead, or the impossibly smooth chicken mousse, served warm in port sauce. Damilano shops daily for fish, and specials of the day can be rewarding. A recent find: fresh tuna grilled with artichoke, garlic, and fresh tomato. Red snapper is poached and served in a bright yellow saffron sauce with sweet red peppers. Chocolate desserts are rich and just bitter enough; the apple tarte Tatin is superb, served upside down and flamed with calvados. The wine list is carefully chosen, with interesting French wines in the $25 to $50 range. For an unusual show, order a bottle of champagne and ask Damilano to open it for you. His favorite party trick is slashing off corks with a military saber, his record being 80 in one evening.

Chiyoda

Near the corner of
Burrard and Alberni,
(604) 688-5050
1050 Alberni Street,
Vancouver
Moderate; full bar;

In a town full of sushi restaurants with robata grills on the side, Chiyoda is a robata restaurant with a sushi bar. Built on a generous scale, Chiyoda was meticulously designed (right down to the graceful little beer glasses) in Japan. Robata selections are arranged in wicker baskets on a layer of ice that separates the customer's

AE, MC, V
Lunch Mon-Fri,
dinner every day

side of the bar from the cook's side. Order from the simple menu: it lists a score of dishes, including snapper, squid, oysters, scallops, eggplant, and Japanese mushroom, with no space wasted on adjectives. The cook prepares your choices and hands the finished dishes over the bar on the end of a long wooden paddle. Seafood is excellent, but don't miss a foray into the cross-cultural world of robata—cooked garlic, potatoes, and corn.

Delilah's

Corner of Haro and
Gilford, (604) 687-3424
1906 Haro Street,
Vancouver
Moderate; full bar;
MC, V
Dinner every day,
brunch Sun

Tiny bites of pretty food are about all we can cope with in a place so entertaining, and that's what Delilah's offers: a place without constraint. Tucked away under the old Buchan Hotel and resembling nothing so much as the salon of a 19th-century bordello (oversized red plush banquettes, painted cherubs on the ceiling), this is a hip little spot catering to young, uninhibited West Enders, some of whom seem challenged to live up to the decor. Food comes in small portions, but is good and reasonably priced. And what better to eat than wild rice pancakes with chicken and an apricot-rosemary demi-glace while watching the evening unfold?

Your menu is your bill; just check off your selections and hand it to your waiter. The corn-and-crab chowder with bourbon is a good choice, and so is the New York steak with shallots and pommes frites (stacked in a little pile like cordwood and drizzled with mayonnaise). There's a decent wine list, but the house specialties are the 20 varieties of martinis, which you shake (or stir) yourself. Expect a wait to get in—it's a popular neighborhood drop-in and reservations are accepted only for groups of six or more. (By the way, there is a Delilah, and you'll know her when you see her.)

El Mariachi

Between Robson and
Georgia on Denman,
(604) 683-4982
735 Denman Street,
Vancouver
Moderate; full bar;
AE, MC, V
Dinner Tues-Sun

El Mariachi serves the most-authentic Mexican food in the city. Sure, you can have enchiladas, but husband-and-wife team Arcelia and Giovanni Vagge (she's Mexican, he's Italian—which may explain the dash of Parmesan on the refried beans) offer much more. Try crab-stuffed puff-pastry tortillas, sole in a coriander sauce, or prawns cooked with smoky-tasting chipotle peppers. Of the chicken dishes, the mole poblano is best; the mole sauce is made from 28 ingredients, including nine types of nuts, four peppers, and bitter chocolate. It's a thick, dark, and hauntingly spicy concoction.

Fish & Co.

Corner of Burrard and
Georgia, (604) 687-6543
Hyatt Regency Hotel,
Vancouver
Expensive; full bar;
AE, DC, MC, V

You expect to find legendary seafood restaurants clinging like barnacles to rustic seaside wharfs, not located on the mezzanine floors of large convention-style hotels; but given just a little more imagination and sense of adventure, Fish & Co. could be the premier seafood place in the city. As it is, we have no complaints about the qual-

*Lunch Mon-Fri, dinner
every day, brunch Sun*

ity of the fish or the expertise of chef Othmar Steinhart's executions.

When you enter the restaurant, your menu is torn off a large brass roller holding what resembles a giant roll of paper towels. It lists starters and entrees in three different categories: Favorites, such as oysters on the half shell or, yes, Surf and Turf; Classics like French onion soup or lobster (steamed, broiled, or thermidor), and Contemporaries. The last is where the kitchen experiments a little, with hot scallop salads and braided salmon and snapper (a dish invented for the '86 visit of the Prince and Princess of Wales). On the whole, the kitchen seems much more comfortable with the favorites and classics and simple dishes than with the attractive-looking specials on the brass-bordered blackboard. The stortebeker soup (a Scandinavian version of bouillabaisse) is hearty and filling and won't disappoint. Desserts are good here, particularly the iced chocolate mousse (they sneak a little spoonful of Advokaat into the middle).

Hermitage
*Between Burrard and
Thurlow in the Robson
Galeria, (604) 689-3237
115-1025 Robson Street,
Vancouver
Moderate; full bar;
AE, DC, MC, V
Lunch Mon-Fri,
dinner Mon-Sat*

Hermitage is one of those restaurants that, despite good food and sincere effort, have a difficult time attaining popularity. Whatever the reason—its rather obscure location on Robson Street, too much powerful competition nearby, or an attitude on the part of diners that Vancouver doesn't need yet another French restaurant—it's a pity that more attention isn't being paid to this deserving little place.

Owners Herve Martin and Luc Verschelden, formerly of the Pan Pacific Hotel, bring a great deal of worldly expertise to their venture. Try as they might to create a casual bistro atmosphere, the food wants to be big-hotel grand. If that's your pleasure, you won't find it done any better than here. Herve is a master with the saucepan, creating artistically appealing dishes napped in richly flavorful sauces. You'll find appetizers of shrimp won ton swimming in a vanilla cream sauce (a surprisingly tasty combination) or a petite souffle of pike with asparagus and basil butter. And the sauces progress into the entrees: a poached trout with eggplant sports a curry cream, and a boneless breast of duck is flambeed with Armagnac. We found the dessert had spent too long in the refrigerator.

Hoshi Sushi
*Near corner of Keefer and
Main, (604) 689-0877
Unit 201, Goldengate
Centre, 623-645 Main
Street, Vancouver
Moderate; full bar;*

One of the few redeeming features of the ugly new Goldengate Centre on the fringes of Chinatown, Hoshi Sushi is powered by the reputation of its owner-chef Tsutomu Hoshi. His 18 years' experience in Tokyo restaurants (followed by 11 years at Aki Japanese restaurant in Vancouver) attracts a largely Japanese clientele. There's an extensive specials list, and young

AE, MC, V
Dinner every day

Japanese waitresses eager to learn English while explaining it. The crisp soft-shelled crabs (when available) with a daikon, green onion, and soy dipping sauce are a treat. Desserts include "Japanese-style jello," a slightly goofy combination of sweet red beans and vanilla ice cream—believe it or not, not bad.

Il Giardino di Umberto

Corner of Pacific and
Hornby, (604) 669-2422
1382 Hornby Street,
Vancouver
Expensive; full bar;
AE, DC, MC, V
Lunch Mon-Fri,
dinner Mon-Sat

In the ongoing debate over which of Umberto Menghi's five Vancouver restaurants is the best, Il Giardino continues to hold the lead. Certainly it is the most romantically attractive, with its Tuscan-villa decor: high ceilings, tiled floors, winking candlelight, and vine-draped terrace for dining alfresco.

Once the darling of the well-heeled social set, then abandoned by them, Il Giardino is experiencing a popularity comeback. Evenings, tables are filled with Maui-tanned, expensively dressed patrons who wave at each other across the room. Movie stars make frequent appearances (Sean Penn recently punched out a local diner here), and the barrel-chested chef works the room, chitchatting with the regulars and flirting with the ladies—presumably leaving much of the cooking to a clamor of young cooks visible through a window to the kitchen.

The emphasis is on pasta and game with an "Italian nuova" elegance. On our last visit we tried the evening special, breast of pheasant. The farm-raised bird itself was on the bland side, but its roasted pepper stuffing and port-wine sauce made up for any deficiency. An accompanying slice of pan-roasted polenta added a comforting homey touch. We were similarly pleased with a dish of tender veal served with a melange of lightly grilled wild mushrooms that added a fine earthy flavor without overwhelming the meat. For dessert, go for the tiramisu, a light Italian specialty of thin layers of chocolate cake, layered with cream and drizzled with coffee liqueur—the best in town.

One word of warning: the daily specials are particularly enticing, but ask the price: they tend to be much more expensive than the regular menu offerings.

Jean-Pierre's Restaurant

Opposite the Hyatt near
the main Sky Train
station, (604) 669-0360
1055 Dunsmuir Street,
Plaza Level, Vancouver
Moderate; full bar;
AE, DC, MC, V
Breakfast, lunch Mon-Fri,
dinner Mon-Sat

Located in the heart of the business district, Jean-Pierre's toney ivory-and-rose-colored dining room with outdoor terrace is a magnet to the town's power lunchers. Hence, owner Jean-Pierre Bachellerie's dinner trade benefits from his license to innovate and to pass on a few good deals to the customers. On Thursday nights he offers his French provincial dinner—a four-course set menu ($18.50). The rest of the week, the dinner menu concentrates on French-accented seafood specialties, spit-roasted meats, and traditional entrees like chateaubriand with three sauces, rack of lamb, veal kidneys a la moutarde, and sole amandine. Jean-Pierre's is also one of the few French restaurants to serve breakfast, and morning can be one of the nicest times to be there. The mood is quiet, the service is unhurried and attentive, and you can gear up for the rigors of the day with a comforting plate of les oeufs Benny.

Kilimanjaro

2 blocks east of the Sky Train station in Gastown, (604) 681-9913
332 Water Street, Vancouver
Moderate; full bar; AE, DC, MC, V
Lunch Mon-Sat, dinner every day

Like East Africa itself, Amyn Sunderji's place is an intriguing melting pot: African masks and batiks mix with the deep pink walls, French provincial prints, and the swirling ceiling fans of the location's former tenants to create the atmosphere of a chic Nairobi restaurant. A smaller bistro downstairs is appealing for lunches, late-night snacks, or private parties.

The menu is based upon an Indian cuisine, reflecting the subtle alterations of the African diet—curries, for instance, are enlivened with the chiles, coconut, and peanuts of Africa as well as the usual Indian spices and herbs. Try the coconut fish soup, a recipe from Zanzibar of amazing complexity and depth; a Swahili specialty of curried goat; the famous prawns piri piri; or the uniquely African (specifically Zairean) combination of chicken in ho-ho peppers, palm oil, and garlic. "Burning spear," lamb served flaming on a sword in honor of Jomo Kenyatta, is the house specialty. The samosas (stuffed savory pastries) are the best in town. Desserts bring a fittingly exotic finale, from a rich homemade saffron ice cream topped with Frangelico to a safari mango mousse.

La Brochette

A 5-minute walk east of downtown in Gastown, (604) 684-0631
52 Alexander Street, Vancouver
Moderate; full bar; AE, V
Dinner Mon-Sat

Sit near the antique French tourne-broche and you get theatre with your dinner as chef-owner Dagobert Niemann does his intricate ballet of stoking the hardwood fires, putting racks of lamb and duck breasts on the rotisserie, sauteeing vegetables, and arranging plates. Downstairs is quieter and has an attractive bar, with seating on wide benches around a huge stone fireplace. Choose grilled veal, quail, pork, beef, lamb, or duck, or the usually reliable fish of the day. Especially good here are duck breast with gin and juniper berries, and Fraser Valley duckling. Fresh local vegetables in various preparations (potatoes mashed with a hint of blueberry; spinach mousse) appear with the main course. The wine list includes some superb (if pricey) selections, including a fair number of California reds.

La Palette

Between Robson and Alberni on Denman, (604) 681-6844
774 Denman Street, Vancouver

Two years ago, Tsugio Yachi, a French-trained Japanese chef, bought Bistro La Palette, a little enclave of French cuisine on Denman Street. Zen what happened? A cultural mix: French food, Japanese feeling. The menu includes every overly familiar dish from the country-French

Moderate; full bar;
AE, MC, V
Dinner every day

tradition. If you felt like it, you could eat escargots in garlic butter, onion soup, duck a l'orange, and the obligatory creme caramel. But the food makes up in quality what the menu lacks in imagination, and is handsomely presented, with every vegetable cooked exactly right. The rich and velvety crab bisque is a good start; follow it with roast rack of lamb or sweetbreads in green-and-pink-peppercorn sauce. Then sit back and soak up the gentle atmosphere of tranquility and ease. No wonder this is a favorite little romantic nook, with plenty of finger-nibbling going on in the corner banquettes.

Malinee's Thai Food

Between Arbutus and
Yew, (604) 737-0097
2153 W Fourth Avenue,
Vancouver
Moderate; full bar;
AE, DC, MC, V
Lunch Mon-Fri,
dinner every day

Easily the most elegant Thai restaurant in a city that is quickly taking to Thai food, Malinee's is also the most painless introduction for anyone new to the cuisine. The exterior, still bearing signs of a former life as a Greek restaurant, isn't impressive, but inside there's a serene room with Bangkok-style tablecloths, linen napkins, and good-quality china and flatware. Co-owners Ted Hamilton and Stephen Bianchin work the front, offering diners a sophisticated knowledge of Thai food gained during two years in Bangkok. Chef Kem Thong works behind the line, creating authentic northeast Thailand fare—something she began doing in Bangkok at the age of 12.

Daily specials, carefully explained, are almost always worth ordering: a whole steamed red snapper marinated in oyster sauce, red chile peppers, ginger, and cilantro, or a green curry (based on green chile peppers) of chicken and green beans in a coconut sauce. From the regular menu, choose the attractive appetizer assortment: clams or mussels, satay chicken, spring rolls, and cashew nuts spiced with red peppers. Basil/shrimp stir-fry is one of the ultimate Thai dishes, an exemplary demonstration of the Thai way with fresh herbs and the freshest of seafood. You'll be asked how hot you want your food. If there's no consensus, you can always order a side dish of green and red chiles to satisfy those who are going for the burn. Western desserts are available—ice cream or the cake of the day—for those who don't want cassava root in coconut cream at the end of a meal.

Phnom Penh Restaurant

Close to Chinatown, near
the corner of Main and
Georgia, (604) 682-5777
244 E Georgia Street,
Vancouver
Inexpensive; beer and
wine; MC, V
Lunch, dinner daily
except Tues

The Cambodian kitchen is a melting pot for the cuisines of Thailand, China, and Vietnam. Not as hot as the cooking of Thailand, not as sophisticated as the cooking of China, nor as light as Vietnamese cuisine, but positioned somewhere in between all three. Phnom Penh, Vancouver's best Cambodian restaurant, has a gentle and dignified hospitality to match its food. It is a family-run operation—which is only suitable, considering that in Cambodia the type of food it offers is considered home cooking and is not usually served in restaurants.

A pale glass of tea arrives at your table for you to sip while perusing the menu. Canh Chua Ga, Canh Chua Ca, and Canh Chua Tom (hot and sour soups containing fish, prawns, or chicken, flavored with cilantro, lemon grass, and ginger) are the best starters. There are many robust dishes to choose from—barbecued chicken with lemon grass; barbecued pork chops served over rice; and marinated beef, half barbecued, half satay—but a definite lack of vegetarian ones. Distinctively Cambodian desserts include the durian fruit (sometimes referred to as "eating sweet blancmange in the lavatory" because of its nasty smell), whipped into a custard and served over a bed of glutinous rice cooked with coconut milk. The alcohol list is limited to a small selection of beers, so order a refreshing glass of lemonade instead.

Piccolo Mondo

On Thurlow 1 block
south of Robson,
(604) 688-1633
850 Thurlow Street,
Vancouver
Moderate; full bar;
AE, MC, V
Lunch Mon-Fri,
dinner Mon-Sat

Conflicting reports persist here. A few people think it is the best Italian restaurant in the city, but others, like ourselves, are yet to be convinced. Service is uneven—sometimes warm and accommodating, at other times unfriendly and self-impressed. Certainly the food remains the most consistent factor: well-prepared, country-style food that is in strong contrast to the elegance of the restaurant's beige-and-brown interior.

Flavor, not looks, is what counts. The kitchen has a "real man" attitude towards garlic, onions, and olive oil and a macho disregard for presentation. Too many dishes come heaped onto the plate like Mt. Vesuvius, with a clashing green combo of snow peas, asparagus, and broccoli clinging precariously to the edges. The choices are just as overwhelming. The regular menu alone lists over 100 dishes, and the photocopied sheet of daily specials is so crammed with items that your eyes could become permanently crossed from the effort of trying to read it all in the dim lighting. You will find every type of Italian dish imaginable, plus some surprises, such as sole in aquavit with Danish caviar (from chef Gildo Casadei's days as a chef in Sweden), as well as some decidedly French items such as frogs' legs Provencal. We can enthusiastically recommend the radicchio alla griglia (an appetizer of radicchio, studded with garlic cloves, oven-broiled, and splashed with olive oil, lemon juice, and salt); the tortellini alla nonna (homemade tortellini in a delicate mustard cream sauce) and the osso buco (veal shank bones cooked to the meltdown point in a sauce of tomatoes and saffron). Avoid the risotto, which had a watery tomato-rice-souplike consistency. This is the place for lovers of Italian wine; Piccolo Mondo has the most comprehensive and most sophisticated selection in Canada.

Send us your opinions and tips on the report form at the back of this book.

The Pink Pearl

Hastings and Clark,
(604) 253-4316
1132 E Hastings Street,
Vancouver
Moderate; full bar;
AE, MC, V
Lunch, dinner every day

At 650 seats, the Pink Pearl is certainly the biggest Chinese restaurant in Vancouver, and some say that, for Cantonese food, it's the best. Fresh seafood tanks out front are a clue that the menu is especially strong on seafood, with a list of preparations for live shrimp, clams, crabs, lobsters, geoducks, oysters, abalone, rock cod, and scallops. The crab sauteed with five spices is not the expected star-anise taste, but a spectacularly good take on a dish sometimes translated as "crab with peppery salt," crisp, chile-hot and salty on the outside, moist on the inside.

Pink Pearl serves an excellent dim sum every day (be sure to arrive early on weekends to avoid the lineups). Here size is a distinct advantage: the busier the kitchen in a dim sum restaurant, the fresher the food when it reaches your table. Cart jockeys here always seem to have time to smile and wait for you to make your selections among such dishes as sticky rice wrapped in a lotus leaf, stuffed dumplings, and fried white turnip cakes. The table-clearing system makes an amusing scene. The "tablecloth" is actually a stack of thick white plastic sheets; when you finish eating, a waiter will grab the corners of the top sheet, with a quick flip, scoop everything up, dishes and all, and haul the mess away.

The Prow

At the north end
of Burrard Street,
(604) 684-1339
Canada Place, Vancouver
Moderate; full bar;
AE, DC, MC, V
Lunch, dinner every day,
brunch Sun

To avoid view restaurants as nothing more than stunning showcases for mediocre food is to miss out on restaurants like The Prow. Its location at the bow of the cruise-ship-shaped Vancouver Convention Centre affords it one of the most arresting outlooks in this view-rich city, but the creations of chef Denis Blais easily hold their own. His appetizers range from the traditional (Caesar salad) to the nouvelle (ginger prawns in black bean sauce with watercress tempura). A range of culinary influences is exhibited in the menu—a little Italian (roasted half duck with blackberry port sauce, served with Gorgonzola polenta), a little Oriental (a sizzling clay pot of marinated beef, straw mushrooms, Oriental greens, and chiles with broad noodles and sake). But somehow, that endless blue vista of Burrard Inlet makes seafood seem the only appropriate choice. We recommend the mahi mahi, pan-fried and draped with an amazing grapefruit and sorrel yogurt sauce, or halibut (in season) with hazelnuts and ginger creme fraiche. By all means reserve a window seat, but bring along a sweater; window tables can be drafty.

Rubina Tandoori

In south Vancouver, near
the corner of Victoria
Drive and Kingsway,
(604) 874-3621
1962 Kingsway,

Son Shaffeen Jamal is the amiable maitre d'; mother Krishna cooks the authentic East Indian fare. Rubina's menu is built around tandoori dishes, South Indian seafood, Punjabi and Mogul dishes, and many more. Tandoori breads are especially good here. Try the fish masala,

*Vancouver
Moderate; full bar;
AE, MC, V
Lunch Mon-Fri,
dinner every day*

Santa Fe Cafe

*Between Fir and Pine
on W 4th,
(604) 738-8777
1688 W Fourth Avenue,
Vancouver
Moderate; full bar;
AE, MC, V
Lunch Mon-Fri,
dinner every day*

Sawasdee Thai Restaurant

*Corner of Main and
27th, (604) 876-4030
4250 Main Street,
Vancouver
Moderate; full bar;
MC, V
Dinner Tues-Sun*

a dry curry with potatoes, or any of the dishes that include the Rubina's homemade paneer cheese. If the coconut barfi (a puddinglike dessert) is still warm, it's delicious. Rubina has separate smoking and nonsmoking rooms. Nonsmokers get the older and funkier room, smokers get the newer, plusher one. Whom do they prefer?

The cooking of the American Southwest has been trendy for so long now that we keep expecting it to blow out of town like a tumbleweed. The fact is, people love it, and what they love they hang on to, no matter what the culinary dictators decree. The Santa Fe Cafe has been around for two years now, and it is just as popular as when it first opened. A bright box of a room with tables too close together, an open kitchen, and a changing gallery of striking art for sale, it doesn't look particularly Western. Foodwise, though, it sticks pretty close to the chiles-and-salsa theme (with some Cajun and Californian influences thrown in).

Hong Kong–born and California-trained owner-chef Eddie Cheung (a shy, bespectacled fellow you could never imagine under a ten-gallon hat) offers both a typed menu of regular items and a handwritten sheet of daily specials. On the regular menu rest our favorites: the crab chimichanga, a neat tortilla package encasing spicy crab in New Mexico–style red and green chile sauce; unclassical Caesar salad (whole romaine leaves under a dusting of Parmesan cheese and homemade croutons); the linguine with prawns is a rich, spicy, but not too hot, coating of garlic, olive oil, cilantro, and black beans; and the homemade Yucatan sausages, stuffed with pork and chicken, seasoned with allspice, cumin, jalapeno, and parsley. Grilled fish is a familar choice on the specials list; the corn and crab chowder is a welcome one.

Side dishes and desserts show less imagination, and over the past two years service has swung back and forth between excellent and appalling. But then, no one else in town dares make Southwestern cuisine this good, so you take your chances.

The oldest of Vancouver's Thai restaurants has aged well. Sawasdee doesn't offer the most sophisticated Thai food you can eat in Vancouver, but it might be the most fun place to go. The authentic Thai feel, mostly supplied by the staff, is of genuine happiness.

The mee krob appetizer—crisp noodles with shrimp, bean sprouts, dried tofu, and shredded red cabbage—will be either too sweet or addictive, depending on your taste. Seafood is very reliable: try the clams with green pepper, onions, and fresh basil in a rich brown sauce, or the prawns sauteed with garlic, broccoli, and black pepper, fragrant with just-cracked peppercorns. You'll be asked how hot you want the dishes: unless you're Thai, two stars out of four is probably enough.

The new Sawasdee at 2145 Granville Street, (604) 737-8222, is open for lunch during the week and for dinner daily except Sunday. The menu's the same.

Shijo Japanese Restaurant

*1 block west of Burrard
on W 4th,
(604) 732-4676
1926 W Fourth Avenue,
Vancouver
Moderate; full bar;
AE, MC, V
Lunch Mon-Fri, dinner
every day (except holidays)*

With its uncluttered modern design (short on Japanese restaurant cliches and long on comfort), Shijo is a pleasant sushi bar, with excellent sushi and robata food. Don't miss the grilled oysters on the half shell, painted with a light miso sauce, or the "shiitake foilyaki," shiitake mushrooms sprinkled with lemony ponzu sauce and cooked in foil. Orange sherbet, served in a hollowed-out orange, is a refreshing end to the meal.

Tai Chi Hin

*Corner of Smithe and
Burrard, (604) 682-1888
888 Burrard Street,
Vancouver
Moderate; full bar;
AE, MC, V
Lunch, dinner every day*

There was a time when going out for Chinese food in Vancouver meant bopping down to Chinatown to a noisy, cavernous place with steamy windows and spotty tablecloths. No longer. The big Asian money shaking up the town has created a demand for restaurants like Tai Chi Hin, upscale and located in the downtown business district. Here the decor is postmodern: glass-block and pastel. The chairs are ebony, the tablecloths white damask, and the china a pretty blue-and-white. New-wave music plays on the sound system, and the tuxedoed waiters give the same polished service as Swiss hotel-school graduates. The look is so glamorous, it makes the food appear to be more expensive than it actually is. Northern and Mandarin cuisines prevail here, which means you will find dishes commonly found in Beijing, Shanghai, and Sichuan province, with some modification to suit Hong Kong (Cantonese) palates.

We recommend the fried smoked duck (served in crisp chunks with coriander and dumplings); the crab and white asparagus soup; and the garlic eel in a smooth brown sauce. Even the simple dishes like crisp rice and chow mein Shanghai style (mixed with thick, fried noodles) are well prepared and distinctive. The rock cod comes to your table live in a plastic case for your pre-meal inspection. If that sort of thing puts you off, tell them you will pass on the preview. For something special, the Peking duck (served in two courses) does not need to be ordered in advance, but the Beggar's Chicken does. It's worth the extra trouble to do so: the whole chicken, stuffed with an aromatic filling, wrapped in lotus leaves, and baked inside a two-inch coating of dough (the original recipe called for river clay) for several hours, is a dramatically different dish for four. Ask them to remove the rock-hard crust at the table—it requires some skill and is fun to watch. Tsing Tao beer makes the perfect accompaniment, especially with the many spicy Sichuan dishes.

Tasca
Near the corner of Nicola and Robson, (604) 681-5015 1508 Robson Street, Vancouver Moderate; full bar; AE, MC, V Lunch Tues-Fri, dinner every day

★ ★

Dining out in Vancouver offers a vast range of international cuisines, including some not often encountered. Here's a vote for Portuguese food: Tasca, a seafood place that calls to mind the tiny, sun-speckled cafes of Lisbon. For starters try the barbecued chorizo (served aflame) or the spicy, lightly fried octopus. Main courses include national dishes of Portugal: bacalhau (salt cod with potatoes); carne de porco a alentejana (a saucy combination of marinated pork and fresh seasoned clams, steamed in their shells); sardinhas en escabeche (fried sardines in a spicy marinade), and, on a lucky day, caldo verde soup (potatoes and greens). The crab in coriander and garlic served with Portuguese-style fried potatoes is a popular dish. Wash it all down with a good vinho verde, and you'll swear you hear fado singers sighing over the good life in the Algarve.

The Teahouse Restaurant at Ferguson Point
Enter Stanley Park from Georgia Street and continue to Ferguson Point, (604) 669-3281 Stanley Park, Vancouver Moderate; full bar; AE, MC, V Lunch Mon-Fri, dinner every day, brunch Sat-Sun

★ ★

This is one of the loveliest places to eat in Vancouver, and certainly the one most in demand on Mother's Day. In the original section, the soft peach-and-leaf-green decor is that of an English country home; the newer glassed-in wings look out over the water and garden, giving you the feeling of dining in a conservatory.

If only the food could rise to the setting. The ingredients are certainly of the best quality, but the menu is dominated by old-fashioned, vaguely French continental entrees. Granted, there have been some welcome innovations since our last visit. The duck a l'orange has been updated to duck in cassis sauce; the lamb chops, formerly basted with mustard, are now served in a Martini & Rossi sauce; and the chicken supreme has taken on a Spanish accent with its Andalusian sauce of red pimientos, tomatoes, mushrooms, and black olives. The simple dishes can be the best: the lamb chops are cooked perfectly medium rare, the fish of the day is grilled simply and well. Vegetables get the attention they deserve.

With the exception of the rarely-seen-nowadays baked Alaska, the desserts tend toward the same teahouse-tourist mode and could be more interesting. But, with the sun setting and the prospect of a walk along the seawall before you, perhaps you could forgive this restaurant almost anything. Weekend brunches are popular, and reservations are necessary at all times.

Looking for a particular place? Check the index at the back of this book for individual restaurants, lodgings, attractions, and more.

Umberto Al Porto

*In Gastown near
the Steam Clock,
(604) 683-8376
321 Water Street,
Vancouver
Moderate; full bar;
AE, DC, MC, V
Lunch Mon-Fri,
dinner Mon-Sat*

★ ★

Large parties order wine by the magnum and take the empties home for their change collections; more serious students of Italian wine come to the basement of a Gastown warehouse to choose from pages of listings, divided by region. Umberto's least expensive restaurant, Al Porto has a lively, color-splashed decor and good pasta (in spite of the fact that Menghi gives this place very little attention). We recommend the antipasto plate or the excellent carpaccio as a starter, and suggest you then move right into pasta (though some of it is made off-premises, it's exactly right). Try the fettuccine with smoked salmon, the clam and garlic linguine, or the cannelloni stuffed with seafood and spinach and topped with a mild cream sauce. A good but seasonal entree is the salmon.

Vong's Kitchen

*Corner of Fraser and
E 44th, (604) 327-4627
5989 Fraser Street,
Vancouver
Inexpensive; no alcohol;
no credit cards; no checks
Dinner Wed-Sun*

With new upscale Chinese restaurants cropping up all over the city, one could get positively nostalgic about Vong's. It seems to have been around forever: the same tiny place on unfashionable Fraser Street, the same steamy windows and kitchen-table decor inside. If you are serious about food and not into making impressions, then Vong's is the choice. The place is owned and run by the Vong family, who maintain high standards and prepare each dish with loving attention. No possibility here of the chef running off to another restaurant and taking along with him the recipes for all your favorite dishes.

The easiest Chinese menu in town to read contains about 70 items, thematically listed. Everything is excellent. The spicy hot noodles are chewy, satisfying, and not unbearably hot. The chile sauce prawns—WOW—are another matter altogether. The atomic rice does not refer to chile power but to the process of pouring rich broth on top of the crisp-cooked rice and vegetables, producing a loud, sizzling racket. Milder palettes will enjoy the jade chicken (nice little pieces of marinated chicken served on a light bed of deep-fried spinach) or the orange beef (almost-sweet strips of tender beef in a rich orange sauce). Vong's daily specials are often a treat. Your bill is accompanied by deep-fried banana fritters. If you don't plan on arriving before 6pm, reservations are essential—even then, be prepared to wait for your table. It's worth it.

Yuen Tung

*Between 23rd and 24th
on Fraser, (604) 873-1931
3944 Fraser Street,
Vancouver
Moderate; full bar;
MC, V
Dinner every day
except Tuesday*

Yuen Tung is one of the secretive Chinese restaurants. There's no view in from the outside, no clue that what's going on behind the closed blinds is the Cantonese wall-of-sound effect, a restaurant full of people eating and talking at maximum intensity. The specialties here are the shark's-fin soup and the squab, roasted until its skin crisps and then served with salt for dipping. Lobsters greet you at the door (live, in tanks) and once again on your plate, delicious with ginger and onions. Don't shy from the large oysters with green onions, garlic, and cilantro or from the deep-fried, battered sole bones, served with flesh of the fish on top.

Yuen Tung is expensive by Chinese restaurant standards, with a chef who made his name as a cook at the Hong Kong Stockbrokers' Society club restaurant.

The Amorous Oyster

Corner of 16th and Oak,
(604) 732-5916
3236 Oak Street,
Vancouver
Moderate; beer and wine;
AE, MC, V
Lunch Mon-Fri,
dinner every day

It calls itself "a casually elegant bistro," but we consider it more of an Australian seafood house. Oysters are the reigning delicacy, with as many as eight variations on a given day (from the classic oysters Rockefeller to the exotic oysters in green-chile pesto). But the selective menu is suffused with the love of fresh food that owner-chef Sue Adams brought with her from Australia, and the wine list (all available by the glass, half-litre, or bottle) is especially strong on down-under entries. Daily offerings are chalked up on a large blackboard. For dessert, try the limey lime mousse.

Beijing

Corner of Smithe and
Hornby, (604) 688-7788
865 Hornby Street,
Vancouver
Moderate; full bar;
AE, MC, V
Lunch Mon-Fri,
dinner every day

The Beijing broke ground in Vancouver as the first upscale downtown Chinese restaurant. Now it has lots of competition, including the Tai Chi Hin, less than a block away on Burrard, and the Kirin on Alberni. The restaurant looked a bit shabby on a recent visit, but the food is still good. Seafood dishes are outstanding, especially the abalone, the sea cucumbers with mushrooms, and the geoduck stewed in onion-redolent broth. Lovers of hotness will not be disappointed, provided they choose wisely.

Cafe de Paris

Denman and Robson,
(604) 687-1418
751 Denman Street,
Vancouver
Moderate; full bar;
AE, MC, V
Lunch Tues-Fri,
dinner Mon-Sat

The bistro may be located on Denman Street in Vancouver's West End, but in spirit it's somewhere on the left bank of the Seine. Gallic as a croissant (right down to the waiters, who can be glacial or perfectly charming, depending on how they feel that day), it's a dim space with small tables, a blackboard menu, and a cast of regulars. Some prefer weekday nights, when a subdued mood prevails and you can actually *hear* Aznavour singing on the sound system; others prefer weekends, when the tempo and noise level soar, the air gets thick and smoky, and there's a theatrical buzz in the air. Chef Patrice Suhner matches the almost-French atmosphere with almost-French food—and gets raves from some. It's a classic bistro menu (rabbit, calf brains, onion soup, sweetbreads, mussels) and he is famous for his pepper steak (a tender cut of meat in a no-nonsense peppercorn sauce). But, in our opinion, the place is waning. The mussels and the crisp pommes frites are probably the most reliable things on the menu. On a recent visit, our duck breast in a peach sauce was a stringy bit of duck and a couple of pallid (could they have been canned?) peach slices. We accept half—but only half—the blame for ordering something made with peaches in March. (It *was* on the specials list.) The "hot" potatoes with the herring salad were tepid. No, Cafe de Paris isn't the great place it once was, but those pommes frites are still to die for.

Cafe Kokken

Corner of W 12th and Granville, (604) 732-3013
1485 W 12th Avenue, Vancouver
Inexpensive; full bar; MC, V
Lunch, dinner Mon-Sat

Co-owners Norman Galdstone and Birgit Westergaard (the latter a native of Hans Christian Andersen's birthplace, Odense) have given the place an atmosphere as bright and fresh as Scandinavian springtime, with a white-and-blue interior, Danish country murals, and perky little red Danish flags poking out here and there. The lunch menu at Cafe Kokken (pronounced Cookin) lists all the obvious things that come to mind when one thinks of Denmark: open-faced sandwiches, Danish pastries, and, of course, herring. But there are other things too: Danish hot dogs; a Baltic borscht; and a Danish omelet topped with bacon, tomato, and onions and called a Hamlet. At dinner the menu expands to more-substantial items such as oven-roasted chicken with apricot and walnut stuffing; a pecan-breaded turkey schnitzel; and Frikadeller, minced veal and pork patties accompanied by red cabbage and potatoes—the national dish of Denmark. The specialty is Bof med Spejlaeg (minced sirloin steak topped with egg and onions), a dish that's fun to eat and even more fun to pronounce. Good food, affordable too—and that's no fairy tale.

The Cannery

East on Hastings, left on Victoria Drive, then right on Commissioner,
(604) 254-9606
2205 Commissioner Street, Vancouver
Expensive; full bar; AE, DC, MC, V
Lunch Mon-Fri, dinner every day

Who says you can't eat the view? From The Cannery's upstairs tables, amid old beams and lobster pots, the vista of the industrial end of Burrard Inlet is one of the best in the city. Fresh fish is barbecued or poached quite carefully, and vegetables are treated with respect. It's a difficult place to find, but very easy to digest.

Chef and the Carpenter

Robson and Denman,
(604) 687-2700
1745 Robson Street, Vancouver
Moderate; full bar; AE, DC, MC, V
Lunch Mon-Fri, dinner every day

The original chef and his partner, the carpenter, are long gone, but the grip of tradition on this reliable Robson Street restaurant is firm: those seeking a meal just like the one they had last time will not be disappointed. Decor is pleasant French provincial: flowered fabric walls, simple tables, a minimum of fuss. The trim menu echoes the design. The chef has a light Mediterranean touch, particularly with fish. The spicy Louisiana gumbo is a good, hefty starter. Regular items include Caesar salad and fresh mussels. For an entree, try the scallops in a creamy leek and vermouth sauce. Daily specials are recommended. The frozen coffee parfait is a refreshing dessert.

Dos Amigos

5 blocks west of MacDonald at W Broadway and Trutch, (604) 731-5444 3189 W Broadway, Vancouver Inexpensive; wine and beer; AE, MC Lunch Tues-Sun, dinner every day

Installed in a former Swensen's ice cream parlor on West Broadway, Dos Amigos makes no claim to be an authentic Spanish tapas bar, and in fact seems more than a little influenced by chef Maureen Brazier's years of cooking in Greek restaurants. Along with the spicy potatoes and six-inch Spanish sardines on the menu, you'll find a Greek salad and grilled skewers of chicken or lamb with yogurt sauce. But the spirit of tapas translates well enough, and the food is exemplary for its freshness. The wine list is small and very inexpensive; beers include Okanagan Spring and Key Lager, both unpasteurized brews from small BC breweries. No reservations accepted, so expect a wait on weekends.

English Bay Cafe

Corner of Beach and Denman, on the beach, (604) 669-2225 1795 Beach Avenue, Vancouver Moderate; full bar; AE, DC, MC, V Lunch Mon-Sat, dinner every day, brunch Sun

The classic view of the sun setting over English Bay can be found a few blocks closer to Stanley Park in the bar of the Sylvia Hotel, but anyone who wants to eat while the glow spreads over the water is well advised to choose the English Bay Cafe instead. Downstairs is a loud "tapas bistro" featuring the Top 40 of international-trendy snacks: nachos, fried calamari, Oriental salads, Cajun crab cakes, and light entrees, along with a large choice of imported beers. Upstairs, where the view of the water doesn't battle the foreground interference of Beach Avenue traffic, the kitchen is more serious. It offers seafood, pasta, and other continental specialties, which might include rack of New Zealand lamb, fresh venison in Dijon sauce, or duck breast saute in brandy sauce. Brunches are very popular, but the best deal is the January and February lobsterfest, when you can get one big lobster with all the trimmings for $12.95. Mid-May to mid-September there's patio seating when it doesn't rain, with a separate barbecue menu of grilled fish, ribs, and burgers. Finding parking around here is very difficult, so we always spring for the cafe's $3 valet parking service (free at lunch and Sunday brunch).

Grand View

On W Broadway at Manitoba, (604) 879-8885 60 W Broadway, Vancouver Moderate; full bar; AE, MC, V Lunch, dinner every day

Chiang Kai-shek's former chef has been overtaken by yet another Chinese revolution: there are now far tonier Chinese restaurants in Vancouver serving essentially the same Northern Chinese fare. But the restaurant on Broadway, with its view to the mountains over the city's industrial center, is still worth a visit. In the hot and sour soup with seafood, scallops, squid, and shrimp share a nicely balanced broth with tofu, egg, Chinese mushrooms, tomatoes, peppers, and scallions. Try the spicy stir-fried eggplant, or the shrimp with hot garlic sauce. The mushu pork can be chancy: at one meal it came garnished with deep-fried won ton wrappers and sesame seeds and was missing one of the traditional ingredients, tiger-lily pods. Service can be very slow.

Greenhut Vietnamese Cuisine

Outside the Granville Island Market, across from the main gates (604) 736-9688 1500 W Second Avenue, Vancouver Moderate; full bar; AE, MC, V Lunch, dinner every day

One of the best new restaurants to have appeared along the suddenly revitalized approach to Granville Island emphasizes the French end of the Vietnamese spectrum. Here you can get escargots, frogs' legs, chicken grand'mere farci (a boneless chicken stuffed with meats, vegetables, and seafood), and a rack of lamb; but don't ignore the more characteristically Vietnamese dishes. One of the best is the hot and sour seafood soup, its sourness provided by cumin and tamarind rather than the usual chile and vinegar. Desserts are worth trying, especially the banana "cake," a warm, custardy bread pudding made with coconut milk.

Many of the Vietnamese restaurant cliches have been left behind in this bright upstairs room with its pink faux-marble columns. The big color photographs aren't travel posters, but clever images, like the one of a monk in a phone booth. "Calling heaven," our waiter said. "No answer." There's another, more traditionally decorated Greenhut at 1429 Robson Street, (604) 688-3688.

Isadora's

Next to the Kids Only Market on Granville Island, (604) 681-8816 1540 Old Bridge Street, Granville Island, Vancouver Inexpensive; full bar; MC, V Breakfast, lunch, dinner every day, brunch Sat-Sun

Parents with young kids bless Isadora's for its children's menu (clown-faced pizzas and chicken drumsticks with raw vegetables), its in-house play area, and its tables next to the outdoor water park in the summer. Isadora's wholesome menu also features more grown-up items, such as smoked salmon, stuffed croissants, salads, burgers, and plenty of choices for vegetarians. Open at 7am weekdays for early-morning business meetings over good coffee, Isadora's is busiest at Sunday brunch. Service is generally slow.

Japanese Deli House

Corner of Powell and Dunlevy, (604) 681-6484 381 Powell Street, Vancouver Inexpensive; beer and wine; no credit cards; no checks Lunch, dinner Tues-Sun

This is the bargain beauty of the sushi crowd, right in the middle of old Japantown. Although it has never recovered from the forced relocation of Japanese citizens during the Second World War, Powell Street still has Japanese grocery and fish stores worth visiting. The Deli is an old high-ceilinged room with big windows and an all-you-can-eat philosophy applied to sushi. Start with eight pieces of nigiri sushi, four pieces of maki, and soup for $7.95; if you can eat more than that, it's yours for free. Quality is surprisingly good, especially if you arrive early: sushi is made in quantity at 11am for the 11:30 opening. The Deli House is open until 8pm weekdays, 6pm on weekends.

Would you like to order a copy of Best Places *for a friend? There's an order form at the back of this book.*

Koji Japanese Restaurant

*Corner of Hornby and
Georgia, (604) 685-7355
630 Hornby Street,
Vancouver
Moderate; full bar;
AE, MC, V
Lunch Mon-Fri, dinner
every day*

Koji wins the landscaping award for the most beautiful garden in a downtown Vancouver restaurant: an island of pine trees and river rocks on a patio several stories above Hornby Street. The best seats in this bank-building outlet (there's another Koji, this one with a view of False Creek, on West Broadway) are the nonsmoking seats by the windows looking out on the garden, or at the sushi and robata bars. The rest is a crowded, smoky room often full of Japanese tourists. Sushi is not the best in town. Selections from the robata grill are dependable; the grilled shiitake mushrooms, topped with bonito flakes and tiny filaments of dry seaweed, are sublime. The Japanese boxed lunch (or makunochi tray) might contain chicken kara-age; superb smoked black Alaska cod; prawn and vegetable tempura; two or three small salads; rice with black sesame seeds; pickled vegetables; miso soup; and fresh fruit—for only $7.95. Finish with green tea ice cream.

La Bodega

*½ block north of
Granville Street Bridge,
between Davie and Drake,
(604) 684-8815
1277 Howe Street,
Vancouver
Inexpensive; full bar;
AE, DC, MC, V
Lunch Mon-Fri,
dinner Mon-Sat*

La Bodega is, in theory, just the bar and tapas lounge of the Chateau Madrid restaurant upstairs. But the dark, cozy, red-bricked cellar with its oddly endearing bull's head mounted on the wall is, in fact, a busy restaurant in its own right. Along with the night's specials, diners can order from a standard dozen hot tapas and 15 or so soups, salads, vegetables, and cold tapas plates. Patatas bravas (fried potatoes with a spicy dressing) are essential, along with clams marinera, prawns in garlic oil, slices of chorizo sausage and—oh—the white bean salad with herb dressing.

Las Tapas

*Between Robson and
Georgia on Cambie,
(604) 669-1624
760 Cambie Street,
Vancouver
Inexpensive; full bar;
AE, MC, V
Lunch Mon-Fri,
dinner every day*

The elegant "fast food" of Spain is offered here in this sunny tiled and whitewashed room, where those in search of delicately spiced and marinated lamb, chicken livers, or charbroiled eggplant mingle over big glasses of earthy Spanish wine. We like the intensely spicy chorizo, chunks of crusty bread to dip in the little pans of garlicky shrimp, and the calamari (particularly good with the sauce that accompanies the potatoes). Most dishes come in three sizes—small, medium, and large—so you can indulge in a big way with familiar favorites and have an experimental taste of something new. Close to the Queen Elizabeth Theatre, Las Tapas is an excellent spot to stop for a quick pre-concert meal. Mind the garlic, though!

Memories on Thurlow

*Just south of Robson on
Thurlow, (604) 681-6366
833 Thurlow Street,
Vancouver
Moderate; full bar;
AE, MC, V*

Swiss-born-and-trained Bernard Weber (a gold-medal winner at the Frankfurt Culinary Olympics) and his partner Carlos Cardoso opened this intimate little place smack in between two of the most popular restaurants in Vancouver, Le Crocodile and Piccolo Mondo. They furnished the walls with jazz instruments, old photographs, and

Lunch Mon-Fri,
dinner Mon-Sat

other memorabilia of Vancouver's turn-of-the-century past and created a menu around such items as saffron mussel bisque, glazed salmon in sorrel sauce, capon breast with sweet bell pepper sauce, and grain-fed pork tenderloin in apricot-ginger sauce.

Unfortunately, they have failed to create a restaurant that is as pleasing as its neighbors. Why is rather hard to pinpoint. Much of the food has a certain flatness, although the sauces can be well prepared, the chef is undeniably accomplished enough, and it is all quite pretty in a nouvelle sort of way. Maybe it's because the diners seem subdued, afraid to raise their voices, and no one seems to smile. It's a shame, because there is good potential here and the owners are seriously dedicated to creating a first-rate dining spot. Perhaps too seriously. The menu lists a lot of policies on coupons, tips, and so forth. What it doesn't tell you, but should, is that the ordering of two or three appetizers in place of a full meal including an entree is strictly forbidden.

Milieu Cafe
Between Thurlow and
Bute on Robson,
(604) 684-1244
1145 Robson Street,
Vancouver
Moderate; full bar;
AE, MC, V
Breakfast, lunch, dinner
every day

Downstairs it's a patisserie and cappuccino bar. Upstairs it's "the Independent State of Milieu," a determinedly modern restaurant with a Berlin-in-the-'30s-as-brought-to-you-by-the-movies decor: rose gray concrete walls, concrete floor, black tables, black metal chairs, triangular lights poised over wall mirrors, every surface designed to bounce noise around. There's no better place to feel slightly decadent over brunch or while having a late-afternoon pick-me-up of excellent pastries and coffee. The rest of the menu can be chancy. The grilled zucchini slices fanned out on top were the best part of our layered pasta with mushroom sauce; it was tepid when served, and the sauce was gummy.

New Seoul
E Broadway and
Commercial,
(604) 872-1922
1682 E Broadway,
Vancouver
Inexpensive; full bar;
MC, V
Lunch Mon-Sat,
dinner every day

The best Korean food in Vancouver comes from this unprepossessing restaurant squeezed between a blank-faced drugstore and a Chinese movie theater. Every table has a gas barbecue. Customers cook their own marinated beef, pork, chicken, and prawns while nibbling on the dozen or so side dishes included with the entree: bean sprouts; zucchini in garlic and chile; shredded daikon; and, of course, the Korean national pickle, spicy, chilled kim chee. Stick with the barbecue; tempura dishes can be leaden. The New Seoul is too busy to encourage loitering over coffee and dessert, so you can avoid that temptation.

Noor Mahal
Between 27th and 28th
on Fraser, (604) 873-9263
4354 Fraser Street,
Vancouver

A haven for big appetites on small budgets, the Noor Mahal is also one of the very few restaurants in Vancouver that specialize in the snack foods of southern India. Decor is basic truckstop, with an overlay of spectacular bead-

Inexpensive; full bar;
AE, MC, V
Lunch Wed-Sun,
dinner every day

ed chandeliers and flashy Indian art. A television set in the corner plays Indian movies and soap opera.

The Noor Mahal's specialty is the dosa: a large, light, lacy crepe made from a batter of rice and wheat flour and cooked on a griddle. It is then stuffed with a variety of fillings (choose from 14, including chicken and spinach or homemade cheese) and served with coconut chutney and a bowl of thick, flavorful lentil-like soup. Order a mango milk shake to cool the flames of an extra-hot curry, or one of the garishly colored but flavorful homemade ice creams.

Nyala Restaurant

Near the corner of
W 4th and MacDonald,
(604) 731-7899
2930 W Fourth Avenue,
Vancouver
Inexpensive; full bar;
AE, DC, MC, V
Lunch, dinner every day

What with the six o'clock news, fund-raising record albums, and multimedia rock concerts constantly reminding us of Ethiopia's current lack of food, it is easy to understand why so many people are unaware that Ethiopia, like other African nations, has a cuisine all its own. In the last year, two family-run Ethiopian restaurants have opened in Vancouver—the other, Lalibela Ethiopian Cuisine at 2090 Alma Street, (604) 732-1454, is just as good. Both represent well the unique and exotically rich cuisine of their country. The food is served in traditional Ethiopian style—no knives, forks, or spoons. The injera (a big plate-sized flat bread with a honeycomb texture) is all the utensil you need. Just tear off a little bread, fold it around bite-size portions of food, and pop the whole thing into your mouth. In Ethiopia, where most food is served in communal bowls, it's not only correct, it's sensible. The food, mostly soft stew or currylike preparations of savory beef, lamb, chicken, fish, or vegetables, is served communally at each table on a large metal platter accompanied by an assortment of condiments (spicy sauteed cabbage, golden herbed bulgur wheat, gingered lentil puree). The only thing impolite is using your left hand.

Olympia Fish Market & Oyster Co. Ltd.

Robson and Thurlow,
(604) 685-0716
1094 Robson Street,
Vancouver
Inexpensive; no alcohol;
no credit cards; no checks
Lunch, dinner every day

Five years ago, Robson Street fish merchant Carlo Sorace decided that what the street really needed was a good place to get fish and chips. His store is still a functioning fish store, but push on into the back, where you'll find one of the contenders for top fish and chips in the Lower Mainland. Whatever is on special in the fish store is the day's special at the fish and chips bar, which might mean scallops, catfish, or calamari, along with the standard halibut and cod. Eat in at one of 10 stools at the counters or take out.

The Only

Corner of Main and
Hastings, (604) 681-6546
20 Hastings Street,

Everything stays the same at Vancouver's favorite greasy spoon—a good place to go if you like simple, pan-fried fish and Manhattan-style clam chowder served with lots of buttered brown bread.

Vancouver
Inexpensive; no alcohol;
no credit cards; checks ok
Lunch, dinner Mon-Sat

There's no booze and no public bathrooms, and you'll probably have to line up along the back wall to wait for a stool at the counter. In the meantime, you can check out the pile of fresh fish reposing on chipped ice in the restaurant window, eavesdrop on the street-wise conversation, or watch the grill chefs shouting back and forth in Cantonese amid the sizzle and steam. The skid-row location and no-nonsense service complete the picture.

Pho Hoang
20th and Main,
(604) 874-0810
3610 Main Street,
Vancouver
Inexpensive; no alcohol;
no credit cards; no checks
Lunch, dinner every day
except Wed

Vietnam's equivalent of the hamburger, pho is a quick lunch, dinner, or snack. Pho Hoang has been packing in crowds at its modest location on Main Street for the past four years. A bowl of fragrant broth with rice noodles and your choice of flank, rump, brisket, tripe, or a dozen other beef cuts and combinations, it is accompanied by a plate of bean sprouts, fresh basil, lime, and hot chile peppers for individually tailored soup. A cup of strong Vietnamese coffee, filter-brewed at the table, is the only other thing you need.

Quilicum West Coast Native Indian Restaurant
Between Bidwell and
Denman on Davie,
(604) 681-7044
1724 Davie Street,
Vancouver
Moderate; beer and wine;
AE, MC, V
Lunch Mon-Fri,
dinner every day

The original Northwest Coast restaurant, Quilicum serves what qualifies as "roots food" for enthusiasts of the region's cuisine: native Indian specialties. Downstairs in the Davie Street "longhouse," among totem poles, Indian masks, and art (for sale), diners consume alder-grilled salmon and local vegetables from handcarved ceremonial bowls. Our favorite is a dish called "succulent parts": the tail, head, neck, and belly of the salmon. Accompaniments include rice with seaweed, a dish of baked sweet potato and hazelnuts, and sweet bannock bread. Other unusuals include steamed herring roe on a bed of kelp, caribou stew, and big bowls of oolichan grease, prepared from the oil of a native fish. Although it sounds like "novelty food," there's a lot of sincerity in this kitchen, and results can be superior.

Raga
3 blocks west of Oak,
(604) 733-1127
1177 W Broadway,
Vancouver
Moderate; full bar;
AE, MC, V
Lunch, dinner daily

The Raga transcends most of the usual Indian restaurant cliches: a comfortable restaurant with upholstered banquettes, restful colors, and a pleasant collection of Indian musical instruments mounted on the walls. The food here is light and fresh, given an extra lift by touches like the long slivers of fresh ginger sprinkled on the potato-and-cauliflower dish called aloo gobi. There's a wide choice of tandoori breads; try the onion kulcha, delicately flavored with dry mango, or the Raga's special naan, filled with chicken and nuts. Vegetarians have plenty of choice here. Service can be erratic.

Settebello
Robson and Thurlow,
(604) 681-7377

Like much of the new Robson Street, Settebello sometimes seems overly impressed with its own casual sophistication. The name of Umberto Menghi's seventh

*1131 Robson Street,
Vancouver
Moderate; full bar;
AE, DC, MC, V
Lunch, dinner every day*

restaurant means "beautiful seven" (from an Italian card game), and it's a departure from his other establishments in its attempt to cash in on the "grazing" trend of the city's younger dining crowd. Settebello is best on sunny days, as a respite from shopping, when you can sit out on the rooftop patio nibbling at pasta or a collection of Italian tapas-style dishes. Most of these fall into the $4 to $10 range and consist of hot and cold appetizers and tasty individual "designer" pizzas cooked in wood-burning ovens and served with matching salads. Try the salsiccia pizza: hot Italian sausage, spinach, sun-dried tomatoes, and chile peppers. For purists there's the classic Settebello: tomatoes, mozzarella, basil, and olive oil. Too bad the food is inconsistent, and the service can be a little too casual.

**Shanghai Palace
Restaurant**
*Near 64th and Granville,
(604) 261-6328
8012 Granville Street,
Vancouver
Inexpensive; full bar;
MC, V
Lunch, dinner Wed-Mon*

When they moved to the Marpole neighborhood, the Ge family left behind the pizza-parlor decor of the old Shanghai Palace on Commercial Drive and joined the world of modern Chinese restaurant design: pink tablecloths, gray-and-pink carpet, and mirrors the entire length of one wall. There's even that sine qua non of current Chinese restaurants, a live fish tank.

But the excellent cooking that made the Shanghai Palace one of the best places in the city for Northern Chinese food hasn't changed. Order mu shu pork, with hoisin sauce and little crepes, or black-bean pork shredded with spinach and Chinese vegetables. Chicken with peanuts is a well-prepared dish typical of the North, and if you must have chow mein, try the Shanghai-style—thick noodles mixed with pork and Chinese cabbage. Despite the live fish tank, fish is not the best option here.

The Topanga Cafe
*1 block west
of MacDonald,
(604) 733-3713
2904 W Fourth Avenue,
Vancouver
Inexpensive; full bar;
MC, V
Lunch, dinner Mon-Sat*

The name comes from LA's Topanga Canyon and reflects the westernized Mexican fare that can best be described as "Mexicali." It's a plain, soulful little place with a few wooden tables and a closet-sized kitchen. The only decorative touch is provided by a multitude of menu covers, hand-colored by restaurant patrons and hung on the walls. It is so popular with the Kitsilano neighborhood crowd, with lineups at the door such a regular feature, that other restaurants have opened in the vicinity hoping to catch some of the overflow.

The food never changes; portions are generous, prices low, and quality high. Chicken enchiladas are made with moist, tender breast meat, meat dishes are made with shredded beef (not hamburger), and the pork tenderloin taco is stuffed with large chunks of pork. Extra-garlicky salsa and home-fried tortilla chips could satisfy any vaquero.

Woodlands Natural Cuisine

W Broadway and
Trafalgar, (604) 733-5411
2582 W Broadway,
Vancouver
Inexpensive; beer and
wine; MC, V
Breakfast, lunch, dinner
every day

Five minutes from downtown Vancouver, this restaurant goes well beyond the usual limitations of vegetarian dining. In fact, the menu is almost international. We enjoyed a moist and filling eggplant casserole with a special cream topping and textured soy beneath. The honey-glazed baked tofu over basmati rice was delicious. Fukumeni was a Japanese-style stir-fry over thread noodles. The dal was mild yet flavorful and the salads outstanding. You select from the buffet and pay by weight (dieters take note). There is a separate dining room for those who would prefer to be served.

Yang's

26th and Main,
(604) 873-2116
4186 Main Street,
Vancouver
Moderate; beer and wine;
MC, V
Dinner Thurs-Tues,
brunch Sat-Sun

David Yang is not a teenager anymore, and now that he owns the family restaurant he grew up in, Yang's has been spruced up with new carpets and more comfortable lighting. The orange vinyl booths still line one wall, and the kitchen is still the province of David's father, Danny Yang, who gave Vancouver its first taste of authentic Northern Chinese food in 1973. Weekend brunches are special. Saturdays it's handmade noodles—Danny Yang kneads the dough on a wooden table in the restaurant and magically draws it out into delectable threads. The thick, chewy noodles are then mingled with beef or spinach, delicious fiery sauce, vegetables, and a sweet bean sauce. Sunday is a day for sweet bean-curd soup and the long, savory doughnuts called "oilsticks" in Chinese. With them, opt for the best pot-stickers in town, and a plate of hot and sour Chinese cabbage, a chilled salad that's simultaneously spicy, sour, sweet, cold, and crisp—the best thing that could ever happen to a cabbage.

The New Diamond Restaurant

In Chinatown,
(604) 685-0727
555 Gore Avenue,
Vancouver
Inexpensive; full bar;
MC, V
Breakfast, lunch, dinner
every day except Wed

Contrary to popular opinion, you *can* still get a good Chinese meal in Chinatown. Seek out the New Diamond, which was an institution long before the new stars of the Chinese restaurant world started looking for lower rents in the suburbs. A large, airy upstairs restaurant, with a modest decor—except for a large gold dragon covering the entire back wall—it's very popular with the Chinese. Daily specials are translated into English on the fresh sheet and are usually worth ordering. The dim sum served at lunchtime is great, with a vast and exotic selection. Dumplings come in a greater variety here than anywhere else; the stuffed duck feet are a must. At dinner, Peking duck is about as authentic as it can get on this side of the Pacific (order a day ahead). The crab braised with orange skin and green onion is a fiery delight.

If you've found a place that you think is a Best Place, send in the report form at the back of this book. If you're unhappy with one of the places, please let us know why. We depend on reader input.

Orestes

West of Broadway and MacDonald, across from the Hollywood Theatre, (604) 732-1461
3116 W Broadway, Vancouver
Moderate; full bar; AE, DC, MC, V
Lunch, dinner every day

Orestes is a party restaurant, with enough nooks, levels, and patios so even parties of two can be comfortable. The place exudes an infectiously young atmosphere, particularly on the weekends (which start on Thursday nights). The fare is standard Greek and the cooking is fine, especially if you order the simpler dishes such as souvlaki, roast lamb, and seafood. Most people make an evening of Orestes, meeting people and eyeing the belly dancer.

Seasons in the Park

Queen Elizabeth Park, (604) 874-8008
33rd and Cambie Vancouver
Moderate; full bar; AE, MC, V
Lunch, dinner every day, brunch Sat-Sun

(unrated)

It may be too soon for time-tempered judgments, but it's not too soon to pop the champagne corks and toast the return of good food to Queen Elizabeth Park. Arguably the city-park restaurant with the best view—a sweeping vista north over the city lights to the North Shore mountains and west to Burrard Inlet—Seasons has now been taken over by Brent Davies, who already runs the Teahouse at Ferguson Point. The menu here owes a lot to the Teahouse, but has a stonger emphasis on fish and is more adventuresome. The hot wild-mushroom salad is a knockout.

LODGINGS

Le Meridien

Corner of Smithe and Burrard, (604) 682-5511, toll-free (800) 543-4300
845 Burrard Street, Vancouver, BC V6Z 2K6
Expensive; AE, DC, MC, V

Le Meridien is the most elegant hotel in Vancouver. The large pinkish stone building holds the refined, patrician decor that you would expect in an aristocratic European hostelry. The place is fairly big—397 rooms—and well suited to its address, close to the Vancouver Art Gallery and the fashionable browsing district of Robson Street.

The modest-sized lobby—decorated in soft shades of coffee and peach, with Asian-inspired rosewood furniture and dramatic flower arrangements in glazed pottery urns—sets the tone for the whole place. Rooms are adorned in soothing shades of beige and cream, and some have city views out of floor-to-ceiling windows. Prices in season are high—$185 to $240 for a standard-sized double, up to $1,000 for the presidential two-bedroom suite—but include twice-daily maid service, a downtown limousine at your disposal, and membership in Spa Sante (a fitness and beauty salon complete with pool and sun deck). Of the restaurants, the dark, polished, publike Gerard's Lounge is the current after-work gathering place for locals; Cafe Fleuri offers a good breakfast, pleasant Sunday brunches, and weekend chocolate buffets; and Gerard's is the French gourmet restaurant (see review).

Pan Pacific Hotel

At the north foot of Burrard, across from Stanley Park,

Destined to become as visual a landmark for Vancouver as the Sydney Opera House is for that city, the 505-room Pan Pacific was opened in 1986 by the Japan-based Tokyu Corporation just in time for the crowds of EXPO. As part

(604) 662-8111, toll-free in Canada (800) 663-1515, in the US (800) 937-1515 300-999 Canada Place, Vancouver, BC V6C 3B5 Expensive; AE, DC, MC, V

of Canada Place in the heart of Vancouver's harborfront, it stands in all its white magnificence overlooking the docking cruise ships and the whole expanse of the inner harbor. The multilevel lobby takes full advantage of that view: after a ride up two central escalators (taking you past an awkward, convention-hall–like entrance), you emerge into a huge, open atrium where a glass roof towers over your head and hotel rooms (arranged in tiers of floors around the outside of the inner court) surround you. The main floor features the Cascades Lounge with its marvelous water views, the five enormous sculptured sails poised on the outside deck (made to resemble a flotilla of sailboats racing up Burrard Inlet), and a waterfall. Other restaurants are Cafe Pacifica, a casual place serving continental cuisine and dim sum lunches; Suntory, with Japanese food; and the Five Sails, a glamorous French restaurant. All are overpriced.

Rooms are smallish and pretty, with light wood armoires and marble bathrooms. They range in price from $160 to $180, and the biggest difference is size. All have views—on the west side toward Stanley Park and the Lions Gate Bridge, and on the east looking over the city. Studios, though a little pricier than standards ($205), don't offer that much more in the way of space; suites ($300 to $1,200) are spacious and lovely. Service is first-rate, and health facilities are endless: an outdoor lap pool (heated to 86 degrees) and hot tub, saunas, a running track, high-tech exercise equipment, squash and racquetball courts, indoor hot and cool pools, and, in keeping with the hotel's Asian connection, shiatsu massage.

Delta Place

Dunsmuir and Howe, (604) 687-1122, toll-free (800) 268-1133 645 Howe Street, Vancouver, BC V6C 2Y9 Expensive; AE, DC, MC, V

The original investors lost their shirts on this beautiful hotel simply because it's so elegant. Mandarin International, kings of luxury hotels, spared no expense with design and fixtures, making this space the most regal, snooty, extravagant, and expensive hotel in Vancouver. Unfortunately, Vancouver (or her economy, at any rate) wasn't ready for such a royal centerpiece. Within a few years the hotel (then named the Mandarin Oriental) was sold at a rock-bottom price to a local investment group, and Delta was brought in to manage. Since then business has picked up, primarily because prices have dropped considerably (weekend specials can start at $130 for a double), although regular summer rates still hover at the ceiling (doubles start around $200, suites at $225).

Located in the center of Vancouver's financial district, Delta Place has ample facilities for the business traveler (board rooms, secretarial services, and fax, among others). For plush surroundings, the Place stands alone: wool carpeting, solid oak cabinetry, marble shower stalls and cast-iron bathtubs, Thai silk wall coverings, balconies off most rooms, a health club (sauna equipped with color TV and towels on ice), a cafe on the second floor, and on and on. The formal dining room, Cristal, is no longer.

The Four Seasons

Howe and Georgia,
(604) 689-9333, toll-free
(800) 268-6282
791 W Georgia Street,
Vancouver, BC V6C 2T4
Expensive; AE, DC, MC, V

Ongoing renovations, and the departure of chef Kerry Sear, leave us uncertain about the future of the Four Seasons. However, it's still at once comfortable and sophisticated, posh but not pretentious. After leaving your car in the porte cochere, you take an escalator up to a lively and elegant lobby, filled with marble, plants, and people. The atriumlike Garden Lounge, off to one side, provides a bosky retreat for cocktails and conversation and serves an excellent buffet brunch on Sundays. An informal restaurant, Seasons Cafe, is open almost all day for casual meals; in summer, light lunches are served around the outdoor swimming pool. Chartwell (which replaced Le Pavillon a few years ago) is a clubbier dining room offering some of Vancouver's most innovative cuisine (see review).

Our room on an upper floor had a grand view of the downtown area, including Arthur Erickson's Law Courts complex and the glittering city beyond. Furnishings (which will all be new by mid-1990) were tasteful, and the many small amenities that are offered as a matter of course—outstanding 24-hour room service, terrycloth robes, hair dryers, mini-bars, fresh flowers—make this place a refined and welcome refuge.

The Georgian Court Hotel

Cambie and Beatty,
(604) 682-5555, toll-free
(800) 663-1155
773 Beatty Street,
Vancouver, BC V6B 2M4
Expensive; AE, DC, MC, V

The exclusive, brick-clad hotel combines the business amenities traditionally associated with a "name" hotel with the luxury and personality of a small one. Exceptional meeting facilities, three phones in each room, a health club (with whirlpool, sauna, and exercise room), and a prime location across from BC Stadium and BC Place are practical advantages (along with the Ving card security system, whereby door locks are changed with every new guest).

The amiable lobby is small and appealing, in tasteful green with peach and gray accents. Doubles (starting at about $115 a night) and one- and two-bedroom suites (around $350) are smartly furnished with mahogany, antiques, and Audubon prints—more reminiscent of a fine home than of a hotel. For these prices, however, we'd expect a little more precision: sounds of the heating system found their way into our room on a recent visit, and the bathroom was curiously understocked with towels. Service—particularly room service—is first-rate.

Perhaps the biggest plus is the city's best continental restaurant, The William Tell, just down the stairs (see review). Rigney's is a more casual, less pricey alternative, and the club lounge provides entertainment.

Westin Bayshore

*Georgia and Cardero, just south of Stanley Park,
(604) 682-3377, toll-free
(800) 228-3000
1601 W Georgia Street,
Vancouver, BC V6G 2V4
Expensive; AE, DC, MC, V*

The setting is one of the grandest you'll ever find: gaze out over a small harbor, with Stanley Park beyond and the mountains beyond that. The city is just behind you, but as you look north from your room, you have the feeling you're at the edge of a wilderness. A great round pool fills up the courtyard, so in the summer you can sunbathe in this secluded setting. Or you can rent a boat for a little tour, or go jogging in Stanley Park. There is also an indoor pool for the cooler months. Unbeatable.

A recent renovation updated the lobby and rooms to a much more contemporary look in muted pastels and earth tones ($150 to $188 for a double). Harbor-view rooms are the best. If you've a boat, moorage at the nearby marina is cheap and allows for full use of the hotel facilities and room service. The Garden Restaurant, a pleasant, open area facing the pool, serves modest breakfasts, lunches, and suppers. The big-deal restaurant is Trader Vic's.

Coast Plaza Hotel

*From Denman and Comox, head east on Comox, (604) 688-7711,
toll-free (800) 663-1144
1733 Comox Street,
Vancouver, BC V6G 1P6
Expensive; AE, DC, MC, V*

This tall hotel, located in a pleasant residential neighborhood, has seen a few owners (former names: Ramada Renaissance, the Denman) and is currently being operated by the Coast Hotel chain. The pastel lobby and rooms in shades of gray, beige, and burgundy reflect the Ramada company's $8 million upgrade a few years back; Coast plans more renovations soon. Because this was originally an apartment building, rooms are larger than average and have individual balconies with wonderful views. All have mini-bars and some have kitchens. Upstairs floors constitute Limited Edition, a private businesspersons' territory where guest rooms have more personal service. All guests enjoy membership privileges in the newly renovated Club Cardio next door—*the* place to play squash in Vancouver.

Granville Island Hotel and Marina

*Take 4th onto the island; at the far east corner,
(604) 683-7373, toll-free
(800) 663-1840
1253 Johnston Street,
Vancouver, BC V6H 3R9
Expensive; AE, DC, MC, V*

The Granville Island Hotel is a bold combination of an old stucco building (now pink) and a dramatic new complex of glass and corrugated iron, the latter reminiscent of the industrial flavor of Granville Island's past. A glass atrium, extending toward the water like the bow of a ship, splits the building down the middle and lets in a stream of natural light all the way to the first floor. The lobby area displays the now familiar postmodern smoky pinks, deep greens, and purples, while a whimsical, brightly colored sculpture, the Cyrus P. Windless Kite Flying Machine, fills the atrium space. The small 54-room hotel has a lot to recommend it: the custom-furnished rooms are decorated in muted tones with light wood accents, and some have shutters that open out onto small balconies. Avoid rooms that face the atrium: the disco sounds can make for a sleepless night. Prices range from $135 for a double to $250 for a one-bedroom suite. Boats can hook up to the dock and connect with the hotel's television and telephone system, power and water lines, and even use its room service.

Hotel Georgia

Howe and Georgia,
(604) 682-5566, toll-free
(800) 663-1111
801 W Georgia Street,
Vancouver, BC V6C 1P7
Expensive; AE, DC, MC, V

It may not have the flash of some of the newer hotels in town, but this old, familiar face has much to recommend it, including a central downtown location and prices competitive with the other major hotels ($120 to $140). The pleasant rooms are adorned with new oak furniture and done in a calming gray palette. In all, it's a cozy, unpretentious place.

The Cavalier Grill features a casual breakfast and lunch menu as well as fine dining in the evening; two other popular spots are the Night Court Lounge, with lunch, Thursday night jazz, and dancing on weekends; and the raucous George V pub with sing-alongs in the evenings (Thursday through Saturday) and authentic pub lunches.

Hotel Vancouver

Georgia and Burrard,
(604) 684-3131, toll-free
(800) 268-9143
900 W Georgia Street,
Vancouver, BC V6C 2W6
Expensive; AE, DC, MC, V

Built in the French chateau style favored by the Canadian railways, this grand hotel comes complete with a steep green copper roof, BC stone exterior, menacing gargoyles and griffins, and rich ornamentation. You don't suspect until you see the lobby that the dowager (whose guests have included King George VI and the Aga Khan) has been made into a convention hotel, owned and managed by Canadian Pacific. Its location is the best in town, near the big stores, the Law Courts complex, and the other major hotels. The 508 rooms are moderately sized, sophisticated, and quiet; and service is good. A brandnew health club adds a modern touch to the old place.

Dining is not the high point of staying here, but the Roof Restaurant and Lounge has a grand view and some interesting French food; it is one of the very few places in town that still offer the dinner dance. The Timber Club, with decor designed to honor BC's timber industry, is a favorite haunt of lunching businesspeople, and Griffin's—a good spot for breakfast—offers views of the passing parade on Georgia and Hornby.

Hyatt Regency

Burrard and Georgia,
(604) 687-6543, toll-free
(800) 233-1234
655 Burrard Street,
Vancouver, BC V6C 2R7
Expensive; AE, DC, MC, V

Located in the city's core, the Hyatt is popular for conventions and business meetings, with over 25,000 square feet dedicated to this purpose. But this is also a good spot for the vacationer: one block to Robson Street shopping, a 15-minute walk to Stanley Park. Harbor-side rooms with a terrific view onto busy Burrard Inlet and the surrounding mountains run $150 to $200. Suites cost $300 to $800. Each room comes with its own electronic safe. A fitness club and pool round out the amenities.

Cafes and lounges abound, but most noteworthy is

the casual Fish & Co., which under chef Othmar Steinhart is earning a reputation as one of the best seafood restaurants in town (see review).

Ming Court

Davie and Thurlow,
(604) 685-1311, toll-free
(800) 663-1525
1160 Davie Street,
Vancouver, BC V6E 1N1
Expensive; AE, DC, MC, V

For warmth and value, this is the best hotel buy in town. Formerly the Miramar (before it was purchased by an Asian chain and totally renovated), it's lovely and coolly sophisticated. The marble lobby is all pastels—peach and dusty rose—and the garden court lounge is particularly fine. Rooms are large and nicely furnished; each has a balcony, and from ours, on the 18th floor, there was an incomparable view of English Bay and the islands beyond. Extras include sauna, outdoor swimming pool, exercise room, and secretarial services. Prices are competitive.

You're a few blocks (a 15-to-20-minute walk) from the hub of the city, but the lively street life right outside your door in Vancouver's West End is a show in itself. Free parking is available for guests.

The Sylvia

Beach and Gilford,
(604) 681-9321
1154 Gilford Street,
Vancouver, BC V6G 2P6
Moderate; AE, DC, MC, V

This charming and rather shabby brick landmark, completely covered with ivy, offers one of the best locations in the city: right on English Bay in the heart of the West End. Families with children especially enjoy its proximity to the beaches and playgrounds of Stanley Park, but the major attraction is its incredibly low prices. Doubles run $50 to $70, triples (an extra bedroom for the kids) are $66 to $78, and suites are $65 to $88. Children under 18 traveling with a parent stay free. Avoid the cheaper rooms, which tend toward the tacky, and opt for a room with a view of the bay or for one of the 16 new rooms—pleasant and less dowdy, although somewhat characterless. Ask to see the room first; the difference in price doesn't necessarily mean much difference in rooms here.

The bay-view bar can get rowdy in the evenings with neighborhood apartment dwellers. The dining room, Sylvia's, offers great sunset- and people-watching but mediocre food.

The Wedgewood Hotel

On Hornby between
Smythe and Robson,
(604) 689-7777, toll-free
(800) 663-0666
845 Hornby Street,
Vancouver, BC V6Z 1V1
Expensive; AE, DC, MC, V

Veteran hotelier Eleni Skalbania (the Devonshire, the Georgia) virtually custom-ordered this hostelry, which emerged like a butterfly out of the wrecked and gutted Mayfair in the center of town. Skalbania exudes a tangible presence here, with her effort and care stamped on almost every facet of the operation. Businesspeople may prefer the commercial atmosphere of the bigger properties, but the Wedgewood is the place Vancouverites recommend to their friends.

Doorkeepers usher you into a plush lobby decorated handsomely with antiques and Oriental fixtures. The 93 bedrooms don't quite come up to this lavish standard, although the suites are decorated in shades of dusty rose and cool green, and many of them include fireplaces. Doubles start at $140. All the rooms have flower-decked patios, remote-control TVs, stocked mini-bars, and morning newspaper delivery. Recent reports indicate that careless service can be a problem here—curious for such a small place run by such an exacting taskmaster—and not all rooms are up to Skalbania's flawless reputation. Guests enjoy membership privileges at the Chancery Squash Club next door.

The 70-seat Wedgewood Room has never been particularly exciting, despite the parade of renowned chefs who continue to come and go. At press time a new French chef, Andre Fagant, had the helm. In the Bacchus Ristorante, the 150-seat oyster bar and bistro, Peter Isacu, a Rumanian with a classic Italian background, serves "rusticiana" (country-style) cuisine created from local, organically grown foods.

West End Guest House
1 block south of Robson, between Jervis and Broughton,
(604) 681-2889
1362 Haro Street,
Vancouver, BC V6E 1G2
Moderate; MC, V

Here's an alternative to the big expensive hotels: a turn-of-the-century Victorian home nestled amid the newer and larger architecture of the last few decades. The place is bright pink, so you can't miss it. There are seven bedrooms, all with private baths, ranging in price from $65 to $80 for a double (depending on size). Most have writing tables and queen beds. Each wears a different theme: ours had a pinkish, Oriental motif, the old master bedroom is done in stately blues, another has a '30s Art Deco flavor. Breakfast is an intriguing display: things like banana pecan waffles and fresh fruit or spinach cream cheese pie.

GREATER VANCOUVER: WEST VANCOUVER
RESTAURANTS

Chesa Seafood Restaurant
22nd and Marine,
(604) 922-3312
2168 Marine Drive,
West Vancouver
Moderate; full bar;
AE, MC, V
Dinner Tues-Sun

After a shaky start, this offshoot of the popular Chesa restaurant has finally found its feet, and its food. The only seafood that isn't at the peak of freshness is the marlin stuffed and mounted on the wall. The rest is very reliable, from a salad of smoked red snapper on a bed of mache, or a warm leek salad with Belgian endive and scallops, to a stir-fried spinach fettuccine with black beans, tomatoes, and a generous serving of crabmeat. Daily specials are indeed special: a salmon fillet stuffed with scallop mousse and served on sorrel sauce, for example. No entree costs more than $10; only one wine on the modest list breaks the $20 barrier. Chocophiles should be aware of the addictive warm chocolate sauce served with ice cream. Unless the fierce fluorescent streetlights outside have been changed, don't sit by the windows.

La Toque Blanche
On Marine near Keith,
(604) 926-1006
4368 Marine Drive,
West Vancouver
Moderate; full bar; AE,
MC, V
Dinner Tues-Sun

In a small strip mall on the way to Horseshoe Bay, you can find the sort of things you'd forgotten you used to love: beef stroganoff, chicken cordon bleu, pork loin en croute, profiteroles with chocolate sauce. And that's okay because they do it well and at reasonable prices. The veal medallions come in a creamy anise sauce, the noisettes of lamb with crushed mustard seeds and Burgundy sauce. Desserts are good too: souffle glace pistachio with B&B sauce; charlotte russe with raspberry sauce and a little grappa hidden in the middle. The decor—mirrors and cedar—is simple (an interior designer would probably say period '70s), and the entrance is actually around the back where the cars are parked.

Salmon House on the Hill
21st Street/Folkestone exit
off Highway 1 West,
(604) 926-3212
2229 Folkestone Way,
West Vancouver
Moderate; full bar;
AE, MC, V
Lunch, dinner every day,
brunch Sun

Every Vancouverite's favorite place to take the out-of-towners (the location, high on a hill in West Vancouver, offers a superb panoramic view of the downtown skyline) now has a bigger menu with a less exclusive emphasis on the West Coast Indian theme. Salmon, barbecued over green alder to infuse it with a delicate smoky flavor, remains the house specialty (and deservedly so), but other items, such as the West Coast shrimp and salmon won tons and the Alaska black cod are worth investigating.

Capers
From downtown
Vancouver travel north
over Lions Gate Bridge,
then west, (604) 925-3316
2496 Marine Drive, West
Vancouver
Moderate; beer and wine;
MC, V
Breakfast, lunch every
day, dinner Wed-Sat
(closes 8 pm); brunch
Sat-Sun

After a brief attempt to join the fine-dining scene, Capers has returned to its first identity: health-conscious meals. Why not? It's a blood brother to Capers' health-food grocery next door. And it's Vancouverites' choice feed spot for breakfast, lunch, and brunch. Egg dishes are highly recommended: only free-range eggs are served. With all this fuss over ingredients, we don't understand why they continue to use prepackaged stock in their soup preparations.

LODGINGS

The Park Royal Hotel
6th and Clyde,
(604) 926-5511
540 Clyde Avenue, West
Vancouver, BC V7T 2J7
Expensive; AE, DC,
MC, V

Every city should have a hotel like this one: 30 spacious units surrounded by a couple of acres of lovely gardens and only 10 minutes from downtown. There's more: a rollicking English pub in the basement, a fine dining room, and a garden lounge (The Terrace) with gazebo for drinks and lunch. It's tough to get a reservation here, since it has become an "in" place for Californians and other fun-loving travelers. If you do make it, ask for one of the 11 ivy-clad riverside rooms, overlooking the gardens and the river (even though reservations in these rooms cannot be guaranteed); rooms facing the parking lot are too noisy. Prices range from $82 to $132 for a double and include a morning newspaper and tea and coffee with your wake-up call. A note of caution to light sleepers: the pub tends to be quite noisy into the night.

The dining room serves continental fare and host Mario Corsi will take good care of you. He is always happy to point out your way to the city's attractions as well. You drive into Vancouver over Lions Gate Bridge, which means adjusting your schedule to avoid rush hours.

GREATER VANCOUVER: NORTH VANCOUVER

RESTAURANTS

Cafe Roma
Corner of Semisch and Esplanade,
(604) 984-0274
60 Semisch Street,
North Vancouver
Moderate; full bar;
AE, DC, MC, V
Dinner every day

Cafe Roma bills itself as "not a fancy restaurant, not a pizzeria, but an Italian experience." Certainly, with its checked tablecloths, red-white-and-green color scheme, glistening cappuccino machine and substantial menu, it comes close to being that. Owner Antonio Corsi (also of the Park Royal Hotel and Corsi Trattoria) has rejected trendiness to create a big, casual, family sort of place with food that a real Italian can recognize. A very good focaccia bread appears at your elbow while you contemplate the menu crammed with over 50 pasta dishes alone. Some, like the bigoli ciociara (in a sauce of potato and minced Italian sausage), are rarely seen outside the old country. There are several choices of Italian designer pizzas, as well as many nicely prepared fish and meat dishes. A light outing? Opt for the halibut cooked on a slate with fresh herbs and olive oil. In a quandary? Eight tasting menus allow you to sample several pastas, pizzas, or entrees.

Corsi Trattoria
Across from the Lonsdale Market, by the water,
(604) 987-9910
1 Lonsdale Street,
North Vancouver
Moderate; full bar;
AE, DC, MC, V
Lunch Mon-Fri, dinner every day

Mario Corsi, owner of the Park Royal Hotel and restaurant, and his brother own this trattoria at the bottom of Lonsdale. Their family ran a trattoria in Italy, so they know what it's all about. The 20-odd pastas are all homemade, with the specialty being rotoli—tubes of pasta stuffed with veal, spinach, and ricotta and topped with cream and tomato sauces. Another good one is the trenette al salmone affumicata (pasta with smoked salmon, cream, olives, and tomatoes). Big appetites will want to take on l'abbuffatta, an orgy of four pastas, salad, lamb, veal, prawns, zabaglione, and espresso. Those who can't resist a challenge should take on the spaghetti trasteverini (labeled "for Italians only"), loaded with garlic, hot peppers, chicken, black beans, and olive oil. It's good, but prepare to be a social outcast for the rest of the week.

Cafe Norte
In the Edgemont Village,
(604) 255-1188
3108 Edgemont Blvd,

A roaring success since the day it opened. You can get enchiladas and burritos, of course, but the imaginative Mexican menu includes Sante Fe pizza, smoked turkey quesadillas, and blue corn tortillas filled with spinach.

*North Vancouver
Moderate; full bar;
MC, V
Lunch, dinner every day,
brunch Sat-Sun*

Daily specials are even more out of the ordinary. The black beans served with the entrees or in a smoky chipotle chile dip are as rich as chocolate and, because they're made without lard, less heavy than refried beans. Pint-sized tacos, pizzas, and hot dogs are available for "little amigos."

Cafe Norte is cheerfully loud, with tables squeezed together around the central fireplace. The Mexican curios will keep your eyes diverted during what is usually a bit of a wait for your food.

La Cucina Italiana
*Corner of Marine Drive
and McGowan,
(604) 986-1334
1509 Marine Drive,
North Vancouver
Moderate; full bar;
AE, MC, V
Dinner Mon-Sat*

La Cucina is a contemplative Italian restaurant, stuck rather incongruously in the middle of North Vancouver's strip of car dealerships and video shops. The little white stucco building looks as though it might dispense Greek fast food, but inside, it's pretty and elegant, with Italian opera playing at exactly the right volume. When it's available, try bresaola—air-dried beef imported from Switzerland—as an appetizer, or the cold antipasto. Pastas range from traditional spaghetti with tomato and meat sauce to black fettuccine with squid and sweet red peppers. Fish specials are usually good; or try pollo alla diavola, a grilled chicken breast with black-pepper-crusted skin. Don't leave without sampling the homemade ice cream.

The Tomahawk
*Marine Drive and Philip,
(604) 988-2612
1550 Philip Avenue,
North Vancouver
Inexpensive; no alcohol;
AE, MC, V
Breakfast, lunch,
dinner every day*

Part museum of Indian kitsch, part tourist trap, and part restaurant, the Tomahawk, now in its 63rd year, must be the original inspiration for all those hokey, totem-pole theme restaurants on highway intersections across North America. In Vancouver, it's an institution, deservedly famous for its hungry-man-sized meals. The Yukon Breakfast, for instance, gives you five slices of Yukon-style bacon, two eggs, hash browns, and toast for $5.50. Or try the excellent French toast, buttermilk pancakes, or mountainous muffins. At lunch there are several hamburger platter combinations (named after Indian chiefs), hot dogs, sandwiches, fried chicken, fish 'n' chips, and even oysters on toast to choose from. The pies (lemon meringue, Dutch apple, banana cream) are homemade on the premises, and they will even wrap one up in a box to go. For children, there is a special breakfast menu for braves and princesses.

LODGINGS

Lonsdale Quay Hotel
*Lonsdale and Carrie
Cates Court,
(604) 986-6111
123 Carrie Cates Court,
North Vancouver,
BC V7M 3K7*

North Vancouver now has its own market complex with two levels of shops and produce stands right at the seabus terminal. Above this somewhat sterile version of the Granville Island Market rises the Lonsdale Quay Hotel, a small (57-room), two-floor hotel that looks quite dramatic from the shore. Rooms, done in soft shades of pink and gray, offer queen-size beds, stocked bars (not

Expensive; AE, DC, MC, V

complimentary), and remote-control cable TVs. Aim for a room in the southern part of the complex where the views are better: from east-facing rooms you gaze on water and tugboats; west-facing rooms look toward the sail-shaped Canadian Pavilion from lovely balconies. It's an active place, with the sea-bus arriving and departing and the constant buzz of the market (open till 9pm on weeknights, 6:30pm on Saturday and Sunday), so quiet-seeking souls might look elsewhere. A dining room, Loops, is undistinguished.

GREATER VANCOUVER: RICHMOND

RESTAURANTS

Steveston Seafood House
Corner of Moncton and #1, (604) 271-5252
3951 Moncton Street, Richmond
Moderate; full bar; AE, DC, MC, V
Dinner every day

Appropriately located near the Fraser River and the fishing docks, the Steveston Seafood House continues to earn its reputation as "that great little seafood place in Richmond." The decor is funky-rec-room, with a nautical motif featuring overhead nets, glass floats, and those corny little made-from-seashells knickknacks.

Simply prepared and generously served on large fish-shaped plates, the seafood delivers all it promises. You are safe with any of the house specialties—even ones with names like Jonathan Livingston Seafood (a mixed seafood platter)—but we have been most pleased with the simple dishes, like the moist, meaty pan-fried halibut with lemon butter. Unfortunately, the alder-smoked salmon has been replaced by a poached version; apparently the chef got tired of stoking the wood stove. Accompaniments are crisp vegetables and rice or boiled potatoes. It isn't cheap, but on a nice day it's well worth the 30-minute drive from Vancouver.

LODGINGS

Delta River Inn
Follow signs to the airport; Cessna is just before the entrance, (604) 278-1241, toll-free (800) 268-1133 in Canada, (800) 877-1133 in the US
3500 Cessna Drive, Richmond, BC V7B 1C7
Expensive; AE, DC, MC, V

This big (416 units) hotel is near the airport, but you can get a room overlooking the Fraser River and a small marina if you'd rather not gaze at jets. Prices for a double range from $99 to $135; rooms are comfortable and spacious. The 10-story hotel has plenty of facilities: a nearby jogging trail, a sauna, and summer barbecues for lunch around the pool. One of the hotel's best features is its main dining room, the Pier, where chef Ron Gibbs serves up French cuisine.

If you've found a place that you think is a Best Place, send in the report form at the back of this book. If you're unhappy with one of the places, please let us know why. We depend on reader input.

GREATER VANCOUVER: LADNER

RESTAURANTS

La Belle Auberge

Corner of 48A and 48th,
(604) 946-7717
4856 48th Avenue,
Ladner
Expensive; full bar;
AE, MC, V
Dinner every day

If this were Europe and not Canada, every afternoon would see the parking lot filled with Mercedes Benzes and Peugeots that had brought their owners out from the big city for a long, leisurely lunch in the country. Here in North America, though, we don't like to be too far from our office towers during the day, so La Belle Auberge is open only for dinner; and only on the weekends does it really draw the Vancouver crowd.

Locating his restaurant in an old, shuttered Victorian manse in Ladner, owner Bruno Marti seeks to preserve and enshrine the cuisine of the traditional French school. In typical European fashion, the place is run as a family enterprise. Marti (who became well known to Vancouverites as a member of the gold-medal-winning team at the '84 Culinary Olympics) is the chef, and his wife oversees the operation of the dining room. You'll find the menu predictable—rack of lamb, milk-fed veal, and some game dishes. But it will be superb if Marti's behind the stove.

The duckling in blueberry sauce is, deservedly, his most popular dish. Many items, such as the salmon mousse in lobster sauce, the rack of lamb in a pastry crust, and a very successful spinach salad with hot bacon dressing, are well worth trying but must be ordered for two. It's a nice stop on the way to the Tsawwassen ferry, but allow enough time to relax and enjoy.

Uncle Herbert's Fish & Chip Shop

Next to the Delta
Museum on the corner
of Delta and Bridge,
(604) 946-8222
4866 Delta Street,
Ladner
Inexpensive; beer and
wine; MC, V
Lunch, dinner Tues-Sun

Most British-style fish 'n' chip houses in this country are long on photographs of the royals but short on the essentials: fresh potatoes and super-fresh fish. At Uncle Herbert's, the walls are covered with tea towels from every English town big enough to print one and with royal memorabilia dating back to George V. But the fish (ling cod or halibut) and chips are top quality, and no older than yesterday. The roster of pub food includes English pork pies, Scotch eggs, sausage rolls, New England clam chowder, and Yorkshire fishcakes (two slices of large potato with fish between them, like a sandwich, battered and deep-fried). Owner Ken Mertens imports as many English beers as he can get. Wheelchair-accessible.

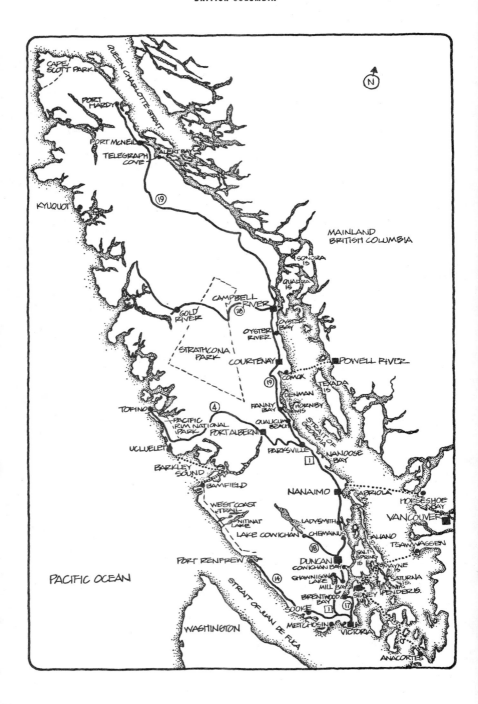

VANCOUVER ISLAND

▲

From Victoria and environs—westward to Sooke, northward to Sidney—
up-island along the east coast to Parksville. From there a short jog inland to
Port Alberni (and access to west coast towns); then back to Qualicum Beach and
north along the coast to Port Hardy. Finally, the Gulf Islands, north to south.

VICTORIA

Author Rudyard Kipling went a bit overboard when he described Victoria, the small urban jewel that dangles from the southern tip of Vancouver Island. "To realize Victoria," Kipling wrote in the early 20th century, "you must take all that the eye admires in Bournemouth, Torquay, the Isle of Wight, the Happy Valley at Hong Kong, the Doon, Sorrento, and Camp's Bay—add reminiscences of the Thousand Islands and arrange the whole around the Bay of Naples with some Himalayas for the background." Romantic as Victoria may be, with its delightful natural harbor and the Olympic Mountains of Washington State on the horizon, the provincial capital of British Columbia is less a museum piece nowadays than it is a developing tourist mecca. With faster and better access available from Seattle, visitors pour in to gawk at huge sculptured gardens, ride London double-decker buses, shop for Irish linens and Harris tweeds, sip afternoon tea, and soak up what they believe is the last light of British imperialism to set on the western hemisphere. Raves in the travel press have brought in a new crop of younger residents to upset Victoria's reputation as a peaceful but dull sanctuary for retiring civil servants from eastern Canada. The quality and variety of restaurants here is improving as a result, and no longer are Victoria's downtown streets silent after 10pm. Rudyard Kipling might not approve, but the "Garden City" is growing up.

Getting There. The *Princess Marguerite* and her sister ship, the *Vancouver Island Princess*—taken over last year by Sweden's BC Stena Line—steam from Seattle to Victoria and back again daily ($39 round trip, $98 car and driver). The *Princess Marguerite* has the 8am run from Seattle and leaves Victoria at 5:30pm (early June to early September). The *Island Princess* leaves Seattle at 10am and Victoria at 4pm. Both offer food, drink, and slot machines (year-round); (604) 388-7397 or (206) 624-4922. A faster sea alternative is the *Victoria Clipper*, the jet-propelled catamaran that makes its 2½-hour voyages up and back twice daily, all year round ($69 round trip). No cars; (604) 382-8100 or (206) 448-5000. Air transportation, the fastest link from Seattle (Lake Union) to Victoria (Inner Harbour), is provided several times daily for about $100 round trip on Lake Union Air, (800) 826-1890. Ferries to the Victoria area also leave from Anacortes (destination Sidney, 27 kilometers north of Victoria), one of the most scenic routes in the Pacific Northwest; (206) 464-6400 or (604) 381-1551; from Port Angeles, a 1½-hour voyage (year-round) on which cars are allowed but for which no reservations are taken (call

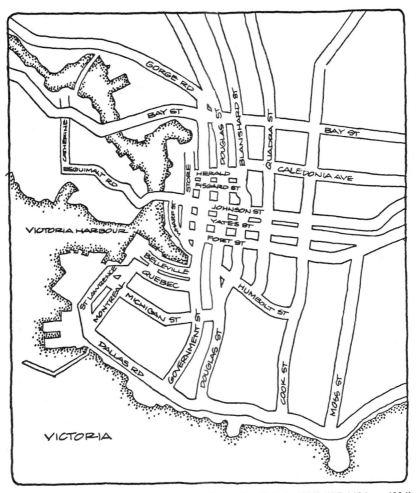

a day in advance to find out how long the wait will be); (206) 457-4491 or (604) 386-2202, $44 round trip car and driver; and Tsawwassen (destination Sidney, 27 kilometers north of Victoria), every hour from 7am to 10pm in summer, following a scenic route through the Gulf Islands; $41 round trip car and driver; call BC Ferries at (604) 386-3431.

   Attractions. First stop should be Tourism Victoria, a well-staffed office dispensing useful information on the sights, 812 Wharf Street, (604) 382-2127. The Esquimalt and Nanaimo (E&N) Railway leaves early in the morning from a mock-Victorian station near the Johnson Street bridge and heads up-island to towns with fine resorts. The trip is slow but scenic; no food service. For an autoless vacation, take the ferry to Victoria and the train from there. Call Via Rail; (800) 665-0200 or (604) 383-4324. The **Royal British Columbia Museum** (the renamed BC Provincial Museum) is one of the finest of its kind in the country, offering dramatic dioramas of natural BC landscapes and full-scale reconstructions of Victorian storefronts. Of particular interest is the Northwest Coast Indian exhibit, rich with spiritual and cultural artifacts. Open every day, Belleville and Government, (604) 387-3701. The **Art Gallery of Greater Victoria** houses one of the world's finest collections of Oriental art (including the only Shinto shrine in North America), with special historical and contemporary exhibits on display throughout the year. Open every day, 1040 Moss Street, (604) 384-4101. Macpherson Playhouse, a former Pantages vaudeville house done up with baroque trappings, offers evening entertainment throughout the summer. The box office, (604) 386-6121, also has information about plays and concerts at the Royal Theatre and other sites. *Monday Magazine* (free, from yellow boxes at numerous locations downtown) offers the city's best weekly calendar of events. Spreading out over 184 acres, **Beacon Hill Park** provides splendid views of the water, but the real interest here is in the landscaping (much of it left wild) and the hand-holding couples who stroll the walkways and give retirement a good name. A lovely spot to get away from the shopping mania downtown. **Crystal Garden** is a turn-of-the-century swimming-pool building converted into a glass conservatory with a tropical theme (lush greenery, live flamingos and macaws) and a palm terrace tea room that is preferable to its counterpart at the Empress. It's a fine place to spend a rainy day; admission is $5.50. Open every day, 713 Douglas Street, (604) 381-1213. Just across the street is the new **Victoria Conference Centre**, linked to the Empress by a beautifully restored conservatory and accommodating 1,500 delegates. (The city's previous convention limit was 300). **Butchart Gardens**, 27 kilometers north, shows what can be done with dug-out limestone quarries (with help from a small army of Chinese workers). The 50 acres of gardens are beautifully manicured, lovely displays in many international styles; they're lighted after dark. Take the time to look beyond the profusion of blooms to the landscape structure and its relationship to the setting of rocky bays and tree-covered mountains. In the summer it's best to go late in the afternoon, after the busloads of tourists have left. Concerts, a surprisingly good afternoon tea, and light meals provide diversions. Open every day, (604) 652-5256. **Craigdarroch Castle** puts you back into an era of untrammeled wealth and ostentation. Vancouver Island coal tycoon Robert Dunsmuir built this 19th-century mansion to induce a Scottish wife to live in faraway Victoria. Open every day, 1050 Joan Crescent, (604) 592-5323. **Victorian heritage homes**. You can visit three of the better restored old-Victoria homes (all free): Helmcken House, behind Thunderbird Park, east of the Provincial Museum, (604) 387-3440; Point Ellice House, off Bay Street at Point Ellice Bridge, (604) 387-5953; and Craigflower Manor, 110 Island Highway, (604) 387-3067.

Specialty Shopping. For British woolens, suits, and toiletries, the downtown area north from the Empress on Government Street is the place to shop despite construction on the new Eaton Mall, set to open sometime in late 1989. **George Straith Ltd** is the best of the clothing stores, and you can be measured for a suit here that will be tailored in England; **Piccadilly Shoppe British Woolens** specializes in good-quality woman's clothes; **W & J Wilson Clothiers** for English wool suits and women's clothes; **Sasquatch Trading Company, Ltd** offers some of the best of the Cowichan sweaters; **E.A. Morris Tobacconist, Ltd** for a very proper, Victorian mix of fine pipes and tobaccos; **Campbell's British Shop** with its unique British collectibles and imports; **Munro's Books**, a monumental 19th-century bank-building-turned-bookstore, with a thoughtful selection of books; **Murchie's Tea and Coffee**, with the city's best selection of specially blended teas and coffees; and **Roger's Chocolates and English Sweet Shop** for chocolates, almond brittle, blackcurrant pastilles, marzipan bars, Pomfret cakes, and more. Farther north, on

Yates and lower Johnson streets, are the trendier shops and designer boutiques. **Market Square** is a restored 19th-century courtyard surrounded by a jumble of shops, restaurants, and offices on three floors. A few blocks farther on at Fisgard Street, the entrance to Victoria's small and seemingly shrinking Chinatown is marked by the splendid, lion-bedecked Gate of Harmonious Interest. Visit the tiny shops and studios on **Fan Tan Alley** and check out **Morley Co. Ltd,** a Chinese grocery. Antique hunters should head east of downtown, up Fort Street to Antique Row— block after block of shops, the best of which are **The Connoisseurs Shop** and **David Robinson, Ltd,** with excellent 18th-century English pieces. Visit **Bastion Square** for sidewalk restaurants, galleries, the Maritime Museum, the alleged location of Victoria's old gallows, and a great gardener's shop called **Dig This; Trounce Alley** for upscale clothing; and **Windsor Court** (formerly Nootka Court) for boutiques and gifts.

RESTAURANTS

Larousse
Between Pandora and
Fisgard, (604) 386-3454
1619 Store Street,
Victoria
Moderate; full bar; AE,
MC, V
Dinner Wed-Sun

Chef-owner Girard Hivon takes special pride in the fact that he's responsible for the stippled pastel finish on the walls of this small but interesting waterfront restaurant. For him, the walls seem to complete the experience that he presents to his patrons—an engaging amalgam of intellectuals, artists, and professionals who lend a slightly heady air to the place.

Hivon, a purist in the highest degree, offers a menu that is eclectic and changes seasonally, but it always includes a few African- and Indian-inspired creations, such as a tender breast of chicken in a spicy Senegalese peanut sauce. Soups are a high point, particularly the classic lentil soup, and an imaginative puree mongole: puree of peas and cream of tomato with basil and nutmeg. An Oriental influence is revealed in some preparations: the Escalope de Veau Pandora comprises two large cuts of local range veal in a rich sauce earthily flavored with Chinese mushrooms. Hivon is careful about presentation (another Asian touch) and has a flair for the dramatic: one salad of finely shredded, bright purple red cabbage flavored with blackcurrant liqueur and cilantro came atop two crisp leaves of deep green spinach with an orange nasturtium flourish. Unfortunately, this dressing needed less vinegar and more cilantro, which points up one quibble: does he care as much about how a dish tastes as about how it looks? Desserts are consistently excellent, especially the fresh berry finishers (we liked the sparkling raspberry mousse). His sorbets—pear, apricot, cranberry—are the best in town. The chocolate and orange cake, surrounded by a moat of light chocolate sauce, is a Larousse standard and worth a taste.

Chez Daniel
Dallas and Beach,
past Sea Land,
(604) 592-7424
2522 Estevan Avenue,

In a city overpopulated with mediocre French restaurants, this small exception, tucked a long way off the tourist track in Oak Bay, stands out. It's been around a long time, and quality here has a reputation for being consistently

Victoria
Expensive; full bar;
MC, V
Dinner Tues-Sat
(summer, Mon-Sat)

high, thanks to the attention of chef Daniel Rigollet. Recently, though, Rigollet has not always been on the scene, and we've started to hear reports of low-quality mussels and indifferent service. Still, the decor in a restrained rose/burgundy/peach scheme serves as a pleasant backdrop for the food, and the deep, thoughtful wine list with many French labels needs no improvement; what's left is to determine whether this high-butterfat cuisine works as well today as it did before the onslaught of nouvelle.

The answer is yes—at Chez Daniel, anyway. The chef's lavish, richly creamy sauces notwithstanding, a few nouvelle touches find their way into some presentations: tender pieces of lamb cooked just enough, sauced in reduced cream, and finished with shreds of fresh ginger, for instance. The menu, though conservative, is wide-ranging: salmon in vermouth and cream sauce, fresh young rabbit, New York steak with peppercorns, duck in a chestnut sauce. The food can be very rich, but the accompaniment of crisply cooked vegetables is a good antidote.

It's expensive, and service ranges from understandably slow (this type of food takes a while to prepare) to condescending. Plan to make an evening of it.

Futaba

Quadra and Pandora,
(604) 381-6141
1420 Quadra Street,
Victoria
Moderate; full bar;
MC, V
Lunch Mon-Fri, dinner
every day

A curious sort of Japanese restaurant without tatami rooms or kimono-clad waitresses, the recently relocated Futaba is nevertheless a good place to try some Japanese dishes that you won't find elsewhere in Victoria. The sushi is okay, but the most interesting and varied selections are listed under "Appetizers." We constructed a satisfying meal of herb- and garlic-flavored vegetarian dumplings, deep-fried tofu with sesame sauce, and teriyaki salmon. Notable features here are the tofu and vegetable broths that are staples in Japan. Futaba serves only brown rice. In fact, the whole menu has a distinctly vegetarian, health-food tone that will appeal to some and not to others.

The Grape Escape

Between Government and
Wharf, (604) 386-8466
506 Fort Street, Victoria
Moderate; full bar;
MC, V
Dinner Tues-Sun

The continued success of this stylish restaurant seems to rest squarely in the hands of owner Luke Harms, once a maitre d' at Deep Cove Chalet and one of the town's foremost wine experts. Consequently, the list here is well conceived (if not the town's best), includes an eminently drinkable house red (Parducci zinfandel), and can be used as the structure around which to build a meal. The a la carte list reads like a catalogue of West Coast specialties—a crock of steamed mussels, coho salmon poached in a scallop and vanilla sauce (very nicely executed), veal with tender chanterelles—but includes a few wanderings: a filet mignon uniquely seasoned with calvados, chutney, and curry, for instance, or venison from

New Zealand with Chinese five-spice. Unfortunately, entree portions tend to be small. One appetizer, a fiery prawns Sichuan in fermented black bean sauce over snow peas, was exceptional; indeed, teamed with an expertly dressed Caesar salad, a soup (our mildly curried butternut squash possessed an elusive, haunting tartness), and a plank of savory focaccia bread, it made a memorable dinner. The table d'hote presents a better value: $11.95 for the Caesar salad, lemon chicken, and lime souffle. The souffles, by the way, should not be missed, in whatever fruit incarnation is offered that night; they're glorious finishers—brought hot to the table, punctured by the waiter, and infused with a splash of warm liqueur.

Herald Street Caffe

Government and Herald,
1 block past Chinatown,
(604) 381-1441
546 Herald Street,
Victoria
Moderate; full bar;
AE, MC, V
Lunch, dinner every day

It's significant that the Herald Street Caffe has maintained its integrity long after the in-crowd has migrated to newer places. Herald Street's owners take their business seriously, and the menu reflects their concern for fresh, wholesome food prepared with delicacy and flair. The essential approach remains "Italian continental," with a range of salads, frittatas, and fresh pastas (the last embellished with a choice of sauces—pesto, clam, marinara, or cream). It's a place where the art on the wall changes more often than the menu does, and we find we favor the specials, which can often reach into the three-star category. Visits have turned up a boneless breast of chicken dusted with ginger and Dijon, and excellent spaghetti alfredo (prepared differently every time we've visited—but well every time). The satisfying dessert list includes daily specials such as papaya mousse.

We've had some reports of poor service here, and the lines that form for dinner can be irritating. But Herald Street keeps late hours (till 3am on weekends), and it's one of the best places in town to people-watch, amid airy, modern decor with cool grays and chic natural wood.

India Curry House

Where Gorge,
Government, Douglas,
and Hillside meet,
(604) 384-5622
2561 Government Street,
Victoria
Moderate; full bar;
AE, DC, MC, V
Lunch Tues-Thurs,
dinner every day

For a restaurant of such a high regard, it's surprising to find the India Curry House in a corner shopping complex. But then this was once a fish 'n' chips joint, a fact hidden nicely by the dense, dark colors, Indian graphics, and subdued lighting that now decorate its interior and lend it an intimate atmosphere. The menu is a shade conservative and includes the standard meat, fish, and chicken curries, but the kitchen takes its work very seriously. Everything is made fresh daily: cooks grind spices, make breads, and prepare chutneys. The food is excellent and the service extremely gracious. Light, crumbly popadums and a small plate of chutneys precede the gently flavored curries, and side dishes of spinach and dal provide a satisfying variety of tastes and textures. Accompany it all with a glass of cooling spiced yogurt lassi.

La Petite Colombe

Off Government, 2 blocks north of the Empress Hotel, (604) 383-3234
604 Broughton, Victoria
Moderate; full bar;
AE, DC, MC, V
Lunch Mon-Fri, dinner Mon-Sat

If it's possible, the lunch served here has improved over the last couple of years, and this was already the best midday spot in Victoria. The menu is simple and French: a selection of hot and cold appetizers, four soups, an array of crepes, an omelet and a croquette of the day, and some salads. The soup might be a shrimp bisque—a lovely, hot, thick puree; the omelet, a smoked salmon and artichoke concoction with a few nicely done vegetables on the side. A recent visit rewarded us with two exceptional crepe preparations: crab crepes served in a tangy bisque sauce, and a light lemon sauce over a seafood crepe that featured shrimp, scallops, and salmon—all of them perfectly cooked, which, considering their variety of textures, is no easy task. The sorbets top our list among dessert choices. Try the pear sorbet with kiwi and strawberries, accompanied by three brilliant sauces: raspberry, apricot, and a coconut concoction with a hint of almond. Dinners are a loving (if less memorable) set of variations on classical French cuisine featuring seafood, chicken, and veal. Service is kind but sometimes troubled. We've heard that long-time patrons were put off by La Petite Colombe's recent expansion and its new black walls. That's fine, because it means we have a better opportunity to find a table on short notice.

Metropolitan Diner

Between Herald and Fisgard, (604) 381-1512
1715 Government Street, Victoria
Moderate; full bar;
MC, V
Lunch Mon-Fri, dinner every day

A diner in name only, this is a small, stylish restaurant with an out-of-the-ordinary menu. How about a salad that combines duck, spinach, green beans, apple slices, and mango chutney dressing? Or a hot salad of assorted cooked vegetables, bean sprouts, and almonds, pan-fried and tossed in a spicy, Indonesian-style dressing? Lunch includes turkey burgers, and for dinner there's rabbit in cream sauce with juniper berries, prawns Pernod, Indonesian satay, fresh fish in tomato Bearnaise sauce, and even duck and pink peppercorn pizza topped with chile sauce. This kind of thing can get out of hand, but here it works. The pan-fried oysters in our Caesar salad were tender and lightly breaded, and our chilled melon, mint, and tomato soup was an unusual but delicate blend of flavors. Service is chummy if somewhat harassed, but everyone's having a good time.

Pagliacci's

Between Fort and Broughton on Broad next to Eaton's Center,
(604) 386-1662
1011 Broad Street, Victoria
Moderate; full bar;
MC, V

A friend from Long Island who had recently eaten at Pagliacci's came home raving about it. But what about the long lines outside the restaurant, we asked? She just ignored our grumbling and instructed us to order the wonderfully spicy cappelletti. So we did. And then we retried some of the dishes that we'd enjoyed here before: the chicken in Marsala sauce, tossed with three colors of fettuccine, and the crepes stuffed with pine nuts, mushrooms, and fried onion. We finished off with a white

Lunch Mon-Sat, dinner every day, brunch Sun

hazelnut chocolate raspberry cake that was as tasty a mouthful to eat as it was to say.

Owner Howie Siegel is a mile-a-minute talker and first-rate eccentric who drifted into Victoria a few years ago from New York via Los Angeles and Lasqueti Island. He bought the old Red Swing tea room, turned it into a Jewish-flavored Italian restaurant, and quickly created what has become a Victoria institution. Howie is a movie buff who names his fresh, hearty salads after such mediagenic types as Veronica Lake, and saddles entrees with punny monikers like "Last Chicken in Paris." Photos of Hollywood stars and wannabes decorate the strange orange walls, with big-band hits casting a vague presence over the din of chatter in this small establishment. Service can be slow, but the food is reasonably priced and worth waiting for. Go for Sunday brunch and you might meet the whole Siegel family, including Howie's very own Jewish mama.

Prima's on Wharf

8th and Wharf next to the Regent Hotel,
(604) 381-2112
218 Wharf Street,
Victoria
Moderate; full bar;
AE, MC, V
Dinner Mon-Sat

Prima's unprepossessing exterior gives no hint of the elegance that greets you as you step through the front door. The tiled foyer is actually a mezzanine, where a white baby grand piano overlooks the candy-colored dining room below (there's entertainment six nights a week). You descend a broad staircase to a high-ceilinged room lit by a wall of windows with a view of the Inner Harbour that would be lovely if the Regent Hotel weren't in the way. This is, however, a gem of a restaurant for decor and authentic Italian cuisine. The pasta menu includes several varieties of linguine, as well as manicotti stuffed with spinach and ricotta and topped with a rich cheese and tomato sauce. In addition to half-a-dozen veal and chicken entrees, there is an important seafood selection that includes salmon, shrimp-filled fillet of sole, and succulent crepes stuffed with scallops, shrimp, and crab in a superb Newburg sauce. The salad of sliced cucumbers in garlic-yogurt sauce is refreshingly cool and crisp, and the spinach salad comes with a vinaigrette and mustard dressing that makes a satisfying blend of flavors. This is rich, filling food, so you probably won't want dessert, but it's almost impossible to pass up the whole-wheat dinner rolls served with a mini-tub of whipped herb-garlic butter. Reports have been heard that waitpersons were not adequately informed about the dishes or wine list, but that hasn't stopped us from enjoying the food.

Spinnakers Brew Pub

Travel west over the
Johnson Street bridge
to Catherine,
(604) 386-2739
308 Catherine Street,

Spinnakers has everything a decent pub should have: excellent cottage-brewed draft ales; a cheerful, noisy atmosphere; a great waterfront view; friendly staff; a dart board; hearty, casual food; and no minors. This is as near to the real thing as you'll find in Victoria, and it's only

Victoria
Inexpensive; full bar; no
credit cards; no checks
Lunch, dinner every day

10 minutes from downtown, in a district that's sprouting condos now almost as fast as weeds. Parking can be a problem and so can seating, thanks to British Columbia's peculiar seat-restricting licensing laws, which also require pubs to shut down at 11pm. But the turnover is fairly fast, and the combination of a frothy pint with a thick juicy burger, traditional steak and kidney pie, or deep-fried halibut and chips is too good to pass up. The clam chowder here is excellent, as are the oysters Rockefeller and the Caesar salad. If you're not sure which of the unique tap brews to sample (we favored the Mt. Tolmie Dark, by the way), ask one of the bartenders for tastes of each—their job seems to be to educate drinkers as much as serve them.

Szechuan

Across from the
Memorial Arena parking
lot, (604) 384-5651
853 Caledonia Avenue,
Victoria
Moderate; full bar; AE,
MC, V
Lunch, dinner Tues-Sun

Joseph Wong turns out some excellent dishes, particularly if you let him know in advance that you like spicy food. Try the Pon Pon chicken as an appetizer—a tender chicken breast with thick sesame sauce. For the main course we recommend the very crisp whole rock cod, served with hot bean, sweet-and-sour, or fermented rice sauce. Other reliable entrees are the chef's spicy chicken with a hot garlic-soy sauce, mandarin pork, and shrimp. But ask the chef what he suggests. Decor is generic Chinese-restaurant. The Szechuan is right across from the Memorial Arena, so it's best to schedule your visit when there's no hockey game or rock concert.

Taj Mahal

Between Douglas and
Government,
(604) 383-4662
679 Herald Street,
Victoria
Moderate; full bar; AE,
DC, MC, V
Lunch Mon-Sat, dinner
every day

The oldest Indian restaurant in Victoria, Taj Mahal deserves its reputation for consistent quality. The excellent food here is influenced by the owners' African-Punjabi heritage. Formerly from Uganda, the Adaatias are friendly, conscientious hosts who are genuinely concerned about whether you enjoy your meal. The buffet lunch offers variety, but it's a rather anemic experience; dinner, however, easily matches or surpasses the other Indian restaurants in town, though at somewhat higher prices. The fish and lamb curries are good and a shade sweeter than you might be used to. We also like the vegetarian side dishes, especially the spiced spinach and the black-eyed peas in a delicately seasoned coconut-milk sauce. If the papier-mache dome exterior is a bit tacky, at least the interior is airy with a pleasant motif of sky blue, a nice departure from the usual Indian maroons and purples.

Yoshi Sushi

In Gateway Village Mall
just outside of town
on Highway 17,
(604) 383-6900

Yoshi makes sushi. Whether you sit at the sushi bar, the robata bar, or in one of the 12 tatami rooms, you'll get consistently excellent service and very fresh traditional Japanese food. The shabu shabu (sliced beef and vegetables in a delicate broth) is a good alternative to

771 Vernon Avenue,
Victoria
Moderate; full bar;
AE, MC, V
Lunch Mon-Sat,
dinner every day

 ★★

Barb's Place

At Fisherman's Wharf,
(604) 384-6515
310 St. Lawrence Street,
Victoria
Inexpensive; no alcohol;
no credit cards; no checks
Breakfast, lunch, dinner
every day

 ★

Cafe Francais

Oak Bay Avenue and
Fort Street,
(604) 595-3441
1653 Fort Street,
Victoria
Moderate; full bar;
MC, V
Dinner Tues-Sat

★

Chez Pierre

Yates and Wharf,
(604) 388-7711
512 Yates Street,
Victoria
Moderate; full bar; AE,
MC, V
Dinner Mon-Sat

 ★

Demitasse

Corner of Blanshard and
Johnson, (604) 386-4442
1320 Blanshard Street,
Victoria
Inexpensive; no alcohol;
no credit cards; no checks
Breakfast, lunch, dinner
Mon-Sat, brunch Sun

 ★

sushi. All entrees (including tempura, teriyaki, sukiyaki) are preceded by miso soup, sunomono, and an appetizer of yakatori or sushi.

For a good grease-up, this floating fish and chips joint anchored at Fisherman's Wharf is a great choice. You can't top the atmosphere: the fishing fleet bobs nearby as you sit at open-air picnic tables eating your fish and chips out of a greasy piece of newspaper. The fish is fine, tender halibut encased in crisp batter, and the chips are real potatoes, fried with the skins on. Help yourself to vinegar and ketchup from large vats on the counter.

We continue to give this spacious-feeling restaurant high marks for its consistently fine French food. The bouillabaisse is very popular (some say it's the best in town), and so are the crepes, of which there is a good variety. Owners Phillip and Valerie Bures do their own cooking, offering such delicious weekly specials as couscous, curried chicken, veal Provencal, and ratatouille. The Bureses serve fresh vegetables and excellent fresh fruit desserts, which also change weekly. Service is friendly and discreet.

Jean Pierre Mercier has been operating this small, rustic downtown restaurant long enough to render it the oldest French restaurant in Victoria. To a standard menu of French classics—tournedos, veal in cream and mushroom sauce, duck a l'orange, rack of lamb—chef Gilbert Leclair has added fresh seafood, including mussels and free-swimming scallops on the half shell served with a cream and white wine sauce, a wonderful dish. Service can be condescending, but still the tourists pack the place—so reservations are necessary.

Finding an excellent cup of espresso in Victoria is the spiritual equivalent of discovering a drinking fountain three days out into the rolling Sahara. This is very much a tea town, with coffee a young and too-often-neglected contender on menus. So it's no wonder that since it opened in 1981, Demitasse, with its good selection of coffees (by the cup and by the bag), has become a favorite haunt of the committed local caffeine-and-croissant set. Lunch is popular, with homemade soup (try the borscht), thick sandwiches, and excellent desserts. But the real Demitasse fan comes for breakfast, when you'll find buttery stuffed croissants—filled, perhaps, with scrambled eggs, Portuguese sausage, spinach, or avocado and artichoke hearts. Continental breakfast features a heated croissant with a plate of fresh fruit and a wedge of Camembert. Pleasant service and quiet, tasteful decor make this tiny coffee shop a winner.

Eugene's Restaurant and Greek Snack Bar

Kitty-corner from the Victoria Eaton's Center,
(604) 381-5456
1280 Broad Street,
Victoria
Inexpensive; beer and wine; no credit cards; no checks
Breakfast, lunch, dinner Mon-Sat

Fans of Eugene Vassiliadis' original Greek snack bar were delighted when he opened the Broad Street location, offering the same good, cheap Aegean food in a roomier space than the former Royal Bank Mall spot. The lentil and bean soups are both excellent (though often sold out by dinner time), and the tzatziki (sour cream, garlic, and cucumber sauce) is addictive either served on its own with hot pita bread or slathered over grilled souvlaki. All the other Greek classics are here too—moussaka, Greek salad, kalamarakia, spanakopita, tiropita—even gyros, a spicy Athens street-food staple. For dessert, skip the baklava and try instead the bougatsa, an incomparable confection made of vanilla custard wrapped in flaky phyllo.

John's Place

Douglas and Pandora,
(604) 389-0711
723 Pandora Avenue,
Victoria
Inexpensive; beer and wine; MC, V
Breakfast, lunch, dinner every day, brunch Sun

It's clear that breakfast is serious business at John's. Okay, so maybe this little place is a bit chi-chi, a tad too in for everybody's taste. It still serves up some of the fluffiest Belgian waffles in town, and innovative omelets (try a lamb, feta cheese, and mushroom combination) that are accompanied by satisfyingly thick wedges of potato. Lunch has its attractions too: lots of different burgers, pastas, salads, homemade soups, and pies—all at low prices. Our spinach salad with ginger vinaigrette dressing was great, and big enough for two, but the clam sauce on the linguine was bland and stodgy. Maybe there was just too much of it.

La Ville d'Is

Behind the main post office in town,
(604) 388-9414
26 Bastion Square,
Victoria
Moderate; full bar; AE, MC, V
Lunch Mon-Fri,
dinner Mon-Sat

Michel Duteau, a native of Brittany, operates this cozy, two-floor French restaurant specializing in seafood, just off Bastion Square. On nice days, tables are set out on the sidewalk. Prices are good and the service is very friendly. We've had the halibut braised with peppercorns and mustard, and frogs legs Provencal—pan-fried with tomatoes, garlic, mushrooms, and cognac. There are a few rabbit, veal, and lamb preparations; the lobster souffle proves the restaurant's commitment to fresh seafood. The lunch menu offers more standard crepes, quiches, and omelets, plus some simpler concoctions of seafood and meat.

Six Mile Pub

Colwood Exit off Island Highway, (604) 478-3121

This jolly pub/restaurant at the Sooke turnoff boasts the longest-established liquor license in British Columbia and a fiercely loyal clientele that continues to crowd the place.

494 Island Highway,
Victoria
Inexpensive; full bar;
MC, V
Lunch, dinner every day

It has a dark, smoky Tudor interior, so we like it best on a sunny day when you can select a courtyard table under a patio umbrella. You stand in line to order your delicious beer accompaniments from a take-out window: garlickly Caesar salad with big homemade croutons; mammoth savory roast beef sandwiches au jus served on slabs of fresh French bread; and rich French onion soup. Lots of international beers.

Southside Pizza

Between Government and
Broad, (604) 383-6273
608 Yates, Victoria
Inexpensive; beer and
wine; MC, V
Lunch, dinner every day

When the original Southside on Broad Street closed its doors in the mid-'80s, Victorians thought that was the last they'd seen of the avant-garde Wolfgang Puck school of pizza making in their town. Not so. The Southside is back with a vengeance, housed in a dark but high-ceilinged space and offering what may be this city's most eclectic selection of dinner music—segueing from Dylan to Diana Ross to Mexican marimba tunes. The new and substantial menu includes such oddities as a pesto and pistachio pizza, and another that carries prawns and scallops on its deck. If you don't like fruit on your crust, you'll be missing out on some of the best varieties. The duck and papaya pizza is a favorite here. Bacon and fig may not seem like the most logical combination, but it proved to be rich and flavorful. Our Capone Melone, covered with cappocolla sausage and melon, rewarded us with a wonderful mixture of assertive spicing and sweetness.

Desserts come in two varieties: fattening and more fattening (Grand Marnier poppyseed cheesecake, for instance). The espresso can be very weak. And the beer selection was niggardly, even if it did lean admiringly toward Northwest brews. A good late-night nosh.

386-Deli

Between Fort and
Broughton on Blanshard,
(604) 386-3354
1012 Blanshard Street,
Victoria
Inexpensive; beer and
wine; V
Lunch Mon-Fri,
dinner Fri

Owner Judith Stuart seems determined to make every lunch hour at the 386 an occasion for fine dining at remarkably reasonable prices. The service is warm, and the lively red, green, and white decor adds to the pleasure of a meal prepared with fresh, natural ingredients and all the skills of a practiced cook. The daily soup is always rich and creamy smooth with a hint of some surprise flavor, such as mild curry with a tinge of apple. This is a good place for antipasti, or for a slice of thick cheesy pizza with a side salad of tomato and crisp leaf lettuce. Stuart's specialty is pasta, made fresh each day and served with a choice of sauces: a four-cheese blend, seafood, marinara, or a heady pesto. Many people come back later in the afternoon for cappuccino and one of her splendid desserts, or to buy fresh pasta, sauces, or salads for take-out. Stuart's special Friday night dinners feature any of the pastas, plus distinctive seafood and chicken dishes.

The facts in this edition were correct at press time, but places close, chefs depart, hours change. It's best to call ahead.

Wah Lai Yuen

Government and Fisgard,
(604) 381-5355
560 Fisgard Street,
Victoria
Inexpensive; beer only; no
credit cards; no checks
Lunch, dinner Tues-Sun

Have a glass of excellent tea while poring over the 136-item menu in this bright, shiny-clean spot in Victoria's small and shrinking Chinatown. The decor is so spare as to be almost nonexistent, but you won't mind: the staff is helpful and efficient, the food delicious, and the prices extremely reasonable. The menu lists soups and vegetables, noodle dishes and barbecued meats, rice specialties and bakery items. Our lunch featured barbecued pork—moist and flavorful, a rarity—and a savory chicken curry garnished with green onions, as well as rice and tea; the tab for two came to less than $10. And we didn't have room for dessert.

Grand Central Cafe

Between Wharf and
Government on Johnson,
(604) 386-4747
555 Johnson Street,
Victoria
Moderate; full bar;
MC, V
Lunch, dinner every day,
brunch Sun

The Pagliacci's people have done a wonderful job of transforming the 1920s Grand Central Hotel bar into an elegant restaurant that blends the spacious proportions of an earlier age with the modern taste for big windows, tile flooring, exposed brick, and back-alley ambience—very chic. We haven't had much luck with the dinners, though: our blackened snapper was incorrectly prepared, and the pasta special with fresh vegetables in cream sauce was undistinguished. You might want to select instead from the appetizer menu (pate, a couple of seafood dishes, a peanut satay), then finish with dessert (best is the magnificent, dense chocolate mousse cake), and enjoy the thoroughly pleasant surroundings.

King Solomon's Studio Cafe

Between Government and
Broad, (604) 381-2545
615 Johnson Street,
Victoria
Inexpensive; no alcohol;
no credit cards; no checks
Lunch Mon-Sat, dinner
Mon-Fri

The half-a-dozen tables at King Solomon's are often occupied by the owner's artist friends. Jim Lindsay is a painter and a cook who knows a lot about Middle Eastern fast food. The atmosphere is art-school bohemian, while the falafel and the Greek salads are filling and inexpensive. The felafel is a meal in itself, served in pita bread with Greek salad and yogurt-feta dressing, hummus, or sesame sauce. For a light touch that includes all the right tastes, try the combination salad plate: tabouli, hummus, Greek salad, falafel, and pita bread. The menu also includes extras such as pita pizza, thick home-style fried potatoes, and espresso. It's a daytime place, closing at 7pm.

Le Petit Saigon

Between Fort and
Broughton,
(604) 386-1412
1010 Langley, Victoria
Moderate; full bar; AE,
MC, V
Lunch Mon-Fri, dinner
every day

This Vietnamese restaurant is small, attractive, and always quiet. Its beautifully presented meals are fine, if not exciting. Our crab, asparagus, and egg swirl soup was excellent, and the Imperial rolls were light and delicious. Although crisp and colorful, the sauteed vegetables can be oversalted. Individual dishes here are fairly pricey, but the combination dinners offer a more economical way to experience the variety necessary for a fully enjoyable Vietnamese meal.

Maddie's Restaurant and Tea House

Newport and Windsor,
(604) 595-3135
2540 Windsor Road,
Victoria
Inexpensive; beer and
wine; MC, V
Breakfast, lunch, dinner
every day

This is the place to take your mother on special occasions: it's clean, cozy, and charmingly old-fashioned. More than any other tea room in the Garden City, Windsor Park looks and feels like those in English country villages; it's even located on the far side of the "tweed curtain" that separates Victoria from ultra-British Oak Bay. The scones, pies, and trifles here are all homemade and delicious, as are the soups, Cornish pasties, and steak and kidney pie. If you want to sample the atmosphere without the sugar, the new owner (a Frenchman named Yvan Couture) has added a full-course dinner menu with things such as veal cutlet in hunter sauce, sole amandine, and New York steak. There are only 56 seats, and it closes at 8pm, so reservations are recommended, especially on the weekend.

Ocean Phoenix

At the bottom end of
Chinatown,
(604) 382-2828
509 Fisgard Street,
Victoria
Moderate; beer and wine;
AE, MC, V
Lunch, dinner every day

We don't think we've ever been waited on quite so anxiously as we were here. Our waitress checked every minute or so to be sure that we were actually eating and not just picking at our dinner between articles in *The New Yorker*. But anxiety is the mark of a new place, which the Ocean Phoenix certainly is. The menu is fairly standard as Chinese restaurants go, but quite well done. Just look out that you're not ordering too much, because portions tend to be large. The Harmonious Meal for one (egg roll, won ton soup, and three of these four: chicken chow mein, chicken chop suey, barbecued pork fried rice, and sweet and sour pork) would easily satisfy two hungry adults. The Eight Treasure Soup is a find.

The Re-bar

On Johnson between
Wharf and Government,
(604) 361-9223
549 Johnson Street,
Victoria
Inexpensive; no alcohol;
no cards; local checks only
Breakfast, lunch, dinner
Mon-Sat, brunch Sun

The Victoria counterpart of Seattle's techy and trendy Gravity Bar, The Re-bar caters to an allegedly health-conscious crowd that's big on almond burgers and bee pollen. Fortunately, most of what you'll find on the photocopied menu is tasty and filling enough to make you forget that you're sitting in a room decorated with corrugated metal walls. Especially good and spicy are the bean and cheese enchiladas, served with a multi-vegetable and sprout salad. Also worth ordering (and a lunchtime bargain at $4.95) is the cream of asparagus soup, which comes with a homemade-tasting corn muffin. Cookies and fruit breads are baked on the premises. The shots of wheatgrass juice, a thick green liquid that's squeezed from plants raised right on the premises, are supposed to cure a plethora of digestive ills.

Wondering about our standards? We rate establishments on value, performance measured against the place's goals, uniqueness, enjoyability, loyalty of clientele, cleanliness, excellence and ambition of the cooking, and professionalism of the service. For an explanation of the star system, see the Introduction.

LODGINGS

Abigail's

Vancouver and McClure,
(604) 388-5363
906 McClure Street,
Victoria, BC V8V 3E7
Expensive; MC, V

The feminine counterpart of the Edwardian Beaconsfield, just two blocks away, the Tudor Abigail's is all gables and gardens and crystal chandeliers, with three floors of odd-shaped rooms, each with a shiny-tiled bathroom. Not a lavish detail is missed: guest rooms are decorated in restrained tones (rose, peach, periwinkle, mint); crystal goblets sit in each room; chandeliers have dimmer switches; the halls smell faintly of good coffee and beautiful women. Practicalities, too, are all well in place—there are electrical outlets wherever you might need them, a light shines in the shower, the walls are well soundproofed (light sleepers, however, may want to request a room as far from noisy Quadra Street as possible). In short, Abigail's combines the beauty of the Old World with the comforts of the new. Third-floor guest rooms are grandest: the Foxglove Room has a canopy bed, and a few of the bathrooms are equipped with Jacuzzis. Prices range from $75 to $155. A note of caution: We've heard reports that late-night arrivals (even when expected) have difficulty checking in.

Breakfast—perhaps toasted whole-wheat croissants topped with eggs and cheese sauce, with orange juice—is served from 8 to 9am in the sunny downstairs dining room. The sitting room is inviting in the sort of way that makes one want to linger, with a glass of port and a hand of whist, after a day of traipsing about Victoria.

The Beaconsfield

Vancouver and Humboldt,
(604) 384-4044
998 Humboldt Street,
Victoria, BC V8V 2Z8
Expensive; MC, V

Of all the imitation England spots, this is the best. The Beaconsfield opened its Edwardian gates in 1984 and since then has quietly and capably assumed its place at the forefront of Victoria's accommodations. Tree-lined Humboldt Street is closer to the hub of downtown than its quiet demeanor would suggest, so the Beaconsfield's location here just a block and a half from Beacon Park is prime. Owner Bill McKechnie named the inn after the posh London hotel where King Edward VII reputedly pursued his liaisons, and it's meant to convey a sense of romance and hideaway. That it does, with twelve antique-filled bedrooms, all with private baths and down comforters. The Attic Room occupies the entire top floor, features its own Jacuzzi and wet bar, and is exceedingly private. Lillie's Room is a little more feminine, with inlaid mahogany pieces and an unusual wood-enclosed period bathtub. The antiques are offset by convenient modernities like steam-heated towel racks.

Public areas, particularly the lobby and the library, are elegantly crafted with so much dark, gleaming mahogany that one can feel a bit cloistered on a sunny day. A fine remedy is the sun room/conservatory, always awash in filtered light. The place is so popular for breakfast that you sign up for your morning meal when you check in—adieu to the annoying waits.

Holland House Inn
2 blocks behind the Parliament buildings at Government and Michigan, (604) 384-6644 595 Michigan Street, Victoria, BC V8V 1S7 Expensive; AE, DC, MC, V

When your eyes start to glaze over at Victoria's endless Olde England theme, this magnificent "modern art" B&B in the cheerful James Bay neighborhood provides just the right antidote. The house is a beauty, decked with rose trellises and a picket fence outside, skylights and stark white walls inside. Fine art and sculpture, many by owner Lance Olsen, fill the 10 sparkling guest rooms. The result is startlingly chic and about as avant-garde as you're likely to find in Quaintville. The Lilac Room has an intriguing, Art-Deco-inspired headboard. Rooms 20 and 30 have fireplaces, the former with a unique lace-draped bed. All of the rooms have immaculate private baths (the fixtures in Room 11 are equipped for wheelchair access); all but one of the rooms have their own balconies. This is consistent with the inn's other orientation, a healthy one: Olsen's wife, Robin, is an occupational therapist. No smoking in the rooms, natch.

A full breakfast is served either in the Gallery Lounge downstairs with the other guests or in the sitting area or balcony of your own room. Owners and the managers are always at the ready with hospitality, but the service is never fawning. And most of the art is for sale.

The Bedford
½ block north of Fort Street, (604) 384-6835 or (800) 661-9255 1140 Government Street, Victoria, BC V8W 1Y2 Expensive; AE, MC, V

We probably could have done without the liveried doorman escorting us inside the lobby *every* time we entered the place, but it's hard to knock a hotel that offers carefully maintained flower boxes, thick and pillowy bed quilts, private Jacuzzis, and a dozen rooms with fireplaces. In a renovation that proved frogs can still become princes, Victoria's reigning dukes of hospitality, Bill McKechnie and Stuart Lloyd (who masterminded the Beaconsfield and Abigail's), transformed what used to be downtown's shoddiest hotel, The Alhambra, into a small showcase of European elegance and then sold the place in the fall of 1988 to Heathwood Resorts Ltd. Most of the 40 rooms don't boast much of a view, and they're pricey ($120–$170 in season), but the hotel's central location—smack in the middle of the shopping district—is hard to beat. There's no room service, but afternoon tea and continental breakfast are included in the price.

Laurel Point Inn
2.5km northwest of the Inner Harbour ferries, (604) 386-8721 680 Montreal Street, Victoria, BC V8V 1Z8

The inn, a massive brick ziggurat on a point overlooking the harbor, is very modern—a refreshing change in a city of antiques. You get many amenities: indoor and outdoor tennis courts, heated indoor pool, hot tubs, and saunas. The angular construction of the lodge means that all of the rooms have good views of the harbor or the ship chan-

Expensive; AE, MC, V

nel. Rooms on each floor can be arranged to connect in-to two-room suites, a particularly nice touch if you are traveling with children. A standard now runs about $125.

The grounds are nicely landscaped, and you can spend hours on your patio or lounging around the pool. The dining room is a wicker-and-fern place called Cafe Laurel, with superior food that is also available in room service. Sunday brunch is the best in town. The lounge has big windows to capture the view. Service is swift and impeccable at all times—the icing on the cake.

Oak Bay Beach Hotel
Near the corner of Oak Bay Avenue and Beach Drive, (604) 598-4556 1175 Beach Drive, Victoria, BC V8S 2N2 Expensive; AE, MC, V

Presiding over the Haro Strait, this Tudor-style hotel is the loveliest—and most British—part of Anglophile Victoria, a nice place to stay if you want to be removed from downtown. Even so, it's a very busy spot—especially its bars. Yet it still evokes another world: handsome antiques dot the comfortable public rooms, and the private rooms, lavishly furnished, are full of nooks and gables. The best rooms are those with private balconies and a view of the sea, but the price runs up to about $150.

The dining room is prettily done, overlooking the gardens, but isn't up to the rest of the place. Instead, opt for the Snug—quite possibly the coziest bar in the whole city—where you can sit before the fire and feel for all the world as if you have successfully penetrated the inner circle of this most class-conscious city. For more status assurance, walk across the street and play a round at Victoria Golf Club, a Scottish-style links with windswept holes dramatically bordered by the sea. And don't forget the hotel's afternoon tea—a proper affair where you might feel a wee bit conspicuous dressed in jeans.

Victoria Regent Hotel
Corner of Yates and Wharf, (604) 386-2211 1234 Wharf Street, Victoria, BC V8W 3H9 Expensive; AE, DC, MC, V

For those with a taste for very luxurious condo living, the modern Victoria Regent is a posh apartment-hotel with grandstand views of the harbor from the north. Don't let the unadorned exterior put you off; inside, huge, nicely decorated one- and two-bedroom suites range from $125 to $190 per night for two people. Each apartment has a living room, dining room, deck, and kitchen, and most have two bedrooms and two bathrooms. All are furnished with quiet taste, and most have views of city and harbor. Even larger suites (three bedrooms and three bathrooms, fireplace and large deck) are available for $570 a night.

"Apartment" is the operative word here: there is limited meal service (a cafe serves lunches and break-fasts), no lobby, no newsstand. You can live in the grand style, however, and if you double up with another couple, the tab becomes almost within reach, especially if you do your own cooking.

Looking for a particular place? Check the index at the back of this book for individual restaurants, hotels, B&Bs, parks, and more.

The Captain's Palace

2 blocks west of the
Empress Hotel,
(604) 388-9191
309 Belleville Street,
Victoria, BC V8V 1X2
Expensive; AE, DC,
MC, V

What was once a charming one-guest-room B&B with a mediocre restaurant is now a charming 10-guest-room B&B with a mediocre restaurant—and a lot more to recommend it. The B&B outgrew the handsome 1897 mansion across the street from the *Princess Marguerite* dock and spread into the adjacent property, where the quarters are newer and decorated in florals and muted pastels. Some have balconies; most have private baths with cute claw-footed tubs. You eat breakfast in the main dining room downstairs (but you'd do better elsewhere in Victoria). Prices range from $75 to $145, the latter offering views of the water and Beacon Hill Park.

Craigmyle Guest House

1.6km up Fort Street
from city center; look for
the castle, (604) 595-5411
1037 Craigdarroch Road,
Victoria, BC V8S 2A5
Moderate; MC, V

Built as a guest house early in the century, the Craigmyle stands next to Craigdarroch Castle (a grand, well-preserved mansion). The 19 rooms are quaint and simple, with papered walls a la Laura Ashley and shared baths; best are those with views of the neighborhood castle. A large breakfast with homemade preserves and good coffee is served in the dining room, and the main lounge features traditional wainscoting, lofty ceilings, an enormous fireplace, and (on our visit) annoying easy-listening music. Rooms are quite reasonable ($45 Canadian for a single, $65 for a double), but you're 1½ kilometers from city center.

Heritage House

Highway 1 north, right
on McKenzie, left to 1100
Burnside Road W,
(604) 479-0892
3808 Heritage Lane,
Victoria, BC V8Z 7A7
Moderate; MC, V

This 1910 beauty is far (five kilometers) from the center of town, but the four rooms are enchanting: the pale blue Dormer Room offers three adjoining sleeping compartments; the Antique Room is pretty and floral, with period furnishings; the Twin Room is turned out in peach and taupe. Our favorite is the Sun Room, with its three walls of windows and off-white, country-style decor. The two bathrooms are shared. Downstairs, the fireplace parlor makes a cozy place to linger; in warm weather a wraparound porch provides ample seating for garden appreciators (Heritage House's is splendid).

Huntingdon Manor Inn

Downtown across from
the harbor,
(604) 381-3456
330 Quebec Street,
Victoria, BC V8V 1W3
Expensive; AE, MC, V

A comfortable antique-furnished parlor with a blazing log fireplace, an indoor whirlpool and sauna, and a location just steps from the *Princess Marguerite* dock make the Huntingdon a pleasant hotel. Unfortunately, it's behind the *very* touristy stuff hard by the dock, and views can be rather odd. Rooms are nicely furnished, some with four-poster beds, and the spacious two-story gallery suites have bedroom lofts. Many rooms have full kitchen facilities. Kids under 12 stay free in their parents' suite.

Mt. Douglas Park Resort

Take the Royal Oak Drive
exit off Highway 17,

Gustav Klimach has entirely revamped his secluded waterfront motel, formerly the Seaview Resort, to a more European ambience: chalet-style units, a staff aestheti-

(604) 658-2171
4550 Cordova Bay Road,
Victoria, BC V8X 3V5
Moderate; AE, MC, V

cian, and a separate dining room where guests can enjoy (extra) continental breakfasts. Now there are 18 units—six with kitchens, two with fireplaces—that feature excellent proximity to Cordova Bay and the wooded trails of Mount Douglas Park. Regulars book early.

Rose Cottage

West on Gorge from
Douglas, (604) 381-5985
3059 Washington
Avenue, Victoria,
BC V9A 1P7
Moderate; MC, V

If ex-Londoners Bob and Vicky Smith seem to bring a most comfortable humor and conviviality to their roles as B&B owners, it's because they're used to entertaining. He credits himself as a ventriloquist, singer, and comedian; she sings; and they can often be seen together on the boards at the Pig & Whistle pub downtown. Where they find the energy to also run this romantic hideaway is anybody's guess. A 1912 Victorian edifice, well appointed with leaded-pane windows and high ceilings, Rose Cottage offers four guest rooms ($43–$45 single, $54–$58 double) and a couple of shared baths. A four-course breakfast includes eggs, sausages, tasty heart-shaped scones, and Vicky's homemade jams (definitely try the plum), as well as coffee and fresh juice. There's not much of a view, but Rose Cottage is located only about a mile and a half (or a good postprandial stroll) from the Inner Harbour. There is also a cat named Eric, who thinks he owns the joint but will leave amorous couples in peace if they request it convincingly. No smoking; no small children.

The Empress

Between Humboldt and
Belleville, (604) 384-8111,
toll-free (800) 268-9411
721 Government Street,
Victoria, BC V8W 1W5
Expensive; AE, DC,
MC, V

(unrated due to renovation)

The hotel that once stood as the quiet, ivy-clad dowager of the Inner Harbour was rocking on our last visit with the noise of jackhammers. While there was talk in 1965 of razing this historic edifice (it was opened in 1908), today owner Canadian Pacific Hotels is finishing up a $45 million refurbishment instead. It's about time: even adoring longtime visitors were saying the hotel looked a bit shabby. A separate guest entrance pavilion has been added, the Palm Court and the Crystal Ballroom have been polished up, and 50 new rooms have been added, bringing the total to 470. The grounds are being re-landscaped, and a restored conservatory at the rear of the hotel connects it to the new Victoria Conference Centre.

When staying at The Empress, remember that you're in one of Victoria's authentic tourist meccas, so don't expect any quiet strolls through the lobby (except very early or very late in the day) or immediate (or good) tea service in the Palm Court. Our refuge has always been the Library Bar, where high prices drive off the gawkers and you can enjoy fresh oysters and other seafood for lunch.

If you've found a place that you think is a Best Place, send in the report form at the back of this book. If you're unhappy with one of the places, please let us know why. We depend on reader input.

METCHOSIN

RESTAURANTS

Fernie Farm
Head west on Metchosin Road and continue 1.6km after it becomes William Head, (604) 478-1682
4987 William Head Road, Metchosin,
Inexpensive; no alcohol; no credit cards; no checks
Tea Wed-Sun (closed September)

Thirty kilometers west of Victoria is an elfin farmhouse where you can consume a luscious afternoon tea (between 3pm and 5pm) in a magical setting. It's all in a state of amiable disrepair, but on nice days you don't mind: you sit outside at brightly painted tables amid a blooming English garden. Tea consists of rich buttermilk scones, Devonshire cream from Jersey cows, fresh pies, cakes, and cookies. The place is quite popular—partly because of the lovely drive from Victoria—so you'll likely have to take a number from a peg on the gate and stand in line. No reservations.

SOOKE

This relatively undiscovered area, half an hour west of Victoria, offers spectacular beach scenery and seclusion. The road at Port Renfrew peters out into the famous West Coast Trail, one of the greatest (and most demanding) hikes in the Northwest. Botany Botanical Beach, just south of Port Renfrew, has exceptionally low tides in the early summer that expose miles of sea life and sculpted sandstone. The entire coast has excellent parks, with trails to the beach or into the forest and good waves for surfers.

Royal Roads Military College, on the road to Sooke, is a Dunsmuir family castle turned military college; the beautiful grounds are open to the public each day 10am–4pm; call (604) 380-4660 or (604) 380-4526.

East Sooke Park, a wilderness park, offers hiking trails in the forest, spectacular views, and good swimming beaches.

Sooke Region Museum mounts some interesting displays of logging and pioneer equipment, Indian artifacts, and a fully restored historic cottage showing turn-of-the-century lifestyles. The museum is also the home of BC's largest juried fine arts show, held every August. Museum open daily 9–5. Call (604) 642-6351 for more information.

Between Sooke and Port Renfrew are dozens of trails leading down to ocean beaches, all of which offer fine beachcombing possibilities. Ask at the Sooke Region Museum for details.

Lester B. Pearson College of the Pacific, on Pedder Bay, has been open since 1974 with a two-year program to foster international understanding; the setting and the architecture are both worth seeing. Call (604) 478-5591.

RESTAURANTS

Sooke Harbour House
At the very end of Whiffen.Spit Road, on the water, (604) 642-3421
1528 Whiffen Spit Road, Sooke
Expensive; full bar;

Perched upon a bluff in the unassuming hamlet of Sooke, this white clapboard farmhouse gives little indication that it is one of the best restaurants in the British Columbia. Complementing the food is truly exquisite lodging. Owners Sinclair and Frederica Philip have thoughtfully expanded the original 1931 inn—which houses three

MC, V
Dinner every day

suites and the light, airy dining room—to include a new house only steps away. The 10 rooms in "new house" are so graciously designed you feel you are merely visiting some well-heeled friends who have given you a time of quiet privacy in their own home. Each is unique: the Mermaid Room creates a theme of grace and whimsy with its pastel hues ($154); the Herb Garden Room, in shades of mint and parsley, opens out through French doors onto a private patio ($230); the vaulted-ceiling Longhouse Room features Northwest native accoutrements and an enormous bathtub positioned before a breathtaking view ($212); and the Underwater Orchard spoils you with a fireplace (stacked with more wood than you could burn in a year) and a whirlpool on a deck at the coast's edge ($154). All of this would be first-rate even without the warm, artful extras that include Frederica's bursting bouquets of fresh flowers in every room, a decanter of fine port, and terrycloth bathrobes. Breakfast and a light lunch (from marinated sauteed tofu to pasta salad to steamed gooseneck barnacles) are included in the cost of a night's stay.

But dinner is the crowning experience. The Philips, along with a team of four chefs, display rare dedication to the freshest natural ingredients, blended with a good deal of energy and flashes of searing innovation. Often, just before dinner, Sinclair will go diving in search of free-swimming scallops, octopus, sea urchins, whelks, and red rock crabs. Fresh local rabbit, meaty Muscovy duck, eggs from free-range chickens, and pheasant all come from local farmers. Beautifully manicured gardens around the property yield French sorrel, pineapple sage, Mallorcan rosemary, and some 200 other varieties of herbs year-round; the brilliant violas, chrysanthemums, wild onions, tulips, and honeysuckle you see growing on the steep banks and behind the house will likely end up as fragrant, edible punctuation to your wild greens salad.

These ultra-fresh ingredients show up in creative combinations. Large Sooke oysters might be baked in a puff pastry and served in a butter sauce made with BC hard cider and alaria seaweed; octopus emerges in a curry and caraway salad. One night we were served braised shoulder of veal (locally and organically raised) with ginger and fennel cream sauce accompanied by Belgian endive, mustard greens, and pasta; another dish was a delightful melange of trout, squid, and mussels. Another evening (when we encountered an uninteresting blackberry sauce on the breast of quail and overcooked salmon) left us wondering if four chefs in the kitchen is just too many. The wine list is impeccably selected.

Request a corner table on the porch for the best view in the house—sea otters are frequently seen playing in the water just below the window. The service is well paced and attentive. Casual dress is encouraged, since many guests like to explore stretches of the beach before or after meals.

Margison House

In the center of Sooke Village, hidden by trees; look for signs,
(604) 642-3620
6605 Sooke Road, Sooke
Inexpensive; beer and wine; V
Lunch, tea Thurs-Sun (May-Oct)

An elegant cottage just off the highway in downtown Sooke serves up the best afternoon tea in these parts, along with light lunches of seafood chowder, raisin scones, sausage rolls, and the like. The view is fine, the grounds are pretty, and amiable owner Sylvia Hallgren has a charming B&B cottage next door with a bathroom and full kitchen. Ms. Hallgren stocks the fridge with freshly laid eggs and breakfast goodies from her garden.

LODGINGS

Malahat Farm

Anderson Road .4km up from West Coast Road, 15 minutes west of Sooke,
(604) 642-6868
Mail: RR2, Sooke, BC V0S 1N0
Moderate; no credit cards; checks ok

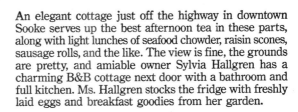

A 1919 farm cottage has been restored to dollhouse condition by owner Diana Clare, who rents the whole place to one group at a time. Three bedrooms and one bath make the place ideal and cozy for small families, especially families unacquainted with the simple satisfactions of feeding cows and geese and gathering eggs—tasks Diana will patiently share with younger members of your group. She has recently opened two new rooms upstairs in her own farmhouse. A separate entry leads the way to the charming country-style rooms, each with private bath. Breakfast, served in the cottage or the farmhouse, is an abundant spread of homemade sweet rolls and muffins, apple or rhubarb sauce, granola or porridge, fresh orange juice, bacon, fried potatoes, and those eggs. The tranquil setting provides sweet rejuvenation.

Burnside House

.5km past Sooke stoplight on Highway 14, turn right to 1890 Maple Street, (604) 642-4403
Mail: Box 881, Sooke, BC V0S 1N0
Moderate; MC, V

The second-oldest house in Sooke is a good place to know about if the Sooke Harbour House is full. This beautifully restored circa 1870 home was recently purchased by a gracious German couple, Gisela and Heinz Kappler. It's directly across the street from Government Wharf. Three of the five rooms have views of the harbor; all five share two baths. You can often sight seals from the window of the blue room. Turn the other way and perhaps you'll spot a deer in the large yard.

Point No Point Resort

Highway 14, 24km west of Sooke, (604) 646-2020
West Coast Road, RR2, Sooke, BC V0S 1N0
Moderate; no credit cards; checks ok

The Soderberg family owns a mile of beach and 40 acres of wild, undeveloped, quintessentially Northwest coastline facing the Strait of Juan de Fuca and west to the Pacific. They rent 11 cabins ($52–$84 for two) among the trees on or near the cliffside, catering to those who eschew TV and telephones and seek remote beauty and tranquillity. The only distractions here are the crashing of the rolling swells and the crackle of the fireplace. Firewood is supplied, but stop on the way to Point No Point and buy your own food. All the cabins have newly redone kitchens, new carpet, and new fireplaces. Trail access to the shoreline and rough benches promote a relaxed appreciation of the area, including tidepools with all manner of marine life to discover. Afternoon tea (with mediocre pastries) and light, soup-and-sandwich lunches are served in the afternoon in a dining room that is both worn and convivial.

BRENTWOOD BAY

LODGINGS

Brentwood Bay Bed & Breakfast

Corner of Stelly and W Saanich, (604) 652-2012 7247 W Saanich Road, Brentwood Bay, BC V0S 1A0 Moderate; no credit cards; checks ok

Inside this restored Victorian you'll find nine guest rooms and a cottage (summers only) with antique furniture, glossy wood floors, lace curtains, colorful braided rugs, and hand-crafted coverlets. A suite designed especially for the handicapped has a kitchenette and a full bath. Most rooms have en suite bathrooms. Ask for a room away from the fairly busy highway. Owner Evelyn Hardy serves spicy sausage and pear cobbler for breakfast in a glassed-in sun porch. No smoking.

Little Thistle Bed & Breakfast

Follow the signs to the Brentwood/Mill Bay ferry terminal, (604) 652-9828 7212 Peden Lane Mail: Box 88, Brentwood Bay, BC V0S 1A0 Moderate; MC, V

You could almost walk to Butchart Gardens from this five-room bed and breakfast on Brentwood Bay. The best room, though small, is upstairs with its own deck. You'll find '50s architecture, dainty flowered wallpaper, spanking-new shared baths, and tea served in proper china cups. Start your day with a full Scottish breakfast served up by the cheerful owner, Mary O'Donell. No smoking.

SIDNEY

RESTAURANTS

Deep Cove Chalet

40km north of Victoria on the Trans-Canada Highway, (604) 656-3541 11190 Chalet Road, Sidney Expensive; full bar; AE, MC, V Lunch, dinner Tues-Sun

Scrupulously manicured lawn rolls down to the cove. Even in winter the fragrance of an extravagant English flower arrangement greets you at the door. This romantic restaurant is suffused with candlelight from tall tapers, the view from each table is postcard-perfect, and the food is exquisite. The service is professional without being stuffy, although sometimes it can be forgetful (especially on busy Saturday nights).

Pierre Koffel is one of the most gifted chefs on Vancouver Island—and one of the most entertaining. He's not above taking on whatever task needs attention in the

Chalet: on any given night he might be spied clearing a table, ceremoniously decanting a bottle of wine, or greeting a guest with the warmest of welcomes. As eccentric as he is, regulars know he's a stickler for freshness and quality: he uses squab and seafood from Vancouver Island and imports truffles from France, vegetables and exotic fruits from as far away as Africa. The wine list is thoughtful, with lots of high-priced California bottlings.

The traditional menu has a light contemporary touch. You may choose from a prix-fixe menu, which ranges in price from $35 to $70 (the latter for the Beluga and Atlantic lobster extravaganza). Or you can put together your own meal, starting with a smooth clam bisque, rich with cream, a splendid avocado salad with perfectly cooked scallops and prawns dressed in an intense curry vinaigrette, or a well-seasoned, beautifully textured duck pate. The lamb roasted in mustard sauce is exquisite in flavor and texture; the rare duck is served with a seductive green peppercorn sauce. Entrees may come with a freshly cooked artichoke heart topped with a tomato coulis and two sizzling puffs of potato. Finish your meal with classic crepes suzettes, prepared with a flourish at your table—an appropriate Koffel finale.

The Latch

4km out of Sidney on Harbour Road,
(604) 656-6622
2328 Harbour Road,
Sidney
Moderate; full bar;
AE, DC, MC, V
Lunch Mon-Fri, dinner every day, brunch Sun

The Latch—rough logs outside, refined wood paneling inside—was built for the provincial lieutenant governor in 1926 and converted to a restaurant half a century later. Fancy dining rooms feature views of the peerless gardens and the harbor yachts, but the food is not consistently good enough to justify the prices.

Dinner is usually more reliable than lunch. The menu runs the gamut from beef Wellington to orange Ruffian with Cajun pecans. Recent reports tell us of generous portions (especially the oysters Rockefeller), a well-dressed brandied shrimp and papaya salad (though the papaya could have used a few more days in the sun), and a pedestrian iceberg lettuce salad with the island's ubiquitous horseradish dressing. The rack of lamb Provencal—though succulent and properly cooked—was overbreaded. The wine list is not extensive, but The Latch does offer any selection by the glass. The place remains Saanich Peninsula's most accessible dress-up restaurant and it's packed for brunch. The Latch is busy in winter months especially, due to the $10.95 four-course specials.

MILL BAY

LODGINGS

Pine Lodge Farm Bed & Breakfast

Here's a Canadian rendition of a French country farmhouse, and the result looks like a slice of the American

Merideth and Mutter,
(604) 743-4083
3191 Mutter Road, Mill
Bay, BC V0R 2P0
Moderate; MC, V;
checks ok

Old West. The lodge, a massive house with an uncommonly rich interior, sits on 30 rolling acres of working farmland. Antique dealers Cliff and Barbara Clarke built the place and filled the rooms with the best of their collection. Grandest is the enormous living room, where Oriental rugs, sumptuous early-century furnishings, and the massive fieldstone fireplace lend a regal feel. Seven smallish guest rooms open off a hall above—rooms 1 and 7 have the best views out over the trees to Satellite Channel.

The farm provides a fresh-air balance to all that culture inside: a walkable trail rings the property and there are horses to pet and hens clucking about. The big breakfast includes Barbara's raspberry jam for the toast and fresh eggs from those hens.

SHAWNIGAN LAKE

In summer, Shawnigan Lake is the favored swimming hole in the area. A good spot to get a lunch to go is **Jalna's Diner** in Shawnigan Village, serving huge pieces of fish on a mountain of fries, or a hamburger in the shape of a hot dog.

RESTAURANTS

Jaeger House Inn
Take the Shawnigan/Mill
Bay Road off Trans-
Canada Highway, 6.5km
to Renfrew,
(604) 743-3515
2460 Renfrew Road,
Shawnigan Lake
Moderate; full bar; MC,
V; no checks
Lunch, dinner every day

An informal pub-style eatery in a massive building, with a big stone fireplace and a charming outdoor beer garden. The menu is just as substantial, with German standbys like a mushroom-laden veal cutlet with brown gravy and a bratwurst or two, side by side with teriyaki chicken and seafood casserole. Situated on the skirt of pretty Shawnigan Lake.

COWICHAN BAY

RESTAURANTS

The Bluenose
40km north of Victoria
off Trans-Canada
Highway, (604) 748-2841
1765 Cowichan Bay
Road, Cowichan Bay
Moderate; full bar; AE,
DC, MC, V
Breakfast, lunch (coffee
shop), dinner (restaurant)
every day

Have breakfast or lunch at the coffee shop—either indoors at its horseshoe-shaped counter or out on the deck, where one waitress handles the whole place with savvy. For dinner, the restaurant is the local favorite in Cowichan Bay, with a menu of steaks and seafood (go for the seafood—ask the waitress to tell you what's fresh), and a great water view. While you're there, check out the Wooden Boat Society's new museum next door.

LODGINGS

Caterham Bed & Breakfast
Take the first Cowichan Bay turnoff on the Trans-Canada Highway from Victoria, (604) 748-6410 2075 Cowichan Bay Road, Cowichan Bay, BC V0R 1N0 Moderate; V

Don't be discouraged by the Astroturfed stairs. Inside you'll find three comfortable rooms furnished in overdone Laura Ashley style (the canopied beds are a little girl's dream). Ask for one of two rooms facing the bay. Claire Killick, with years of experience in the hotel industry, serves a full English breakfast and offers little boats you can row in the bay.

Inn at the Water
About 45 minutes north of Victoria on Trans-Canada 1, watch for signs to Cowichan Bay, (604) 748-6222 1681 Botwood Lane PO Box 58, Cowichan Bay, BC V0R 1N0 Moderate; AE, DC, MC, V

The offending brick edifice with HOTEL lettered boldly across the top belies the dandy suites inside, all with views over picturesque Cowichan Bay. Originally built as a timeshare property, it's composed of 56 modern units, each of which has a bedroom, living room, bath, and unfurnished kitchen. Swim in the indoor heated pool, play tennis on nearby grass courts, or enjoy the Jacuzzi and sauna.

DUNCAN
RESTAURANTS

Richard's Restaurant
Kenneth and Canada, (604) 748-5702 161 Kenneth, Duncan Inexpensive; full bar; V Lunch, dinner Tues-Sat (Wed-Sun in winter)

We look forward to Richard's: the rose-garden terrace in summers and Richard's jovial personality. Not to mention the food, all of which is prepared by the bearded California transplant himself, right down to the bread. His chatty menu is part Italian, part Jewish, and part Middle Eastern: calamari marinated in lemon juice and olive oil, babaghnouj and hummus, a fresh pasta dish tossed in a "sexy, spicy tomato sauce," a homemade minestrone. Or just stop in for an espresso and his mmmmm cheesecake or new chocolate pasta with ricotta orange sauce—sinful! Duncan's first "clean-air" restaurant.

The Inglenook
8km north of Duncan, (604) 746-4031 7621 Trans-Canada Highway, Duncan Moderate; full bar; AE, MC, V Dinner Wed Sun

The traveler may well have grown a little weary of Vancouver Island's fascination with restaurants in Tudor houses, but the food at this one is careful and a notch above standard. You eat in one of several tastefully decorated rooms amid scores of dressed-up Duncanites, choosing among items like lamb medallions with cream, vermouth, and butter; fish pot pie; and prime rib with Yorkshire pudding. Desserts showcase chef Doug Hughes' best work: apple crumble with maple sauce or a fine

English trifle. Co-owner Mary Hughes staffs the front of the place. There's a cozy downstairs pub that calls for an after-dinner brandy.

LODGINGS

Grove Hall Estate

Turn east at first set of lights in Duncan, continue to Lake Road, go north 1.6km,
(604) 746-6152
6159 Lakes Road,
Duncan, BC V9L 4J6
Moderate; no credit cards; no checks

It's all very seclusive, although it's not always open and there isn't a sign out front. Captain Frank and Judy Oliver want it that way. Tough for the curious, but an undisturbed retreat for guests. Seventeen wooded acres surround this 1912 Tudor-style manse near Lake Quamichan. The waterfront garden paths are a good place for a stroll. From the outside it looks as if there would be far more than three rooms—until you see the size of the rooms. Each room has an Oriental theme (Indonesian, Malaysian, Thai), magnificent rugs (you're provided with slippers), and no private bath; the master bedroom, decorated with pieces from Jakarta and Bali, expands into a sitting area and then onto a balcony. There are 2½ baths in the mansion. Play tennis on the private court or games in the billiard room.

Fairburn Farm Inn

11.3km south of Duncan,
(604) 746-4637
331 Jackson Road,
Duncan
Mail: RR 7, Duncan,
BC V9L 4W4
Expensive; no credit cards; checks ok

Once an Irish millionaire's country estate, now a 130-acre organic farm and country inn, Fairburn Farm is a humble retreat that adds new meaning to the term "getaway." You're literally at the end of the road here, but as roads go you can't do much better, winding as it does through rolling green acreage reminiscent of English farmland.

The aged farmhouse occupies a sloping dale, and the working-farm orientation is the charm of the place, especially for families. Six large guest rooms feature comfortable furniture; they share three baths, although private baths are in the works. There's also a cottage in summer that will house six comfortably. Guests are welcome to use two downstairs parlors (family reunions often book Fairburn) and to roam the grounds, where a sheepdog minds the lambs and a creek flows idly by.

The bed comes with a hearty breakfast that always begins with porridge. For a more replete vacation, you can include three meals with the cost of a night's stay. In this modern-day Eden you can witness a stunning example of how it is still possible to live off the land: most everything you eat is organically home-grown.

CHEMAINUS

A logging town that, faced with the shutdown of the mill in 1981, bucked up and hired artists to come paint murals all over everything telling the story of the town, and is now a tourist attraction. What it lacks in inspired art, it more than makes up for in good, old-fashioned small-town chutzpah.

LADYSMITH
LODGINGS

Yellow Point Lodge
*Yellow Point Road,
14.5km east of
Ladysmith,*
(604) 245-7422
*Mail: RR3, Ladysmith,
BC V0R 2E0*
*Expensive; MC, V;
checks ok*

On a rocky promontory overhung with tall trees is Yellow Point Lodge, perhaps the most serene of all the classic British Columbia resorts. A fire razed the original lodge in 1985, but owner Richard Hill and innkeeper Ron Friend took care to restore the place to its creaky, delightful old self, and except for the spiffy new sprung dance floor the feeling is close to the same. The hours still pass with six meals a day—of standard but wholesome quality—as if you were on a cruise ship. In truth, it's a little more like summer camp for grown-ups (though it's popular year-round): you eat family style at shared tables in the lodge, with no kids under 16 to detract from the mood.

A few improvements came with the rebuilding of the old lodge: the guest rooms are somewhat larger, and many now have private baths. Rooms 4 and 5 have balconies. You'll want a cabin, however; newest are the small White Beach cabins with wood stoves and delightful beds with tree-trunk bases. There are two kinds of cabins: those on the beach (the Cliff Cabin is most remote, and the nicest) and the field cabins (Eve's is the most private). And there are the beach barracks, ramshackle quarters with thin walls, but built right on the shoreline rocks and very popular; a feature here is a "tree shower," in which water shoots up into the branches of a tree and falls on a wooden platform at the base.

Best of all is the site: two good tennis courts, a huge seawater pool, 130 acres of meadow and forest for strolling, a hot tub, a sauna, windsurfing gear, a classic 32-foot boat for picnic cruising, and big slabs of rock jutting into the sea for sunbathing. All rooms are on the American plan (topping out at $145 for two, including three full meals and three snacks a day).

Inn of the Sea
*14.5km east of
Ladysmith,*
(604) 245-2211
*3600 Yellow Point Road,
Mail: RR3, Ladysmith,
BC V0R 2E0*
Moderate; AE, MC, V

Inn of the Sea is the most modern facility on Yellow Point. Its nicest feature is still the scenery, especially the long stretch of beach along Stewart Channel. Half of the 60 rooms are smaller than standard. Deluxe suites have fireplaces, kitchens, and balconies; large parties can request rooms that connect vertically via spiral staircase. Play tennis, or swim in the large heated pool at the water's edge. A pier out front allows for boat moorage, with water and power hookup. In the dining room, chefs arrive and depart almost as often as guests, so play it safe in your own suite.

If you've found a place that you think is a Best Place, send in the report form at the back of this book. If you're unhappy with one of the places, please let us know why. We depend on reader input.

Manana Lodge
*4.8km north of
Ladysmith,
(604) 245-2312
4760 Branton-Page Road,
Mail: RR1, Ladysmith,
BC V0R 2E0
Moderate; MC, V*

Manana Lodge is permeated with the atmosphere of an old family beach house: the rooms are furnished with family throwaways, and the beams are shaved logs reminiscent of a Maine lodge. There are just three guest rooms. Two are small with tiny adjoining sitting rooms (ask for the one facing the harbor), and only the wee Blue Room has its own shower. The price of the room includes a mediocre continental breakfast and a decanter of sherry in your room. If you want a wake-up call, bring your own clock; the service is reluctant to help. Avoid the dining room, but enjoy a beer in summer on the delightful deck. The view of Ladysmith Harbour might include a glimpse of a bald eagle or a docking seaplane.

NANAIMO

This onetime coal city has some interesting sights. Some are new, like **The Lighthouse**, a shiny, multi-tiered restaurant, pub, and seaplane terminal jammed up against the harborfront like continental drift from EXPO. Or, for $3, ferry over to the **Dinghy Dock Pub**, a very nautical floating bar off Protection Island. Other attractions are old: **The Bastion**, one of the few Hudson's Bay Company forts still standing, was built in 1853 as protection against marauding Haida Indians. **The Nanaimo Centennial Museum**, 100 Cameron Road, (604) 753-1821, has a full-size

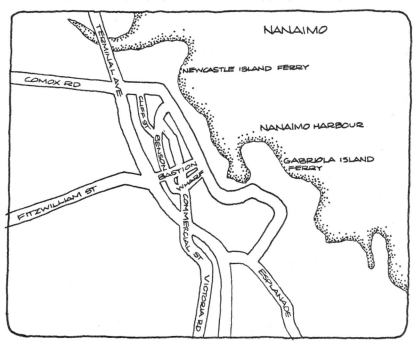

replica of a coal mine, among other displays.

Parks: Pipers Lagoon, northeast of downtown, includes a spit that extends into the Strait of Georgia, backed by sheer bluffs for bird watching. **Newcastle Island** is an autoless wilderness island reached by ferries that leave hourly from behind the civic arena; it has a long shoreline trail and some fine old-growth timber.

Wandering. Bastion Street Bookstore, 76 Bastion Street, (604) 753-3011, houses an impressive collection of guidebooks, natural history texts, and small-press publications by Canadian authors. For a little local flavor, buy a rich **Nanaimo Bar** at the Scotch Bakery on Commercial Street.

Nanaimo Golf Club, five kilometers north of the city, is a demanding 18-hole course with beautiful views of the water; (604) 758-6332.

Gabriola Island. A 20-minute ferry ride from Nanaimo will take you to this rural spot, where you'll find the area's best lodging (see The Gulf Islands).

RESTAURANTS

Crow and Gate Neighbourhood Pub
About 13km south of Nanaimo, (604) 722-3731 2313 Yellow Point Road, Inexpensive; full bar; MC, V
Lunch, dinner every day

This magnificent English country pub makes a nice destination for a lazy afternoon. It is set back from the road with a rose-arbor entrance, a back-yard patio, a duck pond, and a noisy peacock. The homesick fellow who built it remembered the English original well, re-creating it scrupulously from beamed ceiling to Oriental rugs, with a blazing hearth and a dart board. The pub food is top-notch, especially the pasties encased in flaky crusts, steak and kidney pie, and the buttery Yorkshire pudding. The staff is chatty, the draughts are foamy, and at night everyone's having a ruddy good time.

Old Mahle House
Corner of Cedar at Heemer Road, (604) 722-3621 Site 01-6, RR 4, Nanaimo Moderate; full bar; MC, V Dinner Wed-Sun

It's intimate: three elegant, airy rooms done in a country motif seat 55 people. The affable and intelligent owners emphasize fresh, locally produced ingredients. A dozen daily specials fill a whiteboard: thick, savory carrot and ginger soup; homemade pasta tossed with salmon and cream, capers and scallions providing a tart counterpoint; or a succulent beef tenderloin in a green peppercorn sauce. The regular menu competes with fresh-caught prawns in a Pernod sauce or meaty lamb chops with a rosemary glaze (ask about these—ours were tough). End the meal with one of a battery of homemade desserts—the silken chocolate banana cheesecake alone was worth the drive. Visit during the summer months and you could possibly encounter a three-star evening.

Gina's Cafe
1 block up from the waterfront, (604) 753-5411 47 Skinner Street, Nanaimo Inexpensive; full bar; MC, V Lunch Mon-Fri, dinner every day

Gina's is a comfortable place with all the down-home ambience of a Tex-Mex roadside cafe. A healthy imaginative menu reflects Don and Gina Korfield's vegetarian leanings. We enjoyed the daily special, a ricotta and spinach enchilada lavishly smothered in salsa, and barely had room for dessert—a fruit burrito topped with ice cream.

Maffeo's

Prudoe and Wentworth,
(604) 753-0377
538 Wentworth, Nanaimo
Moderate; full bar;
AE, MC, V
Lunch Mon-Fri,
dinner Mon-Sat

Once the home of former mayor Pete Maffeo, this Victorian just outside of downtown now houses Nanaimo's newest, most *real* Italian restaurant. The main floor is a deli: made-on-the-premises pasta and Italian cheeses and meats (where else on the island are you going to find Bel Paese, prosciutto, or cappócolla). You dine upstairs in one of the two rooms prettied with antiques: pastas are what they do best here. Of course, this is Nanaimo, so don't be surprised to see "steak and prawns" on the menu.

The Grotto

On the waterfront next to
the BC ferries,
(604) 753-3303
1511 Stewart Avenue,
Nanaimo
Inexpensive; full bar;
AE, MC, V
Dinner Mon-Sat

The Grotto, a Nanaimo perennial for over 20 years, has completely outgrown its wharfish name. It has recently added sushi to an already ample menu of proven favorites —fresh salmon and Zum Zum (a seafood platter)—and cafe entrees such as gourmet burgers, veal, and pasta dishes.

LODGINGS

Coast Bastion Inn

Bastion and Island,
(604) 753-6601 or toll-
free (800) 663-1144
11 Bastion Street,
Nanaimo, BC V9R 2Z9
Expensive; AE, DC, MC, V

All 179 rooms of this swanky hotel have views of the restored Hudson's Bay fort; all are tastefully styled in postmodern hues. A trio of formula eateries—the Ramparts Gourmet Room, family-style Cutters Dining Room, and Offshore Lounge and Bistro—plus sauna, hot tub, and cool tub make the Bastion a self-sustaining entity. It's right in the middle of things downtown.

PARKSVILLE

The town offers good sandy beaches, lovely picnic sites on Cameron Lake, Englishman River Falls, and Little Qualicum Falls, and fine fishing. **MacMillan Nature Park**, 32 kilometers west of Parksville on Route 4 heading for Port Alberni, has preserved Cathedral Grove, a haunting old-growth forest of Douglas firs and cedars ranging up to 200 feet high and 1,000 years old.

RESTAURANTS

The Judge's Manor

Take the Island Highway
north to the Port Alberni
Highway, head south
to Memorial,
(604) 248-2544
193 Memorial Avenue,
Parksville
Moderate; full bar;
AE, MC, V

The manor, former home of a Parksville judge (hence the name), is embellished with antiques. It's family run, with John Hellum reigning capably in the kitchen, father Arvid supplying fresh seafood from his commercial fishing operation, and mother Lenore supervising the dining room. The trio provides genuinely friendly service and inviting preparations of regional and international cuisines. All this, and a marvelous ocean view.

We've had wonderful, imaginative meals here: locally raised squab with a spicy sweet-and-sour sauce, or the rolled lamb with duxelles stuffing. Salads were fresh

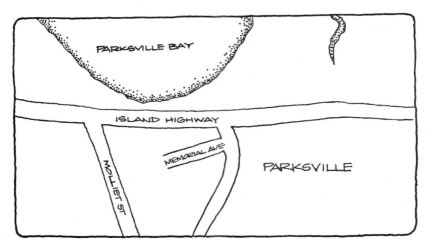

Lunch Tues-Fri,
dinner Tues-Sun

and artfully arranged. Off-season, though, standards are less exacting and service inexcusably slow. If each season got its own rating, summer would get three stars and winter two.

Ma Maison

25 minutes north of
Nanaimo, (604) 248-5859
393 Island Highway N,
Parksville
Moderate; full bar;
AE, MC, V
Dinner Mon-Fri (Oct-
Mar), every day (summer)

Ma Maison is an attractive and serious beachside French restaurant ideal for spending a long, pleasant evening—especially if you can get a table by the window or on the deck, where there is a splendid view of the Strait of Georgia. The entrance to the renovated house is a striking prism-shaped greenhouse; the restaurant then divides into three tastefully decorated small rooms. There's a salon bar and a balcony for an aperitif. The wine list is good and the bottle labels well displayed in an album.

If only the menu could be as inspired. Jean Merlet presents a large menu with virtually all the classics, which in the past were right on the mark. We've had superb roast rabbit, simmered to tenderness in a gooseberry-cream sauce, and we've generally encountered fine meat preparations: filet mignon in Bearnaise, a rack of lamb redolent of mustard. But lately the meals have been consistantly uninspired: our steak was overcooked and the sauce on the rabbit too heavy and bland. We're docking a star because we know Merlet can do better, and we're waiting for the day when he does.

LODGINGS

Tigh-Na-Mara

2km south of Parksville
on Island Highway,
(604) 248-2072

Owners Jackie and Joe Hirsch's complex of rustic log cottages is no longer so rustic and is always busy. They've acquired more acreage and last year added a condominium (all units have views of the Strait of Georgia and some

Mail: RR1, Site 114, C
16, Parksville, BC V0R 2S0
Moderate; AE, MC, V

have their own Jacuzzis). The 30 log cabins are spread among the now-22 acres of natural arbutus and fir. The 12 suites in the lodge are surprisingly cozy, and although none has a view, each has a fireplace, fridge, full bath, and a few have their own kitchens.

Reports on the new log-cabin restaurant have been favorable, though perhaps not yet up to par with more established restaurants in the area. With the new indoor pool and Jacuzzi, outdoor tennis courts, volleyball, and 700 feet of beachfront, you should have no problem working up an appetite.

PORT ALBERNI

The *Lady Rose*, Argyle Street Dock, voyages from Port Alberni to Bamfield on Tuesdays, Thursdays, and Saturdays, with a special Sunday trip during July and August. Round-trip fare is $25. June 1 to September 30, she sails for Ucluelet on Mondays, Wednesdays, and Fridays. Besides being a better way to reach these remote towns than over rough roads, the four-hour cruise down Alberni Inlet and through the Broken Islands Group is breathtaking. Breakfast and lunch are served. (604) 723-8313. Or take along a loaf of cheese bread from The Flour Shop, (604) 723-1105.

BAMFIELD

Bamfield is a tiny fishing village heavily populated by marine biologists. The boat from Port Alberni comes on Tuesdays, Thursdays, and Saturdays (and Sundays in summer). You are better advised to take the *Lady Rose* than the bumpy dirt road, which has some frightening logging traffic. For hikers, it's the end (or the start) of a five- to six-day beach trek along the West Coast Trail from Port Renfrew (see Pacific Rim National Park under Ucluelet). It is one of the premier places for finding a wilderness beach all to yourself, all week long. Photographers, bring your cameras. In Bamfield you can rent boats for fishing or exploring the islands.

Whale watching. During March and April, pods of migrating gray whales can be seen off the coast: whale-watching trips can be booked through Ocean Pacific Whale Charters Ltd., Box 590, Tofino, BC V0R 2Z0, (604) 725-3919, or SeaSmoke Sailing Charter & Tours, Box 483, Alert Bay, BC V0N 1A0, (604) 974-5225.

LODGINGS

Aguilar House
Will meet guests at the
point of arrival,
(604) 728-3323
Bamfield West, Bamfield,
BC V0R 1B0
Moderate; MC, V

The view out over Barkley Sound and the offshore islands is magnificent, so we were thrilled when longtime Bamfield visitors Linda and Larry Myres bought this humble little lodge in 1988 and gave it the care and attention it sorely needed: a new coat of paint, carpets, and—thank heavens—new beds. Still, a few things remain the same: the five rooms in the house are plain and small, the bath is down the hall, and the outsides of the cottages still need painting. We suggest you request one of the two rooms with a view of the wild and inspiring beach—where we spend most of our time anyway. If the weather's unfavorable (there are 110 inches of rain here in the winter), the living room is a comfortable spot to relax.

In the evening, Larry often barbecues fresh oysters as starters for one of Linda's lovingly simple, often inventive family-style meals. Dinners range from chicken Kiev to tarragon spring salmon. Lunches are warming and simple; corn chowder and seaweed (kombu) are two favorite soups. Breakfast is large, except before whale-watching trips (Linda's learned some pre-seafaring tricks).

Lodge rates, including all meals, are $100 per person per day. If you stay in one of the three cottages, which are $80 for two people, you cook your own meals or join the guests in the lodge with advance notice and an extra charge (cottages are available year-round). Closed November through February.

UCLUELET

Pacific Rim National Park, the first National Marine Park in Canada, comprises three separate areas—Long Beach, the Broken Islands Group, and the West Coast Trail—each conceived as a "platform" from which visitors can experience the power of the Pacific Ocean. Long Beach, an 11-kilometer expanse of sand and rock outcrops backed by forest and mountains, can be reached by car from Port Alberni over a winding mountain highway. The Broken Islands Group—more than 100 in all at the entrance to Barkley Sound—is accessible only by boat. This area is famous for sea lions, seals, and whales, and is very popular with fishermen, skindivers, and kayakers. The West Coast Trail is a rugged 45-mile stretch that was once a lifesaving trail for shipwrecked sailors. It can be traveled only on foot and it's a strenuous but spectacular five- to six-day hike for hardy and experienced backpackers. For more information on the park, go to the information center at the park entrance on Highway 4, or contact the Superintendent, (604) 726-7721, Pacific Rim National Park, Box 280, Ucluelet, BC V0R 3A0.

The Wickaninnish Interpretive Center has interesting oceanic exhibits and an expansive view: (604) 726-7333, 16 kilometers north of Ucluelet off Highway 4. The same building houses The Wickaninnish Inn (see review).

RESTAURANTS

Whale's Tale
*Behind the Thornton Motel, 4 blocks from downtown, (604) 726-4621
1861 Peninsula Road, Ucluelet
Moderate; full bar; AE, MC, V
Dinner every day
(Feb-Oct)*

Perhaps because it doesn't have a view, locals regard this as the best dinner house in town. Built on pilings that shake on windy evenings, the Whale's Tale is intimate and quiet. Fresh, simply cooked seafood is on the menu; we found the halibut, sauteed in butter, to be refreshingly clear-tasting.

The Wickaninnish Inn

*16km north of Ucluelet
in the Wickaninnish
Interpretive Center,
Pacific Rim National
Park, (604) 726-7706
Box 939, Ucluelet
Moderate; full bar;
AE, MC, V
Lunch, dinner every day
(closed mid-October
through mid-March)*

We would recommend this place for the location alone: where else can you dine on saffron-laced bouillabaisse, fresh halibut with pesto, or lamb with a rosemary-mint demi-glace on a three-kilometer-long beach touched only by tides and toes? It's a dramatic setting, in a dramatic building with glass on three sides, a beam-and-stone interior, and a rock fireplace setting off white linen tablecloths and pastel-cushioned chairs. And ever since the Oak Bay Marine Group, which operates other British Columbia fishing resorts (including Painter's Lodge in Campbell River), appropriated a four-year lease from the park, we'd recommend it for the food, too.

The menu may look somewhat familiar if you've been to this group's other Vancouver Island establishments, but what they do, at least, is usually well done. The Wickaninnish Salad sprinkled with a raspberry vinaigrette is a superb starter: smoked salmon, three kinds of greens, red onions, artichoke hearts. On our most recent visit we found the halibut lightly cooked and the chowder heavily clammed, but the crab bisque was disappointing. If you're a meat-lover, don't let the draws of the ocean sway you from trying the tender veal draped in a savory blackcurrant and mushroom sauce. The wine list even includes a few selections difficult to find in British Columbia.

LODGINGS

Bed & Breakfast at Burley's

*1078 Helen Street and
Marine Drive,
(604) 726-4444
Mail: PO Box 550,
Ucluelet, BC V0R 3A0
Inexpensive; MC, V*

Located on the inlet of Hi-Focus Island, linked by causeway to Ucluelet proper, and boasting spectacular scenery, this B&B has six bedrooms and a large living room. Hosts Michelline Riley and Ron Burley (he used to be the mayor of Ucluelet; now he's the coroner) fix simple morning meals and stay out of your way. No children under 10.

Canadian Princess Fishing Resort

*In the Boat Basin,
(604) 726-7771
Mail: PO Box 939,
Ucluelet, BC V0R 3A0
Moderate; full bar;
AE, MC, V
Breakfast, lunch, dinner
every day*

★

A retired 235-foot survey ship in the Ucluelet Boat Basin has been converted to 30 cabins for lodging and a below-deck dining room for meals. The accommodations are comfortable but not at all luxurious: small cabins have from one to six berths and share washrooms. If you want something a little more spacious, ask for the captain's cabin with adjoining bathroom. The nautical gear has been left in place—the ship's mast goes right through the dining room—but the conversion is rather spiffy. The newer 46 shoreside units, a little roomier and more modern, are for dry-land sailors. The galley serves reasonable food, with steaks and seafood predominating, and opens at 4:30am for breakfast during the fishing season. A small ship's bar and a roomier stern lounge are pleasant places; there's a fine supply of cold beer.

The *Canadian Princess* serves as a base for scuba divers and fishermen who flock to the Barkley Sound area. You can charter boats for fishing and diving trips as well as nature and sightseeing excursions to Long Beach, the offshore sea-lion rocks, and Pacific Rim National Park.

TOFINO

Literally at the end of the road on the southwest coast of Vancouver Island, Tofino is quietly becoming a favored destination for many Northwest and European travelers alike. It's probably the only town on Vancouver Island where the head of the chamber of commerce is against logging. Recently, local environmentalists and artists have banded together to suspend destruction of one of the last virgin timberlands on the west coast of Vancouver Island and halt the rapid development for which the area is prime, with its miles of sandy beaches, islands of old-growth cedar, migrating whales (March–April, September–October), natural hot springs, colonies of sea lions, and a temperate climate.

Even if you don't have your own boat, you won't be landbound in Tofino. There are more than enough **water taxis** to port you around the innumerable islands and inlets of Clayoquot Sound: Seaforth Charters, based in the back of the Tofino Laundromat, uses a 28-foot Apollo cruiser and a 19-foot Campion; 448 Campbell Street, (604) 725-4252. If you don't mind getting wet, Inter-Island Excursions zips around in Zodiacs, which are fun for warm weather and short trips; Box 393, Tofino, V0R 2Z0, (604) 725-3163.

Tofino Air Lines, located at the First Street Dock, employs some of Canada's best sea- and beach-plane pilots to fly mail, loggers, and tourists in and out of the west coast's otherwise inaccessible logging and Indian villages; you can arrange to be dropped off anywhere and picked up anytime; (604) 725-4454.

Eagle Aerie Gallery. Discover or pay homage to the exclusive showcase of silkscreens and carvings by Roy Henry Vickers in his longhouse of hand-hewn logs— a work of art in itself; (604) 725-3235.

Tofino Sea-Kayaking Company. Experienced guides will paddle with you along the fjordlike shorelines of Clayoquot Sound. The espresso bar in the back of the store is a comfortable spot to sit and chat with other travelers; (604) 725-4222.

RESTAURANTS

Alley Way Cafe
Behind the bank,
(604) 725-3105
Box 439, Tofino
Inexpensive; no alcohol;
no credit cards; checks ok
Lunch, dinner every day
(closed in winter)

Christina Delano-Stephens thinks the way of life in Tofino is the closest thing to her Latin American roots she'll ever see in Canada. In 1986, Christina livened up a little sun-filled house with some pink and turquoise paint, put two picnic tables outside and cactus-shaped balloons in the window, and opened one of the most heart-filled spots north of Victoria.

The menu above the counter, at a glance, is filled with burritos, clam burgers, and—WHAT?—pickled geoduck. We looked again, and then we tasted...and tasted. First the unbeatable geoduck: clean, thin slices of this Northwest mollusk marinated in vinegar, onions, and red peppers. Next came the very garlicky, very lemony hummus dip with tortilla chips. An extraordinary vegetarian burrito followed, bulging with sauteed corn, mushrooms, carrots, tomatoes, and zucchini, all delicately seasoned with fresh basil and tossed with sour cream and salsa. And all, *all*, right down to the mayonnaise on the clam burgers, is made by Christina herself.

Blue Heron Dining Room at the Weigh West Motel

Just south of town on the west side of Route 4,
(604) 725-4266
634 Campbell Street,
Tofino
Moderate; full bar;
AE, MC, V
Breakfast, lunch, dinner
every day

Not all the new motels in town have won the respect of the locals; was it the invitation to the opening-night dinner that drew their favor to the Weigh West, or was it the view of beloved Meares Island? Whatever the reason, it's not the rooms they recommend, it's the restaurant and the bar. Weigh West is not perfect, and the locals know it—and forgive it. We're awarding a star on the basis of the belief that time and a supportive clientele will do this place well.

The view is an immediate hit: a working marina backed by Meares Island, where old-growth forests grow and bald eagles nest. At least once during your meal the restaurant's long-winged namesake will probably swoop by your window. You can get the same view from the bar. Dinner's a bit less striking: a Caesar salad generously doctored with crab and avocado, a tender charbroiled steak au poivre, and an overcooked halibut fillet (billed as halibut steak).

The motel is neither on the beach nor right in town, but its 75 rooms are clean and well equipped. Reserve a room with a kitchen: they're the ones with the views, and the refrigerator will come in handy for lunch.

Common Loaf Bake Shop

1st and Main,
(604) 725-3915
131 First Street, Tofino
Inexpensive; no alcohol;
no credit cards; no checks
Breakfast, lunch, dinner
every day (in winter,
baked goods only)

A town meeting place where save-the-whale buttons are at the cash register and save-the-trees pleas on the bulletin board. Most of the year it's just a bakery with wonderful cheese buns and healthful peasant bread. Come summer, the bread dough becomes pizza dough and it's the busiest nook in town. A fabulous seafood combo pizza is topped with smoked sockeye salmon, shrimp, and mushrooms; a European version has beer sausage and cheese. Staff is young and easily distracted.

LODGINGS

Chesterman's Beach Bed and Breakfast

1345 Chesterman's Beach Road; call ahead for directions, (604) 725-3726
Mail: PO Box 72, Tofino,
BC V0R 2Z0
Moderate; V; checks ok

With its location on Chesterman's Beach, you can't go wrong: miles of beach stretch out at low tide to nearby islands, with ever-changing tidepools. Joan Dublanko designed her home around driftwood and travelers. Each space is different and very much the traveler's own: a romantic nook with a comfortable bed, small bath, and a beach-view sun deck (Joan brings hot muffins in the morning; you make the coffee and might want to bring your own real cream); a separate one-bedroom cabin with a kitchen, living room, and bath (no view, sleeps up to four); or the main floor of the house with its own entrance, two bedrooms, kitchen, bath, and sauna. Showers should be quick: the hot water sometimes runs low. In the evening, you can stay on the beach and have bonfires long into the night.

Paddler's Inn
Bed and Breakfast
Main just above the Front Street dock,
(604) 725-4222
322 Main Street, PO Box 620, Tofino, BC V0R 2Z0
Inexpensive; V

★ ★

Ahh, simplicity. White 100 percent cotton sheets, down comforters, clean-lined Scandinavian-style furnishings. The five rooms in Tofino's original hotel are as basic and lovely as Tofino itself: no phones, no TVs, no distractions but the ocean breeze and friendly conversation. Owner Dorothy Baert (whom you'll often find in her Tofino Sea-Kayaking Company downstairs) drops in to cook you a fitting breakfast in the kitchen—and lets you take over for dinner.

Ocean Village
Beach Resort
4km south of Tofino; look for signs, (604) 725-3755
555 Hellesen Drive, Tofino
Mail: PO Box 490, Tofino, BC V0R 2Z0
Moderate; MC, V

It's too bad this motel—like all the other large motels on the Esowista peninsula—doesn't live up to its setting: one mile of marvelous beach with a tiny island reached by sandbar at low tide and secluded rocky coves a short walk away where you can gather mussels. Just north of Pacific Rim National Park, Ocean Village is the best of the three big on-the-beach resorts. It has three rows of cedar-shake housekeeping units (48 total), each accommodating a family of four for about $70 a night. The rounded A-frames are a bit odd but very well equipped; all face the beach and those glorious northern-summer sunsets. The heated indoor pool and hot tub are nice in cool weather. In July and August, minimum stay is two days.

Tofino Swell Lodge
341 Olson Road, off the main road in town,
(604) 725-3274
Mail: PO Box 160, Tofino, BC V0R 2Z0
Inexpensive; no credit cards; checks ok

You'll be tempted to spend a lot of time on the front lawn: grilling your day's catch, or soaking in the hot tub admiring the view of the inlet and snow-covered mountains across the water. The seven rooms are nothing fancy, but we like the comfortable communal kitchen and the put-your-feet-up living room with a fireplace. The more private rooms are on the ground floor facing the ocean. It's a great spot for friends—but not for newlyweds.

QUALICUM BEACH
RESTAURANTS

Old Dutch Inn
110 Island Highway,
Qualicum Beach,
(604) 752-6914
Mail: PO Box 1240,
Qualicum Beach, V0R 2T0
Moderate; full bar;

It's a funny place, a motel and dining room done in a Dutch motif with a spectacular view of the expansive Qualicum Bay. The 36 rooms that make up the hotel portion of the inn are comfortable enough, and each features a fine view of the water across the street, but the real draw is the Dutch cuisine of chef Leo Teijgeman. We liked

MC, V
*Breakfast, lunch, dinner
every day*

the *uitsmyter*—an open-faced sandwich topped with Dutch smoked ham and Gouda cheese—and *lekkervekje*—Dutch-style fresh fish and chips. The food can be a little pricier than that of competitors, but it's consistently praised.

FANNY BAY
RESTAURANTS

The Fanny Bay Inn
*In the center of town—
you can't miss it,
(604) 335-2323
7480 Island Highway,
Fanny Bay
Inexpensive; full bar; V
Lunch, dinner every day*

Ever wonder what a real roadhouse looks like? It's called the "FBI," an unassuming haunt with Ma-and-Pa vibes, a fine fireplace, the obligatory collection of tankards, a dartboard, and hearty pub fare (steak and kidney pie, Black Forest ham sandwiches on brown bread, Cornish pasties, sausage rolls). Low-key and lovely. Stop in for a pint, but please maintain the anthropological integrity of this classic slice of Canadiana.

COURTENAY/COMOX

The Comox Valley has skiing in winter, water sports in summer, the best restaurants around, and scenic access to Powell River on the Sunshine Coast via the *Queen of Sidney*, which leaves four times daily from Comox, (604) 339-3310. Cross-country and downhill skiers flock to a pair of surprisingly decent hills: **Mt. Washington**, where four chair lifts operate over 140 days of the year, (604) 338-1387, and **Forbidden Plateau**—named for an Indian tale—a half-hour from downtown Courtenay; (604) 334-4744.

RESTAURANTS

La Cremaillere
*Take the 17th Street
Bridge road off the Island
Highway, (604) 338-8131
975 Comox Road,
Courtenay
Moderate; full bar;
AE, MC, V
Lunch Wed-Fri,
dinner Wed-Sun*

One of the few area restaurants capable of answering the challenge of The Old House, La Cremaillere, a two-story Tudor with a charming Puntledge River view, relies on the culinary skills of Michel Hubert, a menu that transforms the region's delicacies into fine French cuisine, and an ambience that offers more intimacy than the bigger restaurant down the road. Start your meal with Huitres Vladimir (locally harvested oysters with shallots in a white wine sauce) or an extraordinarily delicate pheasant pate. Our favorite entree is the pheasant breast, deboned and filled with savory mushrooms, rice, and vegetables—enjoy it in a plush, private dining room for two if you like. Emphasis on regional products stops at the wine cellar—La Cremaillere features an excellent selection of French wines.

The Old House Restaurant
*Turn right on 17th from
Island Highway north,
take the first right*

For years this was the uncontested favorite in these parts. At press time, however, chef Ferdinand Bogner was on his way to Germany—leaving the restaurant in the hands of the two remaining chefs, Loretta Moretto and Mark

before the bridge,
(604) 338-5406
1760 Riverside Lane,
Courtenay
Moderate; full bar;
AE, DC, MC, V
Lunch, dinner every day

★★

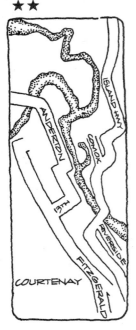

Duncan. A carefully restored pioneer home is set amid lovely trees and colorful flower gardens. Cedar shakes cover the outside; inside, the exposed heavy beams, large stone fireplace, copperware, and old porcelain combine to create an air of simple, rough-hewn charm.

The Old House was one of the first restaurants in the area to divide into distinct formal and casual areas (others are following suit, competently). It features—upstairs—linen, fresh flowers, a pricier menu, and more of the fruits of chef Bogner's innovation (they're continuing his menu for the time being); and—downstairs—an informal restaurant with a latticed deck and simpler fare: sandwiches, salads, pastas (which are also served upstairs at lunch). Both levels are extremely popular, placing heavy burdens on a generally competent serving crew; lunch can be disastrously slow. The seafood fettuccine with squid, shrimp, and scallops and a mushroom-basil sauce was fine, but our Old House Salad was a platter of ordinary vegetables and fruits on iceberg lettuce.

The upstairs menu changes every six months, reflecting the freshest of local seafood, fruit, vegetables, and herbs; however, recently we've encountered signs of skimping on quality. You'll do best to stick with the time-tested French classics (more and more of which seem to be appearing on the menu): a savory quenelle of escargots, milk-fed veal medallions with basil and wild mushrooms, a full-bodied pepper steak. You'll discover a number of unusual sauces—mango curry on the shark, vermouth and leeks on the mousse-stuffed squid, raspberries and ginger on the Dijon-marinated local rabbit. The wine list is well chosen.

The Homestead

Near the corner of
Cumberland and
Fitzgerald,
(604) 338-6612
932 Fitzgerald Avenue,
Courtenay
Moderate; full bar; MC, V
Lunch, dinner Tues-Sat

★

Margaret and John Bowie, charming former owners of the popular Bay Moorings in Comox, have resurfaced in Courtenay. The Homestead is an unassuming restaurant (it's right behind the bus terminal) that's developed a following in town among folks who say it's like dining in the home of friends. They crowd the place at lunchtime, then return for dinner. The Bowies maintain generous portions and a light, informal atmosphere fragrant with the scent of home-baked breads. Try the West Coast Fish Pot, in a savory veloute sauce topped with mozzarella, or the Chicken Alexander, enlivened with fresh herbs. At Christmastime there's fresh grog.

Leeward Pub

Take Comox Avenue to
Anderton Road,
(604) 339-5400
649 Anderton Road,
Comox

Distinctly hoppy Leeward Lager, Leeward Ale, and Leeward Light (the only reduced-calorie cottage brew we know of) are pumped from the pub's own brewery through a pipeline straight to the bar. Try the wide range of fresh seafood dishes (from crepes to chowder) and the popular

Inexpensive; full bar; MC, V
Lunch, dinner every day

14-bean soup. The place is packed and friendly, a fine
establishment for a pint and a bite on the way to or from
the ferry.

LODGINGS

Greystone Manor

5km south of Courtenay,
1km north of Royston on
Island Highway, watch
for signs, (604) 338-1422
4014 Haas Road, Courtenay
Mail: RR6, Site 684/C2,
Courtenay, BC V9N 8H9
Inexpensive; no credit
cards; checks ok

Pharmacist by day, hosteler by night, Mary Nelson bought
into a gold mine when she acquired her bed and breakfast
a few years ago. Conveniently close to the booming ski
scene at Mount Washington and Forbidden Plateau, midway between boaters' havens of Nanaimo and Campbell
River, her elegant four-room B&B is a welcome alternative to a night in a featureless Island Highway hotel.
Authentic Victoriana (Nelson is only the third owner of
this 70-year-old home) and other splendid period furnishings, a lawn that gently slopes to an unobstructed view
of the water, and an amiable mutt named BJ are just a
few of Greystone's winning attributes. Nelson serves a
hearty breakfast—fresh fruit, homemade muffins, fruit
pancakes, or quiche—at about 9am. She also photographs
each of her guests, sends them a copy, and keeps a
duplicate for her scrapbook.

Kingfisher Inn

8.1km south of
Courtenay, (604) 338-1323
4330 South Island
Highway, Mail: RR6, Site
672, Courtenay, BC
V9N 8H9
Moderate; AE, DC, MC, V

Set off the highway among a grove of trees, five minutes
south of Courtenay, this motel with its clean lines, cedar-
shake roof, and white stucco walls is pleasing to the eye
after the dozens of run-of-the-mill places that line the
route. The lobby invites with a large fireplace, skylight,
and hanging plants; and the rooms are spacious, with
striking, simple furnishings, refrigerators, and decks
overlooking the heated pool and the Strait of Georgia.
Diversions include a tennis court, sauna, and whirlpool.

OYSTER BAY

RESTAURANTS

Gourmet-by-the-Sea

14.5km south of
Campbell River on
Discovery Bay,
(604) 923-5234
4378 South Island
Highway, Oyster Bay
Moderate; full bar;
AE, DC, MC, V
Dinner Wed-Sun (Oct-May);
Tues-Sun (June-Sept)

They've surprised us with a strong comeback since the
place was razed by a fire in 1986. The new incarnation
is larger than the old—and all tables look out to the same
magnificent view. A bistro section is a nice addition, with
four or five lighter specials; the main dining room offers
14 or so entrees.

Chef Michel Rabu has made a name for himself with
townspeople and travelers alike, who return for the fresh
leeks wrapped in prosciutto and served with a cheese
sauce, a simple watercress salad sprinkled with a lovely
raspberry vinaigrette, and a mousseline of scallops in a
sauce of pureed lobster reduced in whipping cream and
accented with cognac. His seafood specialties are utterly fresh—don't miss his bouillabaisse.

LODGINGS

Bennett's Point Resort
*15.3km south of
Campbell River; watch for
signs, (604) 923-4281
4283 South Island
Highway, Oyster Bay
Mail: RR1, Campbell
River, BC V9W 3S4
Moderate; AE, MC, V*

The 26-unit motel has all the necessary facilities but no pretensions to elegance. It is set on a beautiful wooded point that lends itself to beachcombing and barbecues, as well as boating and fishing for salmon. There are an indoor pool, tennis court, a Jacuzzi and sauna, and some kitchenettes. The owners are very helpful. Gourmet-by-the-Sea is right next door.

CAMPBELL RIVER

A town of over 16,000 people, Campbell River is big as island cities go. It's completely ringed with shopping malls, yet the city center still looks and feels as it undoubtedly did in the '50s. Here you'll find some of the best fishing outfitters on the island, and during the Salmon Festival in July the town is abuzz with famous and ordinary fisherfolk. For an introduction to the region's wealth of short trails and dive sites, pick up a copy of the comprehensive *Guide to Day Hikes* ($2 at the Chamber of Commerce); (604) 286-0764.

Strathcona Provincial Park, to the west, is a park of superlatives. It has Canada's highest waterfall and Vancouver Island's highest mountain and offers a wide variety of landscapes to explore, including alpine meadows and lakes and large forests of virgin cedar and Douglas fir. Easily accessible by road (take Highway 28 from Campbell River), the park has campgrounds and boat launching facilities at Buttle Lake, and a surprisingly deluxe lakeside accommodation, Strathcona Lodge (see review). The park also has fine trout lakes and an extensive trail system for backpacking.

RESTAURANTS

Koto
*Behind the Bank of BC
building, (604) 286-1422
80 10th Avenue,
Campbell River
Moderate; full bar;
AE, MC, V
Lunch, dinner Tues-Sun*

★★

It makes sense: a very fresh sushi bar smack in the middle of fishing country. Still, it's tough to find essential Japanese ingredients where most people opt for loggers' cuisine. In his pleasant Campbell River restaurant, Takeo (Tony) Maeda is single-handedly turning that around. Locals are becoming familiar with (and fond of) his sushi specialties and other Japanese fare from teriyaki to sukiyaki. It's a nice meal, especially if you pull into town late. There's only one sushi chef—so when it's busy (especially in summer) the service can be slow.

Royal Coachman Inn
*2nd and Dogwood,
(604) 286-0231
84 Dogwood Street,
Campbell River
Inexpensive; full bar;
AE, MC, V
Lunch, dinner every day*

★★

We like everything about this place, from the hearth bearing soccer trophies to the savory aroma of the soup du jour (if it's French onion, order it) to the practiced pouring arm of the bartender. A steady stream of regulars crowds the Coachman from lunch into the wee hours, and Swiss-trained chef Marcus Hediger meets demands with a hard-working kitchen staff of three. A blackboard menu changes daily. Meals include surprisingly ambitious dishes that you don't expect to see in a pub: crepes, schnitzel cordon bleu, sole topped with asparagus, shrimp, and hollandaise. Tuesday night is prime rib night—come early.

LODGINGS

Painter's Lodge

Just off Island Highway
at 1625 McDonald Road,
4km north of
Campbell River,
(604) 286-1102
Box 460, Campbell River,
BC V9W 5C1
Expensive; AE, MC, V

You'd never know this was a 60-year-old fishing lodge. Due to a fire in 1985, the place is brand-spanking new. Old photos of big-name types and their award-winning fish line the plush lobby, lounge, and dark Tyee Pub, where unkempt fishermen seem almost out of place— but aren't. If you're not up here to fish, *you'll* soon feel like a visitor from another planet, particularly when pandemonium breaks out at 4am as the seaplanes and 50 Boston whalers zoom in to pick up the anglers and shatter your sleep. Rooms are $209 a night, which includes eight hours of fishing.

At press time there were two buildings totaling 61 rooms and two more in the works. Best are rooms in the main lodge (sorry, these are for anglers only), with two steps down into the bedroom and a porch overlooking Discovery Passage and Quadra Island.

In the evening, appetizers in the lounge are our choice: try the moist smoked salmon marinated in a honey-mustard-seed and lime vinaigrette. Dinners are inconsistent and service incompetent.

Strathcona Lodge

At the edge of Strathcona
Park, 45km west of
Campbell River, radio
phone H688568, or
(604) 286-3122 or
(604) 286-2008
Mail: PO Box 2160,
Campbell River,
BC V9W 5C9
Moderate; full bar;
MC, V

A week-in-the-woods experience: canoeing, day hikes, lake play. Stay in one of the 50 attractive cabins with kitchens or one of the modest motel units—a bit overpriced for what you get, but you couldn't ask for a better location. There are lots of outdoor activities, perfect for families seeking fresh-air fun. Family-style buffet meals at strictly regulated hours feature healthful food—plenty of vegetables and limited amounts of red meat. Don't be late.

GOLD RIVER

The *Uchuck III* will take you for a magnificent 10-hour chug from Gold River to the remote settlement of Kyuquot. You spend the night at a bed and breakfast and return the next day ($123 all-inclusive); PO Box 57, Gold River, BC V0P 1G0; (604) 283-2325.

Books in the Best Places *series read like personal guidebooks, but our evaluations are based on numerous reports from local experts. Final judgments are made by the editors. Our inspectors never identify themselves (except over the phone) and never accept free meals or other favors. Be an inspector. Send us a report.*

PORT McNEILL

The major asset of this remote outpost is proximity to all things wild and wonderful—great boating, diving, whale watching, salmon fishing, and tidepooling.

The U'mista Culture Center in Alert Bay, an inspiring Kwakiutl museum, is a short ferry ride from Port McNeill. This one examines cultural origins and potlatch traditions. Seasonal hours, closed Sundays, (604) 974-5403.

Whale watching is superior (July through September only) from Telegraph Cove, 16 kilometers south of Port McNeill. Stubbs Island Charters, (604) 928-3185, takes groups out for afternoon cruises to view the cetaceans on their migration down the Johnstone Strait, and can accommodate groups of five or more in a cluster of modest harborfront cabins with kitchens.

RESTAURANTS

The Cookhouse
In Pioneer Mall on
Highway 19,
(604) 956-4933
Moderate; full bar;
AE, MC, V
Lunch, dinner Tues-Sat

The minimalism of Port McNeill makes the polished amenities of The Cookhouse shine all the brighter. Located in the Pioneer Mall, Walter and Sue Schinner's elegant restaurant and carry-out delicatessen/bakery features tasty continental fare prepared on the spot in a central kitchen midway between deli counter and dining room. The Schinners' subtle Eastern European influence is evident (try the Chicken Budapest). More traditional fare, served on brown stoneware, includes Chateaubriand, filet mignon, and crab Bearnaise, or veal Oscar. Eat hearty—it could very well be your last high-quality feast before plunging into the North Country.

PORT HARDY

You'll feel as though you're on the edge of the world in Port Hardy—venture any farther north and you'll have to go by boat. It's a town full of loggers, fishermen, miners, and travelers stopping in long enough to catch the 18-hour ferry to Prince Rupert, (604) 949-6722. The boat leaves every other day in summer and once a week in the winter.

The famous Edward S. Curtis film *In the Land of the War Canoes* was filmed in nearby **Fort Rupert**, still one of the best places to purchase authentic Indian art.

Cape Scott Park. An hour-and-a-half's drive on a dirt road west of Port Hardy and then a short hike on a rickety boardwalk through old-growth forest bring you to spectacular San Josef Bay. For exact directions or information on other hikes at the northernmost tip of the island, contact the Chamber of Commerce, (604) 949-7622.

THE GULF ISLANDS

The Gulf Islands, a 240-kilometer string of small islands in the Strait of Georgia, are British Columbia's more remote version of the American San Juans to the south. Similar in geography and philosophy, the Gulf Islands also enjoy the same rain-shadow weather and offer wonderful boating and cycling opportunities. The best-known and most populous islands, the Southern Group, stretch from Campbell River to Victoria: Gabriola, Valdes, Galiano, Mayne, Saltspring, North and South Pender, and Saturna. North of Nanaimo are Lasqueti, Texada, Denman, Hornby, Quadra, Cortes, Sonora. Ferries from Tsawwassen on the mainland and various spots on Vancouver Island service the islands. For more information, call BC Ferries, (604) 669-1211.

THE GULF ISLANDS: SONORA

LODGINGS

Sonora Lodge
48.4 km north of Campbell River (accessible by boat or plane only), (604) 662-0280 Mail: 625-B 11th Avenue, Campbell River, BC V9W 4G5 Expensive; full bar; MC, V

We're sure it's not the *best* fishing lodge in British Columbia (that's got to be April Point), but it's possibly the second-best and certainly the most expensive. Even so, the $1395 you shell out for two nights and three days includes everything. *Everything*: airfare, guided fishing, meals, drinks, rain gear, fishing rods, five hot tubs and two steam rooms. The place is impeccable—especially considering this multi-million dollar spot has been open under the current owners for four seasons (and it's only open when the fishing is). There are three buildings with 33 very luxurious suites (some have their own Jacuzzis). Other amenities include a world-class billiard table, a small convention center, and five fully stocked self-service bars open 24 hours. Special needs are catered to here.

The kitchen is competent and serves a well-selected variety of, of course, fresh fish. Occasionally a special chef is brought in for a fete around the *teppan* cooker.

THE GULF ISLANDS: QUADRA

Quadra is a 10-minute ferry ride away from the salmon-fishing mecca of Campbell River. A lot of artists and craftspersons live here, so it makes a fine place to sleuth around for pottery and other wares. You can pick up a detailed map of the island at the **Kwakiutl Museum**, an outstanding collection of Native American art. Their masks, blankets, and carvings rival those of the Indian displays in the finest international museums. Three kilometers south of the ferry dock on Green Road, (604) 285-3733.

LODGINGS

April Point Lodge
3km north of the ferry dock (follow signs), (604) 285-2222 April Point, Quadra Island Mail: PO Box 1, Campbell River, BC V9W 4Z9

Between April and October this famous resort draws serious fishermen and celebrities from all over the world for the extraordinary salmon fishing: bluebacks in April and May, tyee July through September, coho throughout the summer. The staff, nurtured by generations of experience, expertly pair guides with fishermen. After a day of fishing, they may take you to feed the bald eagles with the spare bait. About eight kilometers in either direction are exceptionally lovely beach walks: the lighthouse

Expensive; AE, DC, MC, V;
Open April-October

to the south, the Rebecca Spit Provincial Park to the east.

The cabins facing west are spacious, attractively furnished, and graced with large fireplaces; they're also expensive. Facing north are thin-walled cabins overlooking the marina; you might be kept awake most of the night by late-drinking or early-rising fishermen in adjoining rooms. There's a seawater pool, but if you're not here to fish—really fish (the cost of which is *not* included in your already hefty fee)—you will probably feel like a tolerated outsider; there are no other amenities. Reserve at least three or four months in advance.

The main lodge is sunny and cheerful. The dining room is decorated with authentic Northwest Coast art, and the food is always good (though sometimes the steak is overdone) and occasionally outstanding—especially when Eric Peterson barbecues fresh fish from the tanks outside.

THE GULF ISLANDS: DENMAN AND HORNBY

Tranquil and bucolic, the sister islands of Denman and Hornby sit just off the coast of Vancouver Island. Denman, the larger (10 minutes by ferry from Buckley Bay, south of Courtenay) is known for its pastoral farmlands and its population of talented artisans. Its relatively flat landscape and untraveled roads make it a natural for cyclists. Hornby (10 minutes by ferry from Denman) boasts **Helliwell Park**, with dramatic seaside cliffs and forest trails, as well as a lovely long beach at Tribune Bay.

LODGINGS

**Denman Island
Guest House**

*4km from the ferry dock,
(604) 335-2688
Denman Road,
Denman Island
Mail: PO Box 9, Denman
Island, BC V0R 1T0
Inexpensive; no credit
cards; checks ok*

One of the original farmhouses on Denman Island, this pleasant, antique-filled bed and breakfast offers hearty country dinners in addition to lodgings. (The dinners—and full licensing—attract nonresidents as well.) A friendly young couple, the Okrainecs, rent five bedrooms (one has a porch for those who want to bring a pet); bathrooms are shared. On this small farm the rooster may crow a little too early in the morning, but the hens deliver some wonderful eggs for breakfast. Open May through September.

Sea Breeze Lodge

*From ferry, drive across
the island, turn left at
the co-op store (approx.
9.7km), Tralee Point,
(604) 335-2321
Hornby Island,
BC V0R 1Z0
Moderate; no credit cards;
checks ok*

Sea Breeze Lodge may have a reputation among islanders for being posh and exclusive, but off-islanders will find it quite unpretentious. Catch the ferry from Denman before 6pm (or 10pm Fridays) and find 11 warm and comfortable cottages on the beach, some equipped with fireplaces and kitchens. Guests gather in the main lodge for Gail Bishop's home cooking (June 15 to September 15 only), which is fresh and inventive, and for the convivial atmosphere around the rustic oak tables. Beach alternatives here include tennis on a grass court, a soak in the new hot tub (enclosed in winter, open in summer), or a trot on the Bishops' pony around the tiny island.

THE GULF ISLANDS: GABRIOLA

Although this most accessible island has become a bedroom community for nearby Nanaimo (20 minutes by ferry), it manages to remain fairly rustic and beachy. Highlight of the fine beach walks along the west shore is the **Malaspina Gallery:** weird rock structures and caves carved by the sea.

LODGINGS

Surf Lodge
5km north of the ferry on Berry Point Road,
(604) 247-9231
Site 1, Berry Point Road
Mail: RR 1, Gabriola Island, BC V0R 1X0
Moderate; MC, V

A striking rock-and-log resort on Gabriola's south shore, Surf Lodge features nine lodge rooms and eight rustic cottages, along with recreational options: swimming, tennis, badminton, horseshoes, and tidepooling, to name just a few. The food in the dining room is surprisingly good and hearty, and vegetarian meals are available. Views from the lodge are peerless. The Hallidays will meet you at the ferry on request; children over four are welcome.

THE GULF ISLANDS: GALIANO

Galiano Island is a narrow strip of land 22 miles long with fewer than 1,000 permanent residents. Hike or bike the length of the eastern coast and catch glimpses of Vancouver Island on the way back from the west side. Or canoe under high cliffs off the western shoreline, broken only by secluded coves. **Montague Harbour Marine Park** has moorings available and can provide you with most of your vacation supplies; (604) 539-5733. A ferry from Tsawwassen arrives in Sturdies Bay twice a day. The Swartz Bay ferry on Vancouver Island sails into Montague Bay two or three times a day.

RESTAURANTS

La Berengerie
On the corner of Clanton and Montague Harbour roads, (604) 539-5392
Montague Harbour Road, Galiano Island
Moderate; full bar; no credit cards; checks ok
Dinner every day, Fri-Sun Sept-June

This quaint 40-seat restaurant boasts devoted fans on the island. Owner/chef/hotelier Huguette Benger, who learned the trade running a small hotel in Paris, offers a $15 set menu of soup, salad, main course, and dessert. Items change daily and may include cold avocado soup, boeuf bourguignon, salmon mousse, couscous, chestnut mousse, or perhaps something experimental. Many of the vegetables come from the restaurant's own garden. Reservations are a must.

Upstairs are three modest guest rooms, one with a private bath. They're fine if you don't require a spotless bathroom, a dust-free night table, or peace and quiet (the walls are paper-thin). But the hot tub on the deck is an added comfort that makes up for everything. Breakfast for guests is yogurt with fruit and granola, fresh croissants with marmalade, baked eggs, slices of Camembert, and cafe au lait.

Looking for a particular place? Check the index at the back of this book for individual restaurants, lodgings, attractions, and more.

The Pink Geranium

*22.5km north of the
ferry, (604) 539-2477
Porlier Pass Drive, North
Galiano Island
Moderate; full bar; no
credit cards; checks ok
Dinner Sat-Sun*

Look for the pink mailbox; otherwise, you might never find this seven-table restaurant stashed in Ken and Sylvia Mounsey's living room. Dinner starts at 6pm, but if someone needs to catch a ferry an early meal can be arranged. First stop is a cozy nook next to the massive stone fireplace, where you'll be served drinks on comfy chintz chairs, instructed by your jolly hostess to relax, and left to soak up the very civilized, very British atmosphere.

Once seated at your table, you'll find that the food, too, is typically English: simple and basic. Dinners are prix-fixe: $17.50 for hors d'oeuvres, entree, vegetables, and dessert. A starter of smoked herring, taken fresh from Trincomali Channel, was quite tasty but served on dry, tasteless slices of bread that in no way resembled the homemade sourdough billed on the menu. A stuffed chicken entree filled with cubes of herbed bread and doused in white sauce followed, accompanied by mashed potatoes and sauteed carrots generously sprinkled with fresh herbs. Dessert was a sweet, undistinctive meringue pie with berry topping.

The Mounseys run the restaurant by themselves, and as a result the service is not as satisfying as the ambience. Even so, it's an extraordinarily popular place where reservations are often required far in advance.

LODGINGS

Bodega Resort

*Follow Porlier Pass Drive
22.5km north of Sturdies
Bay, (604) 539-2677
Porlier Pass Drive and
Cook Road
Mail: PO Box 115,
Galiano Island,
BC V0N 1P0
Moderate; MC, V*

For owners Steve and Elizabeth Ocsko, this resort represents a labor of love: they're constantly adding on to it themselves. They now have six spacious chalets furnished with care: you might find lace country curtains, custom cherry cabinets, or a cast-iron stove in the living room. Each unit has three bedrooms, two baths, a fully equipped kitchen, and two view decks. There's also a ranch-style unit with three bedrooms, kitchen, living room, bath, and a large sundeck surrounded by a rose garden—perfect for family getaways. A lodge with a conference room also has a few rooms available. For fun there's horseback riding, a trout pond, and hiking trails amid the 25 acres of meadows and trees. Prices are remarkable for such generous accommodations.

Sutil Lodge

*Follow signs for
Montague Harbour; after
long steep hill, turn left
on S Wind; last drive on
left, (604) 539-2930
Montague Harbour,
Galiano Island,
BC V0I P0N*

Upon speculation, this place probably deserves at least two stars, but at press time, Ann and Tom Hennessy were in the midst of renovating the rambling 1928 clapboard building, situated on 20 secluded acres of private waterfront. The Hennessys bought it in 1986 after it had done time as an artists' colony in the '70s. From the looks of it, their labors—which include removing, restoring, and replacing each room's original fir paneling and filling the

Moderate; MC, V

(unrated due to renovation)

rooms with authentic 1930s furnishings—will not be in vain and will be completed just about the time this book goes to the printer.

Travel there with someone you like to be close to; the eight guest rooms are tiny, but not cramped. Front rooms have stunning water views; the others face lush cherry blossoms and the expansive back lawn. A communal living room and dining area both have fireplaces. Among Hennessy's seagoing vessels is a 40-foot catamaran, on which he takes guests on tours of the islands, followed by picnic suppers on the beach. Fabulous off-season rates.

THE GULF ISLANDS: SALTSPRING

Named for the unusually cold and briny springs on the north end of the island, Saltspring is the largest and most populated of the Gulf chain, and its population is growing steadily. It's accessible by ferry from Tsawwassen (to Long Harbour, 2½ hours); Crofton, near Duncan on Vancouver Island (to Vesuvius, 20 minutes); or Swartz Bay (32 kilometers from Victoria) on the Saanich Peninsula (to Fulford Harbour, 30 minutes). All roads lead to Ganges, as the natives are fond of saying. A 20-minute drive from Fulford Harbour, it's the largest town on the island, with a colorful Saturday-morning farmers' market, several pleasant cafes, a new condominium development overlooking the harbor, and a flurry of retail development.

Camping facilities are available at St. Mary Lake, Ruckle Park, and Mouat Provincial Park on the southeastern tip of the island, where you'll find a spectacular mixture of virgin forest, rock and clamshell beach, and rugged headlands. Or drive Cranberry Road up to the top of Mount Maxwell for a panorama of the archipelago from Saltspring to the American mainland. For information, call the tourist bureau, (604) 537-5252.

RESTAURANTS

Bay Window Restaurant (in the Booth Bay Resort)
3.2km north of Ganges on the main road; look for signs, (604) 537-5651
375 Baker Road, Ganges
Mail: PO Box 247, Ganges, BC V0S 1E0
Moderate; beer and wine; MC, V
Lunch, dinner Wed-Sat, brunch Sun

On a protected bluff overlooking pretty Booth Bay, the wood-paneled Bay Window dining room with deck gives the English-country-manor tradition a Pacific Coast accent. Former Hastings House chef (and the owner's brother) Steven Lynch presides in the kitchen now; he's consciously trying to present a more accessible menu than that in his former venue and seems to do well with the seafood standards common to Gulf Island cuisine, and with the local specialty, lamb. Steven's Sunday brunch is worth the drive if you're staying elsewhere on the island.

There are also 11 rustic cabins sprinkled among the madronas. Gay Utter and Bob Lynch, former owners who sold the place a few years ago so they could travel, have returned and taken over again. In their absence, the cabins suffered a decline. Once all the new furniture is in and the field mice out, the cabins will likely regain their cozy comfort. For a while, at least, the owners' joking comparisons to "Fawlty Towers" seemed to have some basis in fact.

Sweet Arts Patisserie-Cafe

In the exact center of town across from the firehall, (604) 537-4127
112 Lower Ganges Road, Ganges
Inexpensive; full bar;
MC, V
Breakfast, lunch Mon-Sat, dinner Fri-Sat, brunch Sun

Like many businesses in the Gulf Islands and in Washington's San Juans, this cafe shows the lingering influence of the countercultural movement of the '70s. In this case, it's a positive force. Sweet Arts specializes in natural foods, such as whole-wheat pastries, bran muffins, and the like, but also translates this wholesomeness into some exquisite napoleons, delicious tortes and mousses, and fresh fruit tarts. Try lunch specials such as the light, creamy shrimp salad, or a fruit bowl with a blackberry muffin. Dinners include seafood and meat preparations, fine fresh salads, and other specials. At breakfast, the excellent pastries go well with homemade granola and the best espresso drinks on the island. This is also a good place to get a midmorning look at the folk who actually live and work in Ganges—it's a sort of Saltspring version of the Chatterbox Cafe.

Vesuvius Inn

At the northwest point of the island,
(604) 537-2312
Vesuvius Bay Road, Ganges
Inexpensive; full bar;
MC, V
Lunch, dinner every day

The big draws at this rebuilt version of a turn-of-the-century loggers and fishermen's inn are the variety of brews and the spectacular view from the waterside porch of the ferry dock with Crofton in the distance. Also good at Vesuvius is the food—Caesar salads (ubiquitous on Saltspring), fish 'n' chips, burgers, Northwest Mex—and entertainment. A very casual place—order at the bar as you go in and find a good spot on the porch.

Luigi's

The only 3-story building in Ganges,
(604) 537-2777
134 McPhillips Avenue, Ganges
Inexpensive; full bar;
AE, MC, V
Lunch, dinner every day

Since moving to a bigger space (in what is known locally as The Inn), Luigi's can accommodate more people both inside and out—there's a wonderfully large patio. The house specialty is pizza, a very fine, thick and chewy example of the genre, which can be taken out if you'd like. Burgers, good Caesar salads, and a decent selection of beer and wine round out the menu. Some weekend nights in high season this is a jumpin' joint, with live entertainment.

LODGINGS

Hastings House

160 Upper Ganges Road, Ganges, (604) 537-2362
Mail: PO Box 1110, Ganges, BC V0S 1E0
Expensive; AE, DC, MC, V

Nestled among fruit trees, gardens, and rolling lawns that overlook a peaceful cove, Hastings House Resort goes a long way toward satisfying the hideaway fantasies of most people. The place is said to have been Admiral Warren Hastings' farmland retreat as he conceived plans for the Normandy invasion. It was bought in 1981 by the Cross family, who invested $1.5 million to renovate the estate. Now it stands in all its gentrified splendor, imbued with a palpable, almost formidable air of genteel hospitality.

The accommodations consist of 12 suites within four revamped farm buildings, plus the recently renovated Cliff House. Each is furnished with down quilts, antiques, and thick carpets. Our favorites are the Hayloft, with its bay window seat, Franklin stove, and quaint folk art; and The Farmhouse, a charming stucco and half-timbered house with two suites—ideal for two couples. Although service here strikes some as just a little too *too* (new towels are supplied every time you leave your quarters; a personal note, thanking you for your stay, follows the visit), the guest gradually discovers that in spite of that, the stiff tariffs ($215–$345 Canadian in high season, including a morning wake-up hamper, breakfast, and afternoon tea), and the almost palpable air of formality, Hastings House is a remarkably warm place, thanks to a friendly staff. And relaxing: you can stroll the farm grounds and pasture, where quaint footpaths bridge little streams; wander down to the beach to watch the sailboats; or borrow the house bikes for a spin around the island.

In the morning, a hamper of coffee and muffins is delivered to your room; later you breakfast in the dining room on farm-fresh eggs and produce. Saturday night stays include an outstanding Sunday brunch. Chef Geoffrey Couper, formerly of Vancouver's William Tell, recently took over the kitchen and is assembling a new staff, so menu changes can be expected in the near future. He will continue to offer a nightly $40 five-course table d'hote dinner, beginning promptly at 7pm with sherry on the lawn or drinks in the parlor. A recent meal began with a luscious, creamy spinach soup decorated with a delicate swirl of sour cream, followed by scallops in a piquant wine sauce, warm asparagus salad, and a perfectly grilled fillet of salmon with tiny red potatoes cut to look like mushrooms and lightly browned. Dessert was a huge, heavenly Grand Marnier souffle. If you're seated next to a window during this genteelly presented feast, chances are good your gaze will fall on some of the Northwest's most beautiful waterfowl in the bay beyond. Lunches are served a la carte; both dinners and lunches are open to nonguests by reservation.

Southdown Farm

9.7km south on Beaver Point Road from Fulford Harbour, (604) 653-4322 1121 Beaver Point Road, Fulford Harbour, Mail: RR1, Fulford

An alternative to the Saltspring-by-the-sea experience can be had at this working farm, owned by English expatriates Jonathan and Sue Yardley, in a quiet valley five minutes from Fulford Harbour. The Vine House ($65) is a self-contained mother-in-law apartment with one bedroom (queen-size bed) and a potbelly stove, decorated

Harbour, BC V0S 1C0
Moderate; AE, MC, V

in English contemporary style. We give two stars, however, on the merits of the Jonathan-designed Cottage ($95), a thoroughly modern, quintessentially Northwest accommodation. It has two bedrooms (one with a queen-size bed, the other with two twins), French doors between all the rooms and onto a wraparound porch, a huge bath with a two-person Jacuzzi and floor-to-ceiling windows, and wonderful lofted ceilings. The Yardleys stuff the fridge with breakfast fixings such as eggs from the farm, home-cured bacon, and their own homemade jam. You can bring your horse along to Southdown, if you have one.

Weston Lake Inn B&B
3.6km east from Fulford
Harbour, (604) 653-4311
813 Beaver Point Road,
Mail: RR1, Fulford
Harbour, BC V0S 1C0,
Moderate; MC, V

This contemporary farmhouse overlooking Weston Lake has been open for several years, and in that time owners Susan Evans and Ted Harrison have become experts at fading into the background and letting their guests enjoy the comfortable space. Their touches are everywhere, though: in Ted's petit-point embroideries, framed and hanging in the three guest rooms; in Susan's excellent, hearty breakfasts; in the blooming results of their gardening efforts. Susan knows and loves her island and is a fount of knowledge about activities, eating places, and quiet entertainments such as swimming, biking, and fishing. Guests have access to a comfortable lounge with fireplace, library, TV, and VCR (including a decent collection of cassettes). Open all year.

THE GULF ISLANDS: MAYNE

Rolling orchards, sheep farms, and warm, rock-strewn beaches abound on this rustic eight-square-mile island. It's small enough for a day trip but pretty enough for a lifetime. By ferry it's usually the second stop from Tsawwassen (1½ hours), and the fourth or second from Swartz Bay (1½ hours).

RESTAURANTS

Five Roosters
Turn left off the ferry in
Village Bay, go 1.6km
to Miners Bay,
(604) 539-2727
Village Bay Road,
Mayne Island
Inexpensive; full bar;
MC, V
Breakfast, lunch, dinner
every day

Don't let the funky-living-room decor throw you, especially since this is one of the only places on the island to have lunch. We sampled a good, if not exactly authentic, Caesar salad, tossed with crisp lettuce, fresh croutons, and a tasty dressing that lacked only the zing of anchovies. A meaty burger was served on a sourdough bun with fries that might have been delicious had they not been so thoroughly drenched in seasoned salt. The seafood club sandwich—shrimp salad, bacon, lettuce, and tomato on hearty toasted wheat bread—was a winner, as was the prompt, friendly service.

If you've found a place that you think is a Best Place, send in the report form at the back of this book. If you're unhappy with one of the places, please let us know why. We depend on reader input.

LODGINGS

Fernhill Lodge

*Left onto Village Bay
Road from the ferry
terminal, go about 2.5km
to Fernhill Road, turn
right, (604) 539-2544
Fernhill Road
Mail: PO Box 140,
Mayne Island, BC,
VON 2JO
Moderate; MC, V
Breakfast,
dinner every day*

If it's comfort and serenity you're after, a visit to this lovely lodge will do you. We'd love to linger here for a week—and never move. The Crumblehulmes' impeccable taste permeates every corner, from Mary's vast collection of English pewter to the eclectic selection of books in the library to the six delightful guest rooms, each decorated around a period theme—Jacobean, 18th-century French, Victorian, Oriental, Canadian, and Farmhouse. Each room has its own bath stacked with plenty of thick cotton towels. Cats roam the five-acre grounds, and guests should do the same; you'll find a spacious solarium, a wood-fired sauna under the trees, an Elizabethan knot garden, discreetly placed benches peppering the hillside, and a huge rope swing.

Brian Crumblehulme's passion is historical cookery. Much of the food he uses is home-grown, and all of it is enhanced by the multitudinous herbs grown in the garden. The extraordinary evening feast is prepared on prior notice (the first party to reserve gets to select one of five menus) and draws Canadians year-round. We had Hadrian's Dinner: oyster stew, grilled lamb in coriander sauce, Pottage Julian, peas, asparagus, and squash in white wine, bread and cheese salad, warm herb bread, and pears in cumin/wine sauce. Breakfast consisted of a copious fruit platter, warm scones and orange muffins with fresh cream and jam, an herb-and-mushroom egg puff and a folded cheese omelet, fresh-squeezed juice, and good, dark coffee.

Food aside, the real treat at Fernhill is the Crumblehulmes' boundless hospitality—from loaning bikes to sharing a soothing cup of tea. They attend to their guests' every need with genuine interest and memorable warmth.

Gingerbread House

*Consult a Mayne Island
Chamber of Commerce
map on the ferry ride
over, (604) 539-3133
Campbell Bay Road,
Mayne Island,
BC VON 2JO
Moderate; MC, V*

As its name suggests, the decor is strictly story-book at the Gulf Islands' only Victorian home, built in Vancouver in 1898 and ferried to Mayne only a few years ago. Perched high on a grassy knoll overlooking Campbell Bay and an abundant shellfish beach, accessible by a short trail, the inn rents four elaborately ornamented bed-and-breakfast rooms March through October. Despite the odd mix of lovely antiques and tacky furnishings (linoleum floors and orange velour chairs), our favorites are the spacious Yellow Room, with private French doors opening onto a rose-rimmed lawn and a spectacular bay view, and the small, charming Peach Room on the main floor—the only room with hardwood floors, a divan, a picture window, and an antique claw-footed tub.

Come morning, dieters beware. Karen Somerville

redefines "full breakfast," beginning with coffee and bran muffins smeared with honey butter, moving on to grapefruit halves grilled in sherry and brown sugar (actually quite delicious), and culminating with almond French toast, bacon, and slices of kiwi and orange. A bit sugar-heavy, but you're on vacation.

THE GULF ISLANDS: NORTH AND SOUTH PENDER

Green, rural North and South Pender islands are separated by a canal and united by a bridge, from which you get lovely views of both Browning and Bedwell harbors. The ferry lands at the dock at Otter Bay on North Pender.

LODGINGS

Cliffside Inn-On-The-Sea
Follow signs to Hope Bay government dock, turn on Clam Bay Road to Armadale,
(604) 629-6691
Armadale Road,
North Pender Island,
BC V0N 2M0,
Expensive; MC, V

You're perched at the edge of a bluff beside a staircase leading down to the sea, with a sweeping view of the channel, the islands, and Mount Baker beyond. The emphasis here is on privacy: each of the four Laura Ashley bedrooms has its own entrance, a deck, and a view—either of the manicured English garden (almost always in some sort of bloom) or of the sea. Even the bathrooms have ocean views, and two rooms feature fireplaces. The hot tub on the cliffhanger deck with the 280-degree view can be reserved for private sessions well into the night.

Hostess Penny Tomlin—a third-generation resident of this property—is eager to please. She will prepare gourmet dinners for guests or arrange boat excursions and island cookouts; she'll even transport you to and from the ferry (bike and all if you'd like). Breakfast, served in the solarium dining room, might be stewed rhubarb with yogurt and homemade croissants, or fresh oyster quiche. Two entrees, usually seafood or lamb, with salad from her garden and soups (Brazilian black bean, outstanding gazpacho), are available nightly in The Conservatory—a dining room with more of that view. The two-day packages ($120), which include two breakfasts and a four-course meal, are a splendid deal—and if you stay more than two days Penny will even do your wash.

Corbett House B&B
Call ahead for directions,
(604) 629-6305
Mail: RRI Corbett Road,
North Pender Island,
BC V0N 2M0
Moderate; MC, V

In April 1989, John Eckfeldt and Linda Wolfe took over at this heritage house and farm. They inherited, along with a beautiful setting and cozy rooms, the previous owners' reputation for running a fine bed and breakfast. The Yellow, Red, and Blue rooms are all equally cozy, though the first is the only one with a full bath (though water pressure is minimal) and a private balcony. The parlor is open to guests, who often gather round the fireplace for evening coffee or quiet reading. The hosts provide an ample breakfast of fresh baked goods, fruit, coffee, and varying entrees, all generally from local sources. Long country walks fit in well here.

Pender Lodge

Immediate left after ferry exit, continue .5km, (604) 629-3221
Mail: RR1, North Pender Island, BC V0N 2M0
Moderate; full bar; MC, V

The new owners of this old property go out of their way to provide a satisfying holiday. Oh, it's still a bit worn in places and the tennis court has seen many harsh-weathered days, but the lodge is getting prettier all the time. Yvon and Nadia Danduran have added nice touches such as hanging flowerpots. The ongoing but unobtrusive renovations have modernized the lodgings, but they still retain an intrinsic rustic feeling (we favor the lodge rooms over the schlockier cabins). The lodge is not on the water, but the view is gorgeous (though not from all nine rooms). Best of all, the turquoise-and-white restaurant is casual, friendly, and open when you want it to be. Non-guests often drop by for a bowl of mussels meuniere or a hearty tourtiere (a meat pie made with delicately spiced ground beef and pork). Desserts are simple creations from locally picked berries. After dinner indulge in a horse-drawn carriage ride. The ferry's only a half mile away.

THE GULF ISLANDS: SATURNA
RESTAURANTS

Boot Cove Lodge and Restaurant

Follow the signs from the ferry, (604) 539-2254
Mail: Box 54, Saturna Island, BC V0N 2Y0
Moderate; beer and wine; no credit cards; checks ok
Dinner Fri-Sun (two seatings per night)

Proprietor Peter Jardine triples as the maitre d', waiter, and sommelier, and he doesn't let a detail slip by him. This lovely frame house high on a hill overlooking an inlet and an oyster farm serves a wonderful five-course meal. Entrees change with the seasons—you'll often find salmon, prawns, or oysters in the summer and some lamb variations in the fall. The five-course menu is different every week. Your only choice is the appetizer: wild nettle soup or a bouillabaisse with Pernod (both were pleasing). The rest just appears at your table, perfectly timed: a papaya-prawn salad on a bed of spinach and wildflowers; a savory (though slightly overcooked) entree of lemon garlic beef and spring vegetables; a mango sorbet with strawberry sauce garnished with a sugared pansy. Reservations are a must.

There's a large fireplace (crackling warm when it's cold outside) in the oak-trimmed waiting room (which doubles as a living room for the inn's guests). A pretty banister leads the oak-and-peach theme upstairs to the three bed-and-breakfast rooms ($55). Call ahead if you need a ride from the ferry.

Wondering about our standards? We rate establishments on value, performance measured against the place's goals, uniqueness, enjoyability, loyalty of clientele, cleanliness, excellence and ambition of the cooking, and professionalism of the service. For an explanation of the star system, see the Introduction.

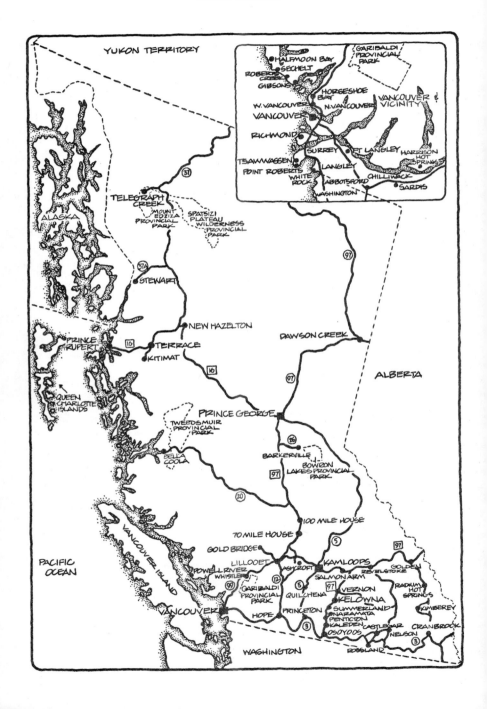

MAINLAND BRITISH COLUMBIA

First, north from White Rock (skipping Vancouver) along the Sunshine Coast to Powell River, then inland to Whistler, continue north to Prince George and eastward to Prince Rupert and the Queen Charlotte Islands. The second route begins eastward out of Vancouver, through Harrison Hot Springs, then north to Kamloops. A third loop starts with the Okanagan Valley at Osoyoos and heads north along Lake Okanagan, east to the Rocky Mountains, turning westward again along the southern rim of the province.

WHITE ROCK
RESTAURANTS

Cosmos
Corner of Elm and Marine, (604) 531-3511 14871 Marine Drive, White Rock Moderate; full bar; MC, V Dinner every day

★

Right near the border, Cosmos is pure Greek taverna, with an atmosphere that can be so electric it can make you forget the food. The food is very Greek and quite good. We enjoyed the taramosalata, the spanakopita, and the dolmathes. Among main courses are rack of lamb and calamari; the moussaka and the tender and flavorful grilled quail (they come two to an order) were excellent. Desserts are luscious: choose between rich baklavas and bougatsas, or opt for the more slimming orange sponge cake (ravani), creme caramel, or Greek yogurt. Greek dancers and belly dancers entertain on weekends.

THE SUNSHINE COAST

Situated inside the rain shadow of Vancouver Island, this blue-sky coast begins just west of Vancouver at Horseshoe Bay and follows a scenic path north to Powell River. The drive takes you through lush, wooded areas, along lovely coastline, and onto two ferries as you journey north. Highlights along the way include a pioneer museum at Gibsons, a local arts center in Sechelt, and the **Saltery Bay Provincial Park** near Lang Bay.

HORSESHOE BAY
RESTAURANTS

Bay Moorings
Across from the ferry

Gus Tsogas has been serving some wonderful meals at this restaurant—seafood plus Greek and Italian specialties

terminal, (604) 921-8184
6330 Bay Street,
Horseshoe Bay
Moderate; full bar;
AE, MC, V
Lunch, dinner every day

Ya Ya's Oyster Bar

Take the Horseshoe Bay
turnoff from the Trans-
Canada Highway,
(604) 921-8848
6418 Bay Street,
Horseshoe Bay
Inexpensive; full bar;
AE, MC, V
Lunch, dinner every day

such as souvlaki, lasagne, and calamari. The preparations are careful, and the service is top-notch. They also have take-out, but once you see the dramatic ocean view, you won't want to leave.

The name came from a nasty joke (which owner Alex Von Kleist wouldn't tell us), and the idea came from the natural surroundings: what else to have in the midst of all this fresh seafood and shellfish than an oyster bar, for goodness' sake? For six years Alex and his wife Barbara have been surprising folk with fresh oysters served in zesty Portuguese broth, on spinach and garlic, or maybe with pernod or bechamel sauce. If oysters aren't your bag, there are clams, mussels, and even a chicken dish or two. It's all rather casual, with entrees including a large basket of French fries, and Alex's special brew, Ya Ya's Oyster Ale, conditioning in the background tanks. The place has been recently remodeled in mahogany and copper ("I'm so sick of oak and brass!" says Alex), and the deck has a great view.

GIBSONS

RESTAURANTS

Ernie and Gwen's Drive-In

In the middle of town,
(604) 886-7813
Highway 101, Gibsons
Inexpensive; no alcohol;
no credit cards; no checks
Lunch, dinner every day

If burgers and fries and homemade milk shakes (the kind that use real milk—remember those?) are your thing, stop at Ernie and Gwen's after your trip on the Langdale ferry. You can adorn your burger with multitudinous condiments. It all tastes real.

ROBERT'S CREEK

RESTAURANTS

The Creek House

Robert's Creek Road and
Beach Avenue,
(604) 885-9321
Robert's Creek
Moderate; full bar; MC, V
Dinner Wed-Sun

Here's a restaurant with continental cooking, by which we mean the continent of today, not the one enshrined in hotel cooking of 50 years ago. This restaurant is owned and operated by Yvan Citernesch (former owner and chef at Le Bistro in Vancouver). He does the cooking, and Yvonne Mounsey still bakes fresh desserts daily. Situated in a house with a view of a tree-filled garden, the restaurant is simply decorated inside with white walls, light wood floors, flowers on the tables, and original contemporary art on the walls. On a given night, you may choose from ten entrees that change seasonally: pork and clams Portuguese, rack of lamb Provencal, or baked boneless rabbit stuffed with herbs and served in a cream sauce. Fresh local seafood is usually offered too. Desserts include mango mousse.

LODGINGS

Country Cottage Bed and Breakfast

Robert's Creek Road,
(604) 885-7448
Mail: General Delivery,
Robert's Creek,
BC V0N 2W0
Moderate; no credit cards;
no checks

The hand-painted sign at the ferry terminal directs you to this charming butterscotch farmhouse, surrounded by a cherry orchard and over 100 rose bushes. At Loragene and Phillip Gaulin's bed and breakfast you stay in a one-bedroom cottage with an antique iron bed, a pull-out couch for kids, and a wood-burning stove. Or you can stay in the Gaulins' sunny Rose Room with your own bath and solarium and a view of the grazing sheep that Loragene raises for wool. In the morning, your uncommon, genial hostess will prepare you a breakfast from what's in season: garden-fresh asparagus crepes with croissants, cheese, and fresh fruit on our visit. A full afternoon tea in the garden or parlor is a new addition. Dinner is just up the road at the Creek House (Loragene reserves your table). You're a pleasant five-minute stroll from a sandbar beach, and the Gaulins have bikes to borrow. No smokers or kids under 10. Reserve well in advance.

SECHELT

RESTAURANTS

Casa Martinez

3.2km south of Sechelt
at Davis Bay,
(604) 885-2911
Highway 101, Sechelt
Moderate; full bar; MC, V
Dinner Tues-Sun

Mrs. Martinez is the reason this Spanish-accented restaurant has been one of the best on the Sunshine Coast, but these days she leaves the cooking mostly in the hands of her son, Jose. He goes to considerable lengths to get fresh vegetables, bread, seafood, and dairy products (his paella meets his mother's standards), but, try as he might, Spanish cooking doesn't quite succeed here anymore, and the menu reflects a more Northwest flavor, full of fresh crab, snapper, and prawns, along with continental dishes. Jose's wife runs the dining room quite convivially.

HALFMOON BAY

LODGINGS

Jolly Roger Inn

Highway 101, 5 minutes
from Halfmoon Bay at
Secret Cove,
(604) 885-7184
Mail: Box 7, RR1,
Halfmoon Bay,
BC V0N 1Y0
Expensive; AE, MC, V

This seasonal (mid-March to mid-November) resort is a cluster of one- and two-bedroom townhouses with fireplaces, kitchens, and decks; most have sweeping bay views. Boaters and fishermen find this spot enchanting: good fishing, a first-rate marina, pleasing accommodations, and a decent steak and seafood restaurant.

POWELL RIVER

RESTAURANTS

The Seahouse
Courtney and Marine,
(604) 485-9151
4448 Marine Avenue,
Powell River
Moderate; full bar;
AE, MC, V
Lunch Mon-Fri, dinner
every day, brunch Sun

Your best bet for dining in Powell River is this spot, overlooking the arriving and departing Vancouver Island ferry. Our bouillabaisse was exceptional—seasoned just right—and the Greek dishes and pasta dishes are gratifyingly authentic. Decor is countrified.

LODGINGS

Beach Gardens Resort
Hotel
A half-hour north of
Saltery Bay Ferry,
(604) 485-6267
7074 Westminster
Avenue, Powell River,
BC V8A 1C5
Moderate; AE, DC, MC, V

★

Sitting on a protected section of the Georgia Strait, the Beach Gardens Resort is a sort of mecca for scuba enthusiasts, who come for the near-tropical clarity of the water and the abundant marine life. It's good for other endeavors besides, with tennis courts, a sauna, an indoor swimming pool, a marina, a dining room (with good breakfasts and a smorgasbord), and a neighborhood pub. The rooms are comfortable—with nothing sensational to recommend them except the views of all that clear water. Cabins without views, less expensive, are popular with divers.

WHISTLER

Highway 99, running north from Vancouver to Whistler, is an adventure in itself. The aptly named Sea to Sky Highway hugs fir-covered mountains that tumble sharply into island-filled Howe Sound. The grandeur and the views are breathtaking, and the curves of the road often demanding. The drive to Whistler from Vancouver takes approximately two hours, depending on road conditions and photo opportunities.

Whistler Village has the makings of a world-class vacation resort. Complete with underground parking, the European-style grouping of lodges, restaurants, and shops nestled against 7,000-foot mountains is tasteful, accommodating, and permeated with a terrific ambience and energy.

The **Whistler-Blackcomb ski area**, at the edge of Whistler Village, comprises two mountains and boasts some of the finest skiing in the Northwest. The Seventh Heaven T-bar, which ran to the top of Blackcomb, has been replaced by a high-speed quad. Two additional T-bars have been added, providing access to glacier skiing (a truly lunar experience) and the opportunity to ski throughout the summer. The two mountains now offer over 180 runs from 26 lifts; the ski area also offers a number of ski classes including all-day supervised skiing for children (Kids' Kamp) and special ski clinics for women; (604) 932-3141 (Blackcomb), (604) 932-3434 (Whistler). **Heli-skiing** is available from private concerns; 15 kilometers of **cross-country ski trails** begin just outside the Village; 50 kilometers of groomed trails can be found 20 minutes to the south of Whistler; (604) 932-5128.

Lodging can be arranged through the Whistler Resort Association; (604) 685-3650 or (800) 634-9622. We recommend planning well in advance, particularly in the winter months. Many lodgings now require 30 days' cancellation notice, with a 3-day minimum stay. Summer activities at Whistler might include hiking, skiing, windsurfing, mountain biking, tennis, and golf. A 2,000-person conference center is available year-round. Note: Increased popularity and an unprecedented construction boom at Whistler have brought attendant growing pains. Even established hotels and eateries sometimes seem unable to handle the crush efficiently. Inexperienced help abounds, and managers are typically frazzled on Friday nights in January. Prices are spiraling upward. The 340-room Canadian Pacific Chateau Whistler Resort, a 10-story development at the foot of Blackcomb, is due to open in November 1989.

RESTAURANTS

**Rimrock Cafe
and Oyster Bar**
*1 block north of the
gondola in the Highland
Lodge, (604) 932-5565
Highway 99, Whistler
Moderate; full bar;
AE, DC, MC, V
Dinner every day
(winter and summer
only), brunch Sun*

At last, Whistler has a restaurant that breaks into our three-star rating. This intimate cafe, housed in an unsuspecting hotel, is remarkable proof that fresh seafood and haute cuisine are not anomalies in the mountains. It offers an exquisite menu of innovative entrees at surprisingly moderate prices. To order here, however, close the menu. The Rimrock's specialty is seafood, and it's all listed on the blackboard against the far wall: fresh oysters, Thai seafood curry, fish soup, and sunomono. On our visit we began with a generous romaine salad with julienned Gruyere and a cream Caesar dressing. The Boston bluefish, marinated and wrapped in well-seasoned vine leaves, was tender and moist; our salmon and scallops were cooked perfectly in a light cream and lemon sauce, then topped with tasty sheets of smoked salmon. Thin stalks of asparagus, carrots, and zucchini were the accompaniments. We plan to return for the shark.

Service was top-drawer. The wine list is comprehensive, if overpriced—as at all the better Whistler eateries. Make reservations early, or you might get stuck at a cocktail table in the lounge instead of at one of the 12 mahogany tables prettied with thin white candles near the stone hearth.

Il Caminetto di Umberto
*Across from the Crystal
Lodge, (604) 932-4442
Whistler Village
Moderate; full bar;
AE, DC, MC, V
Dinner every day*

The ubiquitous Umberto Menghi is at Whistler, too. Not surprisingly, it's *the* place to go in the Village; few things can top fresh pasta and a bottle of red wine after a day of climbing up or schussing down mountains. This perennial favorite is also busy; the tables are too tightly packed together, and noise from the bar and cabaret interferes with table talk. Aim for the specials, such as New York strip with mushroom sauce or poached salmon with passion-fruit cream sauce. Umberto's newest addition, the less expensive Trattoria di Umberto in the Mountainside Inn, appeals to the more informal crowd for pasta and items from the rotisserie.

Sushi Village

2nd floor of the
Westbrook Hotel,
(604) 932-3330
Whistler Village
Moderate; full bar;
AE, MC, V
Lunch, dinner Wed-Sun
(weekends only off-season)

Sushi Village is a welcome reprieve from the boundless activity that Whistler offers. A civilized hush hovers over this refreshingly modest Japanese eatery, where the staff is knowledgable and gracious. Delicious sushi and sashimi plates are prepared by animated experts at the counter. Straightforward and dependable, although the beer, as at most places in Whistler, is quite expensive. Reservations accepted only for parties of four or more. Tatami rooms available.

LODGINGS

Delta Mountain Inn

Whistler Village,
(604) 932-1982, toll-free
(800) 268-1133
Mail: PO Box 550,
Whistler, BC V0N 1B0
Expensive; AE, DC, MC, V

The Delta is currently the queen of hotels in Whistler Village, with 300 rooms; it's the only one with room service and the only one accepting pets. The inn has two indoor tennis courts, an outdoor pool, and a 250-person convention center. The staff is capable, efficient, and downright personable (we've heard the maids will even walk Fido for you—they're particularly fond of golden retrievers). Many of the larger rooms, and all of the suites, have fireplaces and Jacuzzis. You can cook meals in your suite's kitchen or enjoy continental food in the hotel's restaurant: two lounges provide drinks and entertainment.

Carleton Lodge

Whistler Village,
(604) 932-4183
Mail: PO Box 519,
Whistler, BC V0N 1B0
Expensive; AE, MC, V

The boom-or-bust air about Whistler seems to be taking its toll on even the more established hotels in the Village: we've come to expect a flurry of inexperienced service at some of the spanking new spots, but not here, at one of Whistler's first resorts. Its eight years of existence add up to a grandfather's age in Whistler years, yet we've encountered a few kinks in an otherwise excellent hotel. You'll never go wrong with the proximity—it's so close to the mountain you could almost ski in your pajamas. The views are terrific, and the complex houses a hub of shops, lift-ticket sales booths, and the infamous Nasty Jack's (which can generate an awful lot of noise late into the night). Sitting at the base of Whistler and Blackcomb mountains, the Carleton has spacious condominium units, each of which includes a fully equipped kitchen, a washer and dryer, and a capacious bathtub that doubles as a Jacuzzi. The problem lies in the service: the maids sometimes skimp on their duties, and the front desk is not always on the ball.

Haus Heidi

Whistler Way and
Nesters, (604) 932-3113
7115 Nesters Road,
Whistler
Mail: Box 354, Whistler,
BC V0N 1B0

A short drive from Whistler Village, this eight-room, owner-operated pension is a refreshing change from the resort scene at the base of the mountain. Hosts Trudy and Jim Gruetzke will make your stay comfortable—a personal touch often lacking at the large resorts. The rooms have private baths, and guests have access to a Jacuzzi overlooking the mountains. Two of the rooms are located

Moderate; MC, V

a few minutes' walk away in a condo with a fully equipped kitchen and sauna. One awakes to a marvelous complimentary breakfast of fruit, croissants, and omelets.

Pension Edelweiss
1.6km north of Whistler Village at White Gold Estates, (604) 932-3641 7162 Nancy Green Way Mail: Box 850, Whistler, BC V0N 1B0 Moderate; MC, V

If you arrive late, hosts Ursula and Jacques Morel will probably leave directions to your room on the front door and chocolates on your pillow, and expect you late for breakfast. As accommodating as the hosts are, you'll probably be awakened by the guests who clomp about in their ski boots come morning. This casual, six-room guest house is run in European fashion. The rooms are simple and spacious, with double beds, down comforters, and private baths. Jacques (a former competitive skier) and Ursula cook ample breakfasts. Fondue dinners ($30 extra) are optional, as is spending an hour or two in the sauna. If your legs are strong, Pension Edelweiss is within walking distance of the Village.

LILLOOET

Two hours north of Whistler on a gravel road, you'll happen upon Lillooet—mile zero of the Cariboo Gold Rush Trail. The best thing about Lillooet is getting there. The **BC Rail** line between Lillooet and Vancouver is a vital link to the outside world for the loggers, miners, and farmers who live in remote areas of the Coastal Range. It's also one of the most scenic stretches in British Columbia, along pretty Howe Sound and into the jagged mountains. The route links Vancouver with Whistler, Lillooet, and Prince George; only the deluxe car requires reservations: (604) 984-5246.

GOLD BRIDGE
LODGINGS

Tyax Mountain Lake Resort
From Lillooet, follow signs toward Gold Bridge, (604) 238-2221 Tyaughton Lake Road, Gold Bridge, BC V0K 1P0 Expensive; AE, MC, V

Tumbleweed is the manager's son's favorite horse: "You can use him for anything from riding to monkey bars." This spanking-new resort folded into the wilderness of the Chilcotin Range about a hundred miles north of Vancouver is as fun-oriented and versatile as Tumbleweed himself—that is, if scruffy Tumbleweed were a streamlined racehorse. It's the kind of place that attracts wealthy Europeans: float planes are seen dropping incoming guests off at the dock and taking fishermen up to Trophy Lakes; a helicopter out back lifts thrill-seekers to enjoy heli-*anything* (heli-skiing, heli-hiking, and even heli-fossil-hunting). But it's not all a high-tech adventure: you can be just as happy canoeing, gold panning, ice skating, horseback riding.

Stay in one of three chalets (each with three to four bedrooms, kitchen, loft, and a balcony overlooking

Tyaughton Lake and the mountains) or in one of 28 suites (the view rooms are the best, with beamed ceilings, balconies, and down-filled quilts) in the freshly hewn spruce log lodge. Other amenities include a sauna, a large Jacuzzi in the front lawn, a game room with a ping-pong table, aerobics classes, and workout rooms. They've got it all here; the only thing you might run out of in this activists' paradise is energy (or money). The energy, at least, is easily replenished after a day of sunbathing at the lake's edge. There's a lounge that doubles as a dining room, and unless you're in a chalet, this is where you eat.

To get to all these new amenities, you drive a pretty rough road, so you might consider the train to Lillooet, where your hosts can pick you up.

70 MILE HOUSE
LODGINGS

Flying U Guest Ranch
20km east of 70 Mile House on North Greenlake,
(604) 456-7717
Mail: Box 69, 70 Mile House, BC V0K 2K0
Moderate; AE, V

It's a working ranch, ideal for families who like to ride horses on their own. There are 25,000 acres to explore, and cattle to round up if you wish. Back at the lodge, you can stay in log cabins, do a little canoeing on the nearby lake, and dine at the over-140-year-old main building. Movies, bonfires, hay rides, or square dancing often follow the meal. A new saloon offers a full bar and snacks. Rates are $75 per day or $450 per week per adult, all-inclusive (three meals a day, all you can chow).

100 MILE HOUSE
LODGINGS

108 Golf and Country Resort
Highway 97, 13km north of 100 Mile House,
(604) 791-5211
Box 2, RR1, 100 Mile House, BC V0K 2E0
Moderate; AE, MC, V

At what seems like the edge of civilization, a full-scale resort covers thousands of acres of rangeland. The resort has been purchased by a Japanese family, but it's still managed by the Red Coach Inn. The guest rooms have been remodeled, and doubles run between $75 to $95, depending on the season. There are horseback riding, a large pool, five tennis courts, and a top-flight 18-hole golf course. In winter, the cross-country skiing is some of the best in the Northwest, with over 200 kilometers of well-maintained trails. The restaurant has a fine view of the golf course and two lakes, and a cheerful atmosphere, but the menu is limited to the expected steaks and seafood.

Wondering about our standards? We rate establishments on value, performance measured against the place's goals, uniqueness, enjoyability, loyalty of clientele, cleanliness, excellence and ambition of the cooking, and professionalism of the service. For an explanation of the star system, see the Introduction.

BARKERVILLE

Billy Barker found lots of gold here in 1862, whereupon the town became the largest city north of San Francisco; then it became a ghost town, and now it's a place revived for the tourist trade. It's not bad, really: restored old buildings, a stage for melodrama, and a general store full of five-cent jawbreakers and lots of retro '60s (that's 1860s) goods. The whole place shuts down after the summer season (May–September).

Bowron Lake Park. Six lakes form an amazingly regular rectangle, a scenic and challenging setting for a 120-kilometer canoe trip (with a number of portages in between). Plan on spending a week to 10 days. For outfitting, a couple of lodges offer canoe, paddle, and life-belt rentals. Becker's Lodge also has campsites, cabins, and a dining room; contact them at mobile phone N698-552, Wells YP, or in winter at (604) 492-2390; PO Box 129, Wells, BC V0K 2R0.

RESTAURANTS

Wake Up Jake's
Barkerville,
(604) 994-3259
Inexpensive; beer and
wine; AE, MC, V
Breakfast, lunch, dinner
every day (May-September)

There's nothing about this old-time saloon that isn't 1870s authentic: they don't serve French fries (which hadn't been invented); they don't use processed anything. Instead, it's all real: soups, caribou stew, sourdough bread sandwiches, pot pies, steaks, even the specials—pheasant or perhaps cheese and onion pie—amid saloon decor.

PRINCE GEORGE

Prince George is the hub of north and central BC, and the jump-off point for brave souls heading up the Alaska Highway. The city sits amid two mountain ranges on a dry plateau. Forestry is the main industry here, and loads of logging roads

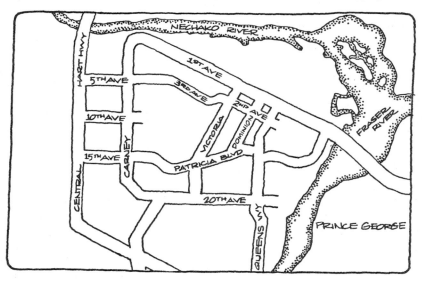

take hunters and fishermen back into remote and bountiful spots. The **Stellako River**, west of Prince George near Fraser Lake, is famous for its record trout. For recreational types, the **Cottonwood Island Nature Park**, along the Nechako River, has an extensive trail system suitable for hiking in the summer and cross-country skiing in the winter. Adjacent to the park is the **Prince George Railway Museum**. Two city galleries are of interest: **Prince George Art Gallery** features regional and national exhibits monthly; **Native Art Gallery** exhibits local native arts and crafts.

Railroads. BC Rail will roll you through 462 miles of some of the most beautiful scenery in BC, from Vancouver to Prince George in 13 hours; (604) 984-5246. Transfer to the Via Rail passenger run to Prince Rupert, where ferries to the Queen Charlotte Islands, Vancouver Island, and Alaska depart regularly; (800) 665-8630.

RESTAURANTS

Cafe New York
5th and Dominion,
(604) 564-1100
1215 Fifth Avenue,
Prince George
Moderate; full bar;
MC, V
Lunch, dinner Mon-Sat

A friendly spot, Cafe New York prides itself on an eclectic menu of entrees collected from a number of countries. The menu includes dishes such as veal Marsala, chicken martina (prepared with garlic, capers, mushrooms, and vermouth), and pasta primavera (with hot Italian cappocolla, basil, garlic, and fresh veggies). All the seafood is remarkably fresh. Lunches are on the lighter side, which provides room for a slice of unbelievable cheesecake (they have over 100 different recipes).

The Achillion
4th and Dominion,
(604) 564-1166
422 Dominion Street,
Prince George
Inexpensive; full bar;
AE, MC, V
Lunch, dinner every day

Authentic Greek lunches and dinners can be found at Kostas Eliopulos' spot on Dominion Street. The combination plate is a good choice for two: you get pan-fried shrimp, beef shish kabobs, roast leg of lamb, potatoes, rice, and Greek salad or soup, all for $28.

LODGINGS

Esther's Inn
Off Highway 97 at 10th,
(604) 562-4131
1151 Commercial Drive,
Prince George,
BC V2M 6W6
Moderate; AE, DC, MC, V

Oh, why not. Bring your swimsuit to Prince George, even in the middle of winter, and pretend you're in the tropics. This Polynesian-style hotel comes complete with palm trees, swaying philodendrons, and waterfalls landscaped around a warm indoor swimming pool. For this dose of tropicana, rates are reasonable (about $50 a double); there are also three Jacuzzis, two indoor water slides spiraling into a separate pool, and a sauna. So they lay it on a little thick. The Tradewinds Dining Lounge and the Papaya Grove Coffee Garden are your dining alternatives.

PRINCE RUPERT

Prince Rupert began as a dream. Founder Charles Melville Hays saw this island as the perfect terminus for rail as well as sea travel and trade. Unfortunately, on a trip back from Europe, where he was rustling up money to help finance his vision, he met with an untimely death aboard the *Titanic*.

Seventy-five years later, a number of local folks rekindled Hays' dream. By the mid-'80s Prince Rupert had two major export terminals and a booming economy. With this newfound prosperity have come culture and tourism.

The **Museum of Northern British Columbia** has one of the finest collections of Northwest Coast Indian art you're likely to find anywhere. First Avenue E and McBride, (604) 624-3207.

Ferries. Prince Rupert is called the gateway to the north, but it's also a place where ferries can take you west (to the remote Queen Charlotte Islands—see listing) or south (through the Inside Passage to Vancouver Island). The Alaska ferry winds north through the panhandle to Skagway.

RESTAURANTS

Smile's Seafood Cafe
Follow 3rd Avenue into
George Hills Way,
(604) 624-3072
#1 George Hills Way,
Prince Rupert
Moderate; full bar;
MC, V
Breakfast, lunch, dinner
every day

Since 1935, Smile's Cafe has been tucked unobtrusively among the fish-processing plants by the railroad. It recently came under new ownership, but about all that's changed is the subtraction of corn from the chowder recipe. Favorites still include the fresh Dungeness crab, halibut, and cod; the French fries are a perfect nongreasy, brown-skinned complement to the fish. The service is small-town friendly.

QUEEN CHARLOTTE ISLANDS

A microcosm of the British Columbia coast, the Galapagos of the Northwest, these sparsely populated, beautiful islands (150 in all) offer an escape to a rough-edged (and often rainy) paradise. There are countless beaches, streams, fishing holes, coves, and abandoned Indian villages to explore. Many unique subspecies of flora and fauna share these islands with the 6,000 residents.

On Haida Gwaii are the Haida Indians, who carve argillite—a rare black slate found only on the islands—into Northwest figurines. The **Haida Gwaii Watchmen** are experienced naturalists who guide wilderness tours in the area—including six-day trips to South Moresby in a 50-foot Haida canoe; (604) 559-8225.

Pacific Synergies offers sailing excursions in the area; (604) 932-3107. Or explore the island via kayak with the help of **Ecosummer**; (604) 669-7741.

Transportation. There are only 75 miles of paved roads in the Queen Charlotte Islands. Take the six- to eight-hour ferry from Prince Rupert, fly in to the small airstrip on Moresby Island, or take a seaplane. Food and lodging are available, mainly on Graham Island, but most people who come camp. Tourist information through the local Chamber, (604) 626-5211, or the Visitors' Info Bureau in summer months, (604) 626-3995.

QUEEN CHARLOTTE ISLANDS: MASSET
LODGINGS

Copper Beech House
Right by the fishing boat

The garden's a bit tangled, and so are all the memorabilia and collectibles inside this turn-of-the-century home, but

docks at Delkaplah and
Collison, (604) 626-3225
1526 Delkaplah, Masset,
BC V0T 1MO
Moderate; no credit cards;
checks ok

come spring the garden smells wonderful and come morning so does breakfast. David Phillips cans his summer
fruits for breakfast year-round and smokes his own
seafood, which—if you request dinner—will probably be
one or more of the six appetizers. Upstairs there are two
guest rooms decorated with Mission Oak furniture; one
has its own living room. Phillips also caters dinner for
groups.

QUEEN CHARLOTTE ISLANDS: QUEEN CHARLOTTE CITY
LODGINGS

Spruce Point Lodge
5.6km west of ferry, left
after Chevron station,
then second left to 6th,
(604) 559-8234
609 Sixth Avenue, Queen
Charlotte City, BC
V0T 1S0
Inexpensive; no credit
cards; checks ok

First it was just a lawn and a shower offered to the occasional kayaker needing a place to stay. Once guests
became more the norm than the exception, Mary Kellie
and Nancy Hett opened up a three-room lodge to fill the
obvious need. After a fire a few years ago, Mary, Nancy,
and their children held a barn raising. Thirty people came
and during four weekends put up a larger version of the
original lodge on the Skidegate Inlet. That's the spirit
of this cedar-clad building encircled by a balcony, a place
which attracts families and couples alike. There are six
clean rooms—each with a full bath, cable TV, and locally made pine furnishings. Price ($45) includes a continen-
tal breakfast and an occasional barbecue of whatever
seafood the local fishermen bring by.

The lawn's not up for grabs anymore, but kayakers
and adventurers on a budget will appreciate the bunk
room (sheets and pillowcase provided) for $10 a night,
which includes use of the kitchen and laundry. Kayaks
for rent. Pets and kids welcome.

FORT LANGLEY
RESTAURANTS

Bedford House
On the banks of Fraser
River in downtown Fort
Langley, (604) 888-2333
9272 Glover Road,
Fort Langley
Moderate; full bar;
AE, MC, V
Dinner every day,
brunch Sun

A lovely place with a picturesque view of the Fraser River,
this restored 1904 house is furnished with English antiques and has a pleasant, countrified elegance. Choose
from a menu rich with fancy continental cuisine: roast
duckling with a fruit sauce, broiled filet of salmon with
hollandaise, or scallops and prawns served on puff pastry
with a creamy champagne sauce.

All places in this book are recommended; even "no stars" are worth knowing about.

LINDELL BEACH
LODGINGS

Ranch Park Estate B&B
1.6km south of Lindell Beach at 1615 Robinson Road, (604) 858-5459 Mail: PO Box 1, Lindell Beach, BC V0X 1P0 Inexpensive; no credit cards; no checks

Robert and Ilse Wilmsmeier take landscaping seriously. Rhododendrons, roses, and hanging fuchsias set off their low, modern ranch-style home. Guests stay in the separate guest house (connected to the main house by a vine-covered arbor), with its own living room, wood stove, and kitchen. There are five sparkling bedrooms (some adjoining, some with private baths) furnished with functional tubular and blond wood furniture, fluffy comforters, and platform beds. The breakfast isn't much. Especially recommended for families with children in tow—there are a jungle gym, swings, and plenty of grass for running around. Cultus Lake is just two miles down the road.

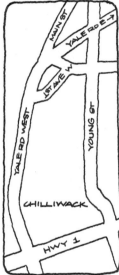

CHILLIWACK

The name's not the only thing curious about this prosperous farming and dairy center: speakers set along the downtown portal blare easy-listening music, and antique cars seem plentiful. Local landmarks include an offbeat military museum at the **Canadian Forces Base** (open Sundays all year, mid-week during the summer), **Minter Gardens**, 10 large theme gardens (14 kilometers east at the Highway 9 junction), and **Bridal Falls Provincial Park**, 15 kilometers east on Highway 1.

RESTAURANTS

Le Pique Assiette
On the corner of Kipp and Main, (604) 795-5616 9256 Main Street, Chilliwack Moderate; full bar; MC, V Lunch Mon-Fri, dinner Mon-Sat

You'll rarely find a more authentic soupe de poissons than in this modest country restaurant in the heart of Chilliwack, partly because one of the owners hails from St. Tropez. The rich broth, redolent of saffron and a splash of Pernod, is a splendid carrier for the traditional toasted slices of baguette, which you spread with garlicky rouille and float on top. Add a cold leek salad with thickened vinaigrette, a slice of the peppery house pate (or seafood pate with scallops, shrimp, and salmon); finish with a creme caramel. Voila—a wonderful meal! Crepes, both entree and dessert, are another specialty. Lunch is the busy meal; dinner is lonely.

Would you like to order a copy of Best Places *for a friend? There's an order form at the back of this book.*

The New Yorker Steak House

Near Ontario at Yale,
(604) 795-7714
45948 Yale Road W,
Chilliwack
Moderate; full bar;
AE, MC, V
Lunch, dinner Tues-Sun

This popular city-center steak house serves up enormous portions and consistently good quality. Charcoal-broiled Alberta grain-fed beefsteaks come in four different cuts and seven sizes, the most expensive being $13.95. You'll appreciate the whole sauteed mushrooms arranged on top. Chilliwack residents swear by the mushrooms Neptune (baked with cream cheese, shrimp, and crab meat) and the hefty seafood platter. For a lighter lunch, order the Greek salad, prepared in true Greek fashion with tomatoes, cucumbers, lots of crumbled feta, and no lettuce. The decor is BC casual, with the usual fringed cloth lamp shades.

Sergio La Mansione

Near Nowell at Yale
(604) 792-8910
46290 Yale Road E,
Chilliwack
Moderate; full bar;
AE, MC, V
Lunch Tues-Fri,
dinner Tues-Sat

Owner-chef Sergio Rabisi and his wife provide a menu of mixed delights in this handsome mock-Tudor mansion with leaded-glass windows and a warm fireplace for winter evenings. (Beware the air conditioner in summer; sitting near it can easily ruin the meal). We sampled a delicious seafood chowder, brimming with shrimp, crab, and clams. An entree of gnocchi Napoletana, in a tomato sauce well seasoned with basil, was mouth watering. The veal, pan-fried in butter, lemon juice, white wine, and capers, was good and tangy. The dinner menu offers a wide variety of seafood dishes, and other specialties include chateaubriand, rack of lamb, and veal scaloppine Sergio. This is a good place to sample wines by the glass: Sergio is an aficionado and carries an extensive selection. Service is efficient.

HARRISON HOT SPRINGS

Situated at the southern end of Harrison Lake, the town is a small, quiet row of low buildings facing the sandy beach and lagoon. The hot springs themselves are

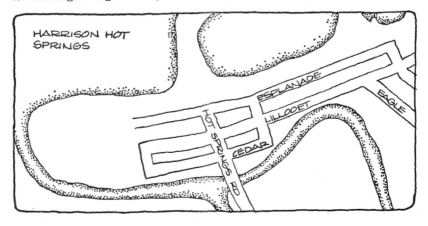

in a strangely enclosed temple with sulfur steam billowing out and Coke cans strewn along the bottom of the pool. But don't be dismayed; the public soaking pool (which has cooled hot-spring water pumped into it) is large, wonderfully warm (100 degrees average), and deep enough to dive into. In addition, there are windsurfers and bikes to rent, hiking trails nearby, helicopters to ride, and a pub or two. In winter, skiers use Harrison as their spa after a day on the slopes at Hemlock Valley (a 40-minute drive).

RESTAURANTS

Black Forest

1 block west of Highway 9 at Esplanade,
(604) 796-9343
180 Esplanade Avenue,
Harrison Hot Springs
Moderate; full bar;
AE, MC, V
Dinner every day
(closed Thurs off-season)

Bavarian food seems a staple in BC, and here's an authentic restaurant serving more than just schnitzels. Mr. and Mrs. Helpmueller run this family place, and the decor reflects their heritage; if you're a fan of goulash soup, schnitzel, and beef rouladen—sirloin stuffed with onions, pickles, mustard, and bacon, braised in red wine, and served with red cabbage and spaetzle—then you'll warm to the ambience too. Mr. Helpmueller and his nephew, Mr. Fethermann, cook as fine a German meal as their strong accents might suggest. We chose the wiener schnitzel, topped with mushrooms, sauteed in wine, and generously covered with Bearnaise sauce. A not-too-sweet mocha cake makes a nice ending. The place is popular, so stop by on your evening stroll and make a reservation.

Conca d'Oro

Next to the public pool on Esplanade,
(604) 796-2695
234 Esplanade Avenue,
Harrison Hot Springs
Moderate; full bar;
AE, MC, V
Lunch every day (summer),
Sat-Sun (winter),
dinner every day

This dark, brooding restaurant serves the familiar continental fare (schnitzel, seafood, veal), but you'll also find very good cannelloni and lasagne and great pizza. At dinner, opt for the upper dining room with patio and lake view. Afterward, if you have room, try the moist, homemade cassata, layered with creamy ricotta cheese, and then boogie it all off at the adjacent Lido cabaret. Avoid lunch: the midday menu is a small-scale offering of grilled cheese and fish 'n' chips.

LODGINGS

The Harrison Hotel

West end of Esplanade,
(604) 796-2244
100 Esplanade Avenue,
Harrison Hot Springs,
BC V0M 1K0
Expensive; AE, DC, MC, V

★

Located at the southern shore of long and beautiful Harrison Lake, this legendary hotel is really a better place to view than to visit. The first hotel was built here in 1885 to take advantage of the hot springs; it burned down, and the present "old" building dates back to 1926. Since then two additions, and a third in the ground-breaking stages, have changed the hotel into a sprawling mishmash of unrelated architecture. The good news is that, with the addition of the eight-story wing, the whole hotel will undergo a revamp, classing up, we hope, the aging babe. Grounds are quite lovely and spacious, with tennis courts and exercise circuit, but the best part about the place is definitely the hot-spring water: two indoor pools (103 and 90 degrees) and one outdoor (90 degrees). A scenic golf course is three kilometers away.

Staying here is expensive (there are extra charges for almost everything), so you need to know what you're doing. The rooms in the old hotel look a shade shabby, but may be expanded into suites with the upcoming remodel. Still, few of them have views of the lake (the hotel won't guarantee lake views), so a safer bet is to book a room in the tower, where you'll have modern, spacious quarters with a view of the lake or the grounds and mountains. But even our tower room had a lumpy bed with a tacky floral spread, and the noise from the pool kept us awake (there's no air conditioning as yet, so you need to keep windows open or ask for a fan). The restaurants are nothing special. Our advice would be to use the place for a short stay, arriving in time to enjoy the excellent pools and have a pool-side drink, and then promenading down the road to one of the village's interesting restaurants.

Harrison Hot Spring Villa Hotel and Restaurant
1 block west of Highway 9 at Esplanade,
(604) 796-9339
270 Esplanade Avenue,
Harrison Hot Springs,
BC V0M 1K0
Moderate; AE, MC, V

For about half the price of staying at the Harrison Hotel, you can have a quiet, clean room with a private balcony right across from the beach and right above one of the best restaurants in town. The Hot Spring Villa is nothing special, but it's got what you need. There are 17 rooms, five with balconies and lovely views. They don't serve breakfast in the dining room, but you can get bacon and eggs, pancakes, or French toast in your room with a night's notice.

The restaurant is fine: lots of greenery and white lace (a welcome change from the darkness of the other restaurants in town), an open patio in the summer. Swiss chef Joseph Ziendler's French-Swiss fare is a treat. We tried the salmon Picasso (poached salmon topped with a creamy mushroom, wine, dill, and shrimp sauce) and the linguine Neptune (fresh pasta with a mushroomy seafood sauce). Both were delicious and not too heavy. The wine list is select, and the service, in both hotel and restaurant, is gracious.

MANNING PARK
LODGINGS

Manning Park Resort
Just off Highway 3 in Manning Provincial Park,
(604) 840-8822
Manning Park,
BC V0X 1R0
Moderate; AE, MC, V

Situated within the boundaries of this pretty, provincial park, the lodge gives you easy access to both gentle and arduous hiking trails. With a short drive, you can be paddling a rented canoe on Lightning Lake or riding a horse through the surrounding country. Besides the lodge (41 rooms), the resort includes a restaurant, a coffee shop, cabins, and triplexes—all in the same plain, functional style. If you have 39 friends, however, book the Last

Resort a few yards down the highway, a real old-fashioned '40s charmer that sleeps 40. Reserve the resort well ahead, especially in winter (two-day minimum then), when the park turns into cross-country and downhill ski heaven.

PRINCETON
RESTAURANTS

The Apple Tree Restaurant
Vermilion at Dixie Lee,
(604) 295-7745
255 Vermilion Avenue,
Princeton
Moderate; full bar; MC, V
Lunch Tues-Fri;
Tues-Sun (July-Sept),
dinner Tues-Sun

The big crab-apple tree across from the Esso station marks the site of Douglas and Mary Rebagliati's excellent small restaurant, in a house filled with greenery and fussy wallpaper. Expect such appetizers as escargots in mushroom caps (an Okanagan favorite), and good, hearty, homemade soup (such as Slovak sausage and sauerkraut); hope for the deceptively simple oregano chicken, marinated in olive oil and herbs and broiled. Desserts receive just as much attention (the reputation of the Louisiana mud pie has spread to Vancouver). The thoughtful wine list focuses on Okanagan Valley wines and BC ales and cider. A new patio for English cream teas will be open for the summer. You can have an early supper here and make Osoyoos by nightfall.

QUILCHENA
LODGINGS

Quilchena Hotel
Take the 2nd Merritt
exit off Coquilahalla
Highway, (604) 378-2611
Highway 5A, Quilchena,
BC V0E 2R0
Moderate; full bar;
MC, V
Breakfast, lunch, dinner
every day

Remote Quilchena Hotel (mid-April through mid-October only) captures the ambience of southwestern BC's cattle country, and it attracts a motley assortment: moneyed urbanites who fly over (the Quilchena has its own landing strip) in search of relaxation; cattle barons who come to buy livestock; gentlemanly senior citizens in search of the perfect golf course; and cowboys, Canada style (French accents belie their Texan appearance). It's a delightful stew, and meant to be that way: there are no phones or TVs in the rooms; guests share bathrooms and dine together in the parlor.

There are 14 rooms in the hotel and a three-bedroom ranch house on the grounds. The rooms are decorated with the original iron bedposts and printed wallpaper. It's not elegant, but there's a worn comfort about the place, which was built in 1908 as a hotel to serve cattle ranchers who traveled between Merritt and Kamloops. The main attraction in the parlor is a piano that was shipped around Cape Horn; guests often gather here for an impromptu recital. At night, in fact, there's not much else

---

Looking for a particular place? Check the index at the back of this book for individual restaurants, hotels, B&Bs, parks, and more.

to do. Daytime finds you riding horses, playing tennis, golfing on the adjacent course, or searching the nearby fossil beds.

The food has improved with the new chef, as has the kitchen's reputation; there is still lots of beef on the menu, but the chicken Irish Mist (breast cooked in Irish Mist, soy sauce, and cream) is a good addition. The old saloon is now open and features appetizers and local wines.

MERRITT
LODGINGS

Corbett Lake Country Inn
16km south of Merritt on Highway 5A,
(604) 378-4334
Mail: Box 327, Merritt, BC V0K 2B0
Expensive; full bar; no credit cards; checks ok
Breakfast, lunch, dinner every day (closed November, March-April)

French-trained owner and chef Peter McVey first came from England to British Columbia on a fishing trip—and it must have been good. McVey's country inn caters to lovers of fly fishing in the summer and cross-country skiers in the winter. There are three nondescript rooms in the lodge, but most choose to stay in one of the 10 simple cabins, each with its own kitchen. The three new duplexes all have fireplaces and separate bedroom/living rooms. Aside from the outdoor activities, the food's the thing here. Dinner (by reservation only, guests and non-guests) is something different every night and is included in the price of a night's stay. McVey creates wonderful four-course evenings starting with soup (perhaps fresh mushroom), a salad (Caesar, hot German, or cucumber), and continuing to an entree which could be anything from loin of pork with Dijon mustard to beef Wellington with Yorkshire pudding. Corbett Lake bears plenty of fish, but an extra $25 fee gains you the privilege of angling in two private lakes stocked by McVey himself. You can catch as many full-sized trout as you'd like, but only one goes home.

KAMLOOPS
RESTAURANTS

Old Battle House
Corner of 2nd and Battle,
(604) 828-0077
172 Battle Street, Kamloops
Moderate; full bar; AE, MC, V
Lunch Mon-Fri, dinner Mon-Sat

Folks come from miles around for Alfred Zanesco's rack of spring lamb, made with garlic, mustard, and fresh herbs from his garden. But that's not the only draw. This lovely house is old and grand on the outside, bright and modern on the inside (a 1985 fire destroyed much of the interior). A sweeping view of the city sets the stage for a meal that may include coquilles St. Jacques to start, veal scaloppine or seafood for the main course, and a chocolate fondue for two to finish.

The facts in this edition were correct at press time, but places close, chefs depart, hours change. It's best to call ahead.

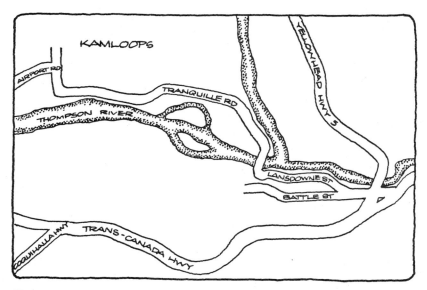

Minos

*1km north of Overlander Bridge, (604) 376-2010
262 Tranquille Road, Kamloops
Moderate; beer and wine; AE, MC, V
Lunch Mon-Sat, dinner every day*

★

Minos is a family-owned operation, with owner-chef Mike Frangiadakis' family living overhead. Wooden furniture and lively-colored tablecloths create a warm atmosphere. Service is exceptionally friendly and prompt; our waitress was painstakingly patient and well informed. We enjoyed the chef's special, Mike's mezethes: bite-size pieces of chicken, pan-fried with mushrooms, onion, and wine, served with pita bread and tzatziki. Also good are the various souvlaki of lamb, chicken, and seafood. Minos' desserts are quite tasty; try a piece of honey-sweet baklava with a strong cup of Greek coffee.

LODGINGS

Lac Le Jeune Resort

*Off Coquihalla Highway, Lac Le Jeune exit, 29km southwest of Kamloops, (604) 372-2722
Mail: PO Box 3215, Kamloops, BC V2C 6B8
Moderate; AE, MC, V*

★

Well equipped and pleasant, this lodge puts you right on the lake for fishing and at the edge of the wilderness for hiking. You can stay in the lodge, in self-sufficient cabins (perfect for families, and you can bring your pet), or in a chalet. The resort includes an indoor whirlpool and sauna, meeting rooms for up to 200, and a restaurant featuring breakfast and an evening buffet. Adjacent is a downhill ski area; 160 kilometers of cross-country skiing trails wind through the property. Boats and canoes are available for rent (the famous Kamloops trout are great to catch—and eat). Large tour groups tend to book the place en masse during the summer months, so reserve early, or take a chance on a last-minute cancellation.

Inspectors for the Best Places series accept no free meals or accommodations; the book has no sponsors or advertisers.

ASHCROFT

RESTAURANTS

Ashcroft Manor Teahouse
9.5km south of Cache
Creek on Trans-Canada
Highway, (604) 453-9983
Trans-Canada Highway,
Ashcroft
Inexpensive; full bar;
MC, V
Breakfast, lunch, dinner
every day

A beautiful, airy roadside tearoom (open March through November) now sits just behind the original Ashcroft Manor, which was built in 1862 to accommodate travelers on their way to and from the gold fields. For breakfast, owners Tom and Susan Saunders offer a fresh fruit platter with hot scones, eggs any way you want, or huge, fresh cinnamon rolls (a meal in themselves). Lunch fare includes seafoods, salads, and fresh pasta dishes; dinners range from T-bone steaks to red snapper poached in orange sauce. The changeable chicken is most popular (a boneless breast prepared differently each night—120 recipes and growing). Outdoor seating in summer under the flowering trees.

LODGINGS

Sundance Ranch
8km south of Ashcroft off
Highland Valley Road,
(604) 453-2422
Mail: Box 489, Ashcroft,
BC V0K 1A0
Moderate; MC, V

Here's a dude ranch set in high plateau country, with the Thompson River cutting a deep gorge just to the west. Low-lying buildings of dark-stained wood contain handsome pine-paneled rooms and public rooms which, once cheerful, are looking a tad run-down these days. Children can stay in their own wing or with their parents. For a real family retreat, stay in the nearby fully equipped lodge (holds up to 20), complete with wrangler to show you the saddle.

The pool is quite grand, though the tennis court is not. The real attraction is the corral, where 96 good horses await you for the two daily rides, morning and late afternoon. It can get very hot here during the day, but if the sun is not too brutal, the rides are simply wonderful. Over a dozen buffalo live in the adjacent fields. During the evening, the excellent meals are often served on the barbecue patio, and rustic rooms set the scene for drinks, parties, and games. You'll sleep very well, breathing the cool, sage-scented air.

Off-season here is November through February; the ranch stays open for some spotty cross-country skiing and—yep—more horse riding. This is a wonderful time to go: it's less crowded; the whitened scenery is pristine; and the price goes down to $79 per night, including all meals and riding (from a top in high season of $94). It also makes a first-class spot for a conference or a retreat.

THE OKANAGAN VALLEY

The Canadian Okanagans, from Osoyoos at the border to Vernon to the north, have grown into a full-tilt summer playground. **Wine-making** is a hot ticket in the

Okanagan and the great hope for making tourism a class act. British Columbians have long taken inordinate pride in their wines—even when those mostly came from a few largish factories like Kelowna's **Calona**, on Richter Street, (604) 762-9144, and Penticton's **Casabella**, on Main Street, (604) 492-0621. In the 1970s, however, British Columbia gave premium, small-scale productions a boost by authorizing "estate wineries." Since then, many of these small wineries have popped up, 13 to date. Some of the best estate offerings come out of **Gray Monk**, 8 kilometers west of Winfield off Highway 97, (604) 766-3168; **Cedar Creek** (formerly Uniacke), 14 kilometers south of Kelowna in the Mission, (604) 764-8866; and **Sumac Ridge**, off Highway 97, just north of Summerland, (604) 494-0451. One to watch is **Gehringer Brothers**, 4 kilometers south of Oliver off Highway 97 on Road 8, (604) 498-3527. Other wineries to visit: **Mission Hill**, south of Kelowna in Westbank off Boucherie Road, (604) 768-5125; **Chateau Ste. Claire** (the oldest of the estate wineries), between Westbank and Peachland on Trepanier Bench Road, off Highway 97; **Lecomte**, 5 kilometers southwest of Okanagan Falls on Green Lake Road, (604) 497-8267; **Brights Wines**, between Oliver and Vaseaux Lake on Highway 97, (604) 498-4981; **Divino**, 5 kilometers south of Oliver off Highway 97, (604) 498-2784; **Okanagan Vineyards**, 5 kilometers south of Oliver on Highway 97, (604) 498-6663; and also **St. Laslo**, 1 kilometer east of Keremeos on Highway 3, (604) 499-2856. Most offer tastings and tours; call ahead for times and dates (tours are seasonal).

Skiing is still the biggest hook the Okanagan swings. The local climate is a powdery medium between the chill of the Rockies and the slush of the Coast Range, and the slopes are distributed along the valley. **Silver Star**, east of Vernon, has full resort facilities, (604) 542-0224. **Last Mountain** is the nearest stop from Kelowna for day schussing, (604) 768-5189, but **Big White**, (604) 765-3101, to the east has many more runs (44, up to 1,850 vertical feet), full facilities, and even cross-country trails, and claims the greatest altitude of all the ski areas in the province. **Apex Alpine**, Penticton's full-facility resort, has lately added a batch of "family" runs to complement its harder stuff; (604) 292-8222. Southwest of Penticton on Highway 3A, the **Twin Lakes Golf Club** doubles as a cross-country course in winter; (604) 497-5359. There's more downhill at **Mount Baldy** west of Osoyoos; (604) 498-2262.

OSOYOOS

Osoyoos bills itself as "the Spanish capital of Canada," but not because of any pioneer ethnic roots. In 1975 the city fathers realized they needed a gimmick, saw the Bavarian motif had been pre-empted elsewhere, so decided to slap up some fake red tile roofs and goofy matador billboards and "go Spanish." The climate (Canada's driest, with 10 inches of rain a year) and the pervasive stucco building style abetted the conversion.

RESTAURANTS

Chalet Swiss Restaurant
½ block off Main, behind the hardware store,
(604) 495-7552
8312 74th Avenue,
Osoyoos
Moderate; full bar; MC, V

There's at least one place in Osoyoos that hasn't gone Spanish. The cool, dark interior of this Swiss restaurant features tasteful murals and high-backed booths. The schnitzels are a little highly seasoned, but they're still the best in the region (ask the waitstaff to hold the sauce on the wiener schnitzel, though, or it will be soggy), and the

Lunch, dinner Tues-Sat
(closed Oct-Nov)

homemade spaetzle can't be beat. That regional anomaly, the Greek salad, puts in an appearance and, as it turns out, goes very well with schnitzel.

Diamond Steak
& Seafood House
Main near 89th,
(604) 495-6223
Main Street, Osoyoos
Moderate; full bar; MC, V
Dinner every day
(closed February)

Just about everyone in Osoyoos likes this casual steak, seafood, and pizza house on the main street of town. The decor carries off the town's ersatz Spanish theme better than most, with brick window arches and black leatherette chairs with shiny silver buttons. The pizzas are quite good, if you like crust that's crisp enough to snap, and the requisite Greek salad is the best in town. No wonder—the owner is Greek. The wine list shows a collection of labels (literally) from several valley wineries, and there are refreshing Okanagan apple and pear ciders too.

LODGINGS

Plaza Royale Motor Inn
Highway 3 (Lakeview
Shopping Center),
(604) 495-2633
Mail: Box 610, Osoyoos,
BC V0H 1V0
Moderate; AE, MC, V

Here is the place to stay if you're just passing through town: no charm to speak of, but spanking new and squeaky-clean, with all the current motel comforts, including cooking units and a pool. It's not on the lake but in a shopping plaza off Highway 97.

KEREMEOS

LODGINGS

Cathedral Lakes Resort
Call ahead for directions,
(604) 499-5848 (or
Kamloops radio phone
off-season N6-99700)
RR1, Cawston,
BC V0X 1C0
Moderate; no credit cards;
checks ok

To say this resort is remote is more than an understatement. First you have to get to base camp, which is a 13-mile gravel road journey off Highway 3 along the Ashnola River. Once you're there, a four-wheel-drive vehicle from the resort picks you up and takes you on your one-hour, nine-mile "exciting, safe journey to the lodge." Happily, you kiss motor vehicles goodbye as soon as you reach your destination: a resort centered around the beauty of nature, heavy on recreation (hiking, canoeing, fishing), light on modern conveniences (such as phones and TVs).

Located inside the Cathedral Lake Provincial Park, the entire area is a protected wildlife refuge and a unique geological region. At 6,000 to 8,000 feet, the air is cool and dry, the views of surrounding Cascade mountains spectacular. Mount Baker, Mount Rainier, the Coast Range, and the Kootenays are all visible from Lakeview Mountain, a day hike from the lodge.

All rooms have hot water and views of the lakes and peaks that surround the resort. Choose a cabin (which can accommodate up to eight) or a room in the chalet

---

Looking for a particular place? Check the index at the back of this book for individual restaurants, hotels, B&Bs, parks, and more.

or the lodge. Showers and toilets are shared. Two big meals are served (breakfast and dinner), so pack extra vittles if you get hungry midday (box lunches are available upon request). Make reservations early, since the season is short and space is limited.

KALEDEN

RESTAURANTS

The 1912

At the bottom of Lake Hill Road,
(604) 497-8555
100 Alder, Kaleden
Moderate; full bar;
AE, DC, MC, V
Dinner every day, brunch Sun (summer) (off-season hours vary, no brunch)

The loveliest restaurant outlook in the Okanagan is framed by the sun-porch windows of this intimate country restaurant in quiet Kaleden, 11 orchard-filled kilometers south of Penticton. You can sip an Okanagan Valley riesling while you look out at the lawn, garden, and Skaha Lake beyond.

Okanagan Vineyards recently bought this restaurant housed in a former country store; Robert Jackson the new chef, dedicated to keeping the same style and quality of food as former owners Ron and Judy Smith. The menu remains relatively unchanged, offering the dishes Okanaganites seem to have relentless appetites for—escargots, pate, filet mignon with Bearnaise, seafood with hollandaise. The roasted quail with tarragon is still a big seller. Light eaters can make a meal of a trio of hot or cold hors d'oeuvres, with soup or salad and a loaf of hot cracked-wheat bread thrown in for free.

LODGINGS

Ponderosa Point Resort

Off Lake Hill Road at 319 Ponderosa Avenue,
(604) 497-5354
Mail: Box 106, Kaleden,
BC V0H 1K0
Expensive; no credit cards;
Canadian checks only

Ponderosa Point's compound of 26 individually owned rental cabins on a peninsula extending out into Skaha Lake is an ideal spot to take a thick book for three days in the off-season or a week in the summer (minimum stays respectively). The most attractive units are the one- and two-bedroom Pan Abodes set on a ponderosa-pine-covered bluff above the lake, where the front decks are sited perfectly for watching the sunset. There's a 600-foot sandy beach, boat rentals, tennis courts, a playground, and a big grassy central compound. The cabins, named after trees, are all individually furnished by the owners. They're not plush or contemporary, but they're universally comfortable and clean. Try Greasewood if there are two of you—the furniture has a hand-hewn look that's perfect for the setting. When you don't feel like cooking, The 1912 restaurant is an easy walk up the road.

Wondering about our standards? We rate establishments on value, performance measured against the place's goals, uniqueness, enjoyability, loyalty of clientele, cleanliness, excellence and ambition of the cooking, and professionalism of the service. For an explanation of the star system, see the Introduction.

PENTICTON

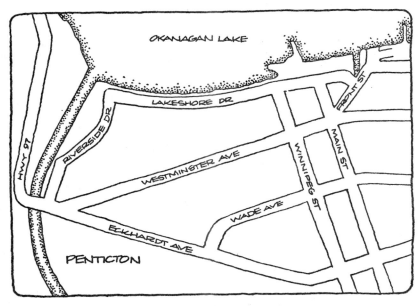

RESTAURANTS

Granny Bogner's
*2 blocks south from
Main, (604) 493-2711
302 Eckhardt Avenue W,
Penticton
Expensive; full bar;
AE, MC, V
Dinner Tues-Sat*

Touted up and down the Okanagan Valley as perhaps the best restaurant in the province is Granny Bogner's. Chef Hans Strobel, a German-trained perfectionist whose credentials include a stint as saucier at Henri Soule's famous New York restaurant La Cote Basque, has a solid reputation and may well be the best in the Valley. And we've often seen what he's capable of—meltingly tender sweetbreads, pan-fried in butter; perhaps a fragrant goulash soup, and expertly herbed salmon. Occasionally, there's an off night—but rarely will you find flaws with the seafood. The menu remains admirable—poached halibut, duck in its own juices, beef filet with Bearnaise, excellent Russian eggs as a starter—and the preparations are consistently infused with creativity if not exactitude. Desserts remain outstanding, especially the fresh, lightly sweet strawberry tart.

Ambience is number one, with substantial old wooden chairs, cloth-covered tables well spaced throughout the rooms, and Oriental carpets and a brick fireplace to remind you that this was once a home. It's all just shy of precious, with fancy lace curtains and waitresses in floor-length paisley skirts. The bar with its comfy chintz chairs overlooks the lawn and invites brandy and dessert. The wine list does a grand job of representing the best local estate wineries.

Theo's
Near the corner of Main and Eckhardt,
(604) 492-4019
687 Main Street,
Penticton
Moderate; full bar; AE, DC, MC, V
Lunch Mon-Sat, dinner every day

The ever-popular Theo's has to be one of the prettiest restaurants anywhere: a series of sun-dappled interior patios, roofed with heavy rough-sawn beams, floored with red tile, walled in white stucco. There's a two-sided fireplace to cozy up to in winter, healthy greenery, and lots of Greek memorabilia. The bar is hung with copper vessels and bunches of dried herbs. Patrons say Theo's cooks a mean steak. We want to believe them, because the Greek salad is no better than any other served in the Okanagan and the taramosalata is like mayonnaise. That said, by all means go in the late afternoon for an aperitif and a plate of excellent fried squid, or late at night to eat moussaka and watch the belly dancer.

Tiffin Tea House
Corner of Eckhardt and Winnipeg,
(604) 493-5997
689 Winnipeg Street,
Penticton
Inexpensive; beer and wine; MC, V
Lunch Tues-Sat, supper Tues-Sat (summer only)

Kitty-corner from the famous Granny Bogner's, an old-fashioned, vine-covered house quietly presents an old-fashioned idea: tea. Go there for lunch, with quiche, crepes, steak and kidney pie, and homemade soup; or for afternoon tea in fancy cups, served with fluffy, delicious scones, fancy sandwiches, or pastries (divine cream cheese and pumpkin custard pie, mocha layer torte, hazelnut torte, pecan fudge pie). They're all made by the proprietor and served at little lace-covered tables. A little homespun, but the real thing.

Three Mile House
6.5km north of the Delta House,
(604) 492-5152
1507 Naramata Road,
Penticton
Moderate; full bar; MC, V
Dinner Tues-Sun

Since George and June MacLeod took over this dinner house two years ago, the menu has seen some changes, and the place's reputation is improving. George serves up lots of seafood dishes, as well as game specialties (wild boar, rabbit, venison) and beef. The food is good, though not excellent (our baby salmon was a bit oily), and the menu is in keeping with the local continental tastes. But the real treat here is the house itself: once a blacksmith shop, the place is cozy-old, with a fireplace in one of the dining rooms and grand views of lake and vineyard from the larger room and balcony. Spend the entire evening; if you sip your coffee and nibble on your cheesecake under the stars in the garden, you might be lucky enough to spot some of the local wildlife.

LODGINGS

Delta Lakeside Inn
Main and Lakeshore,
(604) 493-8221
21 Lakeshore Drive W,
Penticton, BC V2A 7M5
Expensive; AE, DC, MC, V

The Delta Lakeside is the flagship of the Lake Okanagan shore. It's the most expensive place in town, but it's unusually comfortable—hailed by locals, conventioneers, and tourists alike. There are 204 light, airy rooms with balconies, half of which have lake views, and two better-than-average restaurants. One of those, Peaches and Cream, makes an exceedingly pleasant breakfast spot; the other, Ripples, features continental dishes plus—surprise—a teppan table and such deliriously unusual (for the Okanagan) items as sake mushrooms and chicken yakitori.

NARAMATA

RESTAURANTS

The Country Squire
1st Street and 3rd Avenue, (604) 496-5416 Naramata
Moderate; full bar; MC, V
Dinner Wed-Sun

Every meal becomes an event at this clubby old house; dinner might take up to four hours. Master of ceremonies is Ron Dyck, who owns and operates this shrine of Okanagan cookery with his wife Patt. For some, the flourishes are simply too much; for others, the personal greeting and farewell, the endless supply of hot crusty bread wrapped in a snowy napkin, the pretty ramekin of butter, and the perfectly ripe pear more than justify all the fuss.

The opening act of the show takes place when you call for reservations, at which time you are asked to place your order from among several seasonal entrees: stuffed loin of lamb with mint, Bearnaise, and a touch of tarragon; pork fillet with green peppercorn sauce; fresh Dungeness crab cakes with basil; or the ever-popular beef Wellington. Upon arrival at your crisply finished table, you find a formal card detailing the courses to come: perhaps a coarse duck pate surrounded with Cumberland sauce to begin; a soup; your entree; a platter of well-selected cheeses and fruit; and dessert, such as the chocolate ginger pear, poached in sauvignon blanc. The food is good, if rococo, with occasional inexplicable lapses—an inedibly salty leek and potato soup on one visit, an over-done leg of lamb on another. The price is a flat $32—a good deal for Americans, especially since Ron is at your side throughout the meal, decanting one of his 350 wines, flambeing the steak Diane, or carving the Wellington, while assistants quietly fetch and carry. He's also a splendid resource on local wines, many of which reside in his own deep cellar.

LODGINGS

Sandy Beach Lodge
Take the left fork in the road at Mill Road, (604) 496-5765
Mail: Box 8, Naramata, BC V0H 1N0
Moderate; V

Here is the archetypal summer-lodge-on-the-lake, where the same families have signed up for the same two weeks in the same cabin for as long as anyone can remember. The setting is just about perfect: a wide green lawn, breezy with stately pines and shady maples, sloping down to a quiet cove with a sandy beach where Canadian geese raise their goslings in May. A varnished pine-log lodge and a handful of squat brown bungalows are spaced along the lakefront, among an assortment of fruit trees. Tennis courts, a small swimming pool, rental boats, and wooden lawn chairs provide ample diversions.

Unfortunately, the same people have been coming to Sandy Beach for so long that the place has deteriorated without anyone's noticing. The once-extensive flower gardens have gone to seed; the trellises meant to provide leafy awnings for the cabins are sagging and bare of vine; the dining room is closed, except for continental breakfast. Still, the resort has the intrinsic quality that a little neglect can't disguise.

There are seven small rooms upstairs in the lodge, overlooking the lake. The furnishings are old but good: real linen slipcovers in old-fashioned floral prints over big comfy armchairs; heavy drapes and matching fitted bedspreads; wrought-iron-and-glass side tables and dressing tables; and writing desks with matching stools. It's all too period to be tacky. The bungalows, outfitted for stays of a week or more, feature full kitchens, hibachis, picnic tables, and simple pine furniture. The Country Squire restaurant is a stroll away.

Chute Lake Resort
Off Chute Lake Road, about 21km from Naramata (call for directions), (604) 493-3535
Mail: c/o 797 Alexander Avenue, Penticton, BC V2A 1E6
Inexpensive; no credit cards; checks ok
Breakfast, lunch, dinner every day

For outdoorspeople, Chute Lake Resort offers a rustic year-round base camp in the Okanagan Mountains. You have ice-fishing, cross-country skiing, snowmobiling, and apple pie by the fire in winter; in the summer months, the lake is clear, the trout are biting, and the hiking is endless. Accommodations are spare but warm: the six cabins (which sleep 3 to 10) have wood stoves and fridges, but most lack water and therefore baths ($20–$30). Bedding is not provided, so BYO blankets. The nearby log-cabin lodge holds the bathhouse and shower facilities, as well as a full-service dining room and eight more guest rooms ($25). Meals are hearty, and drop-ins are welcome, although you'll need reservations for dinner.

SUMMERLAND
RESTAURANTS

Shaughnessy's Cove
Follow signs from the highway to Shaughnessy's Cove, (604) 494-1212
Lakeshore Drive, Summerland
Inexpensive; full bar; AE, MC, V
Lunch, dinner every day

Built as close to the water as the law allows, Shaughnessy's strong suit is its dramatic view of Okanagan Lake and its airy atmosphere. The restaurant is tiered into four levels, with two outdoor decks, 20-foot ceilings, an old oak bar, skylights, three fireplaces, and pleasant decor. The seasonal menu features fare from fish 'n' chips to chimichangas to a stew served in a hollowed-out loaf of bread. Owner Mark Jones emphasizes service and atmosphere: both are excellent. Watch for the new outdoor margarita bar and firepit for summer evenings.

KELOWNA

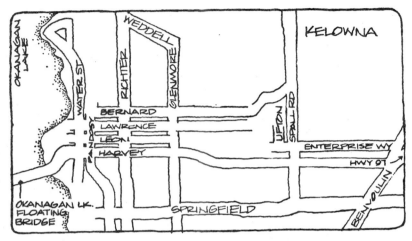

Kelowna is the largest and liveliest of the Okanagan cities, with some noisy nightlife and culture (an art museum and summer theatre), a growing range of continental and ethnic restaurants, a big regatta in July, and an interesting historical preserve at **Father Pandosy's Mission,** (604) 860-8369. It even has its own version of the Loch Ness monster: Ogopogo. Keep a look out for him (or her) while supping on the gaily-decked-out paddlewheeler *Fintry Queen* or touring aboard the *Okanagan Princess*.

Houseboating on 70-mile-long Lake Okanagan is a good three- to seven-day vacation alternative for the entire family—most houseboats sleep up to six ($1200 per week). No previous boating experience is necessary—they'll give you a "Captain's lesson" when you arrive; Shelter Bay Houseboats, (604) 769-4411.

RESTAURANTS

Papillon

Near the corner of Water and Leon, (604) 763-3833
375 Leon Avenue,
Kelowna
Moderate; full bar;
AE, DC, MC, V
Lunch Mon-Fri
(except July-Aug),
dinner every day

Chef Jean Peeters maintains a high profile in his handsome downtown restaurant, wandering out among the diners in his whites, chatting with those he knows and making eye contact with those he doesn't. Consequently, the service isn't exactly swift, but the food is often worth waiting for.

The standard French menu features such appetizers as pate maison, steamed clams and mussels, and escargots; French onion soup and lobster bisque; salmon with hollandaise, steak au poivre, wild duck a l'orange, and veal Marsala—all presented with flair. (The excellent salmon comes on an oversized halibut-shaped glass plate, accompanied by sauteed zucchini fingers and carrot slices and tomato Provencal.) Be sure to check the board outside the front door for dinner specials (a 7-ounce New York steak plus soup, salad, and dessert for $12.95), because they may not appear on the menu or be mentioned; and beware the crab surimi hiding in the seafood gratin. The wine list includes a smattering of everything, from European to local. Decor is contemporary and comfortable.

Vintage Room
(Capri Hotel)
Gordon and Harvey,
(604) 860-6060, ext 229
1171 Harvey Avenue,
Kelowna
Moderate; full bar;
AE, DC, MC, V
Lunch Mon-Fri, dinner
every day, brunch Sun

An elegant old standby, the Vintage Room is loved throughout the Okanagan—for good reason. The service is impeccable, and the restaurant bends over backward to accommodate your whims. Only want a few appetizers, or dessert? No problem—there's no pressure to order more. Light eater? Half orders of all entrees are available. The menu is surprisingly au courant for hotel fare, especially the page devoted to nouvelle cuisine (a welcome relief in the Hollandaise-happy Okanagan) with such items as Louisiana prawns lightly broiled and served with thin slices of cucumber and zucchini. A $16.95 table d'hote menu lists such items as Alberta prime rib, poached salmon with dill, and sweetbreads. Avoid the imported pastries and the runny chocolate mousse. The only other drawback is the tour groups that book here in summer.

Talos Greek Restaurant
Bernard and Water,
(604) 763-1656
1570 Water Street,
Kelowna
Moderate; full bar;
AE, MC, V
Lunch Mon-Fri,
dinner every day

For 11 years now Talos has been turning out superior Greek cuisine, and it just seems to be getting better. Favorites on the menu include: horiatiki salad; very nice, creamy tzatziki with just enough garlic; and a dynamite souvlaki sandwich with thick slices of freshly grilled beef or lamb, stuffed into chewy pita bread. The last comes with a Greek salad, and makes a delicious lunch knocked down with a glass of retsina. All this takes place in a handsome, simple space, cool and pleasant, with checked tablecloths and lots of bare wood—like Greece, only better. Gallons of lemon juice go into the vegetables and grilled meats, and the prawns are reportedly excellent.

LODGINGS

Lake Okanagan Resort
Westside Road, 17km
north of Kelowna,
(604) 769-3511
Mail: PO Box 1321,
Kelowna, BC V1Y 7V8
Expensive; AE, DC, MC, V

You reach the 300-acre resort via a beautiful, pine-clad winding road on the west side of Okanagan Lake. The place shows a little wear and tear (worn flooring here, drunken lamp shade there), and the appointments were never first-cabin to begin with, but it's the only true destination resort in the Okanagan. Open from mid-April to October, it offers sailing, swimming, golf (nine holes), tennis (seven courts), and horseback riding to keep you busy. You can stay in large condominiums or smaller chalets, both with wood-burning fireplaces, or four different inns. All rooms have kitchens and rent by the night. Since the resort is located on a very steep hillside, many of the rooms are a good climb or steep descent away from the activities, but a resort shuttle makes a quick job of it.

The evening restaurant in the white Art-Deco club-house serves fancy continental-resort fare like wrapped and sauced veal and Chateaubriand. The informal Edelweiss Cafe is open all day for salads and sandwiches. A poolside lounge, the Barefoot Bar, makes for an interesting social setting.

Capri Hotel
Gordon and Harvey,
(604) 860-6060
1171 Harvey Avenue,
Kelowna, BC V1Y 6E8
Expensive; AE, DC, MC, V

The Capri, Kelowna's only real hotel (as opposed to motel) on the Highway 97 strip, has been renovated and remodeled. All of the 184 rooms have seen an upgrade, and the old coffee shop has been expanded and renamed the Garden Cafe. The other dining option, The Vintage Room, is outstanding. For relaxation there's an outdoor hot tub and pool, men's and ladies' saunas, and for a taste of nightlife, there's Angie's Pub or Cuzco's Lounge. Tramps, the disco, has been permanently closed.

The Gables Country Inn & Tea House
Off Highway 97 at Old McDonald's Farm,
(604) 768-4468
2405 Bering Road,
Mail: PO Box 1153,
Kelowna, BC V1Y 7P8
Inexpensive; no credit cards; no checks

The Gables sits on Indian land amid vineyards and open space, yet is only 10 minutes from downtown Kelowna. The late-1800s house has been expanded and restored, filled with antiques, and remodeled with salvageable lumber and appointments from other old homes bidding adieu in the area. The three rooms are large and ornate. The largest has a balcony with view of the secluded, sunken garden and pool. In the summer, guests enjoy tea in the garden. Breakfast includes fresh fruit and hot-out-of-the-oven scones.

VERNON

Vernon is the most commercialized tourist center in the Valley, the main jumping-off point for skiers and landing pad for conventions. Nightlife is lively, but the dining scene is uninspired.

O'Keefe Historic Ranch, seven miles north of Vernon, is one of the original cattle ranches from the late 1800s. Now a museum, the compound contains most of the original buildings and equipment from the era. Tours run April–October; (604) 542-7868.

LODGINGS

Villager Motor Inn
At the north end of town, directly across from Village Green Mall,
(604) 549-2224
5121 26th Street, Vernon, BC V1T 8G4
Moderate; AE, DC, MC, V

In terms of plush carpeting, contemporary accoutrements, and upkeep, this half-timbered-and-brick Best Western motel on the Highway 97 strip is the best in town. Some of the rooms open onto the inviting atrium pool and hot tub, but the regular rooms are quieter.

If you've found a place that you think is a Best Place, send in the report form at the back of this book. If you're unhappy with one of the places, please let us know why. We depend on reader input.

SALMON ARM
RESTAURANTS

Orchard House
*Off Trans-Canada
Highway, behind Hill Top
Toyota, (604) 832-3434
22nd Street NE,
Salmon Arm
Moderate; full bar;
MC, V
Lunch Mon-Sat,
dinner every day*
★

A retired British colonel built this lovely house in 1903, planting an orchard and tulips on its surrounding 20 acres. Now it's a restaurant, serving seafood almost any way—baked, fried, poached—but the rack of lamb shipped from Australia is the starring item. Four rooms have been converted into dining areas: try to get into the glassed-in verandah with a view of Lake Shuswap, or the living room with its glowing fire.

SICAMOUS

Houseboating. You and your family can explore the 1,000 miles or so of the Lake Shuswap shoreline at the northern end of the Okanagan Valley on a houseboat—complete with everything from microwave oven to a waterslide. Seven-day excursions run you about $1,500, not including gas (plan on $20 a day extra); Waterway Houseboats, (604) 836-2505.

REVELSTOKE

Heli-skiing. For the serious skier, Revelstoke serves as a base camp to some amazing runs in and around the Albert Icefields. The catch: you need a helicopter to get there. Selkirk Tangiers Helicopter Skiing Ltd., (604) 837-5378, boasts over 200 runs; for a few grand, Canadian Mountain Holidays will take you out, for a week at a time, to one of their three fully staffed lodges in remote hideaways; (604) 837-4204.

RESTAURANTS

Black Forest Inn
*5km west of Revelstoke
on the Trans-Canada
Highway,
(604) 837-3495
Trans-Canada West #1,
Revelstoke
Moderate; full bar;
AE, MC, V
Dinner Wed-Mon,
lunch in summer;
(closed January)*
★

Inside this A-frame you'll find Bavarian glitz, with cute cuckoo clocks and German souvenirs cluttering every spare inch of space. Fondue Provencal, British Columbia salmon fillets, and a variety of beef tenderloins round out a rather extensive menu; we recommend one of the Bavarian dishes such as sauerbraten or schnitzel. Swiss-born chef Kurt Amsler's specialty is rainbow trout from a local hatchery; the servings grow larger as summer and trout progress. Try a glass of schnapps or a slice of Black Forest cake, made locally with cream and kirsch.

The 112
*McKenzie and 1st,
(604) 837-2107
112 E First Street,*

Located in the Regent Inn downtown, The 112 is a unanimous favorite among locals. The masculine decor of dark cedar paneling, historical photographs of the Revelstoke region in the 19th century, and soft lighting

Revelstoke
Moderate; full bar;
AE, MC, V
Lunch, dinner Mon-Sat

blend well with the continental cuisine. Chef Peter Muel-
ler specializes in veal dishes, but the cioppino and lamb
Provencal come with high recommendations. Most of the
seafood is frozen except for the BC salmon. The wine
list has been expanded to include some French and
Australian labels but still emphasizes British Columbia's
own vintners. A variety of after-dinner flaming coffees
are good for show but little else.

GOLDEN

RESTAURANTS

Mad Trapper
1½ blocks north of traffic
light, (604) 344-6661
1105 Ninth Street S,
Golden
Inexpensive; full bar;
MC, V
Lunch, dinner every day

This neighborhood pub is the apres-ski hangout for helicopter skiers in the Purcell Mountain Range (who often
include big-ticket Hollywood types or Olympic competitors on holiday). It's strictly tavern fare, but really
the burgers and ribs are quite good—and predictably a
mess. The hook of the Trapper is that you sign a dollar
bill and staple it to the wall. Autograph hunting is a
favorite activity. It's not uncommon to spot a familiar face.
Cold beer and wine available to-go from the store next
door.

RADIUM HOT SPRINGS

Radium Hot Springs makes an ideal soaking stop at the base of the Kootenay mountain range. The hot springs, open to the public year-round, are equipped with two
pools: one heated, the other cooler for more athletic swimming. If you didn't pack
your bathing suit, don't worry; they'll rent you one for a buck. On Highway 93,
two miles from Radium Junction, (604) 347-9485. Nearby you'll find golfing, camping, lodging, and tennis.

FIELD

LODGINGS

Emerald Lake Lodge
8km north of the Trans-
Canada Highway in Yoho
National Park,
(604) 343-6321
Mail: PO Box 10, Field,
BC V0A 1G0
Expensive; AE, MC, V

In the middle of Yoho National Park surrounded by the
Kootenay Mountains and truly remarkable views is the
Emerald Lake Lodge. The geography is enough to lure
you here, and the comfortably plush log lodge will keep
you here. The owners (who gained their experience from
running the Deer Lodge at Lake Louise) have brought
in all the luxuries of a classy woodsy resort: numerous
decks, three comfortable lounges with large stone
fireplaces, a dining room, a billiards room (with a real
English snooker table), a hot tub, sauna, and weight room.
Stay in a suite (high season: superior $180, deluxe $215,
executive $240); each has a deck, fireplace, and queen-

size bed. The deluxe and executive rooms have "guaranteed" views (do you get your money back if you don't like it?) and a mini-bar.

Breakfast is done well and served buffet style. Dinners are inventive (gold and black pasta with rabbit in a tangy mustard sauce, or pork medallions bathing in morel mushrooms), considering the closest city is an hour away.

The lake is too cold for swimming, so most people opt for horseback riding, fishing for trout, canoeing, or hiking (there's a nice trail around the lake). Come winter, there's access to nearby helicopter skiing, or make the pilgrimage to Banff to cross-country ski out to hot springs. The two foils to tranquil hostelry, smoking and kids, *are* allowed; but at least there aren't any TVs.

INVERMERE

RESTAURANTS

Strand's Old House

In the middle of town,
(604) 342-6344
818 12th Street,
Invermere
Moderate; full bar;
AE, MC, V
Dinner every day

Built in 1912 by pioneer Alexander Ritchie, this house has been converted to an idyllic setting for some of the finest dining in eastern British Columbia. Beyond the beech-tree-lined yard are gardens with panoramic views to the mountains. Chef Tony Wood makes everything from scratch, right down to the mayonnaise served with the steamed artichokes, and prepares a different special each evening (around $16.95). Don't shy away from the elaborate leather-bound menu, though, which features page after page of outstanding appetizers and entrees. A cold, spicy avocado soup started our meal, followed by a well-prepared veal steak with a morel sauce and an exceptional chicken Oscar, stuffed with crab and covered with a cream sauce. Regional wines and beers add gusto to regular evenings of live music. A light menu (smaller portions of the regular fare) is offered after 9pm. Be sure to make reservations in advance. Closed in November.

LODGINGS

Panorama Resort

18km west of Invermere
on Toby Creek Road,
(604) 342-6941
Mail: PO Box 7000,
Invermere, BC V0A 1K0
Moderate; AE, MC, V

More than a resort, Panorama is its own village—a sprawling establishment in the Purcell Mountains that contains a seven-lift ski area, condos and a hotel (even kennels for your dog), lots of restaurants and nightspots, and outdoor recreation aplenty. Eight well-maintained tennis courts, horses, guided hikes, and river rafting on Toby Creek relieve the resort from dependence on the winter ski trade. But ski season is still the time to go. The snow is deep, white powder (World Cup competitions have been held here), and if nature doesn't dispense the white stuff,

---

All places in this book are recommended; even "no stars" are worth knowing about.

machines will. We recommend the condos over the hotel units: they're more expensive, but they all have kitchens. Wherever you stay, you're never more than a five-minute walk to the chair lifts.

KIMBERLEY
RESTAURANTS

Kalamazoo
Highway 95A about 4km south of Kimberley,
(604) 427-2167
418 304th Street, South Kimberley
Moderate; full bar; MC, V
Lunch Mon-Fri, dinner every day, brunch Sun

People drive from as far as Cranbrook to this big cedar building for some of the best wholesome food in the area. The whole-wheat pizza is outstanding, and the Mexican/vegetarian topping (including herb-tomato sauce, broccoli, cauliflower, zucchini, onion, feta, mozzarella, Cheddar, green chiles, cilantro, chili powder, and cayenne) makes your taste buds do the cha-cha. Chef Tami Oakland gussies up the standard spinach salad with a hot (as in temperature) sweet-and-sour dressing that results in delicious, slightly wilted greens. Seafood pasta, quiche, chicken Madagascar, and homemade soups like lemon chicken or Hungarian mushroom round out the menu nicely.

BOSWELL
LODGINGS

Destiny Bay Resort
40 minutes from Creston on Highway 3A,
(604) 223-8455
Destiny Bay, Boswell, BC V0B 1A0
Moderate; beer and wine; MC, V
Lunch, dinner every day (May-September)

German-born Rolf and Hanna Langerfeld brought a bit of Europe to the little town of Boswell on Kootenay Lake. You stay in one of the five cabins which easily sleep two or three (and possibly a close family of five), or in one of the three suites in the lodge. Tall pines shade the view of the lake from the decks. We don't mind the absence of televisions or phones, but we might wish they had kitchens—if it weren't for the reasonably priced good food prepared by Hanna herself. On sunny days, the wrap-around deck on the second floor is the spot—for seafood to schnitzels to herring salads, for the view, and for smokers.

SILVERTON
LODGINGS

Silverton Resort
Coming from the south on Highway 6, first place on the left (lakeshore) in Silverton, (604) 358-7157
Lake Avenue, Silverton,

The road's sometimes washed out in the winter, and it's awfully narrow come summer; but you'll be as pleased with this little resort in the heart of the Hidden Valley as owner Hugh Wilson was when he stumbled upon it (on an exploratory trip from England) a few years ago.

BC V0G 2B0
Moderate; MC, V

Now he windsurfs almost every day and invites guests to share this relaxed getaway. Right now, you stay in one of the new five hemlock-log cabins (more are in the plans)—all spotlessly clean and simple and named after mythological heroes. Thor, at the water's edge, is our favorite. A lakefront resort backed by a glacier in the Valhalla Provincial Park: it's a fine spot to do absolutely nothing.

NELSON

Nestled in a valley on the shore of Kootenay Lake, Nelson sprang up with a silver-and-gold mining boom in the late 1890s and has retained the Victorian character of the era. Its main street has changed little in its 90-year history. Over 350 heritage sites are listed in this small, picturesque city.

A scenic day trip through sleepy villages follows highways 31, 31A, and 6, then loops around to arrive back in Nelson. On the way, there's a short two-hour jaunt (across the lake and back) on the Balfour ferry; Ainsworth Hot Springs, where you can explore a cave of piping-hot waist-deep water or swim in the slightly cooled-down pool; and Kaslo, a town famed for its bakery—Rudolph's Pastries, 416 Front Street, (604) 353-2250.

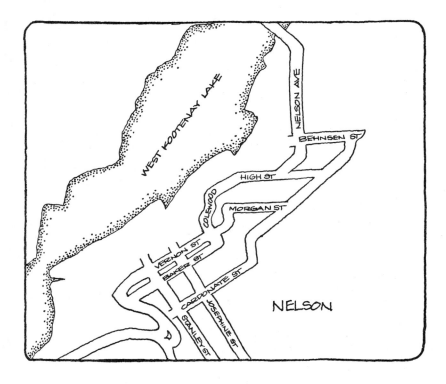

RESTAURANTS

Fiddler's Green
9.7km north of town, just past the Duhamel Store, (604) 825-4466 Lower Six Mile Road, Nelson Moderate; full bar; MC, V Dinner every day, brunch Sun

Oh, do go in the summertime! It's the outdoor dining in the lawn garden we—and so many Nelsonites—love. Inside this old estate house are three intimate dining rooms and one larger area, each serving a huge list of items from the eight-page menu. You'll find favorites from schnitzels to fondue bourguignon alongside an assortment of teriyaki, pasta, steak, and chicken dishes. Better yet, make reservations and go for brunch on a fair-weather Sunday morning.

Le Chatelet
Along the Lakeside Park, (604) 354-3911 903 Nelson Avenue, Nelson Moderate; MC, V Dinner Wed-Mon

It's off the beaten track, but you can find this French restaurant by looking for the spires (Le Chatelet means "little castle"). Chef-owner Eric Eriksen and his wife Essylt, originally from the French Alps, have created an unassuming atmosphere and a country French cuisine. The cornerstone of the menu is a huge brick-lined, wood-burning oven. An Italian influence is also apparent: we sampled a delicate pheasant and liver mousse turnover that very much resembled a calzone). The salads are outstanding: impeccably fresh assorted greens dressed with chopped garlic were delicate and subtle in flavor. Pizza crusts are very thin, crisp, and almost pastrylike, topped with imaginative combinations such as anchovies and vegetables or French ham. Desserts aren't too sweet. Essylt was attentive and always seemed to know what you needed.

Main Street Diner
Across from the Queen's Hotel on the north end of Baker, (604) 354-4848 616 Baker Street, Nelson Inexpensive; no alcohol; MC, V Lunch, dinner Mon-Sat

It used to be Millie's Fish & Chips, so owners Con Diamond and Linda Jameson decided to keep the famed—and still great—fish 'n' chips on what's now a predominantly Greek menu (try the souvlaki or the warm pita bread with tzatziki). We like their Athenian twist on the burger: a thick medium-rare patty with tzatziki and feta.

LODGINGS

Selkirk Lodge
4km north on Highway 3A over Nelson Bridge to Taylor, (604) 825-9411 2211 Taylor Drive, Nelson, BC V1L 5P4 Moderate; no credit cards; checks ok

Sue and Alan Dodsworth make you feel quite welcome in their large rambling 1922 Victorian-style house perched on a hill in the middle of 3½ acres of forested land. The living room has a large stone fireplace. There will soon be four spacious guest rooms, all restored to their original period. Three have window seats—facing an impressive view of the mountains and lake, and one sports a private balcony. A calming half-hour stroll through the woods brings you to a very special place. No smoking is allowed, and reservations are requested.

Send us your opinions and tips on the report form at the back of this book.

Heritage Inn Bed and Breakfast
In the heart of town next to the city parkade,
(604) 352-5331
422 Vernon Street,
Nelson, BC V1L 4E5
Moderate; AE, MC, V

In 1897, the Hume brothers decided Nelson (then a bustling town of 3,000) needed a first-class hotel—so they built one. Over the years the Hume Hotel, as it was known then, became quite run-down. New owners took over in 1980 and began peeling back layers of paint and linoleum to discover hardwood floors and a previously unknown fireplace. Restoration's complete now, and almost everything but the hallways seems polished. The spacious rooms are decorated with floral prints, lace curtains, and antique furniture. Breakfast is ordinary fare, but it's only a short walk to interesting alternatives.

CASTLEGAR
RESTAURANTS

The Doukhobor Village Restaurant
Across from the airport in Castlegar,
(604) 365-2625
Inexpensive; no alcohol;
AE, MC, V
Breakfast, lunch, dinner
Thurs-Tues

The Doukhobors are a Russian ethnic group that emigrated to Canada to flee religious persecution in 1895. This simple cafe reflects the background and creed of the Doukhobor people, who believe in total pacifism and abhor the taking of any life. The vegetarian cuisine on the menu features borscht; pirogi filled with cheese, beans, peas, pumpkin, or sauerkraut; nalesniki (crepes with cottage cheese filling); vareniki (similar to pirogi); and galooptsi (a spicy mushroom mixture wrapped with cabbage and cooked in tomato sauce). Order a combination to sample the unusual fare. No smoking.

ROSSLAND
RESTAURANTS

Sunshine Cafe
In the middle of town on the main street,
(604) 362-7630
2116 Columbia Avenue,
Rossland
Inexpensive; beer and wine; MC, V
Breakfast, lunch, dinner every day

Virtually anybody will feel comfortable in Rossland's favorite little cafe. The new owners have cleaned up the place and slightly rearranged the setup. Food is still creative: you'll do well to start with the mushroom caps with cream cheese and spices or the Malaysian egg rolls (ground beef, coconut, and spices) dipped in a plum sauce. We've heard good reports on the seafood, but we continue to order the budgie burger (boneless breast of chicken with ham and Swiss) or the Indonesian pork with peanut satay. A number of pastas and Mexican dishes round out the dinner menu.

LODGINGS

Ram's Head Inn
Red Mountain Road,
3.2km north of Rossland,
(604) 362-9577
Mail: Box 636, Rossland,

Dave and Doreen Butler's bed and breakfast is the choice place to stay in this mountainous part of the province; it's just a five-minute walk to the unassuming but challenging Red Mountain ski area. The guest rooms are

BC V0G 1Y0
Moderate; AE, MC, V

homey, but the public room is best, with a lofty ceiling, a huge stone fireplace, and big windows looking out to the wooded back yard. Package deals combine lift tickets with a bed and a full breakfast, making a ski weekend nicely affordable. Skiing here is surprisingly good—especially when the Butlers' hot tub and sauna are waiting for you. Kids are quietly discouraged.

CALENDAR

JANUARY

Barbershop Cabaret Shows
Convention Center,
Seaside, OR
(800) 444-6740

Some of the top barbershop quartets in the Northwest harmonize here during the third weekend in January. Come Friday night for dinner and show, Saturday night for the cabaret show only.

Chinese New Year
International District,
Seattle, WA
(206) 623-8171

In late January or early February (depending on the lunar calendar), the International District greets the Chinese New Year with a fanfare of festivals and displays, and a lively parade complete with lion dancers.

Great Northwest Chili Cookoff
Metro Washington Park
Zoo, Portland, OR
(503) 226-1561

For 10 years now, the chili cookoff has benefited the zoo, providing fund-raising for expansion and for the care of the animals. About 34 different chilis are sampled by no less than 3,000 visitors.

Seattle International Raceway
Take exit 142A east off
I-5, Kent, WA
(206) 631-1550

SIR's season begins in January and continues with a busy schedule of races lasting almost the entire year. Though the dirt track for motorcycle races is not much, the nine-turn, 2.25-mile road-racing track (originally built in 1959 for sports car racing) is a very good facility. Open January through November. Tickets are a bargain when purchased in advance.

FEBRUARY

Chilly Hilly Bike Ride
Bainbridge Island, WA
(206) 522-BIKE

Held the third Sunday in February, this 29-mile family ride sponsored by the Cascade Bicycle Club has come to be recognized as the opening day of bike season. 3,500 cyclists fill the morning ferries to Winslow.

Coca-Cola Marathon
Grouse Mountain, BC
(604) 984-0661

Teams of 6 to 12 skiers participate in this 24-hour downhill ski marathon, with all proceeds going to help disabled children in the area.

Fat Tuesday
Pioneer Square, Seattle,
WA (206) 682-4648

Seattle's own week-long Mardi Gras celebration brings a colorful parade and the beat of Cajun, jazz, and r&b music to the streets and clubs of Pioneer Square. Nightclubs levy a joint cover charge, and proceeds from several events benefit Northwest Harvest, a local food bank.

Northwest Flower and Garden Show
Washington State
Convention and Trade
Center, Seattle, WA
(206) 789-5333

This enormous horticultural happening occupies almost five acres at the Convention Center throughout Presidents Day weekend. Landscapers, nurseries, florists, and noncommercial gardeners outdo themselves with over 80 demonstration gardens and booths. Shuttle bus service is available from Northgate and South Seattle. Tickets range from $3 to $6.

Oregon Shakespeare Festival
Citywide, Ashland, OR
(503) 482-4331

An unassuming little college town, set in lovely ranch country, just happens to house the fifth-largest theatre company in the country. Almost 200,000 visitors a year (from February to October) attend the festival and crowd into the three theaters. Lectures, backstage tours, Renaissance music, and dance are other attractions theatergoers enjoy. Last-minute tickets are rare in the summer.

Rain or Shine Dixieland Jazz Festival
Citywide, Aberdeen, WA
(206) 533-2910

Every Presidents Day weekend, rain or shine, Aberdeen hosts top Dixieland bands from around the country. New bands take over every hour and a half. Multiple venues keep the town hoppin'.

Washington State Games
Call for location,
(206) 392-4220

What originated as the Washington Centennial Games is now the Washington State Games, a yearly event held in February, and featuring downhill and cross-country skiing events.

MARCH

Kandahar Ski Race
Forbidden Plateau Resort,
Courtenay, BC
(604) 334-4744

Now in its 41st year, this is possibly the last amateur-status, freefall downhill race in existence. Anyone with the guts and a helmet can register. Generally held the first week in March.

NW Buddy Werner Ski Racing Championships
Call for location,
(206) 392-4220

An alpine ski event designed just for the younger members of your family. About 300 kids from 7 to 12 compete in the frosty event. Come out and watch Olympic hopefuls give it their all. Races are held in Washington, Oregon, or Idaho.

Oregon State Special Olympics
Mount Bachelor, Bend,
OR (503) 382-2442

Disabled athletes compete in ice skating and downhill and cross-country skiing just prior to the big international meet (usually held a few weeks later). Over 400 Olympians compete.

Pacific Rim Whale Festival
Tofino, BC
(604) 725-3414

Migrating gray whales can be observed during March and April just off the shores of the Long Beach section of Pacific Rim National Park. Numerous chartered boats and a seaplane company offer close-up looks at these migratory pods. The actual festival, including dances and education programs, begins the last week in March.

APRIL

Barbershop Quartet International Competition Prelims
Call for location, WA
(206) 788-2436

Every spring, quartets from Alaska to Oregon compete for the honor of representing our region in the Barbershop Quartet International Summer Competition, which is held *somewhere* on this continent. The prelims, however, are held *somewhere* in the Northwest—though definitely not in Alaska. At press time, location was undetermined. (There are local qualifying competitions as well; call for specifics.)

Cherry Festival
The Dalles, OR
(503) 296-2231

This event has parades, cherry tours, dances, a carnival, and golf and tennis tournaments. Held the first and second weekends in April.

Daffodil Festival Grand Floral Parade
Tacoma, WA
(206) 627-6176

The Daffodil Festival, a springtime tradition for over 55 years, celebrates the fields of gold in the Puyallup valley. One of the largest floral parades in the nation visits downtown Tacoma, Puyallup, Sumner, and Orting, all in one day. (In 1990, will be held on April 7.)

Hood River Blossom Festival
Hood River, OR
(503) 386-2000

The coordinators of this event assure us that any similarities between it and the one in The Dalles are purely coincidental. On the whole there are 30–40 different things happening throughout the valley. Tours of the blossoming fruit orchards and wineries are available.

International Wine Festival
Vancouver Trade and Convention Center, Vancouver, BC
(604) 873-3311

The largest and most prestigious wine event in Canada, the five-day festival attracted over 6,800 visitors in 1989. Ten countries were represented by 94 different wineries and 350 wines last year. Future festivals look just as promising.

Longacres Horse Racing
Take I-405 east off I-5, Longacres Racetrack, Renton, WA,
(206) 226-3131

Opening day at this splendid race course is usually in April, and the season lasts until late September. Even kids are allowed on the premises (with adults). Post time is 5pm Wednesday through Friday and 1pm weekends and holidays, and the cost of grandstand and clubhouse admission is $3.00. The Turf Club is now open to the (properly attired) public—$10 includes admission and reserved table for the day. Reservations are accepted two days in advance.

Seattle Mariners Baseball
Kingdome, Seattle, WA
(206) 628-3555

The crowd is predictably loyal—even to a team whose performance is not so predictable. The season lasts from early April through the first week of October (game time is 7:05pm weeknights, 1:35pm on Saturdays). Bring your own peanuts (Kingdome food is too expensive and not too good) and prepare to get lively if you're sitting in the left-field stands. Tickets run from $3.50 to $9.50.

Skagit Valley Tulip Festival
60 miles north of Seattle
via I-5, Mount Vernon,
WA (206) 428-8547

When the 1,500 acres of tulips burst into brilliant color in early April, Mount Vernon seizes the moment and entertains visitors with a street fair and the Taste of Skagit. Makes a particularly nice—and flat—bicycle trip.

Terrific Dixieland Jazz Festival
Victoria, BC
(604) 381-5277

Twenty Dixieland jazz bands from all over the world shake up the town for five days in April. Fifty dollars gets you an event badge good for every concert in every location. Shuttle service is available between participating hotels and the eight concert locations.

MAY

Bloomsday Run
Spokane, WA
(509) 838-1579

Now the world's largest timed road race, Spokane's Bloomsday Run attracts thousands of runners every year (over 65,000 last year) during the area's Lilac Festival, (509-624-1393). Everyone who crosses the finish line gets an official Bloomsday T-shirt and his or her name in the city's major newspapers. Be sure to book hotel rooms well in advance (a year beforehand is advised).

Greyhound Racing
Fairview, OR
(503) 667-7700

You've seen the Kentucky Derby, right? Well, here dogs run instead of horses, the track is smaller (no more than 770 yards), and instead of a jockey urging the dogs on, the dogs chase a little mechanical rabbit. The season runs from May to September. Admission is $1. No children under 12 allowed during evening races.

Hot Air Balloon Stampede
Walla Walla, WA
(509) 525-0850

Four days of hot-air ballooning could make anybody's head spin, and Walla Walla makes a big party of it every year. An arts and crafts fair, fun run, kite expedition, and Blue Mountain Classic car show keep those firmly rooted on terra firma busy while the more adventurous float in the air.

International Children's Festival
Seattle Center, Seattle,
WA (206) 684-7346

This popular event brings in children's performers from all over the world. Puppet shows and musical and theatre performances (some free) entertain kids and their parents for five days in early May.

National Western Art Show and Auction
Ellensburg, WA
(509) 962-2934

For nearly 20 years the three-day event has brought artists from all over the country to this college town off I-90. A hundred display rooms turned into mini-studios offer paintings and sculptures for sale. Three auctions are held as well, including one benefiting Elvien Industries for the community's developmentally handicapped.

Northwest Folklife Festival
Seattle Center, Seattle, WA (206) 684-7300

The largest folkfest in the nation runs throughout Memorial Day weekend and brings many ethnic groups and their folk-art traditions (dance, music, crafts, and food) to stages throughout the Seattle Center. A must.

Opening Day of Yachting Season
Lake Washington/Lake Union, Seattle, WA (206) 325-1000

Boat owners from all over the Northwest come to participate in this festive ceremonial regatta, which officially kicks off the nautical summer. Arrive early to watch the world-class University of Washington rowing team race other nationally ranked teams through the Montlake Cut. Registration is free.

Pole, Pedal, Paddle
Mount Bachelor, Bend, OR (503) 388-0002

This grueling test of endurance is one of Central Oregon's most popular events. In '89, 3,000 people skied, biked, canoed, and ran in teams or by themselves (brave people) past 35,000 cheering spectators. Usually the weekend after Mother's Day, the original small-town run is now a full-fledged two-day event complete with street fair and food.

Poulsbo Viking Fest
Poulsbo, WA (206) 779-4848

In mid-May, Puget Sound's "Little Norway" celebrates Norwegian independence with a weekend of folk dancing and live music, a carnival and parade, and a lutefisk-eating contest (definitely an acquired taste).

Rhododendron Festival
Port Townsend, WA (206) 385-2722

This is the oldest festival in town, and it improves every year. Highlights of this week-long event include a Rover Run (dog and owner), beard contest (scruffiest, longest), adult tricycle race, keg putt, carnival, senior citizen coronation and dance, and more. The "Grand Finale" is a classic parade; the "Anti-Climax Grand Finale" is the 12K Rhody Run. See all of the Rhododendron Queens' cement handprints in downtown Port Townsend.

Sand Castle Day
Cannon Beach, OR (503) 436-2623

Oregon's original and most prestigious sand castle contest is over 25 years old. Buckets, shovel, and squirt guns aid the 1,000-plus contestants in producing their transient creations. Upwards of 40,000 spectators show up to view the masterpieces.

Seattle International Film Festival
Citywide, Seattle, WA (206) 324-9996

Founded in 1976 by Darryl Macdonald and Dan Ireland, the three-and-a-half-week Seattle International Film Festival brings films for every taste—high art to slapstick—to Seattle theaters every May. Fans of the obscure will appreciate the SIFF's archival treasures and independent films. Series tickets go on sale in January.

Ski-to-Sea Festival
From Mount Baker to Marine Park, Bellingham, WA
(206) 734-1330

A Bellingham civic festival over Memorial Day weekend that revolves around a team relay race that includes skiing, running, cycling, canoeing, and sailing.

Slug Races
Old Town Florence, OR
(503) 997-3128

In the Pacific Northwest spring and slugs seem to go hand in hand. During Florence's Rhododendron Festival the main attraction is the slug race. Watch the local gastropods slime their way to victory.

Strawberry Festival
Lebanon, OR
(503) 258-7164

The main attraction at this festive event is the world's largest strawberry shortcake (see the *Guinness Book of World Records*). Standing several feet tall and weighing a couple of tons, it's big enough to give everybody a bite. Served with fresh strawberries, of course.

Swiftsure Race Weekend
Victoria, BC
(604) 592-2441

Held every Memorial Day weekend, this event attracts boats from North America and foreign ports (last year a boat from Russia participated). Three races are held, the longest going out the strait to the Pacific and back. Spectators can watch the vessels coming in from Clover or Ogden points.

Victoria to Maui Race
Victoria, BC
(604) 224-1344

Every two years an exclusive fleet of 20 privately outfitted yachts waits for the Lieutenant Governor of BC to fire the shot that launches them on their way to Lahaina. This internationally recognized race takes years of planning and 12 to 21 days to complete. If you're lucky enough to know one of the sailors, you can board a spectator boat and watch the sendoff. Next sailing is late June or early July 1990.

Washington State Apple Blossom Festival
Citywide, Wenatchee, WA
(509) 662-3616

When the apple trees burst into bloom in early May, Wenatchee hosts an 11-day festival (the oldest in the state) featuring arts, crafts, and plenty of food.

JUNE

B.C. Lions Football
BC Place Stadium, Vancouver, BC
(604) 280-4400

Some people feel that a wider field and one less down than in American ball make Canadian football more exciting. Well, action is the name of the game in this eight-team league, and 38,000 fans demonstrated their agreement on opening day in 1989. The season lasts from late June to late November and culminates in the Grey Cup Game, the Canadian version of the Super Bowl. Regular game tickets cost up to $22.

▼

CALENDAR

Britt Festival
Jacksonville, OR
(503) 773-6077

This musical extravaganza runs from mid-June through August in the hillside field where Peter Britt, a famous local photographer and horticulturist, used to have his home. A handsome shell has been constructed, and listeners sit on benches or loll on blankets under the stars. The season starts with bluegrass and ballet, then presents a full-size orchestra for three weeks, and concludes with jazz and musical theatre.

Canadian International Dragonboat Festival
Pacific Place (False Creek), Vancouver, BC
(604) 684-5151

Everyone comes out to see the dragonboat races and stays to sample the food at the international food fair. Multicultural arts and entertainment round out the day.

Central Washington Dressage Summer Classic
Central Washington Fairgrounds, Yakima, WA (509) 248-7160

Horse enthusiasts will love this free event. About 70 horses and riders from around the state compete for two days. Levels of expertise vary from beginner to world-class Grand Prix precision. Saturday night features a musical *kurs*, classes in which equestrian duos perform to music.

Centrum Summer Arts Festival
Port Townsend, WA
(206) 385-3102

From June through August, one of the most successful cultural programs in the state enlightens thousands with a multitude of workshops held by the nation's leading artists and musicians. For fiddlers, there's the Festival of American Fiddle Tunes. Jazz musicians can hone their skills at the Bud Shank Workshop or listen to the music at Jazz Port Townsend, one of the West Coast's foremost mainstream jazz festivals. Workshops are held at Fort Worden State Park; performances take place at the park grounds or various locations around town. There is also a writers conference and theatre performances.

Chamber Music Northwest
Portland, OR
(503) 223-3202

Portland's nationally acclaimed chamber music festival presents 25 concerts from a widely ranging repertoire. Runs from the middle of June through July.

du Maurier Ltd. International Jazz Festival
Vancouver, BC
(604) 682-0706

Still relatively new to the international music scene, the du Maurier has not disappointed jazz enthusiasts. Last year over 90 artists from Africa, Japan, Europe, and North and South America appeared during the two-wee' festival.

Everett Giants Baseball
Everett Memorial Stadium, Everett, WA
(206) 258-3673

This Class A minor-league affiliate of the San Francisco Giants plays real baseball on real grass in real sunshine from mid-June through August. In 1990, the 1,800-seat Everett Memorial Stadium will be enlarged to 3,000 seats to accommodate the ever-growing number of fans. Tickets are only $3.75 for adults, $2.75 for kids 12 and under. Call for season schedule.

Garlic Fest
Ocean Park, WA
(206) 665-5477

This two-day affair attracts about 7,000 people each year. A street fair, live music, garlic peeling contest, and helicopter rides are just a few of the events that will keep you busy all day.

Mainly Mozart Festival
Meany Hall for the
Performing Arts,
University of
Washington, Seattle, WA
(206) 443-4740

In mid-June the Seattle Symphony presents an annual two-week tribute to Mozart and other late-18th-century composers, in a hall well suited to such music. Tickets for each performance are around $16.

Rose Festival
Citywide, Portland, OR
(503) 228-9411

The Rose Festival is to auto racing what Seafair is to boat racing. Over 80 years old, this 23-day celebration culminates with the running of the CART 200, a race featuring Indianapolis 500–style cars. Don't forget to catch the parade and stop in at the festival center.

Seattle to Portland
Bicycle Ride
(206) 522-BIKE

Traverse the highways and byways from Seattle to Portland on a bike and have a great time doing it. The Cascade Bike Club sponsors this one- or two-day excursion (depending on individual capabilities) every June. Riders don't need to be members of the bike club, but they must register by the first of May. Last year over 9,000 people pedaled the pavement.

Special Olympics
Fort Lewis, Tacoma, WA
(206) 362-4949

In 1968 an act of Congress created the organization known today as the Special Olympics. It has since grown to be the largest single sports training and competition program in the world for the mentally retarded. The June event at Fort Lewis is the biggest competition in Washington.

Umpqua Valley Annual
Arts Festival
Roseburg, OR
'503) 672-2532

Over 100 booths featuring every kind of art imaginable sprout up in the park around the Art Center in Roseburg the last weekend in June. You'll find pottery, silk scarves, jewelry, teddy bears, quilts, folk art, porcelain, woven baskets, and stained-glass items (just to name a few).

JULY

Bellevue Jazz Festival
Bellevue Central Park,
Bellevue, WA
(206) 451-4106

Top Northwest jazz artists entertain outdoors for three days, the third weekend in July. Tickets are cheap ($5) and one concert is free.

Bite of Seattle
Seattle Center, Seattle,
WA (206) 232-2982

A big chompfest, which brings cheap nibbles from over 60 restaurants to Seattle Center in mid-July.

Darrington Bluegrass Festival
Darrington, WA
(206) 436-1077

Every summer on the third weekend in July, bluegrass fans from all over the country turn their attention to the tiny town of Darrington, nestled in the Cascade foothills. Terrific foot-stomping, thigh-slapping bluegrass music is played outdoors by the country's best musicians. Apply early for camping permits ($10); tickets are $25 per person.

Emerald City Marathon
Seattle, WA
(206) 285-4847

It's not the Boston, but this challenging and scenic course gives local—and some nationally known—athletes a run for their money. Approximately 1,600 test their muscles on a circular route that winds its way through some of Seattle's most beautiful parks (Myrtle Edwards, Lake Washington Boulevard, the Arboretum).

Folk Music Festival
Jericho Park, BC
(604) 879-2931

What better way to international peace and understanding than through the universal language of music? Last year over 200 performers from 12 countries came together for three days. A pass for the entire weekend is about $50.

Fort Vancouver Fourth of July Fireworks
Vancouver, WA
(206) 693-1313

The best fireworks in Oregon are across the Columbia River . . . in Washington. Portlanders flock to the National Historic Site of Fort Vancouver for a day of activities and stage entertainment climaxing in the largest free aerial display west of the Mississippi. The bombardment lasts a full hour.

Fourth of July Fireworks
Seattle, WA
(206) 587-6500

Dueling fireworks. Ivar's explode over Elliott Bay and are best viewed from Myrtle Edwards Park. Fratelli's rocket over Lake Union with good viewing from Gas Works Park. A lucky few who think to make reservations for a late dinner at the Space Needle can view them both. The pyrotechnics start shortly after dark.

Frog Jumping Championships
Jefferson, OR
(503) 327-2241

During the Mint Festival, over 200 frogs are brought from home or rented to participate in the Oregon state championship. The frog that jumps the farthest earns a trophy for its owner or lessee.

Goodwill Games (1990)
Statewide, Washington
(206) 622-1990

The world will be watching (via Turner Broadcasting Systems) as 50 countries, most notably the USSR, play for peace from July 20 through August 5, 1990. Twenty-one sports will be represented, including gymnastics, track and field, wrestling, ice hockey, and figure skating. But the 17-day, seven-city event is much more than athletics. A concurrent arts festival and international trade exposition extends the theme of open global relations. Events include performances by the Bolshoi Ballet, the Russian Opera, and the Grand Kabuki Theatre of Japan, and the eagerly awaited "Treasures from Moscow" art exhibit. Tickets will be sold by event or by series for specific sports and will be available through Ticketmaster in mid-September 1989. Patron donations entitle you to advance ticket purchases.

Harrison Festival of the Arts
Harrison Hot Springs, BC (604) 796-3664

During the 10-day event last summer, over 35,000 people visited Harrison Hot Springs to celebrate the musical, visual, and performing arts of Africa and South America. Theatre, lectures, workshops, and live entertainment give visitors many activities to choose from.

IAHA Region 5 Arabian Championship
Central Washington Fairgrounds, Yakima (509) 248-7160

Held every Fourth of July weekend, over 650 horses come to compete for top honors in this five-day equestrian event. Free to the public.

International Classical Music Fest
Victoria, BC (604) 736-2119

Artists from the Northwest gather at the Johanneson International School of the Arts to give concerts, recitals, and ballet performances throughout the months of July and August. Ticket prices can top out at $16 per performance.

International Comedy Fest
Granville Island, Vancouver, BC (604) 683-0883

Watch out, *Improv*, Vancouver has a 10-day shindig with comedians from all over the world that'll knock your socks off. Roving street entertainers and scheduled shows give you the most diverse forms of comedy.

International District Summer Festival
Hing Hay Park, Seattle, WA (206) 623-8171

This extravaganza (second Sunday of July) celebrates the richness and diversity of Asian culture with dancing, music and martial arts performance, Asian food booths, and arts and crafts. A children's corner features puppetry, storytelling, and magic shows.

International Old-Time Fiddlers Contest
Newport, WA (509) 447-4713

Competition is fierce as fiddlers from all over the country try to outdo one another with their renditions of "Soldier's Joy."

King County Fair
King County Fairgrounds, Enumclaw, WA (206) 825-7777

The oldest county fair in the state features five days of music by top country acts, a rodeo, 4-H and FFA exhibits, a loggers' show (remember ax-throwing contests?), crafts, and food. Begins the third Wednesday of July.

McChord Air Show
McChord Air Force Base, Tacoma, WA (206) 984-5637

Come see the real-life *Top Gun* pilots in action as the USAF Thunderbirds do their thing. Afterwards watch military demonstrations of all kinds and get your picture taken in the cockpit of a jet.

Men's USTA Challenger Series and Washington State Open Tennis Tournament
Seattle Tennis Club, Seattle, WA
(206) 324-3200

The top players in Washington and the men's western pro circuit compete side by side during the first week in August at the exclusive Seattle Tennis Club. Tickets range from $1 to $5 ($15 for a season pass), and it's worth the admission just to stroll the idyllic grounds. Order tickets well in advance.

Mid-Summer Jazz Festival
Albany, OR
(503) 926-1517

Bands from Washington, Oregon, California, and even Chicago have participated in this music fest. A prepaid pass gets you into all performances.

Olympic Music Festival
Quilcene, WA
(206) 527-8839

The Philadelphia String Quartet opens its season with one of Puget Sound's premier music festivals, held in a turn-of-the-century barn nestled on 40 acres of pastoral farmland near Quilcene on the Olympic Peninsula. Sit in the barn on hay bales or upholstered pews ($12) or spread a picnic on the lawn ($6). The festival lasts nine weeks.

Pacific Northwest Highland Games
Enumclaw, WA
(206) 522-2874

Kilts are not the only thing you'll find here. Scottish piping, drumming, dancing, and games are the major attractions, not to mention a chance to sample authentic Scottish food and drink. Five dollars gets you in for the day.

Rainier Beer Taste of Tacoma
Point Defiance, Tacoma, WA (206) 232-2982

Another excuse to enjoy all the sinful food your mother warned you about. It's not quite as big as Seattle's Bite, but it is every bit as tasty.

Renaissance Fair
Riverside Park, Grants Pass, OR (503) 479-1602

Local artists display their arts and crafts while the "jousters," knights in shining armor, rescue fair maidens during performances at various times during the day.

San Juan Island Dixieland Jazz Festival
Friday Harbor, San Juan Islands, WA
(206) 378-5509

A three-day festival, $30 for all three days, sponsored by the San Juan Island Goodtime Classic Jazz Association, brings Dixieland fans out to enjoy the jazz of yesteryear, mid- to late July.

Sand-Sations Sand Castle Contest
Long Beach, WA
(206) 642-2400

Hundreds of children and children-at-heart flock to this annual event to build their sand-castle masterpieces. With categories for both sand castles and sand sculptures, cash prizes of up to $1,500 are awarded. At least 10,000 people show up to watch the artists at work.

Seafair
Citywide, Seattle, WA
(206) 623-7000

Seattle's frenzied summer fete has been around since 1950 and—to the chagrin of many locals—isn't likely to go away. The hoopla begins on the third weekend of July with the milk-carton boat races at Green Lake and ends the first Sunday in August when the hydroplanes tear up the waters of Lake Washington. Bright spots include a couple of triathlons, the Blue Angels air show, some excellent ethnic festivals (Bon Odori, late July; International District Festival, mid-July; Hispanic Seafair Festival, late July), and the Torchlight Parade (the Friday before the hydroplane races), which is a full-scale march in the downtown area and a kid's delight. Practically all Seafair events are free.

Sea Festival
English Bay, BC
(604) 684-3378

This festival has everything from puppet shows and sandcastle building contests for the kids to bathtub races and the Vancouver Symphony Orchestra for the adults. Fireworks follow the symphony.

Sweet Onion Fest
Walla Walla, WA
(509) 525-0850

Fort Walla Walla Park celebrates the sweetest onion around with the onion slicing contest, the two-headed onion shotput, the onion hunt, the onion dish recipe and cookoff, and a weekend full of fun.

Vancouver Folk Music Festival
Jericho Beach Park,
Vancouver, BC
(604) 879-2931

Over 200 performers from all six inhabited continents represent an enormous diversity of musical styles. There is a bewildering array of ticket options; the most economical is to form a group of 15 or more to qualify for a discount. Buy early—admission is limited.

AUGUST

The Bite, A Taste of Portland
McCall Waterfront Park,
Portland, OR
(503) 248-0600

Eat to your heart's content and help Special Olympics at the same time. Thirty restaurants and 20 wineries offer scores of delectables while performers at different venues entertain you.

Camlann Medieval Fair
Carnation, WA
(206) 788-1945

Held on Saturdays and Sundays in late August and early September, this fair attracts thousands of people. Dancing, medieval food, performances, and a tournament of knights highlight the event.

Coombs County Bluegrass Music Festival
Coombs, BC
(604) 248-2990

A three-day weekend of gospel, country, and bluegrass. Performers like Rural Delivery or the Rocky Mountain Boys have been major attractions in the past. Tickets are sold for each day. Rough camping is available.

Evergreen Classic Benefit Horse Show
Redmond, WA
(206) 882-1554

Almost 500 horse-and-rider teams compete each year in this six-day A-system hunter/jumper show. Admission is charged during the weekend, but that's all right because proceeds go to Little Bit Special Riders, a program designed to teach disabled kids the joys of riding. And don't miss out on the $25,000 Cadillac Grand Prix of Seattle on Sunday—world-class riding at its best.

Evergreen State Fair
Monroe, WA
(206) 339-3309

For 11 days, late August through Labor Day, the Monroe fair features country music headliners, roping and riding, stock car races, a lumberjack show, a carnival, and a chili cookoff.

Filburg Festival
Comox, BC
(604) 334-3234

A sophisticated arts and crafts show, the Filburg festival continues to grow in reputation as one of the region's finest juried shows. Woodwork, glass, pottery, and woven goods are just a few of the things on display.

Fine Arts Show
Sooke Region Museum,
Sooke, BC (604) 642-6351

Residents of southern Vancouver Island display their paintings and sculptures in this juried show and sale. A $2 admission is good for the entire 10-day event.

Gig Harbor Jazz Festival
Celebrations Meadow,
Gig Harbor, WA
(206) 627-1504

The grassy, natural amphitheater makes a great setting for a festival that draws national jazz artists. Boat owners can sail to the site.

International Airshow/ Airshow Canada
Abbotsford Airport, BC
(604) 859-9211 or
533-3713

Want to see a Russian MiG up close or watch wing-walkers defy gravity? How about the flying acrobatics of the US Thunderbirds and Canadian Snowbirds? Abbotsford Airshow has it all and more. Tickets in advance are $25 per carload.

Mount Hood Festival of Jazz
Gresham, OR
(503) 666-3810

Definitely one of the premier festivals around, this weekend affair has featured in the past such greats as Diane Schuur, Lou Rawls, and the Count Basie Band. Tickets are around $20 a day.

Omak Stampede and Suicide Run
Stampede Grounds,
Omak, WA
(509) 826-1002

The most hair-raising and controversial horse race you're likely to see. No horse has ever been killed since the race started in 1935, but there have been broken bones aplenty. The stampede lasts for three days; ticket prices range from $4 to $8.

Oregon State Fair
Salem, OR
(503) 378-3247

It's everything a fair should be: food, games, rides, horse shows, and live entertainment. For 11 days the people of Salem go hog-wild. Ends on Labor Day. Admission is $5.

Run to Roslyn Antique Car Show
Roslyn, WA
(509) 649-2785

Open to anyone with a special-interest car, this is the perfect opportunity to show off the high school dragster currently stored away in your garage. Five dollars registers your car.

Washington Food and Wine Festival
Woodinville, WA
(206) 481-8300

In late August, Woodinville welcomes food and wine vendors from all over the state. Sample the best in Northwest fare, then kick up your heels in a grape stomp. Admission is $2.50, wine is extra.

World Drag Racing Finals
Spokane, WA
(509) 244-3663

One of the largest outdoor sporting events in the Northwest, this automotive extravaganza attracts over 120,000 spectators each year and over 600 top auto racers from around the US and Canada. Tickets are around $15.

SEPTEMBER

Bumbershoot
Seattle Center, Seattle,
WA (206) 622-5123

The largest multi-arts festival north of San Francisco is a splendid, eclectic celebration of the arts. Select craftspeople, writers, and 500 performing artists (from Robert Cray and B.B. King to Stevie Ray Vaughan and George Thorogood) on 15 stages throughout Seattle Center entertain the hordes over the long Labor Day weekend. A $6 daily pass ($5 if you buy in advance) is all you need to stay thoroughly entertained.

Classic Boat Fest
Victoria, BC
(604) 385-7766

Held every Labor Day weekend, this festival gives boaters a chance to show off their prize vessels. Discovery Reenactment is working up to its 1992 bicentennial of Captain Vancouver's discovery of the island by letting people row an authentic yawl around the bay.

Ellensburg Rodeo
Ellensburg, WA
(509) 925-6144

The biggest rodeo in these parts brings riders in from far and wide for four days of Wild West events over Labor Day weekend. Admission to the big, flavorful event is about $10.

Fall Kite Festival
Lincoln City, OR
(503) 994-3070

Lincolnites love to fly kites of all shapes and colors, and last year so did over 20,000 people who attended the festivities, including the lighted show at night. Prizes are awarded for the most innovative tail and most original kite.

International Film Festival
Vancouver, BC
(604) 685-0260

Similar to the one in Seattle (May), this event at the end of September features over 140 films from 30 countries. Prices are about $6 per movie. Pick up your tickets at the Ridge Theatre by mid-September.

Leavenworth Autumn Leaf Festival
Leavenworth, WA
(509) 548-5807

The last weekend of September is a grand time for a drive through the Cascade Mountains to Leavenworth, a mountain town gussied-up Bavarian-style and home of the festival celebrating the glory of our deciduous trees. A parade, arts and crafts, and Bavarian music are all part of the festivities. Most events are free.

Pendleton Round-Up and Happy Canyon
Pendleton, OR
(800) 524-2984

This four-day rodeo, complete with cowboys, bucking broncos, bulls, and clowns, is said to be one of the biggest in the country. Over 400 contestants and 50,000 spectators make it so. Admission ranges from $6 to $12. A carnival downtown keeps things hopping while the rodeo riders are recovering.

Seattle Seahawks Football
Kingdome, Seattle, WA
(206) 827-9766

The Seahawks may play conservative ball, but the fans' loyalty is steadfast. Consequently, it's nearly impossible to get tickets ($10 to $30) and Kingdome-area parking is a crunch. The season starts in September (pre-season games in August) and runs through December; games are Sundays at 1pm. Best bet is to take a free bus from downtown—and avoid scalpers.

Western Washington State Fair
Puyallup, WA
(206) 845-1771

This 17-day extravaganza begins in early September. It's the rural county fair you remember from your childhood, only bigger. Rodeo, music, barnyard animals, carnival rides, exhibits, and vast amounts of food (including the legendary scones and onion burgers) make for kid—and grown-up—heaven.

OCTOBER

Children's Show
Pacific National Exhibit, Showmart Building, Vancouver, BC
(604) 684-4616

A plethora of activities, such as puppet shows and workshops, geared toward toddlers to pre-teens. A three-day kids' event ($5).

Issaquah Salmon Days
Issaquah, WA
(206) 392-0661

Issaquah celebrates the return of the salmon the first weekend of October with a parade, food, crafts, music, dancing, and displays. At the State Fish Hatchery you can get excellent views of the Chinook and coho thrashing up the ladder.

Portland Winterhawks Ice Hockey
Memorial Coliseum, Portland, OR
(503) 238-6366

See tomorrow's NHL players today in the WHL (Western Hockey League). This developmental league grooms young hockey players for the big time (34 former Winterhawks have already made it). The 72-game season runs from October through March, with prices topping out at about $9.

Salmon Festival
Oxbow Park, Gresham, OR (503) 248-5050

When the salmon come home to spawn, the people of Gresham celebrate with an annual eight-kilometer run, a salmon barbecue, and arts and crafts. The name of the game here is environmental education. Salmon-viewing walks (where you can see the fish spawning in the Sandy River Gorge) and old-growth walks are conducted to teach the importance of our natural resources.

Vancouver Canucks Hockey
Pacific Coliseum, Vancouver, BC
(604) 280-4400

A promising NHL team that is still working on making a name for itself, the Canucks host such teams as the Edmonton Oilers and the Calgary Flames. Season runs from October through April and tickets are between $13 and $27.

NOVEMBER

Model Railroad Show
Pacific Science Center,
Seattle, WA
(206) 443-2001

About 30 different model train setups and clinics on how to make whistles, scenery, and train people bring out the kid in all of us ($5).

Portland Trailblazers Basketball
Memorial Coliseum,
Portland, OR
(503) 239-4422

The Portland Trailblazers are not the most winning NBA team, but their home games are among the most exciting (and earsplitting). They've sold out every home game for the last 10 years! Tickets range from $7.50 to $29.

Rainy Day Film Festival
Douglas County Museum,
Roseburg, OR
(503) 440-4507

For seven years now, the folks at the museum have been showing films on the second Sunday of the month from November through May. Themes in the past have been nature and history, and featured artists have included Buster Keaton and Alfred Hitchcock. $3.50 per family.

Seattle SuperSonics Basketball
Seattle Center Coliseum
and Kingdome, Seattle,
WA (206) 281-5850

From early November to late April, Seattle's home team tears up the courts. In the past, the Sonics have played smart, competitive, and uneven basketball; they have a bright future, so grab tickets early ($5 to $25). Games are at 7pm.

DECEMBER

Christmas Lighting
Leavenworth, WA
(509) 548-5807

Crafts, music, and food are part of the ceremony kicking off the Christmas season. Around 4:45 (usually on the first and second Saturdays of the month) the Bavarian village square is officially lit up for the season. Evening concerts after the ceremony are the only things that require money.

First Night
Vancouver, BC
(604) 669-9894

Downtown Vancouver (the second major North American city after Boston to celebrate First Night) is the happening place to be on New Year's Eve, when virtually every BC theater, arts group, cinema, and church choir entertains the masses for the price of a $5 button. (Vancouver Symphony performances require a separate $5 ticket; advance purchase is necessary.) The Grand Finale and Countdown begins at 11:30pm outside the Vancouver Art Gallery on the Plaza.

Whale Watch Week
Newport, OR
(503) 867-3011

For one week after Christmas, volunteers from the Science Center in Newport report sightings of gray whales from various stations along the coast. Last year the volunteers assisted 11,000 people from all over the world in spotting the whales.

ACTIVITIES INDEX

Editor's note: This is an index to activities specifically mentioned in the book. See also the calendar of events.

INDEX

▼

DID YOU BORROW THIS BOOK?

Northwest Best Places and *Seattle Best Places* are available at bookstores throughout the Pacific Northwest. If you wish to order copies directly from Sasquatch Books, fill out the order form below and return it to us with your payment.

NORTHWEST BEST PLACES 1990-91
Restaurants, Lodgings, and Touring in Washington, Oregon, and British Columbia
by David Brewster and Stephanie Irving

SEATTLE BEST PLACES
The most discriminating guide to Seattle's restaurants, shops, hotels, nightlife, sights, outings, and annual events
By David Brewster and Kathryn Robinson

Northwest Best Places. . . . . $15.95 × quantity_____ = _____

Seattle Best Places . . . . $10.95 × quantity_____ = _____

Seattle Cheap Eats. . . . . $7.95 × quantity_____ = _____

Portland Best Places (April 1990). . . . . . . $10.95 × quantity_____ = _____

Subtotal_____

Washington State residents add 8.1% sales tax . . . . _____

Postage and handling—add $1.50 . . . . _____

Total order = $_____

☐ I have enclosed payment of $_____.
   (Please make check or money order payable to Sasquatch Books.)
☐ Please charge this order to my credit card.

MasterCard #_____ Expiration date_____

VISA #_____ Expiration date_____

Name_____

Address_____

City_____ State_____ Zip_____

Signature_____

Payment must accompany order. All orders are sent fourth-class book rate or via UPS. Please allow three to six weeks for delivery.

☐ Please send me a free catalogue of Sasquatch Books titles.

☐ I would like to use the *Best Places* guidebooks as a fund-raiser for my club or organization. Please send me a discount schedule for bulk orders.

SASQUATCH BOOKS 1931 Second Avenue, Seattle, WA 98101 (206) 441-5555

NORTHWEST BEST PLACES REPORT FORM

Based on my personal experience, I wish to nominate/confirm/disapprove for listing the following restaurant or place of lodging:

_____

_____

_____

_____

(Please include address and telephone number of establishment, if convenient.)

REPORT:

(Please describe food, service, style, comfort, value, date of visit, and other aspects of your visit; continue on overleaf if necessary.)

I am not concerned, directly or indirectly, with the management or ownership of this establishment.

Signed _____

Address _____

_____

Phone Number _____ Date _____

Send to: Stephanie Irving, editor
       Northwest Best Places
       1931 Second Avenue
       Seattle, WA 98101